MORESHET

Journal for the Study
of the Holocaust
and Antisemitism

Claims Conference

This publication has been supported by a grant from the
Conference on Jewish Material Claims Against Germany

MORESHET

Journal for the Study
of the Holocaust
and Antisemitism

Dr. Graciela Ben Dror
Editor

Moreshet, The Mordechai Anielevich Memorial
Holocaust Study and Research Center, Givat Haviva

Alfred P. Slaner Chair in Antisemitism and Racism,
Tel Aviv University

18 | 2021

Moreshet, The Mordechai Anielevich Memorial was established in 1961 by: **Yehuda Bauer, the late Yisrael Gutman, Abba Kovner, Shalom Cholawsky, Ruzka Korczak, Akiva Nir, Yehuda Tubin, and Haika Grossman**

MORESHET
Journal for the Study of the Holocaust and Antisemitism

Editor
Dr. Graciela Ben Dror

Editorial Board
Prof. Yehuda Bauer, Dr. Graciela Ben Dror, Prof. Aviva Halamish, Dr. Ariel Hurwitz, Prof. Guy Miron, Prof. Dalia Ofer, Prof. Dina Porat, Prof. Marcos Silber, Prof. Roni Stauber, Prof. Eli Tzur, Dr. Rafi Vago, Prof. Yechiam Weitz.

Moreshet Director .... Yaakov Asher

Editorial Coordinator ..... Judith Wolff
English Language Editor ..... Naomi Landau

Published by
Moreshet, The Mordechai Anielevich Memorial
Holocaust Study and Research Center, Givat Haviva

The Alfred P. Slaner Chair in Antisemitism and Racism
Tel Aviv University

This publication has been supported by grants from

The Havatzelet Cultural and Educational Institutions

and from the Eta and Sass Somekh Family Foundation

Design
Amy Erani www.multieducator.net

TABLE OF CONTENTS

Moreshet, The Journal for the Study of the Holocaust and Antisemitism • Volume 18

Documentation and Testimony

Book Reviews

Dr. Graciela Ben Dror

From The Editor

We are pleased to present our readers with Volume 18 of *Moreshet, The Journal for the Study of the Holocaust and Antisemitism*, which is being published following a conference celebrating the publication of Issue 100 of the journal's Hebrew edition. *Moreshet Journal* has been a peer-reviewed journal for many years, with each article being read and evaluated by an internal panel of the editorial board and an external panel of experts on the specific topic in question. The Moreshet organization was founded in 1961, and the inaugural issue of *Moreshet Journal* was published in December 1963. Since then, it has been published each year without interruption, up to the present.

Moreshet Journal was initially published twice a year in Hebrew but subsequently transitioned to publication once a year in English and once a year in Hebrew. Since 2011, the journal has been published under the academic sponsorship of The Alfred P. Slaner Chair for the Study of Racism and Antisemitism, which is currently held by Prof. Dina Porat. Over the years, *Moreshet Journal* has also received the support of the Conference on Jewish Material Claims against Germany, and we are deeply grateful to the Claims Conference for its ongoing important patronage.

Since the publication of last year's issue of *Moreshet Journal*, we have had the misfortune of being forced to part with Dr. Esther Webman, who passed away in the summer of 2020. Esther had been a member of *Moreshet Journal*'s editorial board since 2011, contributing significantly to the journal in her own quiet and professional manner. We are greatly saddened by her untimely passing, and we have all lost a dear friend.

Born in Cairo, Esther and her family immigrated to Israel when she was a young girl. She grew up speaking Arabic and French, and she was an excellent student. After completing her compulsory service in the Israeli military, she built an impressive academic career at Tel Aviv University, where she was a senior scholar at the Dayan Center for Middle Eastern and African Studies and an academic advisor for the Program for the Study of Jews from Arab Lands. Her research has dealt with Arab discourse on the conflict with Israel, particularly on its antisemitic aspects and its perceptions of the Holocaust. Her doctoral dissertation focused on Egyptian public discourse regarding the Holocaust between 1945 and 1962, and was awarded a prize by the University of Haifa. Esther was also a visiting scholar at numerous research centers, including Yad Vashem from 2016 to 2017. The English edition of *From Empathy to Denial: Arab Responses to the Holocaust* (2009), which she co-authored with Prof. Meir Litvak, was awarded the Gold Prize in the 2010 book competition of the Washington Institute for Near East Policy. She also edited a number of books, the most recent of which was a collection of articles on antisemitism that was published in Arabic in 2017. Her decorum and her intellectual integrity made her one of the most respected scholars in her field. The members of *Moreshet Journal*'s editorial board are saddened by the great loss of such a prominent professional academic, friend, and beloved colleague. This issue is dedicated to her memory.

The first section contains articles pertaining to a variety of topics related to the Holocaust and antisemitism in different geographical settings and different periods, both before and during the Holocaust. In this section, we offer readers articles dealing with topics such as antisemitism and philo-Semitism in the late nineteenth and the early twentieth centuries; the sociological structure of Jewish Warsaw prior to its occupation by Nazi Germany; the dilemma of the ultra-Orthodox in Hungary and a single ghetto in Upper Hungary; and a Righteous Among the Nations during the Holocaust in Romania. A new subject explored in this issue is the occurrence of genocide in two places in Africa after the Holocaust, which locals have interpreted from the perspective of the Holocaust and regarded as part of a genocide that also draws on the ideology and the means used by Nazi Germany in its effort to cause an entire population to vanish from the face of the earth.

This issue also contains a special section dealing with the research on women in the Holocaust, which was the product of collaboration between *Moreshet Journal* and the Fanya Gottesfeld Heller Center for the Study of Women in

Judaism. The issue also contains a section dealing with documentation and testimony and a section devoted to book reviews.

The issue opens with **Eli Tzur**'s article on Jan Baudouin de Courtenay, who was a world-renowned linguist at the beginning of the twentieth century. Tzur's article deals not with the professional side of Baudouin de Courtenay's work but rather with his public activity, which stemmed from his approach to the nationalist idea that by then had conquered Europe. He opposed romantic nationalism and its emphasis on the linkage between biological origin and geographical origin, or blood and land, which excluded from the political nation all those who did not belong to both categories. In the case of Poland, this meant Catholic Poles, which was a definition that excluded the Jews. But nationalism according to Baudouin de Courtenay was based on multiple belongings and was therefore inclusive. He fought for the provision of equal rights to Jews, not as a benevolent act but as a national right. He also opposed the institution of a Christian Church and worked on behalf of secular and atheistic organizations in Poland. Although his approach was rejected at the time, it serves as the foundation of the liberal nationalism that is customary within the European Union today.

Irith Cherniavsky's article, which also deals with the period preceding the Holocaust, adds a new layer to the discussion by examining a topic that has not previously been explored in the journal: "Residential Living Patterns among the Jews of Warsaw during the Interwar Period." In this article, Cherniavsky examines the residential patterns and the way of life of Jews in Warsaw on the eve of the Holocaust. To this end, she defines the city's "Jewish Quarter," describes the housing conditions in this area, compares the housing conditions of the city's Jews with those of the city's Poles, considers the social and economic disparities among the residents of this area, and examines the changes in the distribution of the Jewish population as opposed to the non-Jewish population between the two world wars. Cherniavsky's article is based on statistical data and newspapers from the period in question, *belles lettres*, and documentary literature.

The two articles that follow both pertain to Hungarian Jewry. **Menachem Keren-Kratz**'s article "A Shepherd without a Flock or a Flock without a Shepherd? The Challenging Dilemmas of Hasidic Rabbis in Hungary during the Holocaust" explores attitudes within ultra-Orthodox Jewry toward the actions of Hasidic "rebbes" from the territory that was controlled by Hungary during World War II. In addition to a number of rebbes who fled Europe early in the war, there were others who refused to abandon their flock, even though their followers and close associates implored them to save themselves and proposed ways of doing so. These religious leaders walked with the members of their communities as they were crowded into the ghettos, consoled them as they boarded the transports, and prayed with them in their final hours in the death camps. Some of the rebbes who survived committed themselves to the rehabilitation of Orthodox and ultra-Orthodox Jewry, despite the suffering and the loss they experienced during the Holocaust. The gap between the confidence in the super-human qualities of the Hasidic Zaddik on the one hand, and the terrible outcome of the Holocaust on the other hand, aroused halakhic and moral questions regarding the conduct of ultra-Orthodox rabbis in troubled times. To whom is the Zaddik obligated first and foremost – to the current members of his existing community who are in mortal danger, or to the Hasidic dynasty that may be established in the future?

Moshe Vered's article "The Nagymegyer Ghetto in Upper Hungary, May-June 1944," which also pertains to Hungary, deals with one of the 150-180 ghettos that were set up in the country in mid-1944. These small ghettos, each of which held only a few hundred Jews, have thus far not been subject to in-depth exploration by the Holocaust research. The article discusses the planning of the Nagymegyer Ghetto in Upper Hungary and the considerations that accompanied the planning process. It also examines the structure of the ghetto in practice, the expulsion of the Jews of Nagymegyer and the surrounding area from their homes, and the conditions in which they lived in the ghetto and, subsequently, in the large pig pen (the *gyűjtőhely*, or "distribution center") to which they were moved. It also depicts the local Hungarian population's attitude toward the Jewish population. From there, the Jews of the ghetto were sent via Fort Monostor, which served as part of the Komaron Ghetto, to Auschwitz-Birkenau for extermination.

Noam Leibman's contribution to this issue deals with another ghetto, that of Warsaw, with an emphasis on two surviving versions of the wartime memoirs of Stanisław Gombiński, a senior officer in the Jewish Police there. A reading of the memoirs reveals a formative difference between the two versions, essentially stemming from their different target audiences. Comparing these two versions enables us to learn about the rewriting process, the reasons for which lie at the heart of the article, and about the subjective point of view of a member of the Jewish Police, which is a topic that still has not been sufficiently explored. Leibman's article also contends with a number of questions regarding the writing of ego-documents, such as: What can we learn from a person's decision to write two versions of such a document? How do changing life circumstances influence the writing? How does the conjectured presence of future readers shape the writing and the story which the author chooses to present to his or her readers? How should we relate to a space that appears self-evident in an ego-document? The article also offers a possible model for reading documents that deal with personal documentation, in which the hermeneutic analysis of the text serves as a major tool for examining how a person understood the reality of his or her life.

A number of scholars engage other aspects of the Holocaust, including the rescue of Jews by Righteous Among the Nations, the Holocaust's impact on subsequent genocide in Africa, and the trial of murderers in Israel after the Holocaust. **Efraim Zadoff** explores the rescue of Jews in Romania during the Holocaust by Chilean consul Samuel del Campo who, while supervising the Chilean diplomatic delegation in Romania between 1941 and 1943, also represented the interests of the Polish Government in Exile. In this capacity he issued Polish passports to Polish Jews who arrived in Chernivtsi, shielding them from deportation to Transnistria. At the end of 1941, del Campo extended his protection to the refugees via his representative in Chernivtsi, Grigore Szymonowicz, and succeeded in preventing the deportation of 250 Jews. In December 1941, he began issuing Chilean passports to local Jews, and later, from 1942 until his flight from the country in May 1943, he continued issuing Chilean protective documents that shielded their bearers from deportation and property confiscation. As he was familiar with the antisemitic policy of his supervisors, he did not report these activities to them. In mid-1943, after being forced to flee Romania, he made his way to Turkey. He did not receive a diplomatic appointment in Switzerland he had been assured, and he was compelled to return to Santiago de Chile to face his superiors.

Yechiam Weitz's article, "The Trials of Murderers from the Holocaust: Comparing the Trials of Eichmann and Demjanjuk," compares the two trials of murderers from Holocaust that were held in Israel. The first was the trial of Adolf Eichmann, the most central figure in the extermination of European Jewry. Eichmann was convicted and sentenced to death by the Jerusalem District Court, and his appeal was denied by the Supreme Court. His execution stands alone as the only execution to be carried out in the history of the state of Israel. The second trial was that of John Demjanjuk, which occurred in the 1980s and the 1990s. Demnjanuk was a "rank and file soldier" – a guard in the death camps in Poland. He too was sentenced to death by the same court, but in this case the Supreme Court upheld his appeal, and he was acquitted of the charges due to reasonable doubt. Weitz's article compares the two trials in terms of their timeframe and the periods in question; the defendants; the courtrooms; the presiding judges; the prosecutors and their opening statements; the defense attorneys; the rulings and sentences in each trial; and the appeals of the defendants. In doing so, it sums up the major differences between them and illuminates the topic as a whole.

As noted above, this issue also contains a special four-article section dealing with the research on women in the Holocaust. It begins with an introductory article by **Judith Tydor Baumel-Schwartz** titled "Why Study about Women in the Holocaust?" On the surface, the research on women in the Holocaust has become a standard field of research alongside topics that have been explored since the establishment of the field. Deeper consideration indicates that, unlike other trends in Holocaust research that were welcomed and nurtured by the broader academic community, the research on women in the Holocaust has sparked controversies and resistance by researchers on the one hand, and public figures and opinion journalists on the other. This section also has a micro-historical aspect, and a few of the articles focus on women in the Holocaust and analyze their situation at extreme moments, their conduct, their desires and aspirations, their limitations, and their decisions within the family unit and in personal contexts.

Aviva Halamish's article "Our Aliyah from Germany to Eretz Yisrael, 1933: The Story of a Family, the Story of an Era" deals with a Jewish family from Germany that decided to immigrate to Mandatory Palestine upon the Nazis' rise to power. This article recounts the story of the immigration and absorption of the members of the Maas family – a father and a mother and their four children – who moved from Germany to Palestine in 1933. It is based primarily on a 14-minute family film and a memorial book for the mother of the family, which together offer information and insights that converge into two genres: autobiography – as the stories of the family's son and three daughters, with an emphasis on the youngest two daughters, are like chapters in the autobiography of each and the shards of a group family autobiography; and biography – as the stories presented constitute tiles in the biographical mosaic of the mother. The article's point of departure is that understanding the story of the family requires knowledge of the historical background of the events depicted in the film. The family story adds to our knowledge of the period and serves as a case study for general phenomena that occurred during it.

Dalia Ofer's article "Transitions in Extreme Situations: Two Women under Nazi Occupation" contends with the question of how to best understand extreme situations in the experiences of women in different stages of the Holocaust. The article makes use of micro-history and focuses on the voices of two women. One is the voice of Sarah Kofler of Vienna, who in 1939-1940 exchanged letters with her daughter who had immigrated to Palestine as part of the Youth Aliyah (*Aliyat Hano`ar*) initiative. The other is the voice of "Ms. C.," which emerges from a 1942 interview with her conducted by Cecilia Slepak of Warsaw. The article presents the ways in which each of the women dealt with their hardships and the mental and practical transitions they experienced by considering the similarities and the differences between the two, which the author regards as characteristic of many women during the Holocaust.

In her article "Out of the Ruins: Establishing Haredi Families after the Holocaust," **Michal Shaul** traces the different stages of establishing a family in the case of ultra-Orthodox survivors. This process occurred among the populations of *she'erit hapleta* in Europe, in the course of the journey to Eretz Israel, and at the initial sites of absorption in the countries to which they immigrated. Each of these familiar stops on the road to the establishment of the religious Jewish family (matchmaking, receiving the halakhic authorization to marry, engagement, marriage, and ultimately bearing and raising children) posed unique challenges, which influenced the shaping of the individual, the shaping of the family, and, ultimately, the shaping of ultra-Orthodox society as a whole. The article places special emphasis on the role played by women in this process.

The Documentation and Testimony section presents three previously unpublished sources. **Leah Langleben** shares poems, songs, and other segments of "A Simchat Torah Celebration," hosted by the Brit Tziyon organization in the Kovno Ghetto. **Nir Itzik** presents a number of pages from the diary that Rachel Ronen wrote in Polish when she was a girl in the Lodz Ghetto, which has not been published until now. **David Golinkin** presents a letter from Rabbi Mordechai Golinkin of Danzig to the President of the Jewish Religious Court in Melbourne, Australia, in which he describes the situation as he understood it in February 1938 and asks whether the Jews of Danzig could expect him to mediate refuge for them.

The Book Review section contains the review of three books that have been published in the past two years. Yechiam Weitz's essay titled "The Trial of Victims" reviews Rivka Brot's *In the Gray Zone: The Jewish Kapo on Trial*, which was published by the Open University Press in 2019. Sharon Geva's "Their Voice is Heard" reviews the book *Let Me Here Thy Voice and the Shadows Flee Away*, which was edited by Batya Dvir and published by Moreshet in 2019. And Eli Tzur's essay "'A Poor Man's Eichmann' or Ivan the Terrible" is a review of Tamir Hod's *Why Did We Remember to Forget? The Demjanjuk Affair in Israel*, published by Resling in 2020.

We hope you find interest in the wide variety of articles offered in this issue.

Eli Tzur

Marching into the Storm
Jan Baudouin de Courtenay's Work
for the Civil Equality of Jews

This article examines the activity of Jan Baudouin de Courtenay, an internationally known linguist whose public work proceeded along two trajectories: 1) the struggle for free thinking unhindered by the interference of structures responsible for "correct" thought and belief, which in Baudouin de Courtenay's case was the Polish Catholic Church; and 2) the struggle for civil equality for all citizens. Though contemporary readers may view his positions as logical and almost natural, his views were highly unusual in the eyes of the inhabitants of Poland at the turn of the twentieth century. Baudouin de Courtenay's courage and intellectual isolation can only be understood after contemplating the system of anti-Semitism he faced.

The Incarnations of Anti-Semitism in Poland

Due to the scope of this article, its discussion on Polish anti-Semitism is relatively cursory and paints a picture primarily of the state of affairs as reflected in Baudouin de Courtenay's polemical articles. It was conventional among Polish Jews to assume that Polish anti-Semitism was as old as Jewish settlement in the country. However, the historical sources reflect that Judeophobia had been only a negligible phenomenon among the Polish population for centuries and had been limited largely to the clergy, which propagated the views of the Church in the West. The first anti-Jewish outburst in Poland occurred in Krakow in 1407 in the context of a blood libel. The very idea of blood libel, it should be noted, was brought to Poland from the West, and the city dwellers of Krakow at the time were mostly Germans. The pogroms and the manner in which they were explained, therefore, can be understood as imported from the West. Anti-Jewish activity intensified during the Church's struggle against the Protestants (most of whom belonged to the aristocracy). As the Church had difficulty taking action against the aristocracy, it turned its attention to the Jews in an effort to do injury to the Protestants through their ties with the Jews. The growth of Judeophobia in Poland prior to the country's partition can be regarded as part and parcel of the Polish Church's struggle against Protestantism, which continued even after the disappearance of this Christian movement in Poland. The frequent usage of blood libels attests to the religious nature of Judeophobia. Tragically, the most severe wave of anti-Jewish pogroms in the First Polish Republic – the Khmelnytsky Uprising (1648-1654) – stemmed from the Jews' role in the economy of eastern Poland as mediators between Ukrainian vassals and Polish estate owners. These pogroms, the likes of which did not reoccur in Poland until the twentieth century, were ingrained in the collective memory of Polish Jewry as *Gzeyres Takh Vetat* – Yiddish for "the Decrees of 1648-1649."

With the exception of the Khmelnytsky era, which was limited to a particular time and place, Polish Jewry generally found its place in the Polish economy, and its fate in light of Poland's loss of independence was similar to that of the other minorities residing in the empires that divided up Poland. Modern Polish anti-Semitism differed fundamentally from the anti-Semitism of the past. I concur with Hannah Arendt's assertion that if it is true that mankind has insisted on murdering Jews for more than two thousand years, then Jew-killing is a normal, and even human, occupation and Jew-hatred is justified beyond the need of argument…The birth and growth of modern anti-Semitism has been accompanied by and interconnected with Jewish assimilation, the secularization and withering away of the old religious and spiritual values of Judaism…In this situation, Jews concerned with the survival of their people would, in a curious desperate misinterpretation, hit on the consoling idea that antisemitism, after all, might be an excellent means for keeping the people together, so that the assumption of eternal antisemitism would even imply an eternal guarantee of Jewish existence.[1]

Unlike Medieval Judeophobia, which was a tool of the Church and served the authorities (of which the Church was a significant component), modern anti-Semitism evolved from the bottom up, out of social groupings that were having difficulty finding their place in society as it developed in light of the Industrial Revolution. Even when the Catholic Church sought to take part in the anti-Semitic activity, as it had in the case of the Dreyfus Affair, it never led the anti-Semitic movement, at least not in the West. The anti-Semitic movement can be defined as a rebellion against the reality of those who failed to favorably situate themselves within the economic and subsequently social changes and who regarded the Jews as the explanation for their personal failure. By and large, it was a movement of city dwellers who feared their decline in social status (declasse) and that portrayed Jews as the party responsible for their situation. According to their worldview, the proper order – that is to say, that in which their status would be maintained – had been disrupted to their detriment by the existence of a population that did it injury: the Jews. In her discussion of the sacred and the impure, anthropologist Mary Stewart describes the impure as material that is not found in its natural place and therefore precludes the system from operating as it is supposed to. According to anti-Semites, the Jews were just such material.

Unlike in the West, the status of city dwellers in Poland was largely limited, and Polish anti-Semitism was born on the eve of the outbreak of the Industrial Revolution. In contrast to the West, the founders of Polish thought came from the lower Polish aristocracy (*szlachta*), which had lost its wealth but not its sense of superiority toward other classes in general and the Jews in particular. The Industrial Revolution reached Poland late, during the final third of the nineteenth century, due to the peasants' emancipation from serfdom at the beginning of the 1860s. Modern anti-Semitism, then, began to emerge in Poland relatively late and was integrated with Judeophobia, which was an outcome of the influence of the Church from the medieval period. This influence, to which historian Alina Cala[2] refers as popular anti-Semitism, existed in Poland at the same time as modern anti-Semitism and found expression both in actions during the Holocaust and in folklore that remains widespread today. Modern anti-Semitism in Poland emerged at the end of the nineteenth century out of the linkage between external influences and the unique Polish reality. It emerged against the background of French and German modern anti-Semitism, and it adopted their terminology. It was also influenced by the institutional anti-Semitism of the Russian Empire. Although pogroms like the ones that occurred in Russia were rare, the Polish anti-Semites inherited their conception of the Jewish conspiracy to achieve world domination and the domination of Poland.

Polish anti-Semitism emerged in Poland relatively late and developed in conjunction with a phenomenon known as the "Litvak Migration." At the end of the 1860s, some of the legal restrictions in the Pale of Settlement were lifted, and some of its Jewish inhabitants migrated westward into Congress Poland, where Jews enjoyed better legal conditions. This migration intensified following the pogroms of 1881. For the Jews of the Pale of Settlement whose native language was Yiddish, Russian was the language of modernization, and in Galicia German played a comparable role.

Polish intellectuals accused the immigrants from the East of two sins: being agents of Russification, which was then the official policy of the authorities, and spreading foreign ideologies associated with Polish Jewry, such as Zionism and Marxist Socialism. The anti-Semitic right wing in Poland called them "social Litvaks" and accused them of being agents of ideologies with the vision of civil government, which was detrimental to the struggle for an independent Poland.[3] It is interesting to note that this kind of accusation, in its various incarnations, also stuck with the Jews during a later period, in the form of accusations of Żydokomuna and being servants of Soviet rule. This political anti-Semitism found organizational expression in the 1920 Warsaw municipal elections, in which it served as a major tool in the election campaign of the Polish right-wing.[4]

Political anti-Semitism stood on the shoulders of ideological anti-Semitism, which was a phenomenon that existed across Europe. It was a manifestation of racism, which was an idea that, in Europe, in the absence of a substantial "other," could be expressed only vis-à-vis the Jews. This racism was based on three foundations: 1) Scientific racism, which assumes the existence of races in a hierarchy of superior and inferior races. This doctrine borrowed the idea of race from contemporary linguistics, which assumed the existence of linguistic groups that developed out of a common ancient language. 2) Race war, borrowed from Social Darwinism, which assumes an eternal war between the inferior races and the supreme race and was translated into scientific racism. 3) Racial exclusivity, meaning, an end to the race war, at which time the superior race rids itself of the inferior races in one way or another and remains the "sole proprietors" of the country.

The move from linguistics to political science and history was enacted by French aristocrat Arthur de Gobineau, who attempted to explain the roots of the French Revolution as a rebellion of the descendants of Gallic slaves against their masters, the Franks. In this manner, the French Revolution became an interracial struggle, a rebellion of the inferior race against their blond, blue-eyed German masters. In Poland, Gobineau's approach was borrowed by Franciszek Duchinski in his attempt to explain the fall of the First Polish Republic and Russia's seizure of its eastern and central regions. In many of his writings, Duchinski argued that, contrary to the Slavic world, of which the Poles were a main element, the Russians were not Slavs but rather belonged to the Tauranic race and the tribes of Central Asia. The border between these two races passed more or less along the border of Poland prior to its partition in 1772.

The Poles, like the rest of the Slavs, were part of the Aryan superior race. Although Duchinski was not an anti-Semite, his conception served as the theoretical source for Felix Koneczny, father of the doctrine of the war of civilizations, according to which the Jews served as an accelerator of the wars of inferior races against the superior Aryans. Koneczny was an ideologue of the nationalist camp, formally known as the "National Democracy" political movement, which was led by Roman Dmowski, who called for establishing a monolithic, hegemonic state in which the Poles would be the "sole proprietors." Whereas territorial minorities such as the Ukrainians, the Belarusians and the Germans could be disposed of by moving the borders, the Jews were dispersed throughout Poland in hundreds of cities and towns. Therefore, only deporting the Jews from Poland could create a homogenous Polish state.

This camp, which was usually referred to as "*Endecja*" (from its abbreviation, ND), was an explicitly anti-Semitic body, and its radical wing was fascist by all definitions. Although Endecja never ruled Poland, it generated the public discourse and was at the center of the cultivation of anti-Semitism. Beginning with independent Poland's initial days of existence, the members of this camp, ND members, and proximate groups were active in universities, where they instituted the "ghetto benches," and in the economy, where they encouraged the exclusion of Jews. The first boycott of Jews was announced in 1912, and although it failed, it provided a good example for similar undertakings down the line. Although the height of Polish anti-Semitism was reached in the 1930s, Baudouin de Courtenay died in 1929, making this development beyond the chronological scope of this article.

Beginning at the end of the nineteenth century, Polish opinion journalism discussed the "Jewish question" in countless articles and societies. The topic's very formulation assumes the existence of a problem known as "the Jews in Poland" and a solution to this problem: Jewish emigration from Poland. The Jews' problem was the absence of a destination for immigration, at least following the imposition of the quotas of the US Immigration Act of 1924. Mandatory Palestine's capacity to absorb immigrants was limited due to its primitive economy, and no other solution for the distress of Polish Jewry presented itself. Nonetheless, the spokesmen of Polish anti-Semitism adhered to the redemptive formula of "steal their property and force them to emigrate."[5]

The Opponents of Anti-Semitism in Poland

According to Cala, it is perhaps surprising, considering the flourishing anti-Semitism in Poland at the time, to learn that there were also thinkers and intellectuals there who opposed treating Jews as an "eternal enemy" and regarded them as partners in the revival of Poland. Practically all of them were writers (in Eastern Europe, writers were considered to constitute the conscience of the nation), and, as such, they depicted the world from which they came: that of the aristocracy. In the iconic poem "Pan Tadeusz" (Master Thaddeus) by Adam Mickiewicz, known as the greatest poet in Polish history, the Jew plays a role that is external to the world of the Polish-Lithuanian aristocracy. In general, during the romantic period of Polish literature, Jews were associated with the realm of exotica that interfaced with the dimension of everyday Polish life, meaning the life of the aristocracy, but were not integrated into it. Prevalent in public discourse in Poland after the failure of the Polish January Uprising (1863-1864) was an orientation that called for improving the reality in Poland not through armed uprising, as in the uprisings of October 1831 or January 1863, but rather via a path of economic and educational progress: positivism. The writers associated with this movement depicted the reality in Poland as it was, relating to two classes other than the aristocracy: the peasants and the Jews. These two sectors were examined with the goal of advancing them, reflecting an internalization of the principles advocated by positivism.

One example of writing that was sympathetic to the modern educated Jew was that of Eliza Orzeszkowa, who depicted a modern, enlightened Jew and a Polish patriot who articulates his views in flawless Polish. Orzeszkowa made a marked effort to get to know the Jewish world and even attempted to learn its language. But in practice, her Jew was as the Poles viewed him from the outside. Indeed, her engagement with Jews was not meant to acquaint the educated Polish public with their world; rather, it was a tool for promoting the principles of positivism among Poles: "If the Jews can, then all the more so the Poles."[6] According to Cala, Orzeszkowa's attitude toward the Jews was fueled by two contradictory ideas: a romantic approach similar to that of Mickiewicz, who regarded the Jews as the bearers of monotheism, similar in spirit to Polish martyrdom, and their view as the initiators of capitalism in Poland, which would create the new Poland that would achieve independence. She therefore supported those Jews who crossed the cultural lines and became agents of Polish culture, alongside the wealthy Jews who became capitalist entrepreneurs.[7] For this reason, she ruled out the Jews whom she regarded as agents of Russification, meaning, the Litvaks. She also loathed Jews who behaved like nouveaux rich – vulgar, ostentatiously displaying their wealth, and derisive of those poorer than themselves, such as members of the aristocracy who had lost their wealth. With views reflecting her perspectives and her sociocultural background as a liberal and modern member of the aristocracy, her books capture the beginning of a process that impacted Jewish society in Eastern Europe: modernization accompanied by migration and secularization. According to Cala, the two decades marking the end of the nineteenth century and the beginning of the twentieth century witnessed the appearance of some 400 literary works discussing Jewish themes.

The positivists also contributed to the casting of Jews as figures who were assuming historical center stage at a time when capitalism, which Jews played an important role in developing, was first emerging on Polish soil. A number of major wealthy figures of Jewish origin conducted themselves with a similar orientation, and in the process of disconnecting themselves from the general Jewish population, they converted to Christianity. However, in order to distinguish themselves from the Polish world, they became Protestants as opposed to Catholics. One of the prominent figures among them, Jan Bloch, established a scientific institute whose publications were meant to prove the importance of the Jews' contribution to the Polish economy, especially in the realm of infrastructure investments. Philo-Semites, like other circles within Poland (including the anti-Semites), believed in a single cultural template: Polish culture, as it had been shaped over the course of generations by the Polish aristocracy. The debate between these groups revolved around the question of the definition of Polishness. The integration of Jews, in their view, required the former's acceptance of Polish culture and of the intellectual codes that were viewed as defining Polishness.

Jan Baudouin de Courtenay

Baudouin de Courtenay belonged to a French aristocratic family descended from Louis le Gros of the Capetian bloodline. Members of this family established branches that spread beyond France, to England, the Middle East (the Crusader kingdoms), and Poland. The founder of the Polish branch arrived in Poland at the beginning of the eighteenth century at the court of August the Strong, king of Poland and the Saxon elector. Like many other aristocratic families, the Baudouin de Courtenay family lost its wealth, and the father worked as a surveyor in a town near Warsaw. Baudouin de Courtenay was born on March 13, 1845 and embarked upon his academic path at the Central School of Warsaw (*Warszawska Szkola Glowna*), the alma mater of many prominent Polish intellectuals. He earned a doctorate in linguistics from Leipzig University in Germany, and his specialization in Slavic languages resulted in his appointment as a lecturer at a number of universities in the Russian empire (Kazan, Dorpat, and St. Petersburg in Russia and Krakow, Warsaw, and Lubin in Poland). In addition to being an internationally known linguist (the Kazan school), he was also a prodigious opinion journalist, articulating views that usually ran counter to the typical schools of thought in Poland. Baudouin de Courtenay regarded himself as non-religious from youth, agnostic in outlook, and atheist in conduct and did not associate Polishness with Catholicism. Indeed, his position on Christianity was the cause of his dismissal from the Jagiellonian University in Krakow, a stronghold of conservatism in Poland.

His position was that of a small intellectual minority in Poland, where the mainstream associated Polishness with Catholicism and regarded the Church as a stronghold safeguarding the values of Polish culture. Only at the beginning of the twentieth century do we witness, in the Polish Diaspora and within Poland itself, secular organizational efforts defining themselves as "free thinking." In 1906, the journal *Mysl Niepodlegla* (*Independent Thought*), edited by poet Andrzej Niemojewski, began to be published in Poland. Baudouin de Courtenay, who defended the poet's work against the harassment of the censors, became one of the journal's prominent supporters. Within a few years, however, this partnership turned sour as a result of a reversal of consciousness on Niemojewski's part. Niemojewski, who started out as an atheist with close ties to the workers' movement, became a devout believer in astrology and a radical and unruly anti-Semite. Many of his publications now dealt with the Jews' supposed rules of conduct – the entire aim of which was to exploit, to cheat, and to enslave the innocent Poles – and their roots in Jewish law (*halakha*). Baudouin de Courtenay regarded Niemojewski's intellectual process as a return to the cultural roots of the Polish aristocracy. In an essay titled "The Anti-Semitism of Progress," Baudouin de Courtenay wrote: "It turns out that when the Polish 'free thinker' remembered that he was a Polish aristocrat…he envisioned himself a Radziwiłłian prince who, with no pangs of conscience, sniped at Jews as if they were quail."[8] After abandoning "free thinking," Baudouin de Courtenay, who continued teaching at colleges in Russia, remained outside the institutional activity of Polish secularism. He returned to this realm only after returning to Warsaw, the capital of independent Poland. On October 5, 1920, a meeting of the "Free Thinkers" was convened in Warsaw under Baudouin de Courtenay's leadership and decided to establish *Stowarzyczenie Wolnomyslicieli Polskich*, the Polish Association of Freethinkers (PAF). The aim of the PAF, which was established and registered with the Registrar of Associations in the summer of 1921, was to fight against sacred elements both in the Catholic Church and in synagogues, and against superstitions that reinforced religious doctrines. In order to prevent the tendency of making anti-religiosity a religion of sorts that became entrenched in Soviet Russia, the PAF defined free thinking as the right of every person to engage in unlimited criticism. In May 1922, the association published the first issue of its journal *Mysl Wolna*, and Baudouin de Courtenay served as its third editor after the resignation of his two predecessors. Baudouin de Courtenay was one of the five members of the PAF's executive chosen in October 1921, in addition to his position as chairman of the association. The executive's make-up reflected the divisions within the PAF and was a harbinger of future splits.

At one extreme of the PAF was Jan Hempel, a Communist activist who strived to turn the association into an alliance of atheist forces within the Soviet Union (*bezbozhniki*) and one of the leading organizations of the Soviet Communist Party. He therefore called for focusing on propaganda among the workers. On the other hand, there was Józef Landau, who called for emphasizing free thinking and regarded the free professions as a natural realm of activity for the association. To balance the centrifugal forces represented by these two men, Baudouin de Courtenay tried to forge compromises and to maintain the unity of the camp. His efforts were met by a counter-attack by each of the two opposing figures. However, whereas his criticism of Landau pertained to the sectarian and purist nature of his position, his argument with Hempel revolved around an assessment of the Soviet regime and of Communism. Baudouin de Courtenay had been in St. Petersburg during the Bolshevik Revolution, and he had borne witness to and suffered from the violence of the Revolution and the barbarity and complete absence of cultural values among those bearing its flag.[9] In his view, Bolshevik ideology was no different than that of the Catholic Church in the dark days of the Inquisition. When attacked by both of the other two figures at once, he announced his intention to cease his work as editor of the journal and to leave the PAF. This resulted in a wave of resignations from the association, transforming it into an organization that accepted Hempel's views. The anti-Communist Polish administration now regarded the PAF as a hostile party, prevented it from publishing its journal, and, in May 1928, announced its closure. Those who had withdrawn from the PAF founded a new association known as *Polski Zwiazek Mysli Wolnej* – the Polish Association of Free Thought (PAFT). Baudouin de Courtenay welcomed the new association but kept his distance from its institutions.[10]

Approximately two years before his death, Baudouin de Courtenay approached the church with which he had formally been affiliated and asked to leave its ranks without delay. Baudouin de Courtenay's request was accompanied by a booklet he authored explaining the reasons for his actions, in addition to the fact that he had been a non-believer for the past 60 years. In the booklet, he presented the principles of his secular view, casting faith in God as an approach that did not further the understanding of reality, as whether or not God existed, reality remained unchanged. Even more intently, he rejected both the belief in a personal God and all the religious doctrines that were shared by the monotheistic religions, such as the eternal soul, the existence of the world to come, and the like. His major criticism was of the conduct of the clergy, which sought to control the devout and served as a focal point of the propagation of xenophobia in general and anti-Semitism of the most violent nature. In this text, Baudouin de Courtenay quoted a publication of the Pallottine Order, which preached expelling the Jews from the citizenry and encouraged physical attacks against Jews based on the association between Judaism and Communism, all in language reminiscent of *Der Sturmer*. According to him, the religious establishment not only demanded complete conformity of the devout with regard to its dogmas but also punished those who deviated from the path it demarcated. There was only one truth: orthodoxy; and whoever deviated from it was to be punished. This was the ideological basis of the Inquisition and the excommunications. In other words, it was a position that was shared by all the monotheistic religions, although the persecution of heretics was subject to varying interpretation and different types of punishment.[11]

Baudouin de Courtenay's Critique of the National Idea

Baudouin de Courtenay's position on anti-Semitism was rooted in his approach to nationalism in principle, and the uniqueness of his national conception cannot be understood without contemplating the social and political environment in which he was active. The ideology of nationalism, based on origin, blood, and land, formed and continued to develop in Germany during the nineteenth century, beginning with the Napoleonic Wars. German nationalism disregarded the religious aspect due to the fact that, in Germany, Catholicism and Protestantism prevailed concurrently, and Germany was almost destroyed by religious wars over the course of more than a century. As a result, it preferred a more inclusive approach when it came to religion. The advocates of German nationalism came from the urban class, and their position was a blow to the aristocracy. The German aristocracy was particularist and loyal to the small political entities that constituted Germany, and the large number of German states endowed the aristocracy with its local power. From a cultural perspective, the German aristocracy regarded France as its intellectual home and preferred the French language; indeed, even Fredrick the Great, the King of Prussia, wrote his essays on military command in French. Its worldview was cosmopolitan, perhaps in compensation for its narrow-minded political world.

Although its perspective on ethnic nationalism was rooted in Germany, Polish nationalism differed from German nationalism in these two realms. The perspective that defined Polishness at the time (it is still problematic at this point to refer to it as a nationalist perspective) was formed in the seventeenth century among the Polish aristocracy. During this period, the Polish city was subject to economic and cultural atrophy and could not serve as a hub of ideological discontent. The Polish aristocracy was part Protestant, with its variety of denominations, and part Catholic. In eastern Poland, the aristocracy, which underwent a process of Polish acculturalization, continued to control the Pravoslav peasants and stressed its superiority to its vassals as a result of the connection between Polishness and Catholicism. The connection between the Catholic religion and Polish nationalism was cemented at the beginning of the eighteenth century, with the aristocrats serving as the mortar. Only in the second half of the nineteenth century was the designation "Polish" applied outside the aristocracy (*szlachta*), first to the urban class and then to the peasants. This expansion of Polishness was the product of two processes that occurred in parallel, stemming from the same cause. Against the backdrop of the Industrial Revolution that had reached Poland, serfdom in the country was terminated and the rural aristocracy migrated to the cities, where they became a bourgeoisie, an intelligentsia, and a source of cultural agitation. Whereas German nationalism excluded anyone whom it did not define as ethnically German, Polish nationalism excluded anyone who was not Polish and Catholic.

Some circles in Poland rejected the Polish model of nationalism, and Marxists such as Rosa Luxemburg replaced national solidarity with class solidarity. But Marxism, too, is an exclusive ideology that distinguishes between exploiters and the exploited. Baudouin de Courtenay did not suggest an alternative solidarity, and he rejected the three legs of early twentieth-century Polish nationalism. Despite his social origins, he derided the Polish aristocracy, as reflected in his above-quoted depiction of Niemojewski, who went from being a secular liberal to being a radical anti-Semite and who regarded himself as an aristocrat. [12] Baudouin de Courtenay's sarcastic description was not a reference to a single individual; rather, it painted a picture of the aristocratic class as a whole as a population of murderous religious fanatics who were living in the past – or, in other words, as a reactionary entity. He opposed nationalism in principle, on both a personal and a scientific level.

Just as monolithic religion rejects other religions and persecutes those within its community who deviate from its path, nationalism denies the existence of other nations residing in the geographical space it regards as its natural habitat. Baudouin de Courtenay viewed the whole idea of nationalism as a mad obsession:

> In recent decades, a general nationalist madness has washed over Europe. This madness has also been manifested in Jewish public life. It has found expression in the birth of Zionism, which effectively fuels the nationalist sense of the Jews, as opposed to other nationalities.

He devoted many pages to a discussion of Jewish nationalism and its Zionist expression. Like Jewish messianism, he believed, Zionism would remain in the realm of daydream. However, unlike others who had rejected Zionism, he had no argument with the national identity of the Jews: "If a Jew feels a sense of belonging to the Jewish nation, he has not only the right but also the duty to declare himself a Jew." Despite the importance of a national language as a basis of national identity, there are national states in Europe (such as Switzerland or Belgium) in which citizens speak more than one language, with these languages crossing the borders with neighboring countries. In these cases, state unity overrides the linguistic fragmentation, and statehood, or the aspiration to statehood, becomes the main goal of nationalism, with the framework being more important than the content. Even in the case of parties advocating a social vision, the vision is subordinated to the dream of political nationalism. For example, Baudouin de Courtenay spoke of the "fighting faction" of the Polish

Socialist Party, whose ranks contained many who believed that before a Socialist regime could be realized the Poles would need to purify their land of all foreign appendages, and that the new regime would be actualized when only Poles resided in Poland.

For every foreigner, for every non-Pole, a bullet in the head. Those who will come to Poland as members of other nations will be able to do so only on a temporary basis, as modest guests with no national aspirations. The earth will be divided into fenced-off national enclosures; to each nation its own enclosure. And each enclosure will contain the prevailing nation – the "proprietors" – and their guests, who lack all national rights.[13]

The Poles saw themselves as the sole proprietors of their country and members of other nations as guests who were reliant on their good will. Roman Dmowski defined the relationship between Poles and the members of other nations as national egoism. The dilemma of Polish nationalists was challenged in the frontier areas of the Polish state, where Poles lived among other national groups: the Ukrainians and the Belarusians to the east of the Polish state, and the Germans to the west and the north. Whereas the mainstream in Poland believed in the country's ability to Polanize the culturally inferior national groups in the east, Endecja was willing to give up this land to safeguard the ethnic hegemony of the state. Whereas the mainstream simply ignored the Jewish question or believed that it would be solved by Jewish emigration, Endecja advocated violent action to cause the Jews to emigrate from Polish soil.

Baudouin de Courtenay rejected both approaches on ethical grounds: "The Pole who persecutes Jews is not entitled to appeal to the conscience of the world's nations when he himself is persecuted by others." However, his principled position regarding the Jews also had scientific roots, stemming from his activity in the fields of anthropology and linguistics. At the beginning of the twentieth century, the Polish mainstream assumed the existence of multiple layers producing the essence of the "true" Pole, who was of ethnic Polish origin (referred to at the time as Sarmaty);[14] of suitable appearance; and a member of the Catholic Church. This definition of identity excluded all those who did not possess these three attributes from the realm of Polish nationalism. In contrast to the nationalists in all national groups who believed in the pure ethnic existence of the nation, Baudouin de

Courtenay assumed the existence of a complex nationalism of "both this and that": "Every Pole with a consciousness and every Jew with a consciousness answers the question of his national belonging in a personal manner…A person with a conscious approach to the question of nationalism, like other cultural connections, can belong not only to a defined nationalist framework but rather to a number of such frameworks, or to none."[15]

As an illustration of this thesis, Baudouin de Courtenay shared an exchange between an anthropologist and a cobbler, both of Lithuania: "What tribe are you from? – I'm Catholic. That is not what I asked. Are you a Lithuanian or a Pole? – I am a Lithuanian and a Pole. That is impossible; either you are a Pole or you are a Lithuanian."[16] His unique view was dictated to a large extent by the reality in which he lived: multinational states that contained deprived minorities, such as Russia, pre-war Austria, and post-war Poland. With the establishment of the new states in Eastern Europe, some of the oppressed peoples became proprietors of their own countries while others continued living in their deprived status. Prominent among these peoples were the Jews, who were dispersed throughout the region – citizens of states that behaved as if they were ethnically homogenous.

From Baudouin de Courtenay's perspective, relinquishing the idea of complex nationalism would lead to two possibilities, both of which were negative: the establishment of a homogenous national state that disregards the reality on the ground, and/or injury to the rights of national minorities within the territory of the state. As an example of the futility of the homogenous national state at all costs, Baudouin de Courtenay drew attention to the Zionist movement, which at the time his article was being written was an ideological notion with little chance of being translated into reality. He rejected the definition of the world's Jews as an anthropological or cultural identity and their definition on a national basis, and he proposed leaving this question to each individual Jew. In his opinion, Jewish nationalism was the product of Jewish persecution:

> The source of contemporary Jews' nationalist and religious over-
> sensitivity is, on the one hand, a religious and tribal uniqueness
> that characterizes them from the distant past and, on the other
> hand, their persecutions and abuse…As a result, the Zionists are

dreaming of the impracticable and have demanded that Russia establish an all-Jewish parliament with legislative powers...A Jew...who proves his Jewish origin...must take part in 'the Jewish state' and be judged by a Jewish court...They want to establish a state with no foundation of land, floating in the air, a wandering state, a 'national autonomy' of Gypsies.

Baudouin de Courtenay engaged in a critically penetrating discussion of the idea of *Gegenwartsarbeit* (work in the present) as accepted by the conference of Russian Zionists in Helsinki at the end of 1906. "Zionism," he wrote,

is understandable on a psychological level, but on a practical level it is harmful and invalid – harmful particularly to Jews. The Zionists want to give the entire Jewish People a charter of rights that endangers its relations with their neighbors in one country or another, and that concurrently sparks the awakening of the rioters and the forces of darkness.

Although he did not mention the Jewish settlement in Palestine, according to his approach the Jews there could expect a similar fate.[17] It is notable that of all the Zionist leaders, Baudouin de Courtenay mentioned only Jabotinsky. Helsinki, he maintained, was the end of a process for the Zionists and the Zionists alone, in their demand for recognition of the suffering of the Jews while simultaneously ignoring the suffering of other national minorities throughout the Czarist Empire. Even though the Jews' suffering increased as a result of the wave of pogroms perpetrated between 1905 and 1907, the Jews' focus on their own suffering, while disregarding that of other minorities, proved injurious to Jews in its relinquishment of possible allies. From Baudouin de Courtenay's perspective, the Zionist position was an incarnation of national egoism according to the school of thought of Dmowski and members of the national-democratic camp.[18]

In contrast to his position that rejected isolationist Jewish nationalism due to its preclusion of the possibility of the complex nationalism that constitutes the basis of Zionism, Baudouin de Courtenay was supportive of Yiddish, the national language of the millions of Jews in Europe, as an expression of "full national liberty," and he advocated allowing the Jews themselves to decide on their own preferred language.[19] His criticism of Zionism stemmed not from a rejection of Jewish nationalism itself, but rather from its totality and from what he regarded as its detachment from the concrete needs of the Jews.

Baudouin de Courtenay's Attitude toward the Jews and Jewish Culture

Another aspect of complex nationalism pertains to the relations between the majority national group and national minorities, which are perceived as dichotomous and as a regular state of affairs between the national groups that constitute state "proprietors" on the one hand, and state minorities on the other hand. Baudouin de Courtenay's assumption was that in the political space of Europe, the large number of national groups in each country was the reality. He therefore invested great effort in planning majority-minority relations in a manner aimed at satisfying both parties. His starting point was that, for historical reasons, as an antithesis of anti-Semitism, the Jews emitted an air of contempt for non-Jews (gentiles, or "*goyim*"): "According to the current situation, regular 'Jews' – the masses of Jewish – regard non-Jews as beasts to be exploited; and without this exploitation, they see no justification for their existence."[20]

In addition to the fact that Jews accounted for one-tenth of the overall population of the Kingdom of Poland, the antagonism between Jews and Poles in practice prevented Jewish assimilation and Jewish integration on an individual level. Although there were figures in Jewish and Polish public life who believed in the possibility of Jewish assimilation in Poland, Baudouin de Courtenay maintained that in Poland this would amount to the mutual assimilation of an "ignorant and fanatical" Jewish multitude into a multitude that is no less ignorant and fanatical." As long as these were the attributes of both national groups, it would be necessary to strive toward arrangements that would enable them to live side by side, while preserving the qualities that could not be brought together and ensuring cooperation for the benefit of both sides. As a man of the academy, Baudouin de Courtenay placed an emphasis on the realm of education. In his plan to establish anautonomy as part of the Russian empire, he proposed two frameworks of study. One was private schools, which could choose its own language of instruction and its own curriculum on the condition that they not have a detrimental impact on morality or on single-language state schools and not engage in religious study. At these schools, the Polish language was a mandatory subject of study, but so was another language, when necessary. He recommended the study of Russian as the language of the state, along with English, French, German, and Esperanto – the lingua franca of the future. In addition to these languages, he recommended the study of languages of national minorities in their population centers. As Poland within its old borders was a multinational state, he proposed setting up research institutes to engage in the study of the linguistics, history, and culture of non-Polish ethnic groups. His description of these institutes also devoted attention to and provided justification for research on Polish Judaism. His aim was to gain an inside understanding of Judaism based on a desire to facilitate closer relations between Poles and Jews. Baudouin de Courtenay was not the only one to propose establishing an institute for the research of Judaism. Eliza Orzeszkowa worked with a rabbi to learn Hebrew but discontinued her studies after a short time. Andrzej Niemojewski initiated the establishment of a Jewish research institute, but with the aim of bringing about the elimination of the Jews. In this way, he preceded Nazi ideologue Alfred Rosenberg, who established the Institute for the Study of the Jewish Question on the eve of Hitler's rise to power, in addition to research institutes that were established during the second half of the twentieth century throughout Europe and North America.

As a linguist, Baudouin de Courtenay emphasized discussion of the research of the Jewish languages. He regarded Hebrew as the language of the pre-modern world and as belonging to the category of ancient languages, such as Latin and classical Greek. On the other hand, he defended Yiddish as the contemporary language of the Jewish People. Many at the time viewed Yiddish as unsuitable "jargon," including Jews among those supporting the acculturation of Jews and among the Zionists who rejected Yiddish for the sake of reviving the Hebrew language. In contrast, Baudouin de Courtenay argued that this contemptible "jargon" was

> …the living language of millions of members of the Jewish People.
> It was the language of families and the language in which children
> conversed with their parents. It was in this language that the dying
> children called out to their parents, who were brutally murdered
> by those known as "Christians." It was a language with value equal
> to that of other languages.[21]

At the turn of the century, Yiddish was not only the language of the persecuted masses, but also a rich literary language and the language of numerous newspapers throughout Eastern Europe. Without a doubt, Yiddish-language literature and journalism was more extensive and richer than that of many languages in Eastern Europe.

Though Baudouin de Courtenay's different suggestions for education were meant to advance the entire population of Poland, including the country's Jews, its fruits would be harvested only years later. In contrast, the political and legal rights of the Jews was, in Baudouin de Courtenay's opinion, an immediate question that could not be put off. In a programmatic article written five years after Poland's achievement of independence, he advocated a relationship between the Jews and the Polish state that would consist of three elements:

> 1) Normalization of the situation of the Jews through the constitution and
> the laws and regulations stemming from it; 2) The treatment of Jews and
> all citizens in accordance with the spirit of the law; 3) The maintaining of
> mutual relations between Jews and Poles in private and social life.[22]

Baudouin de Courtenay began engaging in the issue of Jewish political representation at the conclusion of the Revolution of 1905, when the impression was created in Russian public life that the Czar would be willing to advance democratization within the regime. In a country as massive and multinational as Russia, he held, a parliament elected in nationwide elections was not enough, as the Russians were the largest nation and would deprive all other national groups living in the empire. It was therefore necessary to aspire to the establishment of secondary, nationality-based parliaments, such as the parliament of the Kingdom of Poland, which would send representatives to the all-Russian parliament. However, Poland also contained distinct ethnic groups, most prominently the Jews, who accounted for 12 percent of the overall population of the kingdom. According to Baudouin de Courtenay, all the minorities should be ensured seats in the parliament in proportion to their electoral strength.[23]

Baudouin de Courtenay's Struggle for Jewish Civic Equality

As all hopes for the establishment of a parliamentary regime in Czarist Russia evaporated and the Jews remained inferior under the law, Baudouin de Courtenay and the subjects of his essays were forced to wait until the establishment of the Polish state. Although the sovereign state of Poland was established at the end of 1918, its constitution was approved only in March 1921. The constitution assured equal civil rights for all residents of Poland, as well as the freedom of worship for all religions. However, it also assured preferential treatment of the Catholic religion vis-à-vis other religions. Equal rights for all minorities was imposed on Poland as part of the agreement during the discussions on its sovereignty at the Versailles Conference. From then until 1934, Polish diplomats waged an uncompromising struggle to annul the treaty, which they regarded as limiting Polish national sovereignty. Baudouin de Courtenay regarded the constitution, which also granted the Jews full equal rights, as one of the world's most liberal constitutions. The tragedy of the constitution lay in the fact that its liberal and progressive elements, including the status of the Jews, were forced on the Polish public, at times running counter to what was widely accepted in Polish society.

The Polish constitution was egalitarian and endowed Jews with full equal rights. According to the constitution, Jews could hold any state office, with the exception of the presidency, due to the nature of the oath taken during inauguration. However, implementation of the provisions of the constitution was entrusted to people who were "full of hatred, racism, and prejudice" that caused them to violate it. The Jews were both entitled and obligated to wage a legal struggle to rectify the injustices and deprivation. The only way to fight deprivation and the violation of the constitution by bureaucrats was through cooperation between the Jews and all law-abiding citizens. The struggle was to proceed through legal means and public protest.

Implementing the constitution required the state's adherence to four principles:

1. Recognition of the constitution and of the laws stemming from it that ensure full civil equality, including for Jews.

2. Punitive action against administrators who abuse their powers to do injury to the constitution.

3. In order to imbue society with an awareness of the law and the principles of equal rights, the state must disseminate perspectives based on moderation and consideration as opposed to populism and memories of the past.

4. The principles of equality under the law will remain in existence only if we educate the coming generations in the spirit of social solidarity.

His demands were directed first and foremost at the state and its Polish majority. From the Jews, Baudouin de Courtenay sought primarily overall civil solidarity; that is to say, that they perform their civil duties and refrain from doing harm to Poland on an international level.[24] As far as he was concerned, it was not the constitution that was the stumbling block to ensuring the legal rights of national minorities and other deprived groups, but rather those who were charged with its implementation. The Polish administrators who were charged with running the state and implementing the constitution typically came from the ranks of the lower aristocracy, or *szlachta*, and according to its conception, which was passed down from generation to generation, there was no equality of civil rights. This tendency intensified after the assassination of the first elected president of Poland, Gabriel Narutowicz, who was put into office not only by the votes of deeply rooted Poles but also those of minorities. In the eyes of many, his murderer was elevated to the level of Christian sainthood; and if any official harbored doubts regarding his duties, the murder and the public's attitude toward the murderer signified the path that needed to be taken.

A major factor influencing the legal and constitutional situation of the Jews was their image in Polish society, against which Baudouin de Courtenay fought.

According to the conventional image, the country's multitude of Jews were dirty, did not maintain good personal hygiene, polluted the homes and streets they populated, did not pay taxes, and used services without paying for them (such as when travelling by train).[25] While fighting against anti-Semitic prejudices, he opposed the prevalent relationship between the Jews and the Poles:

> Anti-Semitism is a product of the Bible. Opposition to gentiles gave birth to anti-Semitism in the most ancient of times…Due to lack of time, I will ignore the historical aspect of the Jewish question. However, I will note the national-religious megalomania of the Jewish People, the "chosen people," with its right to exterminate or at least enslave other nations.[26]

One element that was widespread throughout the Polish public was the claim that Jews were undermining Polish culture by trying to weaken it and cause its degeneration. Any diverse nationalism, especially one backed up by xenophobia, makes the shared life of two nations living in the same territory unbearable. In Baudouin de Courtenay's view, this was the situation in Poland during the period in which he was active.

Baudouin de Courtenay defined shared life in the geographical space of the First Polish Republic as Jewish-Polish (*Judeo-Polska*) and presented it in three realms. The first was a millennium-long historical dimension that can be referred to as the Church dimension. The second was the dimension of factionalism, mutual hatred, inciters, and mythical discourse. The third dimension was that of compromise and cooperation – a future dimension of shared civic life that was advocated by the Polish intellectual greats. At the time, however, it was the other Judeo-Poland that prevailed: a land of division and a war of life or death. The radicals on both sides were eliminating or, at best, expelling members of the other national groups. To their disappointment, these aspirations were a daydream, as the Poles could not slaughter the Jews and vice-versa. The expectations of the Zionists were also a daydream, as radical Zionism would also not cause the Jews to leave Poland. Only the third dimension would allow Poland to be Polish in the most noble, pure, and lofty sense. This was the

Poland of civil equality and shared work, the Poland marching in the first row of humanity. It would be a Poland without Judea, and this would make Poland Polish.[27] As a basis for the existence of the enlightened Polish state, Baudouin de Courtenay formulated a paragraph, which he published in the press and conveyed to Versailles, where discussions were then underway regarding the establishment of a sovereign Poland: "I am not satisfied with regular tolerance. I demand unconditional full equality for all citizens, with no exceptions in any countries and for all people of the worldwide republic. It goes without saying that Jews are included in this tally of citizens."[28]

Conclusion: Baudouin de Courtenay's Thinking against the Test of Time

Jan Baudouin de Courtenay belongs to the species of thinkers who were born in the wrong place and at the wrong time. He viewed himself not as a Polish nationalist but rather a Polish patriot. He explained the difference between patriot and nationalist as follows: "Wise national patriotism relies on the protection of the rights of the nation without injuring the rights of others. It is not synonymous with stinging, insulting nationalism."[29] He was aware of the intense nationalism of the Poles, who achieved the independence of their homeland after 150 years of enslavement. He depicted their conduct as that of slaves that were liberated only to be enslaved to others. He preferred multinational states that could develop into multicultural states, in which all peoples enjoyed the same rights. National states, on the other hand, limited the solidarity of citizens to those who are party to the mythos of common origin. In multinational states, based on their own internal interest, the members of different national groups can climb the employment ladder, as had occurred in reactionary Czarist Russia. In national states, the high positions are reserved for the national group of the "proprietors."

In addition to the oppression of minorities by the majority national group, Baudouin de Courtenay identified another danger of nationalism. Among minorities who cannot express their identity using political tools, the solution to the pressure of the majority is addressed by a crowding of the ranks and social pressure to continue to belong to the ethnic community. Baudouin de Courtenay found an extreme example of this tendency within the Jewish community, in which Jewish fanatics used force and even terror against all those who deviated from the domain of the Jewish community. In his view, every person had the right to belong to a particular nation, to a number of nations at once, or to no nation at all. Such a position, he believed, stemmed from every human grouping's right to national self-determination.[30] The basis of all nationalism is language, and although in some states more than one language is spoken and each is considered equal, this is the product of cultural imperialism, as in the case of the French language in the Wallonia region of Belgium. Typically, the first stage of the development of national consciousness is the nurturing and upgrading of the local spoken language and its transformation into a language of culture. In the absence of a common language of culture, the national community cannot grow. This was the basis for the acceptance of the Hebrew language as the language of the Zionist movement around the world and in the Jewish Yishuv in Palestine – a possibility that Baudouin de Courtenay did not believe would be realized. At the same time, majority national groups who tried to assimilate the national minorities in their country took action to do away with the media in their languages and imposed their language on the minority, as in the waves of Russification and the Germanization that were carried out in the parts of Poland that were under their control. Baudouin de Courtenay, a linguist who was aware of the importance of language, understood that in a country with a clear national majority, the language of the majority becomes the language of culture and modern life. As such, even in multicultural countries, the language of the majority serves to eradicate the language of the minority, even if doing so is not the majority's intention. To overcome this obstacle, Baudouin de Courtenay called for adopting Esperanto as the common language of modern life for all citizens of the state, as its artificial nature would prevent the language of one part of the citizenry from dominating the entirety of cultural discourse in the country.

In his book on the October Revolution of 1917, Leon Trotsky recounts the discovery of diplomatic documents signed by Czarist Russia that he "flung into the wastebasket of history." Today, it is clear that history has no wastebasket and that even the most surreal ideas can be revived if a group or a movement is in need of them. Without a doubt, during the initial decades of independent Poland, the ideas of Baudouin de Courtenay were considered to be surreal, non-

people of Jewish identity and Polish culture would regard the idea of a person who had numerous national identities and did not stipulate a hierarchy among them as helpful; it was also natural that they would regard Baudouin de Courtenay as a solution to their intellectual distress. In a poem titled "We Polish Jews" written during the Holocaust, Julian Tuwim, one of the great poets of Poland, wrote:

> I can hear the question immediately: 'Why US?'... Jews ask me, the ones whom I always told that I was a Pole, and now the question will be asked of me by the Poles, for the greatest part of whom I have been and will be a Jew...I am a Pole, because it pleases me...I am a Pole for the simplest, almost the most primitive of reasons, generally rational, frequently irrational, but without a 'mystical' addition. To be a Pole, it is neither an honor, nor glory, nor a privilege. It is the same as breathing. I have not yet met a person that is proud of the fact that he breathes... A Pole also because the birch and the willow are closer to me than a cypress or a palm...
>
> In response to this, I hear voices: 'Good. But then if a Pole, why then 'We, Jews'? To this I respond: BECAUSE OF BLOOD... Blood is twofold: that in our veins and that from our veins...The blood of Jews (not 'Jewish blood') flows through the deepest and the widest streams... Accept me, my brothers, to this honored communion of the Innocently Shed Blood... Then perhaps not 'We, Polish Jews'... but rather 'We Specters, we Shadows of our murdered Brothers, Polish Jews'... We, Shlomos, Sruls, Moishes, we scabs, ritual murderers, curly haired ones — we whose names and epithets will eclipse in honor the fullness of all the Achilles... and Richard the Lion Hearted.[31]

One of the most powerful texts ever written about the extermination of the Jews of Poland, Tuwim's lamentation differs from the suicide note of Szmul Zygielbojm and the poem of Yitzhak Katznelson. The two latter-mentioned texts lament the isolation of the Jews of Poland and their ostracizing by their neighbors. Tuwim understands the Polish Jews according to their dual classifications: Jewish and Polish. This is a powerful expression of the approach of Baudouin de Courtenay, who fought for his conception of nationalism, which incorporates the multiple national affiliations of every individual.

Baudouin de Courtenay's ideas challenged the major nationalist movements both in the course of his lifetime and after his death. His struggle for Jewish equality and for the Jews' integration into Polish society without surrendering their identity, because that was how a civilized state should conduct itself, was foreign to the Polish mindset. The Poles, who were granted sovereignty after decades of oppression, were not willing to have partners in running the state. They regarded themselves as the proprietors of an estate who were willing to exploit their serfs and to refrain from viewing them as equal human beings. Baudouin de Courtenay's ideas are undoubtedly worthy of renewed discussion today, in light of the revival of nationalism in Europe.

Endnotes

1   Hannah Arenndt, *The Origins of Totalitarianism* (London, 2017), p. 7.

2   Alina Cala, *Zyd – wrog odwieczny? Antysemityzm wPolsce I jego zrodla* (Warsaw, 2012).

3   Jan Baudouin de Courtenay, "W sprawie 'antysemityzmu postepowego'," *Miejcie odwagę myślenia... Wybór pism publicystycznych z lat 1898-1927* (Krakow, 2007), pp. 319-320.

4   Theodore Weeks, *From Assimilation to Antisemitism: The "Jewish Question" in Poland, 1850–1914* (Dekalb, IL, 2006).

5   Cala, *Zyd – wrog odwieczny?*, p. 326.

6   Aleksander Hertz, "Obraz Zyda w swiadomosci Polakow," *Znak* 35, Krakow, February-March 1983, pp. 443-444.

7   Cala, *Zyd – wrog odwieczny?*, p. 326.

8   Jan Baudouin de Courtenay, *Miejcie odwage myslenia...*, p.268.

9   Ibid., p. 454.

10   Katarzyna Adamow, "Zarys dziejow ruchu wolnomyslicielskiego w II RP" (2007), *Racjonalista* website, http://www.racjonalista.pl/kk.php/s,5406 (accessed January 2021).

11   See the booklet "Relations with the Church": Jan Baudouin de Courtenay, *Moj stosunek do Kosciola* (Warsaw, 1927), https://commons.wikimedia.org/wiki/File:PL_Moj_stosunek_do_kosciola.djvu (accessed January 2021).

12   Baudouin de Courtenay, "W sprawie 'Antysemityzmu postepowego'," p. 268.

13   Ibid., pp. 296-297.

14   The Sarmatians were a group of tribes that were part of the broader Scythian cultures and that resided in the steppes of central Russia. The Polish aristocracy of the early modern age believed that their roots reached back to this group and created a myth that distinguished it from the other elements of Polish society.

15   Jan Baudouin Courtenay, "Narodowa i terytolialna cecha autonomii," *Miejcie odwage myslenia...*, p. 232.

16   Jan Baudouin Courtenay, "W kwestii narodowosciowej," *Miejcie odwage myslenia...*, p. 371.

17   Baudouin Courtenay, "Narodowa i terytolialna cecha autonomii," pp. 256-259.

18   Baudouin de Courtenay, "W kwestii narodowosciowej," pp. 290-291.

19   Ibid., pp. 259-260.

20   Ibid., p. 304.

21 Baudouin de Courtenay, "Autonomia Polski," *Miejcie odwage myslenia...*, pp. 187-189.

22 Baudouin de Courtenay, " Kwestia Zydowska w Panstwie Polskim," *Miejcie odwage myslenia...*, pp. 330-331.

23 Baudouin de Courtenay, "Narodowa i terytolialna cecha autonomii," pp. 246-247.

24 Baudouin de Courtenay, "Kwestia Zydowska w Panstwie Polskim," pp. 352-353.

25 Baudouin de Courtenay, "W sprawie 'Antysemityzmu postepowego'," pp. 317-318.

26 Ibid.

27 Baudouin de Courtenay, " Kwestia Zydowska w Panstwie Polskim," p. 344.

28 Ibid., p. 323.

29 Ibid., p. 381.

30 Ibid., p. 349.

31 Julian Tuwim, *My Zydzi Polscy* (Warsaw, 1988). English translation quoted from the website of the Montreal Chapter of the Canadian Foundation of Polish-Jewish Heritage, http://www.polish-jewish-heritage.org/eng/rytm_tuwim_eng.htm (accessed January 2020).

Irith Cherniavsky

Residential Living Patterns among the Jews of Warsaw during the Interwar Period

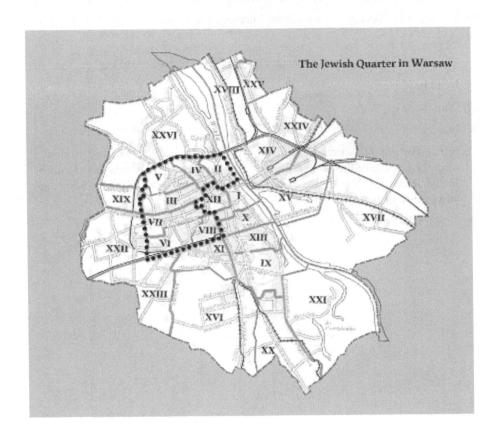

Introduction

We do not want to build our National Home according to the model of Dzika and Nalewki.[1]

Chaim Weizmann, Yitzhak Greenbaum, and many other leaders of the Jewish Yishuv in Palestine were concerned about Jewish Warsaw's possible impact on the building of the future Jewish homeland. Jewish Warsaw has been depicted by writers, scholars, travelers and historians alike, with contemporaries describing primarily its wretchedness and unsightliness, and memoirs tending to remember it with a sense of nostalgia. It is this Warsaw – whose inhabitants were murdered and whose streets and buildings were ultimately razed to the ground, leaving no traces today – that is the topic of the present article. "I relate to a street as a historical, social, and political phenomenon – as an entirety of the material and spiritual aspects that intertwine the fate of buildings and the fate of those living in these buildings," writes Jacek Leociak in the introduction to *Biographies of Jewish Streets in Warsaw*.[2] In this article, I apply the same approach to the city environment and to its material significance.

A significant amount has been written about pre-Holocaust Jewish Warsaw. The research literature has dealt with topics such as the internal politics of the Jewish public, the development of Jewish nationalism, the institutions of the Jewish communities, Jewish literature and the Jewish press, the ultra-Orthodox movements that were active in Warsaw, assimilation, and acculturation. Some writings deal solely with Jewish Warsaw, a few deal with the Jews of Warsaw as part of research on the city as a whole, and others explore Warsaw as part of the research on Polish Jewry. In addition to the research literature, we also have a rich literature of memoir chapters, tourist guides and summations of trips to Warsaw.

Even just a partial reconstruction of the residential housing patterns of the Jews of Warsaw, of the appearance and the atmosphere of the Jewish Quarter, and of the everyday life of its residents shed light on interesting issues that pertain specifically to the Jews of Warsaw but that are also relevant to general issues, such as minority-majority relations, the urban aspect of diverse populations, assimilation and acculturation, national and religious identity, social mobility, social disparities, introversion versus openness, and more.

Pre-Holocaust Warsaw contained the largest concentration of Jews in Europe and the second largest in the world after New York. In 1938, Warsaw was home to 370,000 Jews, accounting for almost one-third of the city's population.

The Jewish population of the city was characterized by a broad diversity of streams, movements and parties: religious, political, social and ideological movements from throughout the entire spectrum, from workers, to artisans, to merchants, to the intelligentsia; the extremely wealthy and the extremely poor; Jews with a Jewish nationalist orientation and the completely assimilated;

Yiddishists, Hebrewists, and Polonists; strict Hassids; and socialists and Communists. These highly varying population groups among the Jews of Warsaw were characterized by varying lifestyles and worldviews.

Residential housing styles and conditions are often among the most central elements of a person's life. The aim of this article is to explore the characteristics of Jewish society in Warsaw and the residential living housing patterns of the city's Jewish population. It also sheds light on this important aspect of the day-to-day life of the Jews of Warsaw prior to the Holocaust. Residential housing patterns reflect the attributes of residents on the one hand, and influence their worldview, their character, and their way of life on the other hand.

The topics examined by this article include: the extent of Jewish segregation and the development, or deterioration, of Jewish identity in the city; the interaction between Jews and Poles and the disparities between the two populations; the tension between nationalism and assimilation and the spread of acculturation throughout the Jewish public; and the economic and social disparities within the Jewish community. These and other issues are explored against the background of an analysis of Warsaw's urban structure and topics such as the role of the Jewish Quarter within the city as a whole, the extent to which the city's Jews were concentrated within this area, the proportion of Jews within the city's population, and the location of the residences of Jews who lived outside of this area. Other issues explored include the residential living conditions of the city's Jews in comparison to those of the inhabitants of the city as a whole, the character of Warsaw during the period in question, and the extent to which these residential housing patterns facilitated the possibility of Jewish integration into the life of the Polish capital.

Ezra Mendelson and Antony Polonski point out that the historiography of Jewish Warsaw, which was written by Jewish researchers, is to a great extent ethnocentric and has ignored the non-Jewish Polish context.[3] One of the goals of this article is to illuminate topics pertaining to Jews in the context of the everyday life of all residents of the city.

Located adjacent to Warsaw's city center, the Jewish Quarter – which occupied a large area of the inner city and to some extent, as we will see below, was part of this center – drew significant attention from city residents and visitors alike. The Jewish Quarter was viewed in different ways, from its perception as a site of cultural backwardness, poverty, and filth that resulted in a hostile attitude toward the neighborhood and its inhabitants, to a romantic and exotic perception of the Jewish "others" who populated it. According to one such description:

> When one enters Nalewki Street, the eye is immediately drawn to a strange, Eastern scented sight of streets, homes, signs, shops, carriages, and wagons – and noise, commotion, tumult, shouting, dirt, and stench…All the inhabitants of the quarter appear to not be residing in their apartments; rather, they can be found with their sheets and their children in the street, where they barter, buy and sell, eat, work, rest, and quarrel incessantly, because all the conversations, whether pertaining to commerce, family, or the declaration of love, sound like stormy altercations, with yelling and foam on the lips, as well as hand motions, twisted faces, and eye rolling. All of this proceeds in guttural cries, quickly and with urgency, as if the world was going to be destroyed at any moment, and there would not be enough time to finish the "*gesheft*" [business deal].[4]

A more favorable description of the Jewish Quarter is offered by an official document of the Warsaw municipality:[5]

> Located beside the cemetery is the liveliest neighborhood in Warsaw: a quarter of small trade and handicraft of many Jewish families. The streets are Dzielna, Gesia, Pawia, Nalewki, Franciszkanska, Mila, Muranowska, and Swietojerska… What traffic. What a pulse of life…Every building is covered with signs, and every courtyard is surrounded by four-story buildings and pulsating with work: ties, wallets, artificial flowers,

containers, bags, haberdashery items…This neighborhood abounds with initiative, ideas, cunning, and work more than other neighborhoods…Rivers of people flow here, and a long chain of freight wagons. The drivers of the cable-cars stuck in the street honk in despair, as stooped laborers carry heavy loads, the veins in their necks almost bursting under the burden… Crowded beside shops with a turnover of millions are wretched shops, and along the sidewalks, at gates, and in courtyards, trade is conducted by peddlers whose entire wealth amounts to five or seven zlotys. Still, there is one day a week on which the tumult of business is silenced: the Sabbath [Saturday]. In the morning the orthodox go to their houses of worship, followed by a short walk and chats with acquaintances in Krasiński Garden. After lunch – a quiet nap, and the benches in the garden are occupied by young romantics. In the winter, when it gets dark early, the shops can still be opened up for a few hours, which is not possible in the summer. Then, a longer walk to Aleje Jerozolimskie, Saski Park, or the new Traugut Park, where youth have been engaged in sports competitions since morning…Anglo-Saxon tourists make haste to visit our "ghetto," but the Jewish Quarter is not a ghetto, which is a symbol of Eastern laziness and filth. It is no worse than the poor non-Jewish neighborhoods.

In the present article, we explore the character of the Jewish Quarter as part of an overall exploration of the city of Warsaw, with an emphasis on urban issues such as building style, infrastructure conditions, transportation, commerce, and the city's administrative, cultural, and economic activity.

The statistical data used here was gleaned primarily from two population censuses, one from 1921 and the other from 1931, and from statistical yearbooks for Warsaw. I also made substantial use of the research literature on Poland and Polish Jewry during the interwar period, and of the extensive memory literature that has been written about Jewish Warsaw.

I. The Jewish Quarter
The Evolution of the Quarter

In the sixteenth century, inhabitants of Warsaw began to settle beyond the walls of the Old City, and the capital was moved there from Krakow. Initially, the city expanded southward to Krakowskie Przedmiescie Street, along which the aristocrats who moved to the new capital built their palaces, which they could not build in the narrow alleyways of the Old City. Over the years, this artery continued to develop southward along Nowy Swiat and Aleje Ujazdowskie streets, with palaces, villas, and magnificent gardens. The city also expanded westward, southward, and northward, and the neighborhood of Praga continued to grow on the right bank of the Vistula River. A dramatic change occurred in Warsaw during World War I, when nearby suburbs and villages were annexed to the city, increasing its territory threefold.

Fig. 1: The borders of Warsaw, before (in gray) and after (in black) 1916.

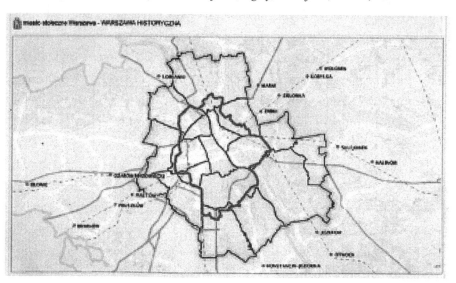

Until the eighteenth century, Jews attempted to settle in Warsaw but were repeatedly expelled. Only from the end of the eighteenth century onward were Jews permitted to settle in specified parts of the city, although the streets on which they were permitted to live changed from time to time. In 1821, the Jews of Warsaw were authorized to build their homes in the city and to register as permanent residents. In 1824, all Jewish residents of the city were directed to move to the area around Nalewki Street and Franciskanska Street, marking the beginning of the evolution of the Jewish Quarter.[6]

As reflected in the Polish meaning of the name, the Nalewki area contained large concentrations of streams, lakes, wells, and marshland and for centuries had constituted a major source of water for Warsaw. Initially, it witnessed the construction of houses and small estates, all of which were Polish owned. In the eighteenth century, the owners of real estate in the area included members of the lower aristocracy, artisans, and merchants. When the area was designated for Jewish settlement, Jews bought many plots. A survey conducted in 1900, which inspected the ownership of homes on 252 streets in Warsaw, found that of the more than 6,000 structures that were surveyed, some 30 percent belonged to Jews. On some streets, most of the homes were owned by Jews. For example, 32 of the 34 homes on Franciskanska Street belonged to Jews, as did 50 of the 65 homes on Gesia Street, 58 of the 69 homes on Mila Street, 44 of the 54 homes on Niska Street, 59 of the 83 homes on Pawia Street, and 46 of the 67 homes on Twarda Street.[7] Jewish merchants and industrialists continued to gradually acquire more properties in the area, and a 1930 ownership register reflects that all the property owners on Nalewki Street at the time had Jewish names. On the other hand, according to the list of owners from 1939, only 62 percent of the home owners on Nalewki Street had Jewish names.[8]

Multistory buildings were constructed on the plots that were purchased, containing apartments for rent. Some of the buildings were planned by the best architects of the day. Over time, the construction became more intensive, and the orchards behind the buildings were replaced by internal courtyards and buildings.

Once people moved into the buildings, the ground floors were used for commercial purposes, including shops and workshops. In the inner buildings, shops, storage facilities, and workshops were opened, transforming some courtyards into commercial streets or squares. The area grew increasingly urban, and the density continued to increase. The demand for commercial space resulted in the opening of additional commercial spaces and workshops on the buildings' upper levels, in courtyards, and in cellars. Nalewki Street and adjacent streets provided a solution for the demand for commercial activity and workshops not only among the Jewish residents of the quarter but for all residents of the city.

At the beginning of the twentieth century, Nalewki Street became part of the commercial artery that crossed Warsaw from north to south; this route focused on elegant Marszałkowska Street and continued to popular Nalewki Street until the massive Simmons' Passage, which was built on the northern section of the street by a German businessman in 1904. This commercial area was considered to constitute the city's Eastern market.[9]

Over the years, Nalewki Street had become the main north-south transportation artery in Warsaw. In 1881, a regular public transportation line of horse-drawn carriages began to operate along the road, and in 1909 a streetcar line began to run. Due to the development of east-west running public transportation lines, Nalewki Street became an important artery on which city transportation ran primarily north-south and east-west. The intersection of Nalewki and Franciskanska streets was the site of the most vehicular traffic in Warsaw (even more than the intersection of Marszałkowska and Aleje Jerozolimskie), with a wide variety of vehicles including streetcars, busses, firefighting vehicles, taxis, carriages, cargo wagons, bicycles, rickshaws, and hand carts used by street merchants to supply merchandise to the narrow inner courtyards.

According to a detailed survey of the businesses on Nalewki Street in 1935, 250 meters of the street contained 700 businesses. The main sectors operating on the street were confectionary and clothing, businesses related to transportation and freight shipment, a few branches of city-wide commercial chains and trading houses, 15 restaurants, hostels and hotels, clinics, law offices, pharmacies, and food shops.[10]

Demarcation of the Jewish Quarter

In 1938, Warsaw's Jewish population numbered 369,332, accounting for approximately 30 percent of the city's total population. Almost 297,000 (80 percent) of them lived in seven adjacent police precincts in the northwestern inner city, and the remaining 20 percent lived in much lower concentrations in other parts of Warsaw.

Table 1. Warsaw police precincts in which Jewish majorities lived, 1938.

Police Precinct	Total Population	Jewish Population	Percentage of all Jews in Warsaw	Percentage of Jews in Precinct
II	49,167	18,388	5.0	37.4
III	94,579	54,383	14.7	57.5
IV	63,929	57,856	15.7	90.5
V	94,898	72,312	19.6	76.2
VI	69,055	18,645	5.0	27
VII	98,727	38,306	10.4	38.8
VIII	69,278	36,717	9.9	53
Total	539,633	296,608	80.3	55.0

Source: Table 1 of Appendix.

In this area, which I refer to as the Jewish Quarter,[11] Jews composed 55 percent of the population. The precinct with the highest percentage of Jews was precinct IV, whose residents were 90 percent Jewish. In precinct V, Jews constituted three-quarters of the overall population, and in the other precincts they made up between one-third and one-half of the local population.

Fig. 2. The Jewish Quarter in Warsaw.

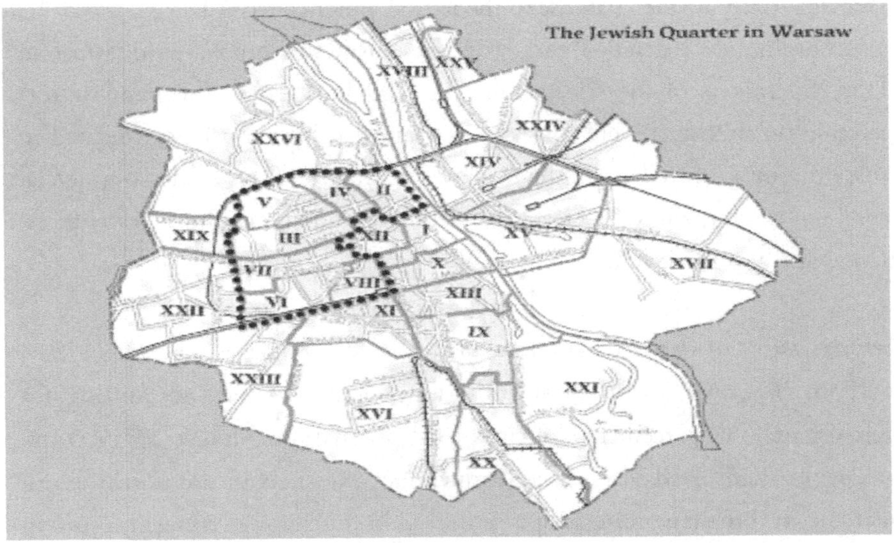

Source: Table 1 in Appendix.

A more detailed view of the concentration of Jews in specific residential areas can be achieved through an analysis of the data by statistical area, as reflected in Table 2.

Table 2. The Jews in the Jewish Quarter by statistical area, 1938.

Police Precinct	Statistical Area	Percentage of Jews	Number of Jews
II	39+41	15	14,658
	40	68	1,853
	42	13	1,882
III	28	79	41,468
	29	38	11,644
	30	8	927
	35+36	88	18,346
IV	37	92	20,952
	38	91	18,581
	31	20	1,375
	32	76	20,761
V	33	91	23,367
	34	76	26,826
	22	53	8,277
	23	23	10,032
VI	24	2	132
	24a	6	205
	25	62	27,520
VII	26	21	6,000
	27	16	4,265
VIII	19	37	8,447
	20	74	20,256
	21	41	8,000

Source: Rocznik Statystyczny Warszawy, 1936-1937 (GUS, 1938), pp. 126-127.[12]

The areas in which the percentage of Jews exceeded half the population had a total population of 228,000 Jews, accounting for 62 percent of all the Jews in the city. The areas in which Jews constituted between 20 and 50 percent of the population contained approximately 45,000 Jews (12 percent of the Jews of the city). A number of statistical areas on the edges of the Jewish Quarter had a combined Jewish population of approximately 22,000 (six percent of the Jews of the city).

Fig. 3. The concentration of Jews in the Jewish Quarter.

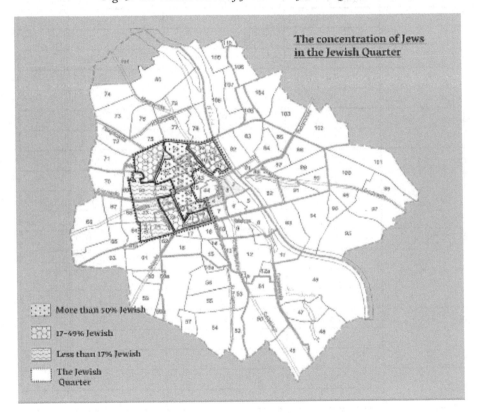

As reflected in Fig, 3, the Jews of Warsaw lived primarily in the eastern section of the Jewish Quarter, whereas the western section of the quarter, beyond Okopowa Street, was home to a relatively small number of inhabitants in general, and a low percentage of Jews in particular.

Jewish Residences outside the Jewish Quarter

Twenty percent of the Jews of Warsaw lived outside the Jewish Quarter, as defined above. Even before Jews were allowed to settle in Warsaw, they settled in

Praga, the neighborhood located west of the Vistula, where they were permitted to do so. Merchants who were not permitted to set up their businesses on the Left Bank of the Vistula established both them and their residences in Praga. Praga initially consisted of small wooden buildings, the population density of which continued to increase over the years, as two or three families crowded into one small apartment. In addition, the area suffered from litter and neglect. As time passed, the wooden buildings were replaced by brick houses, and Praga attracted large numbers of merchants and artisans, Jews and non-Jews alike.[13] In 1938, Praga was home to six percent of the Jews in the city.

During that year, three percent of the Jews of Warsaw lived in police precinct XII, which was located beside the Jewish Quarter. This precinct was ranked highly in terms of socioeconomic and physical factors alike.[14] Another 11 percent of Warsaw's Jews lived distributed throughout the rest of the city in low concentrations.

II. The Residential Housing Conditions of Jews and Non-Jews in Warsaw

Below, I examine all the neighborhoods in Warsaw according to the socio-economic status of their residents and the nature of the buildings and their infrastructure.[15] In 1931, approximately 70 percent of the homes in Warsaw were made of brick, whereas most other homes were made of wood. Only 17 percent of the buildings had four or more storeys, as opposed to 37 with one storey and 46 percent with two to three storeys. By that year, the city's infrastructure had not yet been developed at a level suitable for a big city: more than 30 percent of the homes had no electricity, almost 40 percent had no running water, and more than 50 were not connected to the sewage system.

The average residential density in Warsaw was 2.2 persons per room (the number of rooms included kitchens – in other words, a studio apartment with a kitchen housed 4-5 people on average). More than 40 percent of the apartments consisted of one room, and only 16 percent were large apartments with four or more rooms. More than half of the apartments in Warsaw housed more than one family.[16]

Ten percent of the residents of Warsaw aged ten and older were illiterate, and only 16 percent of those employed were white-collar workers. Also notable was the fact that 6 percent of the households employed domestic help of some kind. The infant mortality rate stood at 10 percent of all births, and approximately 16 percent of all deaths were caused by tuberculosis.

Below is the city's division into three areas based on the socio-economic status of their residents and the physical condition of the buildings in which they lived.

Fig. 4. Warsaw's division into three levels of physical conditions, infrastructure, and the socio-economic status of the residents.

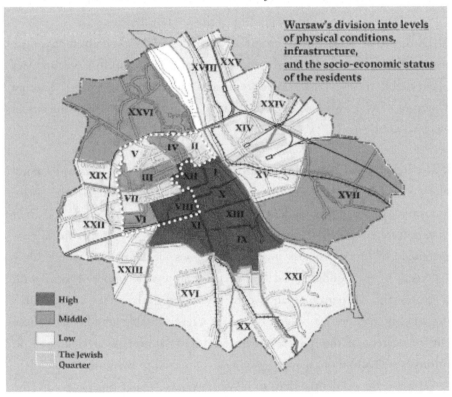

Source: Tables 2 and 3 of the Appendix.

a. The Area Containing the Population of the Highest Socio-Economic Status

This area consisted of police precincts 1, VIII, IX, X, XI, XII, and XIII and included the central part of the inner-city. It was characterized by low residential density, a high percentage of apartments with four or more rooms, and a relatively low percentage of studio apartments. It also had a low infant mortality rate, a very low illiteracy rate, and a high percentage of white-collar workers and live-in domestic help.

More than 90 percent of the homes in this area were made of brick. In addition, the percentage of homes connected to electricity and to running water stood at approximately 80-90 percent, and the percentage of homes connected to the sewage system was also higher than the city-wide average, ranging from 70-90 percent. The high level of this area is indicated by the fact that most of the diplomatic missions in Warsaw, which naturally located themselves in the "best" parts of the capital city, were located there, as reflected in the following figure.

Fig. 5. Location of diplomatic missions in Warsaw, 1939.

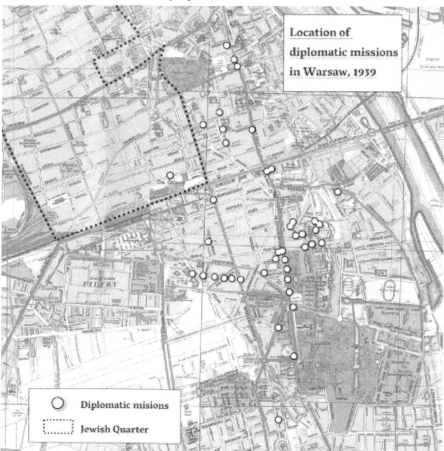

Source: Warsaw telephone book, 1939.

In 1938, 18 percent of the Jews of Warsaw lived in this area, 10 percent lived in the Jewish Quarter (in precinct VIII), and 8 percent lived elsewhere in the city.

b. The Area with a Middle Socio-Economic Population

This area consisted of five police precincts in the inner-city – precincts II, III, IV, VI, and XIV – and two precincts located on the edges of the city – XVII in south Praga and XXVI in northwest Warsaw. The socio-economic characteristics of the residents of these precincts were comparable to the city average, with an infant mortality rate of 7-11 percent; an illiteracy rate of 9-11 percent; a housing density of 2.2-2.5 persons per room; a high percentage of brick houses; a high percentage of buildings connected to running water and electricity (80-90 percent); and a high percentage of buildings connected to the sewage system (65-85 percent). The area was home to 42 percent of the Jews of Warsaw, almost all of whom lived within the confines of the Jewish Quarter.

c. The Area with the Population of the Lowest Socio-Economic Status

This area contained precincts II (the Old City), V, and VII in the inner-city, as well as most of the new areas that had been added to the city. The housing density in these precincts was higher than average (2.4-3.5 persons per room), the percentage of large apartments was low (5-12 percent, in comparison to 16 percent on average), high infant mortality and illiteracy rates, and a low percentage of white-collar workers. The hardest situation existed in precinct V, which was home to approximately 20 percent of the Jews of Warsaw and had an infant mortality rate of 13.7 percent, the highest in the city. It also had an illiteracy rate of almost 19 percent, in comparison to a city-wide average of 10 percent, and a low percentage of white-collar workers – 5 percent, in comparison to a city-wide average of 16 percent. In 1938, it was the area containing the population with the lowest socio-economic status in Warsaw and was home to 39 percent of the city's Jews. Most lived in the Jewish Quarter, and a minority of only 5 percent lived in the peripheral neighborhoods.

Comparing the distribution of Jewish and non-Jewish residences among the lowest and the highest level neighborhoods yields an interesting finding: a similar percentage (around 40 percent) of both populations lived in the city's poorest areas.

In contrast, only 18 percent of the Jews lived in the prestigious neighborhoods, as opposed to 30 percent of the non-Jews who lived in this area. Ten percent of the Jews of Warsaw who lived in the city's highest-level neighborhoods lived in police precinct VIII, which is included in my demarcation of the Jewish Quarter. Three percent lived in precinct XII beside the Jewish Quarter, meaning that only 5 percent of the Jews in the city lived in the prestigious neighborhoods that were located further away. It is reasonable to assume that many of those who were capable of moving to the more prestigious parts of Warsaw declined to do so and preferred to live in the Jewish Quarter, or at least in close proximity to their co-religionists who lived there.

d. The Socio-Economic and Physical Characteristics of the Jewish Quarter and its Inhabitants

The following tables present the socio-economic characteristics of the residents of the Jewish Quarter and the physical characteristics of the police precincts in the Jewish Quarter.

Table 3. Economic and social characteristics of the inhabitants of the Jewish Quarter, 1931.

Police Precinct	Jews in Pop. of Police Precinct (%)	Infant Mortality[17]	Deaths from Tuberculosis[18]	Illiteracy (%)	White-Collar Workers (%)	Those Working in their Homes (%)	No. of Persons per Room
II	37.4	7.4	15.9	10.9	12	4.5	3.5
III	57.5	9.9	14	10.8	12	4.1	3.3
IV	90.5	8.8	8.8	9.8	8	6.3	3.3
V	76.2	13.7	17	18.7	5	6	4.3
VI	27	6.9	16.1	10.5	13	1.7	3.5
VII	38.8	10	15.5	11.2	13	2.2	3.3
VIII	53	6.5	12	7.7	17	2.5	2.7
Avg. for Above Police Precincts[19]	52	9.3	14.4	11.6	11.3	3.8	3.4
All of Warsaw	30	9.4	16	10	16	2.3	3.1

Source: Table 2 in the Appendix.

According to most measures, the socio-economic situation of residents of the Jewish Quarter (Jews and non-Jews alike) was somewhat inferior to that of the overall population of Warsaw: the housing density was higher than the citywide average, the percentage of residents who worked in residential apartments was high in comparison to the city as a whole, and the percentage of white-collar workers was much lower than the citywide average. The infant mortality rate was comparable to that of the city as a whole, but the rate of death from tuberculosis was below average for Warsaw. All of this pertains to all residents of the Jewish Quarter, Jews and non-Jews alike. The lion's share of the Poles who lived in the precincts which I included in the Jewish Quarter lived in its western portion, which was known to be extremely poor. We can therefore conclude that the socio-economic situation of the Jewish residents of the Jewish Quarter was comparable to that of the overall population. This is supported by a study on dietary nutrition in Warsaw prior to World War II, which found that notwithstanding religious differences, the socio-economic level of Jews and Poles in this dietary area were similar.[20]

Table 4. The physical characteristics of the Jewish Quarter, 1931.

Police Precinct	Jews in Precinct (%)	Stone Buildings (%)	Apartments Connected to Sewage System (%)	Apartments with Running Water (%)	Apartments Connected to Electricity (%)	Apartments in One-Story Buildings (%)	Apartments in Buildings with Four Stories or More (%)
II	37.4	93	79	88	82	15	24
III	57.5	83	65	78	80	25	29
IV	90.5	94	84	90	90	10	36
V	76.2	80	60	79	80	21	32
VI	27	81	64	79	79	25	28
VII	38.8	88	68	83	86	21	30
VIII	53	98	92	95	96	6	38
Average for Above Police Precincts[21]	52	87	72	84	84	18	31
All of Warsaw	30	69	46	62	68	37	17

Source: Table 3 in the Appendix.

As most Jews of Warsaw lived in the old inner-city area, the character of the Jewish Quarter was distinctly urban: most of the buildings were made of brick and a large majority of them were multi-story buildings, with only a small number of single story structures. The average level of city infrastructure (water, sewage, and electricity) in the Jewish Quarter was relatively high in comparison to the citywide average, primarily as a result of deficient urban development in the city's newer neighborhoods. Nonetheless, the situation in large parts of the Jewish Quarter was extremely poor.

IV. Social Disparities in the Jewish Quarter

We learn more about the economic disparities within the Jewish Quarter from a ranking of the police precincts in Warsaw based on physical and socio-economic parameters.

Diagram 1. Ranking of police precincts according to socio-economic situation. *

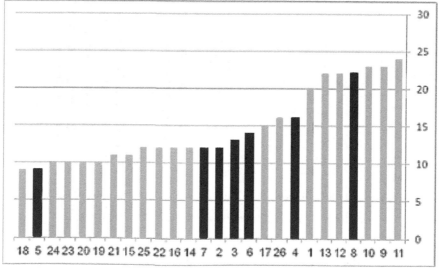

   * *X-axis: number of police precinct; Y-axis: ranking of socio-economic situation (in black: precincts in the Jewish Quarter). Source: Table 2 in the Appendix.*

We can point to a marked disparity in the socio-economic level of the residents of the Jewish Quarter. The precinct with the lowest socio-economic level in the city was precinct V, which was home to 20 percent of the Jews of Warsaw, with a population that was more than three-quarters Jewish. As noted, this precinct was characterized by high infant mortality and illiteracy rates, high residential density, and a low percentage of white-collar workers. Precinct VIII, on the other hand, which was home to 10 percent of the Jews of Warsaw and had a population that was approximately half Jewish, was ranked highest among the precincts of the Jewish Quarter and had relatively low infant mortality and illiteracy rates, low residential density, and a relatively high percentage of white-collar workers.

A ranking of all the police precincts according to physical condition and the location of the precincts of the Jewish Quarter among them reveals a slightly different picture:

Diagram 2. Ranking of the 26 police precincts, based on physical conditions. *

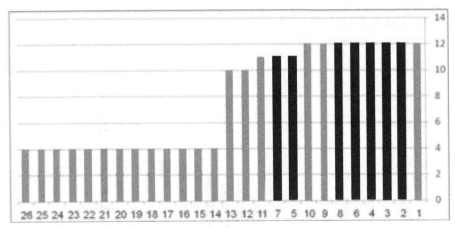

* *X-axis: number of police precinct; Y-axis: socio-economic situation (in black:*
the precincts in the Jewish Quarter).Source: Table 3 in the Appendix.

The Jewish Quarter was part of Warsaw's old urban area. Therefore, the physical state of the buildings and the condition of the urban infrastructure in the quarter was medium-to-high, primarily due to the poor state of the urban infrastructure and the buildings in some parts of the city that had been annexed to the city in 1916. The poorest physical conditions in the Jewish Quarter were found in precincts V and VII: 40 percent of the homes in these precincts were not connected to the sewage system, and 20 percent had neither electricity nor running water. The city infrastructure in the other police precincts in the Jewish Quarter was relatively good.

I have already noted the socio-economic disparities among the inhabitants of the Jewish Quarter, which found geographical expression in the differences between the police precincts in the quarter. Due to the limitations of the statistical data, the picture they provide is only partial. Socio-economic differences were also notable among the locations of buildings in the Jewish Quarter and even on the same street. With regard to east-west running streets, the farther west one went, the worse the conditions were. Below, I will also show that marked class disparities existed within every building and every courtyard: the wealthy and distinguished lived in the apartments at the front of the buildings, and the others lived in the inner apartments. The poorest residents lived in the cellars and the attics of the very same buildings.

IV. Jews and Non-Jews in the Jewish Quarter

No statistical area in the Jewish Quarter was inhabited exclusively by Jews. The most "Jewish" area – statistical areas 35, 36, and 37 – were 88-92 percent Jewish. In the other areas, the Jews constituted a smaller majority. The non-Jews residing in this part of Warsaw were Poles with one of the lowest socio-economic statuses in the city. Other non-Jews living in the Jewish Quarter were housekeepers, wet-nurses, and nannies residing with Jewish families, and the families of the gatekeepers, who played a major role in the Jewish Quarter.

For example, the family of Bernard Singer employed a nanny for their youngest child and a teacher (*Guwernantka*) for their older children. Both women lived with the family. The teacher enjoyed a higher status than the nanny, as reflected in the fact that she was permitted to dine with the family.[22] The servants were of course not permitted to dine with the family, and they worked extremely hard from early morning to nightfall. They were allowed to leave only once in two weeks, on Sunday afternoon. Cooking was a serious problem due to the requirements of Kashrut. Therefore, many servants engaged only in cleaning and in outings with the children and were therefore paid less than those who were also permitted to cook. Wet-nurses, who enjoyed a higher status than servants, were usually unmarried women who, after an unwanted pregnancy, hired themselves out as wet-nurses in the big city. According to Singer, "no one asked about or took an interest in what happened to their natural, unwanted children."[23]

The servants were referred to the homes of their employers by agents who specialized in this sector. As a result of the impoverishment of the Polish village, there was no shortage of this source of labor, which was so inexpensive that even a Jewish family on the verge of poverty could afford to employ them.[24] Most of the servants were teenage girls from poor homes in villages in search of a brighter future in the big city.

An important figure in pre-Holocaust Warsaw that is mentioned in all the memoirs of contemporaries of the time was that of the gatekeeper, who was never a Jew. The gatekeeper lived with his family in the ground-floor apartment of the building or beside the entrance to the building. Only the gatekeeper had the keys to the building, which enabled him to get to know the leisure and nighttime habits of its residents. The gatekeepers had a good knowledge of the Jewish holidays, and they sometimes also spoke Yiddish. They were paid additional wages – Friday wages – by residents for performing tasks that could not be performed by Jews on Saturday, the Jewish Sabbath.

V. The Jewish Residences in the Prestigious Neighborhoods of Warsaw

Some of the wealthy Jews of Warsaw, and some members of the Jewish intelligentsia in the city, did not live in the Jewish Quarter but rather in the most prestigious parts of the city. Three percent of the city's Jews lived in precinct XII, which was located next to the Jewish Quarter. According to the testimony of Lilly Goldenberg, one of the few Jews who managed to immigrate to Palestine after September 1939 and the wife of actor Eliyahu Goldenberg, the elite of the Jewish community in Warsaw lived in a small part of this precinct, which was one of the precincts with residents of the highest socio-economic status in the city. The Jews lived primarily on Leszno, Bielanska, Rymarska, and Tlomacki streets, among a majority of non-Jewish neighbors. In this neighborhood, Wierzbowa Street was the most prestigious. It had a promenade with grand display windows, elegant restaurants, cafés, and movie theaters.[25]

Lilly's father was the general manager of the Great Synagogue on Tlomacki Street, the grandest synagogue in Warsaw. When he was appointed to this position, her family moved from the Polish section of Warsaw (on Wilcza Street in precinct XI, which was also one of the most prestigious neighborhoods in Warsaw) into the service building located next to the synagogue. Lilly described her home at the synagogue site on Tlomacki Street as follows:

The service building had three storeys, and its residents were distributed within it according to their position and status. The beadles and junior officials lived on the ground floor in small apartments. The upper floor was "musical," providing the residences of the two cantors: the well-known chief cantor Moshe Koussevitzky and his colleague Pinhas Sherman. This floor also held the apartment of David Ayzenshtat, the conductor of the choir. His daughter Marysia had an extremely beautiful voice, and her singing could be heard throughout the courtyard in the afternoons when she practiced her vocal training. Later, after the Germans occupied Warsaw and the Jews were moved into the ghetto, Marysia provided the residents with moments of comfort with her singing, earning herself the nickname "nightingale of the ghetto." The middle floor – that is, the first floor – had only two apartments: our apartment, which had three rooms, and the apartment of the chief rabbi of the Jews of Warsaw and the rabbi of the synagogue, Dr. Moshe Schorr, across from us. On the front door of his seven-room apartment hung a sign that read: "Rabbi Prof. Dr. Moshe Schorr." Both our apartment and their apartment had two entrances – one for servants, peddlers, and children coming home dirty from playing in the courtyard, and the other for the masters and their guests…In our courtyard, importance was assigned to the question of who was friendly with whom, who greeted whom first, and who invited whom into their home…The word "unfitting" was an important word in the context of relations and conduct in that house. It was "unfitting" to travel on public transportation on the Sabbath and "unfitting" to play the piano on the Sabbath or to play in the yard with the wife of the beadle who sat there for days on end making pretty handcrafts. It was also "unfitting" to have "balcony conversations" between the apartments. However, what bothered me most of all was the fact that it was "unfitting" for my father's daughter to come home after ten o'clock at night, which was when the gate was locked out of concern regarding "what would the gatekeeper think?"[26]

Another example of a Jewish family living in the prestigious section of Warsaw
was Dr. Mieczyslaw Glass and his son Jurek, who lived at 72 Marszałkowska
Street (police precinct XIII). Although their apartment served as a clinic, it was
a large unit with seven rooms in the most elegant part of the city.[27]

72 Marszalkowska Street

Another Jew, a wealthy wholesaler named Salomon Graff whose iron business
was based at 10 Grzybowska Street in the Jewish Quarter (police precinct VII),
was also the owner of a number of residential buildings in Warsaw, including in
the most prestigious parts of the city. A few years before the outbreak of World
War II, Graf built a stately apartment building at 7 Aleje Roz (police precinct 9).
It was the residential location of the elite of Warsaw, and Graff and his family
moved into one of the apartments in the building. One of the other apartments
was given to Graff's son, who was an attorney. Other apartments were rented to
a Polish engineer, the son of a wealthy industrialist, and a scion of a family of
the lower aristocracy. When the ghetto was established, Solomon Graff and the
members of their families were forced to return to their apartments in the ghetto.

7 Aleje Roz

VI. The Jewish Quarter's Location in Warsaw

A residential area's location in a city is of great importance. Close proximity to centers of urban activity provide residents with opportunities for diverse human encounters, access to cultural, leisure, and entertainment centers, and a rich supply of places of employment and commercial centers. A residential area can be part of the city center or located beside it or far away from it; this determines its urban or suburban character and has an impact on the lifestyle of its residents. Below, I examine the relationship between the location of the Jewish Quarter in Warsaw and the location of the centers of urban activity in the city.

Warsaw's central business district (CBD) at the time was bounded by the following streets: Nowy Swiat, Krakowskie Przedmiescie, Plac Krasinskich, Bielanska, Plac Bankowy, Marszalkowska, Aleje Jerozolimskie, and Miodowa. It was within this area that the city's businesses, offices, commercial representatives, financial institutions, restaurants, hotels, and cultural and entertainment centers were located. North of this center was the business center of the Jewish Quarter, which contained commerce, handicrafts, wholesale enterprises, restaurants, and transportation centers that served the Jews of the city and, to some extent, also the Polish residents of the capital.[28] On this basis, we can say that, on the one hand, the Jewish Quarter was located next to the central business district and that, on the other hand, it was a northward extension of this district.

Fig. 6. The Jewish Quarter and Warsaw's Central Business District.

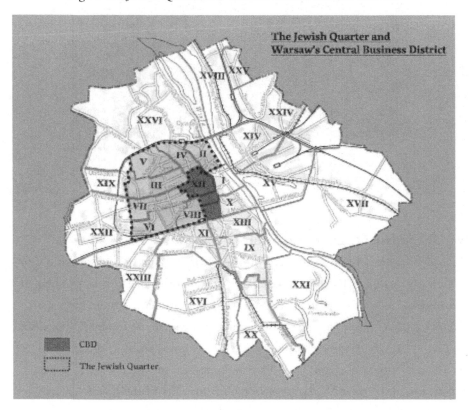

The Jewish Quarter's location adjacent to Warsaw's central business district presented the city's Jews with the opportunity to take part in all the city had to offer in terms of childhood education, higher education, culture, and entertainment. It also resulted in interaction between the Jewish and the Polish populations. The extent of the development of this interaction was dependent on the willingness of both populations to open up to one another. At the same time, regardless of this willingness, the fact that the Jewish Quarter was located adjacent to the center of artistic and intellectual activity in the city facilitated the personal development of residents of the quarter. One example of this dynamic is reflected in the life story of Shalom Rosenberg, the son of a very poor family whose father was a cobbler. The family lived in a small room above the father's workshop, and as a result of the family's inability to pay the tuition fees required, Shalom was forced to discontinue his studies at a *heder*. He signed up at the local library and later enrolled in night school. Over time, following in the footsteps of his big brother who was a laborer, he gravitated toward the literary circles in Warsaw, which at the time included Isaac Bashevis Singer. Shalom used his first wages to buy a ticket to a concert, after which it was "as if he was born again." In later years, his friends included Marek Edelman, Yosl Bergner, and other members of the literary and artistic circles among the Jews of Warsaw.[29] The Quarter's immediate proximity to the cultural center of Warsaw and the residential proximity to members of the other social classes within the quarter undoubtedly helped this son of a poverty stricken family find his place within the city's cultural and political elite.

VII. The Development and the Spread of the Jewish Population, 1921-1938

Under the Warsaw Borders Order of 1916, police precincts XVI-XXVI were annexed to the city. In the following analysis, we distinguish between the inner city (police precincts I-XV) and the peripheral neighborhoods (police precincts XVI-XXVI). The 1930s in particular witnessed the development of residences in the new neighborhoods in the periphery, at the initiative of cooperatives, workers' housing companies, state workers unions, and the like. These projects were almost completely inaccessible to Jews. On the other hand, we know of no organizational efforts of Jews to build residences in the new neighborhoods. During these years, the population of the inner city decreased by 4,000 people, and the population of the new neighborhoods increased by 98,000. As a result of these processes, during the two decades between World War I and World War II, the proportion of the population of the older neighborhoods decreased from 86 percent of the city's total population (1921) to 73 percent (1938).

Table 5. The population of Warsaw in 1921, 1931, and 1938.

	Population (in thousands)			Distribution (as percentage)		
Year	1921	1931	1938	1921	1931	1938
Total	1,745	2,095	2,185	100.0	100.0	100.0
Old Neighborhoods	807.9	923.6	919.6	86.2	78.8	72.7
New Neighborhoods	128.8	247.8	345.8	13.8	21.2	27.3

These were processes that characterized the general population of Warsaw. The picture of the situation of the Jews that emerges, however, is altogether different. The development of the spread of the Jewish and the non-Jewish population is indicative of a marked difference between the two populations. Between 1921 and 1938, the percentage of the non-Jewish residents of the city living in the new neighborhoods increased from 19 to 37 percent, and only a small number of Jews moved into these neighborhoods. As a result, the proportion of Jews within the population of the neighborhoods of the periphery went unchanged, as reflected in the following figure.

Fig. 7. Distribution of Jews and non-Jews in Warsaw (as percentage) among the old and new neighborhoods, 1921 and 1938.

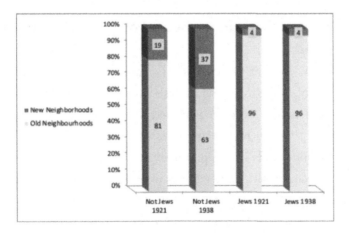

This resulted in an increasing residential density in the Jewish Quarter. The most crowded area was in police precinct V, which was home to the poorest population in the city. The number of Jews in this precinct increased from 52,400 in 1921 to 72,300 in 1938, and the proportion of Jews rose from 71 to 76 percent (respectively). On the other hand, precinct VIII, which had the highest socio-economic status in the Jewish Quarter, was home to only 400 Jews.

Fig. 8. Changes in the proportion of Jews within the general population
(percentage of change), 1931-1938.

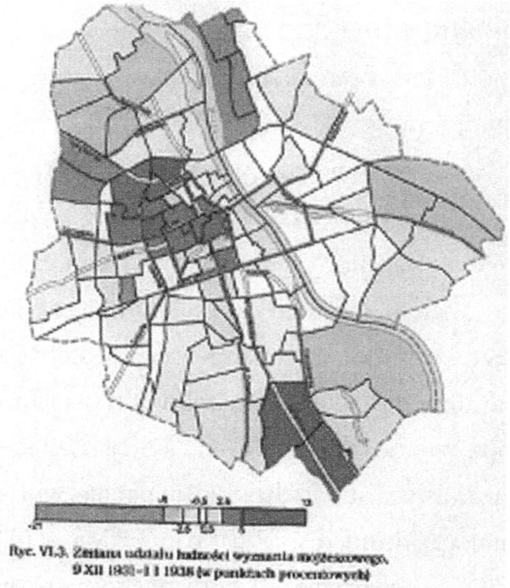

Ryc. VI.3. Zmiana udziału ludności wyznania mojżeszowego,
9 XII 1931–1 I 1938 (w punktach procentowych)

Source: Andrzej, Gawryszewski, Ludnosc Warszawy wXX Wieku,
(Polish Academy of Sciences, 2009), p. 199.

The population density per unit of land in the Jewish Quarter stood at around fifty persons per dunam, although in some statistical areas it reached 100 or even 200 persons per dunam.[30] This density, and the terrible sanitation conditions that existed in part of the Jewish Quarter, have been described as follows: "These people live in the worst sanitary conditions. They are crowded in suffocating conditions and in filth. Many of them are ill…They live in wet, crowded holes and in cellars and in attics. Up to 12 people live in a single room."[31] The workshops increased the crowding problem and the need to engage in work in residential apartments (*Chalupnictwo*) a phenomenon that was widespread among Jews and had a detrimental impact on the quality of residences in Warsaw. Its incidence in the Jewish Quarter accounted for almost 70 percent of the scope of the phenomenon in Warsaw as a whole.

A partial answer to the question of why the Jews of Warsaw dealt differently with the issue of housing than other residents of the city emerges from an examination of the processes of assimilation and acculturation that were underway in Jewish society during the period in question.

Assimilation and Acculturation

The term "assimilation" has been assigned many definitions and meanings. To examine assimilation among the Jews of Warsaw, I employ the definition of the term offered by Gershom Scholem, whose discussion of the assimilation of German Jewry distinguished between assimilation and acculturation, which can be translated as "Germanization" in the German context and "Polonization" in the Polish context. Shalom regarded assimilation as the lifestyle of Jews who had completely severed their ties to Judaism or even converted to Christianity, representing complete and conscious assimilation and detachment from all Jewish elements. Acculturation, on the other hand, was a process of identification with the cultural values of the majority group in the state, in parallel with partial continuation of Jewish tradition and a continued spiritual connection with the Jewish world.[32] These definitions fit the "ideal profile" of both phenomena but are spanned by a continuum of lifestyles and worldviews that differ from person to person and that also change within the same person over time. Both processes were in play among the Jews of Warsaw in the 1920s and 1930s.

These definitions enable us to conclude that the phenomenon that was characteristic of the Jews of Poland during the interwar period was primarily one of acculturation, that only a small portion of the Jews of Warsaw aspired to assimilate, and that the numbers of these Jews continued to decrease throughout the period.

Polonization intensified among the Jews of Warsaw during the interwar period. The primary factor contributing to this phenomenon was the Polish-language education system, which was then being chosen by an increasing number of Jews. Polonization, then, was manifested in Jews' increasing mastery of the Polish language and sense of close ties to the universal culture to which the Jews of Warsaw were exposed, due, among other reasons, to the location of the Jewish Quarter. Still, most of the Jews who experienced Polish acculturation did not adopt an assimilatory worldview and did not advocate full incorporation into the Polish nation.

The assimilatory worldview was embraced by a small group of Jews – most of whom belonged to the wealthy circles or members of the intelligentsia – who viewed social, cultural, and political assimilation into Polish society as a path to a favorable future life for Polish Jews, and who called for the complete integration of Jews into the state and Polish society. This group accounted for a small minority of the Jews of Warsaw, and their ideology was rejected by broad circles within the city's Jewish community. And so, despite the proximity of their residences and the economic interaction between them, the mental distance between the Jewish and the Polish populations of the city remained.

The two populations established separate religious, cultural, and economic organizations, and in addition to the religious disparities, the city also witnessed the development of separate activity in realms such as employment, trade, artisanship, and banking.[33] The mental distance between the two populations is reflected, among other things, in the separate existence of all the artisan and merchant organizations among Jews and Poles.[34] The social separation between Jews and Poles in Warsaw was even manifested in the entertainment venues of the street gangs of both populations. The Jewish youth gangs met up primarily in Saxon Garden and the streets adjacent to it, whereas the Polish youth gangs, whose overall conduct did not differ from that of the Jewish gangs, tended to gather on Aleje Ujazdowskie and Aleje Trzeciego Maja.[35]

The mental distance between the populations and the mutual lack of desire to mix with one another were undoubtedly factors in the increasing concentration of Jewish residences in and in close proximity to the Jewish Quarter.

VIII. The Courtyards of Warsaw

The courtyard was the center of life in the Jewish Quarter. A typical residential building in Warsaw was a multi-story block surrounding, on all four sides, an internal courtyard that was entered through a gate facing the street. Each block had a unique courtyard. During the day, the courtyards could usually be accessed freely and were entered by peddlers, artisans, street singers, organ grinders, and beggars. The visitors proclaimed their wares in booming voices, resulting in a great deal of noise.

Every block was run by a guard, whose job it was, among other things, to clean the sidewalk and the street that ran around the block, to clean the

bagels came out of the oven. The residents of the courtyard were the first customers, who could not pass up the bagels that had just been baked. On the whole, the neighbors lived peacefully with one another, and when conflicts did arise, they did not last long – at the latest, they would be resolved on the following Yom Kippur (Jewish Day of Atonement).[43]

In these courtyards, "everyone knows their neighbor's apartment... They converse via the windows and the balconies, like one big family."[44]

Conclusion

Eighty percent of the Jews of Warsaw resided in the area that this article defines as the Jewish Quarter of the city. Another small concentration of Jews lived in the neighborhood of Praga, on the right bank of the Vistula. Only approximately ten percent of the city's Jewish residents lived dispersed throughout other parts of the city. In the Jewish Quarter, the Jews constituted a majority of just over 50 percent. Even the most Jewish part of Warsaw, Neleviki Street and the surrounding area, was not exclusively Jewish, and even there, ten percent of the inhabitants were Polish. On the one hand, then, the Jews of Warsaw were not isolated from the Polish population and engaged in daily interaction with them, in the markets, in places of employment, and in residential areas. On the other hand, they chose to live in immediate proximity to their fellow Jews. The high concentration of Jews in the Jewish Quarter not only did not decline over the years but rather intensified, in complete contrast to the Poles' trend of geographical dispersion during the period in question. As a result, the residential density of the Jews living in the Jewish Quarter continued to increase, and the most severe crowding could be found in police precinct V, which was home to the city's poorest population. Consequently, the residential living conditions of the Jews of Warsaw continued to decline during the two decades that elapsed between the two world wars.

Integration between any two populations can find expression in residential mixing. The residential pattern in Warsaw, and particularly the fact that Jews refrained from moving out of the Jewish Quarter, is indicative of a low level of integration between Jews and Poles, although the day-to-day relations between the two populations could have encouraged integration and even assimilation. But this is not what occurred. This can be explained by a number of factors, such as the Polish unwillingness to accept Jews in their midst, the Jewish unwillingness to mix with the non-Jewish population, the dominant national identification among both populations, the high percentage of religious Jews, whose lifestyles required them to live in a Jewish area, and the like. All of these factors contributed to the mental distance between the two populations.

An examination of the situation of the overall residents of the Jewish Quarter in Warsaw indicates that only 18 percent of the Jews of the city lived in a police precinct of the highest socio-economic level, as opposed to 30 percent of the non-Jews who lived in these areas. The police precincts in which the socio-economic condition of the overall population was medium were home to 42 percent of the Jews of Warsaw, and 39 percent of the Jews of Warsaw lived in the lowest-level police precincts. Based on most of the parameters, the socio-economic situation of the overall population of the Jewish Quarter (Jews and non-Jews alike) was worse than that of the overall population of the city as a whole.[45] As the Poles who lived in the Jewish Quarter belonged to the lowest strata in the city, we can assume that the socio-economic situation of the Jews of Warsaw was comparable to the average situation among the city's Polish population. Still, the percentage of those who belonged to the highest socio-economic strata was lower among Jews than among Poles.

Marked disparities were found among the police precincts in the Jewish Quarter. Police precinct V – the area of Gesia, Mila, and Smocza streets – received the lowest socio-economic ranking of all the precincts in Warsaw. At the other end of the spectrum, precinct VIII – the area of Zlota, Sliska, and Grzybowska streets – was one of the highest ranking precincts in the city. Nonetheless, both precincts contained a variety of representatives of different groups: Hassidic centers were scattered throughout the quarter, and in many courtyards members of the economic elite, the poor, merchants, Zionists, socialists, and members of the underworld lived side by side as neighbors. In terms of residential location within the Jewish Quarter, no clear separation was established between the different population groups.

The Jewish Quarter in Warsaw was located beside the city's cultural and government center and was part of the city's commercial district. Its location presented residents of the Quarter with the opportunity to be involved in the cultural life of the city.

Appendix

Table 1. The Jewish and non-Jewish population of Warsaw

PRECINCTS	1921			1931			1938		
	TOTAL POPULATIO	JEWS	NON-JEWS	TOTAL POP.	JEWS	NON-JEWS	TOTAL POP.	JEWS	NON-JEWS
1	39,455	3,409	36,046	42,009	3361	38,648	38,830	3,029	35,801
2	43,805	16,713	27,092	50,879	19131	31,748	49,167	18,388	30,779
3	79,171	45,012	34,159	94,299	50450	43,849	94,579	54,383	40,196
4	51,015	47,507	3,508	62,467	55283	7,184	63,929	57,856	6,073
5	70,871	52,387	18,484	90,127	64711	25,416	94,898	72,312	22,586
6	63,689	18,443	45,246	71,672	19495	52,177	69,055	18,645	50,410
7	84,494	31,371	53,123	98,844	35584	63,260	98,727	38,306	60,421
8	67,447	36,291	31,156	72,168	37816	34,352	69,278	36,717	32,561
9	35,097	1,845	33,252	39,007	2223	36,784	38,507	2,118	36,389
10	45,426	3,818	41,608	47,548	3709	43,839	44,571	3,922	40,649
11	59,336	5,233	54,103	55,875	4358	51,517	53,065	5,413	47,652
12	27,939	11,113	16,826	29,987	11995	17,992	28,380	12,714	15,666
13	54,897	5,096	49,801	59,548	5300	54,248	57,412	5,167	52,245
14	45,425	8,878	36,547	56,659	9349	47,310	58,424	9,231	49,193
15	39,820	11,494	28,326	52,494	12809	39,685	60,792	12,766	48,026
Total Old Neighborhoods	807,887	298,610	509,277	923,583	335,573	588,010	919,614	350,968	568,646
16	24,098	2,154	21,944	38,135	2403	35,732	50,222	2,662	47,560
17	5,791	585	5,206	16,925	948	15,977	42,365	1,695	40,670
18	5,805	931	4,874	7,877	1276	6,601	18,214	1,821	16,393
19	5,800	174	5,626	10,138	375	9,763	12,859	399	12,460
20	10,365	886	9,479	17,573	1142	16,431	21,703	1,259	20,444
21	4,432	773	3,659	7,951	1065	6,886	10,938	1,094	9,844
22	20,344	1,701	18,643	29,091	2211	26,880	30,544	2,382	28,162
23	17,848	2,635	15,213	41,525	4485	37,040	42,644	3,070	39,574
24	11,273	237	11,036	21,497	451	21,046	35,490	994	34,496
25	10,534	337	10,197	14,718	618	14,100	18,005	666	17,339
26	12536	1,311	11,225	42384	2501	39,883	62,774	2,323	60,451
Total Old Neighborhoods	128,826	11,724	117,102	247,814	17475	230,339	345,758	18,364	327,394
Tot. City	936,713	310,334	626,379	1,171,397	353,048	818,349	1,265,372	369,332	896,040

1921 – GUS Pierwszy Powszechny Spis Rzeczypospolitej Polskiej z dnia 30.9.1921.Tom XIV .Podzial Warszawy na Obwody Statystyczne I Komisariaty, pp. 4-7.
1931 – GUS Drugi Powszechny Spis Ludnosci z dnia 9.12.1931, Seria C, Zeszyt 49, pp. 286-287.
1938 – GUS Rocznik Statystyczny Warszawy, 1936-1937, Tab. 24.

Table 2. The physical characteristics of police precincts in Warsaw, 1931.

Precinct	No. of Res. Build.	No. of Stone Build.	No. of Build. Connected to Sewage System	No. of Build. Connected to Water System	No. of Build. Connected to Electricity	No. of Build. Connected to Gas	No. of 1-Story Build.	No. of 4-Story Build.	5+ Stories
Total	24,832	17,152	11,400	15,403	16,840	7,863	9,268	3,072	1,152
1	703	657	570	631	619	357	88	125	46
2	882	824	696	774	722	342	132	162	46
3	1,428	1,180	925	1,111	1,138	673	358	339	73
4	770	727	648	696	691	603	77	214	63
5	1,085	867	647	861	872	500	233	262	80
6	1,054	856	672	829	831	395	259	218	78
7	1,372	1,205	937	1,135	1,186	598	284	304	111
8	949	932	872	906	910	664	57	270	93
9	638	565	472	529	541	256	147	114	74
10	823	752	656	712	707	430	142	166	107
11	1,173	1,056	965	1,025	1,073	633	177	281	122
12	525	512	480	487	497	340	46	72	62
13	880	826	733	798	798	483	155	191	83
14	1,173	748	436	835	817	309	388	142	58
15	1,081	652	312	657	680	211	441	75	23
16	1,297	983	360	733	866	295	536	74	22
17	1,084	536	91	271	383	108	704	1	0
18	431	54	5	99	118	5	306	0	0
19	386	156	13	102	175	11	283	0	0
20	801	432	81	283	390	79	496	3	1
21	428	171	28	92	166	18	333	3	0
22	1,057	424	77	288	541	61	726	16	0
23	807	496	37	299	380	55	477	21	9
24	1,023	384	8	155	324	26	709	1	0
25	815	115	20	197	328	45	495	0	0
26	2,146	1,042	699	897	1,087	365	1,200	18	1

Source: GUS Drugi Powszechny Spis Ludnosci Z Dnia 9.12.1931, Seria C Zeszyt 26, Tab. 6,7, 9

Table 3. Socio-economic characteristics of residents of the police precincts in Warsaw, 1931.

Police Precinct	1937		Percentage of Total Population, 1931			
	Infant Mortality,* 1936	Deaths from Tuberculosis, 1937	Illiteracy**	White-Collar Workers	Work at Home	Domestic Help
1	10.1	53	6.3	22	1.6	5.9
2	7.4	78	10.9	12	4.5	3.7
3	9.9	132	10.8	12	4.1	4.5
4	8.8	56	9.8	8	6.3	4.9
5	13.7	161	18.7	5	6	2.3
6	6.9	111	10.5	13	1.7	3.6
7	10	153	11.2	13	2.2	4.7
8	6.5	83	7.7	17	2.5	7.4
9	5.5	61	5.9	24	0.9	7.9
10	7.2	68	4.6	28	1	9.5
11	5.1	64	4.4	33	0.4	10.4
12	2.4	25	5.5	23	1.1	10.6
13	5.4	93	4.8	28	0.8	9.6
14	8.4	119	9.8	17	1.8	3.2
15	11.9	113	12.4	10	1.6	2.6
16	10	87	10.8	17	0.7	4.9
17	11.2	68	8.7	18	1.4	3.3
18	9.8	39	12.9	9	2.1	1.4
19	18.8	27	18.6	4	1.2	1.2
20	10.4	41	13.7	9	1.4	2.3
21	12.4	17	15.2	7	1.2	2.4
22	12.3	66	16.4	7	0.7	1.8
23	12.8	93	18.1	8	0.7	2.6
24	15.7	75	11.6	7	1.4	1.1
25	8.8	39	8.2	9	1	1.3
26	10.2	102	10.8	22	1.6	4.4

* Number of deaths of infants up to the age of 1 year, per 100 live births.
** Illiteracy among persons aged 10 and older.
Source: Infant Mortality: *Rocznik Statystyczny Warszawy, 1936-1937*, Tab. 24.
Death from Tuberculosis: *Rocznik Statystyczny Warszawy, 1936-1937*, Tab. 221. Illiteracy,
White-Collar Workers, People Working at Home, and Domestic Help: GUS Drugi
Powszeczny Spis Ludnosci z dnia,9.12.1931 , Seria C, Zeszyt 49, pp. 286-287.

Endnotes

1   Chaim Weizmann, *Essays and Action: The Memoirs of the President of Israel* (Jerusalem and Tel Aviv, 1962), p. 296 (Hebrew).

2   Jacek Leociak, *Biografie Ulic, O Zydowskich Ulicach Warszawy* (Warsaw, 2017).

3   Antony Polonsky, *The Failure of Jewish Assimilation in Polish Lands and its Consequences* (Oxford, 2000), pp. 5-6.

4   Stanislaw Gieysztor, *Moja Warszawa* (Warsaw, 2010), p. 576.

5   Aleksander Janowski, *Zycie Dzielnic Stolicy* (Warsaw, 1929), pp. 117-118.

6   Zbigniew Pakalski, *Nalewki, z Dziejow Polskiej i Zydowskiej Ulicy w Warszawie* (Warsaw, 2003), pp. 34-38.

7   Eleonora Bergman, *Nie Masz Boznicy Powszechnej* (Warsaw, 2007), pp. 47-49.

8   Spis Wlascicieli domow w M.Stol, Warszawie, Czesc III.

9   Pakalski, *Nalewki*, pp. 38-45.

10   Ibid., pp. 51-86.

11   The Jewish Quarter was also known as the northern or the northwestern quarter. For a more limited demarcation of the boundaries of the northern quarter, see: Gabriela Zalewska, *Ludnosc Zydowska w Warszawie w okresie miedzywojennym* (Warsaw, 1996), p. 63.

12   This data is from the population censuses by police precinct. The classification according to statistical area (2-3 statistical areas per police precinct) in the statistical yearbook of 1936-1937 presented only a small amount of detailed data, making it impossible to analyze the whole style of the residences of the Jews of Warsaw by statistical area.

13   Marian Fuks, *Zydzi w Warszawie* (Poznań, 1992), pp. 211-212.

14   For a ranking of the precincts, see below.

15   Source: Central Statistical Bureau of Poland, the population censuses of 1921 and 1931, the 1936-37 statistical yearbook of Warsaw. The findings of the censuses and the statistical yearbook are presented by city divisions on a number of levels: 12 neighborhoods, 26 police precincts, and 111 statistical regions. I chose the analysis according to the city's division into 26 police precincts, as this division allowed for a comparison between periods and between main parameters. I ranked the police precincts according to the socio-economic level of their residents and according to the level of the physical infrastructure. The statistical parameters that were chosen for examination of the neighborhoods included: housing density, percentage of studio apartments, percentage of four-bedroom apartments, illiteracy rate, percentage of white-collar workers, and the percentage employing domestic help. The physical parameters included: percentage of stone buildings, percentage of one-story buildings, percentage of four-story buildings, percentage of buildings with electricity, percentage

of buildings with running water, and percentage of buildings connected to the sewage system. Each of these parameters were assigned the same weighting, and the police precincts were ranked from highest to lowest. See Tables 1, 2, and 3.

16 Zenon Rogozinski, *Konsumpcja Zywnosciowa Ludnosci Warszawy Przed Druga Wojna Swiatowa* (Łódź, 1959), p. 6.

17 The number of deaths of infants up to one year of age per 100 live births.

18 Instances of death from tuberculosis per 10,000 residents.

19 Weighted average based on the number of residents residing within each of the police precincts.

20 Rogozinski, *Konsumpcja Zywnosciowa*, p. 26.

21 Weighted average based on the number of residents living within each police precinct.

22 Bernard Singer, *Moje Nalewki* (Warsaw, 1959), p. 15.

23 Ibid., pp. 45-46.

24 See Isaac Bashevis Singer's book *In My Father's Court* (New York, 1991).

25 Lilly Goldenberg, *When the Curtains Fell* (Ramat Hasharon, 1992), pp. 9, 47 (Hebrew).

26 Ibid., pp. 16, 17.

27 Aleksandra Domanska, *Ggrzybowska 6/10 Lament* (Warsaw, 2016), pp. 52-54.

28 Marian Marek Drozdowski, *Warszawa w latach 1914-1939*, Vol IV (Warsaw, 1990), pp. 307-308.

29 www.warszawa.jewish.org.pl; https://www.youtube.com/watch?v=lA1f5ng38dk

30 In comparison, the population density in Israel's most densely populated city – Bnei Brak – is 25 persons per dunam.

31 Zalewska, Ludnosc Zydowska, pp. 65-67.

32 Miriam Freilich, Assimilation and Polonization among Jews in Poland between the Two World Wars, 1918-1939: Organizational, Social, and Political Aspects (Jerusalem, 1999), pp. 6-7 (Hebrew). See also Anna Landau-Czajka, Syn bedzie Lech (Warsaw, 2006).

33 Maria Barbaszewicz, Warszawa Perla polnocy (Warsaw, 2014), p. 121.

34 Ibid.

35 Wladyslaw Zaleski, Prostytucja Powojenna w Warszawie (Warsaw, 1927), pp. 45-46.

36 Gieysztor Stanislaw, Moja Warszawa (Warsaw, 2010), pp. 557-563.

37 Jaroslaw Zielinski and Jerzy S. Majewski, Spacerownik po Zydowskiej Warszawie (Warsaw, 2014), p. 150.

38 Alina Cala, Ostatnie Pokolenie (Warsaw, 2003), p. 97.

39 Singer, Moje Nalewki, p. 8.

40 Aliza Witis Szomron, Mlodosc w Plomieniach (Warsaw, 2013), pp. 29-30.

41 Jozef Hen, Nowolipie Najpiekniejsze Lata (Warsaw, 1996), p. 33.

42 Zielinski and Majewski, Spacerownik, p. 270.

43 H. Bauberg, Podworze Przy Ulicy Brukowej 30 (Israel, 2013), pp. 225-233.

44 www.warszawa.jewish.org.pl,http://varshe.org.pl/teksty-zrodlowe/o-miejscach/
341-podworze-przy-ulicy-brukowej-30.

45 The data relates to all the residents of the police precincts in the Jewish Quarter,
Jews and non-Jews alike.

Menachem Keren-Kratz

A Shepherd without a Flock or a Flock without a Shepherd? The Challenging Dilemmas of Hasidic Rabbis in Hungary during the Holocaust

Introduction

In Hasidic eyes, and to a great extent in the eyes of the broader Jewish population, the Hasidic "Zaddik" (a Hebrew term used to refer to a righteous, saintly person according to the Jewish religion) is an exemplary figure with unique supernatural qualities. Many are the Jews who have made use of their blessings in times of need, including some who are not clear-cut Hasidim. In times of crisis for the entire community – for example, in times of war, oppressive pogroms, epidemics, or natural disasters – the presence of a Zaddik has created hope that his prayers would save the community as a whole. As a result of the Zaddik's sanctity, good deeds, and prayers, which many Jews believe open the gates of heaven, God is believed to grant his requests and to protect those around him.[1]

An example of this dynamic can be found in the Jewish public's reaction to a sermon delivered in Budapest by Rabbi Mordechai Rokeach (1901-1949) of Bilgoraj, Poland, before he and his brothers departed for Mandatory Palestine (the formal designation of the Land of Israel at the time). Mordechai Rokeach, and his better-known brother Rabbi Aharon Rokeach (1880-1957) of Belz in Galicia, also known as the Belzer Rebbe, were two non-Hungarian Hasidic rebbes who managed to escape the German occupation and to take temporary refuge in the city of Budapest.[2] Although the two rabbis did not live in Hungary, their names were known there as well. As a result, the following words of Rabbi Mordechai Rokeach left a significant impression and aroused great hope in the hearts of those who heard them:[3]

> The holy and brilliant…Rabbi Mordechai Rokeach – chief rabbi of
> Biloraj, may he live a good life, with the consent and as an emissary

of his brother, the Zaddik of the generation and our teacher Rabbi Aharon Rokeach, the Belzer Rebbe – arrived to deliver a farewell speech before immigrating to Eretz Israel…Almost never has such a large assembly been seen here…the standing crowd listened to his words with great awe …and different expressions began to appear on the faces of the listeners – weeping, despair, and scorn one moment…whereas the next moment rejoicing and happiness prevailed, when the speaker proclaimed loudly, on behalf of our master, his brother the Zaddik of the generation, in whose Beit Midrash a law was enacted that promises and guarantees that the angel of death will no longer rule in our country [meaning, Hungary], and that those who remain will be the last survivors… and the impact on the listeners was so overwhelming that not a single person could be found whose expression did not turn from one of anxiety to one of joy.[4]

The discrepancy between the confidence and the metaphysical virtues of the Zaddik and the terrible outcome of the Holocaust, in conjunction with the fact that many rabbis, such as the Belzer Rebbe and his brother, fled on the eve of the Holocaust, leaving most of their followers behind, raised a fundamental question regarding the role of the Hasidic rabbi in times of crisis. To whom, first and foremost, was the Zaddik obligated? To the frightened members of his community, who were suffering and who looked to him to save them, console them, and imbue them with hope and faith? Or was his fundamental obligation to save himself, thereby saving the unique tradition of the specific Hasidic dynasty he represented? In other words, was the Zaddik obligated to the currently endangered members of his community or to a Hasidic dynasty that may be established in the future?

This question has been discussed by a number of books and essays that have been published in recent decades, whose authors have considered the instances in which Hasidic rebbes were rescued from the killing ravines, whereas most of their followers were sent to the ghettos and subsequently to the death camps.[5] Books and articles by religious and ultra-Orthodox (*Haredi*) researchers have emphasized the role of the rabbis in leading their communities during the Holocaust and in rebuilding ultra-Orthodox Jewry in its wake.[6]

My contribution to this field of research was an article, published in both Hebrew and English, on the actions of Rabbi Yoel Teitelbaum, the Satmar Rebbe, on the eve of the Holocaust, during the Holocaust, and in its aftermath. The article reviewed the Satmar Rebbe's inability to recognize the impending tragedy and to warn his followers. In addition, the zealous rabbi refused to cooperate with various organizations, thwarted local rescue initiatives, and opposed the emigration of his followers to other countries. Nevertheless, during the early years of the war he attempted to escape with his family to Mandate Palestine and the United States but was unsuccessful. Ultimately, Rabbi Teitelbaum was saved after being added to a rescue train organized by Zionist activist Israel Kasztner. After his rescue, he refrained from returning to Satmar to resume leading the members of his community who had returned to the town, and he was not active in the DP (displaced persons) camps, which housed tens of thousands of Jewish Holocaust survivors who were in desperate need of spiritual leadership and religious consolation.[7]

The case of Rabbi Yoel Teitelbaum, who attempted to flee Europe at the beginning of the war and failed to provide assistance to survivors immediately following the Holocaust, represents one extreme of the rabbis' patterns of behavior. The other extreme was represented by the rabbis and rebbes who were beseeched by their followers to save themselves but refused to leave their flock. Instead, they stayed with the members of their communities when they were crammed into ghettos, consoled them when they were loaded onto transports, and prayed with them in their final hours in the death camps. Most of the rabbis who survived took part in the effort to rehabilitate religious and ultra-Orthodox Judaism, despite the great suffering and the loss they experienced during the Holocaust. In doing so, they instilled hope in the hearts of the survivors, who had lost not only their families and their money but, in some cases, also their religious faith.[8]

The actions of the rabbis during the Holocaust raises ethical and theological questions regarding the obligations of religious leaders in general, and of Hasidic leaders in particular. In times of danger, and assuming he has the ability to choose, should a leader remain with his followers, who revere him, long for his consoling words, and pin their hopes on him? Or, alternatively, should he accede to the appeals of those seeking to remove him from harm's way to enable him to set up his rabbinical dynasty elsewhere and to save the Hasidic tradition he represents? Moreover, should the rabbis remain at the side of the members of their community with their heads held high and dressed in rabbinical apparel, thereby publicly sanctifying God's name? Or, are they actually charged with saving their lives, even if this means shaving their beards and their sidelocks and posing as non-Jews? In addition to considering the theoretical question, it is also important to review who among the rebbes were praised and admired after the Holocaust: those who fled, or those who remained with the members of their communities, despite the clear danger this presented?

The decision to engage these questions regarding the conduct of the Hungarian Hasidic rebbes was based on three primary factors. The first is the fact that Hungary was the site of activity of many Hasidic rebbes whose work was documented both during and after the Holocaust. The second reason is the fact that a few of the Hassidic rebbes in Hungary also served as chief rabbis of communities, and were therefore part of the overall Jewish leadership and obligated not only to their followers but also to the other Jewish residents of the town in question.[9] The third reason is the fact that the Holocaust in Hungary occurred a significant time after it began in Poland and Germany and the deportation to the death camps. This left the Hassidic rebbes, like the other leaders of the Jewish public, much more time to consider the appropriate way to respond, both from a public perspective and in terms of Jewish law (Halakha). Nonetheless, the patterns of action employed by the Hassidic rebbes in Hungary during the Holocaust were similar to those that were employed by Hasidic and non-Hasidic rabbis and other public leaders in the other states of Europe, and one cannot identify a specific mode of action that was typical of them in particular.[10]

The Hasidic Rebbes in Hungary

The following sections of this article engage in the history of those who have been referred to as Hungarian rebbes. Although all of these rebbes actually lived outside the borders of Hungary, in the eyes of European Jewry, the label "Hungarian" signified not only a geographical place, but also, and mainly, a worldview.[11] This is because Greater Hungary, meaning Hungary as it existed prior to World War I, was the only country in the world in which the rabbis had succeeded in establishing a clear and formal separation between the Orthodox communities (those that were run based on regulations that were consistent with Jewish law) and the non-Orthodox Jewish communities. The Hungarian rabbis' success in separating their communities almost completely from the non-orthodox communities lent the adjective "Hungarian" an air of separatism, extremism, and piety.[12]

After World War I, almost two-thirds of the territory of Greater Hungary was ceded to other countries. As these areas included most of the Orthodox Jewish communities, the rabbis fought for their right to continue managing separate communities even in the countries to which they were annexed. The success of most of the Jews of these communities in maintaining their Jewish-Hungarian cultural identity on the one hand, and the rabbis' success in maintaining the autonomous status of the Orthodox communities on the other hand, provided the rabbis with the right to bear the designation "Hungarian" with pride, even though they actually lived in other countries.[13] At the end of the 1930s, in the context of the political events that occurred during World War II, Hungary annexed some of the areas that had been taken from it during World War I. These areas included the southern portion of Slovakia and the Karpatho-Rus (both areas had previously been part of Czechoslovakia), the northern part of Transylvania (which had previously belonged to Romania), and territories that had formerly belonged to Yugoslavia and Austria. All of these areas contained particularly large populations of Orthodox Jews and rabbis who had adopted the "Hungarian" way of life and had managed to maintain their social separation by establishing organizations to run the Orthodox communities separately from the non-Orthodox ones. In this way, for example, the communities and rabbis who were known as "Hungarian" only by name were returned to Hungary and once again became Hungarian subjects.

The annexed areas were home to a large number of Hasidic rebbes, much more than many other parts of Europe.[14] The senior rabbis among them also served as chief rabbis of communities, and in this capacity they also held authority over the Jewish residents of their towns who were not their followers or did not observe the commandments at all. A few of these rabbis were also recognized as leaders of Hasidic dynasties with separate identities, but most were family relations of well-known Hasidic leaders ("*banim shel kadoshim*," meaning the sons of a holy person) who established small courts for themselves on the outskirts of a town or a large village.

For a relatively long period, the Jews of Hungary felt fortunate because the war, which had been fought in northern Europe, had thus far passed them over. Because of the relative calm that prevailed in the country, it was a destination of refugees from Poland and Germany, including many Jews.[15] Although these refugees reported the atrocities committed in their countries, to the Jews of Hungary their words sounded exaggerated if not unfounded.[16] Hungary's decision to join the German-led Axis Powers resulted in international political accomplishments when it re-annexed territories that had formerly been under its control.

Following the annexation of Northern Transylvania, Karpatho-Rus, Southern Slovakia, and other territories from Yugoslavia and Austria, the number of Jews in Hungary increased significantly. The Jews were initially glad to return to Hungarian rule, to the bosom of the country in which they had been granted full equal rights and whose culture and language they knew well. The Orthodox Jews had positive memories of Hungary as a benevolent monarchy due to its willingness to permit them to run their own communities with a large degree of independence and separately from the non-Orthodox communities. Unfortunately, their joy and hope were short-lived.

Not long after annexation, Hungary began to institute anti-Jewish policies, including severe economic and social decrees.[17] Tens of thousands of Jews lacked identity documents and the appropriate residence permits; they were arrested and deported to Kamenets-Podolsk in Poland, where many of them were murdered.[18] Later, many Jews were conscripted into the Hungarian labor battalions, in which they were forced to work under difficult and life threatening conditions, in gross contempt of their status as citizens of the state. Many did not survive this difficult service.[19] Following Germany's conquest of Hungary in March 1944, the condition of the Jews declined rapidly, and within a few months approximately half a million Hungarian Jews were sent to the death camps. The vast majority of them were murdered in the Holocaust.

Reevaluating the Flight of the Rabbis and Rebbes during the Holocaust

The flight of Jewish political and spiritual leaders during wartime was not unique to World War II and the Holocaust. Many leaders also fled their communities during World War I, including a large number of rabbis and rebbes.[20] At the time, their flight was typically viewed with understanding, and it was clear that their actions were temporary and that the rabbis did not intend to abandon their flock. This was not the case in Hungary during the Holocaust, when many religious and political leaders from Europe left for Palestine, the United States, and other countries.[21] When members of the Jewish population realized that the rabbis had abandoned them and did not intend on returning they were subjected to public criticism.[22] One rabbi who remained with his community wrote:[23]

> I have observed a scandalous affair within the house of Israel as heavy clouds cover the European horizon. Over the past few days, a rumor has been circulating among Jews that a large portion of our leaders intend on leaving their posts and immigrating to the Holy Land by trying to acquire [immigration] certificates [to Mandatory Palestine].[24]

Words of a similar spirit were articulated by Rabbi Yissachar Shlomo Teichtal (1885-1945):

> ...dread and fear hang over us. At the very moment I write these lines, all of the Chassidic Rebbes of this country are making efforts to flee to *Eretz Yisrael* out of fear of the oppressor. They ignore the fact that this causes Israel to despair. One can hear the masses complain "The Rebbes are fleeing! What will be with us?!"[25]

The Halakhic question was addressed by Hungarian Rabbi Baruch Yehoshua Yerachmiel Rabinowitz (1914-1997), who served as the chief rabbi of Munkács and as the head of the local Hasidic court. Rabbi Rabinowitz held Polish citizenship, and he was therefore deported with thousands of other Jews who did not hold Hungarian citizenship. Their journey ended in the town of

Kamenets-Podolsk, where more than 10,000 of the deportees were murdered.[26] Rabbi Rabinowitz managed to escape and returned to Budapest after facing great hardships. There, he became one of the most important activists in rescue efforts overall, and in the rescue of ultra-Orthodox Jews in particular.[27]

The writings published by Rabinowitz toward the end of his life dealt with the theological significance of the Holocaust, including the question of whether a Jew is permitted to be saved when most members of his community are going to die in the sanctification of God's name (*Kiddush Hashem*).[28] In this context he relied on the ruling of Rabbi Jacob Ben Joseph Reischer (1670-1733). Although the latter ruled that a lenient approach to the matter was permissible based on the importance of "the virtue of saving one's life" (*Pikuach Nefesh*) he also noted that "if one wishes to be strict with himself and give his life in the sanctification of God's name in a way from which others can also learn to do so – he will be remembered positively."[29] Rabbi Rabinowitz explained that when he relied on this ruling to permit others to save their own lives during the Holocaust, he refrained from conveying the second part, which praises those who decided to remain with their community regardless of the mortal risks. He applied a similar standard to himself, and when he felt that danger was imminent, he agreed to accept an immigration certificate to Mandatory Palestine, which had been acquired for him through a special effort.

The willingness of Rabbi Rabinovitch and other rabbis to save themselves, even when they knew that thousands of other Jews did not have the option to do so, was based on Halakhic precedents that stipulated that the students of the wise (*Talmidei Hahamim*) have precedence over others. The most explicit expression of this principle is found in the Mishnaic verse: "A wise student who is a bastard precedes a high priest ignoramus."[30] On the same matter, the Talmud stipulates that if "a man, his father, and his rabbi are prisoners, he precedes his rabbis, and his rabbi precedes his father." Or, in other words, there is no substitute for a bright student, which is why he is the first to be rescued.[31] The Halakhic discussion, of course, is not this simple and offers points in different directions. For example, regarding rescuing someone being held prisoner or facing possible death, in which case some Jewish adjudicators assign preferred status to women, or, according to another interpretation, to widows and to orphans.[32]

The most all-encompassing discussion of the conduct of the Hasidic rebbes during the Holocaust appears in Esther Farbstein's book *Hidden in Thunder*, in which she argues that, with the respect to the saving of the rebbes, "Hasidism considers this a miracle amidst the destruction – a miracle for Hasidism and for the entire Jewish People." At the same time, she adds that "some other people, however, view the matter very differently and ask how leaders could have abandoned their flocks in a time of trouble."[33]

Farbstein concludes the chapter by stating that the term "flight" is inaccurate vis-à-vis the rabbis during the Holocaust,

> because the impulse for their leaving the danger zone came primarily from the Jewish community, which 'pushed' them out... Moreover, unlike the typical "fleer," these leaders never stopped looking back and they took their concern for the community with them wherever they went.

As a result, Farbstein concludes,

> the rescue of rebbes was thus an act of popular rebellion and defiance of the Nazis' war on Judaism, Jewish values, and the representatives of Judaism. It was an attempt to play a role in the future of the Jewish people by saving the Torah. It was also an attempt by Jews to leave an imprint on the future as the threat of annihilation hung over their heads.[34]

The following section examines several individual examples of Hungarian rebbes. A few of them received offers to flee, whereas other took different courses of action to save themselves and their families and succeeded in doing so. The final section of this article considers the connection between the conduct of the Hasidic rebbes during the Holocaust and the manner in which they have been described by the post-Holocaust Hasidic literature. It will also review the connection between their conduct during the Holocaust and the extent of their success in rebuilding their Hasidic dynasties once it was over.

The Hungarian Rebbes and the Test of the Holocaust: Individual Examples

1. Rabbi Aharon (Arele) Roth, Founder of the Shomrei Emunim (Guardian of Faith) Hasidic community: The Only Rebbe who Took Action and Issued a Warning in Time

Of the dozens of Hasidic rebbes who were active in Hungary, only one discerned the impending danger in time and took action. In 1921, Rabbi Aharon Roth established a small Hasidic group in the city of Satmar.[35] In 1925, he immigrated to Mandatory Palestine and settled in Jerusalem, where he established a small Hasidic community. A few years later he again returned to Satmar, where he established the Shomrei Emunim Hasidic community. Due to a disagreement that arose between him and Rabbi Yoel Teitelbaum, who had just started serving as the chief rabbi of Satmar, Roth relocated his center of activity to the city of Beregszász (Berehove), and he established Hasidic communities in other towns as well. At the end of the 1930s, when the severity of the situation in Europe became clear, Roth decided to return to Palestine, substantiating his decision to his Hasidic supporters as follows:

> And suddenly, with its many transgressions, a great gloom emerged in the world, the world grew very dark, and the clouds blackened. And the land shook and its produce melted, etc. I have always thought and told the community that in my heart I am very frightened of the year 5700 (1939/40), and that is why I wished to make my trip there earlier. But suddenly, last week, the tumult of upheaval entered the world, and the resulting fears are great and terrible…And who knows – who knows what the day will bring? Depressed, I entreated my creator to spare his holy people and to have mercy on them, and to not destroy his world.[36]

As a result of his unequivocal decision, his gloomy predictions regarding the future of Europe, and his recommendation that Hasidim make their way to Eretz Israel, a few tried to immigrate to Palestine in his footsteps:[37]

Our rabbi returned to Beregszász and wrote to his students in Jerusalem, telling them to make every effort to send certificates for him and for all the members of their families…And of course, the students that were abroad attempted to speak to the heart of our rabbi to change his mind…But all the requests and efforts were in vain, as our rabbi did not change his mind and was at one with himself when it became necessary to travel back to Jerusalem…And when the students saw our rabbi's determination… they too began to take action to arrange for themselves money and documents so that perhaps they too could make the journey via the indirect route for which a movement had started to organize at the time [meaning, the illegal Jewish immigration to Palestine].[38]

Rabbi Roth immigrated to Palestine in 1940, and from then on he took action to spiritually strengthen his followers who had been left behind.[39] After the Holocaust, he tried to help survivors acquire certificates to facilitate their immigration.[40] His failing health and his sorrow at the destruction of European Jewry during the Holocaust resulted in his death in 1947 at the young age of 53. As most of his followers had stayed in Europe, his dynasty in Israel remained small and without influence.

The members of Roth's family who accompanied him upon his immigration to Palestine included his son Rabbi Abraham Chaim Roth (1924-2012), who, after his father's death, replaced him as head of Shomrei Emunim. Rabbi Aharon's son-in-law was Rabbi Avraham Yitzhak Kohn (1914-1996), a student of Rabbi Yoel Teitelbaum of Satmar.[41] After the death of his father-in-law, Rabbi Kohn founded the Hasidic Community Toldot Aharon, which, with the help of the Satmar Rebbe, became one of the largest and most influential groups in the Edah Haredit.[42]

2. Rabbi Yitzhak Isaac Weiss, the Spinker Rebbe: The Zaddik Who Lost Everything

Rabbi Yitzhak Isaac Weiss (1875-1944), known also by the name of his book "Chakal Yitzchak," was the son of Rabbi Yosef Meir Weiss (1838-1909), who founded a small Hasidic court in the village of Szaplonca (Spinka) in Máramaros County, Hungary.[43] The dynasty's establishment aroused the ire of the rabbis of the nearby city of Sighet (Máramarossziget, Sighetu Marmaţiei), which was the county seat. In addition to their role as the rabbis of the community, the rabbis of Sighet were also the heads of a long-standing thriving Hasidic dynasty whose hegemony was threatened by Rabbi Weiss's new dynasty. Despite this opposition, the new dynasty was successful. Following the death of his father, Rabbi Yitzhak Isaac Weiss assumed his role as leader of the dynasty, and the dynasty became very influential under his leadership.[44]

At the outbreak of World War I, Rabbi Weiss moved his residence to the town of Munkács, where his grandfather, Rabbi Shmuel Zvi Weiss (1814-1879), had served as the presiding judge of the Jewish court. There, his dynasty was joined by additional Hasidim, who established a local community that revolved around the Beis Midrash and the Beis Yosef Yeshiva.[45] In 1930, following confrontations between the Hasidic followers of Rabbi Yitzhak Isaac Weiss and the local followers of the Munkácser Rebbe and after receiving monetary compensation, the former relocated his dynasty to the nearby town of Selish (Nagy-szölös, Veľký Sevľuš), which became the dynasty's main center until the Holocaust. In contrast to the tough and introverted character of Munkácser Hasidism on the one hand and Sighet Hasidism on the other hand, Spinka Hasidism was known for its accepting and uncritical approach toward all Jews everywhere.[46] As a result, this brand of Hasidism was widespread, and local Spinka Hasidic communities were established in dozens of towns in Slovakia and Karpatho-Rus, different regions of Czechoslovakia, and Transylvania in Romania.[47]

After Hungary's annexation of Karpatho-Rus, Rabbi Yitzhak Isaac Weiss ordered the construction of an underground shelter in his home, which he used to hide Jews who had escaped from Poland. He also provided them with forged documents to enable them to live safely in Hungary.[48] When rumors regarding the rescue activities he was conducting began to circulate, Rabbi Weiss fell victim to the abuse of Hungarian soldiers but nonetheless continued his efforts.[49] Thanks to connections with the British royal family enjoyed by one of his followers in London, as well as prayers he had offered years earlier for the health of King George V, the British issued him an immigration visa, but he refused to abandon the members of his community.[50] Instead, Rabbi Weiss remained in the ghetto with them, accompanying them to the extermination camps where they died together. The Hasidim maintain that, by doing so, he fulfilled his desire to ascend to the status of those who sacrificed their lives in the sanctification of God's name (*Kiddush Hashem*). It has also been said that when he was already on his way to the camps, he encouraged those who sought his insight on the grounds that they were going to rescue the messiah. When his time came to die – in a loud voice – he sang "the fire on the altar must be kept burning, it must not go out," which since then has become a Hasidic anthem.[51] In addition to Rabbi Yitzhak Isaac Weiss himself, his two sons and his son-in-law were also killed in the Holocaust, along with many of his grandchildren.

After the war, Rabbi Yitzhak's grandson, Rabbi Yaakov Yosef Weiss settled in Arad, Romania, where he worked rehabilitating the religious life of Holocaust survivors. A few years later, with the rise of the Communist party in Romania and its ban on all religious activity, he moved to the United States where he rebuilt the Spinka dynasty.[52] However, despite the dynasty's reestablishment, and despite the passage of many decades, it never reassumed its prominence and remained on the margins of the Hungarian Hasidic camp.[53]

3. Rabbi Yaakov Elimelech Paneth, the Chief Rabbi of Dej: The Collapse of the Dynasty

Rabbi Yaakov Elimelech Paneth (1889-1944) was a scion of the important Hasidic dynasty based in Dej, in Transylvania. The dynasty was founded by Rabbi Yehezkel Paneth (1869-1930), author of the book *Mar'eh Yechezkel*, who was one of the most important rabbis in Hungary at the time. Rabbi Yaakov Elimelech Paneth, a great grandson of the dynasty's founder, was also one of the most important and influential Hasidic rebbes in Transylvania.[54] In addition to his role as a Hasidic rebbe of a long-standing dynasty, he also served as the chief rabbi of an important city, the head of a yeshiva,[55] and overseer of the Zivinbirgen Kollel, which supported the Jews of Transylvania who immigrated to Palestine.[56] Moreover, Rabbi Yaakov Elimelech Paneth was also a member of the Central Bureau of the Orthodox Jewish Communities in Transylvania, the main organization that ran the lives of the Jews who belonged to the Orthodox community, and he supported Hasidic immigration to Palestine through the Zeirei Agudat Israel movement.[57]

Rabbi Yaakov Elimelech Paneth came to clearly understand the danger of the occupation after his two sons were arrested in 1941 because they lacked documents attesting to their Hungarian citizenship. Along with thousands of other deportees, the two were sent to Kamenets-Podolsk where they were murdered. When the danger awaiting the Jews of Hungary became evident, the leaders of the Orthodox community in Budapest, which was considered to be safer than elsewhere, offered him a rabbinical post there, but he refused. He also refused his younger brother's suggestion that he make himself a flight plan. He reiterated his refusal even after his younger brother, Rabbi Yosef Paneth (1895-1962), managed to escape from the ghetto, and also after a few of his followers who had managed to escape requested his permission to smuggle him out as well. Despite the danger, Rabbi Yaakov Elimelech Paneth refused to abandon his flock, explaining: "I walk with all the members of my community. What happens to them will happen to me. I will not abandon my flock."[58] He and many other members of his family were on the last transport to Auschwitz; there, he was murdered along with his children, other family members, and many other members of his community.[59]

Rabbi Yosef Paneth, Rabbi Yaakov Elimelech's younger brother, who prior to the Holocaust had served as the rabbi of the Jewish community of Ileanda near Dej, managed to escape from the ghetto after finding a hiding place in a nearby forest and receiving the assistance of a number of local villagers, who helped him and his family. After the Holocaust and after he learned of the death of his brother, he returned to Dej, reestablished the family dynasty, and took up efforts to save and to rebuild Hasidic Judaism. When the Communist government in Romania began to put pressure on religious institutions, he immigrated to the United States, where he established the Knesset Israel community in the Brooklyn neighborhood of Williamsburg. There, he also resumed his work on behalf of the Zivenbirgen Kollel in Israel.[60] Like the Spinka dynasty, the Dej dynasty, which had been one of the largest and most influential dynasties prior to the Holocaust, never re-attained its previous prominence and standing.

4. Rabbi Zalman Leib (Yekutiel Yehuda) Teitelbaum, the Chief Rabbi of Sighet: The Town That Was Forgotten

As a result of the death of his father Rabbi Chaim Tzvi Teitelbaum, Yekutiel Yehuda Teitelbaum, known by the nickname Zalman Leib (1912-1944), was appointed chief rabbi of Sighet at the young age of 14. The town of Sighet was one of the most important Hasidic centers in Hungary, and the rabbis of the Teitelbaum family had been serving as its chief rabbis since the 1830s. In the process, they established a dynasty with thousands of followers, headed the largest Hasidic yeshiva in Hungary, operated a separate kollel in Palestine, and served as the Hasidic population's main representatives to the Central Bureau of the Orthodox Jewish Communities of Hungary, and later of Transylvania.

In the initial years following his appointment as the young successor of the chief rabbi of the city, the community's leaders assigned three rabbinical sages the task of educating him. In 1930, upon completing his studies and being ordained as a rabbi, he married Rachel, the daughter of his uncle Rabbi Yoel Teitelbaum, who would later become the Satmar Rebbe. He was also then officially appointed to the city's rabbinate and the post of head of the yeshiva.[61] A few years later, he was appointed to a senior position within the Central Bureau of the Orthodox Jewish Communities of Transylvania.

When the war broke out, Rabbi Zalman Leib Teitelbaum took part in assisting the many refugees who had thronged from Poland to Sighet, hiding many in his home and in the yeshiva building and providing them with forged passes that would allow them to continue on their way to Budapest. When this was discovered, he was summoned by the authorities for an interrogation, but he managed to flee and to go into hiding in a different village. He was ultimately apprehended and imprisoned in harsh conditions for a number of months, but he was released after paying a bribe and numerous fines, only to be arrested again and subsequently released.[62] At the end of 1943, Rabbi Zalman Leib and a group of other rabbis signed a memorandum calling for cooperation with the Zionist movement to prepare escape plans and shelters, but his uncle, Rabbi Yoel Teitelbaum, thwarted the initiative.[63] Despite the younger Rabbi Teitelbaum's involvement in rescue matters and his personal acquaintance with the heads of the Zionist movement in the city, he did not take advantage of his status in order to flee. Instead, he consistently provided encouragement to the members of his community and remained with them even when they were forced into the ghetto and deported to the extermination camps. There, he and the rest of his family were killed, along with most of the Jews of Sighet.

Prior to the Holocaust, Rabbi Moshe Teitelbaum, Rabbi Zalman Leib Teitelbaum's brother, served as the chief rabbi of the Hasidic community in Senta, which was located in the part of Yugoslavia that was annexed to Hungary during the war. During the Holocaust, his followers suggested that he flee. However, like his older brother, he preferred to remain with the members of his community and was taken with them to Auschwitz, where his wife and his children were killed.[64] After the Holocaust he settled in Sighet in place of his deceased brother and renewed the destroyed community. With the rise of Communism in Romania, he immigrated to the United States, where he established a small court and became known as the Sigheter Rebbe. In 1979, after the death of his uncle, Rabbi Yoel Teitelbaum, he was summoned to succeed him, and since then he has held the title of the Satmar Rebbe. Consequently, although the city of Sighet was the home of a long-standing Hasidic dynasty that was one of the most important and influential before the Holocaust, the town's name and legacy ultimately assumed marginal status.

5. Rabbi Yekutiel Yehuda Halberstam – The Sanz-Klausenburg Rebbe: He Lost His Family and Founded a Hasidic Dynasty

Rabbi Yekutiel Yehuda Halberstam (1905-1994) was the son of Rabbi Zvi Hirsch Halberstam (1850-1918), the chief rabbi of Rudnik, and the great-grandson of Rabbi Chaim Halberstam (1797-1876), founder of the Sanz Hasidic dynasty and one of the most important Hasidic rebbes of his time. As a scion of distinguished lineage, it was arranged for the younger Halberstam to marry someone from another important family; his father-in-law was Rabbi Chaim Tzvi Teitelbaum, the chief rabbi of Sighet and the older brother of Rabbi Yoel Teitelbaum. In 1926, shortly after getting married and following the death of his father and his father-in-law, he was appointed by Rabbi Yoel Teitelbaum to replace him as the rabbi of the small Hasidic community in the city of Cluj

(Cluj Napoca), which was known by Jews as Klausenburg. This community, of which Rabbi Teitelbaum had been proclaimed rabbi but in which he never resided, was established in 1922, sparking great controversy after it withdrew from the city's long-standing Orthodox community.[65]

Following the appointment, Rabbi Halberstam moved to the city and led its Hasidic community, which consisted of only a few dozen families, and whose conflicts with the main Jewish community continued for years. Before the Holocaust, he had not served as the rabbi of a large and prestigious community, had not headed an important yeshiva, had not published a single scholarly article, had not been considered an influential Hasidic leader, and had not held any position in the Central Bureau of the Orthodox Jewish Communities in Transylvania. As a result, Rabbi Halberstam received no public recognition, and few knew his name.

At the beginning of the 1940s, Rabbi Halberstam and members of his family were arrested for holding only foreign citizenship and lacking all the required residence permits. Due to the efforts of his followers – that is to say, through their payment of a bribe – they were released and returned to Cluj. When the first refugees from Poland arrived in the city, he hid some of them in his home.[66] At the same time, he tried to acquire certificates for himself and his family to immigrate to Palestine. The policy of the Jewish Agency at the time was to make the issuing of certificates contingent upon a statement of support of the Jewish national institutions and opposition to the anti-Zionist ultra-Orthodox faction. Concerned about the reaction of his extremist patron Rabbi Yoel Teitelbaum, the Satmar Rebbe, Rabbi Halberstam refrained from doing so and his request was therefore denied.[67] When the danger increased, Rabbi Halberstam went into hiding on his own in the city, separated from the rest of his family. As his concern mounted further, he decided to travel alone to the town of Baia Mare (Nagybánya) to join the Hungarian labor battalions and to leave behind not only his followers but also his wife and children.[68] After it became evident that he had been illegally conscripted into the labor battalions, he was sent to the ghetto with all the Jews of the city.[69]

After the Jews of Baia Mare were moved into the ghetto and later, after their deportation to Auschwitz, Rabbi Halberstam was known for his uncompromising devotion to promoting an observant way of life even under the harshest conditions and for his words of encouragement and consolation to the miserable deportees. He continued in this manner even after he joined the large group of prisoners who were sent to loot what remained of the Warsaw Ghetto.[70] Once this assignment was completed, those who were still alive were sent on the death march to Dachau. From there, Rabbi Halberstam was transferred to the Mühldorf concentration camp, where he was put to forced labor until liberation, after which he learned that his wife and all his children had died in the Holocaust.[71]

After liberation, Rabbi Yekutiel Yehuda Halberstam spent time in the DP camps, where he was extremely active in the rehabilitation of ultra-Orthodox Jewry. Through connections he developed with chaplains of the liberating armies, he facilitated the burial of the bodies of the Jewish dead and the provision of kosher food, religious books, and ritual articles for the Jews who had survived. He also set up a system of "Talmud Torah" schools, yeshivas, and schools for religious girls, and he organized all the other religious services – all under the name "The Surviving Remnant" (*She`erit Hapleta*). Approximately one year after liberation, he travelled to the United States on a campaign to raise donations, and although he was offered to remain there, he returned to the DP camps, where he further intensified his activity.[72]

In 1947, after the DP camps began to empty out, Rabbi Halberstam travelled to the United States and settled there. The reputation he earned during the Holocaust, the heavy personal price he paid, and his devotion to the survivors made him a widely admired figure, and stories about him were published regularly in the Jewish newspapers of New York. This reputation helped him raise large donations for the purpose of establishing his Hasidic community in Williamsburg, which was joined by many individuals who knew him from the DP camps.

After establishing his dynasty and becoming familiar with the way of life in the United States and the spiritual dangers it posed to Orthodox Judaism, he moved the center of his court to Israel. The activity of his followers in Israel, in collaboration with Israeli state Jewish immigration and settlement authorities, resulted in the establishment of a separate Hasidic neighborhood on the outskirts of Netanya: Kiryat Sanz.[73] Both the strengthening of his court in the United States and the establishment of the neighborhood in Netanya irritated his former patron Rabbi Yoel Teitelbaum, who had also established a Hasidic dynasty in Williamsburg. Satmar Hasidim persecuted and demeaned the followers of Rabbi Halberstam until they relocated their center of activity from Williamsburg to another location, this time in nearby New Jersey. At the same time, the leaders of the zealous Edah Haredit besmirched those who settled in Kiryat Sanz. As a result, Rabbi Halberstam's community found itself isolated from all other Hungarian and Galician Hasidic groups.[74]

The loss of his large family and his devotion to the refugees of the Holocaust enabled Rabbi Yekutiel Yehuda Halberstam to build a Hasidic dynasty that was much larger than his previous one. Still, Rabbi Halberstam's rivalry with the Edah Haredit and the Satmar Rebbe, and as a result with other Hasidic dynasties in Israel and the United States, limited its growth.

6. Rabbi Chaim Meir Hager, the Vizhnitzer Rebbe: He Went on As If Nothing Happened

Rabbi Chaim Meir Hager (1887-1972) was the son of Rabbi Israel Hager (1860-1936), the Vizhnitzer Rebbe, who led this court's transformation into one of the largest and most influential in Eastern Europe. At the beginning of World War I, Rabbi Chaim Meir Hager joined his father, who had moved his center of activity to the city of Oradea (Nagyvárad, Großwardein) in Transylvania, where most of his followers resided. In 1916, he was selected to serve as the chief rabbi of the village of Vulchovce (Irhocz) in Máramaros County, but he spent most of his time in Oradea, where he helped his father manage the affairs of the court and promote the local activity of Agudat Israel.[75] In 1936, Rabbi Chaim Meir Hager's father died, and the younger Rabbi Chaim Meir replaced him as head of the court in Oradea, as leader of the Hasidic faction within Agudat Israel in Romania, and as a major activist within the Central Bureau of the Orthodox Jewish Communities in Transylvania.

At the end of 1943, Rabbi Chaim Meir Hager made use of his connections in Agudat Israel to acquire immigration certificates to Palestine for himself and his family. He even travelled to Vizhnitz to part with his followers, but for bureaucratic reasons his trip to Palestine did not occur.[76] Shortly after the Germans entered Northern Transylvania in 1944, Rabbi Hager sent a few members of his family to cross the border illegally into Romania, where they settled in the city of Arad.[77] After the Jews of Oradea were moved into the ghetto, Rabbi Hager acquired a permit to leave the ghetto to engage in forced labor in one of the nearby forests. From there, he managed to flee with a small group that crossed the border to the city of Arad, where he joined the rest of his family.[78]

When the war ended, Rabbi Hager returned to Oradea, where he rehabilitated Jewish religious life and, with the assistance of Agudat Israel, worked to repair the religious Jewish institutions in Romania. In 1947, following the intensification of the anti-religious decrees of the Communist regime, he immigrated to Palestine and settled in Tel Aviv. The city was already home to a number of other family members, including his son Rabbi Moshe Yehoshua Hager (1916-2012), who headed the Vizhnitz Yeshiva that had been established by his uncle Rabbi Eliezer Hager (1891-1946) – son of Rabbi Israel Hager – who had died shortly before then.

Rabbi Chaim Meir Hager worked energetically both to promote Agudat Israel in Mandatory Palestine, and subsequently in the state of Israel, and to rebuild his dynasty. He was the first to establish a separate Hasidic neighborhood in Bnei Brak for his followers, thereby helping to make it an ultra-Orthodox city. As a result of his determined work as a social entrepreneur, a political activist, and a Torah educator he became one of Israel's most influential and admired ultra-Orthodox figures. The dynasty he established in Israel was one of the largest, second in size only to the dynasty established by Rabbi Mordechai Abraham Alter (1866-1948), the Gerer Rebbe. Rabbi Alter was his partner in leading the Hasidic camp within Agudat Israel, and, like Rabbi Hager, he had managed to escape Europe while it was burning thanks to his lofty religious status.[79]

7. Rabbi Yoel Teitelbaum – The Satmar Rebbe: He Achieved Immense Success despite His Flight

Rabbi Yoel Teitelbaum (1887-1979) was the son of Rabbi Chananya Yom-Tov Lifa Teitelbaum (1836-1904), the chief rabbi of Sighet and an important and influential

Hasidic rebbe. Although as a child Yoel had not been meant to inherit his father's positions, which were designated for his older brother Chaim Zvi, he nonetheless aspired to reach a position of leadership. Following the death of his older brother in 1926, and decades of political power struggles, Rabbi Yoel Teitelbaum managed to fill all the positions that had previously been filled by his father. He became the chief rabbi of the city of Satmar, served as the head of a major yeshiva and the leader of the Teitelbaum family's Hasidic dynasty, and functioned as one of the heads of the Central Bureau of the Orthodox Jewish Communities in Transylvania.[80]

After the outbreak of World War II, Rabbi Teitelbaum refused to cooperate with parties seeking to plan for the future and refrained from taking even religious measures of self-defense, such as setting days of fasting and prayer. He also refrained from warning his followers about the impending danger and recommended that they not emigrate to other countries. Nonetheless, he himself sought to acquire a certificate to immigrate to Palestine or a visa to the United States on a number of occasions but was ultimately unsuccessful. Although the danger only increased with the passage of time, he prohibited cooperation with Agudat Israel and thwarted the attempts of various rabbis, including members of his own family, to join the rest of the Jewish movements in preparing hiding places and plans of escape.

After the Germans entered Hungary, Rabbi Teitelbaum's followers proposed a number of possible escape plans and hiding places, but he rejected them all. His followers also refrained from fleeing without receiving his blessing, and they were ultimately deported to the extermination camps. When the Jews of Satmar were finally moved into the ghetto, Rabbi Teitelbaum fled with a small group with the aim of crossing the border into Romania and saving themselves. However, when the group reached the town of Cluj, it was apprehended and sent to the ghetto there. When the transports carrying imprisoned Jews to the extermination camps got underway, Rabbi Teitelbaum received an offer to join the rescue train that had been arranged by Zionist activist Israel Kasztner. He accepted the offer even though he knew that the remaining members of the group with whom he had fled, including his closest friend, would not be rescued. A few weeks later, the rescue train, with its 1,700 passengers, arrived at the Bergen-Belsen transit camp, where they resided for a few months in relatively comfortable conditions.

Following liberation, Rabbi Teitelbaum lived in Switzerland. He did not return to Satmar to lead the surviving members of his community who awaited his arrival, and he did not even find it appropriate to visit the DP camps to help the thousands of religious Jews who were in desperate need of spiritual guidance and support. Instead, he attempted to operate within Switzerland itself, but his activities were negligible and had no significant results. A few months later, he immigrated to Jerusalem, where he tried to set up his own Hasidic court. However, as a result of his decisions and his functioning during the Holocaust, as well as his failure to acknowledge the change that had occurred in ultra-Orthodox society in Mandatory Palestine during the period in question and his separatist behavior, he failed to do so, and his institutions racked up substantial debt.

Rabbi Teitelbaum then travelled to the United States to raise funds to cover his debts, but he was unsuccessful. As a result, he decided to remain in the United States and to establish a small community. Although his insistence on sticking to anti-Zionist ideology caused many American Jews and rabbis to keep their distance from him, he had a handful of followers. As a result of his vigorous activity and his charismatic personality, within just a few years his court became one of the largest and most influential Hasidic courts that existed after the Holocaust. Rabbi Teitelbaum also worked to strengthen the anti-Zionist ultra-Orthodox camp, the Edah Haredit in Jerusalem, which after the Holocaust was on the verge of collapse.[81]

Thus, over the years Rabbi Yoel Teitelbaum became one of the world's most familiar and influential Jewish figures. His large dynasty established branches in cities around the world, an extensive education system, significant political connections, and valuable assets. After establishing the Central Rabbinical Congress (Hitakhdut Ha-Rabanim) in the United States and being assigned the title "Gaavad" (*Gaon Av Beis Hadin*) as its chief rabbi and the supreme religious authority of the Edah Haredit of Jerusalem, hundreds of rabbis around the Jewish world came under the Satmar Rebbe's authority. His great success resulted in a deliberate effort to have his attempts to flee and his failings during the Holocaust be forgotten, and books and biographies written by his followers offer various explanations and excuses for his actions.[82]

The Attitude toward the Hasidic Rebbes in the Ultra-Orthodox Holocaust Literature

The above examples reflect two primary patterns of behavior. The first was that of the Hasidic rebbes who, as a result of personal initiative and pressure exerted on them by their followers, took advantage of their senior positions as public leaders in order to flee to other countries by acquiring immigration certificates or visas or by sneaking across the border. The second pattern was followed by those who, whether intentionally or because they had no other option, remained with their followers and with the members of their communities in the ghettos and the death camps. We can also distinguish these two patterns among the rebbes who survived the Holocaust. Some of them worked vigorously in the DP camps or returned to their towns or other towns in order to lead and encourage the survivors who had experienced the horrors, while others avoided doing so.[83]

Ostensibly, it could have been expected that, in light of the criticism of the flight of the rabbis before the Holocaust, different types of behavior would be reflected throughout the ultra-Orthodox literature that was written in its aftermath. However, examining this literature indicates that it actually expresses a supportive view of *both* the rabbis who remained with their communities and ultimately paid for it with their lives, and the rabbis who acted in precisely the opposite manner. There are three possible explanations for this lack of criticism. The first was the need to quickly rebuild Hasidism after the Holocaust and the recognition that no one could do this better than the rebbes who had practical experience, even if their conduct during the Holocaust had been controversial. The second explanation stems from the most basic element of the relationship between the Zaddik and his followers. The Zaddik's followers perceive him as having a holy and perfect personality that cannot err, and therefore – whether he decided to remain with his followers or to flee – it is not their job to ponder the actions of their admired rebbe.[84] The third explanation is the principle of "individual divine providence" – that "no one lifts a finger below unless it is ordered from above."[85] According to Hasidism, the Zaddik has the power to influence what is occurring around him in the spirit of the expression: "the Zaddik decrees and God executes."[86] However, due to his super-human standing, his actions and fate are determined in the heavens. For this reason, his conduct is only an expression of the will of God and is unrelated to his personal virtues, which are not in doubt.

Thus, the Hasidic literature on the Holocaust contains different kinds of texts praising both the rabbis who gave their lives in order to remain with the members of their communities, and those who escaped by the skin of their teeth. For example, the Spinker Rebbe is described as having waited his entire life for the opportunity to sacrifice himself and to enact the commandment of sanctifying God's name through martyrdom (*Kidush Hashem*):

> He burned with flames, and he rose like a wreath on the altar. In truth, the fire did not consume him, just as the maggot did not devour the flesh of Zaddikim. He himself became a flaming fire, and fire does not consume fire. Rather, his pure soul, which was the crown of perfection and the entirety of the glory of the Torah and sanctity, lacked one element: the sanctification of God (*Kiddush Hashem*). His entire life, he yearned and clung to [the question]: When will I have the opportunity to enact it…He went happily to the binding, and, according to the testimony of those who accompanied him, he danced and sang the whole way: "Cleanse our heart so that we may truly serve you." A trustworthy person told me…that he addressed him weeping and with a heartbreaking cry: "Our teacher, light of Israel! Pray for us that a miracle may occur, because we are going to die." The Zaddik looked at him with a merciful smile, placed his holy hand on his shoulder, and said: "Do not fear…We are walking toward the messiah…Yes, the messiah is in Edom, where he is shackled in iron chains and suffering the tribulations of Israel. And the holy one, Reb Isaac, went to redeem the messiah from his suffering and to remove his fetters; he took the iron chains and placed them on his head and walked to the binding, in sanctity and purity, and with joy and enthusiasm. And when his soul parted with his body…he cried, until the very last moment: "The fire on the altar must be kept burning; it must not go out."[87]

Other texts, which articulate a completely different spirit, praised the rebbes for understanding the depth of the political and the military situation and for advising the members of their communities to flee as they did, thereby serving as an example for others to emulate. One example pertains to the case of Rabbi Yosef Paneth, who fled to Romania:

> Our teacher, in his great justice and wisdom – the wisdom of the Torah that he carried within him – did not believe the lure of the Germans. As the heart knows its own bitterness, the Zaddik knew that a terrible danger loomed over all the Jews, that if not now when, and that it was necessary to take all possible measures to escape the clutches of evil, as the time had come. But within this vale of tears…our rebbe did not lose the honorable conduct of a true Jewish leader who sees to the needs not only of himself and his family but rather to the Jewish People as a whole, and whose mind envisions plans and ways of rescuing the miserable families. Our rebbe always spoke about and raised Jews' awareness of the terrible danger looming over them…To escape from the camp in time, before being taken to the camps that had been designated for liquidation, may the All Merciful protect us. But unfortunately, the words of our rebbe had no impact.[88]

At the same time, and in the very same text, the author praised the leaders who refused to flee so as not to abandon their flock. One such figure was Rabbi Yaakov Elimelech Paneth of Dej, brother of Rabbi Yosef Paneth. Here too, the author noted the deep religious and social significance of the fact that the Zaddik accompanied them on their final journey:

> The older brother of our rabbi, the great rebbe bearing the title Zikhron Ya`akkov, may his memory protect us, also resided there in the camp…On numerous occasions, our rabbi implored him to agree to prepare himself an escape plan, but the Zikhron Ya`akov refused. And one of his main reasons was that he did not want to

leave the beloved members of his community, the apple of his eye, in such a time of trouble. Indeed…on the train that took them to Auschwitz's death camps he consoled the members of his community with words of encouragement and awakening and heaped upon them the dew of rejuvenation to enable them to survive and to not lose their confidence in the Holy One, blessed be He.[89]

In the case of rabbis such as Yoel Teitelbaum of Satmar, who began their efforts to flee at the beginning of the war yet did not encourage their followers to do the same, their rescue is depicted as a divine chain of miracles aimed at saving true Judaism from total destruction. The text itself emphasized the tradition of "*Israel Saba*" (the People of Israel of all generations, with an emphasis on the preservation of religion and the observance of the commandments and customs), by which the "holy ancestors" chose not to flee but rather to sacrifice their lives in sanctification of God's name:

Forty years have passed since that great day, the day of salvation and liberation, the 21st of Kislev 5705 [December 7, 1944], the day that divine providence, through a miracle of miracles, rescued the most holy, the rabbi and the leader of the Jews, the sacred pillar of all the Jews, may his memory protect us…While picking up the shards, those pieces of charcoaled wood that were saved from the fire, whose world was destroyed and whose souls had grown dark, our holy rabbi raised up all Jews, tens and tens of thousands of kosher, devout Jews and the children of devout Jews. In a world of heresy and abandonment…we must recount this forever, so that the final generation will know – know and remember that we owe our faith to our holy rabbi, who served as an emissary on behalf of divine providence and was the one who instructed us to follow the path of sanctity…The path of "Israel Saba" that was followed by our sacred ancestors, who bared their necks and were killed in the sanctification of God's name.[90]

In the case of Rabbi Aharon Roth, who fled to Mandatory Palestine during the early years of the war, the Hasidic literature emphasizes his devotion to the Jewish People as a whole through prayer and supplications, and his deep identification with his followers who remained in Europe, which was so intense that it ruined his help:

> From the day our holy rabbi arrived in the Holy Land in the year 5700 [1939/40], he neither rested nor ceased arousing the mercy of the heavens for the Jews who were in the Diaspora facing trouble and hardship, and he always went with his students to prostrate themselves at the holy places, including the remains of our Temple, the Western Wall…The extent of his love… for his students is impossible to describe… He felt sorrow for their poverty and their duress and shared their troubles… The pure heart of our rebbe was broken to bits, which did major harm to his health and his body, as attested to in his holy letter: "I received your letter and it took a great deal of my health, may the All Merciful protect us, and I had to receive an injection to strengthen my heart…I feel the troubles of the Jews, but my strength, my heart, and my senses are exhausted."[91]

As an alternative to the description of the rescue of Rabbi Chaim Meir Hager of Vizhnitz, which may not have been heroic enough, the literature highlighted the work he undertook to rehabilitate his Hasidic court after the Holocaust: in this case, the role of divine providence in his rescue, the fact that he had personal knowledge of the "period of magnificence" that preceded World War I, and the rebbe's role as a living bridge between the eras:

> Our master, may his memory protect us, was chosen by divine providence to be a link connecting the period of magnificence, the generation of the great Jewish sages who lived before World War I, and the new generation, that of the era of the rebuilding of the remainders following the Holocaust…He was the man who saw the distress of his people, devoted his soul to rehabilitating the survivors of the destruction…It was our rebbe who breathed the soul of life into the survivors, encouraged

and strengthened them, led them to the main road of a life of strong faith in the Creator, blessed be his name, and imbued them with the hope for renewed life… Thanks to him, countless survivors rebuilt their lives and began a new chapter…[92]

The accounts reflect that all the Hassidic rebbes – those who remained with their communities and were killed in the Holocaust, those who returned from the extermination camps alive, and those who fled even before they were sent to the camps – were praised, and that all of their choices were deemed correct in retrospect. That is to say, unlike the criticism of the flight of the rabbis that occurred within the ultra-Orthodox camp itself prior to the Holocaust, after the Holocaust even the rabbis' early attempts to flee were justified.

Conclusion

The conclusions derived from the above descriptions can be considered from a number of points of view. With regard to the moral question of the conduct of the rabbis, a distinction must be made between the Hasidic worldview and the perspective that will be referred to below, for the sake of convenience, as the "secular-humanistic" worldview. According to the Hasidic worldview, the Hassidic Zaddik is a super-human figure, and an ordinary person had no way of judging his behavior. This perspective allows praise and glorification of the rebbes who risked and even sacrificed their own lives to remain with their followers on their final journey; to the same extent, it also lauds and exalts the rabbis who escaped with their lives and helped rehabilitate Hasidism after the Holocaust. This perspective also holds that divine providence determines the fate of humans, meaning that the conduct and the fate of the Zaddik is actually in God's hands. Moreover, as one interpretation depicts the Holocaust as part of the redemption and the messianic process dictated by God, all of its participants, regardless of their conduct, contributed to it equally.[93]

The secular-humanistic worldview regards people as accountable for their own decision making and choices. On this basis, the notion that the selection of two conflicting courses of action in the same critical situation can lead to the same moral conclusion is untenable. It is impossible to imagine, for example, two commanders who took part in the same battle being awarded a medal of honor, although one was killed when the force under his command charged the target and conquered it while under fire, thus contributing to the overall victory, whereas the other took advantage of his status to extricate himself from the battlefield on the grounds that his military experience could allow him to replace the commander that had been killed in a unit that would be set up after the war. According to the secular-humanistic view, a public leader's decision to refrain from saving himself and to risk, or even sacrifice his life in order to be no different than other members of the public is viewed as a particularly noble act. In contrast, one who takes advantage of his senior status and connections to save himself and those close to him, but abandons the rest of the population to their own fate without a worthy leader, is condemned with the utmost severity.

Another perspective that emerges from the article is the question of the connection between the conduct of the Hasidic rebbes during the Holocaust and the survival of their dynasties. Based on the sample presented above, we see that the Satmar rebbe, who attempted to flee in the war's early years and who, even after his rescue, did not excel in rescue activity or in providing assistance to refugees and displaced persons, succeeded in establishing one of the largest Hasidic courts after the Holocaust. Similar success was experienced by the Vizhnitzer Rebbe, who smuggled his family members across the border and ultimately joined them, and the Sanz-Klausenburg Rebbe, whose flight left behind not only his followers but his entire large family. One exception was Rabbi Baruch Rabinowitz, the Munkácser Rebbe, who, due to what he regarded as failed leadership during the Holocaust and a change in his religious worldview, refused his followers' proposal that he return to lead the court.[94]

Unlike these rabbis, the Hasidic courts whose rebbes refused to abandon them, remained with their flock, and were therefore killed in the Holocaust paid a heavy price for their decision. Due to their lack of effective and experienced leadership, major dynasties such as Spinka, Dej, and Sighet, which are discussed at length above, and dozens of other smaller Hasidic courts that operated in Hungary, experienced serious decline.[95] As it turns out, human and political nature more generously rewarded the rebbes who did everything possible to survive the Holocaust, and these figures set up immeasurably larger Hasidic courts than they had previously run. On the other hand, the dynasties of the rebbes who died in the Holocaust, which were reestablished by descendants who lacked experience, were left behind, both in comparison to their standing prior to the Holocaust and to the courts established by the rebbes who managed to escape. In any event, after the Holocaust, out of a desire to quickly revive the Hasidic legacy, survivors refrained from addressing the uncomfortable questions surrounding the flight of the rabbis and settling scores regarding the actions of the rebbes during the war.

It was Rabbi Yekutiel Yehuda Halberstam of Sanz-Klausenburg who learned the historical lesson well and implemented it in practice. On the eve of the Six-Day War, at the height of the tension in Israel as the fear of a massive Arab attack mounted, he decided to travel to New York with his family until the danger passed. The flight sparked complaints by a few Hasidim from the other courts, whose leaders remained in Israel despite the concern.[96] Shortly after the end of the war, Rabbi Halberstam joined the victory celebrations.[97] In retrospect, the Hasidic literature concealed the reason for the flight, which was depicted as a trip to help the state of Israel and to set up camps to absorb the defeated Jewish refugees.[98]

Endnotes

1   For example, Gedalyah Nig'al, "On the Figure of the Hasidic Zaddik," *Molad* 7 (35-36) (1975/76), pp. 176-182 (Hebrew); Mendel Piekarz, *The Hasidic Leadership: Authority and Faith in Zaddikim as Reflected in the Hasidic Literature* (Jerusalem, 1999) (Hebrew); Emmanuel Etkes, "The Zaddik: The Interrelationship between Religious Doctrine and Social Organization," in Ada Rapoport-Albert (ed.), *Hasidism Reappraised* (London, 1996), pp. 159-167; Gadi Sagiv, *Dynasty: The Chernobyl Hasidic Dynasty and its Place in the History of Hasidism* (Jerusalem, 2014), pp. 142-161 (Hebrew); Uriel Gellman, *The Paths That Depart from Lublin: The Emergence of Hasidism in Poland* (Jerusalem, 2018), pp. 81-100 (Hebrew).

2   On the Belzer Rebbe, his doctrine, and the dynasty he established, see: Uri Kalt, "Belz after the Holocaust: The Rebuilding of Belz Hasidism after the Holocaust (1944-1957)," master's thesis, Bar-Ilan University, 2009 (Hebrew); Ido Harari, "Atonement for Israel: The Hasidic Leadership of Rabbi Aharon of Belz and Building the Charisma of the Victim," master's thesis, The Hebrew University of Jerusalem, 2012 (Hebrew).

3   In an extensive interview that appeared in a newspaper in 1933, the Belzer Rebbe predicted that Hitler would soon be toppled from power (*Der Moment*, July 16, 1933, p. 6).

4   Nathan Zvi Friedman, *Mashmia Yeshua* (Budapest, 1944), p. 2 (Hebrew).

5   Mendel Piekarz, "The Polish Decrees and Calm and Tranquility for Hungarian Jewry at a Belzer Hasidic Sermon in January 1944 in Budapest," *Kivunim* 11 (1981), pp. 115-119 (Hebrew); Mendel Piekarz, "The Rebbetsin of Stropkov on the Assurances of the Belzer Rebbe and Two Contradictory Perspectives on the Lessons of the Decrees," *Kivunim* 24 (1984), pp. 59-73 (Hebrew); Eliezer Schweid, "The Miraculous Rescue of the Belzer Rebbe: The Belzer Hasidic Leadership's Contending with the Holocaust," *Jerusalem Studies in Jewish Thought* 13 (1996), pp. 587-611 (Hebrew); Bryan Mark Rigg, *Rescued from the Reich: How One of Hitler's Soldiers Saved the Lubavitcher Rebbe* (New Haven and London, 2004).

6   For example, Menashe Unger, *The Rebbes Who Died in the Holocaust* (Jerusalem, 1969) (Hebrew); Esther Farbstein, *Hidden in Thunder: Perspectives on Faith, Halachah and Leadership during the Holocaust* (Jerusalem, 2007); Esther Farbstein, *Hidden in the Heights: Orthodox Jewry in Hungary During the Holocaust* (Jerusalem, 2014); Moshe Yechezkel (Prager), *Rescuing the Belzer Rebbe from the Killing Ravine in Poland – Recounted by Eyewitnesses* (Jerusalem, 1962) (Hebrew); Eliezer Elimelech Stern, *On the Miracle of the Rescue of Our Holy Rabbi: Who Was Rescued from the Evil Enemies on 21 Kislev 5705* (Bnei Brak, 1988) (Hebrew); *Fun tinkelkeyt tsu lekhtigkeyt: The Miracle of the Rescue of… the Belzer Rebbe [Aharon Rokeach] and His Brother* (Brooklyn, 1982) (Yiddish).

7   On Rabbi Yoel Teitelbaum, see Menachem Keren-Kratz, *Hakanai: The Satmar Rebbe – Rabbi Yoel Teitelbaum* (Jerusalem, 2020) (Hebrew). On his actions during

the Holocaust, see Menachem Keren-Kratz, "Hast Thou Escaped and Also Taken Possession? The Responses of the Satmar Rebbe – Rabbi Yoel Teitelbaum – and his Followers to Criticism of his Conduct during and after the Holocaust," *Dapim: Studies on the Holocaust* 28(2) (2014) pp. 97-120.

8   These included, for example, Rabbi Eliezer Zeev Rosenbaum of Kretshniff; Rabbi Moshe Teitelbaum of Senta, nephew of Rabbi Yoel Teitelbaum; Rabbi Abraham Shlomo Hirsch of Beregszász; Rabbi Menachem Sofer of Târgu Mureş; Rabbi Yehoshua Eichenstein of Zidichov; Rabbi Zvi Hirsch Friedlander of Liske; and others.

9   The Sigheter, Satmar, Munkácser, Ratzferter (Újfehértó), and Dejer rebbes, for example, served in this dual capacity.

10 It should be remembered that a number of the "Hungarian" dynasties were established after the Holocaust by rabbis who had not previously observed a Hasidic lifestyle, and they are therefore not addressed in this article. One of them was that of the Pupa (also Pápa) Hasidim, one of the largest dynasties in New York. Its founder, Rabbi Yosef Greenwald (1903-1984), was conscripted into the Hungarian labor battalions during the war and survived. After discovering that his wife and ten children had been killed there, he returned to Pápa and attempted to rehabilitate the community. He then travelled to the DP camps and helped in their rehabilitation, and later spent time in Antwerp, where he led the local community of Satmar Hasidim. When he arrived in New York, he set up his own Hasidic dynasty. On this topic, see Aharon Sorasky, *VaYechi Yosef,* 2 volumes (Brooklyn, 1995) (Hebrew). Other dynasties belonging to this group include Ungvár, Košice, and Erlau.

11 On the meaning embodied in a place name, see Samuel C. Heilman, "What's in a Name? The Dilemma of Title and Geography for Contemporary Hasidism," *Jewish History* 27(2-4) (2013), pp. 221-240.

12 Jacob Katz, *The Unhealed Breach: The Secession of Orthodox Jews from the General Community in Hungary and Germany* (Jerusalem, 1995) (Hebrew); Menachem Keren-Kratz, "The Politics of Jewish Orthodoxy: The Case of Hungary, 1868-1918," *Modern Judaism* 36(3) (2016), pp. 217-248.

13 Menachem Keren-Kratz, "The Politics of a Religious Enclave: Orthodox Jews in Interwar Transylvania, Romania," *Modern Judaism* 37(3) (2017), pp. 363-391; Idem, "The Campaign for the Nature of Jewish Orthodoxy: Religious Tolerance versus Uncompromising Extremism in Interwar Czechoslovakia," *Modern Judaism* 38 (3) (2018), pp. 328-353; Idem, "Keeping up the Separatist Tradition: Hungarian Orthodoxy in interwar Austria, Yugoslavia, and Italy," *Journal of Modern Jewish Studies* 19(4) (2010), pp. 472-489.

14 Marcin Wodziński, "Toward A New Geography of Hasidim," *Jewish History* 27(2-4) (2013), pp. 171-199.

15 Kinga Frojimovics, "The Waves of Jewish Refugees to Hungary, 1933-1944," *Bishvil Hazikaron* 13 (2012), pp. 12-17 (Hebrew).

16 Sari Reuveni, "The Circumstances Promoting and Hindering Rescue among the Jews of Hungary," *Dapim: Studies on the Holocaust* 14 (1997/98), pp. 313-325 (Hebrew); *Livia Rothkirchen*, "Hungarian Jewry during the Holocaust: A General Survey," in Israel Gutman (ed.), *The Leadership of Hungarian Jewry and the Test of the Holocaust* (Jerusalem, 1975/76), pp. 25-60 (Hebrew).

17 Sari Reuveni, "The Nature of the Jewish Laws and Their Implementation in Hungary, 1938-1944," *Bishvil Hazikaron* 40 (2001), pp. 13-16 (Hebrew).

18 On this subject, see Randolph L. Braham and Nathaniel Katzburg (eds.), *The History of the Holocaust: Hungary* (Jerusalem, 1992), pp. 146-149 (Hebrew); Randolph Braham, "The Kamenets-Podolsk and Delvidek Massacres: Prelude to the Holocaust in Hungary," *Yad Vashem Studies* 9 (1973), pp. 111-130 (Hebrew); Nathan Blum, "The Deportation of Non-Citizen Jews from Hungary to Galicia in 1941," *Yalkut Moreshet* 43-44 (1987), pp. 39-64 (Hebrew); Zehava Schwartz, "The Orthodox Community in Hungary, 1939-1945," master's thesis, Bar-Ilan University, 1990, pp. 82-88 (Hebrew); Shlomo Ya'akov Gross and Yitzchak Yosef Cohen (eds.), *The Marmaros Book* (Tel Aviv, 1982/83), pp. 65-100 (Hebrew) (on the deportation of approximately 10,000 of the Jews of Marmaros).

19 Robert Rozett, *Conscripted Slaves: Hungarian Jewish Forced Laborers on the Eastern Front during the Second World War* (Jerusalem, 2013); Yitzhak Peri, "The History of the Jews Conscripted as Slaves into the Forced Labor Battalions," *The History of Hungarian Jewry: From the Roman Conquest of Ancient Hungary (Pannonia) to After the Holocaust*, 4 (Tel Aviv, 2007) (Hebrew); Zvi Erez, "Jews for Copper: Jewish-Hungarian Labor Service Companies in Bor," *Yad Vashem Studies* 28 (2000), pp. 243-286; Sari Reuveni, "Civilian Population and Prisoners: The Case of Jewish Forced Laborers from Hungary in the Camps in Austria," *Bishvil Hazikaron* 37 (1999/2000), pp. 24-28 (Hebrew).

20 The rabbis who fled during World War I included, among others: Yitzchak Friedman of Boyan (1849-1917), who fled to Czernowitz and then to Vienna; Menachem Nachum Friedman of Boyan (1868-1936), who fled to Vienna; Israel Friedman of Czortkow (1854-1933), who fled to Vienna; Mordechai Sholom Yosef Friedman of Sadigura (1896-1976), who fled to Vienna; Yitzchok Friedman of Rymanów (1886-1925), who fled to Vienna; Ben-Zion Halberstam of Bobov (1874-1941), who fled to Vienna; Itamar Rosenbaum of Czernowitz (1886-1973), who fled to Vienna; Yisroel Hager of Vizhnitz (1860-1936), who fled to Oradea; Yissachar Dov Rokeach of Belz (1881-1957), who fled to Munkács; Yitzchak Isaac of Spinka (1875-1944), who fled to Munkács; Avraham Mordechai Alter of Ger (1866-1948), who fled to Warsaw; Shmuel Weinberg of Slonim (1850-1916), who fled to Warsaw; Menachem Kalisz of Amshinov (1860-1917), who fled to Warsaw; and Dovid Bornsztain of Sochatchov (1876-1942), who fled to Lodz. For more details, see Marcin Wodzinski, *Historical Atlas of Hasidism* (Princeton, 2018), pp. 153-159.

21 See, for example, *Bamishor*, July 11, 1946, p. 3 (flight of the ultra-Orthodox leadership from Hungary) (Hebrew); Tzvi Yaakov Abraham, *History of Transylvanian Jewry*, vol. 1 (New York, 1951), p. 159 (Hebrew) (Rabbi Simcha Yoel Fisher of

Deva fled to Kenya, and Binyamin Zitron, vice-president of the Central Bureau of the Orthodox Jewish Communities, fled to Brazil); Zvi Asahel, *In The Open and Underground: The Religious Zionist Youth in Central Europe between Shoah and Revival* (Tel Aviv, 1992), p. 74 (Hebrew) (according to rescue activist and Mizrachi member Moshe Krauss, all the leaders of the movement, with the exception of him, fled Budapest in 1944); Israel Gutman (ed.), *The Encyclopedia of the Holocaust*, vol. 1, pp. 39-40 (flight of the leaders of the Jewish community of Oradea) and vol. 3, p. 310 (flight of the leaders of the Debrecen Jewish community); Naftali Stern (ed.), *Remember Satmar: The Memorial Book of the Jews of Satmar* (Bnei Brak, 1984), p. 44 (Hebrew) (flight of Dr. Ernst Marton, a member of the Romanian parliament from Cluj, to Romania); Shlomo Zimroni and Yehuda Schwartz (eds.), *Eternal Memory of the Sacred Community of Kolozsvár-Klausenburg, Which Was Destroyed in the Holocaust* (Tel Aviv, 1968), p. 50 (flight of the leaders of the Jewish community of Cluj) (Hebrew); Schwartz, "The Orthodox Community in Hungary," p. 118 (Hebrew) (flight of Pinchas [Phillip] Freudiger, the head of the Orthodox community in Budapest, and 70 of his associates from Romania).

22 Isaac Hershkowitz, "'This enormous Offense to the Torah': New Discoveries about the Controversy over the Escape of the Rabbis from Budapest, 1943-1944," *Yad Vashem Studies* 37(1) (2009), pp. 109-136; Farbstein, *Hidden in Thunder*, pp. 55-130.

23 On the possible identity of the author, see Hershkowitz, "'This Enormous Offense to the Torah'," note 25.

24 *Ohel Shem*, Shvat-Adar 5704 (Feb.-March 1944), pp. 4-7 (Hebrew); David Zvi Katzburg, *Tel Talpiot* (Budapest, 1943/44) (Hebrew).

25 Yissachar Shlomo Teichtal, *Eim Habanim Semeiacha* [A Joyous Mother of Children] (Budapest, 1943), pp. 312 (Hebrew). The translation of this excerpt is from the English translation by Moshe Lichtman: *Eim Habanim Sameach: On Eretz Yisrael, Redemption, and Unity* (Jerusalem, 2000), p. 467.

26 See note 18.

27 Farbstein, *Hidden in the Heights*, pp. 139-148, 156-162, 229-234.

28 Baruch Yehoshua Yerachmiel Rabinowitz, *Binat Nevonim* (Petach Tikva, 2012) (new edition), pp. 201 (Hebrew).

29 Jacob Reischer, *Shevus Yaakov*, vol. 2 (Aufenbach, 1718/19), Mark 106, p. 9: 30, 74 (Hebrew).

30 *Mishna*, Horayot 13a (Hebrew).

31 Babylonian Talmud, Horayot, p. 13: 71.

32 On the discussion of whose rescue takes precedence in life-threatening situations, see, for example: Farbstein, *Hidden in Thunder*, pp. 177-190; Yossi Green, "A Man Takes Precedence over Women in Matters Concerning the Saving of Life: Gender Preference in the Jewish Halakha and Implementation of the Ancient Rule in a

Changing Reality," *Netanya Law Review* 10 (2015), pp. 135-179 (Hebrew); Yaakov Navon, "Rescuing Individuals and Groups in General and in Wartime," *Tehumin* 4 (1982/83), pp. 153-172 (Hebrew).

33 Farbstein, *Hidden in Thunder*, p. 55 (quote from the English version, p. 67).

34 Farbstein, *Hidden in Thunder*, pp. 122-123 (quote from the English version, pp. 143-144).

35 On Roth, see Mordechai Hacohen Blum, *Sefer Toldot Aharon* (Jerusalem, 1989) (Hebrew); Avi Ezri Shenkolevski, *Book of Praise for Aharon* (Jerusalem, 2000) (Hebrew); Eliyahu Hacohen Steinberger, *Biographies and Stories of Rabbi Aharon* (Jerusalem, 1985) (Yiddish).

36 Aharon Roth, *Letters of the Guardians of Faith* (Jerusalem, 1941/42) (Hebrew).

37 Blum, *Sefer Toldot Aharon*, vol. 1, pp. 174-177.

38 Steinberger, *Biographies and Stories of Rabbi Aharon*, p. 236.

39 Aharon Roth, *The Book of Letters: Written by Our Rabbi…regarding Questioners among His Students and Friends to Inspire Them to Torah and God's Work* (Dej, 1941/42).

40 Blum, *Sefer Toldot Aharon*, vol. 2, pp. 48-62.

41 On Avraham Yitzhak Kohn, see Zvi Meshi Zahav, *Sefer Aspaklaria Hameira: History [of]…Rabbi Avrohom Yitzchok Kohn* (Jerusalem, 1998) (Hebrew); Meir Brandsdorfer, *Torah and Faith: Chapters in the History of Rabbi Avraham Yitzhak Kohn* (Jerusalem, 2001/02) (Hebrew).

42 On this group, see Menachem Keren-Kratz, "Ha-Edah Ha-Haredit of Jerusalem in the first 25 years after the Establishment of the State of Israel," *Cathedra* 161 (2016), pp. 139-174 (Hebrew).

43 On Rabbi Yosef Meir Weiss, see Aharon Sorasky, "The House of Spinka: A Lively Hasidic Center in Eretz Hager," *Beit Yaakov* 200-201 (1977), pp. 22-25 (Hebrew). On the Spinka Hasidic dynasty, see *Spinka Hasidism and its Rebbes* (Jerusalem, 1957/58) (Hebrew); Aharon Sorasky, *The Spinka Dynasty: The Life and Doctrine of Rabbi Yosef Meir Weiss and His Son Our Rabbi Yitzhak Isaac Weiss* (Bnei Brak, 1989/90) (Hebrew). On the special Jewish atmosphere of Maramaros County, see Menachem Keren-Kratz, *Maramaros-Sziget: Extreme Orthodoxy and Secular Jewish Culture at the Foothills of the Carpathian Mountains* (Jerusalem, 2013) (Hebrew).

44 Gross and Cohen, *The Marmaros Book*, pp. 41-47.

45 Abraham Fuchs, *Hungarian Yeshivot: From Grandeur to Destruction*, vol. I (Jerusalem, 1978), pp. 508-516 (Hebrew).

46 *Spinka Hasidism*, pp. 28-29.

47 On the struggles stemming from the expanded activity in Transylvania between the two world wars, see Menachem Keren-Kratz, "Pashkevils: The Catapult Stones in the War of the Hasidic Admorim," *Magazine of the Jewish Librarians' Association* 25 (2013) https://did.li/nsulC (accessed March 12, 2021) (Hebrew).

48 Unger, *The Rabbis Who Died in the Holocaust*, pp. 145-146.

49 Testimony of Pnina Katz regarding "The Abuse of the Spinka Rebbe," https://lib. cet.ac.il/pages/item.asp?item=16107 (accessed March 12, 2021) (Hebrew).

50 Unger, *The Rabbis Who Died in the Holocaust*, pp. 146-147; Henry Shonberger, *What Saved the King: An Account of the Miraculous Recovery of His Majesty King George V of England* (New York, 1930), pp. 112-127.

51 *Spinka Hasidism*, pp. 32-33; Sorasky, *The Spinka Dynasty*, p. 494.

52 On Rabbi Yaakov Yosef Weiss, see Mordechai Shtub, *Ohevan Shel Yisrael: The Life story of Rabbi Yaakov Yosef Weiss of Spinka* (Bnei Brak, 2002/03) (Hebrew); *Spinka Hasidism*, pp. 66-68.

53 Another contributing factor was the death of Rabbi Yitzhak Isaac Weiss, his sons, and his son-in-law, as a result of which all the remaining descendants viewed themselves as their successors and established many local Hasidic dynasties under the Spinka name. Among these descendants were Spinker rebbes in Jerusalem, Bnei Brak, Beit Shemesh, Queens, Williamsburg, Kiryas Joel, and London, and another approximately 30 rebbes from the past and present who are associated with this dynasty.

54 On Rabbi Yaakov Elimelech Paneth, see Yitzhak Levin, *In Memory: Histories of the Kedushim of 1939-1945*, vol. 1 (New York, 1955-1956), pp. 260-267 (Hebrew).

55 Fuchs, *Hungarian Yeshivot*, vol. 1, pp. 321-331.

56 The following book was published posthumously: *Yaakov Elimelech Paneth, In the Memory of Yaakov…On the Torah and the Moadim* (Brooklyn, 1952/53) (Hebrew).

57 Meir Amsel, *Zichronot Hamaor*, vol. 2 (New York, 1974), pp. 273-274 (Hebrew).

58 Moshe Zeev Friedman, "Kuntres Eileh Masa'i," in *Korban Moshe*, vol. 1 (Tel Aviv, 1986), p. 277 (Hebrew).

59 Yaakov Gerstein, *What Remains of Yosef* (Bnei Brak, 2004/05), pp. 149-150 (Hebrew).

60 Ibid.

61 On Rabbi Zalman Leib Teitelbaum, see Yoel Hacohen Rubin and Yechiel Yehoshua Schon, *Yad Yekutiel* (Brooklyn, 2003/04) (Hebrew); Gross and Cohen, *The Marmaros Book*, p. 10.

62 Ibid., p. 36; Rubin and Schon, *Yad Yekutiel*, pp. 274-281.

63 Keren-Kratz, *Hakanai*, pp. 176-177; Keren-Kratz, "Hast Thou Escaped and Also Taken Possession?"

64 *And Moses Was a Shepherd*, vol. 2 (Kiryat Yoel, 2006/07), p. 281-283 (Hebrew).

65 Mordechai Shaher, *The City of Klausenburg and Its Communities* (Brooklyn, 2012) (Yiddish).

66 Aharon Sorasky, *Torch of Fire*, I (Bnei Brak, 1996/97), pp. 143-145 (Hebrew).

67 Nathaniel Katzburg, "Ultra-Orthodox and Zionists in Hungary in the Shadow of the Holocaust," *Shragai* 3 (1989), pp. 268-277 (Hebrew).

68 Aharon Sorasky, *Torch of Fire*, vol. 1, pp. 156-157. This was in response to a summons issued by Colonel Imre Reviczky of Baia Mare (who would later be recognized as a Righteous Among the Nations) in order to rescue Jews from being sent to the death camps. On Imre Reviczky, see: Adam Reviczky, *Wars Lost, Battles Won* (New York, 1993).

69 Sorasky, *Torch of Fire*, vol. 1, pp. 156-162; Yirmiyahu Tesler, *Remember and Do Not Forget* (Jerusalem, 1968) (Hebrew).

70 Sorasky, *Torch of Fire*, vol. 1, pp. 176-208; Zvi Kratz, "The Concentration Camp in the Warsaw Ghetto and the Death March to Dachau," *Yalkut Moreshet* 77 (2004), pp. 47-64 (Hebrew).

71 According to the different sources, he had between nine and 11 children prior to the Holocaust, all of whom were killed.

72 Sorasky, *Torch of Fire*, vol. 1, pp. 209-389; Esther Farbstein, "Leadership and Rehabilitation: The Role of the Rabbis in the Religious Rehabilitation of She'erit Hapleta," in Moshe Rahimi (ed.), *From Crisis to Growth* (Rechovot, 2014) (Hebrew).

73 Tamir Granot, "The Revival of Hasidism in Israel after the Holocaust: The Ideological, Halakhic, and Social Doctrine of Yekutiel Yehuda Halberstam, the Sanz-Klausenburg Rebbe," doctoral dissertation, Bar-Ilan University, 2008 (Hebrew); Iris Brown, "'For the Sake of Building our Holy Land': The Activist Perception of the Sanz-Klausenburg Rebbe of the State of Israel and the Role of ultra-Orthodox Jews," in Yossi Goldstein (ed.), *Between Religion, Nation, and Land: The Struggle over Jewish Identity in the Modern Period*, vol. 1 (Ariel, 2014), pp. 224-240 (Hebrew).

74 *Panim el Panim*, October 10, 1958, p. 11; June 24, 1960, p. 17; January 13, 1961, pp. 4-5; September 28, 1966, p. 7; *Mishmeret Homateinu* 8 (Sivan 5720, 1959/60), p. 192; 24 (Tevet 5821, 1960/61); *Or Hamizrach*, Elul 5716, 1956/57, pp. 67-68; *Hamaor*, Adar 5720, 1959/60, p. 34; Tamuz 5720, 1959/60, p. 35-48; Tevet 5721, 1960/61, pp. 29-31; *Yedioth Ahronoth*, December 28, 1971, p. 4. All the sources reflect the persecution of the Sanz-Klausenburg dynasty by its opponents.

75 Yitzhak Alfasi, *Tiferet Shebamalkhut*, vol. 2 (Tel Aviv, 1979/80), pp. 528-563 (Hebrew).

76 Nathan Elilyahu Roth, *Meir Chaim*, vol. 1 (Bnei Brak, 1989/90), pp. 290-294 (Hebrew).

77 Alfasi, *Tiferet Shebamalkhut*, p. 533.

78 Roth, *Meir Chaim*, vol. 1, pp. 302-329.

79 Farbstein, *Hidden in Thunder*, pp. 68-71. On this figure, see Daphna Schreiber, "'King of Israel': Rabbi Abraham Mordechai Alter, the 'Imrei Emet'," in Benjamin Brown and Nissim Leon (eds.), *The 'Gdoilim': The Great Individuals Who Shaped Ultra-Orthodox Judaism in Israel* (Jerusalem, 2017), pp. 234-258 (Hebrew).

80 On Rabbi Yoel Teitelbaum, see Keren-Kratz, *Hakanai*; David Sorotzkin, "Redemption of Darkness and Despair: Rabbi Yoel Teitelbaum, the Satmar Rebbe," in Brown and Leon, *The 'Gdoilim'*, pp. 371-401.

81 Israel Rubin, *Satmar: An Island in the City* (Chicago, 1972); Menachem Keren-Kratz, "Rabbi Yoel Teitelbaum – the Satmar Rebbe – and the Rise of anti-Zionism in American Orthodoxy," *Contemporary Jewry* 37(3) (2017), pp. 457-479.

82 Keren-Kratz, "Hast Thou Escaped and Also Taken Possession?"

83 Dan Michman, "The Jewish Leadership during the Holocaust," B*ishvil Hazikaron* 36 (2000), pp. 4-12 (Hebrew).

84 Benjamin Brown, "The 'Da`at Torah' Doctrine: Three Stages," in Yehoyada Amir (ed.), *The Path of the Spirit: The Eliezer Schweid Jubilee Book*, II (Jerusalem, 2005), pp. 537-600 (Hebrew).

85 *Babylonian Talmud*, Chulin, p. 7, 72.

86 *Babylonian Talmud*, Moed Katan, p. 16, 72. There, the principle is phrased as follows: "Although I rule over man, who rules over Me? It is a righteous person. As I, God, issue a decree and the righteous person nullifies it."

87 *Spinka Hasidism*, pp. 32-33.

88 Gerstein, *What Remains of Yosef*, p. 149.

89 Ibid., pp. 149-150.

90 Eliezer Elimelech Stern, *The Miracle of the Rescue of our Holy Rabbi* (Brooklyn, 1984/85), pp. 3-6 (Yiddish).

91 Blum, *Sefer Toldot Aharon*, vol. 2, pp. 24-25.

92 Natan Eliyahu Roth, *Sefer Meir Hachaim*, vol. 1 (Bnei Brak, 1990), p. 13 (Hebrew).

93 Gershon Greenberg, "History and Redemption: Manifestations of Orthodox Jewish Messianism at the End of World War II," in Dan Michman (ed.), *The Holocaust in Jewish History: Historiography, Historical Consciousness, and Interpretations* (Jerusalem, 2005), pp. 537-578 (Hebrew); Menachem Friedman, "Haredi Jewry's Coping with the Holocaust," in Michman, *The Holocaust in Jewish History*, pp. 579-607; Isaac Hershkowitz, " Rabbi Yissachar Shlomo Teichtal's Vision of Redemption: Changes in His Messianic Approach during the Holocaust," doctoral dissertation, Bar-Ilan University, pp. 101-128 (Hebrew).

94 Tali Farkash, "The Zionist Rabbi Whose Followers Abandoned Him and Were Killed," *Ynet*, April 16, 2015 (interview with Rabbi Baruch Rabinowitz's son, in which he explains his father's decision to not return to serve as the rebbe of the dynasty) — http://www.ynet.co.il/articles/0,7340,L4647798,00.html (accessed March 12, 2021). On the relative size of the Hasidic dynasties see: Marcin Wodziński, *Historical Atlas of Hasidism* (Princeton, 2018), pp. 203-208.

95 These included the small Hasidic dynasties of the following rabbis: Yehoshua Eichenstein of Zidichov (1886-1945), who lived in Oradea; Shmuel Gross of Berbeşti (1898-1944); his son Yekutiel Yehuda Gross of Şugatag (?-1944); Avraham Avish Horowitz of Carei (Kroly) (1898-1944); Naftali Horowitz of Budapest (?-

1944); Chaim Yitzkhak Isaac Halberstam of Solotvyno (1899-1944); Chaim Teitelbaum of Tiachiv (Tetsh) (1874-1944); Mordechai Kahana of Neuheisel (?-1944); Aharon Moshe Leifer of Oradea (?-1944); Benjamin Leifer of Oradea (?-1944); Yissachar Ber Leifer of Oradea (?-1944); Reuven Leifer of Oradea (?-1944); David Leifer of Baia Mare (?-1944); Binyamin Zeev Lichtenstein of Bystrica (?-1944); Eliezer Fish of Biksad, Satmar (1880-1944); Tzvi Hersh Friedlander of Liska (1874-1944); Baruch Hager of Oberwischau (1908-1944); Elimelech Freund of Interdam (?-1944); Yaakov Yisroel Ve'yeshurin Rubin of *Szaszregen* (Suliţa) (1884-1944); Yitzkhak Isaac Rubin of Ober Rina (?-1944); Yitzkhak Rosenbaum of Rakhiv (?-1944); Yaakov Yissachar Ber Rosenbaum of Sighet (?-1944); Meir Rosenbaum of Satmar (?-1944); Shmuel Shmelke Rosenbaum of Bitschkov (?-1944); Shalom Eliezer Halberstam of Ratzfert (1862-1944).

96 Menachem Mendel Schneerson, *Torat Menachem*, Vol. 50 (5726/1967, Pt. 3), p. 16 (Hebrew); *Panim el Panim*, June 13, 1967, p. 16 (the flight of the Sanz-Klausenburg Rebbe on the eve of the war); Yair Halevy, "Against the Tide: Resistance to Ultra-Orthodox Enthusiasm Following the Six Day War," in Ofer Schiff and Aviva Halamish (eds.), *Israel, 1967-1977: Continuity and Turning* (Sede Boker, 2017), pp. 221-246 (Hebrew).

97 Yekutiel Yehuda Halberstam, *Shefa Chaim* (Netanya, 1994), Drush 19 (for 5727, 1966/67), pp. 85-89 (Hebrew).

98 Sorasky, *Torch of Fire*, vol. 2, p. 569; Yerocham Landsman and Natan Weiss, "The Rebbetzin Recites Psalms Here and Therefore We Are Victorious There," *Mishpacha – A Special Insert – "Six Days in Iyar,"* Passover, 5767 (2006/07), p. 28.

Moshe Vered

The Nagymegyer Ghetto in Upper Hungary, May-June 1944[1*]

In memory of my grandmother, my aunts and uncles and their children, residents of Nagymegyer and the nearby villages, who experienced the events described below first hand and were murdered in Auschwitz in late June 1944.

Introduction

Over the course of approximately three months, between April and June 1944, 150-180 ghettos imprisoning approximately 430,000 Jews from Greater Hungary (with the exception of the Jews of Budapest) were planned, set up, and liquidated. Although some of these ghettos held thousands or even tens of thousands of Jews, many others, referred to below as "small ghettos," contained less than one thousand Jews each, and in some cases only a few hundred.[2] On the whole, these small ghettos existed for only a few weeks, and their inhabitants were transferred, typically via intermediate stops (referred to as *gyűjtőhely*, or "collection points"), to the large ghettos. From there, they were deported for extermination.

Although the Holocaust of Hungarian Jewry has been the subject of extensive documentation and research, very little documentary and research attention has been paid to most of the small ghettos. For example, the ghetto in the town of Nagymegyer in Upper Hungary,[3] which is the focus of this article, is not mentioned in Randolph Braham's monumental book *The Politics of Genocide*,[4] Yad Vashem's *The History of the Holocaust: Hungary*[5] and *The History of the Holocaust: Slovakia*,[6] or the *Encyclopedia of the Camps and Ghettos* that was published by the United States Holocaust Memorial Museum (U.S.H.M.M.).[7] It receives only three lines in the *Yad Vashem Encyclopedia of the Ghettos during the Holocaust*,[8] and ten half-lines in the *Encyclopedia of Jewish Communities: Slovakia*[9] and the *Geographical Encyclopedia of the Holocaust in*

Hungary.[10] The studies that do address the small ghettos like the one that was set up in Nagymegyer usually treat them in an extremely schematic manner (specification of the number of Jews that lived in the ghetto, where they were concentrated, where they were sent, and when) that does not convey the story of the ghetto. This state of affairs necessarily results in the blurring and omission of the differences between the stories of the different ghettos[11] and therefore misrepresents the reality, as there were "many differences in the ways in which the ghettoization process proceeded."[12]

Few studies have engaged in detailed research of the ghettos of Hungary.[13] Because of the small number of sources regarding everyday life in these ghettos, it has been argued, this everyday life has only infrequently been a subject of scholarly research.[14] Many of these studies address different aspects of the selected ghettos (aspects regarding which we do have information) but do not recount the life of the ghetto itself, from its planning and establishment to its liquidation.[15] This has been particularly true with regard to the small ghettos.

Based on all of the above, it is clear that the small ghettos of Hungary have not yet been the subject of comprehensive, in-depth research, apparently due to the difficulty of devoting research time to them and because of concerns stemming from the paucity of relevant sources. According to Segal, the studies that have been conducted deal primarily with ghettos that were located within the borders of Trianon Hungary and almost not at all with ghettos that were located in the areas that Hitler awarded to his Hungarian allies at the expense of their neighbors.[16] Thus, it appears that in-depth comprehensive research on the small ghettos in Hungary, and in the territories that were annexed by Hungary in 1938, is lacking.

The Aim of the Study

This article seeks to present as in-depth a study as possible on a single small ghetto: the ghetto that was set up in the town of Nagymegyer in Upper Hungary. In addition to recounting the history of this small ghetto, the article demonstrates the viability and usefulness of conducting in-depth research on the histories of numerous additional small ghettos in the country. It does so by offering a detailed account of the range of sources consulted for the present study and by comparing the events in Nagymegyer with parallel events in the history of other small ghettos in Upper Hungary. In the absence of a comprehensive study on such ghettos, the present study can present only a limited comparison with the information contained in the detailed memory books of two small Jewish communities in Upper Hungary: that of Galanta[17] and that of Dunaszerdahely.[18] A similar comprehensive study on even only some of the small ghettos in Hungary could add an important new layer to our understanding of how the Holocaust played out in Hungary.

The Sources for the Study

This study is based on three contemporary Hungarian sources that pertain to the Nagymegyer ghetto. The first is a May 10, 1944 letter from the Deputy Governor of Komárom County (*Komáromi alispán*) to the chief constables of its districts, including the Komárom District, in which the town of Nagymegyer was located. The Deputy Governor's letter contained instructions for setting up the ghetto.[19] The second source is a June 13, 1944 letter from the Chief Constable of the Komárom District (*Komáromi járás főszolgabiró*), who reported to the Deputy Governor of Komárom County regarding the planning of the ghetto in Nagymegyer and the concentration of the Jews there.[20] The third is a June 24, 1944 letter from the Secretary of the Nagymegyer Town Council (*Nagymegyeri jegyző*), which contains an account of the treatment of the Jewish property that was left behind.[21]

For various reasons, particularly the brief existence of the ghettos in Hungary and the discontinuance of postal service between Hungary and the Allies in general and Palestine in particular, letters sent from inside these ghettos to recipients located outside of occupied Europe are rare to find. However, postal service within Hungary, and between Hungary and countries within the German sphere of influence, continued to operate as usual, increasing the likelihood of finding letters that were sent via such routes. One such postcard from the Nagymegyer ghetto that survived the war was written by two children, Laszlo and Eva Span, who were 8 and 6 years old respectively at the time. Laszlo and Eva were living in "safe" Nagymegyer with their grandmother while their parents were in hiding in Bratislava, Slovakia. The children wrote their parents postcards, to which their grandmother added a few lines from time to time. The children and their grandmother were ultimately sent to Auschwitz, where they were murdered. However, approximately 20 postcards, which the children sent and which were kept by their parents, survived.[22] Due to the young age of the children, the postcards contained little information that is relevant to this study. However, the final postcard, which was sent from inside the ghetto, contains interesting information that will be discussed below.

As noted above, we have very few documents and other forms of evidence that depict the Nagymegyer ghetto and the lives of the Jews who inhabited it in the course of its brief existence. Therefore, to learn about and understand the life of the Jews in the ghetto, we must rely on one kind of source in particular: the primarily oral testimonies given by survivors of the ghetto typically many years after the fact. Most of the testimonies at our disposal were found in the Spielberg Visual History Archive and at Yad Vashem and were given 40-50 years after the events themselves. Indeed, one female survivor whose testimony I documented gave her testimony 74 years after the fact.[23]

The methodological difficulties of using extremely late testimonies as a historical source is well known. In her Hungarian Hebrew, Holocaust survivor Tsvonit Sharoni expressed this dynamic in her testimony: "It is far away and there are many things that are not remembered, that have vanished. We rely on what the siblings remember…There are many things I don't remember, that I know from later on."[24] These and other such problems, such as the interviewer's influence on the testimony, have been identified and discussed in the literature.[25] In the event of contradictory testimonies, I apply Christopher Browning's solution of accepting the account of the majority.[26] However, I have also tried here to present the implications of the testimony of the minority.

Many years after the war, two members of the Weisz family who were born and raised in Nagymegyer, Jehoshua Weisz and Sarah Epstein-Weisz, wrote memoirs about their family and about the town's Jewish community.[27] The drawback of these memoirs vis-à-vis the present study stems from the fact that both siblings left the town two or more years prior to the establishment of the ghetto and can therefore provide no first-hand information about it. Their advantage lies in the extensive background material they contain.

One extremely important group of sources for the present study consists of documents that were created or collected three to four decades after the events in question by two non-Jewish Hungarian residents of Nagymegyer. László Varga, a history teacher in the local high school, collected and published a substantial amount of information and documents about the Nagymegyer Jewish community, particularly during the Holocaust.[28] Another source, which is of the utmost importance for our purposes, is a map of the town of Nagymegyer as it existed in 1944, with markings indicating the homes of Jews (before they were expelled into the ghetto).[29] The map was drawn by Sándor Gerháth in 1991 as a result of his "noble and humane interest in the history of Jewry and the local community."[30] In 2004, Gerháth made an expanded version of the map that assigns numbers to the Jewish homes. I make use of this revised map later in this article.

A final group of primary sources pertaining to the background of this study – that is, to Nagymegyer between 1934 and 1943 – consists of diaries of residents of the town of Nagymegyer and letters sent by Nagymegyerian families to their children in Palestine between 1934 and 1942, as well as a handful of postcards that were sent by these families via the Red Cross in 1943.[31]

The research reported on here was made possible by the combined usage of this wide variety of sources.

The Jewish Community of Nagymegyer: Historical Background

The town of Nagymegyer is located in Komárom County in modern-day southwestern Slovakia, halfway between Komárom and Bratislava, the capital city of Slovakia. For centuries prior to 1920, this region, located north-west of the Danube, belonged to Hungary and was known by Hungarians as "upland" (*felvidék*), or Upper Hungary. In 1920, as part of the Treaty of Trianon, which was concluded after World War I, the League of Nations transferred this area to the newly established Czechoslovak Republic. On November 2, 1938, in the First Vienna Award resulting from the Vienna Arbitration, Hitler restored Upper Hungary to Hungary, and after World War II it was returned to Czechoslovakia. Today, it is part of the Slovak Republic.[32]

Like the other Jews in Hungary, the Jews of Komárom County had enjoyed both the equality they were awarded by the Austro-Hungarian Empire in 1867 and the golden age of Hungarian Jewry until the end of World War I. Approximately 40 of Nagymegyer's Jews served in the Austro-Hungarian army during World War I and took great pride in this fact.[33] As noted, however, the region belonged to Czechoslovakia during the interwar period, and during this period its Jewish inhabitants enjoyed the tolerant and egalitarian policies that prevailed there.

Between the two world wars, the Jewish community of Nagymegyer thrived. In 1930, the community had 510 members, accounting for approximately 10 percent of the town's overall population.[34] Most of the local homeowners made a living from business, but some were artisans and members of the free professions. The community was well organized; it maintained a Jewish primary school, a synagogue, a *Beit Midrash* ("house of study"), a *Mikveh* (a Jewish ritual bath), "*Chevra Kadisha*" (a "sacred society" that ensures the bodies of deceased Jews are not desecrated and are properly prepared for burial) and "*Torah Emet*" ("truth of the Torah," i.e., the study of traditional Jewish religious law) associations, as well as a women's association for "*Gmilut Hasadim*" (helping the poor and needy).[35] The Zionist movements were also active in Nagymegyer, especially Hashomer Hatzair and Betar.[36]

The Jews' relations with the Hungarian residents of Nagymegyer were correct, at least until the Vienna Arbitration and the entire region's transfer to Hungarian control. This dynamic is reflected in the diaries of Tereza Wurmfeld[37] and in letters from town residents to their children in Palestine.[38] However, Holocaust survivor Tsvonit Sharoni testified:

> When the Hungarians entered…at that very moment, an anti-Semitism with which we were unfamiliar began. First, they painted on walls in Hungarian: "Stinking Jew" and "Jew, Get Out!" They broke the glass windows of the shop. Still, only property was damaged. Nothing happened to the family except for fear. There was no curfew, but the "*numerus clausus*" began. They entered very aggressively and they subsequently calmed down. [39]

This "calm" included limiting the economic and social freedoms of Jews and conscripting tens of thousands of young Jews into the Hungarian Labor Battalions, most of whom never returned. These measures were of course also detrimental to the Jews of Nagymegyer, whose economic situation had worsened considerably.[40] Young Jews from the town were conscripted into the Labor Battalions, and most of them died there.[41] Still, at that stage, the Jews of Greater Hungary, including the Jews of Nagymegyer, were saved from systematic extermination.

This period of "calm" came to an end on March 19, 1944, the date the Germans seized control of Hungary. On March 23, the anti-Semitic Döme Sztójay was appointed Prime Minister of Hungary and László Endre and László Baky were appointed as State Secretaries in the Ministry of Interior in charge of the country's treatment of the Jewish problem.[42] This issue was dealt with quickly and with extreme efficiency. On April 4, 1944, a meeting run by László Baky, and attended by Eichmann and his associates and representatives of the German Wermacht and the Hungarian army and gendarmerie, was held at the Hungarian Interior Ministry. At this meeting, it was decided to deport all the Jews from Hungary, and the details of the plan to contend with the Jews based on the experiences of the Nazis in other parts of Europe was worked out.[43] By April 7, 1944, the Hungarian Interior Ministry issued a ghettoization order, which was sent to county governors, mayors, and police and gendarmerie commanders around the country to clarify to recipients that the aim of the Hungarian government was to cleanse Hungary of its Jews within a short period of time.[44] The immediate practical measure with which the recipients were charged was to assemble all the Jews of every county and every town at designated locations. On April 20, 1944, on behalf of the Hungarian government, Baky asked Germany to accept the Jews of Hungary, and the Germans willingly agreed (behind the scenes, the Hungarians' request had actually been orchestrated by Eichmann). This marked the beginning of the process of the deportation of the Jews of Hungary,[45] although at the first stage, the deportation order was not sent to county governors or their associates.

The Jews of Nagymegyer and Their Expulsion to the Ghetto

The county governors, in turn, referred the ghettoization order to their subordinates, along with the detailed practical measures they were expected to take. This course of action was also followed by the deputy governor of Komárom County, Dr. Jenő Schmidt, who, on May 10, 1944, conveyed the proper instructions to the chief constables of the county's districts, including the Komárom District, in which the town of Nagymegyer was located. The following is a summary of Schmidt's instructions to the Chief Constable of the Komárom District.

The Jews of the district were to be assembled in the towns of Guta and Nagymegyer in homes that would be allocated for this purpose on defined streets to be specified by the Chief Constable. The Chief Constable was charged with ensuring that the allocation of homes ensured minimal contact between Jews and Christians. The Hungarians living on these streets were not to be forced to leave their homes. Rather, the Jews were to be crowded into the allocated homes at least four persons per room. The Jews were to be permitted to bring their belongings with them, including an unlimited amount of valuables, but should not be assisted with transportation for this purpose. They were also to be permitted to bring money with them, up to a specified amount. The Jewish inhabitants were to organize all the moveable property requiring transport in their former homes, lock their doors, and submit their inventory lists to local officials. The concentration of the Jews was to begin on May 15, 1944, and the completion of the process was to be reported within two days, by May 17.[46]

The instructions betrayed no hints of an intention to subsequently expel the Jews from these homes (in other words, they contained no suggestion whatsoever of the deportation process).

The Chief Constable of the Komárom District carried out the task with which he had been charged by the order of the Deputy Governor and informed the latter of the planning and execution of the undertaking in an orderly and detailed report written on May 16, 1944 – as the Jews of Nagymegyer and the surrounding area were being expelled into the ghetto that had been set up in town.[47] The account provided below is based largely on this report.

The Chief Constable reported that, on May 6, 1944, 543 Jews were living in Nagymegyer itself, and the nearby villages contained another 176 Jews who were to be sent to the Nagymegyer ghetto. According to the Chief Constable's report, there were a total of 719 Jews in Nagymegyer at the time the ghetto was established in mid-May 1944. In actuality, however, the number appears to have been 734 Jews, slightly more than the number indicated in the Chief Constable's report.[48]

According to the instructions issued to him by his superiors, the Chief Constable was charged with the following tasks:

1. Determining and marking the streets of the town that would constitute the ghetto.
2. Allocating specified houses on these streets for Jewish residence.
3. Crowding the Jews at least four to a room.
4. Ensuring minimal contact between the Jewish and Christian residents.
5. Implementing the instructions without forcefully evacuating the homes and shops of Christians located in the area of the ghetto.
6. Marking the homes and shops of Christians as such.

As reflected in his subsequent decisions, the Chief Constable regarded distancing the Jews' homes from main streets and roads and from the majority Hungarian population as a guiding principle of the planning of the ghetto. In his report to his superiors, he noted with satisfaction that he had almost completed the undertaking. Another guiding principle he adhered to was the instruction to refrain from forcibly removing Hungarians from their homes.[49]

The planning of the ghetto was conducted by the Chief Constable of the district on May 13, 1944 during a tour of the town he made especially for this purpose. On this tour, he was accompanied by members of the Town Council, the commanders of the local gendarmerie, the leaders of the Jewish community, and the county physician.

A large number[50] of the Jewish homes in the town were built along segments of main roads, such as Báttanyi St., the main square, and Jókai St. The reason for this was simple: most of the traffic that passed through the town did so on these road segments, making them preferred by businesses. It should be noted that the family business and the family residence were located in the same building,[51] meaning that the preferred location for a business determined the proprietor's place of residence. Ostensibly, each of these segments of road provided a convenient place for concentrating the Jews of Nagymegyer. Such an arrangement, however, ran counter to the Chief Constable's need to remove the Jews from the main roads and intersections, in pursuit of the principle of minimizing contact between Jews and Christians. For this reason, he did not establish the ghetto on any of these segments of road.

Another seemingly natural location for such a ghetto was the area of the synagogue on Jókai St., beside which stood numerous Jewish homes. For clear reasons, a significant number of Jews lived near synagogues, and therefore synagogues were often designated as ghettos or as sites for the concentration of Jews. Indeed, this was the case in Galanta and in Dunaszerdahely.[52] The Chief Constable did not enact this solution in Nagymegyer, apparently due to the fact that, as noted above, the synagogue site was located beside the main road.

To solve this problem, the Chief Constable demarcated a ghetto that was spread out along a number of intersecting segments of road. The route he designated began at Zseller St. and Erdosor St. (on the southwestern edge of town) until they met Vadasz St., which ran eastward to the lower vertex of the main square. From there, the route continued along a short segment of Szent Istivan St. until it intersected with Herceg St. It then ran east to Zrinyi St., north for a short distance to Jókai St., and then northeast to Vasut St. (the road that ran parallel to the railroad) and Bajza St. This collection of intersecting street segments actually constituted the southwest, south, and southeast edges of the town's built area.[53]

In his report, the Chief Constable noted that a number of side streets that connected the abovementioned streets to one another were also designated as part of the ghetto, but he did not mention their names. It is also noteworthy that the Chief Constable wrote explicitly that he wanted to place the synagogue (located on Jókai St., just a few dozen meters from the segment of the street that had been designated for the ghetto) and the Mikveh (located on Báttanyi St.) at the Jews' disposal for religious purposes. He planned on doing this immediately following the ghetto's establishment by finding a route from the ghetto to the buildings in question that the Jews could walk on side streets. According to the testimony of Jonas Bruck, the Chief Constable did indeed come up with such a solution, at least for walking to the synagogue.[54]

The ghetto that was demarcated by the Chief Constable did not comply with all of the instructions he had been issued. It was not a consolidated block of houses (which would have facilitated a single, dense concentration of Jews) but rather a long continuous strip. In addition, this strip included two very short segments of main roads, one of which was explicitly acknowledged by the Chief Constable: the segment of Jókai St. Without this segment the ghetto would have been split in two, an outcome he apparently sought to avoid. In any event, the Chief Constable made a concerted effort to minimize the length of this exceptional segment; indeed, he did not even agree to include the synagogue in the ghetto, even though it was located only a few dozen meters from the designated segment of Jókai St. Another segment of a main street, this time along the main square where Vadasz St. meets Herceg St. (the northern end of Szent Istivan St.), was not even mentioned in the report. The advantage of choosing this layout was its isolation and its distance from Hungarian neighbors, and the fact that it was located along the southwestern, southern, and southeastern edges of the town, as the Chief Constable noted proudly.

This distance, however, existed only in theory, as the street segments that constituted the ghetto were also home to a large number of Hungarians. These residents were not willing to leave their homes, even in exchange for Jewish homes located farther to the north. Their reason was primarily economic: the courtyards of the Jews' homes, they argued, were smaller than their own and were not suitable for the Hungarians' livestock.[55] The Chief Constable had been explicitly prohibited from forcibly evicting Hungarian residents from their homes, and therefore the Hungarians remained, even along and within the "strip" of streets that were designated as the ghetto.

After the streets were marked, the Chief Constable had to determine which homes would be used for Jewish residences and constitute the ghetto itself. These homes clearly had to be homes in which Jews already lived, due to the prohibition on forcing Hungarian residents from their homes; and, as noted by the Chief Constable himself, most of the Christian residents refused to move into the homes of Jews on streets located outside the ghetto.

By integrating the information from Gerháth's map with the information from Jehoshua Weisz's list of the Jews from Nagymegyer who were murdered in the Holocaust,[56] which includes the official addresses of the Jews in question, we can identify and enumerate the homes of Jews that were located along the roads of the "ghetto strip." Overall, the "ghetto strip" contained 27 Jewish homes. In his report, as noted, the Chief Constable also mentioned a number of other side streets that linked these streets to one another that were also designated as part of the ghetto, although we know neither the names of the streets in question nor the number of Jewish homes that they contained. Based on an examination of the map, we can estimate that there were another three such Jewish homes, and that the total number of Jewish homes located within the "ghetto strip" stood at 30.

We cannot be certain of the specific day on which the Jews from the center of town and the nearby villages were expelled from their homes and moved into the ghetto. The Chief Constable's report indicates that the expulsion occurred on May 13, 1944. However, on May 16, the Chief Constable informed his supervisor that the Jews' relocation to the ghetto had met with difficulties and that he intended on travelling to Nagymegyer on May 17, 1944, the following day, to complete the process. We must remember that the Deputy Governor of Komárom County had instructed that the expulsion of the Jews into the ghetto was not to begin until May 15 and was to be completed by May 17. From the postage stamp on the postcard of Laszlo and Eva Span,[57] we also know that on May 19, the Jews were already living in the homes in the ghetto. It is therefore reasonable to assume that the expulsion into the ghetto began on May 15, 1944 and concluded two days later, on May 17.

Some of the testimonies indicate that the order to move into the ghetto came as a surprise to the Jews. According to Edith Adler, "one clear day the Hungarians came and said that all the Jews had to leave their apartments and go,"[58] and Matilda Schwartz from the village of Ekel testified that "one morning the gendarme arrived with a note [that said] to move to a different village."[59] Other witnesses did not mention having been surprised by their move to the ghetto, and reason holds that the move itself was not a surprise, but that some were surprised by the specific date on which the expulsion was carried out or by the dizzying pace of events.[60] The conclusion that most of Nagymegyer's Jews were not surprised by the expulsion to the ghetto itself is based on a number of factors. First, the dignitaries of the local Jewish community had taken part in the visit of the district's Chief Constable on May 13 and were present when he marked the streets of the ghetto. Second, at the order of the county authorities, the Jews were required to compile lists of the furniture and other items they left in their homes, and a letter written by the Secretary of the Town Council[61] indicates that the Jews had prepared such lists. As it cannot be assumed that they made the lists within the brief period of an hour or an hour and a half they were given to leave their homes, it seems likely that they were instructed to make the lists ahead of time, apparently on May 13, and that they therefore had knowledge of the imminent expulsion, although not its precise date. Third, such expulsions had already been carried out in Hungary's eastern and central counties (Nagymegyer, which is located in western Hungary, was one of the last communities to be forced into a ghetto), and at least some of the Jews of Nagymegyer knew about them and knew that their turn would soon come.[62] Ultimately, according to *The Encyclopedia of Jewish Communities: Slovakia*,[63] the Chief Rabbi of the town and its Jewish dignitaries buried the silver ritual articles from the synagogue in the cemetery prior to the expulsion. We can assume that they did so based on knowledge of the impending expulsion (it can also be assumed that some of the dignitaries who helped the rabbi bury these valuables were present during the visit during which the Chief Constable determined the streets of the ghetto). In Galanta, the Jews also knew about the move to the ghetto one day in advance but were surprised by the timing: "… [people] say Good Sabbath… apparently tomorrow we're leaving…On Saturday night at three in the morning, the police began going from house to house and rushing people to leave…"[64] The Jews in Dunaszerdahely, on the other hand, were given relatively long notice: "Within 48 hours the Jews are ordered to evacuate all parts of the town."[65]

The process of moving into the ghetto was described in vivid terms by Edith Adler: "All of 'Megyer',[66] an entire procession, walked to the edge of town almost like Gypsies…from the center to the edge. Those who lived at the edge of town remained there, and those from the center joined them."[67] Edith Adler's description is consistent with the demarcation of the ghetto as described above: the streets of the ghetto were located on the southern outskirts of town, whereas most of its Jews lived in the center. The Jews who lived on the southern outskirts of Nagymegyer remained in their homes, and those who lived in the center moved in with them. Edith Kopel described the move into the ghetto in a similar manner: "Because we lived in the center of town, we had to move to another place that was designated for Jews. We had to move there."[68]

Two testimonies of members of the same family paint a different picture. In a postcard to his parents dated May 19, 1944, Laci (Laszlo) Span wrote: "I am writing this postcard from our new apartment. We did not go very far, just across from our old apartment."[69] Between the lines written by her grandson, the widow Span wrote: "I, Jenő Kohn and Hella, live in the same house." Lily Fleischmann (Span), Laci's aunt, said in her testimony "We had to leave the house. There was a family across the way…where we were given one room."[70] The house in which the widow Span, with whom her grandchildren who wrote the postcards and her daughter Lilly Fleischmann lived, was located at the northern end of Báttanyi St. The house across from hers, to which the widow Span made reference, belonged to Jenő Kohn. These two houses were located on the town's main street, and it seems unreasonable for the Spans and Kohns to be permitted to remain there. I have no explanation for this inconsistency.

Life in the Ghetto

"We had a big house, and we had to leave it," testified Lilly Fleischmann. "Across from us was [the home of] a family with several children in which we were given one room. They allocated [it] – the town, the government, I don't know who it was."[71] According to this testimony, there was advanced planning and the assignment of designated places of residence for the Jewish evacuees in the homes that were allocated to the ghetto. This assignment of families to houses or rooms is not mentioned in any other testimony. According to another testimony: "Other family members also moved to Nagymegyer. They lived with relatives. The family, parents and two daughters, were in the house. They stayed with their family for approximately a month."[72] The preference of residing with relatives appears to be a natural and human one. In this context, it should be noted that in a number of cases, there were entire "clans" living in Nagymegyer. For example, Shmuel Bruck recounted: "My mother had two other brothers in the village. Four married sisters [of the witness] lived in the village."[73] And there were many other instances. Some of the Jews who were sent to Nagymegyer from the nearby villages had relatives in the town. For example, Móric Schwartz from the village of Ekel was a cousin of Mindel Schwartz, who lived in Nagymegyer.[74] It can be assumed that accepting even distant relatives into one's home was, in the eyes of guests and hosts alike, preferable to taking in total strangers. However, the accommodation efforts in this matter were apparently not completely successful, compelling the Chief Constable, on May 16, 1944, to write: "Based on the telephone message I received today, there are still many more who cannot settle in…To get this done, I will go to the town again tomorrow."

The Secretary of Nagymegyer's Town Council was charged with compiling an inventory of the belongings that the Jews left in their homes after their expulsion from the town.[75] According to his letter, the town's Jews had lived in 116 apartments, and the Jews who were expelled from the nearby villages had occupied 44 apartments, for a total of 160 Jewish-occupied homes. It should be noted that the terms "apartment" and "home" are interchangeable in this context, as Nagymegyer had no apartment buildings or buildings with more than one story (there was sometimes a low attic that was used for storage, but not for residential purposes). In the town's 160 Jewish homes, as reported by the Chief Constable above, lived 719 people, at an average density of 4.5 people per home.

After the expulsion, all of these Jews were forced to squeeze into just 30 homes – that is, to live at an average density of 24 people per home, or 5.3 times the average density prior to the expulsion. It is no wonder that even the Chief Constable, who allocated the homes to the ghetto and knew how many evacuees they would need to absorb, was surprised by the crowding in the homes in this area. A substantial number of survivors remembered this aspect of the ghetto for the worse, as reflected in descriptions such as: "We crowded into a large apartment belonging to Jews, a few families together…";[76] "We were crammed in for a few months…[It was] very difficult…because it was crowded…";[77] "We slept on the floor, a large family…"[78]; and others.

To further illustrate the crowded conditions, it is helpful to consider the size of the homes in Nagymegyer – that is, the number of rooms they contained. The town, of course, had large homes, like the home of the wealthy Bruck family.[79] But it also had small, deficient homes, like that of the widow Mindel Schwartz.[80] From various testimonies it appears that most of the homes were typical to this rural region and contained three or four rooms each.

Varga provides a photograph of a family home in Nagymegyer from the World War II period.[81] The home is quite similar to homes that were typical of the rural region even in the surroundings of the town. One home of this kind that remains standing today is the "Old House" in the nearby village of Csicso.[82] This home has an area of 60 square meters (5 x 12), consisting of two rooms, a kitchen, and a pantry. A drawing of a home of a middle-class Jewish family appears in the book of Sarah Epstein-Weisz.[83] This house had two large rooms, another room that was split by a divider into two smaller rooms (a bedroom and a room that was used both as kitchen and pantry and also for making cheese). Assuming that the kitchen was also used for residential purposes during the period of intense crowding,[84] a "typical" home at the time appears to have contained 3-4 rooms that served as living space. In total, then, the 30 homes in the ghetto contained a total of 90-120 rooms, for an average density of 6-8 persons per room. This assessment is supported by Lilly Fleischmann's testimony that "we lived in one room – a mother and three children…and my sister with three children,"[85] or, in other words, eight persons per room. Without a doubt, this was heavy overcrowding. It was also apparently typical of all the ghettos. In Galanta, for example, the ghetto also had "terrible crowding," with "between four and eight families" packed into each home.[86]

The ghetto in Nagymegyer was an "open" ghetto, meaning that it was not surrounded by a wall or a fence. Although the Deputy Governor's above-mentioned instructions required ensuring as little contact as possible between the Jews and the Hungarians, it did not explicitly stipulate that a fence be erected around the ghetto. It is reasonable to assume that the Chief Constable refrained from erecting such a fence because, as noted, many Hungarians lived along the streets he had designated for the ghetto in Nagymegyer and refused to leave their homes. As a result, any fence that surrounded the ghetto would also necessarily surround their homes and cause them great inconvenience. In addition, erecting such a fence would require substantial resources, particularly in the form of building materials, which were in short supply. There was, however, no shortage of laborers; as we will see, young Jewish women were sent from the ghetto and put to forced labor in the agricultural sector.

Soon after the Jews were forced into the ghetto, their freedom of movement was limited. In the initial days of the ghetto, the Jews may have still been able to leave their homes freely,[87] on the condition that they exited from a side door and not directly onto the street of the ghetto from the main entrance.[88] Quite quickly, however, the Jews were placed under curfew and could not leave their homes until 11 am. The Jews of the ghetto used this permission to leave their homes in order to purchase food. Edith Adler maintained that "in the morning they could go out and buy bread and milk,"[89] and Jonas Bruck remarked: "Where could you go? To the synagogue or the market. You could only go out after 11:00, but [by then] all the fresh produce had already been sold."[90] This last point is of particular interest, as although the Chief Constable had planned to allow the Jews access to the synagogue, the market was located far from the ghetto, as reflected in the map. It is therefore unclear whether the Jews were allowed to go to the market to purchase food by special permit, or whether they could walk freely outdoors, at least in the initial days of the ghetto (as asserted by Lilly Fleischmann above).

"It went on like that for 3-4 weeks," stated Jonas Bruck.[91] "Later, you could only go out at night." Jonas Bruck appears to have erred in his assessment of the length of time during which the Jews could also leave their homes during the day, as the ghetto was established on approximately May 15, 1944, and the Jews were already expelled from the ghetto to a collection point which they were not permitted to leave by the end of May or the beginning of June.[92] It is more likely that the permission to leave the ghetto during daylight was in place for approximately 10 days, after which the curfew was extended so that the Jews could only leave their homes during the initial hours of darkness. This situation lasted approximately five days, at which point all the Jews of the ghetto were transferred to the collection point.

The young Jewish population, and especially the young Jewish women,[93] were used as forced labor on the agricultural farms near the town.[94] The women were put to work doing a variety of harvesting and gathering jobs, in accordance with the agricultural season, including harvesting corn,[95] gathering sugar beets,[96] and harvesting beans.[97] It was hard work. "For someone who is not used to it, it is not easy to work a full day," explained Edith Kopel.[98] "We had to do it, there was no choice." In Galanta and Dunaszerdahely, on the other hand, going out to work in the fields was not compulsory. In Galanta, the Jews were permitted to go to work in the fields, apparently at their own request,[99] and in Dunaszerdahely the Jews also sought this work, as they believed it would buy them "some sort of protection and vague patronage" and therefore jumped at the opportunity.[100] It should be noted that the farmers in whose fields the Jews worked and the gendarmes who guarded them were not abusive and did not harm the Jewish girls who were engaged in forced labor.[101]

For unknown reasons, some of the Jewish girls in Nagymegyer were not taken for forced agricultural labor. One was Yaffa Berger, who explained: "We did nothing. They did not give us work, [they] only [had us] pass the time."[102]

This was also the lot of the older women and children; according to one testimony, the "women and children did nothing."[103]

"Every home had a well,"[104] wrote Sarah Epstein-Weisz, and there was no shortage of water in the ghetto. The cesspit in the courtyard of every home served as a toilet, and when the pit was full the residents simply dug another pit, so that the issue did not pose a genuine difficulty.[105] Typical daily hygiene involved washing one's hands and face in a bowl filled with water. People bathed their full bodies once a week in a large wooden bathtub.[106] In the crowded conditions of the ghetto it was difficult to maintain bodily cleanliness, as "you couldn't go over to a non-Jewish neighbor's [house] to bathe."[107]

The Collection Point in Nagymegyer

The Nagymegyer ghetto as defined above existed for approximately two weeks.[108] On an unknown date, the central government's directive arrived regarding the transport of Jews out of the local ghettos, their deportation from Hungary, and fulfillment of the original intention of "cleansing Hungary of its Jews." The plan's first stage called for the Jews' transfer to collection points, such as abandoned factories, empty warehouses, brick factories, and other such sites located near railroad tracks and train stations.[109] At the beginning of June 1944, Jews started to be moved out of the Nagymegyer ghetto to such a collection point.

Just outside the town of Nagymegyer to the northwest stood a factory for the production of sugar and alcohol. The factory was located further down the road that ran alongside the railroad tracks beside the Nagymegyer train station.[110] Also beside the factory was a large farm that, prior to the Jews' expulsion, had employed Miriam Fischer as a forced laborer gathering sugar beets. Among other things, the farm had a large pigsty.[111] According to some testimonies it was a farm for the raising and fattening of pigs,[112] whereas other testimonies describe it as a transit station for trading in pigs, to which farmers in the area would bring the pigs they wished to sell. The pigs were assembled there and then loaded onto trains that brought them to the markets in the nearby large cities.[113] The major advantage of this pigsty from the perspective of the Hungarian government and its intention of deporting the Jews was its location next to the train station. In the eyes of the Hungarians, the area, which was fenced in to prevent the pigs from wandering, was also suitable for assembling the Jews until their transport.

One day in the beginning of June,[114] the Hungarian gendarmes entered the Nagymegyer ghetto, assembled all the Jews, and transferred them to the nearby pigsty.[115] That was the second expulsion of the Jews of Nagymegyer[116] (the first being their expulsion from their homes into the ghetto). The evacuees were permitted to take only a few small belongings with them[117] – primarily only the most essential things,[118] and first and foremost food.

In the pigsty, the Jews were denied "even minimal living conditions," as "the place was not meant for human beings, but rather for pigs."[119] The sty contained a few sheds, but they had low ceilings fit for pigs and were difficult for people to enter,[120] forcing them to remain outside. "Where the cows and the young pigs were…That's where we lived, all the families. They cooked food there,"[121] recounted one witness. "We ate what there was,"[122] explained another, which was apparently not much.

The Jews were held in the pigsty for a few days, and on June 5, 1944, they were sent by freight train to the ghetto in Komárom.[123] This brought an end to the two stages of the Nagymegyer ghetto and to the Jewish community of Nagymegyer.

The Jews of Galanta and Dunaszerdahely suffered a similar fate. Galanta's Jews were expelled from the ghetto in their town to the grounds of the Meyer-Meyerhof sugar factory, where they lived for a few days in the worst of conditions. From there, on June 11 and 13, 1944, they were sent by train to Auschwitz.[124] The Jews of Dunaszerdahely were taken from their ghetto and densely crowded into the Great Synagogue (3,000 people in the synagogue and its courtyard), where they were held for one week. From there, on June 18, they were sent to Auschwitz.[125]

The Hungarians' Attitude toward the Deportation of the Jews

The relations between the Hungarian and Jewish residents of Nagymegyer ranged from hostility, which at times was tangible, to indifference. None of the survivors mention expressions of sympathy or shared grief on the part of the Hungarian population. For example, one survivor's testimony recounted that we did not really feel it [the anti-Semitism] [from] the general population, …they did not show it to us. But there were some who were happy when the Jews were harassed. Members of the Arrow Cross made trouble for the Jews whenever they could. They would beat them, inform on them, and take their property.[126]

According to another testimony, however: "We felt the hostility everywhere. We were Jews, whom they looked at with an evil eye…There were no non-Jewish friends."[127]

During the expulsion to the ghetto, the local Hungarians displayed indifference to the fate of the Jews. They were not abusive to them as they made their way from their homes to the ghetto, and they took no interest in the procession of evacuees. "I did not see the non-Jews on the way to the edge of town."[128] But what *was* very important for the Hungarians was the division of the spoils – the property the Jews left behind: "The non-Jews in the vicinity were waiting for it. I'll take the apartment of so-and-so, and of so-and-so…For them it was a happy occasion."[129] According to another testimony, "the non-Jews came and cleaned out the homes of the Jews"[130] – "They were very good neighbors until they took [our] things."[131]

Only a single compassionate act carried out by a Hungarian during the three-week period during which the Jews of Nagymegyer resided in the ghetto, and then at the "collection point," was recalled, and by only one of the survivors: "One evening, a non-Jew came and gave our family some bread and milk and said that he would come back another day."[132]

The march from the pigsty to the train that took the Jews far away from Nagymegyer, never to return, leaves a different impression. This time, the Hungarians were not indifferent; rather, for "the Christians, it was a happy day to see the Jews being taken away. They applauded when we were taken away."[133] This joy may have stemmed from the local Christians' understanding that after the expulsion, the Jews would not be returning to ask the residents of the town for their property back. The situation in Galanta was similar:

They [a few Jews who were permitted to leave the ghetto, walk to their (former) homes, and bring back a few beds and blankets]

passed through Galanta until the train station. They passed the
closed-up homes next to their shops that had been looted…The
previous time [the expulsion from the Jews' homes to the ghetto],
the neighbors lowered their heads, as if they shared our grief. This
time [from the grounds of the sugar factory to the train that would
take them to another collection point in Nové Zámky and from
there to Auschwitz], they stood with eyes filled with hatred and
shouted derogatory cries…From time to time, someone pushed
down an elderly [Jew] as those watching laughed.[134]

The Attitude of the Hungarian Catholic Church

According to Braham, the Hungarian Catholic Church had "a mixed reaction,
at best,"[135] to the consolidation of the Jewish population within ghettos and
their deportation eastward, meaning, they sometimes expressed sympathy for
the suffering Jews but took no action to thwart the deportation plans. Again
according to Braham, very few sources relate to the views and reactions of lower-
tier clergymen[136] – a few attempted to help the persecuted Jews, but the decisive
majority remained passive, as did the rest of the population.

With regard to the local Catholic Church's attitude to the Jews of
Nagymegyer, I am in possession of one testimony that was written by Mindel
Schwartz on June 6, 1939: "On Sunday, there was a certification of trainee
priests. The Jews feared it greatly, but, amazingly, not a word was said cursing
the Jews."[137] Miksa Bruck attributed this attitude to all the Catholics in the
town. "Thank God, there is nothing unpleasant on the part of the Catholics. On
the contrary, all the good people in their ranks oppose the anti-Jewish laws."[138]

A unique case, apparently, was that of a Jewish woman named Erzsebet
Wurmfeld, who married a Hungarian Catholic man named János Soros[139] in
the village of Csicso on July 6, 1930. In mid-May 1944, the Jews of Csicso
were expelled to Nagymegyer. However, Erzsebet and her four children were
not expelled, and remained in the village, even though she was a Jew (who had
not converted to Christianity) and even though, according to the Third Jewish
Law, her children were also Jewish. According to the family lore,[140] the local
Catholic priest extended his protection to her and her children. The peasants in

the village, who were aware of Erzsebet's origins (she was born in the village in 1906), did not turn her in.

This should not be taken to mean that the Catholic Church and devout Catholics whole-heartedly supported the Jews. On the contrary, the above-noted case appears to have been a positive exception. When asked whether "the Catholic students with whom you went to school had helped," Miriam Fischer answered: "No. They were anti-Semitic. They heard what happened to us. No one in the village helped us or supported us."[141]

We can assume that there were some converts to Christianity in Nagymegyer and the surrounding area, as the rate of conversion to Christianity among Jews in Hungary was relatively high.[142] In his report, the Chief Constable of the Komárom District noted that he had instructed the local authorities "to separate Jews who had already converted to Christianity from the rest of the Jews." Nevertheless, we do not know what this separation actually meant. The only convert to Christianity we know of for certain[143] was murdered at Auschwitz.[144]

The Theft of Jewish Property

The directive sent by the Deputy Governor of Komárom County to the heads and chief constables of the county's districts,[145] which makes clear the Hungarian government's intention to cleanse Hungary of its Jews, assigned importance to the treatment of Jewish property.

> Belongings requiring transport shall not be moved to the Jews' camp. The Jews are required to arrange the movable property in need of transport inside their former homes, to record them in an inventory list in the presence of local officials, and store them in a closed place. No use shall be made of the stored immovable property, even for the purpose of moving residences, and it shall not be conveyed to outsiders.

The intention was clear: the Jews would be forced to leave most of their belongings in their homes, after arranging and recording them in an orderly manner. The lists would be conveyed to local officials, who would be responsible for organizing and safeguarding the property until they received additional instructions from the central government.

In his report to the Deputy Governor of Komárom County, in which he informed him of the implementation of his instructions, including the designation of the roads of the ghetto and the relocation of the Jews, the Chief Constable of the district made no mention of the matter of Jewish property and said nothing about the receipt of inventory lists of the property left in the apartments from which the Jews were expelled.

None of the survivors' testimonies mention making such a list or handing it over to town officials or to anyone else for that matter. This may be because they had no knowledge of these lists. After all, the witnesses whose testimony I consulted were unmarried and relatively young (ages 16-26) at the time of the expulsion to the ghetto, and the heads of the households may have dealt with making the inventory lists without involving the younger family members.

The director of the local office of the Hungarian Ministry of Finance in the county seat of Komárom County charged the Nagymegyer Town Council with preparing lists of the property that the Jews had left in the homes from which they were expelled, in the town itself and in the nearby villages.[146] In a report dated June 24, 1944, the Secretary of the Council explained at length why the council could not complete this task. His explanation includes a detailed assessment of the work force that was formally listed as being at its disposal, as opposed to the staffing in actuality; a review of the other tasks with which it had been charged; and a description of the scope of the task of recording the items in the 160 homes of the Jews who had been expelled. The secretary concluded his argument by asserting that "recording the Jewish property is entirely impossible."[147]

The solution that was found, apparently on August 8, almost two months after the deportation of the Jews from Nagymegyer, was the appointment of receivers to oversee the property in the abandoned Jewish homes.[148] It can be assumed that, by this point, little property actually remained in the abandoned homes and everything had already been looted by the town's Hungarian residents.

According to the testimonies of survivors, the property theft began much earlier, immediately after the Jews' expulsion from their homes. In her above quoted testimony, Yolana Denes noted that "the non-Jews in the vicinity were waiting for it and were dividing up the spoils even before the expulsion."[149] Immediately following the expulsion, explained Lilly Fleischmann, "the non-Jews came and cleaned out the homes of the Jews…They were very good neighbors until they took [our] things."[150] Lea Geron described these developments as follows: "We evacuated the houses and they took everything, even the local population. Whatever they could carry."[151] The local Hungarians did more than just loot the Jewish homes; they moved into some of them. "What did we find in the town?" asked Shmuel Bruck, who returned to Nagymegyer after the war, in his testimony. "Nothing. We found empty homes."[152] Edith Adler, on the other hand, returned to Nagymegyer after the war to search for her family and immediately discovered that "a Hungarian family was living in our home…I saw my coat on somebody else. I kept quiet and did not say a word."[153] All in all, the local inhabitants looted the property and the homes of the Jews, and the letter of the Secretary of the Town Council was meant to explain to the supervising authorities how the property that had been meant to fall into the hands of the Hungarian authorities had disappeared.

In other places, as well, the Jews' neighbors pounced on and looted the abandoned property and moved into the Jewish homes immediately after the Jews were forced out. For example, in Galanta the Hungarians permitted a few Jews to leave the ghetto, walk to their (former) homes, and bring back a few beds and blankets: "When they arrived [at their home], they were surprised to discover that even before 48 hours had passed, the home had been broken into. They also saw the villagers arriving in throngs and moving into the homes they had left… "[154] The situation in Dunaszerdahely was similar: "One passes robbed, destroyed houses…Jewish immovable property, furniture, appliances, and belongings have been found all over the broad area and throughout the villages…"[155]

Two survivors recalled that the Hungarians did not limit themselves to stealing the property that remained in the homes. According to Yolana Denes, "there were rich Jews in the community. They [the Hungarians] took them and beat them [until] they bled to get them to reveal where they hid the property."[156] Lea Geron recounted that "they inflicted murderous blows on the soles of the feet[157] of all the town's [Jewish] dignitaries."[158] None of the other testimonies make any mention of beatings or torture. Even Jonas Bruck – the son of Miksa Bruck, one of the town's wealthiest Jews – and Edith Adler – whose father was the owner of the gristmill and other enterprises and was necessarily a wealthy man – did not mention that their fathers had been beaten in an effort to get them to reveal where they had buried their money. Moreover, Jonas Bruck also explained that they used the money they had with them to purchase food in the Komárom ghetto[159] and recounted throwing gold jewelry into the mud when they were being removed from the pigsty "so that earrings would not be torn off with the ear."[160] According to these testimonies, it appears that at least some of the wealthy Jews were not tortured and succeeded in maintaining possession of the money and valuables which the Hungarians were attempting to appropriate during the interrogations and the beatings.[161]

The End of the Jewish Community of Nagymegyer

After a few days in the pigsty, Hungarian gendarmes and soldiers led the Jews of Nagymegyer and the surrounding area to the town's train station, which was located just a short distance away. There, on June 5, 1944, the Hungarians forced the Jews onto closed freight cars and transported them, crowded and without food or water, to the nearby city of Komárom, the county seat. Komárom, as noted, already had a ghetto in the Monostori fort, in which the city's Jews, and Jews from Nagymegyer and the other small ghettos in the area, were imprisoned. This old fort dated back to the period of Hungary's wars with the Turks, and at this point in time its remains were primarily underground relics, such as tunnels, labyrinths, and catacombs. Two to three thousand Jews were brutally forced into this complex, where they remained for approximately ten days with almost no food or water.[162] From there, on June 13 (22 Sivan) and June 16, 1944 (25 Sivan 5704), they were sent by freight train, again in conditions of extreme crowding and with no food or water, to Auschwitz-Birkenau. Upon arriving at Auschwitz-Birkenau following this unbearable journey that lasted a number of days,[163] the Jews underwent a selection to determine who would be sent for extermination and who would engage in hard manual labor. Of Nagymegyer's approximately 530 Jews, only 110 survived.[164]

Conclusion

This study offers a detailed account of the expulsion of the Jews of Nagymegyer and the surrounding area from their homes and their concentration, initially in conditions of extreme crowding in some 30 homes within a strip of streets on the outskirts of town (the ghetto), and then in inhumane conditions in a large pigsty (the collection point). From there, the Jews of Nagymegyer were sent, via the Monostori fort, which served as part of the Komárom ghetto, to Auschwitz-Birkenau for extermination.

This study demonstrates that through in-depth research, we are capable of painting a detailed picture of the entire life span of a small ghetto in Hungary. It is the type of study from which most researchers have thus far recoiled, due to the fact that it must necessarily rely on a large number of widely dispersed oral and written sources created over many decades that reflect numerous differences and completely different perspectives.

Due to the absence of comparable studies on other smaller ghettos, especially those of Upper Hungary, it was not possible to conduct a detailed comparison between the history of the Nagymegyer ghetto and that of other ghettos. Still, we were able to observe a significant number of elements of the story of the Nagymegyer ghetto in light of parallel events that occurred in the nearby ghettos of Galanta and Dunaszerdahely. This comparison reflects that the history of the Nagymegyer ghetto was not an exception, despite differences in the details of the events that occurred in each of the three ghettos. These differences expand and add depth to our overall understanding. For example, an apparent contradiction between some testimonies maintaining that Jews from Nagymegyer were tortured in order to compel them to reveal where they hid their valuables, and the testimonies of others who did not undergo such torture, can be explained by the understanding that not all wealthy Jews were tortured: in Galanta Jews were tortured based on lists that were compiled ahead of time, and in Dunaszerdahely Jews were selected to be tortured at random.

Conducting similar studies on an additional few dozen small ghettos in Hungary could provide us with a more accurate picture of the Holocaust as it played out in the country's rural communities, enabling us to answer questions such as: Did the Jews of the rural communities in Hungary know ahead of time, even if only a few days in advance, what awaited them? Did the Jews resist the ghettoization and deportation, even if only passively? And how did Hungarian neighbors, junior clergy, and local governments react to the concentration and deportation of the Jews?

Endnotes

1   'This study was conducted within the framework of a seminar paper I wrote as a research student under the supervision of Prof. Havi Dreifuss. I am grateful to her for her assistance and her encouragement.

2   The term "ghetto," which is used by most scholars who have researched the Holocaust in Hungary, was used in official Hungarian documents to refer only to sections of large localities and cities. To refer to the concentration of Jewish populations in small localities, including Nagymegyer, they used terms such as "collection point" (*gyűjtőhely*) or "housing" (*lakótelep*). See Dan Michman, *Jewish Ghettos during the Shoah: How and why did they emerge?* (Jerusalem, 2008), pp. 112-113 (Hebrew). Nevertheless, in accordance with the customary terminology, I too use the term "ghetto" to refer to the first stage of rounding up the Jews of Nagymegyer. To refer to the second stage of this process I use the abovementioned term "collection point," which was used by the Hungarians.

3   Today, this town is named Vélky Meder. It is located in Slovakia, some 65 kilometers southeast of the capital city of Bratislava.

4   Randolf L. Braham, *The Politics of Genocide: The Holocaust in Hungary, Volume I* (Boulder, CO, 2016), p. 797.

5   Randolph Braham and Nathaniel Katzburg, *History of the Holocaust: Hungary* (Jerusalem, 1992) (Hebrew).

6   Gila Fatran, *History of the Holocaust: Slovakia* (Jerusalem, 2015) (Hebrew).

7   Geoffrey P. Megargee, *The United States Holocaust Memorial Museum Encyclopedia of Camps and Ghettos, 1933–1945, Volume III: Camps and Ghettos under European Regimes Aligned with Nazi Germany* (Bloomington, IN, 2009).

8   Guy Miron and Shlomit Shulhani, *The Yad Vashem Encyclopedia of the Ghettos during the Holocaust* (New York, 2010). See the entry for Nagymegyer.

9   Yehoshua Robert Bichler, *Encyclopedia of Jewish Communities: Slovakia* (Jerusalem, 2003), p. 196 (Hebrew).

10 Randolf L. Braham, *Geographical Encyclopedia of the Holocaust in Hungary* (Evanston, IL, 2013), p. 539.

11 Tim Cole, *Traces of the Holocaust: Journeying In and Out of the Ghettos* (London, 2012), pp. 5-8.

12 Miron and Shulhani, *The Yad Vashem Encyclopedia of the Ghettos*. Quote translated from the introduction to the Hebrew edition, p. 22.

13 For example, in "Historical Position of the Hungarian Jewry and untold Ghetto Accounts," published in Eric Sterling (ed.), *Life in the Ghettos during the Holocaust* (Syracuse, 2005), Agnes Kadar presents three brief testimonies describing three small ghettos, although most of the article is devoted to the ghetto in Budapest.

14 Regina Fritz, "Inside the Ghetto: Everyday Life in Hungarian Ghettos," *Hungarian Historical Review* 4(3) (2015), p 608.

15 See, for example, Cole, *Traces of the Holocaust*, which describes a detailed characteristic specific to each of eight small ghettos in Hungary.

16 Raz Segal, *Genocide in the Carpathians: War, Social Breakdown and Mass Violence, 1914-1945*. (Stanford, 2016), pp.14-15.

17 Nitza Esther Kalish, *Restoring the Soul: The Kalish Family of Galanta* (Jerusalem, 2014) (Hebrew).

18 Alfred Engel, *Memorial Book for the Community of Dunaszerdahely* (Israel, 1975) (Hebrew).

19 Komáromi alispán, *A zsidók lakhelyének kijelölése*, 7506/1944, 10.5.1944, Nagymegyer város okirati 1900-1945, Járási leveltár, Komárom [Deputy Governor of Komárom, *Marking the Homes of Jews*, 7506/1944, May 10, 1944, Documents of the Town of Nagymegyer, 1900-1945, County Archive, Komárom]. Hereinafter: Order of the Deputy Governor of Komárom County.

20 Komáromi járás föszolgabiró, *A zsidók lakhelyének kijelölése*, 670/1944, 16.5.1944, Nagymegyer város okirati 1900-1945, Járási leveltár, Komárom [Chief Constable of the Komárom District, *Marking the Homes of Jews*, 670/1944, May 16, 1944, Documents of the Town of Nagymegyer, 1900-1945, County Archive, Komárom]. Appears in: Varga Lászlo, *Velünk éltek*, Komarom – *A nagymegyri zsidóság történte*, (Kómáromi Zsido Hitkozseg, 2010), p. 135 [Varga Lászlo, *They Lived with Us: History of the Jews of Nagymegyer*, the Jewish Community of Komárom, 2010]. Hereinafter: Report of the Chief Constable of the Komárom District.

21 Nagymegyeri jegyző, *Gyüjtőtáborba elhelyezett zsidók vagyonának biztositassa*, 2142/1944, June 24, 1944, *Nagymegyer város okirati 1900-1945*, Járási leveltár, Komárom [Secretary of the Nagymegyer Town Council, Securing the Property of Jews Who Were Transferred to the Collection Sites, 2142/1944, June 24, 1944, Documents of the Town of Nagymegyer, 1900-1945, County Archive, Komárom]. Hereinafter, Letter of the Secretary of the Nagymegyer Town Council.

22 Lászlo and Eva Span, Postcards, 1943-1944, Yad Vashem Archive (hereinafter YVA), RG 0.75, File 3439, Documents 50-91.

23 Edith (Lenka) Adler, Testimony, May 17, 2018 (in the presence of the author, Moshe Vered, at the interviewee's home in Or Yehuda, Israel).

24 Tsvonit Sharoni (Rozi Vays), Testimony 31365, USC Shoah Foundation, Visual History Archive Online, http://vhaonline.usc.edu/login.

25 See, for example, Zoe Vania Waxman, *Writing the Holocaust: Identity, Testimony, Representation* (Oxford, 2006), pp 1-2, 5-6, 167-169; Annette Wievorka, *The Era of the Witnesses* (Ithaca and London, 2006), pp. 129-131.

26 Christopher R. Browning, *Remembering Survival: Inside a Nazi Slave Labor-Camp* (Jerusalem, 2010), p. 25 (Hebrew).

27 Jehoshua Weisz, "Recounting My Life from Nagymegyer to Givatayim," written testimony, Yad Vashem, Document Archive, RG O.33, File 7399, Item 6186983l; Sarah Epstein-Weisz, *I Have Recounted All of Myself* (Israel, 2015) (Hebrew).

28 Lászlo Varga, *Velünk éltek – A nagymegyri zsidóság története* (Jewish Community of Komárom, 2010).

29 Ibid., p.131.

30 Jehosua Weisz, *A nagymegyri zsidó családok tragédiája 1944-45 ben* (December 2000).

31 Tereza Wurmfeld, *Nagymegyeri napló 1933-1934*; Tereza Wurmfeld, *Nagymegyeri napló 1937-1939*. These diaries were written in Hungarian and have not been published. Copies of them are on file with the author (the originals are in the possession of a family member in Slovakia); Yihiel Bruck, Letters from Home: A collection of letters by the Bruck family from Nagymegyer, Hungary, to their son Uri Bruck in Tel Aviv, 1939-May 1943, Yad Vashem, Documents Archive, RG O.75 file 1107; Mindel Schwartz, Collection of Letters from Nagymegyer, Hungary to her children in Palestine, 1939-1943 (unpublished). The letters were written in Hungarian. They were translated into Hebrew by the author and are on file with him. Yehudit Papai, *My Dear Son* (letters between the Schwartz family in Czechoslovakia and their Son Marci who immigrated to Palestine, 1938-1944) (Israel, 2013) (Hebrew).

32 The two towns of Galanta and Dunaszerdahely, which are compared here to Nagymegyer in a number of respects, are located in southwest Slovakia, 37 kilometers and 20 kilometers from Nagymegyer, respectively. Everything stated in this paragraph regarding Nagymegyer is also applicable to Galanta and Dunaszerdahely.

33 Bichler, *Encyclopedia of Jewish Communities: Slovakia*, p. 195.

34 Ibid.

35 Sarah Epstein-Weisz, interviewed at her home on Kibbutz Negba by the author, September 9, 2014.

36 Bichler, *Encyclopedia of Jewish Communities: Slovakia*, p. 196; Schwartz, Collection of Letters, March 1, 1939; Epstein-Weisz, *I Have Recounted All of Myself*, pp. 49-52.

37 Wurmfeld, *Napló*, 1933-1934; Wurmfeld, *Napló, 1937-1939*.

38 Yihiel Bruck, Letters.

39 Atzmon Chana, Testimony 45474, USC Shoah Foundation, VHA. Other survivors testified similarly: Papai, *My Dear Son*, pp. 197-198.

40 The survivors of Nagymegyer testified similarly. For example: "Father could not acquire a work permit" (testimony of Jonas Bruck, Testimony 17137, USC Shoah Foundation, VHA); "They slowly but surely took everything, livestock…" (testimony of Matilda Schwartz from the village of Ekel near Nagymegyer, Testimony 9596, USC Shoah Foundation, VHA); "They took shops, they took permits, they took cars. Every day it was something new" (testimony of Yolanda Denes, Testimony 7679, USC Shoah Foundation, VHA); and many others.

41 On the conscription of young Jews into the Labor Battalions, see Yihiel Bruck, Letters; Schwartz, Collection of Letters. In *Velünk éltek*, pp. 68-74, Varga documents the names of 13 residents of the town who never returned from the Labor Battalions. For more on the Labor Battalions, see Randolph L Braham, *The Hungarian Labor Service System, 1939-1945* (Boulder, 1977).

42 Braham, *Eichmann and the Hungarian Jews*, p. 15.

43 Braham and Katzburg, *History of the Holocaust: Hungary*, p. 243.

44 I know of only one incident in which a recipient of the ghettoization order in Komárom County took action to rescue a Jew. In this case, one of the judges in Komárom sentenced a Jewish childhood friend from Nagymegyer (Lajos N.) to a number of months in prison on false charges. After his release, Lajos returned to Nagymegyer but found no one there from the Jewish community, including his wife and children. During his imprisonment, they had all been sent to Auschwitz. József N. (Lajos's son from his subsequent marriage following the Holocaust), in testimony before the author, March 21, 2018.

45 Braham, *Eichmann and the Hungarian Jews*, p. 21.

46 Order of the Deputy Governor of Komárom County.

47 Report of the Chief Constable of the Komárom District.

48 According to the testimony of Matilda Schwartz (Testimony 9596), the daughter of a Jewish family from the village of Ekel, 15 Jews from her village were expelled to Nagymegyer – not to Guta, as was mistakenly indicated by the report of the Chief Constable.

49 Report of the Chief Constable of the Komárom District.

50 According to a tally of the addresses of Jewish homes that appear in a list preserved by the Yad Vashem Archive, such homes accounted for 48% of the Jewish homes in the town. YVA RG O.41, File 972, pp. 1-6.

51 For example, Atzmon, Testimony 45474: "When someone entered the shop, a bell would ring and grandpa would come in from the apartment, which was next door." According to Shmuel Bruck (Testimony 44364, USC Shoah Foundation, VHA), "the business was at home."

52 In Galanta, "the ghetto encompassed a total of two streets, the ones on which the Beit Midrash and the synagogue were located." Kalish, *Restoring the Soul*, p. 365. In Dunaszerdahely, "three streets located to the east of the synagogue and the enclave between them were designated as the residential area for the Jews." Engel, *Memorial Book for the Community of Dunaszerdahely*, p. 272.

53 See the map of the town in Varga, *Velünk éltek*, p. 131.

54 Jonas Bruck, Testimony 17137: "Where could you go? To the synagogue or to the market. You could only go out at 11:00 [in the morning]…It went on like that for three to four weeks."

55 Report of the Chief Constable of the Komárom District.

56 Weisz, *A zsidó családok tragédiája.*

57 Lászlo and Eva Span, Postcards.

58 Adler, Testimony.

59 Schwartz, Testimony 9596.

60 "It was so sudden and so quick. By the time we woke up, we were already gone." Denes, Testimony 7679.

61 Letter of the Secretary of the Nagymegyer Town Council.

62 "We heard from our older brother who had been conscripted. He wrote to us that they were starting to expel the Jews and that it had started in the east, in Kárpát, in Kassa, and elsewhere." Fisher, Testimony 23706.

63 Bichler, *Encyclopedia of the Holocaust: Slovakia,* p. 196.

64 Kalish, *Restoring the Soul,* p. 362.

65 Engel, *Memorial Book for the Community of Dunaszerdahely,* p. 272.

66 The inhabitants of Nagymegyer and their descendants referred to the town of Nagymegyer as 'Megyer' for short.

67 Adler, Testimony.

68 Edith Kopel, Testimony 21586, USC Shoah Foundation, VHA.

69 Lászlo and Eva Span, Postcards, Doc. 75.

70 Lilly Fleischmann, Testimony, Yad Vashem Collection, RG O.3, Item No. 4416424.

71 Fleischmann, Testimony.

72 Schwartz, Testimony 9596.

73 Shmuel Bruck, Testimony 44364.

74 Alisa Sharon, *Family Schwartz,* April 19, 1999. http://img.tapuz.co.il/forums/2836886.doc

75 Letter of the Secretary of the Nagymegyer Town Council.

76 Elisheva Vays, Testimony 23177, USC Shoah Foundation, VHA.

77 Fleischmann, Testimony.

78 Adler, Testimony.

79 According to Shmuel Bruck, the Bruck family had a "gigantic house." Shmuel Bruck, Testimony 44364.

80 Schwartz, Collection of Letters. A letter dated June 9, 1939 contained the following description: "My room is so small that it is impossible to open the door wide and wheel in a stroller, because of the bed." A letter dated March 13, 1941 read: "We were very scared, because the house should have been repaired last year, and [we] did not manage to do so…"

81 Lászlo Varga, *Béke poraikra*, http://csemadok.sk/files/2013/07/varga-laszlo-beke-poraikra-gyia-25.pdf, Drawing 84.

82 The Jews of this village were expelled to Nagymegyer. See the Report of the Chief Constable of the Kómaron District.

83 Epstein-Weisz, *I Have Recounted All Of Myself*, p. 27.

84 Ibid., p. 11: "The working table in the kitchen was transformed by night into a folding bed, and there she [the Hungarian maid] slept."

85 Fleischmann, Testimony.

86 Kalish, *Restoring the Soul,* p. 365. .

87 Fleischmann, Testimony. "One could walk freely outside in the street."

88 Jonas Bruck, Testimony 17137.

89 Adler, Testimony.

90 Jonas Bruck, Testimony 17137.

91 Ibid.

92 Varga, *Velünk éltek*, p. 66.

93 As noted above, most of the young men were sent to serve as forced labor in the Labor Battalions.

94 Adler, Testimony; Fischer Miriam Alzbeta, Testimony 23706, USC Shoah Foundation, VHA Kopel, Testimon 21586; Schwartz, Testimony 9596.

95 Kopel, Testimony 21586.

96 Fischer, Testimony 23706.

97 Adler, Testimony.

98 Kopel, Testimony 21586.

99 In Galanta "there was a directive that everyone had to work. Some are permitted to leave the ghetto to work for a few hours, especially in the fields…" Kalish, *Restoring the Soul*, p. 365.

100 In Dunaszerdahely, "young adults were given the opportunity to leave for agricultural work…There are some non-Jewish peasants who are the proprietors of large agricultural farms who took pity on us and agreed to accept us for agricultural work on their farms." Engel, *Memorial Book for the Community of Dunaszerdahely*, p. 271.

101 Adler, Testimony; Schwartz, Testimony 9596.

102 Yafah Berger, Testimony 21225, USC Shoah Foundation, VHA.

103 Schwartz, Testimony 9596.

104 Epstein-Weisz, *I Have Recounted All Of Myself*, p. 26.

105 Ibid., p. 31.

106 Ibid.

107 Fleischmann, Testimony.

108 In Galanta and in Dunaszerdahely, the ghetto in its initial format existed for approximately three weeks; in Galanta, from May 7 through May 30, 1944, and in Dunaszerdahely, from May 17 through June 8, 1944.

109 Braham, *The Politics of Genocide*, pp. 533-535.

110 Which, as noted, was located in the northeastern part of the strip that constituted the ghetto.

111 Varga, *Velünk éltek*, p. 66.

112 Fischer, Testimony 23706.

113 Fleischmann, Testimony; Jonas Bruck, Testimony 17137.

114 Fischer, Testimony 23706; Elisheva Vays, "Words Written by Elisheva regarding the Deportation to Auschwitz that Were Found in Her Room," Written on a Notebook Sheet in Hungarian – Translated into Hebrew by Chava and Yosef, YVA RG O.33, File 6896.

115 Adler, Testimony; Fleischmann, Testimony; Elisheva Vays, "Words Written by Elisheva"; Jonas Bruck, Testimony 17137; Vays, Testimony 23177; Berger, Testimony 21225; Kopel, Testimony 21586; Fischer, Testimony 23706.

116 Kopel, Testimony 21586.

117 Elisheva Vays, "Words Written by Elisheva."

118 Fischer, Testimony 23706.

119 Elisheva Vays, "Words Written by Elisheva."

120 Jonas Bruck, Testimony 17137.

121 Adler, Testimony.

122 Berger, Testimony 21225.

123 Varga, *Velünk éltek*, p. 66.

124 Kalish, *Restoring the Soul*, pp. 367-372.

125 Engel, *Memorial Book for the Community of Dunaszerdahely*, 276-281.

126 Geron, Testimony 23026.

127 Denes, Testimony 7679.

128 Adler, Testimony.

129 Denes, Testimony 7679.

130 Fleischmann, Testimony.

131 Ibid.

132 This occurred when the family was residing in the pigsty, where they suffered from a shortage of food. See Sharoni, Testimony 31365. The accounts of the suffering of the Jews of Galanta contain only one case of "a Christian who was friendly…he came to the train station to raise their spirits." Kalish, *Restoring the Soul*, p. 370.

133 Denes, Testimony 7679.

134 Kalish, *Restoring the Soul*, p. 370.

135 Randolph Braham, "The Christian Churches in Hungary and the Holocaust," *Yad Vashem Studies* 29 (2001), p. 194 (Hebrew).

136 Ibid., p. 209.

137 Schwartz, Collection of Letters, June 6, 1939.

138 Yihiel Bruck, Letters, January 18, 1939.

139 This information is based on the couple's marriage certificate, a copy of which is on file with the author.

140 Conveyed orally to me by Magda Fekte, Erzsebet Wurmfeld's daughter, in Komárom, Slovakia, on August 2015

141 Fischer, Testimony 23706.

142 Yehuda Don and George Magos, "The Demographic Development of Hungarian Jewry," *Jewish Social Studies* 45 (3-4) (1983), p. 212, Table 13.

143 The convert was Ignác Deutsch, who converted to Christianity in order to avoid having his land confiscated. See Yihiel Bruck, Letters, October 26, 1939.

144 Varga, *Velünk éltek*, p. 68, entry 11 in the table.

145 Order of the Deputy Governor of Komárom County.

146 Letter of the Secretary of the Nagymegyer Town Council.

147 Ibid.

148 Varga, *Velünk éltek*, p. 66.

149 Denes, Testimony 7679.

150 Fleischmann, Testimony

151 Geron, Testimony 23026.

152 Shmuel Bruck, Testimony 44364.

153 Adler, Testimony.

154 Kalish, *Restoring the Soul*, p. 365.

155 Engel, *Memorial Book for the Community of Dunaszerdahely*, pp. 289, 291.

156 Denes, Testimony 7679.

157 This form of torture was apparently customary for the Hungarians. For example, "Móric Kalish was also taken to be interrogated…Among other things, he was beaten on the soles of his feet, and from then on, until his death, he could no longer stand up." Kalish, *Restoring the Soul*, p. 369.

158 Geron, Testimony 23026

159 Jonas Bruck, Testimony 17137.

160 Berger, Testimony 21225.

161 The theft of money and valuables from Jews, and the torture of Jews to get them to reveal where they had hid them, was built into the process of concentrating the Jews in the ghettos. See Braham and Katzburg, *History of the Holocaust: Hungary*, p. 262. The Jews that were to be tortured for this purpose were either selected by the Hungarians according to lists they already had (see Kalish, *Restoring the Soul*, p. 369) or were selected randomly (see Engel, *Memorial Book for the Community of Dunaszerdahely*, p. 272).

162 Elisheva Vays, "Words Written by Elisheva"; Jonas Bruck, Testimony 17137.

163 Three days according to Jonas Bruck, Testimony 17137; five days according to Denes, Testimony 7679.

164 Varga, *Velünk éltek*, pp. 68-76.

Noam Liebman

Indeed "merely a description of the events"?: The Memoirs of Jewish Warsaw Ghetto Police Officer Stanisław Gombiński as a Model for Hermeneutic Analysis[1]

Introduction

In 1944, Stanisław Gombiński, a senior officer in the Jewish Police of the Warsaw Ghetto, sat down in hiding on the Aryan side of the city and wrote his memoirs. Gombiński was concerned about the cynical smile of future readers. He presumed that the memoirs of an officer in the reviled Jewish Ghetto Police would be received with skepticism. But "the reader should not rush to pass judgement," he cautions. "He should first read these pages, and he should then read thousands of others…And then he should try again, for the hundredth or thousandth time, to understand our reality."[2]

Gombiński wrote two versions of his war-time memoirs.[3] He himself characterized his writing as no more than "an unorganized collection of fragments of memories, a heap of waste, remnants of thoughts."[4] However, in this article, based on a close reading of Gombiński's memoirs, I show how these texts are indicative of writing that was planned and organized.[5] Also indicative of the importance of Gombiński's memoirs is the fact that at least one of its versions has been mentioned by studies on the Jewish Police in the Warsaw Ghetto.[6] Gombiński's memoirs are also quoted in studies dealing with the Warsaw Ghetto from a broader perspective to help researchers convey the organizational structure of the Jewish Police, as well as its attire, its internal hierarchy, and other aspects. Indeed, his memoirs are sometimes the only source of description for organizational aspects of the activity of the Jewish Police[7] and have become an important source for research, despite reservations pertaining to the reliability of a Jewish police officer writing after the liquidation of the ghetto for readers of the future.[8]

This article considers a number of fundamental questions pertaining to Gombiński's writing: Why did he write two versions of his memoirs? How did his changing life circumstances influence his writing? Who were the future readers for whom Gombiński was writing? And in what ways did his appeal to them influence the story he chose to tell? Reading Gombiński's memoirs offers insight into the subjective point of view of an officer of the Jewish Police in the Warsaw Ghetto, which is a subject that has yet to be sufficiently examined by the scholarship. Reading Gombiński's memoirs in this manner can also serve as a possible model for the examination of war-time memoirs in particular, and documents of personal documentation (ego-documents) in general.

I begin by presenting the life story and war-time memoirs of Stanisław Gombiński. Next, I offer an explanation for why Gombiński wrote two versions of his memoirs and attempt to determine which version was written earlier, which is extremely important for understanding the development of his argumentation.[9] I then explain the methodology that guided me in my reading of his memoirs, analyze the differences between the two versions, and consider the significance of the narrative that Gombiński sought to construct for himself and his future readers. Gombiński's target audience, I argue, changed during the transition between the two versions, and as a result so did the content of the text. Through an analysis of Gombiński's memoirs, I also offer a number of methodological conclusions regarding the reading of ego-documents from the Holocaust and in general.

I. Stanisław Gombiński and His War-Time Memoirs

Stanisław Gombiński was born in 1907 in Włocławek, Poland.[10] On more than one occasion, his war-time memoirs express his connection to his Jewish identity[11] and, no less important, to his identity as a Pole.[12] He became a Doctor of Law in 1930, and he was subsequently certified as an appeals court judge. Despite his efforts, Gombiński did not complete his certification as an attorney.[13] He married Stanisława Solnicki and the couple had two children.[14] Before the war, he managed to publish an essay on the different aspects of the death penalty in a professional legal journal.[15] The manner in which he engaged this issue also reverberates throughout my analysis of his war-time memoirs.

When the war broke out, Gombiński was living in Warsaw. He volunteered for the army but was injured, and while he was in the hospital the Germans confiscated his apartment. After the move into the ghetto in November 1940, he joined the Jewish Ghetto Police, where he achieved the status of a senior officer as head of the secretariat of the Jewish Police. His job involved office work for the most part. As a result of his position, and also due to his connections with Józef Szeryński,[16] commander of the Jewish Police in the Warsaw Ghetto, he was privy to the decision-making processes within the Jewish Police and, to a great extent, within the Judenrat. Following the Aktion of January 1943, he left the police and soon after left for the Aryan side of the city, where he went into hiding.[17] He survived the war and moved to Paris, where he lived until his death in 1983.[18]

The two versions of his memoirs were handwritten in Polish, with phrases in Yiddish, German, French, and Latin sprinkled throughout. One version was written in a single thick notebook (actually, a number of notebooks bound together), with pages numbered from 189 to 573. The original of this version is located in the Ghetto Fighters' House Archive.[19] A second version, also located at the Ghetto Fighters' House Archive, is divided into two parts, each containing nine notebooks, for a total of 576 pages.[20] The second version was published in Polish in 2012 along with an introduction and comments.[21] The two versions were written in close chronological proximity to one another, just a few months apart. In both, Gombiński addresses the period of the Warsaw Ghetto.

For many years, uncertainty surrounded the identity of the author of one of the versions – the one that was written in a single thick notebook. Initially, the Ghetto Fighters' House Archive attributed this text to Jewish Ghetto Police officer Josef Rode. However, Pnina Hauser subsequently concluded that it represented an attempt by Gombiński to rewrite the 18 notebooks of the other version, though parenthetically noting that "this still needs to be checked and proven."[22] An identical copy produced using a typewriter is on file at the Yad Vashem Archive, catalogued under the name "Anonymous" and linked to the name "Josef Rode." The file had previously been classified only as anonymous.[23] The Emanuel Ringelblum Jewish Historical Institute in Warsaw also has a copy catalogued under the name anonymous.[24]

Researchers have also drawn different conclusions regarding the author's identity. Yisrael Gutman's book on the Jews of Warsaw attributes it to Josef Rode and makes no mention of Gombiński.[25] In their book on the Warsaw

Ghetto, Barbara Engelking and Jacek Leociak maintain that it was written by an anonymous author who was recently identified as Josef Rode.[26] In her book on the Jewish Police in the Warsaw Ghetto, in contrast, Katarzyna Person refers to the author as anonymous.[27] With the assistance of Noam Rachmilevitch of the Ghetto Fighters' House Archive, Havi Dreifuss was the first to publish the fact that Gombiński was the author of the text in question.[28]

Gombiński's two versions are not identical, and his writing of a second version was not an attempt to simply recreate the same content a second time. In the following section, I discuss the evolution and the content of his memoirs and specify which version, in my view, was written earlier.

II. The Evolution of Gombiński's Memoirs

The evolution of the first version of Gombiński's memoirs began in November 1943, when Hirsch Wasser, secretary of the *Oyneg Shabes* archive, asked Gombiński to write his memoirs.[29] Gombiński began writing during the first half of 1944,[30] and in the summer of that year he entrusted their safe keeping to Basia Temkin-Berman, a member of the Jewish National Committee (Żydowski Komitet Narodowy, ŻKN).[31] In a diary entry dated November 6, 1944, Temkin-Berman notes that his memoirs, which were divided into two parts, had been lost in the numerous moves from apartment to apartment she had made in October of that year for the purpose of remaining hidden. "Oh, how tormented I have been over the fact that I left the bag of texts in my apartment." She writes. "It contains the essays of Barland and Gombiński – the first and second [parts]…and many others."[32] As a result, Gombiński appears to have written another version of his memoirs – the text that was split into two parts, each containing nine notebooks, which were handed over to the Central Jewish Historical Commission in September 1945.[33] The differences between the different versions I point out below establish that it was not just another copy written by Gombiński, as assumed by the editors of the Polish edition,[34] but rather the product of a new writing process. This text, therefore, is the later version of his memoirs.

Temkin-Berman states that Gombiński's memoirs had two parts, allowing us to conclude that the first part – the 188 initial pages that were missing from the thick notebook – had been in her possession and was indeed lost. The second part was preserved and appears to have been entrusted to the Ghetto Fighters' House Archive as part of the Berman Archive. The thick notebook, then, constitutes the second part of the earlier version written by Gombiński.[35]

Gombiński concludes the earlier version with the words "Warsaw, April-June 1944, completed on July 22, 1944, the second anniversary of the deportation."[36] In the later version, Gombiński concludes only the first part with the words: "Warsaw, April 19, 1944, the first Memorial Day."[37] As the date that concludes the first part of the later version is revised to be chronologically earlier than the date that concludes the second part of the earlier version, we can conclude that Gombiński was aware of the loss of the manuscript that he had entrusted to Temkin-Berman. When he rewrote the later version he treated it as the single version that would remain, allowing the conclusion that the dates that Gombiński wrote at the end of the different versions of his memoirs were symbolic and not necessarily accurate.

It is important to note the impossibility of a precise dating of the period during which Gombiński wrote the later version. His activities during the Warsaw Uprising of 1944 are unknown. All that is known is that at some point after the uprising ended, he was sent to the camps at Ożarów and Pruszków. After liberation, in January 1945, he arrived in Lublin.[38] Therefore, the later version was written between October 1944, when the copy in Temkin-Berman's possession was lost, and September 1945, when this version was handed over to the Historical Commission in Warsaw.

In terms of content, in the earlier version Gombiński wrote about the period of the Ghetto until its liquidation. His texts begin with an explanation of the location of the offices of the Jewish Police, the ghetto's division into neighborhoods, and the Jewish Police's command and control structure in the different parts of the ghetto. He also describes some of the departments of the Jewish Police and the logistical roles supporting its everyday operations. He then describes the activity of the police, points of friction with the Jewish population, and relations between the police and the Judenrat. He also extensively addresses the public criticism that was levelled at the police and the Judenrat during the existence of the ghetto, as well as the criticism he anticipates will be directed at these two entities in the future. Later, Gombiński also discusses the armed Jewish resistance and what he regarded as the desired historical memory of Jewish life in the ghetto. The manuscript – that is, the part at our disposal – has no title, although on a number of occasions in the notes Gombiński mentions that the title of the first part – the one that would later be lost – was "The Streets of the Ghetto." He also notes that the first part provides an extensive account of life in the ghetto.[39]

The first part of the later version, both parts of which survived, bears the title it was given by Gombiński: "All Are Equal (The Streets of the Ghetto)" [*Ale głach* (*Ulica ghetta*)].[40] In this chapter, Gombiński provides a chronological review of the history of the Warsaw Ghetto, from its establishment until the outbreak of the Uprising in April 1943. In this context, Gombiński offers a narrative description of the Jewish public in the ghetto, including lifestyle, public figures, the Jewish population's view of reality, the rumors that circulated in the ghetto, and different points of view of the ghetto residents. He does all this from the perspective of someone observing from the side, providing a bird's eye view of ghetto life. The title and the content of this part then, are consistent with Gombiński's description of the lost first part of the earlier version.

The second part of the memoirs is titled "Purgatory (The Ghetto Authorities)" [*Czyściec* (*Władze ghetta*)].[41] Although this title only appears in the later version, this part is comparable to the surviving part of the earlier version and is what it can be compared with. Here, as in the earlier version, Gombiński places an emphasis on characterizing the Judenrat and the Jewish Police while also discussing the Jewish population's relations with these two institutions and contending with criticism of their functioning that had already been voiced or that he expected to be voiced in the future. In this article, therefore, I compare the surviving part of the earlier version and the second part of the later version: "The Ghetto Authorities."

III. A Methodology for Contemplating Gombiński as a Documenter

Gombiński was well aware of what he was putting down in writing. He wrote clearly and fluently, and even sometimes poetically; he wrote so that his words would reach the readers of the future, as he frequently notes explicitly in both versions.[42]

He was an educated man, a fact he thought important that the readers of his memoirs know. He used phrases in Polish, which he spoke fluently,[43] and he peppered his writing with phrases from other languages.[44] He mentions historical events that he felt provided important context for an analysis of European culture;[45] relates to the suffering of other peoples under Nazism or the murders of other peoples throughout history;[46] demonstrates his knowledge of Polish history and culture;[47] and displays his knowledge of philosophy (for example, when borrowing images from Zoroastrianism[48] or referring to Clio, the muse of history).[49]

Gombiński's great awareness regarding his documentation is reflected not only in what he writes but also in what he does not write. We can determine with a great level of certainty that his memoirs are not a spontaneous and unorganized "heap of waste," and that he wrote preliminary drafts before putting it all down in writing. In practice, then, we can also say that these drafts, although they are not in our possession, constituted a third version and the earliest incarnation of his memoirs. For example, the earlier version of Gombiński's memoirs contains only approximately 30 erasures of a few words over hundreds of well-written pages. This small number of erasures in this version is particularly notable in comparison to a single occasion on which Gombiński erased almost an entire page. The planning of the writing is also notable in the differences between the erasures themselves. The full page that was erased leaves the reader no chance of reading what was written, but the style of erasure is not uniform. The two versions reflect that on some occasions Gombiński erased words or sentences simply using a line or an "x," whereas on other occasions he erased text in a manner that prevents the erased text from being deciphered.[50]

Gombiński's awareness of the writing process, his meticulous erasures, and the changes that occurred from one version to the other may raise questions in the reader's mind regarding the writer's reliability. However, it is important to remember that changes are natural whenever there are two texts, each consisting of hundreds of handwritten pages. We must also keep in mind that Gombiński wrote both texts just a few months apart, and perhaps even less, in the extreme reality of living in hiding; it would therefore be unreasonable to expect to find two identical texts.

In his book *On Autobiography*, Philip Lejeune, a pioneer in the study of biographies and diaries, explains that the fundamental condition for the unwritten autobiographical contract between the writer and his or her reader is that the reader knows that the writer is a person who really exists.[51] As the writer proclaims the veracity of his or her existence, the reader tries to find falsehoods and errors in the text. As readers, Lejeune holds, we regard ourselves as detectives in search of "breaches of contract" whose meaning pertains to the identity of the writer.[52] The problem, according to Lejeune, is that when we find what appears to us to be a breach of contract, we immediately tend to ascribe it too much significance. From Lejeune's perspective, we tend to assign a dimension of deeper "truth" to revelations" that we are able to discover even though the writer did not tell us about them.[53]

This common mode of reading is part of the positivist paradigm, which views memoirs as a facsimile of reality. Attempting to read Gombiński in this manner is futile, as he writes in a style that enables every reader to find almost anything they wish to find. This is true with regard to accounts of major events and references to public figures, as well as to views on controversial topics. One example of this phenomenon is his description of the controversial character of Jakub Lejkin,[54] deputy commander of the Jewish Police in the Warsaw Ghetto. Another example is his attitude toward cases in which police members exploited their position of power for their own personal gain.[55]

At this juncture, I pause momentarily to consider the legal essay that Gombiński published in 1938 in which he discusses the arguments for and against the death penalty. The essay reflects continuity in Gombiński's style of writing and highlights the positivist paradigm's limitations in analyzing his writing.

Gombiński begins the essay by reviewing the history of the death penalty, the major justifications for it, and the primary arguments for its annulment.[56] He then clarifies: "The aim of this essay is not to defend one thesis or another, and not even to describe the struggle between advocates and opponents of the death penalty. Its aim is to present an episode from this struggle."[57] From this point on, Gombiński devotes almost the entire essay to quotes from others, the lion's share of which pertain to execution and to the public and legal discussion it elicits. Indeed, of the essay's seventeen pages, Gombiński wrote a cumulative total of only four. Throughout the entire essay, he refrains from expressing an opinion on the subject. He does not even sum up the discussion or point out questions or additional issues to be clarified. Readers can perhaps conjecture that Gombiński opposed the death penalty, as he provided longer quotations from its opponents; this, however, would be an assumption based solely on the number of pages.[58] As in his writings from during the war, here too Gombiński does not offer readers insight into his own views.

For this reason, we are in need of a different approach to reading the text, one stemming from a different paradigm. Here, I propose using a constructivist paradigm based on the premise that people construct their own realities. The major question that needs to be clarified, therefore, is not what exactly happened, but rather how the author understood the reality of his or her life.[59] The main tool employed here is a hermeneutical reading of the text that combines the hermeneutics of restoration (faith) and the hermeneutics of demystification.

In the hermeneutics of restoration, explains Ruthellen Josselson, we begin by attempting to believe the narrator and to convey to the reader what the narrator is trying to say by means of his or her subjective point of view. This approach is important primarily when attempting to give a voice to oppressed or marginalized groups.[60] This idea poses a number of challenges when applying it to a man such as Gombiński, who was an officer in the Jewish Police. As noted by Dreifuss, war-time memoirs reflect "the bias of writers attempting to justify positions or decisions that were reached in the past,"[61] and even more so in the case of officials of the Jewish establishment.[62] We can also assume that their status as victims on the one hand, and people who worked with the system of oppression on the other hand, makes it difficult for them to write their subjective story as they experienced it and as they wish it to be conveyed. One example of this difficulty is the presumed fear, among members of the Jewish Police, of being tried for their actions after the war.[63]

Still, Gombiński appears to have been regarded as a reliable and honest man even during the war, and therefore hermeneutics of restoration plays an important role in analyzing his writing. This is attested to by the words of another police officer, Stanisław Adler. In his war-time memoir, Adler is extremely critical of almost every person from the Jewish establishment he chooses to mention. Although he himself was under Gombiński's command, he did not respect him on a professional level, belittled his abilities, and condescendingly nicknamed him "the law student."[64] On various occasions, he mentions that Gombiński lacked the skills that were required for his job,[65] and asserts that every one of his appointments had been a mistake.[66] Despite his criticism, however, he describes Gombiński as follows:

> Intellectual, bright, intelligent, and, most importantly, a man with rare honesty…He always stood out for his European manners (in the most positive sense of the word), his honesty, his commitment to the truth, his lack of obsequiousness toward Szeryński, and, most importantly, his perception of the gravity of our situation and the need for solidarity with and compassion for the unfortunate members of our community.[67]

The hermeneutics of demystification, on the other hand, relate to language as distorted, multi-meaning, and ambiguous. The experience is not transparent to the subject of the narrator, and therefore the story that is told also encompasses a story that is not told. The self-evident presents itself as that which requires no further analysis, although the interpretive attempt is able to remove masks and reveal illusions of false consciousness.[68] The structure of language reveals a social structure that influences the perspective of the narrator, as, for example, in the cases of gender, status, and power relations. For the narrator, however, this is the realm of the self-evident and, therefore, of the invisible. It is a position that is subconscious.[69] The interpretation involves paying attention to the ways in which the story is structured, how it is organized, what is silenced, and what is emphasized.

Gombiński is a sophisticated writer, but not a manipulative one. I seek not to assess whether or when he erred or lied consciously or subconsciously, but rather to understand his argumentation, which is not necessarily identical to the story he tells. Upon the first reading, both versions appear to tell a similar story with minor changes; however, examining the changes between the versions proves to be of great value. Identifying the differences can help us to understand the processes of consciousness that a person in his position underwent and to hone the questions that need to be asked when examining the ego-documents of life stories.

IV. Gombiński Writes for the World at Large

When comparing the different versions of Gombiński's memoirs, it is important to note that many of the differences appear to be negligible if not meaningless, each in its own right. Even the quantitative accumulation of differences is not enough to reach conclusions of any value. The fundamental difference between the versions becomes a full and coherent story only when the picture of the difference is complete, allowing interpretation of the reciprocal relationship between them. For this reason, stories and descriptions that sometimes appear to be completely banal can later take on substantial meaning when we link and compare them to the other version.

I argue that the formative difference between the two versions of the memoirs written by Gombiński stems from the fact that, though not explicitly stated, each focuses on a different future target audience of readers; it was this change in target audience, I maintain, that resulted in the changes in the stories, the descriptions, and the argumentation.[70]

The earlier version appeals to the world at large that would read his words after the war, when considering who the Germans were and who the Jews were. Gombiński wanted the Jews to be remembered as a people of heroes that unwittingly encountered a terrible tragedy that struck all of them, regardless of the function they fulfilled.[71] The Jews, he maintains, neither understood nor were capable of understanding what was occurring. The element of surprise paralyzed them, reaching its height during the deportations.[72] They also could not resist the Germans, as such resistance would give the Germans an excuse to kill them. Resistance or the violation of directives could cause historians of the future to ask whether the Jews were responsible for their tragedy, and whether "perhaps it could have been entirely different."[73] All the Jews could do was to believe that their behavior had meaning with regard to their survival.[74] In addition, despite the German oppression, the Jews of the ghetto managed to preserve their essential community life and their commitment to work and to cultural production; they also proved that they were a people who observed the eternal laws of morality.[75] Ultimately, when condemned to death, they chose rebellion and died like "a great nation."[76] According to Gombiński, this is the story of the Jews during the war.

There is one aspect of the heroism of the Jewish People, however, that Gombiński found important to explain: the role and the functioning of the Jewish Police in the ghetto, including its relations with the Jewish population. On many occasions, Gombiński tries to respond to the criticism of the police and its actions. For example, in response to the known criticism of corruption throughout the ranks of the Jewish establishment in the ghetto, he describes the efficient work of the Order and Discipline Section of the Jewish Police. He places special emphasis on the great importance that the police and its command echelon ascribed to the expectation that police personnel not abuse their positions[77] but then articulates a reservation, asking cynically: "Does this lofty perfection contain no shadows?" Was everyone truly taking part in the effort to uproot the iniquity and the weeds?" If they were, Gombiński notes, "the reality would be different." There was no denying it,[78] he explains, "the reality was different, but the description is also accurate. There was confusion between good and bad… between light and shadows."[79] At this point, he explains why, in his opinion, the prevalent view among the population was nonetheless one of hostility to the police. He attributes this state of affairs primarily to the fact that its ranks were joined by the downtrodden seeking ways to support their families. They cooperated with smugglers, which was valid but yielded insufficient income. Honest policemen watched others get rich from prohibited business activity while they worked without remuneration, and as a result they began to "grab income for themselves" by collecting payments from business owners.[80] Gombiński also describes the custom, which began prior to World War I, "of Jews giving gifts to policemen on a regular basis." In the past, the police in question were Polish, he explains; in the present, the Jewish police viewed themselves as "the legal heirs" of the beneficiaries of this custom, and justifiably so, in his opinion.[81]

In one instance, Gombiński writes about an order issued by the police to fill quotas of workers for the labor camps. As the lists of names had not been properly prepared, Czerniaków decided that the police should use force to collect those whose names appeared on them. As those who were supposed to be sent away went into hiding, the plan failed and the method was changed; now, passers-by were abducted from the streets and, subsequently, from their homes. The act was met by "dramatic scenes, pleas, curses, and threats,"

Gombiński writes.[82] The population's fury was directed at the police, who had to bear "hatred and the denunciation" for its methods.[83] Immediately following this description, Gombiński clarifies that the police were not the correct target of these charges. First, the lack of order with which the Judenrat operated had an impact on the course of events. Second, Czerniaków believed that if the Jewish Police would not perform the task then the Germans would, and in a much more violent manner. It was therefore preferable for the Jewish Police to implement the directive. Finally, the police was the operational arm of the Judenrat and had to implement the instructions of its chairman.[84]

The two examples presented above reflect the major writing strategy that characterized the earlier version of his memoirs: the adoption of a regime of justification[85] that can be generally described as follows:

> Description of an existing situation (for example, difficult living conditions in the ghetto).
>
> A disputed issue stemming from the existing situation (for example, acts of corruption in the Jewish establishment).
>
> Initial justification of the police activity (for example, the use of an internal system of discipline).
>
> Reservations concerning an action or the exception of individuals (for example, there are exceptions who tend primarily to their own well-being).
>
> Repeated justification of police activity (for example, they were honest people who looked around themselves and saw corruption that was much more severe).

This structure appears dozens of times in the earlier version.[86] In some cases it assumes a somewhat different form in terms of the order of its components, and in other cases a component may be missing. Overall, however, the essence of the structure remains constant.

More than the conduct of the Jews, Gombiński felt it important to highlight the guilt of the Germans as the main issue that needed to be addressed. In the preface to his memoirs he writes, with regard to the Germans, that his words were "an indictment of the only truly guilty parties."[87] Gombiński sought to emphasize the Germans' role as the perpetrators and the disgrace that history would bring to them.[88] His writing portrays the Germans as a murderous people of lords that saw itself as a great and cultured nation but that was actually a nation of obedient [individuals] motivated by orders. He characterizes them as inhumane people who, with level-headedness and no pangs of conscience, hesitation, or pain had already destroyed cultural symbols and murdered masses of people during World War I.[89] The terrible mistake of the Jews was thinking that the Germans were also a people who "believe in certain truths and certain laws and who recognize the duties by which people are obligated."[90]

Gombiński goes beyond general statements regarding the guilt of the Germans by providing future readers with an account of administration within the ghetto. One example is his description of the structure of the German regime in the ghetto and its major officials.[91] His account of the course of the *Grossaktion* details the Germans' organizational structure in the ghetto at that point in time.[92] To enhance his description, he on a number of occasions stresses that the Germans were the lords of the ghetto (*panami ghetta*).[93] Gombiński's description of the Germans also finds expression in the occasions on which he stops the flow of writing to describe an episode. In both versions, this occurs in a few instances that are dispersed throughout the text. In the earlier version, most of the stories are related to direct dynamics with the Germans. In addition, the stories are mostly of incidents that are difficult to process and that are indicative of the impossible reality of the period in question – for example, as in the case of a policeman who feeds his mother poison during the Aktion,[94] or, in a very different context, the case of a Jewish physician and an S.S. officer discovering that they served in the same place during World War I.[95] The large amount of space that Gombiński devotes to the Germans and their actions highlights for readers his own helplessness, and that of others, in light of the reality. The Germans were a force that could not be withstood to change the course of things.

In the earlier version of his memoirs, then, Gombiński writes for the world at large, applies a justification-regime writing strategy vis-à-vis the activity of the Jewish Police, and seeks to place all of the blame on the Germans and the Germans alone. Although the contents of this version appear to be expected and perhaps also necessary, examination of the later version indicates that, quite surprisingly, the Germans are no longer the focus of the story and the world at large is no longer the target audience for his writing.

V. Another version telling a different story?

Unlike in the earlier version written by Gombiński in which the Germans play a central role, the later version relegates the Germans to a negligible role in the story. Indeed, he sometimes mentions the Germans and their murderous intentions almost incidentally.[96] Similarly, in complete contrast to its central role in the earlier version, the *Grossaktion* of the summer of 1942 goes almost unmentioned. The cases recounted in the later version are also not the same as those recounted in the earlier version, and the new stories assume a new character. In the later version, a minority of the stories have to do with contact with the Germans,[97] and most of the stories are more mundane, whether pertaining to the receipt of a bribe while standing[98] in line or to a conversation with Józef Szeryński.[99]

It is not only the Germans who are absent from the later version; so is the regime of justification for the activities of the Jewish Police. In the later version, the above-mentioned structure appears on only a few, negligible occasions to the point of raising doubt about whether it holds any importance whatsoever, except vis-à-vis the earlier version. In the later version, Gombiński actually omits the two major instigators of the story he chose to present to readers in the first version.

In the later version, on the other hand, Gombiński devotes much more space to a description of the organizational structure of the Jewish Police, with an emphasis on police headquarters. He begins this version with an account of his joining the force. He explains how he initially sought a position on the Judenrat, which was a position he felt suited his profession and his education. He received no response for almost a year, and he remembers the "noise of the chaos that prevailed in those days" of October 1940, when he returned to the Judenrat to again submit his request.[100] As he wandered around the offices in an attempt to learn what had happened to his request, he met Judenrat member and attorney Bernard Zundelewicz, whom he "encountered by chance in the hall." Zundelewicz wrote down a few words of recommendation for Gombiński and explained where to submit an application to join the Jewish Police. When Gombiński submitted the request, he was informed that although no new candidacy applications were being accepted, they would make an exception in his case. At this point, Gombiński recounts, "I remembered that a close acquaintance of mine was living in Warsaw…Józef Andrzej Szeryński."[101] He phoned Szeryński, and the two set a meeting for the following day.[102]

Gombiński does not tell us how he learned that he had been accepted by the Jewish Police. However, he characterizes his entry into the force as an almost incidental episode. Although he mentions his connections at senior levels, in his description of the course of events he seeks to give the impression that these connections had only a minor impact on his acceptance for service. The account described above, including Gombiński's acquaintance with Szeryński and, by insinuation, with Zundelewicz, is not even hinted at in the earlier version of his memoirs. I believe that it is the element of coincidence that Gombiński puts forward that needs to be noted here. Later in the article, this element will be considered in conjunction with other aspects of the later version.

In addition to the story of his joining the Jewish Police, the opening of the second part of the later version of his memoirs also reflects the dynamic at play within the Jewish establishment around the time the Jewish Police was established. For example, he recounts the case of Judenrat member Leopold Kupczykier, who was appointed to oversee the police on behalf of the Judenrat. Gombiński describes him as a man who was full of contradictions; on the one hand, he fashioned himself into a "father of the nation," spoke in empty slogans, thought primarily about himself, and could be described as "a hollow man who was full of self-regard, an extrovert, and a vacuous speaker"; on the other hand, Gombiński writes, Kupczykier was also a good and gentle person who helped the needy. Still, he lacked the abilities required to manage the Jewish Police. In practice, then, the person who was supposed to be overseeing the activity of the police did not do so.

Gombiński went on to describe the lengthy and complicated process of joining the Jewish Police,[103] as well as its organizational structure.[104] Unlike the earlier version in which his descriptions pertained primarily to the field commanders or to police elements that came into contact with the Jewish population in the ghetto,[105] the later version of Gombiński's memoirs places an emphasis on headquarters and its senior officials.[106] The process of his joining the police, it should be noted, is absent from the earlier version, as are most of the descriptions pertaining to police headquarters and its staff.

Gombiński's extensive discussion of the evolution of the Jewish Police and its organizational structure reflects an additional attribute of this later version: a focus on the internal Jewish aspect. Another prominent manifestation of this aspect is the space that Gombiński devotes to different parties within the Jewish establishment. For example, he describes Szeryński's hesitations before taking on the position, his many fears, and his personal story – a brief biography of the period prior to his appointment as commander of the Jewish Police.[107] None of these appear in the earlier version. For Gombiński, biography was a means of putting a face to a name, presenting complexity, and using it to create empathy. In Szeryński's case, for example, Gombiński recounts that although the suggestion that he serve as commander of the Jewish Police attracted him, as it would enable him "to work in his profession openly, without disguising it and without concealment," he viewed the position as something that was "dangerous and extremely difficult." The job "instilled fear in him," and its distance from Jewish life filled him with concerns.[108] Szeryński's concerns were long-term, and from the outset he preferred to split his authority with a senior public figure.[109] He was forced to assume responsibility for all aspects of police activity due only to Kupczykier's lack of suitability for the job.[110] In this way, Gombiński attempts to help his readers understand the role of the officials. Neither the *Grossaktion*, nor the Germans, nor the friction with the Jewish population were critical; rather, the story that needed to be told was that of the coping of the people.

Szeryński's biography is not the only one to which Gombiński devotes space in the later version of his memoirs. Other police officials, some of whom are not even mentioned in the earlier version, also receive biographical description. The descriptions are sometimes critical and sometimes sympathetic. Most important, however, is the fact that these figures appear in the later version not only in their capacity as police officials but also as ordinary people. For example, Marian Händel,[111] Maximilian Schönbach,[112] Rafael Lederman,[113] and others (including Abraham Gancwajch, founder of the "The Thirteen")[114] are extensively described.[115] Biographical description also enables Gombiński to describe the system matter-of-factly. An interesting example of this dynamic pertains to his description of Händel. In the earlier version, Gombiński writes that "Josef Rode headed the 'Community' Company."[116] In the later version of the text, on the other hand, Gombiński makes absolutely no mention of Rode. The Community Company, he writes, "was under the personal supervision of Händel (although the day-to-day service was implemented by the Company commander)."[117] In this way, Gombiński strengthens Händel's position, and parenthetically yet explicitly ignores the field command, which is a major topic of his account in the earlier version.

Another individual for whom Gombiński provides a much more in-depth biographical description than what appears in the earlier version is Adam Czerniaków, chairman of the Judenrat in the Warsaw Ghetto. In the later version, Gombiński not only analyzes Czerniaków, his actions, and his character, but devotes the text's 32 final pages to this undertaking.[118] It is an empathetic analysis that highlights the democratic aspect of his actions and his great commitment to the public, even if his indecisiveness proved to be an error.

> In the ghetto, we saw the man behind the desk. We saw many great attributes of the private person; the public figure was not without flaws. But these flaws are precisely what brings him closer to Jews and to the Jewish way of life – sometimes too sensitively. Adam Czerniaków will be recorded in the pages of history as a wonderful and perhaps excessively weak, excessively submissive man, proudly representing the dignity of the Jews in his own way. His life and his death are indicative of his Jewish connection and his belief in democracy – the unforgettable chairman of the Council of Jews in Warsaw.[119]

For good reason, Gombiński devotes the entire end chord of his text to Czerniaków. His writing about Czerniaków also appears, to a great extent, to be his way of writing about himself. Like Czerniaków, Gombiński viewed himself as a man who, like others, was not perfect,[120] but who possessed great sensitivity to the Jews and their way of life.[121] Even more important is the fact that, like Czerniaków, Gombiński's role was to be the man behind the desk. That is to say, even at the most difficult points of friction with the Jewish public, such as the *Grossaktion*, neither man hurt a soul on his own.

Comparing the closing words of the later version with those of the earlier version reflects the major change in the story that Gombiński chooses to tell. In the earlier version, it was the April uprising that summed up his text:

> The Jewish reality was not extinguished in those April days, when the test of the souls that were withstanding the difficulties materialized. At that point, the Jewish reality moved directly from the gray alleyways of the ghetto to a legend of heroism. Fire emerging from the mouths of the fallen of April and the flames of homes burning like altars will burn perpetually among Jews, as an eternal flame. A great deal of blood saturated the ground. A thriving yield would come forth and grow. There, in the ghetto, there was life and there was death. There was body and there was blood. The sowing occurred at a time of weeping; the harvest will occur at a time of joy.[122]

Unlike the conclusion of the later version, which is devoid of pathos, here, at the end of the earlier version, Gombiński concludes his memoirs with the story of the Uprising, which he characterizes as a "legend of heroism." This ending suits his desire to emphasize Jewish heroism to the world. In addition to an account of the April Uprising,[123] the same version of Gombiński's memoirs also mentions the Jewish resistance during the January Aktion[124] and the murder of Jewish police by Jews.[125] Still, it does not mention the Jewish Combat Organization (*Żydowska Organizacja Bojowa*) by name.

Gombiński's treatment of the April Uprising is particularly interesting due to the fact that although it constituted the crowning glory of the earlier version, in the later version the Uprising is absent not only from the conclusion but also from the entire section titled "The Ghetto Authorities." In this section, the

Uprising is recounted solely as an opportunity to incidentally and critically mention the murder of a Jewish policeman on the first day of the Uprising.[126] It is important to note that, in the first chapter of the later version of his memoirs (*The Streets of the Ghetto*), Gombiński writes explicitly about the Jewish Combat Organization.[127] In the same section, he also characterizes the Uprising with great pathos in his statement that it constituted "heroism that stands alone."[128] The positive approach to the Uprising, then, exists in the earlier version of the memoirs and in the first and more literary section of the later version; it does not exist in the section of the later version that offers a description of the ghetto authorities.

How should these disparities between the two versions be understood? I believe that the major explanation for the differences lies in the change in the target audience of future readers. The later version was no longer an appeal to the world at large, but rather to the Jewish public, which, after the war, would settle accounts with its own people, including members of the Jewish Police and the Judenrat.

VI. The Change in Writing as an Expression of a Change in Target Audience

As long as Gombiński was appealing to the world at large, it was important to him to explain to those who were not there who the true guilty parties were. It was also important to emphasize the helplessness of all the Jews, regardless of the function they fulfilled; they also included all those who were part of the Jewish establishment as a whole and the Jewish Police in particular. The regime of justification he employed vis-à-vis the activities of the Jewish Police was an expression of the writing strategy that furthered this narrative.

It is also reasonable to assume that in defining the Germans as the only truly guilty parties, Gombiński was seeking to concretely address the Poles. As a person who was well connected with his own identity as a Pole, this held significant importance. By making his blame for the Germans the heart of his account he seeks to emphasize that he did not regard the Poles as responsible; in return, he asks them not to blame the Jews for their own tragedy. His appeal to the Poles also finds expression in his use of an ethos of a heroic uprising. For example, he combines a description of the Jewish uprising with the use of culturally significant concepts that were also instilled in him as a Jew who integrated into Polish society prior to the war.[129]

On the other hand, when he writes for the Jewish population in the later version as a former senior officer of the Jewish Police, he has no reason to present himself as a later victim of the Germans as a way of contending with the criticism leveled against the Jewish Police. All Jews who were not part of the ghetto police could claim that they too were living under German oppression but nonetheless had not taken part in the police activity. For the Jewish target population, and certainly for anyone who had experienced the reality of the period, blaming the Germans and offering an account of their murderous actions is a declaration that goes without saying. As a result, the designated purpose of the Germans was no longer relevant, leaving him no reason for them in his later version.

Along with the Germans, the *Grossaktion* also vanishes from the story and ceases to be the focus, as discussing the Aktion without discussing the Germans highlights the question of the guilt of the Jewish establishment and the Jewish Police or their collaboration with the Germans. This is a dramatic point in his writing and in the difference between the two versions. The *Grossaktion* was the most significant point of conflict between the Police and the population of the Warsaw Ghetto. Although this conflict does not vanish altogether, it takes on a much smaller and almost negligible dimension.

In the new narrative in which the Germans and the Aktion are relegated to the sidelines, it is not nearly as necessary to justify the actions of the Jewish Police. As a result, the structure of the regime of justification that characterizes the first version is no longer required. Still, it is important for Gombiński to present himself not as an agent[130] but as a victim of circumstance. To do this he needs to present a different structure, one that highlights his limited ability to maneuver in his position, or at least to present it as having only minor influence. The incidental nature in which he received his position, the power struggles, the bureaucratic entanglement, and the other position holders all played a role in limiting his agency and stressed the Jewish establishment as a mechanism that became stronger than those who, like him, took part in it.

The substitute he chose was not complete. In actuality, there were alternative structures reflecting other possibilities for taking action in reality.

One example was the Jewish Combat Organization. To contend with such an organization, which offered a possible alternative to his actions, Gombiński leaves the narrative-chronological aspect intact in the first part, but permits only a critical hint of it in the second part.

It is important to emphasize that these are not two contradictory versions and that the change is not a binary one. In addition to the similar main general points noted above in section II, each version also contains an element of the major emphasis of the other version. For example, Gombiński is also critical of the Jewish establishment in the earlier version, as exemplified above with regard to filling the quotas for the labor camps. Another example of this attribute is the description of Szeryński's character, which is also part of the earlier version.[131] In the later version, we cannot ignore the fact that the epilogue of the first part deals clearly with the Jewish heroism during the Uprising and with the fault of the Germans, which are two aspects that are discussed prominently in the earlier version:

> [The Germans] will enter the pages of history forever…as those who murdered human ashes, a defenseless nation, in the gas chambers…murderers of children and burners of women, the elderly, and the defenseless – this is their name in history. This is the truth. And this name – this truth – has been signed by the Jews of the ghetto, the last defenders of the public. Everyone falls in order to resist; in order to convey this truth onward.[132]

In the first part of the memoirs, which is written in a more literary manner and given a title that deals less with the ghetto authorities, Gombiński appears to also have left a place for these aspects.

There are also elements that appear in both versions with little or no change. Prominent from a biographical perspective is Gombiński's recurring choice to neither mention his family nor relate to their fate. This decision suits his writing style, which seeks to represent the Jewish population as a whole and not the individual case of Gombiński himself. Another example of the continuity in Gombiński's writing is his mention of the Jews' historical difficulty attaining self-rule.[133] And still another is his emphasis on the fact that the pace of events made it impossible to understand the reality and to process this understanding into actions that were more appropriate than those of the Jewish establishment.[134]

The change in Gombiński's target audience between the first and second versions of his memoirs required changes in its writing. It had become redundant to place blame on the Germans as the earlier version so notably did. Instead, in the later version, he sought primarily to address the methods of the Jewish establishment and the criticism it sustained.

Conclusion

"These writings are merely a description of the events,"[135] writes Gombiński in his memoirs. But in ego-documents , writings are never "merely a description." While Gombiński was composing the first version of his memoirs, he was apparently motivated by his lack of confidence and his inability to survive to convey a message to the world on behalf of the Jewish People. He wanted history to remember the Germans as the guilty party, and instead of Jewish forlornness he wanted the world to remember Jewish heroism. It may also be the case that the world for which it was written was first and foremost the Polish population, which constituted a target audience that would be open to accepting German responsibility and the helplessness of their victims.

The loss of the first version of his memoirs led him to write them again from his perspective. It may also be the case that he was trying to reconstruct the original text. However, although he wrote about the same period, the few months that had elapsed had changed his role as a documenter, and the experience he reported changed accordingly. When writing the later version of his memoirs, Gombiński understood that he needed to hone his messages. The experience of the Polish uprising in Warsaw had concluded, the war was about to end, and his chances of surviving had improved. The day after the war, it would no longer be enough to blame the Germans. He sensed that he needed to produce a different message aimed at a new audience. He now sought to speak not to the world at large but primarily to the Jewish population that would seek to settle accounts with him. As a result, the uprising was assigned a marginal and, to some extent, a qualified role, making it necessary to retell the story of the Jewish Police and the story of the Judenrat. The timing of the second writing, which ultimately occurred over a period of just a few months if not less, reshaped not only the details in the text but also its essence.

As the later version of Gombiński's memoirs was handed over to the Central Jewish Historical Commission only in September 1945, as noted in Section II above, the text could also have been revised even after the war ended, in accordance with what Gombiński thought should be written in the new reality. In this sense it may be necessary to treat this version like a testimony, albeit an early one, and not in the manner in which it has been classified in various archives and in the research literature thus far – that is, as a diary or a war-time memoir.

The elements that appear in both versions, such as the processing of the experience in such a short time and the Jews' difficulty achieving self-rule, were also fundamental components of the message Gombiński sought to convey and of his regime of justification. However, in these cases there was no need for change, as they also served the new argumentation he sought to advance: placing an emphasis on the internal Jewish aspect. Gombiński played down his role as an agent by adapting a writing strategy addressing a different potential target audience. But in places that played down his role in any event, there was no need to make changes.

The two versions that Gombiński wrote emphasize the need to look beyond the events, the stories, and the autobiographical details conveyed by ego-documents from the Holocaust – that is, to look beyond that which the authors themselves do not manage to write about themselves. Comparing the two versions of Gombiński's memoirs beckons us to understand the change in perspective, as well as the changes in emphasis and in active and passive agents – for example, with regard to the role of the Germans. The change in versions teaches us that there is no place in ego-documents that can be related to as self-evident. His assertion that this was no more than a "description of the events" may indicate that the role of historians is not only to present or to replicate the story of documenters but rather to attempt to extricate them – of course, while maintaining their humility as historians – from their own story. As I see it, the changes between the versions, as well as the sections that are comparable in both, point to a need to emphasize the documenter's experience of time. It is a hermeneutics of time – an invitation to examine how time elapses in a subjective manner and the ways in which it structures how people understand their own experiences.

Endnotes

1   This article is based in part on my MA thesis, "Perception of the Role of Jewish Police in the Warsaw and Otwock Ghettos as Reflected in war-time Memoirs," which was written at the University of Haifa's Department of Jewish History under the supervision of Prof. Marcos Silber and Prof. Avihu Ronen. I would like to thank Prof. Silber for his helpful comments on this article. I, of course, am solely responsible for its content.

2   Stanisław Gombiński (Jan Mawult), *Wspomnienia policjanta z warszawskiego getta* (Warsaw, 2012), p. 179.

3   I employ Havi Dreifuss's (Ben-Sasson) definition of "war-time memoirs" as "summaries, generally composed between 1943 and 1944, which describe events during the war from the vantage point of a few years." Havi Dreifuss (Ben-Sasson), *Relations Between Jews and Poles during the Holocaust: The Jewish Perspective* (Jerusalem, 2017).

4   Gombiński, *Wspomnienia policjanta z warszawskiego getta*, p. 30.

5   On the advantages of close reading, see, for example, Amos Goldberg, *Trauma in First Person: Diary Writing during the Holocaust* (Bloomington, IN, 2017), p. 20.

6   See Aharon Weiss, "The Jewish Police in the *Generalgouvernement* and in Upper Silesia during the Holocaust," doctoral dissertation, The Hebrew University of Jerusalem, 1973 (Hebrew); Aldona Podolska, *Służba Porządkowa w getcie Warszawskim* (Warsaw, 1996); Katarzyna Person, *POLICJANCI- wizerunek żydowskiej służby porządkowej w getcie warszawskim* (Warsaw, 2018).

7   See, for example, their mention in Yisrael Gutman, *The Jews of Warsaw, 1939-1943* (Jerusalem, 2011) (Hebrew); Dreifuss, *Warsaw Ghetto*; Barbara Engelking and Jacek Leociak, *The Warsaw Ghetto: A Guide to the Perished City* (New Haven, 2009).

8   See, for example, the following comment by Zvi Shner: "Despite the author's subjective, structured approach, his essay constitutes one of the most important sources for getting to know the organization and the nature of the Jewish Police." Jan Mawult, "The *Ordnungsdienst* in the Warsaw Ghetto," *Ghetto Fighters' House News* 22 (April 1960), p. 35 (Hebrew). See also Aharon Weiss's comment: "Using this source requires extreme caution, but its contents stand to make a contribution to both fact and assessment." Weiss, "The Jewish Police in the *Generalgouvernement* and in Upper Silesia," p. 106. Jan Mawult is Stanisław Gombiński's nom de plume.

9   The term argumentation as used in this article is based on sociologists Werner Kallmeyer and Fritz Schütze's distinction between narration, description, and argumentation. Narration is a continuum of events from the past that are either temporarily or permanently related to one another. The primary element that distinguishes description from narration is the fact that description depicts a

static situation, whereas argumentation encompasses abstract elements located outside the directly reported sequence of events, such as theories and statements regarding a general idea that are indicative of the views of the narrator. See Gabriele Rosenthal, "Reconstruction of Life Stories: Principles of Selection in Generating Stories for Narrative Biographical Interviews," *The Narratives Study of Lives* 1(1) (1993), pp. 59-91.

10 Gombiński, *Wspomnienia policjanta z warszawskiego getta*, p. 9. According to a number of other sources, Gombiński was born in 1906. See, for example, Arolsen Archives, Gombinski Stanislaw, TD card 972600.

11 For example, he makes multiple usage of the expression a "Jewish heart" (*Jidisze harc*) to refer to the merciful heart that has historically characterized the Jews. See ibid., p. 227; Stanisław Gombiński, *The Memoirs of Stanisław Gombiński (Jan Mawult) on the Jewish Police in the Warsaw Ghetto*, Ghetto Fighters' House Archive (GFHA), Collections Dept. 2557, Part 6b, p. 234. Gombiński also sometimes quotes from the Jewish scriptures, such as Psalm 137 from the Book of Psalms. See also ibid., p. 258. Elsewhere, he offers an analysis of the developments in the nature and attributes of the Jewish community that have occurred throughout history. See Gombiński, *Wspomnienia policjanta z warszawskiego getta*, pp. 228-231.

12 For example, he views "a correct understanding of Polish-ness" during the war as a matter of great importance. Gombiński, *The Memoirs of Stanisław Gombiński*, Part 6b, p. 47. On the meaning of Polish identity as far as Gombiński is concerned, see below.

13 Gombiński, *Wspomnienia policjanta z warszawskiego getta*, pp. 9-10. A few days before he was meant to take the certification exam, a directive known as the "Grabowski law" went into effect. According to this directive issued by the Polish minister of justice, the rolls of attorneys in the country were closed.

14 In his memoirs, Gombiński makes no mention of his wife or children. However, according to the editors of the Polish edition of his memoirs, they apparently went into hiding on the Aryan side of Warsaw during the initial stages of the war. They all survived. See Gombiński, *Wspomnienia policjanta z warszawskiego getta*, p. 309 (note 28).

15 Stanisław Gombiński, 'Victor Hugo a kara śmierci', *Palestra* 7/8 (July-August 1938), pp. 735- 751.

16 Józef Szeryński (1893-1943) was a converted Jew who, by the eve of the war, had reached the rank of colonel in the Polish police force. He was appointed commander of the Jewish Police in the Warsaw Ghetto in October 1940 by Judenrat Chairman Adam Czerniaków.

17 Gombiński, *Wspomnienia policjanta z warszawskiego getta*, pp. 10-11.

18 Ibid., pp. 13-14.

19 Gombiński, *The Memoirs of Stanisław Gombiński*, Part 5a-5c. This version was also translated into Hebrew by the Ghetto Fighters' House Archive. See Part 6b of this source itself (translation by Pnina Hauzer and Zvi Nathan).

20 Ibid., Sections 1-4.

21 Gombiński, *Wspomnienia policjanta z warszawskiego getta*. This publication also contained a two-page preface from the Jewish Historical Archive in Warsaw. See Jan Mawult (Stanisław Gombiński), Archive of the Jewish Historical Institute in Warsaw (Archiwum Żydowskiego Instytutu Historycznego, or AŻIH), 302\38.

22 Gombiński, *The Memoirs of Stanisław Gombiński*, Part 6a; Ibid., preface. Josef Rode was a refugee from Włocławek who fought with the French army and the Polish army in World War I. During the ghetto period, he commanded the "Community" (*Gmina*) Company, which was responsible for security in the Judenrat offices. During the *Grossaktion*, he was appointed deputy commander for the Jewish Police at the *Umschlagplatz*.

23 Josef Rode (?) [in original] "The Diary of Attorney Josef Rode, a Refugee from Włocławek and an Officer in the Jewish Police," Yad Vashem Archive O.6/156. This item was previously titled "The Diary of John Doe (*ploni almoni*) of the Jewish Police in the Warsaw Ghetto." There is no documentation explaining who decided to change the name of the item or why. The file also contains the Hebrew translation that was undertaken by the Ghetto Fighters' House Archive, in addition to revisions.

24 NN [John Doe], AŻIH 302/129.

25 See, for example, Gutman, *The Jews of Warsaw*, p. 126 (note 7).

26 Engelking and Leociak, *The Warsaw Ghetto: A Guide to the Perished City*, pp. 191, 197.

27 Person relates to Gombiński in the footnotes and to this source as two different sources. See Person, *POLICJANCI*, p. 64 (note 14).

28 Dreifuss, *Warsaw Ghetto*, p. 60. Dreifuss does not explain the decision and notes only that it was Rachmilevitch who recognized the author's identity.

29 Anonymous, "Request for Urgent Assistance for 18 People in Hiding Who Are Subject to Extortion, November 23, 1943," GFHA Collections, 5823. On November 23, 1943, Gombiński and others who were in hiding with him on the Aryan side of Warsaw asked Wasser for financial assistance. At the same time, they acceded to Wasser's request that they document their experiences in memoirs.

30 Gombiński's name does not appear in the list of texts that was compiled by Wasser on January 15, 1944. However, in a June 1944 letter to Ludwik Hirszberg, Wasser thanks Gombiński for agreeing to write his memoirs. See Hirsch Wasser, "List of Original Texts Written by Jews in Hiding," GFHA, Collections, 6142; Hirsch Wasser, "Letters to Arnold Majorek (May 1, 1944) and to Ludwik Hirszberg (July 7, 1944)," GFHA, Collections, 5994.

31 Basia Temkin-Berman was born in Warsaw in 1907. In her youth, she was active in socialist organizations and then joined the Po'alei Zion – Left party. During the

existence of the ghetto she managed an underground library, took part in mutual assistance activities, and maintained close relations with Emanuel Ringelblum. After leaving for the Aryan side of the city in September 1942, she worked in conjunction with her spouse Adolf Berman as part of the Council to Aid Jews. (*Żegota - Rada Pomocy Żydom*) and the National Jewish Committee. Today, the committee's archive on which the Bermans were working, known as the Berman Collection, is held by the Ghetto Fighters' House Archive. See Basia Temkin-Berman, *Underground Diary* (Tel Aviv, 1956), pp. 233-237 (Hebrew).

32 Ibid., p. 127.

33 Michał Czajka, *Inwentarz Zbioru Pamiętników* (Warsaw: Jewish Historical Institute, 2007), pp. 36-37; Gombiński, *Wspomnienia policjanta z warszawskiego getta*, p. 13.

34 Gombiński, *Wspomnienia policjanta z warszawskiego getta*, pp. 304-305.

35 Hauser, therefore, was correct in her identification of the author but erred in her assessment that the thick notebook was the later version.

36 Gombiński, *The Memoirs of Stanisław Gombiński*, Part 5c, p. 573.

37 Gombiński, *Wspomnienia policjanta z warszawskiego getta*, p. 161.

38 Ibid., pp. 11-12.

39 See, for example, Gombiński, *The Memoirs of Stanisław Gombiński*, Part 5b, pp. 370, 380, 389.

40 This is how it appears in the original. In the Polish-language edition of these memoirs, the title was revised to "*Ale glajch.*" See Gombiński, *Wspomnienia policjanta z warszawskiego getta*, p. 32. See also Gombiński, *The Memoirs of Stanisław Gombiński*, Part 3, p. 2.

41 Gombiński, *The Memoirs of Stanisław Gombiński*, Part 1, p. 2.

42 See, for example, Ibid., Part 6b, pp. 29, 37, 47; Gombiński, *Wspomnienia policjanta z warszawskiego getta*, pp. 179, 192, 254.

43 For example, he uses the Polish expression "*od rzemyczka do koniczka*" ("from a leash to a horse"), meaning that someone who begins perpetrating minor crimes will ultimately move on to major crimes. See Gombiński, *Wspomnienia policjanta z warszawskiego getta*, p. 203.

44 Such as French, Latin, and Italian. See, Gombiński, *Wspomnienia policjanta z warszawskiego getta*, pp. 233, 259, 264.

45 Ibid., p. 160.

46 Gombiński, *The Memoirs of Stanisław Gombiński*, Part 6b, p. 256.

47 For example, Gombiński relates to major battles in Polish history as a source of inspiration. See Gombiński, *Wspomnienia policjanta z warszawskiego getta*, p. 159.

In other places, he uses the figure of Józef Piłsudski or the stories of other popular heroes as models to emulate. See Gombiński, *The Memoirs of Stanisław Gombiński*, Part 6b, p. 46, and *Wspomnienia policjanta z warszawskiego getta*, p. 168.

48 Gombiński, *The Memoirs of Stanisław Gombiński*, Part 6b, p. 246.

49 Ibid., p. 252.

50 See, for example, ibid., p. 518; ibid., Part 1, pp. 77, 108.

51 Philippe Lejeune, *On Autobiography* (Minneapolis, 1989), pp. 11-12.

52 Ibid., p. 14. According to Lejeune, the "breach of contract" pertains to the identity of the writer. Here, I expand this definition somewhat to also include other revelations discovered by the readers, even if they are not directly mediated to them by the author.

53 Ibid.

54 Prior to the war, Jakub Lejkin (1906-1942) was a lawyer and an officer in the Polish police force. In the Jewish Police, he initially served in the services and training department and was subsequently appointed as deputy commander of the Jewish Police in the Warsaw Ghetto. After Szeryński's arrest, he served as acting commander. He was shot to death by the Jewish Combat Organization on October 29, 1942. According to Gombiński, Lejkin was "a rough and cruel man" who, on the one hand, took part in all the Aktions, instilled terror in Jewish policemen with the demand that they bring him "skulls," and worked in perfect coordination with his German superiors. On the other hand, he explains that his actions stemmed from a true and sincere belief that they would save many lives. Like many others, he notes, Lejkin did not know, nor could he know, the truth about the exterminations. See Gombiński, *Wspomnienia policjanta z warszawskiego getta*, pp. 188-191.

55 Gombiński does not attempt to conceal or deny the existence of cases in which Jewish police personnel abused their powers. Indeed, he himself provides accounts of them, from collecting an excessive share of the profits from smugglers, to demanding payment from business owners, to using violence with contempt for the population. On the other hand, he highlights the poverty of most members of the Jewish Police and describes it at length, emphasizing their moral right to seek sources of livelihood for themselves and their families. See Gombiński, *The Memoirs of Stanisław Gombiński*, Part 6b, pp. 30-33.

56 Stanisław Gombiński, „Victor Hugo a kara śmierci," pp. 736-737.

57 Ibid., p. 737. Gombiński's decision to write about the death penalty as a philosophical and legal issue is interesting in itself and may also attest to his character. This, however, is a matter that lies beyond the scope of the present article.

58 Gombiński devotes approximately 10 pages to quotations from opponents of the death penalty, as opposed to some three pages devoted to quotations from advocates.

59 On the constructivist paradigm, see, for example, Peter L. Berger and Thomas Luckmann, *The Social Construction of Reality: A Treatise in the Sociology of Knowledge* (London, 1966).

60 Ruthellen Josselson, "The Hermeneutics of Faith and the Hermeneutics of Suspicion," *Narrative Inquiry* 14(1) (2004), pp. 4-6.

61 Havi Dreifuss, *Warsaw Ghetto*, p. 34.

62 Ibid. As an example, Dreifuss offers the war-time memoirs of Stanisław Adler, who was also an officer in the Jewish Police in the Warsaw Ghetto.

63 Person, *POLICJANCI*, p. 229.

64 Stanisław Adler, *Żadna blaga, żadne kłamstwo: Wspomnienia policjanta z warszawskiego getta* (Warsaw, 2018), p. 73.

65 Ibid., p. 98.

66 Ibid., p. 114.

67 Ibid., p. 73. Adler was not the only one to mention Gombiński in a positive light. According to Hillel Seidman, Gombiński was one of the "few honest people" in the Police at its beginnings. See Hillel Seidman, *The Warsaw Ghetto Diary* (New York, 1957 [1946]), p. 136 (Hebrew).

68 Josselson, "The Hermeneutics of Faith and the Hermeneutics of Suspicion," p. 13.

69 Ibid., pp. 226-234.

70 For a definition of these terms, see note 9 above.

71 See, for example, Gombiński, *The Memoirs of Stanisław Gombiński*, Part 6b, p. 36.

72 Ibid., pp. 164-165.

73 Ibid., p. 245.

74 Ibid., p. 244.

75 Ibid., pp. 226-234.

76 Ibid., p. 249.

77 Ibid., pp. 26-29.

78 Ibid., p. 29.

79 Ibid., p. 30.

80 Ibid., p. 31.

81 Ibid., p. 31.

82 Ibid., pp. 54-55.

83 Ibid., p. 56.

84 Ibid., pp. 56-57.

85 This concept is borrowed from the work of Boltanski and Thévenot, in which social agents are not forces that are unknowingly controlled by social structures but rather maintain a regime of activities in places where there is lack of agreement and where it is necessary to provide justification for certain actions. These agents are working for the common good, which is nobler than working for personal interests. They rely on a number of worlds of justification and make use of words that are representative of them. For example, in the world of inspiration, they use terms such as creativity and vision. In the civil world, they use words such as identity, commitment to certain values, and collective will. These agents also use different tools for justification. One is anticipatory justification, meaning the kind of justification offered prior to a disagreement. They anticipate the possibility of criticism and negate it by relating to elements of it, among other things. Another example is multi-world justification, through which interests or intentions are justified by relating to other realms or to as many figures as possible. See Richard Giulianotti and Tommy Langseth, "Justifying the Civic Interest in Sport: Boltanski and Thevenot, the Six Worlds of Justification, and Hosting the Olympic Games," *European Journal for Sport and Society* 13(2) (2016), pp. 133-153.

86 See, for example, Gombiński, *The Memoirs of Stanisław Gombiński*, Part 6b, pp. 16-17, 37-41, 153-155.

87 Ibid., preface. It is important to note that the editors of the Polish edition of Gombiński's memoirs thought that these pages belonged to a different version, which I have identified as the later of the two. See Gombiński, *Wspomnienia policjanta z warszawskiego getta*, pp. 30-31. However, as I show below, relating to the Germans in this manner was actually distinctly characteristic of the earlier version of his memoirs. Gombiński also repeats this sentiment exactly, making it more reasonable to assume that these pages actually belong to the earlier version. See, for example, Gombiński, *The Memoirs of Stanisław Gombiński*, Part 6b, p. 220.

88 See, for example, ibid., pp. 243-246, 249.

89 Ibid., pp. 194-200.

90 Ibid., pp. 62-66.

91 Ibid., pp. 62-66.

92 Ibid., pp. 121-126.

93 Ibid., pp. 145, 147, 148, 153.

94 Ibid., p. 176.

95 Ibid., 127.

96 See, for example, Gombiński, *Wspomnienia policjanta z warszawskiego getta*, pp. 282-284. Although Gombiński wrote about the Germans' murderous intentions, the more the text advances the clearer it become that the explanation regarding the Germans is meant to address the Judenrat's role in the reality of the period.

97 See, for example, ibid., pp. 210-211, 264-265.

98 Ibid., pp. 201-203.

99 Ibid., pp. 165-166.

100 Ibid., p. 162.

101 Ibid., p.163.

102 Ibid., p. 165.

103 Ibid., pp. 175-177.

104 Ibid., pp. 173-175, 180-183.

105 Gombiński, *The Memoirs of Stanisław Gombiński*, Part 6b, pp. 1-5.

106 Gombiński also mentions himself and describes his position among the headquarters staff with no additional comment. This is the first and last time that Gombiński mentions himself in the context of the official position he held. See Gombiński, *Wspomnienia policjanta z warszawskiego getta*, p. 181.

107 Ibid., pp. 163-168.

108 Ibid., p. 166.

109 Ibid., p. 167.

110 Ibid., pp. 171-172.

111 Ibid., pp. 169-170. Marian Händel was born in Lviv in 1908. Before the war, he engaged in commerce relating to the film industry and had a good command of the German language. After the Jewish Police was established, Händel was appointed its deputy commander. Unofficially, he was one of the main elements serving to liaise between the Judenrat and the Germans. In the summer of 1942, with the onset of the *Grossaktion*, Händel left for the Aryan side of the city. He survived the war, immigrated to Venezuela, and died in 1983. See also: ibid., p. 352 (note 348); Person, *POLICJANCI*, p. 29; Weiss, "The Jewish Police," p. 45; Adler, *Żadna blaga, żadne kłamstwo*, p. 59.

112 Gombiński, *Wspomnienia policjanta z warszawskiego getta*, pp. 183-184. Maximilian Schönbach (?-1942) was an officer in the Polish army during World War I. He was a well-known and well-respected attorney in Warsaw, as attested to by his position in the Warsaw Bar Association and his selection for its disciplinary court. See Michał Grynberg (ed.), *Words to Outlive Us: Voices from the Warsaw Ghetto* (New York, 2002), pp. 40-41; NN [John Doe], "Z Rady Adwokackiej w Warszawie," *Palestra* 4 (1937), pp. 361, 369.

113 Gombiński, *Wspomnienia policjanta z warszawskiego getta*, p. 186. Rafael Lederman (1899-?) was an officer in the Polish army who fought in the Polish-Soviet War. Following this war, he served as an instructor at the police training school, worked as the deputy district attorney in Piotrków, and then worked as

an attorney in Warsaw. In the ghetto, he was a deputy of Alvin Fleischman at "Reserva" and was subsequently appointed head of the training department of the Jewish Police. See Person, *POLICJANCI*, p. 45 (note 128); Adler, *Żadna blaga, żadne kłamstwo*, p. 64 (note 51).

114 The Office to Combat Usury and Profiteering (*Urząd do Walki z Lichwą i Spekulacją*) was nicknamed the "Thirteen" due to its location at 13 Leszno Street. For more on the Thirteen, see Aharon Weiss, "The Thirteen in the Warsaw Ghetto," *Yalkut Moreshet* 21 (June 1976), pp. 157-180 (Hebrew).

115 Gombiński, *Wspomnienia policjanta z warszawskiego getta*, pp. 250, 256-259. Not all of Gancwajch's history from before and during World War II is sufficiently clear. It is known that he was born in Częstochowa in 1904, was religiously educated, and was certified as a rabbi. Prior to the war he was a Zionist activist, a Hebrew teacher, and an editor of a number of newspapers in Vienna and Lodz. From there, over the course of the war, he made his way to Warsaw. There is no clear indication of how he achieved his standing among the Germans; one possibility is that he was a relative of Moshe Merin, head of the regional Judenrat in Zagłębie. During the existence of the ghetto, Gancwajch sought to increase his influence to the greatest extent possible, attempting even to replace Adam Czerniakow as chairman of the Judenrat. The reasons for his fall from grace in the eyes of the Germans are unclear. According to some versions his name appeared on the list of wanted individuals on St. Bartholomew's Day Eve, on April 18, 1942. According to other versions, Gancwajch already left for the Aryan side of the city in August 1941, and at this point he may have been functioning as a Gestapo informant. The circumstances surrounding his death also remain unclear, but he may have been shot by the Germans at Pawiak in April 1943 along with his wife and son. See also: Gutman, *The Jews of Warsaw*, pp. 181-186; Person, *POLICJANCI*, p. 55; Engelking and Leociak, *The Warsaw Ghetto: A Guide to the Perished City*, pp. 218-226, 821.

116 Gombiński, *The Memoirs of Stanisław Gombiński*, Part 6b, p. 2.

117 Gombiński, *Wspomnienia policjanta z warszawskiego getta*, p. 194.

118 Ibid., pp. 289-303. This count of 32 pages is based on the original manuscript.

119 Ibid., p. 303.

120 Ibid., p. 249.

121 See for example, Gombiński, *The Memoirs of Stanisław Gombiński*, Part 6b, p. 234.

122 Ibid., pp. 258-259.

123 Ibid., pp. 248-249.

124 Ibid., pp. 214-215.

125 Ibid., pp. 166, 209-210.

126 Gombiński, *Wspomnienia policjanta z warszawskiego getta*, pp. 172-173.

127 See ibid., p. 158.

128 Ibid., p. 159.

129 For example, Gombiński describes the heroism of the Jewish struggle and then immediately writes "'zginąć' – może nawet naród wielki." This Polish sentence – meaning that even a great nation can die – is actually a paraphrasing of the following adage by Stanisław Staszic, a member of the Polish intelligentsia who lived in the eighteenth and the nineteenth century: "A great nation may fall: only a corrupt one can perish." See Gombiński, *The Memoirs of Stanisław Gombiński*, Part 6b, pp. 248-249.

130 The term "agent" as I use it here is borrowed from the field of sociology. An agent is a pragmatic person who feels that he or she is able to change the social reality in which he or she is operating. That is not to say that this individual will definitely succeed in implementing the changes that he or she desires, or that he or she is capable of influencing all aspects of life. Despite the limitations of reality, agents regard themselves as sovereign persons with free will who can actively choose from different possible courses of action. The opposite of the position of the agent is that of structure. Structure can be cultural, class-based, religious, and so on. Within a structure, individuals act primarily according to the category to which they belong, and structure shapes their actions. It is important to note that structure does not "exist" but rather is an analytical tool that assists in the examination and analysis of stances and behaviors. See Chris Barker, *The SAGE Dictionary of Cultural Studies* (London, 2004), pp. 4-5, 191-192. For a broader and more complex definition of the concepts of agent and structure, see Pierre Bourdieu, *Outline of a Theory of Practice* (Cambridge, 2013).

131 See Gombiński, *The Memoirs of Stanisław Gombiński*, Part 6b, pp. 25-26.

132 Gombiński, *Wspomnienia policjanta z warszawskiego getta*, pp. 160-161.

133 See Gombiński, *The Memoirs of Stanisław Gombiński*, Part 6b, pp. 33-34; Gombiński, *Wspomnienia policjanta z warszawskiego getta*, pp. 228-232.

134 See Gombiński, *The Memoirs of Stanisław Gombiński*, Part 6b, p. 38; Gombiński, *Wspomnienia policjanta z warszawskiego getta*, pp. 238.

135 Gombiński, *The Memoirs of Stanisław Gombiński*, Part 6b, p. 241.

Efraim Zadoff

Samuel del Campo and the Rescue of Jews in Romania during the Holocaust

Introduction

This article is part of a comprehensive study pertaining to the efforts of Latin American consuls in Europe to rescue Jews from extermination during the Holocaust. These diplomats issued passports of the countries they represented[1] to Jews in Poland, Holland, and perhaps also other countries that were occupied by Germany. The Jews who were issued these passports and protective documents enjoyed a degree of protection against persecution and murder, as the documents made them candidates for a prisoner-exchange deal between Germany and the Allies.[2]

These cases differ fundamentally from the case I present below, due to the fact that it concerns events that occurred solely in Romania and the conditions that developed there and, with greater intensity, in Bukovina. The conditions in question were also different, as the diplomat who issued the documents – Samuel del Campo – also took measures, with a local partner, to have them recognized and to protect their Jewish bearers. Del Campo was the only Latin American diplomat to take such action in Romania, and his country – Chile – was the only Latin American country mentioned in this rescue effort.

Chilean Passports

In May 2012, Mr. Uly Kotzer contacted the Chilean Embassy in Israel bearing a copy of a Chilean passport that was issued in Bucharest, Romania on January 14, 1942 and signed by Chile's diplomatic representative in the country (*chargé d'affaires*, or in Spanish: *encargado de negocios*). The passport was issued to Rose Kiesler, the wife of Kotzer's father, and to Ulrich Kiesler, who later changed his name to Uly Kotzer. Some years later, Kotzer found another passport, this one issued on December 8, 1941, bearing the name of his father: Avraham Kiesler.

Kotzer had no knowledge of the circumstances in which his father had acquired the passport, as he was only a boy at the time. However, he was well aware of the fact that the passport had saved them from being deported from the Chernivtsi (Czernowicz; in Romanian, Cernauţi) ghetto to Transnistria. He therefore contacted the Chilean Embassy in Israel to express his gratitude to the country for its act of rescue and to the consul who was responsible for saving his life.[3]

At the Chilean Embassy, Mr. Kotzer was received by diplomat Oscar Alcaman, who knew nothing about the matter and was unable to provide him with any information. He did, however, make an effort to find information about Samuel del Campo, whose signature appears in the passport. The matter was referred to the Ministry of Foreign Affairs in Santiago, and another ministry employee named Jorge Schindler was charged with investigating it. Following a search through the ministry's historical archive, Schindler confirmed that there had been a Chilean diplomat named Samuel del Campo and that his last post had been supervising the Chilean consulate in Bucharest between 1941 and 1943.

In the archive's files of correspondences, Schindler found a lengthy, detailed report dated January 1, 1942, which Samuel del Campo had sent to his superiors in Santiago and which contained an update regarding his activity during the months since his arrival in Romania. In this report, Del Campo explained his work to protect Polish citizens, "without distinction based on religion" (*sin distinción de religión*), in an effort to rescue them from Romanian state persecution. In the course of his efforts, he noted, he had appealed to the office of Ion Antonescu, president of the Council of Ministers of Romania. He also recounted the work in which he had engaged in the city of Chernivtsi through a local attorney, whom he appointed as his representative to intercede with the authorities and to entertain the complaints of persecuted locals.

According to this account, Del Campo asked the president's office to send instructions to Chernivtsi stipulating that Jews bearing foreign citizenship should not be harmed, as Romanian law pertaining to anti-Jewish laws did not apply to foreign citizens and as all detrimental treatment of them required the authorization of the Ministry of Foreign Affairs. According to Del Campo, they acceded to his request, but the instructions never reached the officials on the ground, who subsequently resolved to deport 250 families to Transnistria. Del

Campo's last-minute intervention prevented the deportation and resulted in the decision that the candidates for deportation would return to their homes and that a sign would be hung at the front of each dwelling stating that they were protected by the government of Chile. He also wrote that he was continuing to protect Jews in a variety of situations, such as when their property was being confiscated. He concluded by asking his superiors if they consented to his activities.[4]

In addition to providing important information concerning his activity, Del Campo's report raises numerous questions and highlights the need to find evidence that clarifies his actions in Chernivtsi. Before we turn to an account of the events based on all the known details, we will first consider Del Campo's character and the background of the events depicted in the report.

Samuel del Campo y Candia was born in 1882 in the city of Linares in the Chilean Central Valley, some 300 kilometers south of the capital city of Santiago. He was born into the wealthy family of Abelardo del Campo y Palma and Carolina Candia de del Campo, and he studied engineering at universities in Paris, France and Liège, Belgium. In 1918, he began working in Chile's Ministry of Foreign Affairs supervising the publicity for promoting the sale of salts (*salitre*) at the embassy in Paris. In 1926-27, he served as the trade attaché at the Chilean embassy in Belgium, and beginning in 1940 he served as an honorary economic advisor to the Chilean embassy in France. In June 1940, his summer home was bombed by the Germans and all of his servants were killed, although Del Campo saved himself by hiding in the cellar. On January 11, 1941, he was entrusted with Chile's diplomatic mission to Romania, holding the rank of consul and the official position of chargé d'affaires.[5] He arrived in Romania on May 9, 1941, and on May 18 the Romanian government recognized his appointment.[6]

At the time Del Campo arrived in Romania, the conditions in the Bukovina region and in the capital city of Chernivtsi, overall and for Jews in particular, continued to worsen.

Between June 1940 and the end of June 1941, the entire region was under Soviet control. On July 5, 1941, Romania assumed control of the city, which, the following day, was entered by a unit of the Romanian army, and then by *Einsatzkommando* 10B of Germany's *Einsatzgruppe* D. Pogroms and the organized murder of Jews by police and military forces got underway immediately. Toward the end of the month, discriminatory restrictions were instituted regarding the places where Jews were permitted to live and the food supply.

On August 1, *Einsatzkommando* 10B left the city and were replaced by a special unit comprised of 15 administrators and 15 soldiers of *Einsatzgruppe* D. This force began their attacks immediately, killing 682 Jews. The same month, the Germans ordered Corneliu Calotescu, the governor-general of Bukovina, to consolidate the Jews in a ghetto. Chernivtsi Mayor Traian Popovici tried to delay implementing this decision on the grounds that he needed to learn from experience that had accrued in Poland and Germany regarding how to move Jews into ghettos. In the meantime, additional restrictions were placed on Jewish life. On October 9 forces of the Romanian army surrounded the city, and the following day Popovici was informed that the president, General Ion Antonescu, had decided to immediately implement the Romanization policy he had instituted in the country and to deport the Jews to Transnistria.[7] Popovici opposed the deportation, on the grounds that the Jews held occupations that were essential to life in the city, and demanded that all those who held such professions and their families not be deported. He was authorized to release up to 120 people from the deportation, according to a detailed list that specified their occupations.

Popvici continued to engage in extensive activity aimed at rescuing Jews from deportation to Transnistria, and was dismissed from his position as a result. For this reason, Yad Vashem recognized him as a Righteous Among the Nations in 1969. Rescuing people from the deportation to Transnistria was extremely important, as although there were no extermination camps there, the prevailing conditions during the journey and in the locations to which the Jews were sent were extremely harsh, and most of the deportees died.[8]

In addition to the possibility of being rescued from deportation due to an occupation that was deemed essential in the city, Del Campo's report explained that the Romanian regulations included a presidential directive that Jews with foreign citizenship were not to be deported.[9] This was the legal basis of the application to the Romanian authorities, made by the Swiss and the Spanish diplomatic missions to Bucharest, to protect people with Spanish citizenship and any other foreign citizenship from deportation and from the imposition of special taxes.[10]

These conditions provided Del Campo with two possible avenues for rescue. One stemmed from the fact that in 1940, after Germany invaded Poland, Chile assumed responsibility for the affairs of the Free Polish Government in Exile vis-à-vis Italy and Romania. As a result of this status, the Chilean mission could issue and renew Polish passports for Jews who had been living in Romania prior to the war or who fled there when the Germans invaded. In addition, Samuel del Campo began issuing protective documents to Jews from the Republic of Chile, which Jews hung at the entrance to their homes.[11]

The other possibility was to extend them Chilean protection or citizenship in order to protect them from deportation. In more than 600 cases, including the case of the Kiesler family, Del Campo issued Chilean protective documents and passports.[12]

These actions, which began in mid-1942 and are documented in the archives of the Romanian Ministry of Foreign Affairs and of Chernivtsi Oblast in Ukraine, were carried out approximately half a year after the submission of Del Campo's report to the Ministry in Santiago.

On June 9, 1942, through the Ministry of Foreign Affairs in Bucharest, Del Campo contacted the military cabinet for the administration of Bukovina and Bessarabia in an effort to bring back 100 Polish citizens from Transnistria, including Christians and many refugees from the days of the fighting between Poland and Germany (1939), who had been transported via the train station in Chernivtsi. He also requested that the military cabinet intervene to change the decision to deport them, and that "if they think they need to be moved elsewhere, that a place of settlement in a different city in the country be determined."[13]

Del Campo's appeal, the fact that the Romanians knew that these Polish Jews held Chilean-issued protective documents, and the internal discussions within the Romanian government that highlighted these facts, were of no avail. During the second week of June 1942, Bukovina's Governor-General Corneliu Calotescu ordered the deportation of additional Jews from Chernivtsi to Transnistria, on the grounds that they were non-productive Polish refugees who were suspected of Communism and were not connected to the affairs of the country. On June 23, 1942, the Romanian

Ministry of Foreign Affairs conveyed to the Council of Ministers a complaint by a Chilean representative, who held that approximately 100 Jews entitled to his protection had been deported to Mogilev (Transnistria) in two groups, one on June 7 and the other on June 14, 1942. As a result of the deportations, the Chilean diplomat requested that his representative in Chernivtsi, Grigore Szymonowicz,[14] be permitted to compile a list of the property of Jewish subjects of Chile who had been deported to Transnistria and to secure their residences with the seal of the Consulate to prevent their property from being confiscated and looted.[15]

In September and October 1942, Del Campo again approached the Romanian Council of Ministers in Bucharest by means of its Ministry of Foreign Affairs; he also approached Bukovina and Bessarabia's Governor-General Calotescu through an attorney named Grigore Szymonowicz. He requested that they prevent deportation to Transnistria of the Jews on the lists they submitted, which consisted of holders of Chilean passports. Del Campo submitted his lists on September 11, 1942, and Szymonowicz submitted his on October 3. Together, the lists contained more than 600 names.[16]

These appeals were preceded by an assessment submitted by the director-general of Romanian intelligence on August 7, 1942 to the Ministerial Council's committee on the administration of Bessarabia and Bukovina. In this assessment, the director-general of Romanian intelligence determined that 770 Polish Jews[17] held passports issued by the Chilean consulate. This included 42 who "had not been baptized" and who are not mentioned in the immigration department data, but rather only in the documents that were submitted by Szymonowicz, Chile's representative to Bessarabia and Bukovina. He also noted that a number of the passports had been issued by Dr. Josef Trink, secretary of the Peruvian consulate in Bucharest,[18] in cooperation with a local Jew named Kafeman Heimich. Others had been issued by Grigore Szymonowicz, based on personal information forms that had been filled out and signed by Del Campo. In addition to the passports, the Jews were also provided with certificates of Chilean protection to prevent their deportation to Transnistria.[19]

The work of Del Campo and Grigore Szymonowicz appears to have achieved positive results in September 1942. On the 11th of the month, the presidency of the Council of Ministers provided its representatives in the province of

Bukovina, Bessarabia, and Transnistria with a list of Chilean citizens and authorized them to prevent their deportation to Transnistria. On September 12, 1942, the same recipients were instructed to bring all those holding Chilean passports from the Tulchyn district to the capital city.[20]

In addition to this firsthand evidence regarding the activity of Samuel del Campo and his associates, we also possess information from second-hand sources. One example is a January 7, 1943 letter sent by a Jewish man named Samuel in Chernivtsi to the director of RELICO (Relief Committee for the War stricken Jewish Population), Abraham Silberschein, who was based in Geneva. In the letter, Samuel attributed recognition of the legal status of an acquaintance to a Polish passport he had received from the Chilean consulate.[21]

In a report on the situation of the Jews in Bukovina in August 1942, Silberschein wrote that, in Chernivtsi, 250 Jews had been loaded onto trains for deportation to Transnistria and then, apparently without reason, were removed from the train and returned to their homes. The following day, Romanian policemen abducted 250 other Jews at random, loaded them onto trains, and deported them.[22] Based on the identical number of Jews noted, it may be possible to assume that this testimony pertains to the events of October 1941, and not to the occurrences of June 1942.

This evidence can be considered alongside the summary of two trials that were held immediately after the war. The first was conducted against Calotescu, the governor-general of Bukovina, and against Sterie Marinescu, apparently in May 1945. In this trial, a Jewish witness by the name of Ghertner accused Marinescu of deporting him to Transnistria in the deportations that were carried out on January 7, 1942, despite the fact that he was a Polish citizen holding a Chilean passport and that the Chilean government's representative, Dr. Szymonowicz, had intervened on his behalf.[23]

The second trial was conducted in Bucharest on August 18, 1947 against Romulus Cojocaru, the Romanian commissar in Chernivtsi during the war. The trial was intended to be conducted in absentia, as the defendant had fled. Cojocaru was charged with arresting Jewish and Christian Polish refugees who crossed the border from German-occupied territory and handing them over to the S.S., who subsequently executed them. The witnesses in the trial, who included

Szymonowicz's secretary Eugen Apter, described the acts that were committed in March 1943, arguing that the behavior and actions of the defendants ran counter to the agreement that the Romanian Ministry of Foreign Affairs had concluded with Chile's representative in Romania: Samuel del Campo. According to their testimony, the refugees who had been driven across the border should have been tried in Romania by a military court, and not handed over to the Germans. Szymonowicz explained this to the defendant during the incident, but the defendant had not listened to him. He also confiscated their passports.[24]

It is difficult to determine all the practical consequences of the actions taken by Del Campo to rescue Jews. However, these testimonies clearly establish that, on many occasions, the protective documents were not effective and that Jews were deported from Chernivtsi in any event.[25] The rest of his testimony indicates that this activity caused him many difficulties.

Two years after assuming his post, Del Campo was forced to depart Romania. On February 12, 1943, his superiors in Santiago informed him that he needed to leave the country because Chile was about to sever its diplomatic relations with it. Indeed, on May 18, 1943, Chile severed its diplomatic ties with Vichy France, Romania, Hungary, and Bulgaria. As a result, Switzerland assumed representation of the affairs of Chile and the Polish Government in Exile vis-à-vis the governments of Romania, Bulgaria, and Hungary. When, in February, Del Campo was informed that he needed to leave Romania, he was told that he was being transferred to Switzerland to fill the post of consul-general in Zurich and to represent the acquisition department of the national railway.[26]

At the same time these messages were being conveyed, efforts got underway to acquire Del Campo a visa to enter Switzerland and to secure the country's agreement to his appointment (*exequatur*). On April 21, 1943, Chile's representative in Bern informed the Swiss Ministry of Foreign Affairs that Del Campo had been appointed consul-general in Zurich and requested that both he and the Catholic official with the mission in Bucharest be issued visas.[27] Ten days later, René de Weck, the Swiss consul in Bucharest, reported that Del Campo had visited him and had informed him that he was being transferred to Zurich to serve as the consul-general and the representative of the National Bank of Chile. He also requested a visa for his secretary, Casimir Szymonowicz, who was "supposedly" (in the words of De Weck) a Catholic Pole. De Weck maintained that Del Campo was a suspicious character and that Romania's foreign minister, Mihai Antonescu, had asked him to personally update him about Del Campo's dealings regarding the Polish passports.

The following day, de Weck informed the Ministry of Foreign Affairs in Bern that Del Campo had a terrible reputation among the Romanians, the Poles, and the diplomats in Bucharest. He therefore recommended not approving his appointment as a consul in Switzerland and denying the request for a visa for him and his secretary, who was actually a Jew posing as a Catholic Pole using a Chilean service passport. A few days later, an internal memorandum of the Swiss Ministry of Foreign Affairs stated that Del Campo had been involved in selling Chilean and Polish passports to individuals who were not entitled to them. It also maintained that, according to an investigation of the federal foreigners' police, a Romanian Jewish man named Roberto Grief, who had fraudulently entered Switzerland with a Chilean passport issued by Del Campo, was present in Zurich and had become friendly with another Jew named Fleischmann, who had previously served as Romania's consul-general in Zurich. In conclusion, leading up to April 1943, the Swiss Ministry of Foreign Affairs informed the Chilean consulate in Bern that it had not approved Del Campo's appointment to the position of consul in Switzerland and that a visa would not be issued.[28]

At the same time, through the services of Carlos Morla Lynch, the Chilean representative in Bern, Del Campo informed the Foreign Ministry in Santiago that on May 13, 1943 he had met with General Antonescu, the president of the Romanian Council of Ministers with whom he was friendly, and that the latter had told him that Germany was demanding that Romania sever ties with Chile. Antonescu recommended that Del Campo leave Romania immediately, as he could no longer guarantee his safety. He also told him that the only good way for him to leave the country was via Turkey, as Germany would not allow him to travel to Switzerland by way of Hungary or Italy.

Del Campo felt threatened and that his life was in danger, and under these conditions he quickly left Romania after burning the confidential material found in the consulate's archive and sending a request to Santiago to ask Briones Luco, the Chilean representative in Ankara, to arrange him the status of secretary of the diplomatic mission there. On May 28, 1943, Del Campo sent Morla Lynch a telegram from an unknown location outside Romania and asked if a response regarding his appointment in Turkey had been received.[29]

The position of the Ministry in Santiago is revealed in two telegrams to Morla Lynch in Bern. The first, dated May 25, 1943, announced the decision to rescind Del Campo's appointment in Zurich and to summon him back to Chile. The second, written six days later, informed him that on May 27, 1943 Del Campo had arrived in Turkey, but that the Ministry had decided not to appoint him as an advisor to the mission in Ankara and reiterated the directive that he return to Chile. In June 1944, an entry in Del Campo's service file in the Chilean Ministry of Foreign Affairs stated that his previous position had been declared "*vacante.*" The use of this term indicated that he had been removed from his position, and this is the last information we have about him.[30]

To understand the circumstances surrounding Del Campo's dismissal, we need to consider the questions raised by the events. Among other things, it is notable that the officials of Chile's Ministry of Foreign Affairs did not respond to Del Campo's question of whether it consented to his activity to rescue Jews in Chernivtsi. It can be assumed that the Ministry would have agreed to his intervention on behalf of Polish Jews who were entitled to the protection and defense of the Chilean government, as this stemmed from his representation of the affairs of Free Poland.

However, nowhere do we find evidence that Del Campo informed the Ministry in Santiago that his efforts to provide Jews with protection involved the issue of Chilean passports, such as the passports that were issued to the Kiesler (or Kotzer) family,[31] to Roberto Grief, and to Casimir Szymonowicz.[32] He also did not report that he had issued Chilean citizenship certificates and official protective documents to Jews, as attested to by archival documents of the Romanian Ministry of Foreign Affairs and the local archive of Chernivtsi in Ukraine.

There is no clear answer to the hypothetical question of how Chilean Foreign Ministry officials might have responded to Del Campo had they known he had issued Chilean passports and protective documents to Jews who were not natives of Chile or citizens of the country. However, indications of an answer can be gleaned elsewhere. In the abovementioned case of Romanian citizen

Roberto Grief, when the diplomatic mission in Bern asked how to deal with the Chilean passport he held, the answer was unequivocal: as there was no evidence that the passport had been issued with the Ministry's authorization, it should be confiscated from him immediately.[33] To this we can add the Foreign Ministry's directives to the mission in Bern, which explicitly stated the Ministry's position that the Swiss mission, which was representing the affairs of Chile, renew the Chilean passports of native-born Chileans alone.[34]

This policy of the Chilean Ministry of Foreign Affairs regarding recognition of the passports that were issued under various conditions was particularly stern when Jews were involved. Studies on Chile's immigration policy beginning in 1933, and more notably after 1937, clearly indicate discrimination against Jews requesting immigration visas and transit visas. The statistics regarding Jewish immigration to Latin American countries between 1933 and 1945 indicate that between 10,000 and 12,000 Jews arrived in Chile during this period, accounting for approximately ten percent of all the Jews who entered the sub-continent.[35] However, many Jews were turned away on racist grounds or due to a failure to meet economic or professional requirements.[36]

This policy, and its outcome for consuls who ostensibly violated it, is reflected in the punitive action taken by the Ministry in Santiago against two consuls who had served in France and Japan and were suspected of issuing visas to Jews. These cases also shed light on the risk that Del Campo had taken.

The first instance concerned Enrique Turri, Chile's consul in the French port city of Marseilles between 1939 and 1941. During the first half of 1941, Turri worked on submitting requests to the Ministry for the issue of a number of travel visas to Chile. According to standard procedure, Turri sent the applicants' relevant information to Santiago, where it would be decided whether or not to approve the requests based on the information he sent. In the case of the Benesra family, the Ministry approved the family's visa request on the condition of confirmation that the recipients were not Jews. As a result, Turri did not issue the visa.[37]

In other instances in which Turri was authorized to issue visas by what appear to have been falsified telegrams, he was asked why he had submitted the visa request for Jews contrary to instructions. In response, he maintained that the Haymann, Lustig, and Wassertheil families had "stated that they were not of the Jewish race but rather were Catholic" ("*[ninguno] manifestó, en ningún momento, ser de raza judía, sino católicos los tres primeros*"), and that Zubin Hiller "stated that he is Orthodox" ("*declaró ser ortodoxo*"). On August 26, 1941, the Ministry decided to dismiss Turri. Apparently, he was aided by the explanations he had provided – that he had received telegrams from the Ministry (which turned out to be falsified) approving the visas – and on September 9, 1941 his termination was suspended pending the results of a police investigation of the telegrams. In the months that followed, Turri continued handling visa requests in accordance with the instructions he received from the Ministry. On November 6, 1941, Gabriel González, head of the Chilean mission in Vichy, informed the minister of foreign affairs in Santiago that the findings of the police investigation proved that the telegrams had in fact been falsified by Jews wishing to help the applicants receive the visas.[38]

The second case was that of Alfredo Hernández Camus, Chile's honorary consul to Kobe, Japan, who was dismissed from his position on August 29, 1941 for working contrary to the instructions he had received from the Ministry regarding the issue of entry visas to Chile.[39] According to a complaint submitted by Jorge Rosselott, the Chilean consul in Yokohama, Hernández issued visas to a number of individuals without indicating them in the monthly reports, including a few of Jewish extraction. According to the debate that was conducted between the two consuls, and the explanations the consul in Kobe sent to the Ministry in Santiago, the visas were used solely for transit purposes in order to reach Bolivia, or as assistance visas issued to people in emergency situations. The consul in Kobe also explained that in some cases he had issued visas to residents of Japan who had lived there for approximately two decades and who had relatives in Chile. In his defense, he maintained that they had not included any Jews or refugees ("*No son ni israelitas ni refugiados*"). These clarifications were submitted a few weeks before Hernández's dismissal, following warnings from the Ministry's Consular Department in February 1941 to refrain from issuing visas to Jews.[40]

Another clear and direct manifestation of the discriminatory policy in the issue of immigration visas to Jews, also reflected in the occurrences involving the consuls in Marseilles and Kobe, can be found in the letters from Marcelo Ruiz, a senior official at the Consular Department, to Rosselott in Yokohama during the first half of 1941. In February of that year, Ruiz accused Rosselott of having issued tourist visas, three months earlier, to nine people based on the clarification that they were Catholic Poles, even though it was quite clear that they were Semites ("*semitas*"). Two months later, perhaps in order to refute Rosselott's claims, Ruiz explained that the ban on the entry of Jews into the country was based on their racial appearance, not on their nationality or religion. One could be a Pole of the Catholic religion and also a pure-race Jew ("*la prohibición de entrada de israelitas al país se debe más bien a su aspecto racial y no a la nacionalidad o religión. [...] un ciudadano es de nacionalidad polaca y de religión católica pero eso no puede dar margen a suponer que no sea judío de pura raza*"). In such situations, the consul could require the applicants to produce certification of their racial origin ("*certificado de origen racial*") issued by the consulates of different countries. He also reprimanded Rosselott for attaching certificates bearing the fingerprints of individuals "of Polish nationality and European origin" ("*de nacionalidad polaca y de origen europeo*") to a visa application he submitted in January 1941, even though it was clear that they were undoubtedly of Jewish origin" ("*son de innegable origen judío*").[41]

An issue that came up later, after his dismissal, regarding the Chilean consul in Kobe was the fact that he had issued Chilean passports to serve as protective documents for Jews. In September 1943, the Ministry of Foreign Affairs in Santiago instructed Morla Lynch, its representative in Bern, to ask the Swiss representative in Berlin to not recognize the validity of any Jewish passport that was issued by Hernández, the former Chilean consul in Kobe, "unless they present Chilean documents that confirms its legality" ("*desconozca validez todo pasaporte israelita otorgado ex-Cónsul Kobe Sr. Hernández a menos envíen a US. documentación chilena que permita confirmar su validez*").[42]

This instruction may have been in reference to the three known instances in which Hernández had issued passports to Jews. The first was issued in the name of Rabbi Aron Lewin, regarding whom the representative of the Polish Government in Exile in Chile, Ladislas Mazurkiewicz, contacted Chilean Foreign Minister Joaquín Fernández at the beginning of 1943. In this interaction, Mazurkiewicz requested that the Chilean passport be recognized, as Rabbi Aron Lewin, who had formerly served as the president of the Council of Polish Rabbis and as a delegate to the Polish Sejm, had been issued a visa to

Argentina and was only in need of a transit visa. The passport had been issued in Kobe on December 31, 1940; Izaak Lewin, the rabbi's son, had purchased it and sent it to Lviv, where the rabbi and his wife were living. As already noted, the request was denied.[43]

A similar instance presented itself a few months later. In May 1943, Chile's representative in Bern was asked by the Swiss diplomatic mission in Berlin[44] how to respond to requests to renew Chilean passports that were issued on May 19, 1941 in Kobe in the names of Ara Frumkin and Eugenia Gorlin, two native residents of Warsaw. The Chilean Ministry of Foreign Affairs responded by saying that the passports should be confiscated "without prejudicing the ability to return them, in the event that their citizenship is subsequently proven" ("*sin perjuicio que posteriormente comprueben los interesados su nacionalidad*").[45]

All this helps explain the fundamental change in Chilean Foreign Ministry officials' approach to Samuel Del Campo upon the conclusion of his service in Romania – from one of support, and appointment to the post of consul-general in Zurich in March 1943, to a negative attitude, reflected in the denial of his request to be appointed secretary of the diplomatic mission in Turkey in May of the same year and, ultimately, his dismissal from the Ministry due to his conduct in Romania (where he had issued Chilean passports to Jews, Poles, and Romanians) and the Ministry's total objection to these actions. We can also conjecture that had his actions been discovered earlier he would have been removed from his position immediately, while he was still in Romania.

Conclusion

Samuel Del Campo, Chile's representative in Romania between 1941 and 1943, was in Romania during the severe persecution of the Jews that occurred there. In his capacity as representative of the Polish Government in Exile, he became aware of the suffering of the primarily Jewish refugees from Poland, who had arrived in Bukovina in general and the city of Chernivtsi in particular, and who suffered from brutal deportations to Transnistria. According to his report, Polish refugees in Chernivtsi began to request his help around the time he arrived in Bucharest.[46]

He took advantage of his ability to protect them by issuing them Polish passports belonging to people who had not taken documents with them when they fled Poland and by renewing the passports of people who had already been in Romania beforehand. Nonetheless, he contacted the Romanian Ministry of Foreign Affairs and attempted to establish Chilean protection of hundreds of Jews through various agreements. However, he appears to have quickly realized that this method was not enough and began issuing Chilean protective documents to save them from deportation.

Del Campo reported only some of his actions to Santiago, particularly those in which he acted on behalf of the Polish government, and he asked for the opinion of his superiors. His requests received no response, but he was warned against reporting actions in which he provided Jews with the direct protection of Chile or regarding the issue of passports and protective documents, including service passports. Samuel Del Campo was most likely quite familiar with the policy of his government, and of the Chilean Foreign Ministry in particular, regarding the issue of citizenship documents or visas to Jews, and it was clear to him that they not only would have not consented to his activities but would also have taken punitive measures against him. Indeed, this had occurred in much less severe cases – for example, in the cases of the consuls in Marseilles and Kobe.

Based on various correspondences of the Ministry, we can conclude that Del Campo's superiors were unaware of his actions and, had they known about them, would not have allowed them to continue. They would not have authorized the issue of Chilean protective documents and passports to individuals who were not entitled to receive them under law. Had they known about these activities when they occurred, they most likely would have sanctioned him. Samuel Del Campo conducted himself in a manner that he knew was not in accordance with the explicit policy of his superiors.

The Swiss government was the first to take action against him for his efforts to rescue Jews in Romania; it did so by not approving his appointment as consul-general in Zurich and refusing to issue him a visa. The Swiss decisions were followed by a second punitive measure, this time by Chile's Ministry of Foreign Affairs. When the Chileans received information regarding the reasons for the non-approval of Del Campo's appointment as consul-general, the government decided not to appoint him to the position of secretary of the Chilean mission in Turkey, or any other diplomatic mission, and instructed him to return to

Chile. Based on this information regarding his efforts to rescue Jews, he appears to have been removed from all positions in his country's foreign service in June 1944. I possess no other information about Del Campo's subsequent actions, except for the fact that he returned to France at the end of the war and remained there for the rest of his life.

On February 24, 2016, on behalf of Uly Kotzer and Eliyahu Rosenthal, I submitted a request to Yad Vashem's Righteous Among the Nations Department to recognize Samuel Del Campo as a Righteous Among the Nations. On May 22, 2017, we were informed by the Committee for the Righteous Among the Nations that it had decided to bestow upon Del Campo the title of Righteous Among the Nations due to the assistance he provided to Jews during the Holocaust at risk to his own life. On October 22, 2017, a medal of honor was presented to members of his family.

With this decision, the Jewish People expressed its gratitude to one more individual who, on humanitarian grounds, took action to rescue Jews and prevent their suffering during the Holocaust, despite the risk he knew he was taking by doing so.

Endnotes

1   * This study was undertaken in part while I was a research fellow at Yad Vashem's International Institute for Holocaust Research, in 2014, and at the Hebrew University of Jerusalem's Liwerant Center for the Study of Latin America, Spain, Portugal and their Jewish Communities, between 2010 and 2015.

    The main countries on behalf of which these consuls acted included El Salvador, Ecuador, Guatemala, Honduras, Haiti, Paraguay, and Peru.

2   For a more extensive account of these activities and a discussion of the consul of Ecuador in particular, see: Efraim Zadoff, "Ecuadorian Passports as Protective Documents for Jews during the Holocaust: The Case of Consul Muñoz Borrero," *Moreshet, The Journal for the Study of the Holocaust and Antisemitism* 13 (2016), pp. 121-156.

3   See the recorded testimony of Uly Kotzer, which featured as part of an exhibition titled "Stories of Rescuers and Rescued: Diplomats from Latin America who Rescued Jews during the Holocaust," held by the Jerusalem House of Quality, April 12-28, 2014 (a copy of the exhibition and the testimony is on file with the author). See also Kotzer's oral testimony to the author.

4   Letter from Del Campo (Bucharest) to the minister of Foreign Affairs (Bucharest), January 1, 1942, Archive of the Chilean Ministry of Foreign Affairs (hereinafter CMFA Archive), Historia 2080.

5   CMFA Archive, Relación personal y Hoja de servicios del Señor Samuel Del Campo, file 857-881, Dirección del Personal, Antecedente ex funcionario.

6   CMFA Archive, Misión de Chile en Europa – Consulados 1942, file 1971.

7   The policy of Romanization was aimed first and foremost at the Roma, who were more detrimentally impacted than the Jews. On this topic see Stefan Cristian Ionescu, *Jewish Resistance to "Romanization", 1940-1944* (New York, 2015). Ion Antonescu's Romaninzation policy was intended to expel "foreigners" such as the Roma and the Jews from the local economy, in an effort to protect members of the Romanian ethnic group, whom he regarded as "loyal citizens" of the state. This policy included the confiscation of "foreigners'" property, their deportation to Transnistria or areas under German control, and their murder. On this topic in particular, see ibid., pp. 55-60. See also Jean Ancel, *The History of the Holocaust: Romania* (Jerusalem, 2002), pp. 685-694 (Hebrew).

8   For a detailed account of the history of the Jews of Czernowitz, from the withdrawal of the Soviets and Romania's occupation of the city in July 1941 through the end of the war, see Ancel, *The History of the Holocaust: Romania*, pp. 653-696. For an account of the deportations to Transnistria in November 1941, see Ancel, *The History of the Holocaust*, pp. 672-676. On Popvici's activity to rescue Jews see Ancel, *The History of the Holocaust*, pp. 677-685. On the resumption of the deportations from Chernivtsi on June 7, 1942 see Ancel, *The History of the Holocaust*, p. 1201.

Also see the entry for Czernowitz/Cernăuți in *The Yad Vashem Encyclopedia of the Ghettos during the Holocaust*, pp. 131-136.

9   See Ionescu, *Jewish Resistance to "Romanization"* (p. 55), which argues that this policy was paradoxical to some extent, as it gave disproportionate rights to Jews who had acquired foreign citizenship and discriminated against those who were only citizens of Romania, while at the same time accusing these Jews of disloyalty to Romania. Ionescu notes that the Jews conducted a legal struggle against Romanization in order to highlight their allegiance to the state and to avoid giving traction to the official charge of disloyalty. In doing so, maintains Ionescu, the Jews prevented approximately ten percent of the confiscations of their property. See Ionescu, *Jewish Resistance to "Romanization"*, pp. 147-161 pp. 147-161, p. 234, note 1; and especially p. 149.

10 See the February 5, 1942 letter from José Rojas y Moreno, Spain's representative to Romania, which emphasizes that Jews with Spanish citizenship were exempt from deportation (see the collection of documents of the Romanian Ministry of Foreign Affairs at the Yad Vashem Archive (hereinafter YVA), JM/13732, pp. 27-28; the letter from the Swiss consulate stipulating that the authorities were prohibited from imposing special taxes on foreign citizens due to their origins, in apparent reference to Jews with Polish citizenship, ibid., pp. 276-277; letters from the Swiss diplomatic mission to Romania (October 26 and November 2, 1943) stating that it was prohibited to classify citizens of foreign countries as Jews (see the collection of CMFA documents referred to above in this note, pp. 151-152).

11 An example of such passports can be found in a collection of documents on file with Eliyahu Rosenthal of Rehovot, which contain a copy of the original authorization of Chilean protection – in Spanish, German, and Romanian – that was hung at the front of Jewish homes or next to the entrance on the inside. The collection also contains passports in the name of Rozenthal's father, who was a Polish citizen, had lived in Bucharest since the 1920s, and would renew his passport at the Polish consulate in the city. Upon the establishment of the Polish Government in Exile, the passports were renewed by Consul Samuel del Campo and his predecessor Miguel Ángel Rivera, and later by Swiss Consul René de Weck, who were representing the affairs of Poland. According to the personal testimony of Eliyahu Rosenthal, his family was not deported and his property was not confiscated, thanks to the Chilean protective document that hung at the entrance to their apartment. Also see his testimony at the Shoah Foundation Institute, University of Southern California, Testimony 25099. A copy of a similar document – issued in the name of Samuel Maibruch, who held Chilean passport no. 1361/c (this name, along with the same passport number, is found in the list of passport holders discussed below), which was issued on July 1, 1942 – can be found at the Romanian Ministry of Foreign Affairs' Archive Service, Main Collection, "Problema 33: The Issue of the Jews," 1942, Vol. 20, p. 19.

12 We can assume that all 617 people appearing on the list, which contains last names in alphabetical order and is nine pages long, were issued the same documents as the members of the Kiesler family. For another description of this list, and of another

list made by a representative of the Chilean consulate in Chernivtsi, see note 16 below. For Del Campo's list, see "Problema 33: The Issue of the Jews," 1942, Vol. 20, pp. 11-18. This material was photographed in Bucharest by the United States Holocaust Memorial Museum (USHMM). Copies of the photos can be found in the Jean Ancel collection of the Center for Research on Romanian Jewry at the Hebrew University of Jerusalem. I would like to thank Miriam Caloianu for providing me with a copy of this material. These documents can also be found at YVA, JM/13735, pp. 12-42, but a few are unreadable. I would also like to thank Etty Hershkowitz and Lucian Hershkowitz, who assisted me in translating Romanian-language documents from these files into Hebrew.

13 See "Problema 33," p. 20.

14 On Grigore Szymonowicz, see below.

15 Del Campo's petition can be found in the abovementioned file "Problema 33: The Issue of the Jews."

16 Del Campo and Szymonowicz compiled separate lists. The list submitted by Del Campo consisted of item numbers and names alone, whereas Szymonowicz's contained a table with item numbers in alphabetical order, the name of the bearer of each passport and his or her family members listed in the documents, home address, passport number, and ID number (apparently local). Del Campo's list can be found in the abovementioned file "Problema 33." For the letter sent by Szymonowicz and the partial list, see the collection of documents from Chernivtsi Oblast, Ukraine, YVA JM/11345, pp. 10-11. The almost complete list can be found at the Elie Wiesel National Institute for Studying the Holocaust in Romania (Institutul Național pentru Studiarea Holocaustului din România "Elie Wiesel"). I am grateful to Romania's consul-general in Toronto for providing me with this list through the offices of the Israeli consulate there.

17 This number appears to be quite accurate. The list submitted by Del Campo contained 607 names, and the list submitted by Szymonowicz contained only 508. The lists with which I was provided, however, are incomplete and missing pages.

18 The mention of Josef Trink in this context is interesting and significant in that it indicates cooperation between the Chilean consul and José Gambetta, the Peruvian consul in Bucharest, on whom I conducted a separate study. Based on my research on Gambetta, I petitioned Yad Vashem to recognize him as a Righteous Among the Nations in April 2019.

19 See "Problema 33."

20 "Problema 33," pp. 7-8.

21 YVA, Abraham Silberschein Papers, M.20/145, pp. 35-36.

22 In his report, Del Campo wrote that there were 250 families, and not individuals, as is written in the report that Silberschein received. YVA, Abraham Silberschein Papers, M.20/103, p. 72.

23 See *Scanteia*, the official journal of the Communist Party in Romania between May 10, 1945 and June 3, 1945, which published the protocol of the initial trial held in Bucharest against the first group of war criminals: Issue 227, May 19, 1945, p. 5. http://czernowitzbook.blogspot.de/2015/06/moarte-criminalilor-de-razboi-death-to.html (accessed and downloaded on August 3, 2016). I would like to thank my son Jonathan Zadoff for translating this Romanian-language document into Hebrew.

24 See Jean Ancel (ed.), *Documents Concerning the Fate of Romanian Jewry During the Holocaust, Vol. 6: War Crimes Trials* (New York, 1986), pp. 252-255 (Romanian). I am grateful to my son Jonathan Zadoff for translating this Romanian-language document into Hebrew.

25 This conclusion is also supported by Ancel's words regarding the deportation of 120 Jewish bearers of protective documents issued by the Chilean consulate in Bucharest in the first transport of June 1942. Ancel, *The History of the Holocaust*, p. 1205. See also ibid, note 77.

26 CMFA Archive, Telegramas a Legación en Suiza 1943, Ministry of Foreign Affairs in Santiago to the Consulate in Bern, telegrams from April 6, 1943; April 22, 1943; and May 20, 1943.

27 See the Archive of the Swiss Ministry of Foreign Affairs in Bern: *Schweizarisches Bundesarchiv* (hereinafter BAR), Chilean consulate (Bern) to Foreign Affairs Division, Federal Policy Department, File E2001D#1000/1553#1798*, April 21, 1943.

28 BAR, internal memorandum signed by Weber, April 20, 1943, Chilean Consulate (Bern), April 21, 1943; de Weck to Chilean Consulate (Bern), May 1, 1943 and May 2, 1943; internal memorandum, May 6, 1943; BAR, Swiss Ministry of Foreign Affairs to Chilean Consulate (Bern), May 24, 1943. On the episode surrounding Roberto Grief, see CMFA Archive, Legación Chile en Suiza, File 2166, telegram from Morla Lynch to Ministry of Foreign Affairs (Santiago), July 26, 1943.

29 CMFA Archive, Historia – Legación Chile en Suiza, File 2166.

30 CMFA Archive, Historia – Legación Chile en Suiza, File 2166, Fernandes – Foreign Minister, to the representative in Bern, May 25 and 31, 1943. See Del Campo's service file at CMFA Archive, Relación personal y Hoja de servicios del Señor Samuel del Campo, File 881-857, Dirección del Personal, Antecedente ex funcionario.

31 As already noted, the first passport was issued three months before the report was sent, and the second was issued one week later.

32 Casimir Szymonowicz was the son of Grigore Szymonowicz, Del Campo's representative in Chernivtsi.

33 CMFA Archive, Chilean Ministry of Foreign Affairs (Santiago) to Mission (Bern), July 29, 1943.

34 CMFA Archive, Telegramas a Legación en Suiza, File 2165, Telegram of March 25, 1943.

35 For a comprehensive assessment of the number of Jews who immigrated to the countries of Latin America between 1933 and 1945, see the table in Haim Avni, "Los países de América Latina y el Holocausto," in *SHOÁ – Enciclopedia del Holocausto* (Jerusalem, 2004), pp. 85-94, especially p. 93.

36 For an example of these studies, which provide additional bibliography in this realm, see Irmtrud Wojak, *Exil in Chile: Die deutsch-jüdische und politische Emigration während des Nationalsozialismus, 1933-1944* (Berlin, 1944), especially Ch. III.2.1, pp. 106-114, and Ch. III.2.2, pp. 115-125; idem, "Chile y la inmigración judeo-alemana," in Avraham Milgram (ed.), *Entre la aceptación y el rechazo: América Latina y los refugiados judíos del nazismo* (Jerusalem, 2003), pp. 128-173, especially pp. 162-173; Moshe Nes-El, "La actitud de Chile frente a la inmigración judía durante la Segunda Guerra Mundial (1933-1943)," in *Estudios sobre el Judaísmo Chileno* (Jerusalem, 2009), pp. 51-66, especially pp. 60-65.

37 CMFA Archive, Turri (Marseilles to Ministry (Santiago), Consulados de Chile en Europa y Asia 1941, File 1882-a, June 6, 1941.

38 CMFA Archive, Turri (Marseilles) to Ministry (Santiago), Consulados de Chile en Europa y Asia 1941, File 1882-a, September 9, 1941; telegrams between the minister (Santiago) and González (Vichy), Legación en Francia 1941, Cables File 1908, September 6, 1941 and November 6, 1941; telegrams between the minister (Santiago) and Turri (Marseilles), September-December 1941.

39 CMFA Archive, Japón – Legación Chile, Tokio, File 1939, Chilean Legation in Tokyo to Hernández (Kobe, Japan), August 19, 1941.

40 CMFA Archive, Sección Clave, Archivos confidenciales, Vol. 1, File 1908, Marcelo Ruiz, Consular Department (Santiago) to Hernández (Kobe), February 11, 1941; Hernández (Kobe) to Rosselott (Yokohama), June 26, 1941; Hernández (Kobe) to Ministry (Santiago), July 19, 1941 and August 13, 1941.

41 CMFA Archive, Consulados de Chile en Europa y Asia 1941, File 1883, Ruiz (Santiago) to Rosselott (Yokohama), February 11, 1941, April 2, 1941, and June 16, 1941. Emphasis in original.

42 CMFA Archive, Telegramas a Legación en Suiza, File 2165, Ministry (Santiago) to the Legation in Bern, September 8, 1943.

43 CMFA Archive, Misiones residentes en Chile, File: 2096 A – Polonia, correspondence between Ladislas Mazurkiewicz and Joaquín Fernández, February 5 and 19, 1943. On the receipt of the Chilean passport of Rabbi Aron Lewin in Kobe, see the testimony of his son Izaak Lewin, who acquired it for his parents while he was in Kobe (Izaak Lewin, "Hour of the Holocaust," *Jewish Tribune*, September 29, 1978, p. 6; October 27, 1978, p. 5). Izaak Lewin recalls paying much more than 400 dollars for the passport. According to his account, after his parents were murdered by the Germans, a Gestapo member sold the passport for a high price to another Jew who used it to make it to Bergen-Belsen. Indeed, the list of prisoners at Bergen-Belsen

contains the name Aron Lewin, who appears to have survived. See Gedenkstäte Bergen-Belsen, *Gedenkbuch–Häftlinge des Konzentrationslagers Bergen-Belsen*, April 2005, p. 644. In a different article, Izaak Lewin describes the consul in Kobe as anti-Semitic. See Izaak Lewin, "Probyratowania Zydow europejski chprzypomocy polski chplacowek dyplomaty cznychpod czasdrugiej wojnys wiatowej," *Biuletin Zydowskiego Instytutu Historicznego W Polsce* 4(120) (1981). I am grateful to Dr. Edna Green for her assistance in translating the article from Polish into Hebrew. Zerach Warhaftig wrote that Izaak Lewin actually acquired two passports, based on various aspects of the son's own testimony, which he quotes. See Zerach Warhaftig, *Refugee and Survivor during the Holocaust* (Jerusalem, 1984), p. 336 (Hebrew).

44 Beginning in April 1943, following the severing of relations between Chile and Germany, Switzerland assumed responsibility for representing Chilean affairs to Germany and its allies.

45 CMFA Archive, Legación de Chile en Suiza, File: 2166, Carlos Morla Lynch (Bern) to the Ministry (Santiago), May 8, 1943; CMFA Archive, Telegramas a Legación en Suiza, 1943, File: 2165, Ministry (Santiago) to the mission in Bern, May 12 and September 8, 1943.

46 At the beginning of his January 1, 1942 report to the Ministry in Santiago, he stated that he had already written about it in a previous report dated October 25, 1941, which appears to have been lost. See CMFA Archive, Historia 2080, Letter from Del Campo (Bucharest) to Minister of Foreign Affairs (Bucharest), January 1, 1942.

Irit Back

From Biafra to Darfur:
The African and Global Discourse on the Holocaust

In 2011, while visiting the Ethiopian city of Gondar, I came across a group of youths selling used books on a blanket spread out on one of the city's sidewalks. Among the books, I spotted an Amharic-language edition of *The Diary of a Young Girl* by Anne Frank. When I spoke with the kids about the book, it became evident that they were well informed on the particulars of Anne Frank's biography and that they regarded her as a heroic figure and attributed her fate to the fact that she was Jewish.

The story of Anne Frank has always occupied a special place in my heart. Her history and personality offered parallels with the life and character of my mother. Both were condemned to a childhood of imprisonment in close quarters and almost complete isolation from the events going on around them. Young Anne hid in an apartment in central Amsterdam with her family and a number of other children and adults, and young Rachel (known as Shela) Schout (later Qedar) lived in a small room in the Mogilev Ghetto in Ukraine, along with her mother (her father was killed during the Nazis' invasion of her town) and a few other adults. Both remained optimistic, each in her own way, and refused to abandon their belief in the good of man, even in light of the horrors around them. After the death of my mother, I was motivated by a strong desire to explore references to the history and the character of Anne Frank in the discourses of the different nationalist movements of Africa.

In a 1994 speech marking the opening of an exhibit titled "Anne Frank in the World," South African President Nelson Mandela stated that Anne Frank's diary had been a source of inspiration for him and his associates on Robben Island, the prison in which he had lived for 18 of the 27 years of his incarceration.[1] He recalled that a copy of the book, worn and torn due to its popularity among the inmates, "kept our spirits high and reinforced our confidence in the invincibility of the cause of freedom and justice."[2] He also stated that "by honoring her memory as we do today, we are saying with one voice: Never and never again!"[3]

During this process, I learned that the discussion of Anne Frank's memory was part of a broader discussion of the relationship between the Holocaust and the history of South Africa – a subject that has been considered extensively in the context of the construction of post-Apartheid South African history and identity. In some cases, this discussion has even advanced the claim that Apartheid South Africa perpetrated a genocide against its black majority population.[4] On this basis, I decided to expand the discussion to other countries on the African continent to examine the ways in which the events and lessons of the Holocaust have been represented in the context of two formative events in the history of post-colonial Africa: the war between Nigeria and Biafra, fought between 1967 and 1970, and the unremitting civil wars in Sudan – between the north and south from 1955 to 1972 and 1983 to 2005, and between the north and the west, in the Darfur region, from 2003 until the present. In this article, I also consider aspects of the African, international, and Israeli discourses on the relationship between the Holocaust and international events. We begin by briefly reviewing the manner in which the major developments in the fields of Holocaust Studies and Genocide Studies have incorporated the discourse on conflicts in post-colonial Africa.

How is Africa reflected in the fields of Holocaust Studies and Genocide Studies?

The field of Genocide Studies began to develop in the 1980s and 1990s. Still, the distinction between the explicit desire to eradicate a group in its entirety on the one hand, and ethnic, religious, and other kinds of tensions on the other hand, remains unclear, and the debates surrounding the question of when we can classify a specific conflict as genocide have increased.[5] As the field continued to evolve, the connections between genocide and the Holocaust began to emerge, as noted by Amos Goldenberg:

Another process on which the history of the Holocaust has had decisive influence is the development of the field of genocide. The term "genocide" was coined in 1944 by Jewish-Polish legal expert Raphael Lemkin after he fled from Poland to the United States at the beginning of the 1940s…His book on the Axis countries' rule in occupied Europe…was written with regard to the immediate context of the Holocaust, in which dozens of his relatives were killed by the Nazis. Interest in the topic faded, and it was only in the 1990s that it emerged as a major independent field, due to the dominance and the fruitfulness of the field of Holocaust studies, the events that occurred in the Balkans and in Rwanda, and the activity of the international courts that were established in their wake.[6]

Indeed, the events that occurred in Rwanda (1994) and Srebrenica (1995) sparked discussion of their relationship to the events and lessons of the Holocaust in the evolving field of Genocide and Holocaust Studies.[7] For example, this field engaged in the discussion of the connections between the Holocaust and the processes of decolonization and post-colonialism in Africa and elsewhere.[8] In the context of this article, the events of the genocide in Rwanda in particular, which have been discussed extensively elsewhere,[9] served to sharpen questions regarding the relevance of the events and the lessons of the Holocaust to defining genocide in post-colonial Africa, as has been argued by Mahmood Mamdani in light of the events that occurred there in 1994:

> While the impulse to destroy the enemy is ancient, the technology of genocide is constantly evolving. The Nazi Holocaust was a state-of-the-art mass extermination. Jews were branded for the purpose of identification and subjected to experimentation by Nazi doctors. The killing took place in industrial compounds where the killers – the attendants – simply sprinkled Zyklon-B crystals into the gas chambers. The whole genocidal apparatus functioned with bureaucratic efficiency. The Rwandan genocide, on the other hand, was rather old-fashioned. It was carried out with machetes rather than chemicals; street corners, living rooms, and churches became places of death. Whereas Nazi Germany made every attempt to isolate those

most guilty of its crimes from their victims, the Rwandan genocide was a much more intimate affair. It was carried out by hundreds of thousands of people and witnessed by millions. A Rwandan government minister I met in 1997 contrasted the two horrors: "In Germany," he said, "the Jews were taken out of their residences, moved to distant, faraway locations, and killed there, almost anonymously. In Rwanda, the government did not kill. It prepared the population, enraged it and enticed it. Your neighbors killed you.[10]

To some extent, the research has considered the ways in which the events and lessons of the Holocaust were reflected in the Rwandan genocide. According to René Lemarchand, the two events were among the most horrifying occurrences in twentieth century human history. Although we must take care to avoid projecting a carbon copy of the events of the Holocaust on those that occurred in Rwanda, considering the lessons of the Holocaust can provide a theoretical framework for studying the case of the Rwandan genocide regarding parameters such as accusing the "other" of anti-national revolutionism – for example, the Jews through Communism and the Tutsis through anti-State revolutionism. In both cases, he maintains, these charges encouraged xenophobic trends and demonization of the "other."[11]

The genocide in Rwanda and the discussion sparked by the events and lessons of the Holocaust are especially interesting with regard to the cases discussed in this article. If the war between Nigeria and Biafra and the first civil war in Sudan took place before the discipline of Holocaust and Genocide Studies had evolved, the second civil war in Sudan and the events in Darfur occurred in parallel to the development of the field. For this reason, a review of these instances also facilitates examination of the development of and changes in the research engaged in by Holocaust and Genocide studies.

"After all, you experienced a similar fate.": Discussion of the Significance and the Lessons of the Nigerian-Biafran War

The war between Nigeria and Biafra was fought between 1967 and 1970, just a few years after most of the Sub-Saharan African countries achieved independence. Like most of the political entities on the continent, the colony of Nigeria, formed from the unification of two separate entities in 1914, was more a product of European imperial considerations than a reflection of local geopolitical realities. Nigeria was the most populated colony on the continent (upon independence, its population was estimated at 45 million) and remains so today. Its borders artificially brought together approximately 250 ethnic groups, including three dominant regional ethnic groups that have been classified as "core peoples":   the Hausa-Fulani in the north, the Yoruba in the southwest, and the Igbo (which previous studies refer to as Ibo) in the southeast. In addition to the ethno-regional division, there was also a religious element, including the separation of a prevalently Muslim north from a largely Christian south and significant development gaps between the south, which was close to the center of colonial interests, and the remote north. The initial tensions surrounding the regional, religious, and ethnic divisions within the young country that began to emerge shortly after Nigeria became independent from British colonial rule (1960) were intensified during the second half of the decade, when oil was discovered as a significant resource in southeast Nigeria.[12] Members of the Igbo, the major ethnic group residing in this region, demanded greater political and economic representation in the country. This demand exacerbated fears of the ultimate dominance of members of this group, who were viewed as a threat not only due to their military advantage (the roots of their dominance reach back to the colonial army) but also due to their perception as competitive and as having an advantage in education and employment. These fears began to actualize when a military coup, led largely by members of the Igbo leadership, was staged in January 1966.[13] The same year, the pogroms against the Igbo throughout Nigeria increased, leading approximately one million of them to migrate to the country's eastern region. In May 1967, after the Igbo lost their political dominance in a counter-coup, and after their demands for broader autonomy for the country's eastern region were rejected, Col. Odumegwu Ojukwo, leader of the eastern region, declared the establishment of the independent republic of Biafra, named after the Bight of Biafra on the Atlantic coast. In response, Nigerian government forces invaded the seceding region. Later, the Nigerian army imposed an air and land blockade against the Biafran enclave, which created conditions of shortage and starvation. The Biafran leadership's refusal to accept humanitarian aid by land and the demand to be provided with air assistance alone significantly worsened the situation on the ground, resulting in many deaths from starvation and the illnesses that accompany it. The overall number of lives lost in the war is a source of contention, with estimates ranging from one million to three million deaths. The war continued until Biafra's surrender in 1970.[14]

The coverage of the Nigerian-Biafran War was the opening shot in what has been referred to as the "age of televised disaster," referring to the fact that during this period, television sets began to be increasingly prevalent in private homes. Photos of Biafran children dying of starvation became a symbol of the period and an icon of the suffering of the Third World. The war also symbolized the dashed hopes for a better future following the end of the colonial era and for a turning point in the history of non-government humanitarianism, which emphasized the moral obligation to the victims of human-made tragedies and led to the development of an activist and more aggressive conception of humanitarian intervention. The emergence of organizations such as the French *Comité de Lutte contre le Génocide au Biafra* (the Committee of Struggle against Genocide in Biafra, out of which the well-known organization Doctors without Borders sprouted) was practical evidence of the activism of this period. The starvation that came to be associated with the war raised for discussion a state's responsibility for the starvation of its own inhabitants, especially when it is systematically aimed against a group the state regards as illegitimate.[15] The image of a small, starving Biafran David battling a murderous Nigerian Goliath created immense sympathy throughout broad populations around the world. The lessons and imagery of the Holocaust were used prominently within the intellectual activist discourse of the period. Advocates of the comparison between the lessons of the Holocaust and the events in Biafra included figures such as writer Günter Grass, who argued that "as Germans…the knowledge of Auschwitz, Treblinka and Belsen obligates us to speak out publically against the culprits and accessories of the genocide in Biafra…[S]ilence – we had to learn that as well – turns into complicity."[16] Bernard Kouchner, one of the founders of Doctors without Borders, linked his humanitarian obligation to Biafra to the fate of his grandfather, who died in Auschwitz. Images of concentration camps, such as "Buchenwald for Children" and "Mauthausens of famine," repeatedly popped up in the global media, mobilizing additional recognition and sympathy for the fate of the Biafran People.[17] Journalist and writer Frederick Forsyth, author of the best-seller *The Biafra Story,* explained that Britain was guilty of supporting Nigeria, which was conducting a genocide against the Biafran People that resembled what had been experienced by the Jews during World War II.[18]

On the other hand, in the postcolonial world in which many nation states fought for the legitimacy of their existence and Cold War considerations often defined alliances and rivalries, many countries in Africa and elsewhere in the world decided to support Nigeria against Biafra.[19] In many cases, the policies of the different governments stood in stark contradiction to domestic public opinion. In some studies, images and lessons of the Holocaust were part of the discourse of support for Biafra. This phenomenon was prominent primarily in the Israeli discourse of the period.

In August 1968, Nathan Alterman published a column titled "Indeed Prague, but Nevertheless..." Its thrust was its focus on the charge that the discussion on Biafra had been pushed to the sidelines of public consciousness, especially in light of the intensive discussion surrounding another event that occurred during this period – the Soviet invasion of Czechoslovakia. Although his column placed blame on the world as a whole, Alterman was also critical of Israel for disregarding its Holocaust-related moral duty to raise discussion about Biafra:

> Following an extensive discussion, [the Knesset] approved the wording of a [resolution of] protest that expressed the unique Jewish concern regarding this crime of genocide and the horrible Jewish memories by virtue of which Israel regards itself as obligated to not remain silent in face of the atrocity. Nonetheless, the protest, as we know, refrained from all "extremism" and from any words that would place blame on "one side" alone, and from any "physical recommendations"... The entire protest was an expression of a position of responsibility and gravity by the majority of the Knesset against the minority faction...[20]

Indeed, the Biafran case had considerable reverberations in Israeli public discourse. The discussion focused largely on the moral obligation of the Jewish People in Zion to take action on behalf of the people of Biafra.[21] The conception that the inhabitants of Israel must serve as a moral spearhead in the global discourse regarding support for Biafra was espoused by figures with varying and sometimes polar opposite political views – religious and secular, activists and thinkers, and the like. The mounting sympathy of the media and the public regarding Biafra resulted in increased pressure on the Israeli government and its institutions to increase its aid and to recognize Biafra. After the surrender of Biafra, even Abba Eban, Israel's foreign minister at the time, who was criticized for representing Israel's failure to recognize Biafra, maintained: "We stretched ourselves to the point that were another dozen or twenty countries, of different dimensions, to mobilize themselves for the matter like us, it is highly doubtful that the Holocaust would have occurred."[22]

Israel was not only forced to fall in line with the countries of the Western bloc, most of which were supportive of Nigeria (or at least declared neutrality); it also aspired to establish its standing and cultivate relations as much as possible with the countries of the Third World – especially those countries that did not pursue anti-Israel policies. At this stage, when most African countries south of the Sahara still maintained full diplomatic relations with Israel,[23] Nigeria was viewed as a key country with significant influence on the African continent. If the Nigerian nationalist movement's legacy during the anticolonial struggle was to a large extent a sense of identification with the Jewish People, its fate, and the establishment of Israel, the polarization between the predominantly Muslim north and the predominantly Christian south over relations with the state of Israel became apparent in the initial years of Nigerian statehood. Thus, in the face of the Muslim north's hostility toward Israel, which prevented many possibilities for cooperation, many Igbos identified deeply with the Jewish People and its fate and venerated the state of Israel even before the outbreak of the war with Nigeria. These feelings intensified during the war.[24] In his recollections from a previous aid delegation he led to Biafra (in conjunction with Abie Nathan and Israeli physician Yoram London), Col. Yitzhak Shani, the director of Magen David Adom at the time, wrote:

> When the Biafrans discovered us, people from Israel, they were especially happy. It was their first encounter with Israelis. They hoped, and still hope, that Israel will extend its hand to them. They pinned many hopes on us, and they said so openly. **After all, you experienced a similar fate**. You are the only ones who can understand our suffering and our desire for independence. And you are also the only ones who can help us. [25]

Here, it is helpful to elaborate somewhat on the roots of the Igbo People's deep identification with the Jewish People and the state of Israel.

Since the beginning of the nineteenth century, a number of groups among the Igbo have identified themselves as members of the lost tribes of the Jewish People. Various scholars have noted the distinct linguistic motifs that are derived from Hebrew,[26] as well as more focused historic contexts, such as ties between a certain Igbo clan and an ancient Jewish tribe or the performance of Jewish customs such as circumcising boys eight days after their birth.[27] One example of this relationship was articulated by Nnamdi Azikiwe, known as "Zik," who was the mythological leader of the Nigerian national movement and a northern-born Igbo who was elected to serve as the first president of the independent Nigerian state. Azikiwe deeply identified with the history of the Jewish People, from biblical times up until the present, and he related to the establishment of the state of Israel as a formative event in the history of the twentieth century. Later, the leaders of independent Biafra also identified with the fate of the Jewish People. They observed parallels between the Jews' fate and the pogroms that were conducted against Jews in the modern era – such as the Cossacks' pogroms against the Jews of Russia – and the fate of the Biafrans, who were also the targets of pogroms before the war. Biafra's leader, Col. Ojukwo, even proclaimed: "Like the Jews…we saw in the birth of our young Republic the gateway to freedom and survival."[28]

In this context, it is interesting to consider the role played by Holocaust imagery in constructing the identity of the Biafran homeland. In many senses the Biafran homeland was imagined, and its construction began around the time of the outbreak of the war itself.[29] Approximately half of the 14 million inhabitants of the republic were not Igbo, meaning that ethnic identity could not provide a common denominator for the Biafran "melting pot". Its territorial basis of identity was also not sufficiently solid, as the region had not contained a defined political entity in the past. Moreover, some of the Igbos themselves had lived in other parts of Nigeria for a number of generations and had only fled to eastern Nigeria around the time that Biafra was established, as a result of the ongoing pogroms there, especially in the north. As the sense of separation played a central role in the experience of the young homeland, Holocaust imagery was perceived as promoting the concept of the Biafran melting pot. According to Edith Bruder, "the Jews of Africa" envisioned their state as the "African Israel," a new nation born of the violence of genocide.[30]

The war concluded not only with Biafra's surrender to Nigeria and with the ongoing political suppression of the inhabitants of this area from the end of the war until today,[31] but also in the ongoing debate over whether or not the events that occurred during the war constituted genocide. In many ways, the Nigerian-Biafran war was a war over representation, as Michal Givoni explains: "The tragedy of Biafra, which at the time was labelled alternatively starvation, civil war, and genocide, is in many ways a given name – an unclassified event revolving around a struggle for representation and the inability to settle it."[32] Furthermore, when Robert Melson, an influential researcher in the field, claimed in 1992 that "the Nigerians were not Nazis, and the Ibos were not Jews,"[33] his views influenced many, both due to his personal experiences as a child in the Holocaust in Poland and the fact that he was a researcher of Nigeria whose notable sympathy for the Biafran case was palpable in the way he covered what occurred there. His coverage included a comparison, during the war itself, between the fate of the Biafrans and the European Holocaust. However, he later argued that the only case that could be compared to the Holocaust was the Armenian Holocaust, and that comparing it to other cases served to trivialize these other holocausts.

The dimension of chronological proximity and distance from the events of the Holocaust, and its impact on the discourse regarding them, was also significant in the case of the civil wars in Sudan. These wars broke out approximately one year before Sudan's independence and to a certain degree continue up to the present, although their geographical focus has changed.

Furthermore, like the events of the Nigerian-Biafran war, the civil wars in Sudan – particularly between the north and the south – were also characterized by geopolitical and ethno-religious polarization that helped shape the discourse regarding the events and the lessons of the Holocaust in a meaningful way. Although this discourse is more complicated in the case of Sudan due to factors such as geographical location, participant diversity, and numerous periods of internal struggle, there are many similarities between the cases of Nigeria and Sudan, as described below.

"We thought the Jews were an extinct race.": Civil Wars and the Discourse on the Holocaust in Sudan

The political maps of Sudan since its colonial conquest by Britain in 1898 illustrate the paradoxes that accompanied their creation. The lines that were drawn, typically using a ruler, reflect their artificial nature, and the massive size of the country (which until 2011, when it was split into two separate countries, was the largest country on the continent) emphasizes the lack of logic underlying the assembly of such diverse regions and groups into a single political entity. Moreover, as most of the British interests revolved around the Nile Valley region where the Blue Nile meets the White Nile, and the remaining regions were gradually annexed for reasons pertaining primarily to European competition in the conquest of Africa, vast disparities in development emerged between the north and the rest of Sudan.[34] One of the impacts of colonial conquest was the strengthening of a group whose presence gradually changed the texture of ethnic and racial relations in Sudan. This group consisted of traders of Arabic origin, particularly from the region of the Nile Valley between Aswan in Egypt and Khartoum. With British encouragement, they continued to migrate to different parts of the colony of Sudan and became an elite that determined the norms of "Sudanese-ness" – primarily those associated with Islam and Arab identity; however, they were excluded from the identities of national discourse that were perceived as African and non-Muslim. The preferential treatment of the north and of certain groups associated with it resulted in intensified ethno-religious division along class lines. These characteristics resulted in chronic instability and ongoing struggles between the north and the rest of the country, with the civil war between the north and the south constituting what was known and familiar.

The first manifestations of the civil war emerged approximately one year prior to Sudan's achievement of independence in 1956.The war between the dispossessed south, populated largely by Christians and the adherents of traditional faiths, and the primarily Arab-Muslim north continued until 1972. Problems of under-development and the pronounced disparities between the center and the periphery were accompanied by chronic problems of political instability. Sudan became independent as a democratic multi-party state and, like in Nigeria (and the other countries of post-colonial Africa), democracy in Sudan collapsed in a matter of a few years. The first military coup occurred in 1958, and in 1969 another coup was carried out under the leadership of Jaafar Nimeiri, who ruled Sudan until 1985. Although a ceasefire between the north and south was reached in 1972 under the tyrannical military rule that Nimeiri instituted, it gradually became clear that the government in Khartoum intended to implement it only partially. Moreover, President Nimeiri and his successors cultivated a discourse of Arab hegemony both in their foreign policy, which strengthened Sudan's relations with the Arab world and made use of pan-Arab rhetoric, and in their domestic policy, including fostering the use of the Arabic language and displacing African languages from political systems such as the education system, the media, and Sudanese national historiography. For example, the claim that Islam reached Sudan from the Nile was reinforced, despite extensive evidence proving that the influences penetrated the area primarily from the Sahelian kingdoms (the border with the Saharan Desert), which were characterized as "African." In 1983, Nimeiri proclaimed the institution of Shari'a law (Muslim religious law) as state law, which was perceived as a declaration of war against the south. The civil war resumed that year, continuing until 2005. It was the longest war in the history of independent Africa and took a heavy toll, resulting in approximately two million dead and four million refugees and displaced persons.[35]

The Igbo in Nigeria had been close to the center of interests of the colony's colonial power, and some were educated in Western educational institutions and joined the modern workforce and the colonial administration.[36] In contrast, as a result of the distance of the inhabitants of South Sudan from the colonial center of interests and the neglect of the periphery even after the end of the colonial era, the young South Sudanese who joined the liberation movement were not familiar with the global discourse on the Holocaust, unlike the leaders and members of the movement in Biafra, who highlighted the similarities between their fate and that of the Jewish People and the significance of the "Holocaust and the Resurrection" (*hashoah ve'ha-tekuma*) for their national identity. They also used these ideas to mobilize international support for their interest. Most leaders of the Anya Nya – the liberation movement of South Sudan, which was established in 1963 – did not possess an in-depth knowledge of the fate of the Jewish People during World War II and certainly did not make use of it for building national identity or mobilizing international support.

Furthermore, whereas in many senses the Nigerian-Biafran War became a symbol of the period as described above, the civil war of Southern Sudan was initially perceived as an internal matter of the Sudanese state and at the time was not the subject of international interest or support. This is an important point, as the Israeli government stepped into this vacuum of lack of interest and support and for a number of years became the primary supporter of the struggle of the Southern Sudanese People.[37] Joseph Lagu, the founder and leader of the Anya Nya, faced many difficulties in mobilizing military support, training, and weapons for the young movement. His appeal to representatives at Israel's embassies in Kenya, Uganda, and Ethiopia yielded positive results as far as he was concerned. The state of Israel at the time was cultivating an "Alliance of the Periphery," a plan that advocated political, economic, and security cooperation with the non-Arab countries of the region; in this spirit, it regarded cooperation with Southern Sudan as extremely desirable. Lagu was invited to Israel to meet with the heads of the governments of Levi Eshkol and Golda Meir, who promised their support to the struggle of the Southern Sudanese people.[38] At the initiative of then Mossad Chief Zvi Zamir, David Ben-Uziel (known to Anya Nya fighters as "Tarzan" or "General John") was sent to Southern Sudan, where he provided significant assistance in setting up and arming the movement's army.[39] In an interview, Ben-Uziel noted that during his many conversations with Lagu, there had been no direct mention of the common fates of the Jewish People during the Holocaust and the Southern Sudanese People. There had been, however, a number of indirect references to the fact that the Israelis were the only ones capable of helping the Southern Sudanese, who, like the Jews had been, were being persecuted, abducted, and exterminated.[40]

Despite the close ties between the state of Israel and the Southern Sudanese liberation movement, the discourse on the events and the lessons of the Holocaust appear to not have constituted a significant element of the fabric of these relations. Support for this assessment can be found in an excerpt from Dave Eggers book *What Is the What: The Autobiography of Valentino Achak Deng.* This book documents the life history of Valentino Achak Deng, a boy from Southern Sudan who fled his village upon the outbreak of the second civil war, and his tumultuous journey until his arrival to the United States (and afterward). Among other things, it describes the extended period during which he lived in the Kakuma refugee camp in western Kenya. The book depicts a conversation between Deng and his friend Gop regarding fear of the extermination of the Dinka, one of the two dominant ethnic groups in Southern Sudan:

> This seems very much like what they did to the Jews, Gop said. People spoke a lot about the Jews in those days, which was odd, considering that a short time before, **most of the boys I knew thought the Jews were an extinct race**. Before we learned about the Holocaust in school, in church we had been taught rather crudely that the Jews had aided in the killing of Jesus Christ. In those teachings, it was never intimated that the Jews were a people still inhabiting the Earth. We thought of them as mythological creatures who did not exist outside the stories of the Bible.[41]

At one stage, the camp contained 12,000 unaccompanied minors from Southern Sudan with educational needs for which a diverse array of education systems sought to provide. Some of these systems also discussed the events and lessons of the Holocaust. Elsewhere in the book, Deng recounts a rumor that spread through the camp following the erection of tall fences on its grounds:

> Soon even the best educated among us bought into the suspicion that this was a plan to eliminate the Dinka. Most of the Sudanese my age

had learned of the Holocaust and were convinced that this was a plan much like that used to eliminate the Jews in Germany and Poland.[42]

It must be remembered that Eggers' book is a historical novel that combines fact and fiction, making it difficult to establish the accuracy of these excerpts. Future research involving individual interviews with people who resided in the Kakuma camp and in other refugee and displaced persons camps will engage in deeper discussion of the issue.

Somewhat paradoxically, discussion of the context of the Holocaust actually gained momentum during Sudan's war against its western region: Darfur. This paradox stems from the Muslim religious character of this war. Most of the inhabitants of the Darfur region, which had a long history of existence as an independent kingdom and was annexed by Sudan in 1916, were Muslim. In a sense, the inhabitants of this region were perceived as more integral to the Sudanese state than the inhabitants of the south who were Muslims or who adhered to traditional faiths. Still, with the inhabitants of the south, the inhabitants of Darfur shared the injustices of exclusion and lack of development. When the initial signs of protest began to spread throughout Darfur in the 1990s, due to factors such as the spread of starvation because of climate change and underdevelopment, and the protest escalated into armed struggle beginning in 2003,[43] the Sudanese government responded with extreme violence, According to Gerard Prunier: "In Khartoum the government panicked because it suddenly felt that the Muslim family was splintering, potentially with enormous consequences [for Sudan]."[44] Despite their common Muslim identity, many inhabitants of Darfur (for example, the Fur, the region's namesake) were identified as "Africans" and, as a result, as inferior to the "Arabs" of the North. The sense of superiority harbored by the Arabs of the North toward the inhabitants of Darfur resulted in the former's reference to the latter as "'abid" (slave), a derogatory term that cast doubt on the very Muslim-ness of the person and that is often applied to black-skinned people.[45] The onset of regional rebellion and its ethno-racial association resulted in an extremely brutal attack by the Sudanese government against the inhabitants of Darfur, including air strikes and ground attacks using cavalry companies known as Janjaweed (Arabic for "mounted gunman"). These forces burned villages and murdered and raped many Darfur inhabitants. The immense number of casualties (some estimates place the number of dead at 600,000, or approximately one-tenth of the population of Darfur), refugees, and people who had been displaced from their homes, in conjunction with the systematic propaganda to eliminate the "Africans" of Darfur, resulted in the Darfur conflict's classification as the first genocide of the twenty-first century.

Actually, the claim that a genocide was underway in Darfur was already being voiced in 2004 by U.S. Secretary of State Colin Powell, for example, who stated: "We concluded that genocide has been committed in Darfur and that the government of Sudan and the Janjaweed bear responsibility and genocide may still be occurring." The evidence that was collected in the camps, he argued, proved that the pattern of violence was coordinated and not incidental.[46] This claim subsequently faded for a variety of reasons, such as: the hope for an end to the long war between the north and the south in Sudan; the resulting unwillingness to recognize the new crisis that had engulfed Sudan at the time; the United States' commitment to the "war on terror" following the attacks of September 11, 2001, which led to cooperation between the governments of the U.S. and Sudan; the discovery of oil as a significant inorganic mineral in Sudan; and more.[47] In a precedential 2005 decision, the United Nations resolved that the events in Darfur constituted "crimes against humanity" and therefore fell under the jurisdiction of the International Criminal Court (I.C.C.). The decision to define this as genocide, however, was not mentioned.[48] Nonetheless, in March 2009, the I.C.C. ruled that Sudanese President Omar al-Bashir was found guilty of charges of crimes against humanity, which were later bumped up to genocide.[49]

With regard to Darfur, as in the case of Biafra, public opinion in the countries of the West was often also at odds with the official position of governments and international organizations. This involvement had a prominent dimension of international institutions engaged in preserving the memory of the Holocaust. For example, in 2007, the heads of Yad Vashem called on U.N. Secretary General Ban Ki-moon to recognize what was occurring in Darfur as genocide:

Chairman of the Yad Vashem Council Joseph (Tommy) Lapid and Chairman of Yad Vashem Avner Shalev today sent a letter to UN Secretary General Ban Ki-moon urging him to do everything in his power to stop the genocide in Darfur. "It is not sufficient for the international community to issue condemnations, and statements via the United Nations, while this Khartoum-sponsored genocide is taking place. Concrete steps must be taken; we must do everything to ensure that the Security Council will decide to send troops to Darfur who will be able to restore security. Every day that passes adds thousands of names to the list of dead," they wrote.[50]

In the United States, the U.S. Holocaust Memorial Museum (U.S.H.M.M.), engaged in prominent involvement at a very early stage of the conflict to raise international awareness of what was occurring. The museum worked in a variety of ways to draw international attention to the subject, including through the activity of the Committee on Conscience (COC), which was established "to alert the national conscience, influence policy makers, and stimulate worldwide action to confront and work to stop acts of genocide or related crimes against humanity."[51] Museum officials acted independently or in cooperation with the umbrella organization "Save Darfur" and other humanitarian groups. To a significant extent, the museum's involvement in the issue was revealed as a result of the activity that was generated with Senator Barack Obama, which continued during his election campaign and after his election as president of the United States in 2008. Among other things, he declared the following: "We can't say 'never again' and then allow it to happen, and as a president of the United States, I don't intend to abandon people or turn a blind eye to their slaughter."[52] In 2008, during a pre-election debate, he asked: "If we could have intervened effectively in the Holocaust, who among us would say that we had a moral obligation not to go in?"[53] Also as president, Obama's government worked in cooperation with the Holocaust Museum to emphasize the connection between the events in Darfur and the legacy of the Holocaust. For example, in April 2012, during a speech at the museum, President Obama announced the establishment of an Atrocities Prevention Board, which was supposed to cooperate with the museum's COC on issues such as early detection and mapping of the areas of conflict that could develop into crimes against humanity and genocide.

The involvement of institutions such as the U.S.H.M.M. in Washington in raising awareness regarding the occurrences in Darfur was also the subject of much criticism. Samuel Totten, for example, spoke of great disappointment with the action of the Obama Administration, and particularly with its cooperation with the Holocaust Museum. Totten's research and public work focus on other centers of violence in Sudan, in the Nuba Mountains and in the Blue Nile State. According to Totten, the focus on Darfur by the Obama Administration and the U.S.H.M.M. diverted attention from the ongoing war between the Sudanese government and these regions, which could also be characterized as involving genocide. Genocide experts and other humanitarian organizations have also maintained that the intervention regarding Darfur constituted paying lip service in a manner that covered up the true interests of the U.S. government.[54] Museum officials, for their part, maintained that projects such as displaying alternating and permanent exhibits exposing the atrocities underway in Sudan to its millions of visitors constituted an important aspect of the notion of "never again," which guides its work. Indeed, the museum subsequently hosted an exhibit depicting what had occurred in Southern Sudan.[55]

To the best of my knowledge, various representatives of the Sudanese leadership did not relate specifically to comparisons between the events and lessons of the Holocaust and the events underway in their own country. Rather, they tended to relate generally to international intervention in Darfur as a neo-imperialist plot, and they accused world Jewry and the state of Israel of creating a conspiracy to draw attention to the events in their country in order to divert attention from the Israeli-Palestinian conflict.[56]

Conclusion

Discourse regarding the events, the lessons, and the representations of the Holocaust also held great significance in time and space in post-colonial Africa. It was especially significant in the case of the Nigerian-Biafran War. The Igbos' sense of identification with the fate of the Jewish People in general, and during the Holocaust in particular, resulted in an appropriation of the ethos of the "Holocaust and the resurrection" to create a unified national identity and, using these images, to mobilize international sympathy and support. Due to the short time that elapsed between the end of World War II and the outbreak of the Nigerian-Biafran war, this appeal appears to have generated significant sympathy for Biafra and was one of the factors that established the suffering of the Biafran People as a symbol of the period. This sympathy, however, did not prevent many countries and international organizations from supporting Nigeria, which helped facilitate the defeat of Biafra.

But despite the significant changes in the field of Genocide Studies from the 1980s onward, the case of Biafra still appears to be excluded from it. A prominent and representative example of the non-inclusion of the case of Biafra is the well-known book by Ben Kiernan, which reviews the history of genocide from Sparta to Darfur but fails to mention the case of Biafra.[57] In the field of Genocide and Holocaust Studies, as well, the events that occurred in Biafra are defined more as an "ethnic struggle" than as a genocide.

Biafra's struggle for recognition ended only in 1970, and many Igbos continue their struggle to classify the events that occurred in Biafra as genocide. They assign great importance to the comparative dimensions between the fates of the Biafran and the Jewish People. In this manner, historian Chima Korieh argues that the starvation of the Igbos leaves no room for doubt regarding the existence of a well-organized and systematic plan for their extermination, and that "the war was indeed a variant of what the Nazis called the Final Solution to the Jewish problem."[58] It would be interesting to ascertain whether today – with the reawakening of the Biafran separatist movement and the renewed violence against its claim[59] – we will also witness the reemergence of discourse that combines the events and lessons of the Holocaust with the case of Biafra, or whether the chronological distance and the emergence of a new generation of activists will lead the discourse into other comparative dimensions.

Whereas most struggles in Sudan did not produce a meaningful discourse regarding the Holocaust, such a discourse did evolve, somewhat surprisingly, in the case of Darfur. In addition to the work of the U.S. Holocaust Memorial Museum described above, director Steven Spielberg also initiated a project to document testimony from Darfur within his Holocaust documentation foundation. The aim of this project, he explained, is to actualize the mantra of "never again" in the context of more contemporary cases of genocide and oppression: "We must ask ourselves how we can give this vision right of way in different countries around the world."[60] Nat Hentoff has referred to the events in Darfur as a "Black Holocaust" and has maintained that since the Holocaust of the Nazis, the civilized world has never faced such a concrete threat to what he calls the fundamental principles of justice, human rights, and the inherent value of the individual.[61] In the opposition Sudanese newspaper *The Sudan Tribune*, Eric Reeves authored an article considering the fate of children in what it referred to as "Darfur's Holocaust." The article contains testimonies regarding the horrors experienced by children in Darfur, including frequent air strikes, the murder of parents and other family members, starvation, disease, rape, and the like. It also highlights the systematic and formative nature of the murder and sums up as follows: "This is Sudan, suffering a long way off; too few care, and far too little."[62]

The charge that the world had abandoned the children of Darfur as it had abandoned the children of the Holocaust is of course reminiscent of attitudes regarding the fate of the children of Biafra a few decades earlier, coming full circle from one of the first struggles in post-colonial African history to one of the best known contemporary struggles. Nonetheless, as ongoing violent struggles continue in many places across the African continent, regardless of how they are defined, there appears to be reason for research examining the discourse on the events, the lessons, and the representation of the Holocaust in the context of these struggles, as well as the global discourse regarding the world's moral obligation to them. Research along these lines could be conducted in fields such as Holocaust Studies, Genocide Studies, and African Studies, possibly in combination with other disciplines, such as literature.[63]

In an interview, Nur, an asylum seeker from Darfur, explains that during his studies in the education system of South Darfur, he learned nothing about the Holocaust and its meaning. Nur fled Marla, his village of birth, in the early stages of the Janjaweed invasion of the area; made it to the Kalma refugee camp in Sudan; and from there continued on to Chad, Libya, and Egypt before reaching Israel in 2008. He notes that, throughout his years of flight and wandering, he never encountered mention of the Holocaust; rather, he was introduced to the subject only after he arrived in Israel.[64] Future research involving interviews – with members of different generations of the Southern Sudanese struggle and the struggle in Darfur – regarding the role of the discourse in the events and the lessons of their struggle could add a new and original layer, from the African perspective, to the evolving field of Genocide and Holocaust Studies.

Endnotes

1 Moira Schneider, "Mandela Looked to Anne Frank for Inspiration while Imprisoned," *The Times of Israel*, January 9, 2014. http://www.timesofisrael.com/mandela-looked-to-anne-frank-for-inspiration-while-imprisoned/ (retrieved on May 2, 2021).

2 Shirli Gilbert, "Anne Frank in South Africa: Remembering the Holocaust during and after Apartheid," *Holocaust and Genocide Studies* 26(3) (Winter 2012), p. 366.

3 Ibid., 378-379.

4 Tali Nates, "But, Apartheid was Also Genocide…What About Our Suffering? Teaching the Holocaust in South Africa – Opportunities and Challenges," *Intercultural Education* 21(1) (2010), 517-526.

5 See, for example, Ann Curthoys and John Docker, "Defining Genocide," in Dan Stone (ed.), *The Historiography of Genocide* (New York, 2008); Dominik J. Schaller and Jürgen Zimmerer, *The Origins of Genocide: Raphael Lemkin as a Historian of Mass Violence* (London, 2009).

6 Amos Goldberg, "The Holocaust and History: Disconnects in the Postmodernist Era," *Theory and Criticism* 40 (2012), p. 124 (Hebrew). For other discussions of the relationship between Holocaust Studies and Genocide Studies, see Alon Confino, *Foundational Pasts: The Holocaust as Historical Understanding* (Cambridge, 2012).

7 Yair Auron, *Genocide – Reflections on the Inconceivable: Theoretical Aspects in Genocide Studies* (Raanana, 2006), pp. 88-111 (Hebrew).

8 See, for example: Michael Rothberg, *Multidirectional Memory: Remembering the Holocaust in the Age of Decolonialization* (Stanford, 2009); Louise Bethlehem, "Genres of Identification: Holocaust Testimony and Postcolonial Witness," in Amos Goldberg and Haim Hazan (eds.), *Marking Evil: Holocaust Memory in the Global Age* (New York and Oxford, 2015).

9 For a comprehensive source in Hebrew, see Benyamin Neuberger, *Rwanda 1994: Genocide in the Land of a Thousand Hills* (Raanana, 2005) (Hebrew). For the translation of this source into English, see Ralph Benyamin Neuberger, *Rwanda 1994: Genocide in the Land of a Thousand Hills* (Sheffield, 2017).

10 Mahmood Mamdani, *When Victims Become Killers: Colonialism, Nativism and the Genocide in Rwanda* (Princeton, 2002), pp. 27-28.

11 René Lemarchand, "Disconnecting the Threads: Rwanda and the Holocaust Reconsidered," *Journal of Genocide Research* 4(4) (2002), pp. 499-518.

12 Michael Crowder, *The Story of Nigeria* (London, 1978), pp. 237-259: Sarah A. Chan, *Nigeria: The Political Economy of Oil* (Oxford, 1994).

13 This year in Nigerian history is known as the "year of long knives" due to the large number of military coups that occurred, leading to the end of the brief period of multi-party democracy and politics in the country.

14 For a brief discussion (containing many bibliographical references) of the main developments that led up to the war, including the number of casualties, see Lasse Heerten and A. Dirk Moses, "The Nigeria-Biafra War: Postcolonial Conflict and the Question of Genocide," *Journal of Genocide Research* 16 (2-3) (2014), pp. 172-176.

15 For one of the most comprehensive discussions on this topic, see Alex de Waal, *Famine Crimes: Politics and the Disaster Relief Industry in Africa* (Oxford, 1997).

16 Quoted in Heerten and Moses, "The Nigeria-Biafra War," p. 179.

17 Ibid.

18 Ibid.

19 For a concise analysis of the map of support for both sides over the course of the war, see Benyamin Neuberger, *Africa in International Relations* (Raanana, 2011), pp. 257-263 (Hebrew).

20 Nathan Alterman, "Indeed Prague, but Nevertheless...," from the Nathan Alterman website.

21 For a comprehensive survey of this discourse, see, for example: Michal Givoni, "Who cares (What's to be done)?" *Theory and Criticism* 23 (Fall 2003), pp. 66-78 (Hebrew) (contains references to many articles from contemporary newspapers); Zach Levey, "Israel, Nigeria and the Biafra Civil War, 1967-1970," *Journal of Genocide Research* 16 (2014), pp. 271-277 (this survey contains numerous government documents from the period in question).

22 Arye Oded, *Africa and Israel: A Unique Case in Israeli Foreign Relations* (Jerusalem, 2011), p. 313 (Hebrew). According to Oded, this statement was detrimental to the Israeli government's relations with the government of Nigeria, which was victorious in the war but was very sensitive to external criticism regarding its role in Biafra.

23 This reality changed gradually during the period in question and dramatically following the war of October 1973, when most of the countries severed their political ties with Israel.

24 Levey, "Israel, Nigeria and the Biafra Civil War," pp. 263-280.

25 Yitzhak Shani wrote the epilogue of the book's Hebrew translation: P. de Bonfil, *Biafra: The Demise of a People* (Tel Aviv, 1969), pp. 145-146 (Hebrew) (emphasis added).

26 Tudor Perfitt, *Black Jews in Africa and the Americas* (Cambridge, 2013), pp. 107-109.

27 Edith Bruder, *The Black Jews of Africa: History, Religion, Identity* (Oxford, 2008), p. 143.

28 Quoted in Levey, "Israel, Nigeria and the Biafra Civil War," p. 267.

29 Heerten and Moses, "The Nigeria-Biafra War," p. 178-181.

30 Bruder, *The Black Jews of Africa*, pp. 142-146.

31 For example, according to the post-war arrangements, Nigeria was divided into 36 states, and the southeastern region, including Biafra, was split into a large number of small states with no political strength.

32 Michal Givoni, "Who cares (What's to be done)?" p. 61.

33 Robert Melson, *Revolution and Genocide: On the Origins of the Armenian Genocide and the Holocaust* (Chicago, 1992), p. xviii.

34 Actually, only in 1916, with the annexation of the western region of Darfur, were the final borders of the colony of Sudan demarcated.

35 Among the many sources that have been written on this subject, see Robert O. Collins, *Civil Wars and Revolution in the Sudan: Essays on the Sudan, Southern Sudan, and Darfur, 1962-2004* (Hollywood, 2005); Ruth Iyob and Gilbert M. Khadiagala, *Sudan: The Elusive Quest for Peace* (Boulder, 2006).

36 See, for example, Elizabeth Isichei, *The Ibo People and the Europeans* (New York, 1973).

37 Scopas S. Poggo. *The First Sudanese Civil War: Africans, Arabs and Israelis in the Southern Sudan* (New York, 2009).

38 Ibid., pp. 155-161.

39 David Ben-Uziel, *A Mossad Agent in Southern Sudan, 1969-1971: An Operational Log* (Herzliya, 2017). Beginning in 1971, with the improvement in relations between the north and the south that found expression in the signing of the Addis Ababa Agreement regarding a ceasefire between the parties, the close relations between Israel and the leaders of the liberation movement of Southern Sudan began to fade. Still, the gratitude toward Israel for the aid it received during the critical periods of its struggle felt by most leaders of the movement and their successors in the Sudan People Liberation Movement Army (SPLM/A) – which led the Sudanese People during the second civil war – was also notable after the independence of South Sudan. See Dana Harman, "Leaving Bitterness Behind," *Haaretz*, January 28 2011. Available at: file:///C:/Users/Eyal/Desktop/'Leaving%20bitterness%20behind'%20-%20Haaretz. com.html (retrieved on December 3, 2012).

40 Personal interview with David Ben-Uziel, October 12, 2020.

41 Dave Eggers, *What Is the What: The Autobiography of Valentino Achak Deng* (New York, 2006), p. 385-386 (emphasis added).

42 Ibid., p. 414.

43 On the developments leading up to this war, see Irit Back, "From Struggles for Existence to Crimes against Humanity: The Case of Darfur," in Yair Auron and Issac Lubelski (eds.), *Genocide: Between Racism and Genocide in the Modern Era* (Raanana, 2010), pp. 22-103 (Hebrew).

44 Gerard Prunier, *Darfur: The Ambiguous Genocide* (Ithaca, 2005), p. xi.

45 Mahmoud Mahgoub El-Tigani. "Inside Darfur: Ethnic Genocide by a Governance Crisis," *Comparative Studies of South Asia, Africa and the Middle East* 24 (2) (2004), pp. 3-17.

46 "Powell Declares Genocide in Sudan," BBC News, 9 September 2004. http://news. bbc.co.uk/2/hi/africa/3641820.stm (retrieved on December 3, 2012).

47 For an extended discussion of international involvement in the Darfur crisis, including the obligation of the African countries in the matter, see: Irit Back, *Sovereignty and Intervention in Africa: Conflict Resolution and International Organizations in Darfur* (London, 2015).

48 Ibid., pp. 98, 126-127. See U.N. Security Council Resolution 1593 (2005). https:// www.un.org/press/en/2005/sc8351.doc.htm (retrieved on December 3, 2012).

49 This was the first time that a sitting president was accused of such a thing. It should nonetheless be noted that al-Bashir continued to serve as president until the revolution that resulted in his removal from power in April 2019. Even as these lines are being written, al-Bashir has still not been extradited to the International Criminal Court.

50 "Today, Global Day for Darfur: Heads of Yad Vashem Call on UN Secretary General to Act to Stop the Genocide in Darfur, Urge Security Council to Send Troops to Region to Restore Security," Press Release, April 29, 2007. https://www.yadvashem. org/press-release/29-april-2007-11-28.html (retrieved on December 3, 2012).

51 https://www.ushmm.org/genocide-prevention/simon-skjodt-center/committee-on-conscience (retrieved on December 3, 2012). This committee also took action in the case of Southern Sudan. See, for example: United States Holocaust Memorial Museum's Committee on Conscience Takes Action to Raise Public Awareness of Sudan Genocide Threat," *PR Newswire* (New York), 15 November 2000, p.1. Still, its involvement in the case of Sudan was limited in comparison to the case of Darfur.

52 Quoted in Samuel Totten, "Paying Lip Service to R2P and Genocide Prevention: The Muted Response of the U.S. Atrocities Prevention Board and the U.S.H.M.M.'s Committee on Conscience to the Crisis in the Nuba Mountains," *Genocide Studies International* 8 (1) (Spring 2014), p. 30.

53 Quoted in ibid., p. 31.

54 Totten, "Paying Lip Service to R2P and Genocide Prevention," pp. 23-57.

55 "United States Holocaust Memorial Museum to Project Wall-Size Images from South Sudan onto Museum," Press Release, October 28, 2010. https://www. ushmm.org/information/press/press-releases/united-states-holocaust-memorial-museum-to-project-wall-size-images-from-so (retrieved on December 3, 2012).

56 For a review of the Sudanese press from this period including an analysis of these views, see Back, *Sovereignty and Intervention in Africa*, pp. 83-97.

57 Ben Kiernan, *Blood and Soil: A World History of Genocide and Extermination from Sparta to Darfur* (New Haven, 2007).

58 Chima J. Korieh, *The Nigeria-Biafra War: Genocide and the Politics of Memory* (New York, 2012), p. 14.

59 This movement attracted international attention following the arrest of one of its most prominent activists, Nnamdi Kanu, leader of the Indigenous People of Biafra movement and director of Radio Biafra and Television in London, upon his arrival in Nigeria. See Onyekachi Wambu, "The Ghost of Biafra," *New African* 557 (January 2016), p. 82.

60 This project also involved testimonies from Rwanda and Cambodia. http://www.haaretz.com/news/spielberg-s-shoah-foundation-to-document-darfur-other-atrocities-1.218913 (retrieved on December 3, 2012).

61 Nat Hentoff, "Darfur: The Black Holocaust," *The Village Voice*, January 12, 2007.

62 Eric Reeves, "Children within Darfur's Holocaust: An Overview of Vulnerabilities Particular to Genocide's Youngest Victims," *Sudan Tribune*, December 23, 2005.

63 Robert Eaglestone,"You Would Not Add to my Suffering If You Knew What I Have Seen": Holocaust Testimony and Contemporary African Trauma Literature," *Studies in the Novel* 40 (1 & 2) (Spring & Summer 2008), pp. 72-85.

64 Interview with Nur, Tel Aviv, October 14, 2020.

Yechiam Weitz

The Trials of Murderers from the Holocaust: Comparing the Trials of Eichmann and Demjanjuk

Introduction

Over the years, three major trials focusing on the Holocaust have been conducted in Israel. The first was the trial of the victim – the trial of Melchior Greunwald, better known as the trial of Israel Kasztner, which was a defamation trial initiated by the Israeli State's Attorney's Office. The two others were trials of the murderers: the first of Adolf Eichmann, who was charged under the Nazis and Nazi Collaborators (Punishment) Law that was enacted by the Israeli Knesset in 1950; and the second of John Demnjanuk, who was charged under the same law.

The aim of this article is to compare the trials of the accused murderers in the latter two trials by considering the following 8 aspects: (1) the timeframe of the trial and the period in question; (2) the defendant; (3) the courtroom; (4) the presiding judges; (5) the prosecutors and their opening statements; (6) the defense attorneys; (7) the rulings and sentences; and (8) the appeals of the defendants. The article also sums up the major differences between the two trials.

A significant number of studies have already been written on the Eichmann trial, with the major book on the subject authored by Hanna Yablonka[1] and a number of articles authored by myself.[2] In contrast, little has thus far been written on the Demjanjuk trial. The fundamental study on the topic is the doctoral dissertation of Tamir Hod, titled "The Demjanjuk Affair in Israel, 1986-1993: History, Memory, Trial."[3] Merav Sagi has also completed a master's thesis on the subject.[4]

I. The Timeframe of the Trial and the Period in Question

The timeframe of the Eichmann trial in broad perspective was just over two years, from Eichmann's capture in Argentina on May 11, 1960 until his hanging in

Ramle Prison in Israel on May 31, 1962. The trial itself lasted approximately four months, beginning on April 11, 1961 and concluding on August 9. The decision and the sentence were read out between December 11 and 15, 1961, and the defendant's appeal was considered at a session of the Court on March 22, 1962. The decision on the appeal was read out on May 29, 1962, and two days later, close to midnight on the night of May 31, 1962, Eichmann was executed.

The Eichmann trial can be regarded as part of the transition that played out in Israel at the beginning of the 1960s, during which Israeli society advanced from its primal stage into a more mature and critical era. It was the twilight of the rule of Israel's founding father and first prime minister, David Ben-Gurion, who played a decisive role in the Eichmann trial. In the midst of the trial Israel experienced the Lavon Affair, which stirred up the political arena and the Israeli public as a whole, and approximately two years earlier, in 1959, the Wadi Salib riots had constituted the first protest against the discrimination and deprivation of Mizrahi Jews in Israel. The Eichmann trial was part of this transformation, marking a turning point in Israeli society's attitude toward the Holocaust. In its wake, the country began its liberation from the mythos of heroism, and legitimacy was given to the everyday survivors who were neither partisans nor ghetto fighters but rather survived the terrors of the Warsaw Ghetto, Treblinka, and Majdanek by the skin of their teeth. The Eichmann trial was the first platform from which survivors were able to present their testimony.[5] In this way, the Eichmann trial can be understood as a powerful formative event.

The Demjanjuk trial was held a generation after the Eichmann trial. It was extremely lengthy in duration, lasting more than seven years, and can therefore be regarded as an "affair." Demjanjuk was extradited from the United States to Israel in February 1986, and his trial began one year later, in February 1987. The ruling was read out on April 18, 1988, and the sentence was read out one week later, on April 25, 1988. The defendant submitted his appeal to the Supreme Court on May 13, 1990, and the decision was read out on July 29, 1993.

This major disparity between the timeframes of the two trials is no coincidence, as the Demjanjuk trial was much more complicated and volatile than the Eichmann trial. The Eichmann trial was conducted within a clear framework, whereas Demjanjuk's trial was exceedingly circuitous and fluctuating and touched on a variety of different issues. The period during which the Demjanjuk trial was conducted was altogether different than the period of the Eichmann trial.

In terms of the governing situation at the time, during the Demjanjuk trial Israel was a country of rapid political change. When the trial began, the ruling government was a unity government headed by Yitzhak Shamir of the Likud party, in 1990 Shamir formed a narrow-majority right-wing government, and in 1992 a new government headed by Yitzhak Rabin of the Labor Party was formed. In the realm of security, the First Intifada that erupted at the end of 1987 also resulted in challenging tensions.

In terms of Israeli society's attitude toward the Holocaust, by the time of the Demjanjuk trial, the Holocaust had moved much closer to the heart of Israeli consciousness than it had been at the time of the Eichmann trial. The subject was covered by the Israeli school curriculum, and youth trips to the death camps in Poland began during this period. Indeed, awareness of the Holocaust had become an inseparable part of everyday life. Earlier on, Israeli society had dealt less with the Holocaust, explains Tom Segev. However, "beginning in the 1980s, not a day has gone by without the Holocaust being mentioned in some context or other in one of the daily newspapers; it is a central subject of literature and poetry, of theatre, cinema, and television."[6]

In 1986, the year that Demjanjuk arrived in Israel, Claude Lanzmann's film Shoah was aired. According to Amos Oz, the film was the opposite of K. Tsetnik's well known phrase "another planet," in that it "perceives the extermination not as occurring outside of history but rather as part of it – not outside of human nature but rather as part of it."[7] The attitude toward the Holocaust during this period was therefore much less stereotypical and polarized, and much more complicated.

II. The Defendants

As noted above, both the Eichmann trial and the Demjanjuk trial were trials of murderers, not victims. However, these two trials also differed from one another in a fundamental manner on two major issues: 1) the position and role of the defendant and the intensity of the proceedings, and 2) the issue of identification.

In terms of position and intensity, Adolf Eichmann was the major executor of the Final Solution to the Jewish Problem: the Nazis' plan to exterminate all the Jews of Europe. He headed the IV B4 Bureau within the Gestapo, which dealt with Jewish affairs and deportations. As a SS-Obersturmbannführer (lieutenant colonel) Eichmann's rank was not particularly high, but he wielded immense power. Eichmann was the main implementer and the moving spirit behind the Final Solution. British historian David Cesarni, the author of Eichmann's biography, has written that "Adolf Eichmann is an icon of the twentieth century, of the Nazi regime and the genocide it waged against the Jews…Along with Hitler, Himmler and perhaps Reinhard Heydrich, he is the face of Nazi mass murder."[8]

Gideon Hausner, the prosecutor in his trial, characterized Eichmann's power and actions as follows:

> Eichmann was personally responsible for the official operation of the extermination program and held vast powers within the German Reich…He operated through district and sub-district police commands, each of which had a supervisor of Jewish affairs who received instructions directly from Eichmann.[9]

Demjanjuk, in contrast, who was Ukrainian as opposed to German, was a "small cog" – a *Wachman* (guard) in one of the extermination camps.[10] Demjanjuk was one of thousands of guards that made up the vast extermination machine. According to Segev, Demjanjuk, unlike Eichmann, was not "part of the decision making that preceded the extermination of the Jews…He was what was referred to in Israel at the time as '*rosh katan*' [literally, 'small headed']: a soldier who did as he was told without thinking, trying his best to avoid taking any responsibility." On this basis, Segev has characterized Demjanjuk's trial as the "trial of the *rosh katan*."[11]

Yeshayahu Leibowitz addressed the trial in a coarse manner: "The entire trial was a terrible mistake. Suddenly locating this vermin at the heart of the extermination of the Jewish People was a major flaw." According to Leibowitz, it was "terribly disproportional,"[12] which makes it totally impossible to compare Demjanjuk to Eichmann.

According to Nahum Barnea:

> Hanging over the Demjanjuk trial on its first day was the sense
> that it was an embarrassing deviation from all proper proportion.
> *Demjanjuk is not Eichmann.* It is doubtful whether he is one of the
> top thousand, or ten thousand fugitives under the Nazis and Nazi
> Collaborators (Punishment) Law.[13]

His trial can be viewed as similar in nature to the dozens of kapo trials that were
conducted in the 1950s and 1960s, about which much has been written in
recent years,[14] but not to that of Adolf Eichmann. In this sense, the difference
between the two trials is unfathomable.

With regard to the identification of the accused, Eichmann acknowledged
that he was Adolf Eichmann immediately after his capture in Argentina.
Although he initially attempted to conceal his true identity, he quickly realized
the futility of doing so. While still in his safe house in Buenos Aires, he told his
abductors: "My name is Adolf Eichmann."[15] In his diary, Ben-Gurion wrote:
"Isser [Harel] has informed [us] that Adolf Eichmann has been identified and
captured." According to the entry, Harel noted that "if there is no error in the
identification, then this was an important and successful operation."[16] Even
before the beginning of Eichmann's trial, the question of identification had
been settled unequivocally and never came up in the trial, which examined his
crimes, not his identity.

In Demjanjuk's trial, the issue of identification played a very different
role. Indeed, the question of whether "Ivan the Terrible" (the nickname of the
wachman who served in the Treblinka and Sobibor camps) was in fact John
Demjanjuk was critical. The two defense attorneys, American Mark O'Connor
and Israeli Yoram Sheftel, argued that there was no disagreement regarding the
shocking nature of the deeds of Ivan the Terrible, who was one of the most
monstrous figures of the Holocaust, but that his identification needed to be
considered, and that perhaps "an error has been made in the identification,
and Ivan the Terrible is not John Demjanjuk."[17] According to Justice Tzvi Tal:
"The defense did not deny the atrocities of Treblinka; the only question was

that of identification – whether or not the defendant is Ivan the Terrible." The defense demanded that the trial be focused on this point alone, but Justice Dov Levin "decided on a broad discussion, as the broad historical background is a condition for the proper evaluation of the evidence."[18] Despite Justice Levin's comment, the court sessions in the Demjanjuk trial – before the district court and the Supreme Court – focused solely on this issue. The difference in the character of the trials, then, also stemmed from the issue of identification.

III. The Courtrooms

The Kastner trial was held in the courtroom of Benjamin Halevi, president of the Jerusalem District Court, in the Russian Compound in Jerusalem. The two subsequent trials, in contrast, were the only two trials in the legal history of the state of Israel to be held in public halls as opposed to courtrooms of the formal justice system.

When Eichmann was captured and brought to Israel, it was believed that his trial would attract great interest. For this reason, efforts were made to seek out a hall with at least 500 seats. It was decided to conduct the trial in the main "People's Hall" – in Hebrew, *Beit Ha`am* – in central Jerusalem, which was typically used for cultural performances of different kinds. Though Justice Minister Pinchas Rosen concluded that this would be the most suitable hall for the trial, the hall was not ready. It was being renovated at the time, and the government awarded the Jerusalem municipality a sum of money to complete the renovations by the trial date.[19] The hall was deemed well suited for the trial because, with 650 seats, it was larger and more spacious than a regular district courtroom. According to Hannah Arendt: "Clearly, this courtroom was not a bad place for the show-trial David Ben-Gurion, Prime Minister of Israel, had in mind…"[20] The hall was the site of both the district court trial and the appeal that was subsequently submitted to the Supreme Court.

A bulletproof glass cubicle, in which the defendant, Eichmann, was to sit during the trial, had been installed in the hall. The cubicle was considered an "essential means of security," based on the assumption that Nazi circles would seek to silence Eichmann, and that survivors would also want to kill him, in the event that the judge did not sentence him to death.[21] "The cubicle was open in the direction of the judges, to enable them to observe the reactions of the defendant directly, without being hindered by a transparent glass barrier."[22] The cubicle was a distinct symbol of the trial. Haim Gouri, then a columnist for the newspaper *Lamerhav*, compiled the articles he wrote during the trial into a book,[23] which became one of the canonical works on the Eichmann trial.

After the trial, the glass cubicle was moved to the Ghetto Fighters' House, where it became a museum exhibit. Just days after Eichmann's hanging, it was placed in one of the halls of the museum, beside a collection of photos and "books and documents pertaining to the trial of the detestable enemy."[24]

The Demjanjuk trial was also held in a public hall instead of the Jerusalem District Court. In this case, the considerations were similar to those in the Eichmann trial. Both Demjanjuk himself and his trial proved to be of major media interest, and when his plane landed at Ben-Gurion airport, dozens of reporters and television crews assembled to cover his arrival. It was therefore decided to hold the trial at *Binyanei Ha`uma* in Jerusalem. In Segev's words: "The trial was held not in a court but rather in a hall that was usually used for the screening of films."[25] Justice Tal explained that it had been decided to hold the trial there because of the great public interest, reflected in the hundreds of people who descended upon the hall and filled it to capacity.[26] In the initial days of the trial, hundreds of students and soldiers made their way to the hall. However, later, when the trial came to concern primarily technical issues, the crowd thinned out somewhat.

In this case too, a glass cubicle was installed where the defendant was supposed to sit.[27] When Demjanjuk arrived in Israel, one newspaper wrote: "In Jerusalem, Eichmann's glass cage is being prepared for the trial of Ivan the Terrible."[28] Although the official reason for the cubicle's installation was to ensure Demjanjuk's own safety, it was also argued that, in terms of security, the glass cubicle was unnecessary. "It can be assumed that the security services would have been able to protect Demjanjuk's life in some other way," Segev maintained. "Like a transparent partition, for example."[29] The unspoken reason for the glass cubicle, in my opinion, was to link Demjanjuk's trial to the previous one – that of Eichmann.

Unlike the Eichmann trial, Demjanjuk's appeal was heard not in the hall where the original case had been heard but in one of the courtrooms of the old Supreme Court.[30] With clear ridicule, Sheftel depicted the dismal nature of the courtroom:

It was approximately ten meters long and six meters wide. The judge's dais, which covered almost the entire width of the room, was made of brown wood, behind which the five chairs of the judges were placed. Tall and old looking…Beside the entrance, on the right-hand side, was the appellant's cubicle…in which Demjanjuk sat, flanked by two policemen.

According to Sheftel, the atmosphere in this courtroom bore no resemblance to "the circus-like atmosphere of Binyanei Hauma."[31] The difference between the courtrooms was reflective of the dramatic difference in the status of the trial.

IV. The Judges

Eichmann was tried by the district court in Jerusalem by a panel of judges headed by a Supreme Court justice. This set a precedent in the legal history of the state of Israel: a Supreme Court justice heading up a panel from a district court. This arrangement emerged not out of legal precedent or principle but rather an attempt to resolve the embarrassing and uncomfortable problem of Jerusalem District Court President Benjamin Halevi's initial decision to appoint himself to head the panel. The decision was problematic because Halevi had been the only judge for the Kastner trial and, in that decision, had asserted that "Kastner sold his soul to the devil" – the devil in this case, of course, being Eichmann. In his memoirs, Yitzhak Olshan, the president of the Supreme Court at the time,[32] described the situation as follows:

Since the establishment of the state, a custom had become entrenched among judges that if a judge had already expressed an opinion, even only incidentally, on an issue that subsequently became a matter in a trial, then that judge would recuse himself from hearing the case.[33]

Both Olshan himself and Justice Minister Pinchas Rosen asked Halevi to recuse himself from the panel for the Eichmann trial. Halevi told them explicitly that he had no intention of honoring their request, and neither had a way of preventing him from including himself in the panel. The authority to determine the constitution of the panels of the Jerusalem District Court lay entirely with the president of the court, and the only way to bypass this obstacle was by enacting a new law. In this context, the Fourth Knesset enacted The Courts (Crimes Punishable by the Death Penalty) Law, 5721-1961, which was nicknamed "the Halevi law." The law stipulated that if a defendant could be subject to the death penalty, the president of the Supreme Court shall be authorized to establish a court consisting of two district judges and a Supreme Court justice to head the panel.[34]

To this post, Olshan appointed veteran Supreme Court Justice Moshe Landau.[35] Olshan noted this in his memoirs, but did not elaborate.[36] One newspaper reported that Olshan had selected Landau for the job due to his "rich experience in criminal trials."[37] According to Michal Shaked, Landau's biographer, Olshan's choice was based on Landau's "distinct skill in conducting trials as complex as the Eichmann trial stood to be," and his ability to "erect an obstacle to prevent the trial from becoming an amorphous mass." According to Shaked, the Eichmann trial changed Landau's public legal standing: "After years of diligent and exhausting daily work, Landau all at once became the most well-known and glorified judge in Israel and abroad."[38]

The two other members of the panel were district court judges. Benjamin Halevi, who would be appointed to the Supreme Court in 1963, appointed himself over the objections in a move that was by no means surprising. The second judge appointed was Yitzhak Raveh (Reuss), a long-time Tel Aviv district court judge who had been appointed to his post in 1952. Raveh was less known than Halevy and has been described by Daniel Friedman as " a top tier judge" who "was worthy of being appointed to the Supreme Court, although this did not occur."[39] In the course of the trial, Raveh's approach was similar to that of Justice Landau: to not deviate from the scope of legal procedure.[40] All three judges had been born in Germany, had immigrated to Mandatory Palestine prior to World War II, and spoke German as their mother tongue.[41]

In the Demjanjuk trial, the panel of judges resembled the panel that had presided over the Eichmann trial. This stemmed from, among other things, a desire to view it as the second Eichmann trial. In his autobiography, Justice Tal wrote that the court that was authorized to deal with crimes against the Jewish

People and crimes against humanity was "a special panel of the district court, headed by a Supreme Court justice…as was the case in the Eichmann trial."[42]

The panel was headed by Supreme Court Justice Dov Levin, whom Supreme Court President Meir Shamgar appointed to the position, noting that "he brought with him years of rich legal experience" and was a "conscientious man…who knows the law."[43]

Unlike Justice Landau the 'Yekke' – a stereotypical term referring to Jews of German origin – Levin was a native-born Israeli 'Sabra'. Born in Tel Aviv in 1925, Levin was appointed to the Supreme Court in 1982, retired from the judiciary in 1995, and passed away in 2001 at the age of 76. Levin had been involved in one of the major previous Holocaust trials – the Kastner trial – not as a judge, but rather as a member of legal defense team of Malchiel Gruenwald, the trials' official defendant, which was headed by attorney Shmuel Tamir. According to Moshe Gorali, this fact "appears to not have deterred him from conducting a show as opposed to a trial."[44] It is noteworthy that, unlike Landau, Levin did not become a well-known figure after the trial, which is another difference between the two trials.

The two other judges were district judges Tal and Dalia Dorner. According to Hod, the two were selected through consultation between Supreme Court President Shamgar and Justice Levin.[45] In my opinion, it was Judge Yehuda Weiss, who was the district court's president at the time, who appointed both to the panel. Unlike Benjamin Halevi, Weiss did not appoint himself to the panel. Tal began serving as a district court judge in 1978, and Dorner was appointed to the Beer Sheva district court but in 1984 moved to the district court in Jerusalem. Both were appointed as Supreme Court justices in 1994, the final year of Shamgar's tenure as president of the Court.[46] Tal retired from the judiciary in 1997 and Dorner in 2004. The members of the panel were announced at the beginning of 1986.[47]

V. The Prosecutors and Their Opening Statements

The lead prosecutor in the Eichmann trial was Gideon Hausner, the Israel's attorney general at the time. He had assumed this position on July 1, 1960, just over a month after Eichmann was captured,[48] and he had a short tenure of approximately two and a half years before resigning in January 1963. During his tenure Hausner dealt with a number of major issues, such as the Lavon Affair; however, most of his time and energy went into the Eichmann trial. Until today, there has been no other attorney general in the history of the state of Israel that has come to be so strongly identified with one particular trial.

Justice Minister Rosen, Hausner's patron and the head of his political party,[49] announced the latter's appointment as prosecutor in the trial as a *fait accompli*. At the government's meeting regarding the appointment of Eichmann's prosecutor, Rosen simply stated that "the chief prosecutor will be Hausner."[50] Hausner very much wanted to serve as Eichmann's prosecutor, and he did all he could to highlight his role in the trial, which helped him promote himself as a historical figure. Hausner was the only participant in the trial who wrote a book about it. It was published in English[51] and only translated into Hebrew after his death, and years after the publication of the English edition.[52] Hausner's conduct was completely different than that of Justice Landau, who limited himself to unpublished memoirs that were read only by his three daughters. Landau did not want to be identified with the Eichmann trial, Shaked explains. He was 49 years old,[53] and he had 20 years of judicial activity ahead of him. According to Shaked, Landau "did not want the spotlight of legal glory to cast a shadow over all of his professional work."[54]

Hausner held senior positions over the years, serving for extended periods as a member of Knesset and a member of the Israeli government.[55] However, he regarded his role in the Eichmann trial as the high point of his life, and others concurred. Haim Cohn, for example, wrote that Hausner had "made this trial his life's enterprise."[56]

The prosecution's opening statement, delivered by Hausner at the beginning of the trial, became one of the most prominent and well-known speeches in Israeli history. According to Gouri, "never before had one man of flesh and blood said to another man of flesh and blood the things that Gideon Hausner said to Adolf Eichmann." He wrote about the speech in almost mythical terms: "This time, the miracle I almost did not believe would occur has occurred in Jerusalem."[57] *Herut*, the newspaper of the Herut movement, articulated a similar sentiment: "It was a powerful speech of accusation, the likes of which have never before been delivered."[58] It began as follows: "When I stand before you here, Judges of Israel, to lead the Prosecution of Adolf Eichmann, I am not standing alone. With me are six million accusers."

These words are considered to be canonical and have not been forgotten. An article on Hausner that was published after his death, titled "Six Million Accusers," reads: "Gideon Hausner will never be forgotten due to the words he spoke on behalf of the 'six million accusers' who stood beside him in the People's Hall that morning in April 1961, facing the murderer Adolf Eichmann."[59]

The prosecution team for the trial was by no means small, and Gabriel Bach was its most well-known member. At the time, he was serving as the deputy state's attorney."[60] Bach questioned the prosecution's witnesses a bit, but Hausner was the prosecution's dominant figure, taking part in most of the sessions and questioning many of the prosecution's witnesses.

For the prosecution's first witness, Hausner wanted to call a prominent historian to speak "generally about European Jewry, what it had encompassed prior to the Holocaust, and what remained in its aftermath." From his perspective as a prosecutor, "such testimony was essential for completing the picture." As the historian he chose Prof. Salo (Shalom) Baron of Columbia University in New York, who was the "author of a monumental work on the history of the [Jewish] communities."[61] Before his testimony, Baron conversed with Ben-Gurion, who told him: "It is important that our youth know the magnitude of the loss of the extermination of six million."[62]

Baron testified on April 24, 1961. In his testimony, it was written, the "Jewish scholarly" historian spoke not of the gas chambers but rather of "the destruction of the Jewish *communities*, the destruction of Jewish culture in Europe, and the annihilation to which the intellectual assets and the grand Jewish federations and organizations had been condemned."[63] Calling on Baron to testify had a clear goal: to imbue the trial with a historical dimension.

In the Demjanjuk trial, the prosecution was led by State's Attorney Yona Blattman. Blattman was the most senior figure in the justice system, but he was not the attorney general.[64] Even before Demjanjuk arrived in Israel, a special legal team was set up in the State's Attorney's office to prepare the material for the prosecution. This team was led by Blattman.[65]

Blattman and Hausner differed from one another in significant ways:

1. Blattman was by no means a political figure. He came into his own in the State's Attorney's Office, first serving as a deputy state's attorney and in 1978 being appointed as the deputy to State's Attorney Bach. He was appointed state's attorney in 1982, and when the Demjanjuk trial began he had already occupied the position for some time. When he retired at the end of 1988, he accepted the position of comptroller of the Hebrew University of Jerusalem, which was a distinctly professional position.

2. Blattman was an excellent and extremely experienced criminal lawyer,[66] whereas Hausner was an attorney who dealt primarily with civil law and had relatively little experience in criminal matters. This point found expression in the Eichmann trial. Shaked noted the problematic nature of the appointment: Hausner "lacked concrete experience in broad criminal law" and lacked expertise in both criminal law and examining witnesses. This was attested to by his cross-examination of Eichmann, which was "long-winded, unfocused, lacking in force, and ineffective, and the judges were forced to come to terms with it."[67]

3. Unlike Hausner, Blattman's role in the trial was not considered the high point of his life, and not even the peak of his tenure as state's attorney. After his death, two roles he fulfilled as state's attorney were singled out as marking the high point of his work: heading a committee that investigated the killing of terrorists who had seized control of Bus 300, and leading the prosecution in the trial of John Demjanjuk.[68]

4. Unlike Hausner, Blattman did not attend all the trial sessions. In practice, the prosecution was managed by Michael Shaked.[69] And Justice Tal wrote that Shaked "assumed the burden of examining most of the witnesses."[70]

5. Shaked's story was exceptional in comparison to the personnel of the states attorney's office. He was born in Jerusalem in 1946, and in the I.D.F. he was a combat soldier, serving in the naval commandos and Sayeret Shaked. He studied law and set up his own private law office, which he closed after the Yom Kippur War when he became the personal aide of information to ministers Shimon Peres and Aharon Yariv. At the beginning of the 1980s, he was appointed senior deputy to the district attorney of Jerusalem responsible for criminal affairs. When the trial began, Shaked was almost unknown.[71] Hod described him as "a Sabra, a fighter, and an eloquent speaker – things that added to his significant role in the trial."[72] He himself asked Blattman to be permitted to join the prosecution team, recounting: "I asked to join the case, and Blattman acceded to my request."[73]

6. At the end of September 1986, Yona Blattman submitted a letter of indictment against John Demjanjuk to the Jerusalem District Court. In it, Blattman stated that the defendant, who had served in the S.S. auxiliary forces in the Treblinka extermination camp, had "committed offenses of immeasurable severity" and that "Demjanjuk's cruelty surpassed even that of his Nazi 'employers'."[74]

7. The trial began on February 16, 1987, and Blattman delivered the prosecution's opening statement the same day (in correspondence with Hausner's speech, although it can be assumed that Blattman knew that his speech would not be canonical like Hausner's). It began as follows: "Before you, judges, stands the defendant John Demjanjuk, who is Ivan Demjanjuk, nicknamed Ivan the Terrible. He is standing trial for taking part in some of the most severe actions that have ever been perpetrated."

8. Blattman intended to imbue his speech with a historical dimension. In addition to the details of the charges against the defendant, he spoke about Treblinka, "one of the most terrible

extermination camps in human history, a camp that was built for the purpose of mass murder, existed for more than a year, and was razed from the earth." With regard to the uprising that took place at the camp, Blattman wrote: "Under inhuman conditions…Jews planned to take revenge and to escape from the camp, with the hope, no matter how slim, that at least some of them would succeed in finding refuge and making the whole world aware of the terrifying story."[75]

He concluded his speech by addressing the significance of the establishment of the state of Israel (which was not directly related to the letter of indictment or to the defendant), which was established "shortly after the end of World War II" and absorbed "multitudes of Jews who were rescued from the inferno." The state of Israel, Blattman emphasized, "has neither forgotten, nor is permitted to forget, the memory of the Holocaust, as memory is part of its essence." It is not at liberty "to not continue trying to locate the war criminals, wherever they may be, and seeing to it that they find no rest." Following these words, Blattman addressed the defendant and his offenses.

During his statement, a deathly silence prevailed in the courtroom, which "which was filled from wall to wall" with "hundreds of spectators who listened to every word uttered by the state's attorney."[76] His remarks made a strong impression on those watching the trial, but no more. They did not create the anticipated impression that his speech was one of historic importance. Unlike Hausner's speech, Blattman's address was completely forgotten, remembered by no one. Moreover, the members of the prosecution team in the Demjanjuk trial corresponded with the words of Hausner, who was on his deathbed at the time. In an interview, Shaked said words clearly echoing Hausner's speech: "I stand in awe and reverence… Though small, I can be a mouthpiece for them, for the slaughtered."[77]

The first witness of the prosecution in the Demjanjuk trial was Dr. Yitzhak Arad, who can be considered a symbol: a Holocaust survivor and partisan, a senior officer in the I.D.F., and a historian who was the chairman of the Directorate of Yad Vashem.[78] He researched Operation Reinhard, which pursued the extermination of the Jews of Poland in three of the death camps: Belzec, Sobibor, and Treblinka. The aim of Arad's testimony was to present the historical background of the trial, and he attested to the "unique role of the Star of Ashes, Treblinka, in the galaxy of this inferno."[79] Many years later, Arad explained that he had needed to be objective in his testimony, and he was. However, from his perspective, the trial was important because his parents were killed at Treblinka.[80] Arad's testimony was noticeably similar to Baron's testimony in the Eichmann trial, although Baron's was much broader in scope.

VI. The Defense Attorneys

One question that emerged immediately following Eichmann's capture was who would defend him. The Israeli government had a distinct interest in the defense of the accused. At a government meeting held in June 1960, approximately three weeks after Eichmann's arrival in Israel,[81] Ben-Gurion announced that a defense attorney needed to be found for Eichmann immediately: "It is essential that it be known that the trial will earn the respect and trust of the world, and that the entire world listen. It is essential that it be known that a trial in Israel is a trial of justice."

For all the parties involved in the Eichmann trial, it was clear that neither an Israeli lawyer nor a Jewish lawyer would be capable of contending with Eichmann's defense, because he would "not succeed in establishing the relations of trust that that must prevail between an attorney and his client."[82] He would also not be able to handle "the tension that would result from the severe collision between his duties as an attorney and his national sentiment."[83] In the meeting of the Israeli government that addressed the question of Eichmann's defense attorney, Rosen suggested the possibility of appointing a German attorney to represent him. Ben-Gurion, from his part, saw "no reason why a German, but not a Nazi, could not serve as Eichmann's defense attorney." Rosen explained the prime minister's position as follows: "No defense attorney would defend Eichmann as a Nazi. This was also not the case at [the] Nuremberg [trials]." According to Rosen, any defense attorney would base Eichmann's defense on the argument that the defendant was "a tool in the hands of a stronger party," but none of the defense attorneys would defend them as Nazis. At the end of the discussion, the government decided "that it was permitted to assign a defense attorney for Adolf Eichmann."[84]

Eichmann's defense attorney was Robert Servatius (1894-1983), who had a law office in the German city of Cologne. In World War II, Servatius had served in the Wermacht as an artillery officer but had not been a member of the Nazi Party. At the Nuremberg Trials, he had served as the attorney of Fritz Sauckel, who had been responsible for millions of forced laborers, was sentenced to death, and was executed on October 16, 1946. According to Rosen, he was "an extremely mediocre attorney," but "in terms of his Nazi past, he is okay."[85]

To make it possible for Servatius to defend Eichmann at his trial, it was necessary to amend Israeli law as it pertained to the practicing of foreign lawyers and law firms in Israel, which prohibited the engagement of lawyers who were not Israeli citizens. The matter was raised at a July 1960 government meeting,[86] at which Minister Rosen reported that the Eichmann family had selected Servatius as Eichmann's attorney, and that this required that the law be changed. He therefore proposed an amendment allowing "the minister of justice…to permit…a person who is not an Israeli citizen" to serve as the attorney of a defendant charged with "an offense for which the sentence is death or life imprisonment." The government approved the justice minister's proposal on November 22, 1960, and the Knesset passed the second and third reading of the Advocates Ordinance Amendment, which permitted the appointment of a foreign attorney to defend Eichmann without any opposition or reservation.[87] As a result, the Fourth Knesset enacted two laws aimed at facilitating Eichmann's trial in Israel.

In terms of the legal costs of the defense attorney, in Eichmann's case the Israeli government paid all of Servatius' fees. At the beginning of the 1960s, this amounted to an immense sum of more than $30,000.[88] In the Demjanjuk trial, the defendant's first attorney was an American named Mark O'Connor who had been retained by the defendant's family. Israeli Justice Minister Moshe Nissim authorized the appointment based on the agreement that had emerged at the time of the Eichmann trial – the appointment of an attorney that was not a citizen of Israel in order to defend a foreign citizen.[89] All those who came into contact with him said that he was a mediocre attorney. Segev described him as a "slim man who was annoying and had a penetrating tenor voice – Perry Mason in caricature."[90] In a different article, Segev offered the following discerning description:

He is not pleasant, but he is not foolish. He is as slippery as an eel, a sycophant with acute senses who is well prepared. His Americanisms, his great love of Israel, and his proclaimed faith in divine supervision radiates shallowness and kitsch. In step with his ingratiating manner, he is very arrogant.[91]

Unlike the defense in the Eichmann trial, in which there was no Israeli attorney whatsoever, the Demjanjuk trial involved a number of Israeli attorneys. This stemmed from O'Connor's desire to add an Israeli attorney to the defense team, although he had difficulty finding one. Justice Levin promised to help him, even stating that "if necessary, the court will appoint a special attorney for this purpose."

Justice Levin brought the issue of an Israeli attorney to Menachem Berger, chairman of the Israeli Bar Association, who proposed Gershon Orion –a veteran attorney who had served as a senior judge in the military's legal system for many years.[92] Berger described Orion as "a high level attorney" who handled the district court decisions on behalf of the Bar Association. Upon receiving the request, Berger noted that the job in question was a thankless one. He was concerned about negative reactions to his agreement to represent Demjanjuk but noted: "We cannot forget that the state of Israel must maintain a regime of law." If a defendant is being judged," he emphasized, "it is necessary to enable a defense attorney to represent him." According to Orion, he was earning nothing from his involvement in the defense – he was appointed by the court, and he would receive "the minimal wage that is paid to an attorney in such cases."[93] Orion resigned from this position just one week later, on the grounds that O'Connor had simply ignored him and was not willing to provide him with the defense material. According to Orion, O'Connor was sidelining him "because he wants to be a soloist."[94]

Then a different Israeli attorney joined the defense: Yoram Sheftel. Sheftel has been characterized as "a man whom even the mind of a particularly unruly script writer would have trouble inventing,"[95] and he became a prominent and unforgettable figure related to the trial of Demjanjuk – much more than Blattman, whose role in the trial was quite minor. According to Hod, the only one to write a book from the Eichmann trial was the prosecutor, and the only one to write a book from the Demjanjuk trial was the defense attorney. This point is extremely symbolic.

Sheftel was born in Tel Aviv in 1949 and studied law at the Hebrew University of Jerusalem. Over the years, he established a reputation as the most prominent lawyer in the field of criminal and constitutional law. On the other hand, he had been convicted of four disciplinary offenses due to "conduct unbecoming of an attorney" in the Israel Bar Association's national disciplinary court. Politically, Sheftel is a member of the radical right wing who tends to represent Israeli settlers pro bono. In his book on the Demjanjuk affair, he provided an extensive account of how he joined the defense team through O'Connor in September 1986.[96]

Many years after the conclusion of the trial, Sheftel said that, from his perspective, his decision to represent Demjanjuk was "the best decision of my life." It stemmed from two considerations: the first was the fact that he was convinced that John Demjanjuk was not Ivan the Terrible; the second was his subversive view of the Israeli justice system and his claim that the Demjanjuk trial was nothing but a farce: "The whole reckless show, masquerading as a proceeding, needed to be dismantled. It was a great privilege to tear apart the proceeding and to turn a death sentence into one of the most sensational acquittals of the twentieth century."[97]

After Sheftel joined the defense team, he became the victim of numerous threats. The most prominent occurrence took place at the December 1, 1988 funeral of Dov Eitan, a member of the defense team in the Demjanjuk trial who took his own life (whom I discuss in greater detail below). Israel Yehezkeli, a 70 year old Holocaust survivor who claimed that all the members of his family had been murdered by Demjanjuk, splashed highly concentrated hydrochloric acid in Sheftel's face, shouting: "They're guilty – This is all because of you." Sheftel's face was burned and his eyes were seriously injured. However, he stated that he had no intention of ceasing his involvement in Demjanjuk's defense, and that he regarded those who had engaged in incitement against him as directly responsible for the incident. It was a "planned slander campaign that went on for 14 months and that resulted in the wave of threats to my life."[98] Even his elderly mother said that she could not get even one day of peace and quiet:

"I am always being threatened," she complained. "The trial has shortened my life."[99] This campaign indicates that the Israeli public refused to accept the Israeli attorney's willingness to defend a Nazi criminal. Hod held that the two most prominent attorneys in the trial were Shaked of the prosecution and Sheftel of the defense. "Each explained the professional aspiration that led him to join the case, in addition to a desire to take part in a historic event." Both had been born in Israel to parents who had immigrated to the country before the Holocaust, and Shaked was pleased that Sheftel had joined the case, as he understood the ins and outs of Israeli criminal law.[100] Another difference between the two trials was the participation of Israeli-born attorneys in the trial of Demjanjuk.

Another notable aspect pertained to the payment of legal costs. Before the trial, the Justice Ministry announced its intention to help pay O'Connor's fees. However, unlike in the Eichmann trial, the lion's share was paid by representatives of the Ukrainian lobby in the United States.[101]

The Dov Eitan Affair

In preparation for the appeal in the Demjanjuk trial, the legal team was joined by Israeli attorney Dov Eitan, whose tragic and dramatic story complicated matters. Eitan was a veteran judge. He had been appointed to the magistrate's court in Eilat in 1967, and in 1978 he was appointed to the Jerusalem District Court. He was also known for uncouth remarks, such as: "I would have burned down the Broadcast Authority building."[102] In 1982, during the First Lebanon War, Eitan took an action that was unusual for a serving judge: he signed the Yesh Gvul organization's petition that called on Israelis to refuse to perform reserve duty in Lebanon.[103] The justice system viewed Eitan's signature with disfavor and sought to take a hard line against him. Yitzhak Zamir, who was serving as Israel's attorney general at the time, stated unequivocally: "A judge must refrain from adopting public positions on controversial partisan or political issues."[104] As a result of Eitan's signature, Justice Minister Moshe Nissim intended to lodge a complaint against him with the Judicial Selection Committee, but Eitan preferred to resign from the court on his own volition, so as not to be rebuked or subjected to a disciplinary trial."[105]

Eitan became a regular attorney and joined the law firm of Roni Baron. In the fall of 1988, in preparation for Demjanjuk's appeal, Sheftel asked Eitan to join the defense team. "[I decided] to try to recruit Dov to work with me," Sheftel recounted. "I wanted him, as a former district judge, to work into his arguments criticism of the court's operating in the theatre. I knew that this would have a huge effect." Eitan agreed enthusiastically[106] and explained his reasons for joining: "The question of his identification was worthy of defense; every defendant, even one convicted under law, is entitled to a defense."[107]

After joining the defense team, Eitan began receiving threats. His wife, the poet Miriam Eitan, recounted that her husband had received phone calls urging him to cease defending Demjanjuk. [108] If he continued representing Demjanjuk, he was told, the fact that he was a bisexual would be exposed. As a result of these threats, Eitan committed suicide by jumping off the roof of a high-rise building in the middle of the city at the age of 53. According to an article published years later, "the sudden and surprising suicide...struck the citizens of the country...The newspapers emphasized the incomprehensible shock, but they did not know what caused such a young and lustrous man to put an end to his life in such a manner." The same article stated that Eitan's "death became an enigma shrouded in mystery, and to the best of our knowledge it remains a riddle until today."[109]

VII. The Decisions and the Sentences in Both Trials

The Eichmann trial ended in the defendant's death through a process that can be seen as ritual. The decision was read out on December 11, 1961, when the judges convicted the defendant on all 15 counts of the indictment and found that an Israeli court was fully within its rights to try Eichmann "under the Nazis and Nazi Collaborators (Punishment) Law." With regard to Eichmann, one newspaper reported: "A final spark of humanity was extinguished in Eichmann's heart."[110]

Two days later, the prosecutor explained the considerations in the sentencing, summing up his remarks in two short sentences: "Standing before you is the annihilator of a people [*mashmid `am*], an enemy of the human race, and a spiller of innocent blood. I hereby request that you rule that this man is mortal." According to Gouri, the prosecutor spoke to "a paralyzed room, at the chilling ceremony in which one man asks the three men seated across from him, black and tall, to put to death another man sitting beside them because he is an annihilating, blood-thirsty predator."[111]

On December 15, 1961, the judges read out the sentence: "This court sentences Adolf Eichmann to death for the crimes against the Jewish People, the crimes against humanity, and the war crime of which he has been found guilty." The court emphasized that the death penalty was not mandatory and was not required under the law, "and we therefore set forth from the assumption that the sentencing in this case was subject to our discretion."[112]

The sentencing was extremely brief – just 16 minutes. The courtroom was packed and the atmosphere was dignified: "No one raised their voice and conversations were conducted in a whisper, reflecting the tension, the emotion, and the courtesy paid to the respected judges."[113] In this context, the Israeli court handed down the death sentence for the first and the last time in the history of Israel.

All the newspapers viewed the sentence as a historic event reflecting the Jewish state's independent ability to conduct a trial of justice for the murderers of the Jewish People. *Davar* wrote that the severe sentence decided on by the court "is the only one that fits the severity of the conviction," and shows that "the arm of historical justice has caught up with Adolf Eichmann."[114] *Lamerhav*, the newspaper of the Ahdut Haavoda party, stated that the court in Jerusalem had handed down "a sentence of justice" that shows that "although there is no atonement for it, Jewish blood is not entirely free for the taking."[115] The National Religious Party's newspaper *Hatzofeh* carried the following words: "The Eichmann affair, from his capture to his sentencing, is, ethically and legally, a mighty Jewish story. A sacrificed people trying the murderer of its children. The Jewish conscience voiced its prosecution and articulated its ruling." Everyone accepts the fact that "there is law, and there are judges."[116]

A handful of people opposed giving Eichmann the death penalty. After the hanging, Gershom Scholem wrote: "Had we wanted to prove that we had conducted a trial of justice and that a major historical account had been addressed, a living Eichmann…is not liable to have disturbed this account. And we should be concerned that Eichmann, as someone killed by the court, will cause a significant disturbance."[117]

In Demjanjuk's trial, the potential death penalty also played a role that was decisive, but also deceiving and full of vicissitudes. On April 18, 1988, the three judges – Levin, Dorner, and Tal – read out their decision. It was extremely lengthy, covering 450 pages dealing mostly with its historical background – Operation Reinhard and the Holocaust of the Jews of Poland – until it reached the actions of the accused.[118] The judges unequivocally found that John Demjanjuk was indeed Ivan the Terrible. In the ruling,[119] the judges emphasized that they were "relying first and foremost on the testimonies of survivors" and addressed the identity of the defendant as follows:

> After meticulously considering and checking all the evidence on this matter, responsibly and with all due caution, we find decisively and without hesitation or doubt that the defendant Ivan John Demjanjuk who is standing trial before us is Ivan…the gas chamber operator at Treblinka, and the perpetrator of the brutal deeds described above.

In *Maariv*, celebratory words were offered regarding the ruling: "The ruling that was handed down yesterday in Jerusalem is one document in the tractate of the Holocaust and the revival of the Jewish People."[120] The weekly *Koteret Rashit* carried words that were less celebratory. Problematic in the ears of professionals "was the combination of regular legal analysis and a broad emphasis on the historical aspect." A ruling could have first been made regarding whether or not the accused was guilty, and the historical side of things could have been elaborated on at the time of sentencing; in the eyes of the judges, however, the trial was a historical trial.[121]

As a result of the decision, a feeling began to emerge throughout the Israeli public that Demnjanjuk was a monster. Journalist Yosef (Tommy) Lapid, who was a Holocaust survivor, depicted him in such terms: "So that's it. That lanky moon-faced slob who knows how to smile is *Ivan the Terrible*. In his free time, he would cut women's breasts open with a scalpel. Throw babies into the gas chambers. Crush skulls."[122]

Over the years, justices Tal and Dorner have resolutely maintained that the decision they authored was worthy and just. Tal addressed this point on a number of occasions. For example, in 2009 he said:

> Justice Dorner and I have no doubt, even today, that Demjanjuk
> was Ivan the Terrible, despite the fact that on appeal to the Supreme
> Court he was acquitted as not proven beyond a reasonable doubt.
> The doubt in his case is not doubt…The Supreme Court thought
> that doubt had been created in its heart, but despite this doubt it
> could have convicted him for his actions in Sobibor.[123]

"Even today, I am certain that Ivan Demjanjuk is Ivan the Terrible from Treblinka," Tal wrote in 2012. "We reached the unequivocal conclusion beyond a shadow of a doubt that the accused was Ivan Grozny. The ruling ended in the defendant's conviction on all counts of the indictment."[124] In 2017, he recounted: "Based on the evidence placed before me, I am still convinced 100% today that he was the man."[125] Dorner has also expressed the conviction that "it was the same man, who was responsible for the murder of thousands of people and who operated the [gas] chambers."[126]

Contrary to the unequivocal view of the judges, others adopted differing positions, and as years passed the decision came under fundamental criticism. The major argument was that the decision was based solely on Demjanjuk's identification by witnesses. For example, after the reading of the decision, Segev wrote that "the decision is well substantiated, but what was ultimately decisive was the testimony of the identifying witnesses; without them, there is no conviction. This touches a sensitive nerve, virtually the final taboo."[127]

In 2005, Moshe Gorali wrote that "Demjanjuk was convicted based solely on witness identification." It was an identification that was legally uncertain due to the passage of time, and particularly because of the witnesses' natural tendency toward a positive identification that would enable them to exact the maximum "retribution" upon the Ukrainian guard.[128]

In 2012, the journalist Dan Margalit wrote that during the Demjanjuk trial, he asked himself why Dorit Beinish was not leading the prosecution for the case.[129] She did not answer this question, but it was clear to him "[that] she has doubts whether it is actually possible to prove that Demjanjuk was not just a regular criminal from Ukraine who was employed in the Sobibor death camp but rather the man known as Ivan the Terrible."[130]

In her biography of Aharon Barak, Nomi Levitsky's writes that "they convicted based on his identification by the witnesses. They were not presented with supporting evidence, and they nevertheless sentenced him to death."[131]

The court handed down its sentence one week later, on April 25, 1988. Blattman, the prosecutor, ruled that Demjanjuk had not been a small cog but rather "a major perpetrator of crimes against humanity and one of the greatest murderers of the Jewish People." Blattman maintained that many Nazi criminals, "and most notably Eichmann, referred to themselves as a small cog in the Nazi killing machine," and he demanded that the defendant receive the maximum sentence: death.[132] The defense, on the other hand, warned "against such a sentence, which if found to be erroneous cannot be rescinded."[133]

The three judges decided on the death sentence unanimously, emphasizing that the death penalty was not mandatory but rather a choice. After the reading of the decision, Nachum Barnea noted: "The court is authorized to sentence Demjanjuk to death. *Authorized but not obligated.* It would be best to leave this status to Eichmann alone," as "Demjanjuk is not a criminal in the same league." According to Barnea, those talking about a death sentence for Demjanjuk are "actually wishing for the gallows that will follow."[134] Even before the trial began, Avraham Sharir, who was serving as justice minister at the time,[135] characterized Demjanjuk as "a cruel human being" who "according to the law must be executed." In Barnea's opinion, the justice minister himself had erred: the court was not obligated to sentence him to death – it could sentence him to a prison term instead.[136]

In contrast to the extremely short sentencing in the Eichmann trial, the sentencing in the Demjanjuk trial took some time. "The three judges needed three hours yesterday to sentence John Demjanjuk."[137] In the process, the judges presented the logic underlying their decision. They emphasized that they had deliberated over the issue of the long period of "almost seven sabbatical (*shmita*) years"[138] that had elapsed since the perpetration of the crimes, which was a reason for leniency. However, unlike most crimes, which could be atoned for and for which there was a period of limitation,

> The crimes committed against humans in the Holocaust...against
> the Jewish People, crimes against humanity, and war crimes. For
> them – there is no eternal absolution. No absolution under law, and

no absolution of the heart…[These] crimes must be regarded as if they are beyond time, as if Treblinka still exists and the multitudes of Jews are choking as one, issuing cries from ragged lungs. [As if] Ivan the Terrible is still standing and poisoning, standing and stabbing. [As if] the old are not respected and the young are not pitied. Cutting breasts and cleaving stomachs. Shooting a youth and drilling into raw flesh.

"Even a thousand deaths would not absolve him of his actions," the judges explained, comparing him to Eichmann in justification of the death sentence he had received.

Though it is true that the defendant is not Eichmann, and that he was not the one to initiate the extermination and to organize the extermination of millions, he served as a chief hangman who, with his own hands, killed tens of thousands, debasing, abusing, treating them barbarically, and persecuting with pleasure.[139]

Unlike the restrained response of the spectators at Eichmann's sentencing, the hundreds of spectators at Demjanjuk's sentencing reacted rowdily, with thunderous applause and dozens of cries of "death to the murderer." Others shouted "vengeance, vengeance," and the Holocaust survivors in attendance wept, uttering "vengeance, vengeance."[140] It was a rare, exceptional occurrence in the courtroom. In an article titled "The Crowd Wanted Blood," Barnea argued that there was a profound difference between the Eichmann trial, which "ended in heavy silence and awesome respect," and this trial, which "concluded in a market-like atmosphere…The day is not far off," he wrote, "when people will demand that the execution be carried out in Kings of Israel Square."[141] Shalom Rosenfeld was also shocked by the unruliness in the courtroom. "The sentencing of Ivan the Terrible should have been received in silence," he wrote: "the silence of death." Unfortunately, a few people "could not control their emotions and burst into applause in the courtroom in Jerusalem." It was a grating chord of the drama at hand.[142]

The death penalty was controversial in this case. *Maariv* ran explicit words in support for the sentence:

> Whoever spills the blood of people due to the fact that they are Jewish people or any other kind of people, whoever abuses and tortures, butchers and murders, whoever is a racist who not only speaks against a people but takes an active part in the attempt to annihilate it, is fated to death.[143]

A number of public figures also supported the death sentence that was handed down to Demjanjuk. According to Hausner, "there are acts of murder so shocking and so awful for which imposing the death penalty is justified."[144] Even before the reading of the sentence, Justice Minister Sharir expressed hope that Demjanjuk would be sentenced to death.[145]

Barnea offered a different view. "Morally," he wrote, "he should be put to death. [But] historically speaking, executing him is a belated and unnecessary act that yields no lesson and no benefit. A demonstration of power that is empty, Herutesque."[146]

Immediately following the sentencing, the weekly *Koteret Rashit* asked five prominent figures their views on the matter.[147] The only figure asked who expressed support of the sentence was the jurist Prof. S.Z. Feller,[148] who maintained that from all perspectives, "death is the only option." Although this penalty has an element of retribution, he explained, it applies to "a category of the most severe offenses that can be committed"; he must be given "the maximum penalty." With a sense of irony, he noted that although Israeli society excelled at conducting festivals, "we are not thinking about the victims."[149]

The others who were asked objected to the death penalty. Prof. Allan Dershowitz, a professor of law at Harvard University, characterized the sentence as "foolish," arguing that the conviction was based on witness testimony, and that "you do not hang someone based only on the words of witnesses." He also raised a moral factor: "The death penalty is brutal and cannot be equitably assigned. It has the potential for inequity, and there is a historical score here – it is not viewed as deterrence." Dershowitz expressed reservations regarding

Justice Tal's assertion that "the blood of the victims is crying out." From his perspective, this statement was "too biblical."[150] Legal scholar Ruth Gavison also opposed the death penalty for two reasons. First, "as a result of the long period of time that had elapsed since the acts were committed, executing him today reflects only vindictiveness and has no symbolic value." The second reason was the fact that the major point dealt with during the trial was the identification of the accused, and that "there are people in the population who have doubts about whether the man in question is indeed Ivan the Terrible." For this reason, she believed it was preferable "to not impose the final, irreversible sentence of death."[151] Gavison noted that because of the human limitation, it was best to refrain from imposing the death penalty.

Prof. Yeshayahu Leibowitz articulated a complex position on the death penalty. In his characteristically resolute manner, he stated that although "there are people who should be killed like stray dogs," he did not want the justice system to encompass the death penalty; rather, he maintained that people like Demjanjuk "should be killed without a trial."[152] These remarks, of course, were extremely unusual.

Justice Haim Cohn opposed the death penalty primarily on principle, unrelated to the sentence in question. The approach of "an eye for an eye" and "a life for a life" was a thing of the past, Cohn argued. "The state does not need to kill and, perhaps we should say, is prohibited from doing so."[153]

This was a major difference between the two trials. The death sentence that was handed down in Demjanjuk's case sparked serious contention and many opposed it, whereas Eichmann's death sentence was met with almost complete overall agreement.

VIII. The Appeals of the Defendants

Eichmann appealed both the decision and his sentence to the Israeli Supreme Court, which was another step in the ritual. The appeal hearing was held on March 22, 1962 before a panel of the five senior Supreme Court justices: President Olshan, Deputy President Shimon Agranat, and Justices Moshe Zilberg, Yosel Zussman, and Alfred Vitkon. This panel was similar to the panel that had been constituted for the appeal in the Kastner trial.[154] The appeal was conducted in the room in the People's Hall where all the court sessions had been held, and, during the trial, defense attorney Servatius denied Israel's right to try Eichmann. When the appeal got underway, Gouri wrote the following:

> In the glass cubicle – Eichmann. In the room and in the gallery – the same crowd…It seems that we were forced to take another, critical step. The defendant-appellant should not be denied the attempt to exhaust the rights he was granted under the law.[155]

On May 29, 1962, the decision in the appeal was read out. The five judges ruled unanimously to deny the appeal and confirm the appealed decision. They justified the death penalty as follows: "We knew very well how meagre and pale this death sentence would be, as opposed to the millions of incomprehensible deaths to which he condemned his victims." *Lamerhav* informed its readers that "the death penalty has been authorized for the chief slaughterer."[156] For Justice Agranat, the confirmation of the death penalty for Eichmann created an internal dilemma. Agranat opposed the death penalty with all his heart but was compelled to join the other justices in the message they conveyed: "The Jewish state will respond to violence with violence in order to prove to itself and to the world that Jewish blood is not free for the taking." The price he paid was "a weakening of the spirit of progress."[157]

After the appeal, the process moved more quickly. On May 29, Eichmann submitted a pardon request to Israel's President Yitzhak Ben-Zvi. On May 30, the government discussed the request and passed a majority decision to deny it.[158] One day later, on May 31, the president denied the request for a pardon, writing on it a verse from the Book of Samuel: "As your sword has made women childless, so shall your mother be childless among women" (I Samuel 15:32). At midnight that night, Eichmann was hanged. As noted, this was the only time the death penalty has been implemented in the history of the state of Israel.

With the exception of the handful of public figures who opposed execution, an overwhelming majority viewed it as a natural and justified conclusion to the Eichmann trial. After the hanging, Eichmann's corpse was burned and his ashes were scattered over the territorial waters of Israel. Hausner regarded this action as coming full circle: "The waves of the Mediterranean Sea washed away Eichmann's ashes exactly 25 years after he had sailed the very same waters as a young S.S. officer on his first important mission in the struggle against the Jewish People."[159]

Newspapers from across the political spectrum viewed the hanging as total justice incarnate. Shmuel Schnitzer wrote that "placing him on the gallows is a moral imperative."[160] In *Kol Ha`am*, it was written that "chief Nazi murderer Adolf Eichmann was hanged on the gallows. A trial of justice was conducted, a decision of justice was reached, and a sentence of justice was given and carried out."[161] The newspaper *Hatzofeh* contained the following words: "All circles within the Jewish People received the implementation of the sentence as a moral necessity, an unavoidable conclusion to the trial as a whole, which raised the saga of the Holocaust in an intense manner."[162]

The story of the appeal in the Demjanjuk trial was altogether different. This is a decisive point, as following the trial, the character, the image, and the historical status of the Demjanjuk trial emerged as new principles that differed from those of the Eichmann trial. A significant amount has been written about the reversal in this case that Demjanjuk's appeal engendered. The story of the appeal is recounted in *Finished But Not Complete*, the autobiography of Meir Shamgar,[163] who was serving as president of the Supreme Court at the time.[164] After the sentencing by the district court, Demjanjuk's attorneys appealed his conviction. They had no argument with the significance of the conviction of Ivan the Terrible; rather, they maintained that an error had occurred and that Ivan the Terrible was not John Demjanjuk. "And that is how his matter came to rest on our desk in the Supreme Court," Shamgar wrote. The President of the Court understood the sensitive and explosive nature of the matter, and he appointed a panel of five justices to hear it, with himself as its chair. Also appointed to the panel were Deputy Supreme Court President Menachem Alon and Justices Aharon Barak, Eliezer Goldberg, and Yaakov Meltz. These were senior justices, but not the most senior.[165] Aharon Barak, himself a Holocaust survivor, preferred to not be on the panel, but Shamgar insisted and Barak accepted his decision.[166]

Before the Supreme Court session pertaining to the appeal, the world witnessed a dramatic event with major legal implications: the fall of the Iron Curtain and the rapid demise of the Soviet Union. This was followed by the opening of the Soviet archives, including archives containing documentation from the period of World War II. In September 1990, Yoram Sheftel visited the Soviet Union "and acquired evidence, including the written testimony of 32 guards and five inmates who testified that Ivan the Terrible's surname was Marchenko, not Demjanjuk."[167]

This decisive point had an impact on the appeal judges. The identifying details of Ivan Marchenko were agreed upon by the prosecution and the defense. In light of the situation, Shamgar found himself facing a possibility which, from his perspective, was intolerable. He truly wanted to convict Demjanjuk, but he understood that this posed a major legal problem and that he had no choice but to acquit him of the charges because they had not been proven beyond a reasonable doubt.[168] "Though it turns my stomach," Shamgar wrote in an apologetic tone, "and despite the clear feeling that the man before us is a war criminal that may go free, all we can do is to rule that reasonable doubt exists with regard to his identification, and we must identify him."

Shamgar's book also provided a brief but important excerpt from the acquittal decision:

> Due to the existence of reasonable doubt, the *wachman* Ivan Demjanjuk was acquitted of the terrible accusations that are attributed to Ivan the Terrible of Treblinka. This is a worthy determination for judges, who are not God and have only what their eyes see and read. Finished – not complete. Completions are not the domain of mortal judges.

It is no coincidence that words from this decision constituted the title of his book. Shamgar did not express emotion in the book. However, he did acknowledge that "this was the most difficult trial on which I have had to rule and to decide and the most difficult trial I have ever experienced. The doubt has not dissipated; it will follow me until my dying day."[169] The decision was read out on July 29, 1993, when the five judges entered the courtroom for the last time during this trial. Their steps were heavy, and their faces were gray. At the end of the day, Ivan Demjanjuk went free.

Daniel Friedman has written about the acquittal on appeal in his analysis of the policy of the Supreme Court during the period in question. The trial took place during the revolutionary age of the Supreme Court, when "the tendency to convict and to disregard the presumption of innocence gained strength, causing the conviction rate in criminal cases in Israel to reach unreasonable proportions." In Demjanjuk's appeal, however, a completely different approach was revealed, and he was acquitted due to the existence of reasonable doubt. According to Friedman, this was "an act of far-reaching liberalism in a trial during a period in which precisely the opposite trend was mounting in the punitive realm."[170]

This decision remains controversial up to the present. "Even in my darkest dreams," wrote Holocaust survivor Noah Klieger, who covered the trial for *Yedioth Ahronoth*, "I could never have imagined that the day would come that I would witness the Israeli Supreme Court rule to free a Nazi criminal." Why, he asked, had the judges reached this decision? "After all, under law, they had other options besides release."[171] On the other hand, lawyer Ze'ev Segal wrote, "the decision, with its 405 pages, is not only a legal document. It is a public, historical, and educational document about the terrors of the Holocaust and about the ability of the judges of Israel to reach unbiased and fearless decisions.[172] According to Haim Cohn, it was "a great day for the Israeli court."[173]

Conclusion: The Major Differences between the Eichmann Trial and the Demjanjuk Trial

To conclude, we again note the three major differences between the two trials. The first is the fact that Eichmann's trial was the trial of a general, whereas Demjanjuk's trial was the trial of a much more junior functionary. It is therefore entirely impossible to use the terms of the general's trial in the trial of a corporal.

The second difference between the trials lay in their historic status. The Eichmann trial is considered a formative event in the history of the state of Israel, a crossroads in Israeli legal history and in Israeli society's attitude toward the Holocaust and its victims. In the words of Nathan Alterman in an article on the opening of the trial:

Revealed here, first of all, are the smallest springs of this mighty
legal machine and also, from within it, a reflection of its visage.

Their minute gleam is also part of the clap of thunder and bolt of lightning that, in this trial, will awaken and turn Israeli history upside down.[174]

Forty years after the trial, Gouri explained its impact on Israeli society:

Many of those who had been paralyzed until that point opened their sealed hearts, as many of those born in Israel were exposed to the terrors of the Final Solution in their full dimensions. It was an Open University that changed the concepts of national memory.[175]

Unlike the impressive success of the Eichmann trial, Friedman has characterized the Demjanjuk trial as a failed attempt to repeat the success of the former through another trial in Israel. The latter trial, he maintains, was a "futile move – despite the mighty effort that went into it."[176] As a result, the memory of the Eichmann trial is alive and well, whereas the memory of the Demjanjuk trial barely exists. This is a third and decisive difference between the two trials.

Hod maintains that states organize their pasts and shape their collective memory based on the needs of the hour, "silencing and repressing pestering past events that are inconsistent with the desired self-image."[177] From this perspective, it would be preferable to forget the Demjanjuk trial. One can argue that the Eichmann trial had a distinct impact on Israeli society in general and on the shaping of the memory of the Holocaust in particular. On the other hand, it was Israeli society that shaped the Demjanjuk affair as it played out, and certainly what remains of it.

Endnotes

1 Hanna Yablonka, *The State of Israel versus Adolf Eichmann* (New York, 2004), originally published in Hebrew under the same title (Tel Aviv, 2001).

2 See, for example, Yechiam Weitz, "In the Name of Six Million Accusers: Gideon Hausner as Attorney General and His Place in the Eichmann Trial," *Israel Studies* 14(2) (2009), pp. 26-49; Yechiam Weitz, "The Founding Father and the War Criminal's Trial: Ben-Gurion and the Eichmann Trial," *Yad Vashem Studies* 36(1) (2008), pp. 211-252.

3 Tamir Hod, "Remember to Forget: The Demjanjuk Affair" (Tel-Aviv 2020) (Hebrew).

4 Meirav Sagi, "The Demjanjuk Trials and Israeli Society: Between Catharsis and Battle for Memory," master's thesis, Bar-Ilan University, 2016 (Hebrew). Sagi wrote her thesis under my supervision.

5 Yechiam Weitz, "The End of the Beginning: Clarifying the Concept of the 'Starting Point' of the State," *Middle Eastern Studies* 31(4) (October 1995), p. 684..

6 Tom Segev, *The Seventh Million: The Israelis and the Holocaust* (Jerusalem, 1991), p. 385 (Hebrew).

7 Amos Oz, "Deeds between Man and His Fellow Men," *Davar*, June 27, 1986 (Hebrew).

8 David Cesarni, *Eichmann: His Life and Crimes* (London, 2004), p. 11.

9 *The Eichmann Trial: Arguments of the Prosecution, A. Opening Arguments, B. Closing Arguments* (Jerusalem, 1974), p. 31 (Hebrew).

10 Sagi, "The Demjanjuk Trials and Israeli Society," p. 12.

11 Segev, *The Seventh Million*, p. 387.

12 Avi Katzman, "For and Against: Death to Demjanjuk," *Koteret Rashit*, April 27, 1988 (Hebrew).

13 Nahum Barnea, "The Crowd Wanted Blood," *Koteret Rashit*, April 27, 1988 (emphasis added) (Hebrew).

14 For example, Itamar Levin, *Kapo in Tel Aviv: Prosecution in Israel of Jews Accused of Collaboration with the Nazis* (Jerusalem, 2015) (Hebrew); Rivka Brot, *In the Gray Zone: The Jewish Kapo on Trial* (Raanana, 2019) (Hebrew).

15 Segev, *The Seventh Million*, p. 307.

16 Diary of David Ben-Gurion (herein, BGD), May 15, 1960, Ben-Gurion Heritage Institute Archive (herein, BGA).

17 Meir Shamgar, *Finished But Not Complete* (Tel Aviv, 2015), p. 173 (Hebrew).

18 Tzvi A. Tal, *Until the Sun Came* (Or Yehuda, 2012), p. 192 (Hebrew).

19 Mordechai Ish-Shalom, *In League with Quarrymen and Builders: An Autobiography* (Jerusalem, 1989), p. 291 (Hebrew). Ish-Shalom was the mayor of Jerusalem between 1959 and 1965.

20 Hannah Arendt, *Eichmann in Jerusalem: A Report on the Banality of Evil* (New York, 1963), p. 2.

21 Gideon Hausner, *The Eichmann Trial in Jerusalem* (Tel Aviv, 2011), p. 308 (Hebrew).

22 Ibid.

23 Haim Gouri, T*he Glass Booth: The Jerusalem Trial* (Tel Aviv, 1962; second edition, 2001) (Hebrew).

24 "Eichmann's Glass Cubicle – To Kibbutz Lohamei Hagetaot," *Hatzofeh*, June 4, 1962 (Hebrew).

25 Segev, *The Seventh Million*, p. 388.

26 Tal, *Until the Sun Came*, p.192.

27 It was not the same glass cubicle in which Adolf Eichmann had sat but rather a new cubicle made especially for Demjanjuk. I am grateful to Lior Inbar, a former student of mine, for providing me with this information.

28 *Al Hamishmar*, February 27, 1986, in Sagi, "The Demjanjuk Trials and Israeli Society," p. 15.

29 Tom Segev, "A Showcase Trial, But A Small One," *Koteret Rashit*, March 5, 1986 (Hebrew).

30 The Supreme Court was located in the Russian Compound until 1992, when it moved to its present location in Givat Ram.

31 Yoram Sheftel, *The Demjanjuk Affair: The Rise and Fall of a Show-Trial* (Tel Aviv, 1993), pp. 313-314 (Hebrew).

32 Olshan served in this position for 11 years, from 1954 to 1965.

33 Yitzhak Olshan, *Law and Reflection: A Memoir* (Jerusalem and Tel Aviv, 1978), p. 315 (Hebrew).

34 Yechiam Weitz, *The Man Who Was Murdered Twice: The Life, Trial, and Death of Israel Kastner* (Jerusalem, 2011), pp. 101-103. The law was enacted in January 1961, approximately three months before the beginning of the Eichmann trial.

35 Landau was appointed to the Supreme Court in 1953.

36 Olshan, *Law and Reflection*, p. 317.

37 Gabriel Strassman, "The Youngest Judge Will Chair," *Maariv*, February 27, 1961 (Hebrew).

38 Michal Shaked, *Moshe Landau – Judge* (Tel Aviv, 2012), p. 172 (Hebrew).

39 Daniel Friedman, *End of Innocence: Law and Politics in Israel* (Rishon Leziyon, 2019), p. 260 (Hebrew). Friedman is an emeritus professor of Tel Aviv University's Faculty of Law. Between 2007 and 2009, he served as Israel's minister of justice.

40 "Judge Yitzhak Raveh," *Davar*, June 16, 1961 (Hebrew).

41 Friedman, *End of Innocence*, p. 172.

42 Tal, *Until the Sun Came*, p. 191. Justice Tal's words are inaccurate: relevant here was the possibility of imposing the death penalty, not the fact that the crimes in question were crimes against the Jewish People and crimes against humanity.

43 Shamgar, *Finished But Not Complete,* p. 152.

44 Moshe Gorali, "The Trial of Folly," nrg, October 12, 2015, https://www.makorrishon.co.il/nrg/online/19/ART/1/1084/994/964.html (accessed November 19, 2020) (Hebrew).

45 Hod, "The Demjanjuk Affair," p. 56.

46 Shamgar served as President of the Supreme Court from November 1983 until 1995.

47 Baruch Meiri, "Demjanjuk Will Be Tried by Dov Levin, Dalia Dorner, and Tzvi Tal," *Maariv*, October 1, 1986 (Hebrew).

48 The government confirmed Hausner's appointment as attorney general on May 8, 1960. However, he officially took on the position later, after closing the law firm of which he was the proprietor.

49 Rosen was the leader of the Progressive Party, and Hausner was a senior party activist. Hausner's appointment was distinctly political in character.

50 Meeting of the 12th Government, June 12, 1960, Israel State Archives (herein ISA). This meeting was held before Hausner began his tenure.

51 Hausner, *Justice in Jerusalem* (New York, 1966).

52 Gideon Hausner, *The Eichmann Trial in Jerusalem* (Bnei Brak, 2011) (Hebrew). Hausner passed away in 1990.

53 Landau was born in 1912.

54 Shaked, *Moshe Landau*, p. 237.

55 Hausner served as a member of Knesset from 1965 to 1974, and from 1977 to 1981. He also served as a minister without portfolio in the government of Golda Meir and the government of Yitzhak Rabin between 1974 and 1977.

56 Haim Cohn, *A Personal Introduction: An Autobiography* (Or Yehuda, 2005), p. 335 (Hebrew).

57 Haim Gouri, "A Speech of Accusation and Lament," T*he Glass Booth*, p. 13 (Hebrew). Gouri's words were published on April 18, 1961.

58 Yitzhak Dish, "Trial Diary," *Herut*, April 18, 1961 (Hebrew).

59 *Maariv*, November 16, 1990.

60 Bach subsequently went on to occupy senior posts in the Israeli justice system, including state's attorney (1969-1982) and Supreme Court justice (1982-1997).

61 Hausner, *The Eichmann Trial in Jerusalem*, p. 299.

62 BGD, April 10, 1961, BGA, Diaries.

63 Shalom Rosenfeld, "The Trial: Servatius Tries to Find a Justification for Eichmann," *Maariv*, April 25, 1961 (Hebrew) (emphasis in original).

64 Attorney General Yosef Harish, who held the post from 1986 to 1993, was not significantly involved in the trial.

65 "Nazi Criminal 'Ivan the Terrible' Will be Extradited to Israel and Will Arrive This Week," *Maariv*, February 25, 1986 (Hebrew).

66 Hod, "The Demjanjuk Affair," p. 58.

67 Shaked, *Moshe Landau*, p. 185.

68 Jonathan Lis, "Former State's Attorney Yona Blattman Has Died," *Haaretz*, February 2, 2012 (Hebrew).

69 "Michael Shaked: On His Toes at the Demjanjuk Trial," *Maariv*, March 6, 1987 (Hebrew).

70 Tal, *Until the Sun Came*, p. 191.

71 "Michael Shaked: On His Tiptoes at the Demjanjuk Trial," *Maariv*, March 6, 1987 (Hebrew).

72 Hod, "The Demjanjuk Affair," p. 59.

73 Yonatan Kramer and Yaniv Vaki, "The Trial of Ivan Demjanjuk in Israel: Conversations with the Prosecutor in the Case, Michael Shaked," *Mishpat Mafteach: Journal of the State's Attorney* (August 2019), p. 128 (Hebrew).

74 Baruch Hameiri, "Demjanjuk Committed Crimes of Immeasurable Severity," *Maariv*, September 30, 1986 (Hebrew).

75 On August 2, 1943, prisoners launched an armed uprising that was planned far ahead of time. Some 200 inmates managed to escape the camp, and only some survived until the end of the war. As a result of the uprising, the camp was dismantled and plowed over.

76 "State's Attorney Yona Blattman's Opening Speech Yesterday," *Maariv*, February 17, 1987 (Hebrew).

77 "Michael Shaked: On His Tiptoes at the Demjanjuk Trial."

78 Arad served as the chief education officer of the I.D.F. from 1968 to 1972. He occupied his post at Yad Vashem from 1972 to 1993.

79 Aharon Dolev, "Ella, Age 15: I suggested to my mother that she come with me to the Demjanjuk trial. She did not have the emotional strength." *Maariv*, February 20, 1987 (Hebrew). It is noteworthy that Arad's memoirs make no mention of his testimony at the Demjanjuk trial. The second edition of his book *Treblinka: Destruction and Uprising* was published in 2013 and makes no mention of the Supreme Court's ruling on Demjanjuk.

80 Dalia Mazori, "The Demjanjuk Trial Showed That Justice Must Be Done," nrg website, March 18, 2012, https://www.makorrishon.co.il/nrg/online/1/ART2/347/494.html (accessed November 19, 2020).

81 Meeting of the Israeli government, June 12, 1960, ISA.

82 Well-known Jerusalem attorney Mendel Scherf was willing to join Eichmann's defense team but did not do so out of fear for his life. However, he did advise Servatius on questions of Israeli law. On this, see Gabriel Strassman, "Servatius's Israeli Advisor," *Maariv*, February 13, 1961 (Hebrew).

83 Hausner, *The Eichmann Trial in Jerusalem*, p. 305.

84 Meeting of the Israeli government, June 12, 1960, ISA.

85 Meeting of the Israeli government, July 24, 1960, ISA.

86 Ibid.

87 See the Knesset proceedings for November 22, 1960, *Knesset Record* 30, p. 306. See also "Servatius Law Passed by Knesset," *Davar*, November 23, 1960 (Hebrew).

88 Segev, *The Seventh Million*, p. 324.

89 Baruch Meiri, "Outgoing Justice Minister Approves Appointment of Attorney O'Connor to Represent Demjanjuk," *Maariv*, April 17, 1987 (Hebrew).

90 Tom Segev, "Foreign Correspondent – Criminal Case 373-86," *Koteret Rashit*, February 25, 1987 (Hebrew).

91 Tom Segev, "Foreign Correspondent – The Defense Attorney Shows His Cards," *Koteret Rashit*, March 4, 1987 (Hebrew).

92 Orion served as the president of the military courts in the West Bank between 1974 and 1976.

93 Baruch Meiri and Aya Orenstein, "Six Attorneys Agree to Represent Demjanjuk," *Maariv*, November 18, 1986 (Hebrew); Baruch Meiri, "I Am Certain that As Demjanjuk's Trial Continues I Will Have Problems of Conscience," *Maariv*, November 20, 1986 (Hebrew).

94 *Maariv*, November 27, 1986 (Hebrew).

95 Shany Littman, "One Defense Attorney Committed Suicide; Another Sustained Acid to the Face," *Haaretz*, November 4, 2019 (Hebrew).

96 Sheftel, *The Demjanjuk Affair*, pp. 17-25.

97 "Sheftel: Representing Demjanjuk – The Wisest Decision of My Life," *Israel Hayom*, October 31, 2019 (Hebrew).

98 Yossi Levy, "'It's All Because of You' Shouted a Holocaust Survivor, and Splashed Acid in Sheftel's Face," *Maariv*, December 2, 1988 (Hebrew).

99 "Mother of Attorney Sheftel: I'm Always Receiving Threats," *Maariv*, December 5, 1988 (Hebrew).

100 Hod, "The Demjanjuk Affair," p. 61.

101 Tom Segev, "Foreign Correspondent – Criminal Case 373-86."

102 *Davar*, May 11, 1983 (Hebrew).

103 "A Disciplinary Complaint May be Lodged against the Judge Who Signed the 'Yesh Gvul' Petition," *Davar*, June 8, 1983 (Hebrew).

104 "Zamir: Judges Must Refrain from Signing Political Petitions," *Davar*, October 3, 1983 (Hebrew).

105 "Judge Dov Eitan Resigns from the Court," *Davar*, September 20, 1983 (Hebrew).

106 "Sheftel: Representing Demjanjuk."

107 "Attorney Dov Eitan Will Meet with Demjanjuk Today in Jail," *Maariv*, September 4, 1988 (Hebrew).

108 Tamir Hod, "Why did we repress and forget about the Demjanjuk affair?" *Ynet*, April 12, 2018 [Hebrew].

109 Moshe Admon, "He Took His Secret to the Grave: The Mysterious Death of Dov Eitan," *Zman Darom*, July 14, 2010 (Hebrew), https://www.ynet.co.il/articles/0,7340,L-5225325,00.html (accessed November 19, 2020) (Hebrew).

110 *Maariv*, December 11 and 12, 1961 (Hebrew).

111 Haim Gouri, "The Mortal," *Lamerhav*, December 14, 1961, in T*he Glass Booth*, p. 257 (Hebrew).

112 "Attorney General vs. Adolf Eichmann: The Sentence," Jerusalem, 1974, p. 285 (Hebrew).

113 Moshe Tavor, "A Trial Diary – The Final Session," *Davar*, December 17, 1961 (Hebrew).

114 *Davar Hayom*, December 17, 1961 (Hebrew).

115 "Trial of Justice – Today," *Lamerhav*, December 17, 1961 (Hebrew).

116 "The Sentence, from the Vantage Point," *Hatzofeh*, December 17, 1961 (Hebrew).

117 Gershom Scholem, "Eichmann," *Amot* 1 (September 1972), in *Explications and Implications* (Tel Aviv, 1975), p. 120 (Hebrew).

118 Hod, "The Demjanjuk Affair," p. 72.

119　Sagi, "The Demjanjuk Trials and Israeli Society," p. 27.

120　"Ivan the Terrible," *Yoman Maariv, Maariv*, April 19, 1988 (Hebrew).

121　Eyal Meged, "Ivan the Terrible: The Moment of Breaking," *Koteret Rashit*, April 20, 1988 (Hebrew). Meged was a close friend of defense attorney Yoram Sheftel.

122　Yosef Lapid, "John Demjanjuk, You Are Not an Extra," *Maariv*, April 19, 1988 (Hebrew) [emphasis in original].

123　"Former Justice Tzvi Tal: An Interview," *Alei Mishpat* 7 (2009), pp. 27-28 (Hebrew).

124　Tal, *Until the Sun Came*, pp.196, 199.

125　Elichay Shilo et al. (eds.), *Without a Robe: Conversations with Supreme Court Justices* (Rishon Lezion, 2017), p. 178 (Hebrew).

126　"Justice Dorner, 15 Years after Demjanjuk's Acquittal: 'Even Today I Know It Was Him,'" *Maariv*, July 24, 2018 (Hebrew).

127　Tom Segev, "The Conviction," *Haaretz*, April 19, 1988 (Hebrew), in Sagi, *The Demjanjuk Trials*, p. 31 (Hebrew).

128　Moshe Gorali, "The Trial of Folly," nrg, October 12, 2005, https://www.makorrishon.co.il/nrg/online/19/ART/1/1084/994/964.html (Hebrew).

129　At the time of the Demjanjuk trial, Beinish was serving as the deputy to State's Attorney Yona Blattman.

130　Dan Margalit, "Justice Was Not Exhausted," *Israel Hayom*, March 2012 (Hebrew).

131　Nomi Levitsky, *Your Honor – Aharon Barak: A Biography* (Jerusalem, 2001), pp. 84-85 (Hebrew).

132　Baruch Meiri, "At the Gates of Hell, He Performed His work with Unparalleled Devotion and Enthusiasm," *Maariv*, April 26, 1988 (Hebrew).

133　Tal, *Until the Sun Came*, p. 197.

134　Nahum Barnea, "Demjanjuk," *Koteret Rashit*, April 20, 1988 [emphasis added].

135　Avraham Sharir, a member of the Liberal Party within Likud, served in this position from July 1986 through December 1988.

136　"Demjanjuk: Sharir's Two Mistakes," *Koteret Rashit*, October 1, 1986 (Hebrew). This point was raised during the Eichmann trial.

137　Baruch Hameiri, "'Justice and Vengeance Has Been Served', Holocaust Survivors Sobbed," *Koteret Rashit*, April 26, 1987 (Hebrew).

138　Seven seven-year periods, or 49 years.

139　Dina Zilber, *In the Name of the Law* (Or Yehuda, 2012), p. 252 (Hebrew).

140　Baruch Hameiri, "'Justice and Vengeance Has Been Served', Holocaust Survivors Sobbed," *Maariv*, April 26, 1988 (Hebrew).

141 *Koteret Rashit*, April 27, 1988 (Hebrew).

142 Shalom Rosenfeld, "You Wept Nicely, Individual Taste," *Maariv*, April 29, 1988 (Hebrew). Shalom Rosenfeld (1914-2008) was the editor-in-chief of *Maariv* from 1974 to 1980.

143 "Demjanjuk: End of Chapter I," *Yoman Maariv*, *Maariv*, April 26, 1987 (Hebrew).

144 "Punishing Every Last One of Them," *Yoman Maariv*, *Maariv*, April 26, 1987, in Sagi, "The Demjanjuk Trials and Israeli Society," p. 39.

145 Arnon Yafeh, "The Justice Minister Hopes Demjanjuk Will Be Sentenced to Death," *Al Hamishmar*, April 20, 1987, in Sagi, "The Demjanjuk Trials and Israeli Society," p. 35. Sharir's remarks were subject to substantial criticism.

146 Nahum Barnea, "The Crowd Wants Blood," *Koteret Rahit*, April 27, 1987 (Hebrew).

147 Avi Katzman, "For and Against: Death to Demjanjuk," *Koteret Rashit*, April 27, 1988 (Hebrew).

148 Schneur-Zalman Feller (1913-2016) was a member of the Faculty of Law of the Hebrew University of Jerusalem. Between 1971 and 1974 he served as dean of the faculty.

149 Katzman, "For and Against."

150 Ibid.

151 Ibid.

152 Ibid.

153 Cohn addressed this topic in his autobiography as follows: "Judicial death, in all its possible forms, is no longer consistent with the modern level of human rights, as reflected in the international treaties and the constitutions of many enlightened states." Cohn, *A Personal Introduction*, p. 207.

154 Two of the justices – Schneur Zalman Cheshin and David Guttwein passed away, and justices Zussman and Vitkon replaced them. Tzvi Berenson, who had more seniority than Vitkon, was not assigned to the panel because his expertise lay in labor law and not in criminal matters.

155 Haim Gouri, "Human Rights," *Lamerhav*, March 23, 1962, in *The Glass Booth*, pp. 272-273 (Hebrew).

156 May 30, 1962.

157 Pnina Lahav, *Judgment in Jerusalem: Chief Justice Shimon Agranat and the Zionist Century* (Berkeley, 1997), pp. 160-161.

158 "In the Nations of the World People Are Executed without Debate," *Haaretz*, July 27, 1962 (Hebrew). Two government ministers argued that Eichmann should be pardoned.

159 Hausner, *Justice in Jerusalem*, p. 447. In October 1937, Eichmann travelled to Palestine to check on the possibility of Jewish immigration.

160 *Maariv*, June 1, 1962. Shmuel Schnitzer (1918-1999) was a senior figure at *Maariv* for many years. He served as its editor-in-chief from 1980 to 1985.

161 "Lost, On the Agenda," *Kol Ha`am*, June 3, 1962 (Hebrew).

162 "The Implementation and the Sentence," *Hatzofeh*, June 3, 1962 (Hebrew).

163 Shamgar served in this position for 12 years, from 1983 to 1995. Justices Shlomo Levin (appointed to the Supreme Court in 1980) and Gabriel Bach (appointed in 1982) were not on the panel.

164 Shamgar, *Finished But Not Complete*, pp. 173-176.

165 Goldberg (appointed to the Supreme Court in 1984) and Meltz (appointed in 1988) were less senior. Bach was not on the panel because he had been on the prosecution team in the Eichmann trial. Levitsky, *Your Honor*, p. 81.

166 Levitsky, *Your Honor*, p. 82.

167 Shamgar, *Finished But Not Complete*, p. 174.

168 Levitsky, *Your Honor*, p. 88.

169 Shamgar, *Finished But Not Complete*, p. 176.

170 Friedman, *End of Innocence*, p. 267.

171 Noah Klieger, "No Justice," *Yedioth Ahronoth*, July 30, 1993 (Hebrew).

172 "This is the Legal Truth, But the Doubt Continues to Gnaw," *Yedioth Ahronoth*, July 30, 1993 (Hebrew).

173 Ibid.

174 Nathan Alterman, "The Seventh Column: The Court," *Davar*, April 14, 1961 (Hebrew).

175 "Forty Years Later," in *Facing the Glass Booth*, p. ii.

176 Friedman, *End of Innocence*, pp. 265-267.

177 Hod, "The Demjanjuk Affair in Israel," p. 275.

This section is dedicated to the memory of Fanya Gottesfeld Heller, Holocaust survivor, author and philanthropist who supported the study of women during the Holocaust. The section is based on a symposium held at Bar-Ilan University in November 2018 sponsored by Finkler Institute of Holocaust Research and the Fanya Gottesfeld Heller Center for the Study of Women in Judaism.

Fanya Gottesfeld Heller
1924 - 2017

Judith Tydor Baumel-Schwartz

Why Study About "Women During the Holocaust" As a Separate Topic?

Introduction

In the beginning there was the Holocaust over the heavens and the earth. And the Earth was without form and void, and darkness was on the face of the deep. And the spirit of the researchers hovered over the face of the waters in search of sources from which to learn about what they would soon be calling the Major Topics of Holocaust Research: the Judenrat, Partisans, Ghetto uprisings and even German Jewry during the 1930s, but, of course, only the men among them.

Then the researchers said "let there be light," and there was light! And the light began to illuminate the Major Topics until the research map, initially white, began glowing in brilliant research colors, with strong emphasis on black, yellow, and blue and white Stars of David. Then the researchers divided the light of the Major Topics from the darkness of all the rest. And the researchers called the light "worthy topics" and the darkness they called "unimportant, trivial and partly dangerous topics." And there was evening and there was morning, and the basis of Holocaust research was set, not only for the first day, but for more than a generation.

And the Land was peaceful for forty years as the Holocaust researchers worked on the Major Topics. But a new generation of female and a few male researchers arose, asking: "Who appointed you officers and judges of the people?" They began to study additional aspects of the Holocaust that they considered as important as the Major Topics: Daily life during the Holocaust, Refugees, Children, DPs, and finally, also the women.

Then the Elders among the researchers arose, along with a few younger researchers crawling after them, and they spoke harshly against those wishing to study women and the Holocaust. And they accused them of strange doings, beginning with breaking the ten commandments of research and ending with

Holocaust Revisionism and Denial. Then they outdid themselves by trying to prevent younger researchers from following the this path and stated: "Blessed is the researcher who did not walk in the path of the ungodly who study women and the Holocaust, nor stand in their way, nor sit in the seat of these scornful people, but delights in the Major Topics and meditates on them day and night." Then they continued by saying that the fate of those embarking on the wrong research path would be like "the chaff which the wind drives away," and that they had no chance of finding academic positions or being promoted. And besides, they would just bring trouble to the Jews.

It was after these things that a small group of young women researchers arose, along with a few who were no longer so young, and dared to challenge the research Elders. And they began studying the fate of women during the Holocaust, and even among the DPs, and they struggled with the research Elders who controlled the academic positions in universities throughout the world. But they continued with their work and received the support of the multitude, and even convinced a few of the research Elders that there was righteousness in their path. And they continued to research, and to write, and to publish, and the shelves began to fill up with books about women during the Holocaust until it was a wonder in the eyes of the multitude who could no longer imagine Holocaust research without this topic. The morning came, and then another, and another, until the time arrived when the women researchers began to rise in the ranks until they were commanders of hundreds and commanders of thousands and even heads of Institutes and Professors. Then the younger women researchers stood and looked at the veteran women researchers, and could not believe that there was once a generation that did not know anything about the study of women during the Holocaust. And there was evening and there was morning, the second day.

This brief tongue-in-cheek description summarizes the basics of how the study of women during the Holocaust developed as an academic topic. Initially, Holocaust researchers concentrated on what they considered to be the "Major Topics," which were actually those that interested the (mostly male) researchers of that generation, and were similar to the topics being studied then in history without any connection to the Holocaust – those dealing with leadership, administration, politics, economics, and the military. An exception to the rule was the *Analles* school, concentrating on social aspects of history, which was a bit past its infancy. Only a generation later did they begin focusing on social and cultural aspects of the Holocaust that had once been considered secondary, or had not been considered as existing at all. As part of this trend, and with the support of the Feminist Movement that made its academic mark from the late 1960s onward, a number of researchers from different disciplines began examining various aspects of Jewish women's lives under the Nazis. Until then, the majority of publications dealing with women during the Holocaust were women's wartime diaries and survivor memoirs.

The first academic studies of Jewish women's lives during the Holocaust were published during the late 1970s and early 1980s. An important turning point in publicizing the newly emerging topic was the "Women Surviving the Holocaust" Conference organized by Joan Ringelheim[1] and Esther Katz[2] at Stern College, NY in 1983.[3] An addition stage in the discipline's development occurred during the 1990s when a number of anthologies, academic studies, and sourcebooks were published, all focusing on women's lives under Nazi rule. The growing awareness of the topic and availability of studies that could serve as reading material, encouraged Holocaust scholars to begin teaching courses about women during the Holocaust, first in the USA and later in Israel and Europe. These courses, in turn, also encouraged graduate students to specialize in the field.[4] As time progressed, it appeared that the study of women's lives during the Holocaust was soon to be located alongside the topics of Holocaust research that had been studied since the discipline developed.

This, however, was an illusion. Unlike other new Holocaust related topics that had been easily accepted by the academic community, the study of women during the Holocaust aroused powerful emotions and elicited forceful reactions among scholars, public figures, and commentators. At the end of the 1990s, the topic became the subject of a fiery public debate that began in the press and continued in scholarly journals. Its ricochets were felt throughout the academic community. The polemic even shaped the professional attitude towards those who chose to research and teach the topic of women in the Holocaust, leaving widespread fallout in its wake for a number of years.

Why did anyone oppose studying Jewish women's lives during the Holocaust? Why did the debate elicit such an emotional response? What was the true agenda behind those posing the question "why study about women during the Holocaust as a separate topic"? Was this not a field that simply "developed" over time, like many other field in Holocaust study such as the Judenrates where the attitude towards the topic change throughout the years? How did the opposition to the topic affect its further development? Can one state today, two or more decades after the public debate on the topic began, that "women in the Holocaust" is now a mainstream topic, a central and accepted theme of Holocaust study?

This article will focus on the development of this polemic and its repercussions throughout the academic world, examining the nature of the debate, the reason it elicited such an emotional response among certain groups of scholars, leaders, and journalist in American Jewry, and the fallout that it left behind.

Research Framework

In spite of the tendency to treat the Holocaust, and anything having to do with its study, as historically unique and unprecedented, on the surface it appears that the polemic being discussed was primarily ideological and possibly intergenerational. In their study of ideological and intergenerational conflicts, psychologists Mark J. Brandt, Christine Reyna, John R. Chambers, Jarett T. Crawford and Geoffrey Wetherell describe the stages characterizing the phenomenon:

1. The dominant group locates the target group whose values they perceive as conflicting with or threatening their own values.

2. It then tries to distance itself from those who do not share their worldview and moral convictions.

3. To do so, the dominant group uses motivated information selectively attending to, ignoring, or distorting information, to confirm pre-existing beliefs about the group and validating their own ideological beliefs.

4. The length and intensity of the dominant group's response towards the conflicting target group is determined by the degree of threat it feels towards its values and moral convictions. [5]

Can the objections to studying Women in the Holocaust as a separate research topic be considered part of the accepted dynamics of intergenerational ideological conflict as described by Brandt and his colleagues? To what degree were the elements that they mention in their study expressed in the polemic against those studying, teaching, and writing about the lives of Jewish women during the Holocaust? Did the public debate include components unusual in such ideological polemics and if so, what were the reasons for their inclusion?

In order to answer these questions, we must first understand the background to the battle that was declared against those pursuing the topic of women during the Holocaust. I will therefore briefly return to the early academic discourse on that topic, following its development until the end of the twentieth century and the beginning of the polemic that developed. I will then analyze the controversy and its effects on the study of Jewish women during the Holocaust, concluding with a discussion of how the discipline developed from then until today.

How it All Began

The first scholars who examined the lives of Jewish woman during the Holocaust did so *in situ*. In 1941 and 1942, Dr. Emanuel Ringelblum, founder of the clandestine "Oneg Shabbat" archive in the Warsaw ghetto, charged journalist Cecilia Slepak with interviewing Jewish women about their ongoing wartime experiences.[6] More than sixty years after Slepak began her research, the handful of completed questionnaires that remained from her uncompleted study, became the basis of Dalia Ofer's fascinating exploration of Slepak and her ghetto-based research.[7]

Soon after the war's end, the first wave of Jewish women's Holocaust publications began to appear. Most were memoirs of women who had survived the war in hiding, in ghettos, camps and underground movements.[8] The credibility of these books, written during or near the end of the war, was relatively high because of the timing of their writing. Some explicitly referred to "female" experiences during the war and even emphasized the centrality of mutual aid among women as an essential component in their survival. Others pointed to the lack of mutual aid among other women. Some of these books were written as a form of psychological catharsis to process trauma through writing about the past, but this was true only for a portion of them. Ultimately, these books became a key for scholars who later sought to explore the unique dynamics of women's wartime survival. [9]

Women's Holocaust memoirs continued to be published during the 1950s and 1960s, with a high proportion of authors who were former members of the underground movements or those who held senior positions in the camps.[10] In those years, the lack of synthetic research on women in the Holocaust was evident, as it was not considered one of the "big issues" worthy of academic study.

Following the growing international interest in the Holocaust, and in the use of social analysis, along with the academic development of women's studies, a third wave of publications dealing with women during the Holocaust began in the mid-1970s. Survivor memoirs[11] and collections of testimonies edited mostly by scholars[12] were now augmented by the first academic studies about women under Nazi rule. Some explored the lives of Jewish women in Germany, such as Marion Kaplan's study, the volume she edited together with Atina Grossman and Renata Bridenthal, or that by Gisela Bock.[13] Another group dealt with refugee women.[14] Additional books, such as that by Marilyn Heinmann, dealt with the literary aspects of women's lives under the Nazis.[15] Yet another group of studies, such as those by Joan Ringelheim, dealt with philosophical and conceptual-social issues.[16]

The transition from memories to research had a disciplinary aspect, but also a generational one. Unlike the memoirs, all of which were written by Holocaust survivors, many of the academic studies were written by researchers who had no first-person connection to the Holocaust. Some had a family connection because they were daughters of refugees or survivors, or they had a close family member who perished in the Holocaust. But there were also those who had no personal connection to the Holocaust and chose the subject out of intellectual identification and academic interest.

A fourth wave of academic publications dealing with women in the Holocaust began in the early 1990s and peaked towards the end of the decade. In 1993, the first academic anthology on the subject appeared, *Other Voices: Women and the Holocaust,* edited by Carol Ritner and John Roth.[17] Two years later, Dalia Ofer and Lenore Weizmann organized a research workshop in Jerusalem on the topic of "Women in the Holocaust" and in 1998 they published a collected volume on this subject.[18] 1998 and 1999 were extremely fruitful years for academic publications about women during the Holocaust. In addition to Ofer Weizmann's compilation, my book on Gender and the Holocaust appeared,[19] along with Marion Kaplan's book on Jewish women in Nazi Germany,[20] a collection of survivors' testimonies edited by Brana Gurevitch,[21] a literary study by Lillian Kramer on women's literature and the Holocaust,[22] Roger Ritbo and Diane Plotkin's book about Jewish doctors and nurses in the camps,[23] and a collected volume of essays edited by Esther Fuchs entitled *Women and the* Holocaust.[24]

Unlike the situation fifteen years earlier, when the conference on women in the Holocaust relied mainly on survivor testimonies and not scientific research, by the end of the twentieth century Holocaust scholars had at their disposal a growing body of academic studies about women during the Holocaust. Not only did this encourage additional research on the topic; It also made it possible to begin teaching the topic of "Women in the Holocaust" at colleges and universities worldwide.[25]

The Polemic

Then came the resistance. In late May 1998 Gabriel Schoenfeld, editor of the conservative (Jewish) journal *Commentary*, published an article in the Wall Street Journal, a widely circulated, conservative leaning daily newspaper, about what he called "The Cutting Edge of Holocaust Studies." In it, he came out against the academic study of the Holocaust and particularly, the study of Women in the Holocaust.[26] Soon after, under the headline "Auschwitz and the Professors," in June 1998 Schoenfeld expanded his arguments, both against the academization of the Holocaust and the study of Women during the Holocaust. This was very different than the attitude towards other topics in Holocaust study, such as the Judenrat, where there had been initial opposition to some of the conclusions which changed over time, but never to the topic's legitimacy. No one had ever claimed that the Judenrates were not worthy of study, only that it was a very problematic topic, albeit a legitimate research topic. Only when it came to "Women in the Holocaust" had voices been raised questioning its legitimacy as a suitable topic of study.

Back to Schoenfeld. After discussing the failed attempts to fill the newly endowed Chair of Holocaust research at Harvard University which was ultimately cancelled, and lamenting the tendency to turn Holocaust studies into a subsection of "Victimology Studies," he moved on to what he saw as the most dangerous trend in the academization of Holocaust research of those days: "the voguish hybrid known as gender studies,"[27] in other words, the study of women during the Holocaust.

Initially, Schoenfeld phrased his criticism carefully. He mentioned Ringelblum's research in the Warsaw ghetto as an example of a legitimate study of women in the Holocaust. "But it is one thing to carry out such work in the name of honest understanding, and quite another to do so in the name of a naked ideological 'agenda'."[28] From herein the article's tone changed and he began to attack almost everyone who had written on the topic. Mentioning a number of prominent researchers who had published studies on women in the Holocaust, he listed their shortcomings: Ofer and Weitzman, whose book presented distortions of research and various dangerous agendas, Joan Ringelheim, who flirted with relativism when creating an equation between Nazi "sexism" and the exploitation of Jewish women by Jewish men, or poor women and minorities, Myrna Goldenberg who "joyfully announcing" her discovery of "feminist values" in the barracks of Auschwitz, Deborah Rene Kaufman who objected to researchers trying to advance their careers in gender and Holocaust research while doing just that in her own field of sociology, and Ruth Linden who furthered a postmodernist ecological agenda in her research on women and the Holocaust.

Some of the problems he mentioned were methodical; Others were ideological. Claiming that the studies were written in feminist jargon that hinted at the researchers' real agenda, he gave examples of how women survivors were asked leading questions that created gender dilemmas in places where they never existed. By attempting to locate the female Holocaust experience within that of universal victimology, he claimed that feminist scholars denied the Holocaust's uniqueness. In order to suit their agenda, they presented phenomena such as women's mutual existence or caring for women for their families as feminist values, and not as Jewish or human values.

Schonfeld linked all these evils to the priorities of those Holocaust researchers, who were trying to raise feminist consciousness more than Holocaust consciousness. Time and time again he argued that these studies broke the continuum of Jewish existence by creating a barrier between the study of women in the Holocaust and the examination of their Jewish families and communities. By doing so, he claimed they were creating a feminist research bubble that had nothing to do with the Holocaust's historical essence. As proof of the validity of his claims, he cited Ruth Bondy's article in Ofer Weizmann's collection. Bondy, a journalist and writer who survived Terezin and Auschwitz, wrote that she believed that death in the Holocaust did not differentiate between men and women, and that she agreed to participate in the project "with grave reservations." Schoenfeld claims that Bondy's testimony proved that the Nazis did not harm Jewish women out of "sexism" but as part of an ideological decision to exterminate all Jews. Atrocities committed against Jewish women were not male sexual abuse of women as some feminist scholars claim, but part of the extermination process.

What really frightened Schoenfeld in the study of women in the Holocaust and how does this relate to "Auschwitz and the Professors," the article's title? Schoenfeld emphasized that the study of women in the Holocaust is the pinnacle of all the dangers inherent in the academization of the Holocaust. While there may be merit in the kind of research that Ringelblum sought to carry out, i.e. historical research about the lives of women in the Holocaust, he argued, the feminist agenda of contemporary researchers plays into the hands of Holocaust deniers. Emphasizing "female connections," "sexist vulnerability," and "feminist consciousness in the camps," they create an alternative narrative that dwarfs or even erases the Holocaust's central feature - the common fate of all Jews, men, women, and children, under Nazi rule.

Schoenfeld's arguments were not new. Ever since the study of women in the Holocaust became an independent discipline, there had been senior scholars who were unenthusiastic about it, to say the least. Some were still immersed in the concept that the study of women in the Holocaust was a very minor topic and did not feel comfortable with sectoral and gender issues. In a 1990 article, Sara Horowitz of York University describes receiving a similar response from a senior and respected colleague in the field who heard about her intention to study writings by women Holocaust survivors.[29] Marion Kaplan's dissertation advisor, Prof. Fritz Stern, initially discouraged her from focusing on women, but ultimately agreed to her writing about the topic. [30]

If Schoenfeld's arguments against focusing on the lives of women in the Holocaust were not new, how did he manage to provoke such controversy? Initially, because of the medium. There was nothing new in the allegations, but this was the first time they had been put in writing, and publicized in a reputable journal. And because he was a reputed editor and writer, writing about a provocative subject, news agencies circulated the article which was later published in dozens of newspapers across the U.S. and Canada.[31] Schoenfeld was not only a mouthpiece for all those criticizing the discipline before him, but far surpassed them by transferring the polemic from the intellectual sphere to the public one.

The response was almost immediate. As soon as the article appeared, various groups within the academic community began debating where and how to respond. A number of Holocaust scholars began to formulate a rebuttal to be published in *Commentary.* Others preferred to respond in the feminist-Jewish journal *Lilith.*[32] A third group debated whether to respond at all, thinking that any response would grant Schoenfeld and his cohorts legitimacy. Myrna Goldenberg recalled: "After reading the Commentary article, I called Joan Ringelheim to discuss our next move. We were concerned that Schoenfeld would distort and take out of context any response we authored…I wrote him personally to tell him that he misquoted me and owed me an apology or retraction or something. He wrote back to apologize!"[33]

In August 1998, two months after Schoenfeld's article was published, the opening salvo of responses appeared in *Commentary.* The first to respond was Joan Ringelheim, a scholar of gender and philosophy, who had been one of his prime targets. Ringelheim claimed that Schoenfeld had distorted her remarks, maliciously quoting them out of context. Unaware of developments in Holocaust research, so she claimed, he cited her early research while ignoring her later publications in which she had re-examined her conclusions.[34] Dalia Ofer and Lenore Weizmann, whose volume Schoenfeld had attacked, claimed that he had distorted their conclusions as well and explained the rationale behind their research. Myrna Goldenberg argued that Schoenfeld not only deliberately distorted what was written in her research, but also falsely presented the way in which she herself had presented her research conclusions. She never "joyfully announced" her conclusions about women in Auschwitz and didn't even employ the methodologies he attributed to her.

Other respondents such as John Roth, who co-edited the first anthology on women in the Holocaust, expressed sympathy with Schoenfeld's concern that the study of women in the Holocaust be conducted according to the highest research standards, but stressed the difference between this concern and his general contempt for the field. Referring to Schoenfeld's claim that the study of women in the Holocaust is ripe with political agendas, Nehama Tec, a scholar and survivor, asked: "In view of his almost wholesale condemnation, I wonder whom Gabriel Schoenfeld would appoint as appropriate guardians of this field. Does he have in mind journalists? Perhaps people with strong political agendas?"[35]

But there were also respondents who supported his approach. Unlike most of the academic responses, a significant number of readers, some of them survivors, supported Schoenfeld's conclusions. Some mocked what they called the "pseudo-academization" of the Holocaust. Others referred to the "vulgarization of the Holocaust by anyone who pushes the 'isms'." One respondent claimed that if Schoenfeld would had replaced the word "feminist" with the phrase "working class," it would have reminded him of the ideological-Marxist education he received as a child in post-war Poland.

Schoenfeld responded to all the allegations, repeating what he wrote in his original article and emphasizing that studies of women in the Holocaust were nothing more than a platform for advancing a political-feminist agenda. The only argument he withdrew was that about Goldenberg, admitting that she did not announce her conclusions "joyfully." However, he reiterated that the very claim that she had discovered feminist values in Auschwitz seemed absurd to him. In other cases where he failed to respond to the writers' claims, he attacked them from either political or personal directions. In total, the journal published 21 responses, two-thirds of which were penned by academics and researchers.

At this point the controversy shifted from the pages of the conservative magazine to a more liberal arena, the Jewish feminist newspaper *Lilith*. Under the headline "Why is the Wall Street Journal now devaluing women's Holocaust experiences?" the editors referred to Schoenfeld's article as well as the summary published in the daily newspaper as "scornful" and "misogynistic." Over the course of two pages, Holocaust researcher Deborah Lipstadt responded to Schoenfeld's claims about Ofer and Weizmann's book. She was followed by four additional responses: one by Paula Hyman, a Yale historian specializing in Jewish women, who accused Schoenfeld of defaming all researchers in the field, another by Ofer and Weizmann who wrote about the importance of preserving evidence of women's experiences in the Holocaust, a third by Marion Kaplan who emphasized how gender research in the Holocaust allows us to understand the multiplicity of voices during that period, and a fourth by well-known writer and Holocaust survivor Lore Segal, who discussed how natural controversies are, and that everyone is looking for what they consider to be the proper way to memorialize the Holocaust.[36]

With the publication of the responses in *Lilith*, the first act in the controversy came to an end. This phase was characterized by widespread publication of Schoenfeld's arguments in the American daily press, and by relatively quick and brief responses by scholars and others.

The controversy now shifted from the public to the academic arena where the main respondent was a researcher that Schoenfeld had not mentioned at all: Sara Horowitz, a literature professor at York University in Canada. In an extensive article published in the literary journal *Prooftexts* in early 2000, Horowitz reviewed developments in gender and Holocaust research, and the claims of those who opposed it: Why did a colleague warn her not to research the subject at all, instead of researching it out of research responsibility and caution? Why do scholars of literature such as Lawrence Langer claim that any study of gender and the Holocaust automatically becomes a competition for the relative endurance of both sexes? How can Schoenfeld claim that anyone working in the field of women and the Holocaust does so out of a desire to raise their readers' feminist awareness? After all, how can one understand the Holocaust without addressing gender issues? "Gender studies thus has the potential to transform our understanding of this terrible past and of our own relationship to it." She states.[37]

"If Schoenfeld did not mention you in his article, what made you dedicate a long article to him in *Prooftexts*?" I asked Horowitz twenty years after the controversy began. Her answer was short and to the point. "Probably some self-destructive impulse!" She wrote to me jokingly. "I think that when I read GS's article, I felt that its thrust was to de-legitimatize the kind of work I do on two levels – as a literary scholar, and as someone interested in issues of gender. *Prooftexts* was interested in my touching on state-of-the-field issues, and GS article so baldly illustrated the resistance to gender work. Also, because he wrote as a journalist, not a scholar, it was a way of pointing to attitudes outside the academy to such work."[38]

As the ball was now back in Schoenfeld's court, he sent a scathing response to the editor of *Prooftexts*, Prof. David Roskies, accompanied by a letter whose language made it clear that he was convinced that he was writing to a person who understood and perhaps even identified with his approach. On the issue of the journal devoted to the field of gender he wrote that it was like "giving the inmates the opportunity to run the asylum for the day."[39] Roskies showed Horowitz Schonfeld's response and his letter of intent, asking if she would like to respond. "I debated about whether to do so or not – whether writing a serious response somehow elevated his critique, which was so poorly founded…But given that GS's critique would be given space in *Prooftexts*, I felt his comments against gender-based works needed to be refuted."[40]

Schoenfeld said nothing new in his response where he once again attacked Ringelheim, Ofer, Weizmann, and Linden with allegations he had made two years earlier. Although he mentioned Marion Kaplan, one of his critics in *Lilith*, as a researcher who dealt responsibly with women in the Holocaust, he immediately added that she was the exception that proves the rule. The study of gender is not research but propaganda, he concluded, as a summary of all his claims.[41]

Horowitz's response followed immediately. There is no problem in Mr. Schoenfeld's opposing gender studies as a whole and not just gender studies in the Holocaust, she argued, which is clear from his contemptuous language almost bordering on hysteria. But anyone who is so vehemently opposed to any field should at least have minimal knowledge of that field. Schoenfeld, she continued, knows nothing about gender studies and prefers to deliberately misquote gender research, including my own, instead of examining issues in context. He does not understand that examining the Holocaust through the gender prism helps us to better understand the lives and deaths of women and men in the Holocaust, and to emphasize their humanity, so she concluded.

Discussion and Conclusions

Horowitz's response sealed the polemic's public discussion. Schoenfeld and others who opposed the study of women in the Holocaust, were occasionally mentioned at academic conferences or articles, but the public bashing came to an end as the arguments on both sides were quite clear and were summarized in eight points:

1) **False purpose:** The study of women in the Holocaust is an outgrowth of gender studies whose purpose was "raising consciousness," i.e. "propaganda" and not research.

2) **Fashion:** The study of women in the Holocaust is a passing fad like women's studies, which will not stand the test of time.

3) **Trivialization:** Holocaust research becomes trivialized when examined through the lens of a feminist agenda.[42]

4) **Misleading focus:** Holocaust research should be focused on race and not on gender. This is how the Nazis examined the Jews.[43]

5) **Survivor Opinions:** Even survivors such as Ruth Bondy, well acquainted with Holocaust reality, feel that there is no point in examining the issue independently.

6) **Holocaust Revisionism:** The Jewish dimension of the Holocaust is dwarfed and minimized when the lives of women in the Holocaust are presented as a gender struggle, i.e., the enslavement of women by men in a patriarchal society, and not as part of the Nazi assault on Jews. Thus scholars play into the hands of Holocaust revisionists.

7) **Destruction of Jewish Solidarity:** A study that differentiates between men and women during the Holocaust disconnects women from the Jewish community at large, creating a competition between the sexes as to which of them coped better

in the Holocaust. In doing so, they create what literary critic Lawrence Langer calls "the mythology of comparative endurance," destroying the concept of Jewish solidarity in the Holocaust.[44]

8) **Historical anachronism**: The study of women in the Holocaust precedes feminism and thus locates feminism in an era in which it did not yet exist historically.

Each claim was met by a counterclaim. The argument about **false purpose** was countered by stating that Schoenfeld was merely reviving an old argument raised by conservative scholars during the Cold War who referred to "consciousness raising" in feminist history as "propaganda." He also did not understand that "raising consciousness" is merely a form of education: to educate a new generation about the experiences of women in the Holocaust. With regard to **fashion,** Schoenfeld's opponents reminded everyone that the discipline has been studied in depth for over twenty years with new scholars constantly seeking to specialize in the topic.

When it came to the claim of **trivialization**, opponents countered that as long as women's Holocaust experiences are examined factually, nothing about the Holocaust is trivialized. To those claiming the issue of **misleading focus,** opponents argued that a gender focus does not supplant a racial focus on race but adds to it. As to **survivor opinions,** those responding reminded everyone despite her initial opposition, Bondy eventually wrote an in-depth study detailing many important facts about women's lives during the Holocaust, thus joining those studying that field.

What about **Holocaust revisionism?** Here scholars argued that critics forget that two trends can exist simultaneously. The Nazis and their accomplices indeed sought to exterminate all of European Jewry, men and women alike, but until the moment of their death, women's lives were often very different than those of men. Even under Nazi rule, and regardless of the ultimate Nazi gold of exterminating all Jews, there were women who functioned in a state of enslavement in a patriarchal society.

The issue of **Destroying Jewish Solidarity** was one of the most serious claims levelled against the academic study of women during the Holocaust. Here it was argued that clarifying the conditions in which women lived and suffered during the Holocaust does not necessarily create competition between the sexes. There are no "better" or "worse" ways of coping and survival, but different methods, both worthy of examination. And in response to claiming **Historical Anachronism,** responders reminded everyone that Ringelblum was researching the topic already during the war, thus proving there were those who considered it a worthy research topic without any connection to the feminist movement that later emerged.

To better understand not only the claims and counterclaims, but the polemic's entire dynamic, let us return to Brandt's model presented earlier that deals with the dynamics of ideological and intergenerational conflicts. Looking deeper, this appears to be a typical conflict of this kind. It ostensibly includes all the elements that Brandt and his associates mentioned: locating a target group whose values they perceive as conflicting with or threatening their own values, demonstrating intolerance towards it, and selectively presenting information about it to convince others of the risk it poses, with the length and intensity of their response being determine by the degree of threat it feels towards its values and moral convictions.

But there are a number of points that cast doubt on whether this is a purely ideological controversy. First the focus. Schoenfeld's article initially dealt with the Holocaust's academization, and only later did he turn his attention to the study of women in the Holocaust. Of the 21 responses that appeared in *Commentary*, 14 referred to the academization argument, two of which also touched upon the study of women in the Holocaust. Why, then, did the debate over the academization of the Holocaust ended there, while the polemic surrounding the study of women in the Holocaust lasted for more than three years, moving from the press to scholarly journals?

Schoenfeld's arguments against academization of the Holocaust were as severe as those he raised against the study of women during the Holocaust. And if one claims that the discussion of the first issue ended as academization of the Holocaust was already a fait accompli, then one can make the same claim regarding the study women during the Holocaust. The topic had been studied in depth for over twenty years, including by research bodies founded in major academic and public institutions such as the International Research Institute on Jewish Women in Brandeis (founded in 1998 and renamed Hadassah-Brandeis Institute), the

Fania Gottesfeld Heller Woman at Bar Ilan University (founded 1998), and the Remember the Women Institute in New York (founded 1997).

A second point to note is the polemic's intensity. Brandt argues that the length and intensity of the dominant group's response is determined by the degree of threat it feels towards it values and moral convictions. As the editor of a popular conservative Jewish monthly, Schoenfeld was a busy man. And yet, he devoted an extraordinary amount of time and effort to publishing repeated personal attacks against women scholars specializing in the lives of women during the Holocaust. Instead of toning down his language over time and adopting a more balanced response, he seemed to react acutely in a way that appears disproportionate to the "threat" at hand. Why was that so?

A third point was the plethora of offensives, in terms of both arguments and platforms. At least eight different arguments were raised against the academic study of women during the Holocaust and pursued on academic, public and literary platforms. Many of the arguments were immediately shown to be factually incorrect: the gendered focus did not eliminate or surpass the racial one; In practice, there was little opposition among the survivors to the study of women during the Holocaust;[45] The study of women in the Holocaust was not a matter of "fashion" but had existed for nearly two decades before the polemic; Scholars have highlighted that the study of women during the Holocaust focused on their lives rather than their deaths, did not necessarily become an endurance race between the sexes, is not anachronistic, and the traditional oppression of women by men did not negate the Nazi persecution of all Jews but rather added a dimension to the double jeopardy facing Jewish women during the Holocaust. These allegations were answered shortly after they were raised, including the claim that those dealing with women during the Holocaust were playing into the hands of Holocaust deniers.

This last argument, which could have been considered threatening and decisive, might have explained the intensity of response according to Brandt's model, and its broad dissemination. But the argument soon proved to be untrue. If so, which argument posed against the study of women in the Holocaust can explain Schoenfeld and colleagues' seemingly disproportionate response to the study of women during the Holocaust?

A careful examination points to only one argument that can explain the response's severity and its scope: the claim that by isolating the study of Jewish women during the Holocaust as a separate topic one is destroying Jewish solidarity. This argument becomes even more significant when we examine the Holocaust's role during the late twentieth century in the three centers of contemporary Jewish life: Europe, the United States and the State of Israel. In Europe, the Holocaust was proof of European guilt vis a vis their historical attitude toward the Jews, towards the war, and even a tool for regulating contemporary public attitudes toward the Jews; In the United States it was one of the two pillars of American Jewish identity at the time, with the other being the State of Israel; In the State of Israel it served as an central argument for the need to establish the state. Anything that could chip away at Jewish solidarity during the Holocaust, thus undermining the use of the Holocaust as a key element of identity, becomes potentially dangerous as well.

There were naturally those who were expressing their concern regarding the topic and thus called it "trivialization," in other words, derailing research from those topics that people considered more important, more scholarly, or more urgently in need of study that had not yet been examined. But this could be said about any of the new topics in Holocaust study. The lack of opposition to the study of such topics, including that focusing on the lives of LGBTQ members during the Holocaust, as opposed to the vehement opposition to studying women during the Holocaust, makes it difficult to accept this as a major claim. Furthermore, some might state that part of the opposition to the study of women in the Holocaust came from the fact that most of the researchers were women who were trying to make their mark in various research disciplines that they had entered. There was, however, no parallel opposition in countries such as Germany, Austria, and other European countries, to scholars studying the topic such as Gisela Bock, Insa Eschebach and others. Nor was there overt opposition to women in the United States who were concentrating on the lives of women during the Holocaust in Germany, such as studies by Marion Kaplan, Atina Grossmann and others, who, other than possibly at a very initial stage, never had to "struggle" for acceptance in researching their chosen topic.

Bearing this in mind, the controversy over the study of women and the Holocaust does not appear to have been ideological or intergenerational, but rather one focusing on identity, which could explain Schoenfeld and company's disproportionate responses. Not a polemic that dealt with the memory of the victims, but one focusing on the struggle to preserve a major component of American Jewish identity.

This also explains the polemic's practical implications. A number of Holocaust scholars were personally tainted by the allegations. Others were professionally harmed. Joan Ringelheim recalled: "At the time, I was chair of the Department of Education at the US Holocaust Memorial Museum, and his [Schoenfeld's] article made people so nervous that they tried to get me out of the position. It took more than a year but the Museum eventually did so, and I returned to being head of Oral History."[46] Ruth Linden was also personally and professionally harmed by what Schoenfeld wrote against her.[47] Myrna Goldenberg recalled that after what Schonfeld wrote about her, she was no longer considered eligible to judge projects at the National Endowment for the Humanities.[48] "I had been a frequent reviewer of proposals, but Lynne Cheney, NEH Director at the time, crossed my name off the possible list of reviewers for any kind of proposals (women's studies, community college, composition, etc.). I was no longer in consideration. At one Community College Humanities Association Conference, she attended a session in which I presented, wrote furiously while I spoke, and walked out when I was finished. Such childish behavior. I couldn't even get angry at such infantile behavior."[49]

European researchers were not mentioned in the article and the situation of Holocaust research in Israel was fundamentally different than that in the USA due to the existence of Yad Vashem, the national Holocaust memorial authority that served as a hub for Holocaust research across the country. Although there were Holocaust scholars in Israel who were not particularly enthusiastic about the study of women during the Holocaust as it was not considered a "major topic," there was no ideological opposition to its study, nor was it seen as a factor that could unravel Jewish solidarity during the Holocaust. Dalia Ofer recalled: "There was no opposition at the [Hebrew] University nor at Yad Vashem although they had discussed it [the article] in depth. They knew about the article, but the majority paid it little attention, including Prof. Israel Gutman when I discussed it with him."[50]

The situation was different in the United States where senior academic figures, journalist and even survivors believed in what Schoenfeld had stressed: that examining the lives of Jewish women during the Holocaust using gender tools harms the Holocaust's essence as a unifying factor, thus undermining American Jewish solidarity. This also explains the polemic's professional and personal ricochets that for quite a number of years, continued to affect a number of academic scholars already engaged in studying the field, some of whom changed direction and even left the profession as a result, especially if they were as yet untenured. In other words, despite the fact that Schoenfeld had left the arena long ago, the damage that he did to a number of women scholars continued to wreak havoc for many years, changing their professional trajectory and lives for over a decade.

Epilogue

Over the years, the radical and cultural feminist approach to the topic has all but disappeared. It is hard to determine how much of this was related to the polemic, or whether it was connected to emerging research trends in gender studies as a whole. At the same time, the study of women in the Holocaust began to take on new directions, both in the social sciences and in the humanities. Scholars began to examine feminist theology of the Holocaust, sexual violence during the Holocaust, women's functioning within the family unit during the Holocaust, and even queer theory and the Holocaust, all of which merited books and articles appearing during the first decades of the twenty-first century.

Now it was clear to most of the scholars, and the public, that despite various polemics, it was very important to study the topic of women during the Holocaust. The depth and richness of the topic that unfolded made it obvious to all that it would be impossible to continue studying the Holocaust through a uniform and seemingly all-encompassing prism which, in most cases, was actually a male prism. Only as time passed and the research on the topic continued, did it become clear that to fully understand the experiences of women during the Holocaust their lives had to be examined separately from those of men.

Historical research about women during the Holocaust has also developed in new directions. These included the commemoration and memory of women during the Holocaust, ultra-Orthodox woman during and after the Holocaust, and monographs devoted to key figures active in the survival and rescue of Jews in occupied Europe and the free world. Forty years after serious academic research on Jewish women in the Holocaust took shape, a book was published that focused not only on the research, but on the researchers, a volume of academic ego-documents written by close to thirty women scholars who had devoted years of their lives to researching the subject.[51] Such a project proves that the study of women in the Holocaust has long become a mainstream topic, attracting young researchers and offers them mentors and advisors who are veteran researchers in the field. Just as the "third generation" era of Holocaust survivor offspring has begun, we are on the brink of the "third generation" era of researchers studying women and gender during and after the Holocaust.

To close the circle, we now return to the beginning. What do those who were part of this formative controversy twenty years ago think about it today?

Even from a twenty-year perspective, Gabriel Schoenfeld did not change his mind on the subject, nor did spare those involved in the field from a tongue lashing:

> It has indeed been a long time since I stirred that particular hornet's nest, but I will try to answer your questions. My objection was and is not in the least to the study of women in the Holocaust; it is an entirely legitimate topic for inquiry. I made that point in my piece itself, noting that the study of the subject is 'hardly without merit.' My quarrel was with the way such study was being carried out. The most serious wrongdoing, in my view, consisted of purveying nonsense and/or of applying highly ideological modes of inquiry to a subject of the utmost gravity. Both in my piece and in my response to my critics, I cited quite a few specific examples…I also objected to the ongoing academization of the Holocaust, and regarded the entrance of the faddish "gender studies" into the realm a disturbing landmark--but not the only such--in academization's progress. I must say that the prospect of a collection of 30 'academic autobiographies' of women scholars makes it sound as if inquiry into the Holocaust has now been replaced by Holocaust scholars

studying themselves....As for how treatment of the topic has evolved in the two decades since I wrote that article...if, as you report, Holocaust scholarship has moved away from the cultural and radical feminism of the 80s and 90s, perhaps I can claim a little credit for that welcome shift.[52]

Although I understood Schoenfeld's intention and concern, as one of the women who had studied and still studies the topic for more than thirty years, I am very pleased that the study of women during the Holocaust has developed in different and multifaceted directions. This feeling was strengthened when I edited a path-breaking study with Dalia Ofer about the journey that close to thirty prominent women scholars had undertaken when choosing to study women during the Holocaust. The conclusions we drew pointed to the fact that although we all come from different places and different disciplines, and each of us have our own opinions and have taken our research to different directions, we had the same goal – to shed light upon an important topic in Holocaust research, one that dealt with more than fifty percent of those who had gone through the Holocaust, the women.[53]

John Ringelheim: "I did not change the tone of my research at all given what he said...I think that Schoenfeld's ideas came at a particular time in the history of that work and institutions were much more sensitive--don't know if he could write that now and get any resonance. This is a complicated subject however. Good that you are writing about this."[54]

Ruth Linden: "What an awful memory! I vaguely recall asking my old friend, Debby Kaufman, if she wanted to collaborate on a letter in response to him to *Lilith* magazine but I don't recall why we... decided not to write it...It was a while ago.[55]"

Myrna Goldenberg: "The few of us whom he cited so negatively felt good that he noticed us. It meant that we, indeed, were a threat. If we hadn't been noticed and insulted, it would have meant that our work was simply disregarded. I, for one, knew I was saying something noteworthy. He never would have bothered with that ill-advised article if he felt that were weren't worth a fight!"[56]

Sarah Horowitz: "I imagined for a moment that my arguments would be persuasive to Gabriel Schoenfeld or to the other diehards. But readers whose minds were open, who were not ensconced or invested in a particular view, deserved to hear the counter arguments. So I do think it worked in terms of future generations of scholars. I think even among many 'old guard' scholars, even if in their heart of hearts they were not entirely persuaded, most see that this is the way the field has gone – that the lens of gender is integrated into the legitimate study of basically everything, and that to be considered current and part of the ongoing scholarly conversation, they have to leave behind an automatic bias against gender studies. I think that Jewish Studies, generally, was more resistant to Women's Studies and Gender Studies that most other academic fields. And that Holocaust Studies was even more resistant than Jewish Studies. But I do think there has been a climate change in both areas."[57]

Marion Kaplan: "It took a while for things to change. I recently saw a letter that a colleague wrote, asking a German historian (in the late 1970s?) to chair a panel of three of us – he found the topics trivial but would have agreed to chair IF one of us happened to be his cousin (he recognized the name). My colleague wrote back that that was an unprofessional reason and thanked him and withdrew the offer. So, not sure the "field" welcomes us. We just charged in!"[58]

Endnotes

1   Dr. Joan Miriam Ringelheim, a researcher of Gender and Philosophy, was then a Kent Fellow at the Center for the Humanities as Wesleyan University, after which she directed the Educational Department and finally the Oral Documentation Division of the United States Holocaust Memorial Museum. Author's correspondence with Joan Ringelheim, August 13, 2018.

2   Dr. Esther Katz was then a historian at NYU. She was deputy director of the Institute for Research in History and today directs the Margaret Sanger Papers Project at NYU. Author's correspondence with Esther Katz, August 6, 2018.

3   Ava F. Kahn, Review of Esther Katz and Joan Miriam Ringelheim, *Women Surviving the Holocaust*, New York: Institute for Research in History, 1983," *The Public Historian* 7(3) (Summer 1985), pp. 104-106; "Focus on Issues: Women Surviving the Holocaust," *JTA*, March 29, 1983.

4   The first academic course about Women during the Holocaust that I could find appears to have been taught by Konnilyn Feig in 1984 at Foothill College in Los Altos Hills in California. See: R. Ruth Linden, "Troubling Categories I Can't Think Without: Reflections on Women in the Holocaust," *Contemporary Jewry* 17(1) (January 1996), pp. 18-33.

5   Mark J. Brandt et al., "The Ideological-Conflict Hypothesis: Intolerance Among Both Liberals and Conservatives," *Current Directions in Psychological Science* 23(1) (2014), pp. 27-34. DOI: 10.1177/0963721413510932

6   Distributing questionnaires as the basis of social research was an accepted social science research method in Eastern Europe following their use by the YIVO Institute during the 1930s in various European Jewish communities.

7   Dalia Ofer, "Her View Through My Lens: Cecelia Slepak Studies Women in the Warsaw Ghetto," in Judith Tydor Baumel and Tova Cohen (eds.), *Gender, Place, and Memory in the Modern Jewish Experience: Re-Placing Ourselves* (London and Portland, OR, 2003), pp. 29-50.

8   These include Olga Lengyl, *Five Chimneys* (Chicago, 1947); Gisella Perl, *I Was a Doctor in Auschwitz* (New York, 1948); Kitty Hart, *I Am Alive* (London, 1946); Mary Berg, *The Diary of Mary Berg* (New York, 1945); Gusta Dranger, *Pamietnik Justyny* (Krakow, 1946); Rozka Korchak, *Flames in Ash* (Tel Aviv, 1946) (Hebrew); Zvia Lubetkin, *Last on the Wall* (Ein Harod, 1947) (Hebrew).

9   Jason Thompson, "Writing About Trauma: Catharsis or or Rumination?" *Philosophy, Psychiatry, & Psychology* 17(3) (September 2010), pp. 275-277. See also Ella Lingens-Reiner, *Prisoner of Fear* (London, 1948); Severyna Szmaglewska, *Smoke Over Birkenau* (New York, 1947); Luciana Nissim Momigliano, *Ricordi della casa dei morti* (Torino, 1946); Liana Millu, *Il Fumo di Birkenau* (Milano, 1947); Raya Kagan, *Women in Hell's Office* (Eretz Israel, 1947) (Hebrew); Shlomo Ahkenazi, *The Heroism of the Women of Israel* (Tel Aviv, 1946) (Hebrew).

10　Grete Salus, *Eine Frau Erzaehlt* (Bonn, 1958); Marga Minco, *Bitter Herbs: A Chronicle* (New York, 1960); Gemma LaGuardia Gluck, *My Story* (New York, 1961); Halina Birnbaum, *Nadzieja umira ostatnia* (Warsaw, 1967); Vladka Meed, *On Both Sides of the Wall: Memoirs from the Warsaw Ghetto* (New York, 1972); Rachel Auerbach, *In the Streets of Warsaw, 1939-1945* (Tel Aviv, 1954) (Hebrew); Basia Berman-Temkin, *Diary in the Underground* (Tel Aviv, 1955) (Hebrew); Helena Sharshevska, *Between the Cross and the Mezuza* (Merhavia, 1969) (Hebrew); Fredka Mazia, *Friends in Upheaval* (Jerusalem, 1964) (Hebrew).

11　Fania Fenelon, *Playing for Time* (New York, 1977); Isabella Leitner, *Fragments of Isabella* (New York, 1978); Charlotte Delbo, *None of Us Will Return: Auschwitz and After* (Boston, 1978); Leesha Rose, *The Tulips Are Red* (New York, 1979); Bertha Ferderber-Satz, *And the Sun Kept Shining* (New York, 1980); Georgia Gabor, *My Destiny: Survivor of the Holocaust* (Arcadia, CA, 1981); Frida Michelson, *I Survived Rumbuli* (New York, 1981); Sara Zyskind, *Stolen Years* (New York, 1981); Gerda Schild Haas, *These I do Remember: Fragments from the Holocaust* (Salt Lake City, 1982); Kitty Hart, *Return to Auschwitz* (New York, 1982); Agnes Sassoon, *Agnes: How my Spirit Survived* (Edgeware, Middlesex, 1983); Aranka Siegal, *Grace in the Wilderness* (New York, 1985); Alicia Appleman-Jurman, *My Story* (New York, 1990); Bela Yaari-Hazan, *My Name is Bronislawa* (Tel Aviv, 1991) (Hebrew).

12　Voices from the Canada Commando (Jerusalem, 1989) (Hebrew). See also: Lore Shelley (ed.), *Secretaries of Death: Accounts by Former Prisoners who worked in the Gestapo of Auschwitz* (New York, 1986); Vera Laska (ed.), *Women in the Resistance and in the Holocaust: The Voices of Eyewitness* (Westport and London, 1983); Ruth Schwertfeger, *Women of Theresienstadt: Voices from a Concentration Camp,* (Oxford and New York, 1989); Karin Berger, Eilsabeth Holzinger, Lotte Podgornik, Lisbeth, Trallor, *Ich geb Dir einen Mantel, dass Du ihn noch in Freiheit tragen kannst: Widerstehen im KZ Oesterrichische Frauen erzaehlen* (Fulda, 1987). A unique Hebrew-language book published during this period was *Lochmat Nashim* (Tel Aviv, 1979).

13　Marion Kaplan, *The Making of the Jewish Middle Class* (New York and Oxford, 1991); Marion Kaplan, *The Jewish Feminist Movement in Germany: The Campaigns of the Judischer Frauenbund, 1904-1938* (Westport, CT, 1979); Renate Bridenthal, Atina Grossmann, and Marion Kaplan (eds.), *When Biology Became Destiny: Women in Weimar and Nazi Germany* (New York, 1984); Claudia Koonz, *Mothers in the Fatherland: Women, the Family and Nazi Politics* (New York, 1987); Rita Thalmann, "Juedische Frauen nach dem Pogrom 1938," in Arnold Paucker, Sylvia Gilchrist, and Barbara Suchin (eds.), *The Jews in Nazi Germany 1933-1945* (Tübingen, 1986), pp. 295-302; Claudia Koonz, "Courage and Choice Among German Jewish Women and Men," in Paucker, Gilchrist, and Suchin (eds.), *The Jews in Nazi Germany*, pp. 295-302; Gisele Bock, *Zwangssterilisation im Nationalsozialismus: Studien zur Rassenpolitik und Frauenpolitik* (Opladen, 1986).

14 Andreas Lixi Purcell, *Women of Exile: German Jewish Autobiographies since 1933* (New York, Westport, CO, and London, 1988); Gabriele Kreis, *Frauen Im Exil. Dichtung und Wirklichkeit* (Dusseldorf, 1984).

15 Marlene E. Heinemann, *Gender and Destiny: Women Writers and the Holocaust* (Westport, CO, 1986).

16 Joan S. Ringelheim, "Women and the Holocaust: A Reconsideration of Research," *Signs* 10 (1985), pp. 741-761; Joan S. Ringelheim, "The Unethical and the Unspeakable: Women and the Holocaust," *Simon Wiesenthal Center Annual* 1 (1984), pp. 69-87.

17 Carol Rittner and John Roth, *Different Voices: Women and the Holocaust* (New York, 1993).

18 Dalia Ofer and Lenore Weitzman, *Women and the Holocaust* (New Haven and London, 1998).

19 Judith Tydor Baumel, *Double Jeopardy: Gender and the Holocaust* (London, 1998).

20 Marion Kaplan, *Between Dignity and Despair: Jewish Life in Nazi Germany* (New York, 1996).

21 Brana Gurewitsch (ed.), *Mothers, Sisters, Resisters: Oral Histories of Women Who Survived the Holocaust* (Tuscaloosa, AL, 1998).

22 S. Lilian Kremer, *Women's Holocaust Writing: Memory and Imagination* (Lincoln, NE, 1999).

23 Roger Ritvo and Diane Plotkin, *Sisters in Sorrow: Voices of Care in the Holocaust* (College Station, TX, 1998).

24 Esther Fuchs (ed.), *Women and the Holocaust* (Lanham, MD, 1999).

25 See note 4 above.

26 Gabriel Schoenfeld, "The Cutting Edge of Holocaust Studies," *The Wall Street Journal*, May 21, 1998, p. 16.

27 Gabriel Schoenfeld, "Auschwitz and the Professors," *Commentary* 105(6) (June 1998), pp. 42-46.

28 G. Schoenfeld, "Auschwitz and the Professors": 43.

29 Sara R. Horowitz, "Gender, Genocide, and Jewish Memory," *Prooftexts* 20(1-2) (Winter/Spring 2000), p. 180.

30 Author's correspondence with Marion Kaplan, August 14, 2018.

31 Author's correspondence with R. Ruth Linden August 18, 2018.

32 Author's correspondence with R. Ruth Linden August 13, 2018.

33 Author's correspondence with Myrna Goldenberg, August 14, 2018.

34 Joan Ringelheim in "Controversy: Holocaust Studies, Gabriel Schoenfeld and Critics," *Commentary* 106(1) (August 1998), pp. 14-25. All responses cited appear in this issue.

35 Nechama Tec, "Controversy: Holocaust Studies, Gabriel Schoenfeld, and Critics," *Commentary* 106(1) (August 1998), pp. 14-25.

36 Deborah E. Lipstadt, "Why is the Wall Street Journal Now Devaluing Women's Holocaust Experiences," *Lilith* (Fall 1998), pp. 10-13.

37 Horowitz, "Gender, Genocide, and Jewish Memory."

38 Author's correspondence with Sara Horowitz, August 12, 2018.

39 Sarah R. Horowitz, "Controversy, A Response to Gabriel Schoenfeld," *Prooftexts* 21(2) (Spring 2001), pp. 279-283.

40 Author's correspondence with Sara Horowitz, August 12, 2018.

41 Gabriel Schoenfeld," Controversy, Feminist Approaches to the Holocaust,"*Prooftexts* 21(2) (Spring 2001), pp. 277-279.

42 Lisa Pine, "Gender and Holocaust Victims: A Reappraisal," *Journal of Jewish Identities* 1(2) (2008), p. 123.

43 Erika Potter, "Feminist Interpretations of Holocaust History," *Mt. Royal Undergraduate Humanities Review* 4 (2017), p. 37.

44 Lawrence Langer, "Gendered Suffering? Women in Holocaust Testimonies", in Ofer and Weitzman, *Women and the Holocaust*, pp. 351-363.

45 Sara Horowitz wrote to me as follows: "One place I never felt resistant to looking at women and gender as issues was the community of survivors. Interesting, no?" Author's correspondence with Sara Horowitz, August 12, 2018.

46 Author's correspondence with Joan Ringelheim, August 13, 2018.

47 Author's correspondence with Ruth Linden, August 13, 2018.

48 The National Endowment for the Humanities is the Federal organization supporting studies of the Humanities in the USA.

49 Author's correspondence with Myrna Goldenberg, August 14, 2018.

50 Author's correspondence with Dalia Ofer, August 19, 2018.

51 Judith Tydor Baumel-Schwartz and Dalia Ofer (eds.), *Her Story, My Story? Writing about Women and the Holocaust* (Bern, 2020).

52 Author's correspondence with Gabriel Schoenfeld, August 12, 2018.

53 Tydor Baumel-Schwartz and Ofer, *Her Story*.

54 Author's correspondence with Joan Ringelheim, August 13, 2018.

55 Author's correspondence with R. Ruth Linden, August 13, 2018.

56 Author's correspondence with Myrna Goldenberg, August 14, 2018.

57 Author's correspondence with Sara Horowitz, August 13, 2018.

58 Author's correspondence with Marion Kaplan, August 13, 2018.

Aviva Halamish

Our Aliyah from Germany to Eretz Yisrael, 1933
The Story of a Family, the Story of an Era

Friday, March 31, 1933. As usual, every Saturday evening, members of the Maass family gathered after candle lighting for Kiddush and a festive meal. They were apprehensive about tomorrow, April 1, the date on which the Nazi regime's declared boycott of Jewish firms, and professionals was to begin. At the end of the meal, the family members moved into the living room of their spacious home, and the father, Alfred-Yitzhak, announced that he and his wife, Lucie, had decided that the family would leave Germany and move to Eretz Israel, as soon as possible. First, their daughter, Mariana (Rushka) and their son, Gerhard (Gershon), aged 24 and 21, would emigrate, and at the end of the school year they would join them along with their younger daughters, Hannah-Ruth, 13, and Eva-Dorothea (Netanya, called Tushi by all), age nine. And so it was. All six members of the family, the parents and the four children, left Germany and immigrated to Eretz Israel in 1933.

In research and public discourse there is no general and unequivocal agreement as to the time frame of the "Holocaust period" (and the brief reference here is to its starting point only). Those who date it early see Hitler's rise to power in Germany in January 1933 as the beginning of the Holocaust, and even some of those who determine it as beginning later tend to accept 1933 as the beginning of the Holocaust in <u>Germany</u>.[1] In any case, it is generally agreed that German Jewry had a relatively long period of time to react to the gradually increasing danger, and had more of an opportunity to choose between various possible responses than Jews in countries occupied by Germany from September 1, 1939 onwards. Furthermore, in matters of definitions and terminology, there is no uniform terminology regarding Jews under Nazi or collaborationist rule, or those who fled to the Soviet Union during World War II (in Germany: since 1933; in Austria since the Anschluss in 1938) and were alive at the end of the war. The most common terms used are: *Sordei Shoah* ("Holocaust survivors"), *Nitzolei Shoah* ("Having been Saved from the Holocaust") and *She'erit HaPleitah* ("The Surviving Remnant").[2] Even if we adopt the definition of "Holocaust survivors," which is more prevalent recently, it might be more correct to use the term *Nitzolei Shoah* for Jews who left continental Europe in the 1930s, including members of the Maass family: they were saved from the Holocaust because they left on time.

Dr. Alfred-Yitzhak Maass had been a Zionist since studying at the Ludwig-Maximilian University in Munich, where he received a doctorate in political economy in 1911. After serving in the German army during the First World War, he joined a Zionist club in Mannheim where he met Lucie (née Friedmann), who had lost her husband Louis Schwartz in 1912. Lucie had joined the Zionist group during the war, probably under the influence of her friend, the painter Herman Struck. Alfred and Lucie married in 1919 and moved to Cologne, where he managed a bank branch. They intended to immigrate to Mandatory Palestine after Alfred turned 50, when he could take early retirement and receive a monthly pension. However, shortly after Hitler came to power, they decided to immigrate as soon as possible. In September 1933 their eldest daughter and son reached Palestine, and they followed in November with their two younger daughters.

The Maass family lived at 21 Virschuwstrasse in Cologne in a three-story house with a basement, an attic, and eleven rooms, surrounded by a beautiful garden. As a well-to-do family, they immigrated under A1 certificates, intended for the wealthy ("Capitalists" in British Mandate immigration terminology), those who possessed at least £ 1,000. The family transferred part of their capital to Palestine under the terms of the "transfer" agreement.[3] Alfred Maass's honest integrity and innocence did not ease his absorption in Palestine. He soon lost all his fortune, and suddenly passed away less than three years after his immigration, from heartbreak, as the family used to say.

I had been familiar with the saga of the family members in Germany and the various stages of their immigration since childhood. Between first and third grade I studied in a second shift, and to compensate me for the fact that I ate lunch alone, five days a week my mother, Hannah kept me company during the meal, telling me stories about her life and that of her family. I listened eagerly, and learned a lot. Years later, on the third anniversary of Lucie's (called "Mutti" by everyone, having passed away in 1976 on her 90th birthday) death the family published a booklet in her memory, from which I re-learned what I already knew about the family history along with a few new details.[4]

Later, I wrote a doctoral dissertation on Zionist immigration policy in the 1930s, and in the introduction to a book based on it I wrote: "How does a person choose his research topic? Clearly in addition to direct academic considerations, and motivations deriving from contemporary Israeli society, I had personal reasons to examine the immigration and absorption policy of the Zionist Organization during the 1930s, even if I was not fully aware of them." I briefly recounted the story of my father's immigration and that of his family from Poland during the 1930s and my mother's and her family's immigration in 1933, and dedicated the book with respect and love to my grandfather Dr. Alfred-Yitzhak Maass (1885-1936) and my grandmother Lucie née Friedmann (1886-1976). While my family history, albeit subconsciously, had caused me to choose my research topic, the research in turn enriched my understanding of the family history, allowing me to view the personal, family story, in a broader, more general context.

In this spirit, the present article is a circular move: from the general story to the family story, and from there back to a re-examination of the broader story. In order to understand the family story that I will relate, based on the video whose details are presented in the next paragraph and on additional evidence, one must be familiar with the historical background of the events described, during the first half of the 1930s, in Germany and Palestine. The video, in turn, enables us to further understand the period, serving as a case study of the broader phenomena of that time, such as the implementation of the "Transfer agreement," and difficulties in learning Hebrew that were common to many German-speaking expatriates. One should naturally avoid sweeping generalizations at the macro-historical level based on discussion of micro-history. As Carlo Ginzburg, pioneer of the micro-historical approach, teaches us, one must move back and forth between micro-history and macro-history, **being meticulous in presenting the text against the context and in** examining the effect of context on text.[5] The following discussion is therefore based on various types of material. Alongside memoirs and testimonies about this period related in hindsight, it also draws on historical research regarding the 1930s, studies of the experiences of Jewish immigrants from Germany during this period, and research about the gendered aspects of immigration from Germany.

Let us now turn to the video that is at the center of this discussion. As we neared the seventieth anniversary of my family's immigration (2003), I decided to make a film about this formative event. I spoke in advance with the four "children" of the family, who were then 94, 91, 83 and 79, and we agreed that they would address four issues: how the decision was made to leave Germany and immigrate to Palestine; The journey to Palestine; Absorption issues during the early years; and finally, a retrospective assessment of the decision to leave Germany and immigrate to Palestine. I interviewed each of the four separately for about half an hour; the photographer, my nephew Gal Nimri, edited the recorded material (a total of about two and a half hours), added stills from the family's vast photo collection, and included background music. Thus we composed a 14 minute video that can be viewed with English subtitles at this link: *https://www.youtube.com/watch?v=k1WTKKsIcsI&feature=youtu.be* The full transcript of the video is provided in the article's appendix.

The segments included in the edited film were selected according to two criteria. The first was essentially technical - the time frame, which we determined would not exceed 15 minutes. The second was content: there were quite a few anecdotes of interest to family members in the recorded segments, but not only did they not have any meaning for a broader audience, they also did not fit the project's delineated framework as phrased in the aforementioned questions. Moreover, more than one family member told the identical story, albeit using a somewhat different style. We therefore chose the most appropriate version in terms of wording and, more than once, also in terms of the ability to combine it with a segment from another interviewee, thus creating a narrative sequence that would be historically accurate (according to the rules of cross-evidencing) while meeting the criterion of presenting a flowing and interesting story.

The information and insights that emerge from the video and the family memorial booklet are grouped into two genres. One is autobiography: the stories of the son and the three daughters, particularly the two younger ones, are chapters in each and every one of their autobiographies while also being slivers of a group and family autobiography; The second genre is biography: the stories are segments of the family matriarch's biographical mosaic.

The stories narrated in the video and those appearing in the booklet are, of course, testimonies given long after the events being described occurred. Such materials suffer from a built-in (immanent) deficiency resulting from the long period of time elapsing between the events and their oral or written reconstruction, and due to the known failures of memory which by its very nature is selective. Thus they raise problems of credibility and issue of how much one can rely on them as a historical source. Recently, there has been a growing tendency to rely on memory in reconstructing the past, raising the fear among some historians that, in the words of historian Yoav Gelber, memory "that emerges somewhere between longing and research, threatens to deprive history of its monopoly on the past." Gelber claims that an attitude towards the past based on memory, individual or collective, is not history but just the opposite.[6] Indeed, every historian wonders how to treat oral history, written or recorded long after the fact. While it often illuminates various issues for the historian and through them, for the readers, from additional angles than those of contemporary sources, adding "color" to the story, it is accepted that they cannot be used as a sole source to study a period and reconstruct its history. It is different, however, when reconstructing a personal or family story.

The video and the family memorial booklet have ego-document characteristics. This term, coined by Dutch historian Jacques Presser in 1958, defines a broad category embracing different types of texts, in which the author is also the subject of the story. These are texts of a biographical nature, such as autobiographies, memoirs, diaries and personal letters. Since 1958, extensive methodological literature has developed on ego-documentation, but it seems that "the question of what makes a text an ego-document is still being debated."[7] For the purpose of this discussion, it is sufficient to define it as: "a text in which the author writes about his or her actions, thoughts and feelings," as well as "documents in which 'Ego' is willingly or unwillingly revealed or hidden."[8]

Although it is customary to consider ego-documents to be self-contained items, a subjective reflection of the past as told by the narrator, in our case the stories told by the video's protagonists are supported by additional sources. The video therefore fits what I call "the Triple Iron Rule" of oral testimony: cross-referencing testimonies of different interviewees, each of whom gave testimony separately; confirmation of what was said in the interview by other sources, in other words, the existence of additional references to issues mentioned in the testimonies, preferably those from the period during which the events took place; and the use of oral testimony simply for the purpose of adding "color" to a story lacking other suitable and reliable sources.[9]

In the years since the video was produced I have presented it to different audiences (in addition to the family circle) and have seen, to my delight, that it is more than a family story. It is also the story of an era, in the spirit of what was written in the memorial booklet for the family matriarch:

Still in Mutti's lifetime I thought that her special personality and life history deserved to be told and broadly described by a gifted author. As much as her personality and fate is unique and special - they also reflect the history of that era, one of many upheavals and events in the life of German Jewry.[10]

Contrary to previous trends in the study of German Jews in general and their immigration in particular, since the 1990s, there has been a movement towards widespread use of oral history and autobiographies,[11] and in Germany, the study of German Jewish immigration based on oral history and autobiographies is flourishing.[12] As time passed, the proportion of essays written by women, and writing based on interviews with women regarding the history of German Jews in Palestine, increased. These studies were initially based on published items, a genre in which men had a quantitative advantage. For example, in Guy Miron's path-breaking book *From "There" to "Here" in the First Person* (in Hebrew), only a few pages are dedicated to women's autobiographies and he found no unique female typology detached from the general, male, one.[13]   A few years later, Miron wrote an article about memoirs of middle-class women who immigrated to Palestine[14] and since then, quite a number of publications have appeared that focus on women who immigrated from Germany to Palestine.

As stated previously, the video is composed of autobiographical fragments of the four children, along with sections of their mother's biography. The discussion here focuses on her story and on those of her two younger daughters. My gendered observation of the family story began with a casual conversation with my mother. I told her that I was going to Jerusalem for a research workshop on immigration through a gender prism.[15] My mother wondered - why should everything be examined from a gender perspective, what is the use of that? I responded with the question: "Mother, who pushed to leave Germany and immigrate to Eretz Yisrael?" Without hesitation she replied: "Mutti." This matter is not explicitly mentioned in the video, but is supported by the other family source, the booklet in memory of "Mutti" in which her daughter Hannah wrote: "After Hitler came to power, Mutti was the driving force to immigrate to Eretz Yisrael without delay. If it is true that Father was somewhat hesitant, as Mutti stated in her later years, it was perhaps because he was more realistic than she was, more aware of the upcoming difficulties."[16] Mutti, as she testified in retrospect, feared for her husband and how he would react if the Nazis conducted a search of his home and rummaged through his Judaica collections. This distinction regarding the mother's role in the decision to immigrate is consistent with research literature in general, and that pertaining to German Jews in particular,[17] which states that women generally more inclined to immigrate than men, because they were less integrated into society and more exposed to the impact of events under the Nazi regime upon the family's daily life, and particularly that of the children.[18]

Although the timing of the decision and its execution was a result of the events in Germany during the first months of 1933, the decision itself did not come as a surprise to the family. Zionism was taken for granted in the Maass family, present in the home's atmosphere, in the library, and in objects such as the JNF's brass box and a map of Palestine. "Zionism was not a issue of debate, a matter of one set of beliefs or another - we grew into it."[19] The children grew up in a Jewish home, with a tradition of making Kiddush on Friday night, Havdalah on Saturday night, and celebrating the Jewish holidays. The parents, as we recall, met at the Mannheim Zionist Club. The younger daughters knew for certain that in due time, the family would immigrate to Palestine. And when they did make Aliya, "it was the fulfillment of a long-standing wish, a kind of dream come true."[20]

Preserving Jewish tradition and Zionist motivations did not spare them from having to deal with economic difficulties, problems of mentality and others, and it was difficult for both parents to adapt to the new country. The father of the family died of a stroke three years after immigrating. Though the mother of the family was imbued with a belief in Zionism and had initiated the decision to immigrate, but could not know in advance, nor guess, what awaited her. As her daughter Hannah wrote in the memorial booklet:

Immigrating to Eretz Yisrael was the fulfillment of a long-standing wish, a kind of dream come true. But a dream that becomes a reality does not remain a dream; it becomes a series of everyday actions and even at best does not resemble its desired image and becomes a disappointment. All the more so when the objective difficulties were great - a sharp decline in the standard of living, of which Mutti was unaware in advance and unready for both emotionally and practically. Adaptation was difficult: a small, cramped apartment, no help in running the household, not the kind she had been used to; None of the products to which she had been accustomed; none of the services she knew and or could imagine living without; climate, different lifestyles; Even Jews were different than those she knew [Eastern European Jews]. [---] There they tried to adapt to the local practice, while here she encountered a completely different dominant mentality and was unable to grasp that we have to adapt ourselves to it.[21]

After immigrating, Mutti was largely a "girl" at a loss, and even more so after her husband's death.[22] When she was widowed she ceased to function as a mother and housewife. She was left with almost no money and no financial backing. At first she received a sort of monthly allowance from relatives who immigrated to the United States, and when they stopped supporting her, she had no other resources. Being on the verge of starvation, she began pawning valuables and works of art she possessed, and was later unable to redeem them all. At the time, she even sold valuable items, including a signed picture of Herzl by Hermann Struck, which she had received from the painter as a wedding present. The positive side of the story is that the buyer was Reuven Hecht, and the picture was on view to the public at the Dagon Silos and today at the University of Haifa.

Sometime after losing her husband Mutti began to recover, overcame her weaknesses, and found a way to make a living. As a book lover, she decided to set up a loan library of German books, later adding those in other European languages (and a few children's books in Hebrew). Men and women from all over Haifa and the nearby Krayot would come to the small library (half a store) at 133 Moriah Street in Ahuza to borrow books. Here we have an example of a woman's ability to overcome difficulties that she was unprepared for and had initially lacked the skills to deal with. Her youngest daughter estimated that establishing and operating the library contributed to strengthened her self-image.[23] In time she also made friends, devoted herself to her hobbies and collections, and corresponded with people abroad.[24]

Mutti went through personal tragedies and economic and cultural hardships, but she never complained, certainly not in Hebrew, which she failed to learn until the day she died, 43 years after making aliyah. She actually lived in a kind of bubble, in the Ahuza neighborhood in Haifa, where it was possible to get by in German without the need for Hebrew, and she also made her livelihood from a German readership. She deliberately ignored the change that took place in her life, as the youngest daughter wrote in retrospect:

Inside she was and remained the same "Frau Doctor Maass" from Germany, who held an honorable status in society. Outwardly, she practiced exactly the same "Yekke" manners to which she was accustomed in the past, and endeavored to cultivate her acquaintances and relationships with new friends in the same respectable "Yekke" format as ever. She just transferred her way of life and culture to Eretz Yisrael, and was hardly influenced by the atmosphere and culture existing here.[25]

Mutti appropriately summarized her immigration and absorption experiences through the verse she asked to have engraved on her tombstone: "Lo, he goeth by me, and I see him not: he passeth on also, but I perceive him not." (Job 9:11; King James Version)

Along with the mother's biography, the video presents autobiographical fragments of her children's life. One can clearly see the generational difference not only between parents and children, but also the difference between the daughter and son who immigrated as adults, and the younger daughters.[26] The older two, who immigrated when they were 24 and 21, never completely mastered the Hebrew language, and their children acquired German at home. When the family published the booklet in Mutti's memory (in the late 1970s), the eldest daughter and son wrote there in German, and the younger daughters in Hebrew. None of their seven children spoke German.

The eldest daughter, who was 24 when she immigrated to Palestine by herself, initially studied at the agricultural school for young women at Nahalal. Two years later she was already married with a daughter. The son found a job immediately thanks to the profession he had learned and the experience he had gained in Germany. The two young girls, who were 13 and 9 years old when they arrived in Palestine, fully acquired the Hebrew language and spoke it fluently (without losing their German). Consciously and stubbornly, they became more native ("Sabra") than the native born. They belonged to the same breed of Jews whose immigration to Palestine was a transition from their country of birth to their homeland, those for whom Eretz Yisrael had been their homeland from time immemorial, and as soon as they set foot on its soil, they felt at home.[27]

Hannah was passionate about the country and everything she found there. She was unaffected by the lower standard of living, on the contrary, she saw it as something positive, "as pioneering fit for the country."[28] At Tushi's funeral, who had been a member of Kibbutz Maagan Michael until the end of her life, they played "The Song of the Companies" [Zemer Haplugot], as per her express request.

The two young girls' lives changed after their father's death. Sixteen-year-old Hannah dropped out of school and tried to find various jobs in order to financially assist the family, and also because as a teenage girl she could not "deal with Mutti's depression."[29] After a year, she moved to the women-workers' farm in Hadera, against her mother's wishes. She distanced herself emotionally from her mother, and only became close with her once again, when she was about to become a mother at age 23.

Tushi, 12, who was an outstanding student, continued her studies at the Reali School and joined the Scout youth movement. She and her mother lived together in one room; the second room was rented to put some cash into the empty family coffers. "It is difficult to say that these were ideal conditions for an adolescent daughter, and indeed we did not have the kind of mother-daughter relationship that should have existed."[30] Moreover, although the mother and daughter lived together, each functioned in a different culture. Tushi's story is in many ways reminiscent of that of Mira Glassheip Ben Ari, and like her "represents the ultimate young immigrant of the Fifth Aliyah. These immigrants came at a very young age, at the beginning of the immigration wave, rapidly integrated into the linguistic and social frameworks in Eretz Yisrael, and basically felt themselves natives."[31]

The Maass family story is consistent with Dorit Yosef's findings regarding narrative strategies in the life stories of German-Jewish women in Palestine. Yosef concludes that:

The older writers who immigrated to Palestine when they already had a family (and mostly lived in cities) tended towards continuum and maintained familiar life patterns from the past, while the younger writers, especially those who immigrated as children, gave 'meaning' more space. These writers grew up in Eretz Yisrael, in local society, and wanted to be part of it, to belong to the generation known as the 1948 generation [...]. During their youth, their parents' German-Jewish culture was a burden and a nuisance for them, and the connection with their parents played a less significant role in their lives during the first years after their immigration.[32]

Thus, in the story of the mother (as described by her daughters) who immigrated at age 48, one can sense her desire to maintain continuity between her life "there" and "here." In contrast, the younger girls' way of life and their retrospective view points to the line of "meaning," which seems to demarcate the family story as a "Zionist Meta-Narrative."[33] The eldest daughter (and also the son), were in a sort of intermediate state. They felt comfortable having made aliyah and gave it meaning, but in their personal and family lives they largely maintained cultural continuity with their country of origin which also continued to serve them as a source of identification.

While the story of the second generation of the Maass family fits into the rich fabric of existing memoires and research about the immigration and absorption of German Jews in the 1930s, adds to it, and even confirms research claims, the mother's story is somewhat unique. Although its German chapter fits the profile and background of the female immigrants of the 1930s, its Eretz Israel chapter is largely unique.[34] Nevertheless, the multi-generational family story deepens and broadens our knowledge of Jewish history during the 1930s, both in Germany and in Eretz Yisrael.

Transcript of the movie
"Our Aliyah to Eretz Yisrael," 1933

The opening slide:

70 years to the immigration of the Maass family to Palestine (Aliyah)

1933-2003

https://www.youtube.com/watch?v=k1WTKKsIcsI&feature=youtu.be

M = Marianne

G = Gershon (Gerhard)

H = Hanna (Hanna-Ruth)

T = Tushi (Eva; Netanya-Dorothea)

M – there had always been a Zionist atmosphere at home.

G – We received Zionist education all along. We were members of a Zionist youth movement.

H – We knew that we would make Aliyah.

T – A map of Palestine was posted on the wall above my bed and I knew how it looked like

G – It was obvious that the grown-up children, Marianne and I, would go to Palestine after graduation and our parents would come once Dad retires.

H – it matured during the first months of 1933.

T – Hitler came to power, the Nazis came to power and we knew it was bad for the Jews.

G – When was the final decision taken? It was on Friday, 31 of March 1933, after we finished eating, our father gathered us at the living room

M – and he said: the situation is bad, we should leave.

G – he said: we made two decisions. 1 – we leave Germany as soon as possible. First Marianne and Gershon and then the rest of us. 2 – Hanna and Tushi will no longer go to a German school; they will move to a Jewish school in Köln.

H – Tushi and I got prepared by playing some kinds of games. For example: One sunny day in June we played on the lawn on Sunday. We pretended we have a beach on the sea shore of Tel Aviv. We brought tubs, all kinds of toys, blankets, easy-chairs, tables and chairs and filled the tubs with water.

We brought some friends and played as we are in Tel Aviv.

M – I was not very impressed. I went to say goodbye to all the people I knew. I also went, and this is interesting, to Dr. Rosenthal, he was a Rabbi in Köln and said farewell to him too, and he said: do you know what you are doing? You are going now to be absolutely primitive. Look, there is no toilet, no bathroom, all the things you are used to. But it did not make any impression on me. I accepted it. I said, yes, that's it. It was a change, but like going on a journey. I was attracted by all the new things.

T – I was fascinated by the travel, the adventure of the something new, that we are moving to Palestine which is the place where Jews should be. That Germany is not our place. It is not our country. I fully consented with it, I was very happy about it. I did not leave behind any important or interesting memories.

G – We left Germany in the middle or end of August, and on 30 August sailed from Trieste to Haifa.

H – Before Gershon left we had a farewell party for him at home. Tushi went to the piano in the other room and started to play "Ha-Tikvah." We all sang "Ha-Tikvah" and then Gershon responded to the greetings in Hebrew!

G – The voyage: our cabin was so hot – it was near the machinery room – so we did not stay down there at all. We slept all the nights up on the deck.

M – We arrived after five days, first to Jaffa and then to Haifa.

G – We stayed awake all night to be the first one to see the land.

M – Gershon found a job while we were still on board, so for him it was no problem. He also found a room right away.

G – On board there was a director of a big forwarding company, I think Marianne had an affair with him. So Marianne told him that her brother studied in Germany marine forwarding, maybe he could find a job with them. So he said to her, tell him to come on the first or second day to my office, and we'll see.

M – In Nahalal it was very difficult. There was a large room of eight young women. I was the last one to join and I could not speak with them at all. They put me first of all to work in the kitchen. I did not understand too much. They gave me a brush to hold in one hand and a radish in the other one so I should clean it for breakfast. Everything worked on kerosene. All the food, everything tasted kerosene.

H – We left Köln on 10 November. We traveled first to Manheim, there we stayed for two days to say goodbye to all the uncles and aunts. One of them said to us, I understand people leaving Germany, it is not good now in Germany. So you should go to Holland, or probably to Paris. But to Asia? Who is travelling all of a sudden to Asia? The journey through Switzerland impressed me very much, the scenery and all. And we went through Sankt-Gotthard-Pass.

T – And when we were up there in Sankt-Gotthard, there was snow. We made a snow ball and we knew that for a very long time it would be the last time.

H – With the ship we went to Venice. We traveled first class and it was not a direct cruising but it took ten days, a voyage.

T – On board it was awfully boring. In one day I finished to read all the books I took with me. There is not too much to do there.

H – At dawn the ship approached the shores of Jaffa so we woke up at daybreak, we saw the sunrise on the east. And we knew – this is Eretz Yisrael. We were very excited.

T – just like the sailors of Columbus who got thrilled when they saw a piece of land so we waited and expected until finally we saw a strip, a strip of land. We knew this is Eretz Yisrael. I remember that we kissed the soil, the holy earth, and we were in Eretz Yisrael.

H – I had no absorption problem. From the very first moment I was happy and I loved everything I saw.

T – It was evident that to be a Jew from Germany was not a matter of great honor. We were all Yekes [=Jews of German descent] and there were many jokes about us. I did everything I could to make people forget that I was a Yekit.

H – Tushi and I decided that between the two of us we'll talk only Hebrew. But we did not know all the necessary expressions. So, it was allowed to insert German words, words that we don't know in Hebrew. But if one of us caught the other saying a word in German, a word she ought to know in Hebrew, she had to pay one mil to the Jewish National Fund from our poor pocket money.

M – I don't think Mutti knew what was in store for her. Mutti was pampered to the point that she had no idea when water is boiling, more or less.

T – Mutti went through a crisis when we immigrated. From the good life she really had there in Germany, with two maids and a laundrywoman and a gardener and all the treats she had, to move to a lousy small apartment.

H – First we lived in Hahermon street. We had there two apartments, two rooms each. We needed what is called in German Dienstmädchen which is actually a maid. From the labor bureau they sent us a "helper." A helper, it means that the work is actually done by the housewife and the helper helps. Who ever heard such a thing? at 4 PM she goes home. How comes? And Mutti asked: and who will prepare supper?

G – For Mutti it was like a tourist voyage. She did not know where she is. And Dad also not exactly understood. He had a problem of career, money. People proposed to him two options. 1 – to buy land. To make land speculation. He said: I will not make business with the land of Eretz Yisrael. I am not ready to do this. Then he was offered to be a clerk in Anglo-Palestine Bank. And he said: How can I? I was a bank manager, a big bank, not the only manager, but how can I sit there as a clerk?

H – So he found that business called "Medidenta." A store for medical and dental equipment, in which he did not have the slightest notion. And there was an expert who was in charge of the business. But the expert was not only an "expert," he was also a crook. And the merchandise he brought was obsolete items, useless. They were just lying in the store. It did not work.

G – There were many problems, and after two years it was clear the company had no future.

H – so, the business was on the verge of bankruptcy.

M – I don't know if Mutti acknowledged that Dad had been cheated. That the money was gone.

G – the problems with the company totally crushed him.

H – Dad, as we all know, had a stroke less than three years after the Aliyah. Sad end.

T – when Dad died, for her it was horrible.

G – He made a mistake not going to the bank. To work. A bank clerk. Not that terrible. He would have gotten a not too bad salary, maybe also some pension. That's it.

M – After Dad died all of a sudden, there were just fifty pounds left. She absolutely did not manage. She got in touch immediately with Bodenheimer [a relative who immigrated to the USA] and demanded they take care of her. She really demanded that. So he, I don't know how, gave her every month a nice amount of money for a year. But later on he said she had to cope on her own.

H – I quit school. I worked in all kind of works and thought that I support myself. Helping the family. I am already grownup.

M – In the meantime Gershon's first wife, Marianne, she was clever. She told Mutti: you know what. You have books, start a library.

G – Mutti accepted it and started with 10 or 15 books, all in German, of course. She started slowly-slowly to build it. Mutti was not a business woman, but it worked very well that eventually she rented a place here in Ahuza. Until today people still mention the name of Lucie Maass. Even these days I here every so often "the white old lady of Ahuza."

M – Look, I was happy here. The atmosphere was totally different. I was content that I have a house, I have children. But let me tell you, I think today that then I did not think too much. I accepted it as it is and I lived the day-to-day without great thought.

G – for me it was really like a dream. Only one thing I missed by leaving Germany. I was a pretty good athlete. I was getting better with my achievements. When I came here I did not continue with it.

T – the home I was raised in was Zionist and we always knew there is Eretz Yisrael. We saw what happened in Germany, what happened to European Jewry. What happened to the friends of my parents.

H – I think we have to conclude it positively. There is no doubt. From six people who came here we became a family of almost 80 people. All are in Israel. Really, the bottom line is only good.

Initiator, interviewer and producer: Aviva Halalmish

Photographer and editor: Gal Nimri

Endnotes

1 See Dan Michman, "The Holocaust in the Eyes of Historians: The Problem of Conceptualization, Periodization, and Explanation," in Dan Michman (ed.), *Holocaust Historiography: A Jewish Perspective, Conceptualizations, Terminology, Approaches, and Fundamental Issues* (London and Portland, 2003), pp. 9-58; Aviva Halamish, "The Yishuv and the Holocaust: Time for Synthesis," in Roni Stauber, Aviva Halamish, and Esther Webman (eds.), *Holocaust and Antisemitism in Research and Public Discourse: Essays Presented in Honor of Dina Porat* (Jerusalem, 2015), pp. 108-110 (Hebrew), and references listed there.

2 See a discussion on this matter in in Dalia Ofer (ed.), *Israel in the Eyes of Survivors of the Holocaust* (Jerusalem, 2014), pp. 7-8 (Hebrew).

3 Regarding the "transfer" agreements and the manner in which they were implemented, see Aviva Halamish, "Capitalist Immigration to Palestine between the Two World Wars," in Devorah HaCohen (ed.), *Ingathering of Exiles: Aliyah to the Land of Israel – Myth and Reality* (Jerusalem, 1988), pp. 193-232 (Hebrew), and especially pp. 207-218, which contains many references to previous studies; and Aviva Halamish, *A Dual Race Against Time: Zionist Immigration Policy in the 1930s* (Jerusalem, 2006), pp. 250-261 (Hebrew). The transfer agreement underwent changes over time and had several channels. In brief: potential immigrants deposited German marks in a special account in Germany, used to purchase German goods which were exported to Palestine and sold there. The "transfer" company would transfer the proceeds in Palestinian Pounds to the immigrant in Palestine after deducting commissions.

4 *Mutti, Lucie Maaz-Friedmann* (Haifa, 1979) (published by the family) (Hebrew).

5 Carlo Ginzburg, "Microhistory: Two or Three Things that I Know About It," *Critical Inquiry* 20(1) (1993), pp. 10-35. Ginzburg is quoted in Judith Baumel, "Bridges between Yesterday and Tomorrow: The Role of Diaspora Culture in the Stories of Fifth Aliyah Heroines," *Cathedra* 114 (Spring 1995), p. 124 (Hebrew).

6 Yoav Gelber, *History, Memory and Propaganda: The Historical Discipline at the Beginning of the 21st Century* (Tel Aviv, 2007), pp. 251-296 (Hebrew).

7 Arianne Baggerman and Rudolph Dekker, "Egodocuments and the Study of Cultural History," in Amir Horowitz et al. (eds.), *The Past and Beyond: Studies in History and Philosophy Presented to Elazar Weinryb* (Raanana, 2006), p. 262 (Hebrew).

8 Baggerman and Dekker, "Egodocumentim," p. 245.

9 Regarding the advantages of combining oral history with traditional sources in order to integrate the private and public dimension into the historical narrative of human experience in general and of women's lives in particular, see: Paula Hyman, "Gender and the Immigrant Jewish Experience in the United States," in Judith R. Baskin (ed.), *Jewish Women in Historical Perspective*, 2nd Ed. (Detroit, 1998), p. 331. On the virtues of autobiography in general and as a source for the history of German Jews in Palestine, see Guy Miron, "Autobiography as a Source of Social History: German Jews in Eretz Yisrael as a Test Case," *Historia* 2 (1988), pp. 103-132 (Hebrew).

10 See Hannah in *Mutti*, p. 8.

11 Viola Alianov-Rautenberg, "Liftmenschen in the Levant: A Gender History of the German-Jewish Immigration to Palestine/Eretz Israel, 1933-1939," doctoral dissertation, Berlin Institute of Technology, November 2017, pp. 11-12.

12 Alianov-Rautenberg, "Liftmenschen in the Levant," p. 12.

13 Guy Miron, *German Jews in Israel: Memories and Past Images* (Jerusalem, 1995), pp. 256-262. On the virtues of autobiography in general and as a source for the history of German Jews in Palestine, see Guy Miron, "Autobiography," *Historia 2* (1988), pp. 103-132 (Hebrew).

14 Guy Miron, "From Bourgeois Germany to Palestine: Memoirs of German Jewish Women in Israel," in *Nashim: A Journal of Jewish Women's Studies & Gender Issues* 17 (2009), pp. 116-140 (Hebrew).

15 The workshop was one of a series of discussion workshops held by the Van Leer Institute in collaboration with the Institute for Contemporary Jewry at the Hebrew University of Jerusalem in 2005 and 2007 on the subject of "Women's Migration." Some of the studies presented in the workshops were published in the collected volume: Pnina Morag-Talmon and Yael Atzmon (eds.), *Immigrant Women in Israel* (Jerusalem, 2013) (Hebrew). This collection does not contain an article about immigrants from Central Europe during the Mandate.

16 *Mutti*, pp. 9-10.

17 Regarding the role of women in making the decision to immigrate and choosing the destination country, see Batsheva Margalit Stern, "Who Will Help the Helper? Gender Differences in Jewish Immigrant Families in Eretz Israel," in Morag-Talmon and Atzmon (eds.), *Nashim Mehagrot Beyisrael* pp. 112-142.

18 See Miron, "From Bourgeois Germany to Palestine," p. 119; Marion A. Kaplan, *Between Dignity and Despair: Jewish Life in Nazi Germany* (Oxford and New York, 1998), p. 63.

19 See Hannah in *Mutti*, pp. 9-10, and also referred to in the video..

20 See Hannah in *Mutti*, p. 10, and also referred to in the video.

21 Ibid. The description of Mutti's difficulties in moving from Germany to Palestine and in adapting to life in a new country are consistent with Guy Miron's general conclusions in his article "From Bourgeois Germany to Palestine," p. 118. See also Dorit Yosef, "Bourgeousie and Zionism in the Home Life of Central European Immigrants in Palestine," *Iyunim Bitkumat Yisrael* 28 (2017), p. 209, which quotes from an article published in the Jüdische Rundschau in November 1933: "Be aware that you will only have a very small apartment and very little household help."

22 Regarding the immigrant who is in the "child position" see Margalit Stern, "Who Will Help the Helper?"

23 See Tushi in *Mutti*, p. 14.

24 See Hannah in *Mutti*, p. 12.

25 See Tushi in Mutti, p. 14. Regarding the fact that the home continued to be run along European lines, see Baumel, "Bridges," p. 122 and Yoav Gelber, *New Homeland: Immigration and Absorption of Central European Jews 1933-1948* (Jerusalem, 1990), p. 613 (Hebrew).

26 Regarding the significance of the immigrant's age in acquiring the Hebrew language see the discussion in Alianov-Rautenberg, *Liftmenschen in the Levant,* pp. 95, 284, and also Baumel, "Gesharim", p. 126.

27 Regarding this matter see Aviva Halamish, "The 'New Jew': Where and When Should His Persona be Molded or Was it Just A Legend?" in Devorah HaCohen and Anita Shapira (eds.), *The Constant Pioneer: In Memory of Zeev Tzahor* (Israel, 2017), p. 244 (Hebrew).

28 See Hannah in *Mutti*, p. 10, and also referred to in the video.

29 See Hannah in *Mutti*, p. 11.

30 See Tushi in *Mutti*, p. 14.

31 Baumel, "Bridges," p. 133.

32 Dorit Yosef, "("From 'Yekiyut' to Zionism: Narrative Strategies in the Life Stories of German-Jewish Women in Palestine," *Israel* 22 (2014), pp. 111-132: 129-130..

33 Ibid., pp. 116-117.

34 See Yosef and Miron, "Bourgeoisie and Zionism." This recent article contains references to many earlier studies.

Dalia Ofer

Transitions in Extreme Situations:
Two Women under Nazi Occupation

This article describes extreme situations faced by Jewish women during the Holocaust. It does not discuss the most extreme situations of deportation or the reality of the concentration camps, but rather the stages in which there were still signs of a familiar routine in Jewish life. I will discuss how women coped and deliberated in such changing realities, in which it was difficult to predict how things would develop and the state of uncertainty was a constant.

My methodological approach is that of microhistory, "which reflects a focused study of phenomena from everyday life — the behavior and experiences of concrete human beings."[1] I will present in detail, as best as the sources will allow, the fate of two women, while mapping out where they lived and how they functioned, addressing the development of historical events in those places that served as the background and the motivations for their decisions and actions. The methodology of microhistory does not discuss the individual or a particular case as an example or illustration, but rather argues that in-depth analysis of the individual's behavior or analysis of a particular case attests to human responses as a whole, highlighting a concrete historical reality and giving us a deeper understanding of the period under study and the human responses that characterized that period.[2]

Specifically, I will discuss two women, who were active during two different periods of the Holocaust in different geographical areas, regarding which different documentation was available to the historian. These women were selected in order to emphasize that despite differences in content and contexts, extreme situations faced by Jews during the Holocaust required similar behavior patterns. Beyond the unique personality and status of each woman, the cultural framework in which she was active, and the means at her disposal, also required was a great deal of flexibility, adaptation, and creativity, without which it would have been impossible to survive. All of these factors indicate the considerable emotional resilience that enabled a constant search for successful activity in view of the harsh reality that the Nazis imposed on the Jews.

I will begin by explaining the concepts in their various contexts, and from there I will move on to the stories of the two women, which demonstrate their coping with extreme situations and how they transitioned from one situation to another. In conclusion, I will emphasize the contribution of such research toward a better understanding of the fate of women during the Holocaust.

The Terms

Extreme Situation

How should we define extreme situations during the Holocaust, a phenomenon that itself is entirely composed of extreme situations and that, as a whole, reflects genocide on an unprecedented scale?

Every war, deportation, expulsion and natural disaster puts people in extreme situations. However, we often tend to contemplate the Holocaust from its conclusion – the mass murders and death camps. As a result, we frequently observe the various stages of the Holocaust backwards, from end to beginning. Knowledge of the extreme — the mass and absolute death — causes us to look differently at various incidents. For example, forced emigration from Austria following the Anschluss in March 1938 may be seen as less extreme than the Zbonszyn deportation or Kristallnacht, since escape routes still existed through immigration or flight to a different country. The yellow badges and ghettoization seem less extreme than deportation to a forced labor or death camp, since despite the isolation and marking, the family remained a unit in the ghetto and did not yet comprehend that death was to be their ultimate fate.

Nevertheless, at the time they occurred, and for the men and women who experienced them, each of the aforementioned events was an extreme reality. This is not only because of the immediate suffering and the emotional burden involved, but because they created a true rift vis-à-vis the past, produced an incomprehensible and frustrating present, and undermined their vision of the future. Sociologists Peter Berger and Thomas Luckmann state that the ability to learn from personal and collective past experiences and to project them onto the present reality helps one understand the here and now and deal with it. It also gives the individual the ability to imagine the future, for better or for worse. By doing so, it enables one to function in a daily routine even when it is difficult and crisis-ridden. Yet in an extreme reality it is difficult to find similar cases in the past, one cannot draw conclusions from the past regarding the present, and thus, it is difficult to envisage a positive or comforting future. One's basic security is therefore undermined. It becomes more difficult to deal with reality and one often feels desperate and helpless.[3]

As Ringelblum states:

> The war changed the lives of Jews in Polish cities very quickly. One day was unlike another and the scenes changed as quickly as those in a film. A Warsaw Jew locked in his shop remembers the ghetto as being heaven, with the time before the ghetto as a true idyll. Each month brought profound changes that fundamentally changed Jewish life. That is why it was so important to photograph every event in Jewish life at the moment it occurred, while it was fluttering and vibrant. The shop before the deportations is as far from the shop after the deportations as east is from west. And the same is true of smuggling and socio-cultural life; even Jewish clothing in different periods was different.[4]

We must, however, emphasize that every adult and child, male and female alike, experienced the aforementioned crises and situations differently, due to their personality, economic situation, social status, age, gender, and the cultural atmosphere in which they lived, and therefore tended to react to, remember, and define the same extreme situations in different ways. The interesting question is whether, despite the differences, we can find similar principles or criteria for behavior and responses.

External Factors

External factors here can be understood as those who were responsible, to varying degrees, for enforcing Nazi rule in daily life. When viewing the past from a distance, everyone appears to be the same: Polish police officers, Austrian and German policemen, SS men, and guards at ghetto exits, all of whom were part of the same external factors. Every one of them was an oppressor, disrupting the Jews' daily lives, endangering them in one way or another. And yet, in the tangible everyday reality they differed from one another, and their activities could be defined in various ways. For example, a permissive oppressor in a forced labor camp cannot be compared to a cruel oppressor overseeing work in the camp. Similarly, a strict or distracted guard looking for bribes at the ghetto gate when goods arc being smuggled cannot be compared to a strict policeman fulfilling his duty to the utmost, who cannot be bribed. Seemingly minor differences can have a big impact. Hence, despite the same overall policy, external factors everywhere had a real impact on the Jewish fate.

Jews found themselves in all of these situations under Nazi rule and they experienced them differently even though they either perished or survived due to the oppressor's arbitrariness. Men and women, children, and the elderly experienced the dangers and attempted to survive in different ways. When it comes to the experience of the individual, it is difficult to generalize. And while we cannot tell the stories of millions of people, we try to tell the stories of individuals or groups and to organize them according to different criteria that allow for generalization. It is important to remember that by doing so, we reduce the depth of the individual's experience, even when basing our work on their testimony and life stories.

Transitions

Transitions can be understood as physical movement, including migration or escape from a ghetto to a camp, to a forest, to a city that did not yet have a ghetto, to another ghetto, or the like. However, there are also transitions of consciousness, relating to activities and the definition of their purpose, as well as transitions in the execution of tasks in daily life, work, family, political affiliation groups, and more. Hence the transitions are both spiritual and intellectual, reflecting change or a reshaping of the individual's self-understanding. From an emotional point of view, adaptation, completion, disagreement and subversion are possible responses to internal transitions.

Transitions are always dynamic and may cause a change in the individual's personality. Historical protagonists often experience an emotional transition, as if they were creating a new self. This can contribute to or impair the will to live or survive; it can also cause them to concentrate on themselves at any cost, even at the expense of others, or, alternatively, to desire to assist others, even at the cost of their own life. All of this is connected, in one way or another, to extreme situations as we have defined them.

The word "women" in the title also reflects a diverse group that consists of women of different ages and different levels of education and professional knowledge. One must also notice class differences; differences in life experiences and relationships; and differences in various aspects of personality, including adaptability, flexibility, and mental resilience. Hence, I have chosen to focus on the life stories of two women who experienced Nazi rule in different ways in almost every sense. They lived in different countries at different times under Nazi rule, and in different social and cultural frameworks. Here, I touch upon only part of their lives.

I am not claiming that the aforementioned factors are typical only of women. Men have also faced extreme situations and transitions as I have defined them. It is both possible and desirable to analyze men's reactions in similar situations and to compare them with those of women. My working assumption is that in view of the different ways in which boys and girls were raised and educated in those years, and due to the different social and cultural expectations from boys and girls, men and women would respond differently but also similarly. Extreme situations may also provoke reactions that are inconsistent with the cultural and social tradition of each gender.[5] However, I will not make such a comparison in this article.

Rather, I will explore the cases of two women: one in 1938–39 Vienna, following the Anschluss and the outbreak of the war; and the other in the Warsaw Ghetto. Using a Microhistorical analysis and based on our understanding of the broader reality in which the events took place, I will describe how each of these women coped with transitions in extreme situations.

Also important to note from a methodological perspective is the fact that I use different documentation, although it is included in what is referred to today as ego documents. In the case of Sarah Kofler of Vienna, my main source is an exchange of letters that were written in German and then translated into Hebrew by Sarah's daughter, Clara Kofler, who is a major protagonist in Sarah's life story. Many of the texts are written in the first person. In describing Mrs. C. of the Warsaw Ghetto, I used material from the Oneg Shabbat archive that was written in Polish and translated into Hebrew, including a report and summary of an interview with Mrs. C penned by Cecilia Slepak, through which I learned about her life during the events described.[6] Unlike in the letters, Slepak mediates between me and Mrs. C, her interviewee, particularly as the interview is written in the third person. This can be viewed as a methodological problem in relation to the authenticity of the interviewee's intentions and self-awareness, as Slepak's voice is heard in the interview. However, the documentation left behind by Slepak is one of the most important and profound sources in existence for understanding the fate of women in the ghetto. Hence, it seems to me that within the limits of the existing personal documentation from the Holocaust period, Mrs. C's story is presented here with a high degree of credibility.

Sarah Kofler

I begin in Vienna, immediately following the Anschluss in March 1938, with the story of the Kofler family's experiences, as related from the point of view of Sarah Kofler, the family's wife and mother. Sarah Kofler, born in 1895, moved to Vienna from the village of Konkolinki near Stanislawow at the end of World War I. In 1921, she married Jacob Kofler (1892) of Buczacz, who also immigrated to Vienna after the war. They had two daughters: Clara in 1922, and Hela in 1931.

The information about the family is based on two main sources: an exchange of letters between Jacob, Sarah, and their daughter Hela, and their other daughter Clara, who immigrated to Palestine (Eretz Israel) as part of the Youth Aliyah movement in January 1939; and a few letters from Sarah and Jacob to Sarah's sister Pepi who immigrated to the United States. A second source is memoirs written by Hedva (Clara's Hebrew name) Yuval (née Kofler), the daughter who immigrated and the only survivor of the immediate family.[7]

The Kofler family lived modestly in a one-room apartment, and despite financial difficulties they managed to maintain a proper lifestyle in a traditionally observant home. Jacob was a men's work-clothes cutter, selling his wares to tailors to sew before they were sold as finished products. It was hard work with long hours and paid a limited income. The parents placed a great emphasis on education, and despite the large expense involved they sent Clara to high school. In her memoirs, Clara describes the family's financial situation as follows: There was always bread to eat but not always clothing to wear. This was through the eyes of a teenage girl who was comparing her family's inferior financial situation to that of her more well-to-do classmates. Sarah had a brother and sister who immigrated to Vienna before her. Her sister, whom she adored and to whom she was particularly attached, died in 1927 while giving birth to her third son, and this had a powerful effect on Clara. Another sister, Pepi, immigrated to the United States where she was widowed and left to raise and support her children on her own. Sarah's third sister immigrated to Eretz Israel in the 1930s; she lived in Rehovot, where she raised her family. Sarah's mother, another unmarried sister, and their extended family remained in Stanislawow. This may be seen as a case study of family dispersal, characterizing many Eastern European Jewish families. Jacob's family — parents, siblings and other branches of the extended family – remained in Buczacz.

Sarah and her husband were not involved in Jewish political activity, despite the fact that in 1934 and 1935 Jacob wanted to immigrate to Eretz Yisrael. However, his wife Sarah and his 12-year-old daughter Clara didn't like the idea. Years later, Clara concluded that in light of the difficult initial years in Vienna, and having finally become somewhat better established there, her mother feared another transition and was unwilling to leave. Clara speculates that the information they received from her sister in Eretz Israel was not encouraging, as these were difficult years for the Jewish community there. She painfully recalled her opposition as a twelve-year-old girl to her father's immigration plans and felt guilty that her position might have influenced the plan's cancelation.

Following the Anschluss, the family's situation worsened drastically. Their income was abruptly halted, their shop was looted, and anti-Jewish legislation now prohibited them from owning it. Clara was forced to drop out of high school, relatives were sent to Buchenwald, and friends and relatives emigrated. Illegal journeys were arranged to various countries, including Eretz Israel, and daily life was permeated by an atmosphere of insecurity and uncertainty.[8]

From the family's correspondences, we can learn that by the summer of 1938, the Kofler family had decided to emigrate. Although Eretz Israel was a prime and preferred destination, they also attempted to obtain an American visa through Pepi, Sarah's sister, and acquaintances who could assist them in getting an affidavit. These efforts failed, and pressure to leave Vienna increased. As daily life got harder and the situation more desperate, the Kofler family was willing to consider any destination, as long as they could leave Vienna. Eventually, when their hopes of obtaining an immigration certificate to Eretz Israel or an American affidavit were dashed and World War II began, the family joined a never-completed odyssey to immigrate to Eretz Israel that has come to be known as the "Kladovo Šavacz affair." In this framework, they were part of a group of approximately 1,200 illegal immigrants who made their way along the Danube River toward Constanza port in Romania, where they could board ships to Eretz Israel. Like most of the immigrants on this expedition, organized by the Mossad LeAliyah Bet, the Kofler family was murdered by the Nazis: the men in the fall of 1941, and the women and children in the spring of 1942.[9]

Here, I will not discuss all of the family's activities until they set out from Vienna on their attempt at illegal immigration; rather, I will focus on the article's central theme and consider how Sarah Kofler dealt with the transitions she underwent in view of the extreme situations she faced.[10]

Sarah Kofler, her husband, and other family members experienced transitions. The first was both physical and consciousness-related, and was a transition of choice: migration to Vienna after World War I. It can be assumed that the war and its ensuing crises were a "push" factor in this transition while her brother and sister's presence in Vienna were a "pull" factor. At the time, many Jews were immigrating to Austria in the hope of improving their daily lives by living in a country that granted Jews a more equal status. Sarah married Jacob, whom she met in Vienna, and as Clara proudly testifies, they were a love-match, as opposed to a product of family introductions and arrangements.[11]

Sarah organized the family's life, helped Jacob run the store, and continued to do so even after Clara was born. Only in the late 1920s, after the Kofler family's financial situation improved slightly, did the family expand with the birth of their youngest daughter. Sarah supported her sister's family after the latter passed away and helped care for her orphaned children. She also maintained close ties with her brother and his family. Based on Sarah's correspondences and Clara's impressions, it appears that she was very stable and goal-oriented, conservative in her approach to family life, and saw her main role as that of a mother and an educator. Clara stated that on matters of religion her mother was less strict than her father. "Mother was more inclined to compromise. She was religious and devout, but it was her practical nature that controlled behavior."[12] In her letters to Clara, she reiterated the need to "believe in the good and benevolent God," and the need to not "forget that until now, the Lord has supported us and we should believe that he will continue to do so in the future." Clara saw her mother as the more dynamic and powerful force in the family, and her father as softer and more lenient.

Clara summed up her mother as follows:

> Mother was active all day long, helping Dad in the store, cooking, ironing, doing almost everything herself. Her demands were modest, I never heard her complain…Just as I wished to dress nicer as a young girl, I really wanted my mother to have beautiful clothes, as I wished her to look young and beautiful and she had all the attributes to do so. But as life was so difficult, she aged prematurely.[13]

Following Austria's annexation, Sarah experienced a sudden severe transition in the family's situation. Problems of income and insecurity became the focus of daily life. Violence escalated and the situation facing the Jews in Vienna worsened as a result of the Nazis' forced emigration policy that was first put into effect there. Kofler's store was impacted and he could no longer run his business. During the first months following the Anschluss, much of the Jewish population realized that it that had to leave Austria as quickly as possible. Such emigration, I believe, could already be viewed as lifesaving at the time and not just in retrospect. It is typical to use the term "rescue during the Holocaust" when discussing escape from existential danger, which also existed prior to the period of the Final Solution. The deportation of tens of thousands of Jewish men to concentration camps in Austria and Germany in the wake of the pogrom of November 1938 posed a true existential danger. The same held true for the Jews of Vienna, who were not deported to concentration camps and experienced the violent policies of forced emigration. As time passed, the situation intensified, claiming many lives even before Jews were deported to the Lublin district and Nisko during the autumn of 1939.[14]

The first extreme transition, which was significantly reflected in our documentation, occurred after Clara immigrated on her own to Eretz Israel to secure her future. Sarah had to contend with the transition between identifying herself as a mother protecting her young ones by her side, to that of a mother sending them off to ensure their existence.[15] This complex transition is documented in her letters to Clara from the moment she boarded the train to Trieste, and from there the ship that set sail for Eretz Israel.

Sarah dealt with the new situation on several levels and adopted different strategies. She needed to maintain the family framework, as Hela, their younger daughter, was 8 years old, necessitating reorganization of her education and special sensitivity to her feelings following Clara's departure, as the two had been quite attached. The Sabbath and Jewish holidays posed a special challenge, but they were also a source of heightened religious belief, strengthening the hope that all was not yet lost. In a letter to Clara, Sarah described a special Sabbath dish that she prepared:

> You know, because I received such an 'important' letter from you that we had long been expecting, I had to cook broad beans for the Sabbath. Of course, Uncle David took a first helping and Goldberg did not refuse either, so there was nothing left. If you were here – no, no, we'd be better off with you (January 20, p. 31).

The text describes a seemingly routine family and social gathering, but Clara is gone. Everything would have been fine had Clara been there and eaten the Sabbath beans, but a sense of reservation is immediately expressed in an almost panicked tone: "no, no, we'd be better off with you." The wording is positive, and the letter asserts that they will be together; however, the implicit text states: "It is good that you are not here; you are in a safe place that we eventually hope to reach." Sarah seemed to be functioning flawlessly. She cooked, cleaned and baked, took care of Hela and Jacob, and kept in touch with Clara's friends who were waiting to immigrate to Eretz Israel. She poured over her letters again and again, reading out passages to Hela. She prepared the family's belongings to be sent to Eretz Israel in hope that they would soon be able to immigrate and that the separation would be brief.

And yet, Sarah felt a void. She missed Clara's presence, her attention, and the moments they spent together side by side lying in bed, chatting about everyday matters. In a sense, the house was empty.[16] She also felt ashamed that she was not a full partner in Clara's experiences and difficulties, as well as a sense that she had abandoned her daughter, which is a harsh term to use in view of the fact that her daughter had taken the right steps to save her own life. Regardless, the longing of a mother who sent her child away for her own protection, and the transition from close mothering to distance mothering this involved, was difficult, deceptive, and frustrating.

As time passed and the family found no way to leave Vienna, the parents' letters began reflecting their concern that they would not be able to do so in an orderly and legal manner. Sarah sensed Jacob's despair over his continuous inability to obtain an immigration certificate. Friends and family had managed to emigrate, while they remained in the city that haunted them and in which they felt an ever-increasing sense of danger. She wrote to Clara: "We miss you every step of the way" (January 30, p. 37).

Clara's mother recalled her daughter's support for her, how she helped her father run the business during the summer of 1938 when she was no longer attending school, and how, as Hela's older sister, she showed her love and attention. Sarah's letters express restlessness and an emotional state reflecting her inner transitions, which swung like a pendulum between hope and optimism and utter helplessness. Their dependence on the authorities and on the Jewish institutions in Vienna and abroad created frustration and a growing sense of insecurity. "Possibilities come and go until the right one comes along, and then we will certainly travel to Eretz Israel. May the Lord grant us a good journey with much luck" (February 13, p.

41). And yet, she was painfully aware of her responsibility, as a wife and a mother, to maintain what exists, noting, as if trying to convince herself: "I'm supposed to be strong" (February 13, p. 41). The appearance of these sentences in the same letter are indicative of her inner turbulence, as well as her own recoiling from it, as she was supposed to remain strong.

Two months later, she stressed to Clara how tiring emigration matters were:

> I am brave, so for me you can be pleased. From what Father writes, you can sense less courage. But have no fear about that – as long as Father sees nothing real in hand, he is pessimistic, and maybe rightfully so. But we must be patient (March 21, p. 56).

This letter reflects Sarah's desire to be strong and practical, which was her role at the time. She not only had to function as a mother and a wife, but to remain optimistic while caring for her daughter, who missed her and faced numerous difficulties, from a distance. She could not be dragged into a sense of hopelessness. She expressed her strength by explaining her daily agenda, which included household chores, volunteering in the community, and helping her husband. They no longer ran the store, but Jacob volunteered with the Mizrachi movement and, with Sarah's assistance, helped organize the Youth Aliyah warehouse. She also maintained contact with the family in Eastern Europe, informing them of their situation, and the family sent food packages to Vienna.

Clara's correspondences are letters from a mother who was aware of her daughter's distress and absorption difficulties. Two decades earlier, she and her husband had experienced immigration themselves, and as parents they wished to help Clara by not burdening her with their problems. Yet, on more than one occasion, they were also in need of her assistance in approaching family and friends in Eretz Yisrael whom they hoped could help them obtain an immigration certificate. They felt compelled to explain the problems involved with obtaining such a certificate in all honesty, in order to prevent her expectations from skyrocketing and keep her realistic. Sarah's correspondence with her daughter, therefore, contains reference to her complex and sometimes conflicting feelings over their separation. It also reflects her feelings of guilt over what she considered to be her abandonment of her daughter, as well as her longing for her, her desire to keep her safe, and her joy that she was no longer in the Vienna that threatened their entire existence.

As the months passed and the immigration certificates did not arrive, and the American consul in Austria asked for additional guarantees even after the affidavit arrived, Sarah's letters expressed deep concern.

Her letters to her sister in the United States revealed more of her distress, which bordered on despair. She wrote about the difficulty of the situation and about their mounting despair and loneliness. She asked her to continue trying to help them obtain the necessary papers, and her sister expressed hope that she had enlisted a Polish Jew from the town of their birth to send them an affidavit. He had promised to support them so that the family would not become a public charge, and Sara repeatedly stressed that they would manage and would not become a burden on him either. Despite the letters they provided from their supporter, the consul demanded more forms. Sara desperately asked her sister to send them as quickly as possible, as time was running out. "Of course, the request should be addressed to him [the person sending them an affidavit, D.O.] in a way that will arouse his compassion so that he will finish the very human act he started and save us from our desperate situation." (August 14, 1939, p. 105). The letter reveals only a trifle of Sarah's emotional state. The situation appeared impassable and their loneliness increased. Friends and acquaintances had managed to emigrate or leave in one way or another, and the reality was growing worse by the day.

Sarah did not reveal these feelings to her daughter, writing that they were surviving in spite of everything that was going on. But she also explains to her why they should consider leaving Vienna for anywhere else, even if it meant foregoing their reunion with Clara (May 26, 1939, p. 80). By that point she had accepted the fact that the ultimate reunion of her family may not happen in the near future, which was no small step for her as a mother. At home, she remained the family's anchor of security. As Clara's father wrote:

> Your dear mother now offers me special support. She is a real hero.
> When I grow weak, she is by my side and says the right thing. That's

a lot for me. I wish I could recall mother's words of encouragement (August 19, 1939, p. 107).

But nothing worked, and on September 1, 1939, war broke out, making the situation of the Jews in Vienna more difficult. In October 1939, Rolf Günther, Eichmann's deputy, told Vienna Jewish community head Josef Loewenhertz about the establishment of a Jewish reserve in the Lublin area in Poland. On October 18, 26, and 29, three groups of about 3,000 men each were sent there to ostensibly establish the infrastructure to settle the Jews of Vienna in Poland. When news of their conditions and fate reached Vienna, a terrible panic gripped the city's Jews, who wanted only to escape. This was also evident in the Kofler family's letters to their daughter Clara from October 30, 1939 onward. Mother, father, and Hela wrote short letters of just a few lines expressing love and longing and happiness about Clara's health, and reporting that they were in good health, but no more than that.[17] They wrote nothing about what was going on in Vienna, their feelings, or their plans, as if the letters were written out of a sense of duty. In fact, the letters hide more than they report. It seems that they either did not want or were afraid to convey the family's plan to immigrate to Eretz Israel illegally, an option the family had already considered in the past. They ultimately joined a voyage that had been organized by the Mossad LeAliyah and that left Vienna for Bratislava on November 18, 1939.

Here, I will refrain from going into all the details of this unfortunate journey, other than the fact that the group included some 1,200 immigrants from Vienna, Berlin, and Bratislava, as well as a few from Poland and Yugoslavia who also joined the voyage. The plan was to reach Eretz Israel within a few weeks, as the Mossad LeAliyah ships had done in the past. However, this journey, which came to be known as the "Kladovo Šavac affair," encountered special difficulties and was never completed. The Mossad LeAliyah was unable to provide a ship to wait for the immigrants in Constanta, Romania, to enable them to continue their journey to Eretz Israel. As the Danube froze early in the winter of 1940, the three ships and their passengers had to wait at the Kladovo port for the ice to thaw. The result was that 1,200 immigrants remained densely packed on the three ships in the cold weather and had to make do with little food until the spring of 1940. At that point, the organizers of the voyage had to return the ships to their owners, and the Mossad LeAliyah was still unable to provide a ship to wait for the group in Constanza.

The immigrants were transferred to the village of Kladovo on the banks of the Danube in the hope that, by summertime, they would find a ship to take them to Eretz Israel. But even this plan did not go well, and in August 1940 the immigrants were transferred to Šavac, located far from the river. Although the conditions there were better, their chances of continuing on to Eretz Israel dissipated. In April 1941, the Germans occupied Yugoslavia, sealing the immigrants' fate. More than 1,000 men, women, and children were murdered by the Germans. Three groups of about 200 children, teenagers, and instructors from among these immigrants reached Eretz Israel through Youth Aliyah, but Hela Kofler was not among them. The Kofler family perished in Yugoslavia, as a result of the German occupation.

Joining an illegal immigration effort and living in harsh conditions on a ship at Kladovo and Šavac for a year-and-a-half exposed Sarah Kofler to new extremes. During this period, she had to cope with the uncertainties of daily life without her home or domestic routine, without a familiar social framework, and without smooth communication with Clara and her family in Eretz Israel and with her sister in the United States. Clara's communication with her parents became infrequent. Mail was extremely slow because of the war, and letters could take weeks to arrive. The new situation and hardships made it more difficult to write, and Clara also had trouble writing to her parents. The infrequent correspondence reflects the extreme emotional and physical transitions that Sarah experienced and how she coped with them. The parents' first letter from the journey that Clara received was dated January 19, 1940, almost two months after they left Vienna. Only then they did write about their departure.[18]

However, on January 2, 1940, Clara received a letter from relatives who had fled to Belgium and who wrote her about her parents' departure. From October 30, the date on which their last letter was written in Vienna, until the beginning of January, Clara knew nothing of their experiences. Her parents had sent her a number of letters and postcards, but they had received nothing from her and assumed that their letters had not reached their destination. The letter from her parents, dated January 19, was sent from the Yugoslav ship "Tsar Nikolai" which had already docked for the winter at the port of Kladovo with about 350 illegal immigrants on board, all observant Jewish adults from families affiliated with the Mizrachi movement, along with children and groups of BaHaD – *Brit Halutzim Dati'im*, or the Union of Religious Pioneering Youth – from Germany.

Neither the parents' letters nor the letters from her sister Hela gave an indication of the difficult situation on the ship, including the overcrowding and the unsanitary conditions. "You do not have to worry about us", Sarah wrote in an optimistic tone,

> we are healthy, and we have enough food. And we hope that God will not abandon us and will help us see you soon [...] We are rid of it all, the daily fear that did not let up, the anxieties about decrees [*geseries*] that might befall us. I am free and can sleep quietly, though not as comfortably as in our home (January 19, 1940, p. 114).

Based on this sentence, and the sentence in which she acknowledges that God did not abandon them and they therefore managed to embark on their journey, we conclude that Sarah (and her husband Jacob) experienced a bearable transition, as they were rid of the extreme situation they had experienced in Vienna due to their fear of deportation to Poland. It is here that we learn how Sarah expressed her relative reference to extremes. Contrary to information provided by other passengers, who spoke of immeasurable difficulties and uncertainties during their prolonged stay on the ship, Sarah described the multiplicity of rumors and lack of information as preferable to what she had recently experienced in Vienna.[19] What made it difficult for them was their infrequent communication with Clara. They received no mail from her until mid-March 1940, which caused them tension and anxiety.

They expressed joy in response to her letter of March 20, but also substantial anxiety regarding the continuation of their voyage. "We have no idea how long we will stay here," her father wrote, adding that there was much he would like to tell her. Her mother explained that there was not enough room on the small postcard to provide details about their lives, but that they "are learning Hebrew and hope to reach Eretz Israel as quickly as possible." Sarah appears to have maintained a positive attitude and to have adapted to the difficult conditions on the crowded ship. Although she could not perform the domestic duties that provided her with a degree of stability and self-confidence in Vienna, she found other ways to express her practicality. After all, one must know Hebrew to live in Eretz Israel. However, is that how she behaved, or only what she wrote to Clara?

The parents' letter dated May 1, 1940 reflects how connected Sarah was to reality, with its many contradictory aspects. "Can you imagine what our mood was when we left W [Wien – Vienna]? We imagined a different situation, and here we are. It's been so long, and we are still waiting" (p. 120). She wrote that although she had an opportunity to learn Hebrew from a well-known Hebrew teacher from Vienna, "I have no patience." This letter reflects a change from the previous letter in which she attested to learning Hebrew. But her motherly responsibilities did not dissipate, and she was full of concern about Hela. Hela had no proper educational framework on the ship, she wrote to Clara, so she was teaching her arithmetic. She proudly wrote that Hela can already compose sentences in Hebrew.

After approximately five months aboard the ship, the Kofler family disembarked at Kladovo. This was yet another transition to a new, contradiction-riddled reality. Daily life was easier in the village, as they lived in a house; she could run a household, cook, clean, and fall into a daily routine, giving them a degree of stability. However, it now became even clearer that the chances of reaching Eretz Israel had diminished. In a letter dated May 12, 1940, about a week after they went ashore at Kladovo and five days before Clara's 18th birthday, Sarah congratulated her daughter, wishing her good health, a good and happy life, and good luck. At the same time, however, she lamented the situation, contradicting her usual remarks in her many letters. "Why do you rarely write?" she asked. "It worries me." She continued: "Don't worry about us. Try to get Dr. Knopfmacher's address and call him. Maybe your father can get an immigration certificate for a veteran Zionist. Try to get it through Klausner (Tel Aviv Montefiore 43) or have your uncle find out and let us know soon" (p. 121). This was not the first time that Clara had been asked to intervene and to expedite their immigration, and she spoke to acquaintances and relatives, asking them to contact influential people. But this time the urgency was more noticeable. She enclosed their new address, and she even signed the letter differently; not "Mother," as in most letters, but rather "from your Mama." May this have been indicative of her troubled mood and her fear that her long-awaited meeting with Clara was fading into the distance?

In May 1940, Sarah wrote a sad, desperate letter to her sister in the United States, asking her to call certain people who might help ensure improved collateral for the affidavit the family had received but could not yet be used. She described their difficult situation, even though they were no longer on the ship and they were living in a house in the village of Kladovo:

> Our lack of knowledge about how long this situation will last, when and if we will ever reach our destination, causes us deep concern. We never imagined that we would be stuck here for so long (May 1940, p. 122).

Later in the letter, she also asked her sister to send her a dollar or two to improve Hela's food.

Sarah was tense, the uncertainty eating away at her. Yet, she concentrated on how to adapt in order to build up her resilience in the new reality. Moving to the village allowed for a more comfortable life but also raised many questions. She tried to return to some type of routine — cooking, caring for family members, hosting friends for a late Saturday afternoon meal — and informed Clara that some form of normalcy had returned to their lives. In a letter dated June 26, more than a month after coming ashore at Kladovo, she wrote: "So you see, it's like home for us, with one difference; we would like to have a real home of our own, we don't know how long this will last, and we miss you terribly (124)." The phrases like a home and a real home reflect the depth of her shame at being a refugee. Sarah wished to ease matters for her daughter but remained faithful to her deep desire to express her inner truth.

During this period, Sarah was pained by not being able to help her daughter, who was facing difficult decisions at the end of her first year in the Youth Aliyah framework. Clara now had to decide where to go – to a kibbutz, to her relatives, or to the city? As long as Clara was in a Mizrachi youth home learning gardening as a profession, it appeared that despite the distance, Sarah could advise her from time to time, expressing her desire to share things with her daughter and support her. However, in preparation for Clara's next stage, that of a program graduate, she had to make weighty decisions about her future. As a mother, Sarah felt lost. Her daughter had just turned 18, and she was alone, without her parents, who were responsible for counseling and supporting her:

> Your words brought me to tears – your having to learn how serious life is at such an early age, far from your parents, who wish to protect you and to encourage and comfort you when needed. May God grant us happiness, and unite us soon with joy in Eretz Israel (July 5, 1940, 125).

At this point, Sarah lost her composure. Thus far, her adaptation to changing situations had been her most prominent attribute. Her mood ranged from joy and satisfaction that Clara was in a safe place, to sadness, longing, and a sense of guilt and neglect. However, now that Clara had completed the first stage of her absorption, she had to move on to the next stage. Although this was a positive transition of increased responsibility, she needed advice and hesitantly shared her deliberations regarding how and what to choose. Her distant parents seemed to have identified a degree of insecurity in her deliberations. What could they do to fulfill their responsibility and desire to help their daughter? How could they guide her from such a distance? Their inability to help was unbearable.

This time Sarah wrote to Clara about how much she wanted to protect her and how she was shedding tears because of her helplessness to do so. Such statements contradicted the approach she employed in letters, according to which she tried to encourage and strengthen Clara rather than upset or weaken her. And yet the letter ends with what can be regarded as a mantra that appeared in all of her letters (albeit in different versions): "May God grant us happiness and unite us soon with joy in Eretz Israel."[20]

On August 2, Sarah again wrote: "I'm annoyed that you write to us so rarely…Write to us every week. The long wait of 3-4 weeks makes us nervous" (125). Two weeks later (August 15), she wrote: "We are very upset that since your postcard of 19.6 – we have had no sign of life from you. I can't even begin to explain what our mood is like." And on August 15, her sister Hela, who had recently turned ten, wrote: "We hope you think of us more than you write. How are you? Are you healthy?"[21]

This volatile shifting – among concern and anger at the lack of letters, helplessness with regard to the rest of their immigration, and the decreasing likelihood of realizing the dream of being together in Eretz Israel – marked all their letters from the autumn of 1940 to March 1941, when the Nazi occupation of Yugoslavia cut off all communication. The letters reflected an improvement in their physical conditions and organization following the move to Šabac. Emotionally, however, the move created immeasurable distress, as their ultimate goal of immigrating to Eretz Israel now seemed more distant than ever. In December 1940, it was clear that winter had arrived and that they had to wait until spring. But what then?

We can perhaps summarize Sarah's despair and her dependence on what she could still cling to as a mother using a short excerpt from her last letter:

> My dear and beloved child, please write to us often and make us happy when we see your lovely handwriting. This is our whole life; it gives us strength and courage to survive, and we feel the long distance between us less acutely. We are always with you in spirit (March 11, 1941, p. 142).

Mrs. C. of Warsaw[22]

Mrs. C from Warsaw was 30 years old, sewed corsets and bras for a living, and was married without children. I first encountered her through Cecilia Slepak's research on women in the Warsaw Ghetto. The information we have about Mrs. C is limited to seven pages in which Slepak describes her actions and her behavior. Slepak's narrative moves from the conversation between the two, and the place where Mrs. C expects to meet a customer, to Mrs. C's life before the war, during the war, and before moving into the ghetto. Despite the brevity of the account, it tells us something about Mrs. C's life and her responses to extreme situations and the physical and emotional transitions she had experienced.

The first encounter with her is dramatic. Mrs. C had been walking back and forth beside the wall on Novolipia Street for over an hour, waiting for a man "from the other side." They met twice a week at this time. Mrs. C did not stand in the same place for long but rather moved back and forth, walking on the narrow sidewalk, then hiding in an entranceway. She was skilled at waiting and aware of the dangers. She had learned to be careful.

Mrs. C was an entrepreneur. She had a profession and initially ran a small workshop for corsets and bras in her home. Over the years her customers increased, and she opened a larger workshop and a shop at the market. When the war broke out, the building where her store was located was bombed and destroyed. However, she managed to save a significant portion of her merchandise. Following the onset of occupation and destruction she rented another shop on the same street. Understanding how fragile her personal status was and that her Jewishness put her shop in danger, she refrained from wearing the Jewish armband when venturing out to her store.

Both the war and Warsaw's terrible destruction were undoubtedly an extreme situation for all the city's inhabitants, including Mrs. C. Although she was aware of her vulnerable status as a Jew, she viewed herself as an inhabitant of a ruined Warsaw and found a way to deal with the adverse change in status. Her adaptation was reflected in the fact that she did not mark herself as a Jew in the public sphere, trusted those who recognized her as a Jew, and assumed that strangers would not notice her Jewishness. Despite the risks, this behavior put her mind at ease. Violating the order to wear the Jewish armband bothered her less, as she trusted the people in her work environment – her customers and the shopkeepers she knew.

How long could she go on like this? Her strategy proved successful during the first year of the Nazi occupation, until she was forced into the ghetto. "Random customers saw me as Aryan, but all my acquaintances knew about my origins and treated me fairly, even sympathetically. Until the ghetto was established, my situation was not bad" (p. 7).

In her first transition in an extreme situation, Mrs. C displayed flexibility and adaptation without relinquishing her main goal. She was content to keep the business going and to continue earning a living. She understood the significance of the change that had taken place in her life, but she estimated that despite the dangers, she had found a solution that provided her and her husband with a reasonable existence. In doing so, she displayed daring and resilience.

The move to the ghetto reflected a new extreme situation.

Tension and anxiety increased during the summer of 1940, as rumors spread of a plan to concentrate the Jews of Warsaw in a ghetto. Reports of ghettos in other cities aroused great anxiety among the Jews, who feared that the same was about to happen in Warsaw. It was difficult to prepare for such a radical change when it was still unclear whether it would actually happen. "Rumors about the future and the uncertainty about life in a ghetto aroused anxiety," wrote Slepak. "Lacking funds or a stock of food, [Mrs. C felt] she must act quickly if she wanted to live." Changes in her extreme situation expressed themselves in two stages: first, the loss of her home and the need to find a place to live in the crowded ghetto; and second, the loss of her livelihood.

Having been denounced as a Jew, her shop was sealed shut by the Nazis, and she could no longer enter. For her this was a severe blow, in addition to her forced transfer to the ghetto. Mrs. C felt she needed to act urgently. "The ground slipped away under her feet," Slepak wrote. Most of the merchandise remained in the sealed shop, necessitating a speedy decision. Mrs. C faced a complex problem; it was difficult to understand the situation correctly, and it was even more difficult to decide how to act quickly. "Unfortunately, the chaos following the changes taking place after the Jews were incarcerated did not enable them to immediately grasp their chances or options of earning a living," wrote Slepak (p. 8).[23]

Moreover, even before moving to the ghetto, the livelihood of her husband, a salesman for a textile company, had been affected. He also became anxious and hesitated to leave the house because of the "seizures," or abductions, of Jews for forced labor that were taking place in the streets.[24] The move to the ghetto did not suit him. The concern of earning a living fell to Mrs. C and forced her to rethink her responsibility for the family's economic situation.

To ensure her livelihood, Mrs. C pursued a different strategy. Her main task was to save the merchandise in her sealed store, which was her only capital. However, having been denounced as a Jew undermined one of her basic assumptions: trust in those with whom she worked. She realized that she had to leave the ghetto in order to try to save her goods, but in the new reality, getting out of the ghetto was difficult and dangerous. And if her former acquaintances would not cooperate with her, it would be a disaster.

To leave the ghetto, she pretended to be a Polish maid who had come to collect her wages from a Jewish home and had to return home. The impersonation was successful, and she made her way to the sealed store. To her delight, she discovered that the Germans had not found the rear entrance and had left it unsealed. But she still had to overcome another obstacle. The gatekeeper, who watched the entrances and exits, feared that the Germans would learn that he had allowed her into the sealed building and refused to cooperate. After bribing him with a hefty 100 zlotys, she entered the store at dusk to remove her goods. In doing so she was assisted by a customer, an ethnic German (*Volksdeutsche*) with whom she was friendly. Together, they removed a considerable portion of the merchandise. Mrs. C stayed overnight at a friend's house.

The next day, she had to move the merchandise into the ghetto. Again, she relied on social ties, this time approaching a Polish policeman who was an acquaintance and shared her plan with him, and he transferred the goods to the ghetto. She returned to the ghetto disguised as a Polish cleaning woman.

We do not know the nature of Mrs. C's relationship with the Polish policeman whom she termed an acquaintance, as opposed to a friend (whereas the ethnic German is referred to as a friend). Did she compensate him in some way?

In her narrative, Slepak revealed Mrs. C's resourcefulness and courage showing both how she adapted to new situations and her personal and social connections with merchants and customers in her workspace. She understood why the gatekeeper was afraid of the Germans; he knew her, and they may have even developed a relationship in the past. Her approach to the situation was matter-of-fact and reflected good judgment in persuading him to assist her.

Despite the bitter experience of having been informed on by a saleswoman she knew, Mrs. C continued to rely on social ties, friendships with ethnic Germans whose status had improved in the new reality and were willing to risk helping their Jewish friend. Even her request from a Polish policeman to transport the goods to the ghetto for her indicates a willingness to take risks along, with clear thinking and good judgement. She knew how to circumvent orders by manipulating those designated to keep the orders in place. Polish policemen were involved in both helping the Jews and turning them over to the Germans. Mrs. C succeeded in getting through another transition while operating in a state of uncertainty. She exercised trust and at the same time took considerable risk, in view of the need to secure her livelihood. Without a doubt, her conduct in this situation reflected inner resilience and decisiveness.

After successfully returning to the ghetto with her merchandise, Mrs. C decided to wait and see how to proceed. In the ghetto, she told Slepak, she sold the lower grade part of her merchandise and bought enough food to meet her family's needs and to ensure their basic subsistence. This waiting period lasted several months. She looked for work in her profession, but the demand for corsets was nonexistent and the pay was meager. Meanwhile, she continued to sell the merchandise in her possession, which by that time was almost gone. On the other hand, food prices continued to rise. During the first quarter of 1941, the demand for food increased further as waves of refugees and deportees reached the ghetto, increasing its population by a third.[25]

"We must live. We want to survive," Slepak quotes Mrs. C as saying.

In the spring of 1941, Mrs. C realized that she needed to reconsider her actions and economize. She came to the conclusion that despite the many risks involved, she had to start smuggling products into the ghetto. Food was highly sought after and ensured the best profits.

We do not know what steps Mrs. C took to implement her plan to become a smuggler. We do not know whether she had friends who were involved in smuggling, other than one other woman, Mrs. P., whom she mentioned in her testimony as someone who accompanied her several times to the Aryan side. However, what is visible in the text is also indicative of what is missing or hidden. She appears to have started on her own. On Easter 1941, Mrs. C made the "professional" transition to smuggling, using her ties with Poles to exit the ghetto safely. This time, her plan was bolder. With the help of the prison steward, who was her acquaintance, she disguised herself as his wife and showed her ID card to exit to the Aryan side (according to Slepak, Mrs. C did in fact resemble the prison steward's wife in the photo on her ID card).

The account of the transition demonstrates Mrs. C's inner strength when dealing with extreme danger. According to Slepak, Mrs. C's anxiety and fear of being caught threatened to paralyze her:

> As she approached the guard post, a growing fervor of excitement and fear enveloped her, her heart pounded, her temples pounding strenuously. Fear of the gendarme. The man [prison steward] showed his identification and in a quiet voice turned to her: "Show the man your document." And at that moment the fear disappeared. There was a cold silence, like petrification, **and the impersonation in front of the Wacha (guard) was successful** [emphasis added].

In the face of extreme danger, Mrs. C was filled with daring and exuded confidence. According to this description, her full cooperation with the Pole, ostensibly her husband, and his quiet instruction to "show the man your document," reassured her, enabling her to make the transition in peace. Her success strengthened her conviction that she had acted appropriately, and her successful cooperation with the Polish prison steward encouraged her to seek out additional support and expand her cooperation with Polish acquaintances. As a first step, she "contacted previous customers and renewed her acquaintance with those necessary for her plans, to find out what was in demand 'on the other side'," where she stayed for three days.

We pause momentarily here to consider this transition in Mrs. C's story. It was, we read, a transition that was twofold: the physical transition of leaving the ghetto and the internal, emotional, consciousness-related, and "professional" transition to a new phase of activity. The worsening reality and the danger of starvation awakened her inner voice: "We must live. We want to survive." This voice encouraged her to take extreme measures. According to Slepak, Mrs. C "pretended and dared to do what she did for her sake and that of her husband." She responded to an extreme situation by adapting herself to it, and incorporated the lessons that she learned during the previous stage. Her relationship with Poles was a cardinal one, as acquaintances and stallholders became her partners in creating a network of contacts for expanding her operations with various commercial companies. This, Slepak maintains, enabled the dangerous smuggling operation. She had to learn not only what food products she could deliver to the ghetto, but also what the demand was on the Aryan side. She summed up what products she would move out of the ghetto and set a date for their delivery. It was important to remain on schedule to ensure her credibility and connections. "The necessity of her actions bolstered her courage," Slepak concludes.

Mrs. C was successful in the smuggling business and expanded the type of goods in which she traded: "Around her body she wrapped bras, belts, and knitted fabrics covered with wide rubber, and inside she sewed foreign currency and smuggled everything possible – gold, watches, and goods – to 'the other side,' and from 'there' groceries." (p. 9)

Once again, we see how she managed to expand her business. She no longer worked alone, and she joined groups of Jewish and Polish smugglers who formed an entire network. In addition to her connections with the customers she knew before entering the ghetto, she conducted transactions with merchants in the Rozycki market in Praga, a neighborhood of Warsaw. "Her profits reached 6-7 thousand zlotys per month." (p. 9)

The ways in which she entered and exited the ghetto became increasingly sophisticated and diverse. She usually used the basements of bombed out houses that connected the ghetto to the Aryan side and were referred to as "headquarters." She knew many buildings and changed her location from time to time. More than once she was assisted by a Jewish policeman who, in exchange for a few zlotys, showed her new places of passage and accompanied her "surfing" to the "headquarters" hide-out.

The connections she made through her business on the Aryan side became contact networks, thus enabling her to change accommodations and making it difficult to track her movements. Initially, Mrs. C stayed on the Aryan side for two nights at a time and sometimes even for a full week, in order to reduce the dangerous entries and exits to and from the ghetto. However, as her business expanded and her confidence increased, she left and returned to the ghetto every day.

Mrs. C engaged in smuggling from the spring of 1941 until the end of the year. In November 1941, the Germans declared that any Jew found outside the ghetto without permission would be executed, and a significant number of executions were carried out.[26]

Slepak recounts three cases that she refers to as "unpleasant adventures." Here, I will present two of the cases and quote from Slepak's text. The first was an encounter with German police that occurred about a month after she began systematically smuggling. She was carrying a bag full of cigarettes, the trading of which was strictly forbidden, on top of which she had placed chunks of meat. Beside her walked a Jewish boy dressed in rags who was also smuggling and who was supposed to show her a new passage. Suddenly, a car stopped beside them, brakes squealing, and four German policemen got out.

"Jew!" the policemen shouted. She smiled. "I don't understand," she replied in Polish. "Not a Jew?" the gendarme repeated. "*Documenten*!!! (documents)" "Ah, documents", she said in a sing-song voice strange even to herself. Panicked thoughts went through her mind, but she overcame them: Courage will save me. "Documents? What woman carries documents! She proclaimed innocently." *"Und was haben Sie hier* (and what do you have here)' the gendarme pointed to the basket. "I bought meat before the holidays," she explained. In a quick motion she opened the lock, revealing the meat piled up. So they gave up on the rest of the inspection. After a moment they returned. "And do you know him? The boy?" They pointed to her guide, who was walking beside her. Mrs. C denied it. "God in heaven, there are so many people." She was defiantly brave, and she succeeded. They released her. (p. 11).

The second seriously dangerous incident occurred in the autumn of 1941, in the Rozycki market in Praga, in close proximity to merchants with whom she was in contact.

Suddenly someone blocked her path, as if it were a bad omen. Instinctively she guessed: an agent. "Jewish?" he asked threateningly. "Of course not! We know, we know — documents, burned during the bombing. Please come with me." "I won't go," she said. "I am not Jewish. I don't know what you want from me." Right beside her stood a merchant woman that she knew. She leaned back against the edge of the stall, and from the competing stall across the way she heard the words of the merchant who, it later turned out, was the informant who informed on her. "Well, what about that? Let the agent earn 100 zlotys. I will not pay, because I have no reason." She was shaking all over but kept insisting. Her mind acted feverishly. In a large bag that was always with her she hid a small purse containing several thousand zloty. She had to save the money. She reached out her hand as if to take a kerchief, deftly removed the purse, put her hand behind the merchant's waist, and handed her the purse. Then she turned around abruptly and whispered an address where the merchant could return her purse. It all lasted a split second, but the agent missed nothing. "What did the lady place in the merchant's hand?" "Nothing." "Give me 50 zlotys." "No." "So please come with me." But at that moment a customer came to her assistance — an acquaintance from a nearby stall. She began a conversation with the agent, engaging him to such an extent that he did not even notice Mrs. C's escape.

She waited until evening, and the merchant from the market returned her purse and all its contents.

In the third incident, she was not at all successful, and she had to pay the informant 1,500 zlotys, a huge sum, but returned home.

In these three cases, two of which took place in the fall of 1941, the Germans had already issued an order proclaiming the death penalty for Jews who left the ghetto without permission, and the tension involved with exiting the ghetto skyrocketed. Once again, her creative and resourceful capacities and her ability to stay calm in difficult situations came to the fore, as she displayed practicality and a correct assessment of the extent of the danger she faced.

Following these three experiences, and news of the arrest and execution of smugglers, Mrs. C decided to stop going to the Aryan side and engaged in smuggling and sales only within the ghetto. In the ghetto, she had a network of clients and brokers through whom she conducted her transactions of goods, money, and food. Her business had shrunk, and so had her profits, and now she had to sell household items to survive. Nonetheless, "the most important thing is life," Slepak quotes Mrs. C as saying at the time. "I would take risks to live: taking risks to die is completely pointless.

We now return to the main topic of the article. With Mrs. C, we experienced a number of transitions and a number of extremes, and during each one she adopted a different tactic. The strategic goal was life and survival. She was aware of extreme situations, reacted, and moved from one situation to another, adapting herself to fluctuations in personal security and family needs. She altered her paths of entering and exiting the ghetto due to the changing dangers. The scope of her work increased, and she felt successful. She planned her actions carefully, checked the "market" and considered how she could operate within it, exploited social connections, and created a network of information within the ghetto and between trusted partners on the Aryan side. She was willing to expand her clientele, and seemed to trust them on the assumption that the business was beneficial both to her and to the merchants with whom she did business. She was manipulative, agile, brave, aware of danger, and resourceful.

Her confidence increased, but so did her alertness to danger. She ironically reported another attempt by the informant to entrap her during a meeting with the agent who tried to blackmail her or turn her in, and this time the informant failed. Mrs. C did not shy away from resisting and outwitting the extortionist, enlisting the help of the other merchants she trusted who indeed treated her with honesty and successfully rescued her from danger. She did not lose faith but remained realistic about the situation, as reflected both in relation to the people with whom she worked and the extent of personal risk she was willing to take.

Toward a Conclusion

In this article, we read about the experiences of two women who lived in different countries and under different conditions but whose fate was sealed following the Nazi occupation. We followed the various problems they faced as they attempted to survive under Nazi occupation, which increasingly undermined their chances of success. The various sources at my disposal allowed for a different look at each of the women. In both cases, the need to use one's historical imagination is crucial for bridging gaps of time and place, and for understanding the everyday horrors that women and their families faced. The methodology of microhistory is concerned with simple people as opposed to leaders or prominent figures in society, and their life stories integrate the routine and the unique. Carlo Ginzburg defines his protagonist as "normal exceptional."

The two protagonists of this article are simple housewives and wives, and one is also a mother. Even before dealing with the reality created by the Nazis, their daily lives were not easy. In Vienna Sarah Kofler was an immigrant, and immigrants face unfamiliar and often difficult situations. But she had chosen to immigrate (albeit due to external constraints) and allowed for a positive future, given the experience of her relatives. The ability to imagine the future as more positive than the present is helpful when dealing with a crisis-fraught reality.

Like many other women from the lower bourgeoisie, Mrs. C studied a profession and faced difficulties earning a living during periods of economic crisis in pre-war Poland. Nonetheless, she was successful. We met these two women in a reality that had no precedent in their practical and emotional world, as they dealt with worsening extremes. For both, uncertainty increased, and the future seemed increasingly unclear. They had to function in a rapidly and unexpectedly changing reality, and the need to adapt, to maneuver, and to create a future vision of hope was becoming increasingly difficult.

Sarah Kofler's letters to her daughter Clara essentially reflected the daily life of a mother dealing with the positive and negative aspects of separation from her daughter. However, this was not a routine case of a mother who missed her daughter who had emigrated — which was a situation experienced by many Jewish mothers in the late nineteenth and early twentieth centuries — as she lived in a reality of worsening danger and existential anxiety for herself and her family. And yet she sought to protect her distant child; not to reveal her true situation, but rather primarily to share her longings and hardships, but without burdening her. Ostensibly, this is a routine situation in a society for whom emigration is a basic element of daily life; however, this was not the case. The danger of living in Vienna grew daily and reached its peak with the first deportations to Nisko. Also relevant was the pain of parting with a life that existed until March 1938, when the Nazis annexed Austria.

Focusing her letters on trying to protect her daughter limited the accounts of how the violence and anxiety that Sarah Kofler and her family faced were manifesting themselves. However, the necessity to leave Vienna forced the mother to divulge more than she concealed. The radical deterioration in Jewish security, including that of the Kofler family, outweighed the mother's desire to protect her child. Although she tried not to sound desperate, cries of desperation appear in the letters, especially those to her sister. When corresponding with her sister in the United States, she did not hide her desperation, suggesting various tactics through which they might obtain an affidavit. Her letters to Clara revealed the waves of hope and disappointment, and the transitions she underwent while trying to function as a mother, tending to her daughter in Eretz Israel; to her family, which was undergoing immense changes; to her younger daughter's schooling; and to the anxiety of her husband, who could no longer fulfill his primary duty as father and spouse.

Reading the letters today, while knowing the ultimate fate of Sarah, Jacob, and Hela, one can identify their survival strategies, how they coped with a deceptive daily life, adapted to changes and internal transitions that allowed for a different view of that reality, and demarcated the boundaries of adaptation. Why was Hela (Clara's younger sister) not sent to Eretz Israel with a Youth Aliyah group? Was it due to the difficulty of saying goodbye to their remaining daughter and their hope of arriving there together, or was it because of Clara's letter about the difficulties Hela would face upon arrival if she came alone that convinced them that it would be better to wait and immigrate together? These are things we will never know. Only Clara would bear a sense of guilt over Hela's death, as she wrote how hard it would be for Hela to immigrate on her own. Our imagination illuminates their tragic end, focusing on their efforts to remain sane and normal. As long as it seemed possible to get through these extreme situations, Sarah adapted to the transitions and displayed resilience. But as soon as the murderer resolved to destroy them, neither resilience nor intention could change the decree. By using our historical imagination and knowledge we have of the events of the period, we can imagine their feelings when the men were deported to be put to death and the women were transferred to the Belgrade camp a few months before their murder.

Mrs. C appears to find herself in an even more extreme situation. We were not able to hear her voice in the first person, but rather only through Slepak's mediation. A careful analysis of Slepak's narrative reveals that it focused on survival rather than the pain of parting or longing for a past life, and that it centered on efforts to maneuver out of an anxiety-ridden situation where one feared the loss of livelihood and hunger, through the use of vitality, wisdom, and courage. This existential state of a determined, calculating, and socially connected woman presents a dynamic, challenging, and suspenseful story. Through a cunning strategy against the occupation and its regulations, the extreme situations became a lever empowering a woman with no small degree of initiative and determination. When we listen carefully to the voice that emerges from Mrs. C in the third person, we appear to be facing a success story.

But this is not a heroic story of success. When we first met Mrs. C we saw a woman walking back and forth in front of a ghetto wall, plagued by significant anxiety and insecurity as she awaited a "Pole from the other side." And at the end of the interview, Slepak tells us, Mrs. C emphasized that all of her efforts were nothing but an attempt to live, to survive. However, it is precisely these sentences at the conclusion of the interview that bring to mind what occurred in Warsaw just a few months later, when the vast majority of the Jewish population was murdered by the Germans.

These two women, and many others, struggled, day by day and hour by hour, to survive and to succeed, evoking our admiration for their determination, their personal redesign, their energy to repeatedly invent new techniques and forge new connections, and, above all else, their adaptation to transitions and extreme situations. However, they were eventually confronted by the ultimate extreme situation, the Nazis' Final Solution, which they were unable to evade.

Notes

1 Yosef Kaplan, "About Carlo Ginzburg and His Writing," in Carlo Ginzburg, *The Cheese and the Worms: The Cosmos of a Sixteenth Century Miller* (Jerusalem, 2005), p. 300 (Hebrew).

2 For an interesting encyclopedia entry about microhistory see: Bill Kte'pi, *Salem Press Encyclopedia* (2016): "Microhistory is...larger issues." See also the introduction to Claire Zalc and Tal Bruttmann, *Microhistories of the Holocaust* (New York and Oxford, 2017). One example of such work is Carlo Ginzburg, *The Cheese and the Worms*.

3 Peter Berger and Thomas Luckman, *The Social Construction of Reality: A Treatise in the Sociology of Knowledge* (London, 1971).

4 Emmanuel Ringelblum, *Final Writings: Jewish-Polish Relations, January 1943-April 1944* (Jerusalem, 1994), p. 11 (Hebrew).

5 For a theoretical discussion of gendered differences between men and women that pertain to women's fates, see the introduction to Dalia Ofer and Lenore Weitzman (eds.), *Women in the Holocaust* (New Haven and London, 1998), pp. 1-18.

6 Cecelia Slepak was a Warsaw-based journalist who was asked by members of the Oneg Shabbat Archive to write a study of women in the ghetto. This was part of a broader study about two years of life under German rule in the ghetto, initiated by members of the archive. Regarding Slepak, see Dalia Ofer, "Cecilia Slepak," in the *Jewish Women's Archive's on-line Encyclopedia of Jewish Women*, at https://jwa.org/encyclopedia/article/slepak-cecila. See also Dalia Ofer, "Her View through My Lens: Cecilia Slepak Studies Women in the Warsaw Ghetto," in Judith Tydor Baumel and Tova Cohen (eds.), *Gender, Place, and Memory in the Modern Jewish Experience: Re-placing Ourselves* (London and Portland, OR, 2003), pp. 29-50.

7 Kofler, *A Cry Before the Holocaust: Letters from Jacob and Sara Kofler and Their Daughter Hella to Their Daughter Hedva in Jerusalem*, 1939-1941 (Jerusalem, 1998) (Hebrew). The letters were translated by Hedva. Her son, Yisrael Yuval, got them published. My citation of the letters will indicate only their date and page number. Kofler, *The Voice of the Days of My Life: Memoirs, 1922-2005* (Jerusalem, 2007).

8 Evan Burr Bukey, *Hitler's Austria: Popular Sentiment in the Nazi Era, 1938-1945* (Chapel Hill, 2000). Regarding illegal immigration to Palestine, see Dalia Ofer, *Escape from the Holocaust: Illegal Immigration to the Land of Israel, 1939-1944* (New York and London, 1990).

9 Regarding Certificates and American immigration bureaucracy, see David S. Wyman, *Paper Walls: America and the Refugee Crisis, 1938-1941* (Amherst, MA, 1968). Regarding the Kladovo Šavacz episode, see: Dalia Ofer and Hannah Weiner, *The Dead End Journey: The Tragic Story of the Kladovo-Sabac Group* (Lanham, 1996).

10 I have already discussed the parents of the Kofler family from a different angle in the article "The Historian and Historical Heroes" (German), which is forthcoming in the *Münchner Beiträge zur Jüdischen Geschichte und Kultur*, 2019.

11 Yuval, *A Cry Before the Holocaust*, p. 2.

12 Kofler, *The Voice of the Days of My Life*, p. 6.

13 Ibid.

14 Regarding deportation from Vienna to Nisko, see Peter Longerich, *Holocaust: The Nazi Persecution and Murder of the Jews* (Oxford, 2010), pp. 150-151.

15 Regarding the difficulty of mothers parting with their children and acting against their maternal instincts, see Dalia Ofer, "Motherhood under Siege," in Esther Herzog (ed.), *Life, Death, and Sacrifice: Women and Family in the Holocaust* (Jerusalem and New York, 2008), pp. 41-67.

16 Yuval, *A Cry Before the Holocaust*, pp. 22, 30-31.

17 Ibid., p. 111.

18 Ibid., p. 114.

19 Dalia Ofer, *Dead-End Journey: The Tragic Story of the Kladovo-Šabac Group* (Tel Aviv, 1992), pp. 40-42 (Hebrew).

20 Yuval, *A Cry Before the Holocaust*, p. 125.

21 Ibid., p. 125-126.

22 Slepak did not indicate the women's name but rather used initials.

23 We know very little about Mrs. C's age, family, and personal history. However, it is important to remember that the adults of the 1930s and 1940s, including the young adults, had experienced hunger, deportation, and deprivation during World War I, whether as adults or children. These were anxiety-provoking memories.

24 This was a reference to the abduction of Jewish individuals, particularly men, during the first months of occupation, for the purpose of forced labor, either inside or outside the city.

25 Lea Praiss, *Displaced Persons at Home: Refugees in the Fabric of Jewish Life in Warsaw, September 1939-July 1942* (Jerusalem, 2015).

26 On smuggling in the ghetto, see Barbara Engelking and Jack Leociak, *The Warsaw Ghetto: A Guide to the Perished City* (New Haven, 2009), pp. 446-529. Regarding executions, see p. 458.

Michal Shaul

Out of the Ruins: Establishing Haredi Families after the Holocaust

Introduction

Matchmaking in the Ashkenazi Haredi (Ultra-Orthodox) world[1] is based on the initiative and organization of parents, with lineage and social and economic standing constituting the paramount factors when agreeing to a match, in addition to the erudition of the groom and the dowry of the bride.[2] During the years immediately following the Holocaust, the vast majority of unmarried survivors had neither parents nor anyone else who was familiar with them or their lineage.[3] The long years of war had kept the men from study and all were destitute; a dowry was out of the question. This raises a plethora of questions: How, then, were matches arranged in Haredi society after the Holocaust? What unique challenges accompanied the process of setting up new Haredi families? Which authorities took responsibility and what initiatives were taken for the purpose of establishing new Haredi homes? How did the results of the Holocaust affect the creation of Haredi families both in the short and the long term? And how did the "orphaned generation" ultimately create a society with one of the world's highest birthrates?[4]

This article tracks the various stages of the process of creating a Haredi family in the aftermath of the Holocaust, whether among the displaced persons (DPs) in Europe, during the journey to Eretz Israel (the Land of Israel), or during the first period of absorption in their new homeland. This includes making introductions, obtaining halakhic approval to marry, engagement, marriage, and finally bearing and rearing children. All of these stages, which are a natural part of establishing a religious Jewish family, were accompanied by special challenges that affected the individual, the family, and, ultimately, all of Haredi society. In this article, special emphasis is placed on the role of women in this process. As sociologist Nancy Chodorow states in *The Reproduction of*

Mothering (1978), the basic assumption in gender research is that the mothers have a great influence upon the formation of their daughters' identity. Unlike a son, a daughter continues to emulate her mother even after she reaches maturity. As many women were separated from their mothers during the war, an entire generation of young girls sought a mother figure to emulate after the Holocaust. This dynamic was even more significant in traditional Haredi society,[5] in which most socialization is effected by the conveyance of traditions from mother to daughter. The absence of a mother during intimate junctures – such as getting engaged, becoming a bride, and being a young mother – and maintaining strict norms of modesty and unique religious prohibitions were all challenges facing Haredi women after the Holocaust, when they sought to build their own family as their life's paramount mission.[6]

Haredi Holocaust survivors were simultaneously part of three groups: Haredi society, Israeli Holocaust survivors, and Holocaust survivors in general. Their activities were influenced by processes that took place within each of these groups, both separately and in parallel to one another.[7]

Establishing a new family after the Holocaust was largely a personal process. However, as a means of dealing with tragedy, it also held social, national, and universal significance.[8] On the personal level, after the hardships they had undergone, the survivors chose life, seeking to create for themselves a space where they belonged and a source of hope for the future. Thus, finding spouses and having children was one of the first steps taken by both religious and non-religious survivors after they were liberated.[9] In light of the recent development in the study of gender and family during the Holocaust and research on the testimony of children after the Holocaust, a number of scholars have begun studying the establishment of post-war families. Noting that the establishment of new families after the war was a sign of healing and rehabilitation, they emphasize that the phenomenon was not simply a "happy ending"; rather, the process of establishing families was accompanied by the cataclysm and the scars it left behind.[10] However, these studies did not focus on Haredi survivors, who comprised some ten percent of all Holocaust survivors. This article focuses[11] specifically on the Haredi survivors, as this society, like all traditional and certainly traditionalistic societies, was and remains family oriented and makes no room for singles.[12] Thus, this study is particularly significant in light of the unique voice of this group, which constituted the founding generation of Haredi society, whose impact on Israeli society has increased over the years.

Certain aspects of the revival of Orthodox Judaism in the DP camps have already been explored by Judith (Tydor) Baumel-Schwartz, who has depicted the politics that characterized the return of religious praxis and its gendered aspects, and by Esther Farbstein, who has emphasized educational and halakhic aspects.[13] Here, I focus on the social-historical perspective, understanding the establishment of new families as one of the ramifications of the Holocaust, but also as part of the rehabilitation of post-Holocaust Haredi society. In this way, therefore, the article contributes to our understanding of the ramifications of the Holocaust, while shedding light on the development of Haredi society.

Our discussion focuses not on demographic, economic, or statistical data, but rather on how the memory of the Holocaust has impacted the values and emotions that are involved in and underlie marriage and married life.[14] In addition to archival documents, I also consulted autobiographies, oral testimony, and halakhic literature. This wide range of primary sources enabled me to uncover the issue's complexity and provided me with a means of crosschecking sources. I begin with an introduction describing the various aspects of establishing a Haredi family after the Holocaust and then describe and analyze the stages of establishing a new family, from matchmaking to child rearing, focusing on how the Holocaust and its aftermath affected each stage. In the article's conclusion, I consider the topic within broader historical context.

The "Wedding Campaign" in Haredi Society, 1945-1949

The Holocaust almost completely wiped out the world that was familiar to the survivors, and their return to life required tremendous efforts. The DP camps in which they were housed in Germany, Austria, and Italy offered poor living conditions and were permeated by overwhelming dynamics of isolation and mourning. Despite this, all who study the lives of Holocaust survivors describe the great vitality that characterizes them.[15] The survivors wanted to look toward the future and rehabilitate their lives. Even in the DP camps, they organized themselves on personal, social, cultural, political, and national levels.

As part of the shared goal of rehabilitating Jewish life, the survivors, in various general groups, had to redefine their goals and their particularistic identity. The ideological division of the DPs, usually according to the movements to which they had belonged before the war, was part of their rehabilitation.[16] According to some estimates, approximately 40% of the DPs in the camps returned to religious life in one form or another.[17]

There was a connection between marriage and the process of returning to religious life. According to many Haredi rabbis and educators, family units acted as a bulwark against the winds of change that drove people away from Haredi life, and marriage was supposed to provide supervision and stability.[18]

The campaign to rehabilitate the family units during the years immediately following the Holocaust required emotional fortitude, especially since it was undertaken without the natural support of family members who had perished.[19] Survivors hoped that this effort would compensate for the families that had been lost on the one hand, and lay a foundation for building a new life on the other hand.[20] The primary motivation for marriage, for the most part, was not to find true love, but rather to establish a family unit.[21] This impulse was noted by Rabbi Yitzchak Izak Leibes, head of the rabbinical court in Bytom, Poland:

> And after the repatriation from eastern Galicia to western Silesia I was appointed rabbi and head of the rabbinical court of the city of Bytom; we were gathered there about twenty thousand people without families, only widows and widowers who lost their children, and they were in a rush to get married in order to build a new home and have children…[22]

In addition to the biological impetus, there was another practical consideration in the DP camps, as marriage entitled DPs to a separate residence within the camp.[23] Migration – legal, and certainly illegal – as couples to different countries eased the travails of travel and resettlement, and therefore many preferred to marry before setting out on a voyage, the results of which were often difficult to predict.[24]

The establishment of new families was required to ensure the demographic rehabilitation of Haredi society, which had been decimated by the Holocaust.

Establishing a home and bearing children is one of the fundamental commandments of the Bible, and according to the Haredi view, the marital relationship is simply the means to that end. This view minimizes the importance of romantic love and focuses marriage on bringing children into the world and providing them with a warm environment in which to aid the family in fulfilling its spiritual purposes.[25] However, after the Holocaust, demographic rehabilitation and the desire to pass on a Haredi lifestyle to future generations, were intertwined with a special socio-ideological mission. As noted by Raphael Stern from Ungvar:

> Perhaps for this reason the Lord let me survive, that I may direct my sons, my house and those of my relatives and friends to follow the path of the Lord, the path that our sacred families followed… To what metaphor can this be compared? To that of an electric wire, which as long as it is not disconnected, can provide light hundreds of miles from its source, but if it is disconnected from its source by even a hairsbreadth, can no longer illuminate.[26]

Restoring the generational chain that was so cruelly torn asunder by the Holocaust was the goal behind establishing new families. Thus, marriage in general, and marriage of the survivors in particular, held special religious, national, moral, and social significance in Haredi society.

Matchmaking

Establishing new families during the years immediately following the Holocaust raised critical halakhic and social problems for the Haredi survivors. The first was how to find matches for orphans in a society where the matchmaking system was traditionally based on the lineage of parents and partners. Z. Asiriya addressed this problem in her memoirs:

> Finding a match is as difficult as the parting of the Red Sea. Devout Jews know that with matchmaking…the hand of Providence can be seen in everything. The Lord makes matches, and the parents

are the emissaries of that Providence in establishing a Jewish home. However, the survivors of the cataclysm who were left parentless have had unprecedented difficulty, since there has been no one to help them in this difficult time with this fateful decision.[27]

In Haredi society, the basic assumption regarding matchmaking is that God designated the couple for one another even before birth,[28] and it was not customary for them to be in unsupervised contact with each other beforehand.[29] The traditional function of rabbis as matchmakers for their students intensified after the Holocaust,[30] when it appears that all rabbis were taking this task upon themselves.[31] Matchmakers traveled back and forth between the Agudat Yisrael movement's training kibbutzim for men and for women in order to match up single survivors. Every matchmaking interview attempted to discern the qualities of the intended, although the lack of such data did not impede the matches. The 'inventory' of singles coming from Haredi homes was very limited, whereas the urgency to marry was enormous, and it was important to not be too selective. Indeed, it was especially urgent for them to marry off those whose religious faith was not particularly strong.[32]

There was special concern regarding the girls and their modesty. Rabbi Avraham Meir Israel, the rabbi of the survivors in Austria, shared the sense of mission he felt in finding proper spouses for the orphaned survivors:

> And I saw the great spiritual and physical destruction…and I had not even a drop of hope that these dry bones, brands plucked from a fire, should return to life. And I said to myself, the Lord has sent me to preserve life, and it was the Lord's will to keep me alive, to give to the members of my city and community who remain few from many, a remnant in the land, and to keep them alive by a great deliverance. I acceded to them, and with the help of God I fulfilled my mission both in the matters of enhancing the community and its institutions, and in the matter of marrying off the miserable orphans who were left without parents or guardians. I made sure that they would not be swept away in the wave of

anarchy that prevailed at the time throughout the land, and with
the help of God I was able to marry them off to proper men, and
I took care of them as though they were my own daughters, my
flesh and blood. Many of them live with their Jewish brethren in
the Holy Land, and also in this land (the United States) they live
peaceful and placid lives, thank God.[33]

Even after immigrating to Eretz Israel, educators continued with their
matchmaking efforts. For the Hassidim, the arena for matchmaking was often the
shteibel (small synagogue), where the singles were more or less known and where
they were approached with proposed matches.[34] In other social and educational
frameworks, such as yeshivot, the homes of women pioneers,[35] or the kibbutzim
of Agudat Yisrael[36] (the ultra-Orthodox political party), counselors and rabbis
continued to engage in matchmaking for their students. The counselors and
rabbis often stood beside the bride or groom during the writing of the "*tnoyim*"
(the prenuptial arrangement that enumerates the mutual responsibilities of the
families of the bride and groom), at the engagement parties, at the wedding,
and as godfathers for the offspring.[37]

Being orphaned and detached from family life, which is what happened to
the survivors during the long years of the war, occasionally raised the concern
that they would not know how to run a proper Haredi household. Israeli-born
children have testified to their parents' hesitations regarding the idea of their
daughter marrying a survivor, with all of his emotional scars.[38] Rabbi Israel Meir
Lau spoke about the difficulties of the process of making the match between
him and the daughter of Rabbi Yitzhak Yedidya Frankel (1913-1986):

My father in law, Rabbi Yitzhak Yedidya Frankel OB"M [of blessed
memory] … was an exceptional man … and the moment I saw
his daughter, I decided to marry her. It did not occur to me to
phone her… I called her brother and told him that, although it is
customary for the father to approach the girl's parents, I had neither
a father nor a mother … I was permitted to arrange a meeting with
the girl…I secretly decided to get engaged. I had not yet met her

father. They finally told me that her father, the rabbi, expects me to visit him on Saturday night, at his home. He was alone, and he served an excellent meal, and then he told me the following: (…) they tell me that you are a gifted student. I shall, however, tell you the truth. For a long time, I hesitated and was deterred from giving my only daughter to a man without father or mother, who never knew normal family life, who doesn't remember his parents. How can he set up a real home when he never knew one?[39]

The fear of a match with a Holocaust survivor existed even in the case of erudite youth or sons and daughters of families with distinguished lineage. Apparently, the disruption the Holocaust caused to the intergenerational transfer of traditions that is described above in connection with the yeshiva world[40] had ramifications on daily life and the functioning of the family and community.

Hava Bronstein related the problems that her friend, a Holocaust survivor from a distinguished family, faced when seeking a proper match:

I had a friend named Malka, a graduate of a teachers' seminary… She was the daughter of a famous Hassidic Rebbe from Romania and sought a learned groom who only studied Torah. I travelled with my aunt from Jerusalem to the secretary of a well-known yeshiva asking that he find Malka a proper match… He listened to us, heard our description…and finally said: "Our yeshiva doesn't have a handicapped youth who can take a new immigrant"… I was shocked to the depths of my soul… My aunt was also shocked… and reacted angrily: "I am happy that you and your family weren't in Europe during the years of horror, but know that the parents of the girl you are speaking of wouldn't have considered entering into the ties of matchmaking with the likes of you."[41]

Bronstein also wrote about one of her friends, a Holocaust survivor and the daughter of a Hassidic Rebbe, who refused to marry someone from a lower social class:

She would not settle for less than a great scholar or a Hassidic Rebbe. This was her aspiration, since her father was a rabbi. It was difficult to admonish her, partly because I was much younger than she was, but I plucked up my courage and answered her: "You can ask the Blessed Lord to order an '*erlicher yid*' [honorable Jew] for you ... after all the suffering you went through in the fires of Europe, on the contrary, you would enable him to learn and rise higher and higher.... What is your conclusion from the story of Rabbi Akiva and his wife Rachel?... Some receive their husband 'ready-made,' a clear scholar, with good qualities, and then there is the woman who has to enable him to study, to relinquish much so that he can become a great scholar." She was not convinced by my words – "I want a husband who is a Rebbe, of great stature, raised above the crowd." As expected, Hinda remained a spinster until the day she died.[42]

Significant age differences between those being matched were commonplace. In 1952, the average age of a Haredi groom was 27.5, whereas the average age of a Haredi bride was 21.6.[43] This phenomenon had social implications for Haredi society for many years, including fertility rates, the percentage of singles, and the percentage of widows.

There was also, however, an opposite trend, and to some extent matchmaking became easier after the Holocaust. The inventory of unmarried men and women was limited, the differences between the proposed grooms and even between the various brides were very minor, and in any event, the choice was limited. In cases where there were very few surviving relatives – even distant – and few survivors from a specific city or region, there was a natural tendency to marry someone from the same city or family.[44] The concentration of women and men from a mixture of origins in the DP camps, kibbutzim, illegal immigration ships, detention camps in Cyprus, and ultimately in Eretz Israel permitted matches that would probably not have occurred in normal times due to geographic and intellectual distances. Thus, for example, in a society where it was accepted to emphasize and preserve national origins, matches were made that could not have been maintained, or were very rare, in the interwar period.[45] Emigrants from Poland married emigrants from Hungary. Emigrants from

Germany married those from Poland, and so on. Even ideological differences were blurred. Sons of Lithuanian homes married daughters of Hassidic homes, and vice versa. Many Haredi homes were established through marriage between survivor-immigrants and long-time inhabitants of the country.[46]

It is clear that the overriding need to marry often overcame prejudices. The lack of a supervising family allowed for matches that in normal times were unlikely to have been approved.[47] Thus, for a number of years there was an intra-Haredi "melting pot," which had significant ramifications on the nature of the families that took shape, the customs that were created or adopted, and the education of the children.[48]

As Haredi society became more established, parents regained their traditional role of finding matches for their children. They could again be fussy about their future sons- and daughters-in-law. From this perspective, then, the initial years after the Holocaust were a "historical enclave" regarding matchmaking in Haredi society, with norms that differed from what was customary in pre-war Europe and what is accepted today. These norms were all ramifications of the Holocaust.

Halakhic Examination of Personal Status

Books of responsa assemble rabbis' answers to questions they have been asked regarding all realms of life. We have at our disposal many responsa from the DP camps that are of great importance.[49] Life in the DP camps raised crucial questions among rabbis, especially regarding marital matters. The primary problem was how to marry couples who wished to start a family but who had known each other for only a short time and had little knowledge of each other's past. It was not always possible to produce two witnesses from each side to attest to the personal status of the couple seeking to marry, which according to Orthodox Halakha is a necessary condition.[50] Religious Holocaust survivors, and even those who were not religious but wanted a court's confirmation regarding their personal status, had to clarify their questions and doubts with a rabbi. This situation caused many Holocaust survivors, who hitherto had not revealed their personal stories, to testify before the adjudicator.[51]

The Holocaust is the only event in Jewish history to have left behind thousands of *agunot* (grass widows) wishing to rebuild their marital lives.

Enabling them to remarry was the most urgent halakhic concern during the initial years following the war.[52] When dealing with this complex and sensitive halakhic matter, rabbis had to delve deeply into the historical details of the Holocaust, leading some to define them as the "first Holocaust researchers."[53]

The matter of "grass widowers" (*agunim*) who wanted to marry was less complex, as the religious ruling against marrying more than one woman was handed down later and was not biblical law, permitting them to marry if they submitted a conditional bill of divorce, which would be presented to the first wife should she return.[54] With regard to permitting the agunot to remarry, the rabbis related to the matter as one of "life or death," in which it is forbidden to be overly strict or to delay resolution.[55] The clear tendency of all the rabbis, from their part, was to find the most lenient rules of proof, which do not exist in any other halakhic field, and to allow the agunot to remarry.[56]

Other halakhic concerns regarding marital matters also arose after the Holocaust, including the matter of married women who were victims of rape. Some female Holocaust survivors testified that after the Holocaust, the burden of proof that they had not used their bodies sexually to survive rested with them.[57] In this context, Rabbi Ephraim Oshry (1914-2003) discussed a question he had been asked:

> A young woman from a respected family in Kovno came to me with tears gushing down her cheeks, She, like many of her unfortunate sisters, had been captured by the Germans and forced into prostitution. The evildoers had not only made free use of her pure body, but they had also tattooed the words "prostitute for Hitler's soldiers" on her.
>
> After the liberation, she was reunited with her husband, who also survived. Their children had been murdered by the Germans, and they hoped to establish a new family on the basis of Jewish sanctity and purity. But when her husband saw these words tattooed on her body he was extremely upset. He decided they must clarify first whether he was allowed to live with her according to halacha, for if she had even once willingly slept with a German she might be forbidden to her husband. Therefore, she came before him to ask

what could be done for her, as her breach was as great as the sea, and her eyes were seeking mercy to bring forth her judgment.[58]

The women therefore came to Rabbi Oshry seeking a solution and seeking mercy. His position was as follows:

> I ruled that there was no need for this woman to try to have the tattoo obliterated. On the contrary, let her and her sisters preserve their tattoo and regard them not as signs of shame, but as signs of honor, pride, and courage – proof of what they suffered for the sanctification of G-d.[59]

Despite this woman's sense of shame and humiliation, she was able to speak freely and intimately with the rabbi who, from his part, demonstrated a deep sense of compassion for her and sought to remind her and other Jewish girls that they were not to blame and therefore could and should return to the bosom of their People, with a sense of purity, honor, and bravery.

Another matter brought before the rabbis after the Holocaust was matchmaking for *Kohanim* (members of the priestly caste). According to Jewish law, a Jewish woman who was captured by gentiles is considered to have been raped and therefore may not marry a Kohen. If she had been married to a Kohen after she was captured, she is now forbidden to him. On several occasions, the question arose as to whether to forbid marriage between Kohanim and Holocaust survivors, and the rabbis who dealt with this problem unanimously decreed that such marriages should be permitted.[60] Rabbi Liebes justified this ruling based on the fact that the racial laws promulgated by the Nazis forbade sexual contact with Jews and on the assumption that these laws were enforced.[61] In another case, heard by Rabbi Tavyomi, the following question was asked: A Kohen's wife, who had been in the Bergen-Belsen camp in Germany for several years, had worked there as a "Polish" woman, and after the war she returned to her husband, who was a Kohen. Was he permitted to continue having sexual relations with her by law, or was the law of captives applicable here?[62] Tavyomi replied that even though strict application of the law ruled out leniency, it was nonetheless necessary –

after their years of suffering, their miraculous survival, and their return to their husbands – to seek out and find some other grounds for permission in order to avoid further compounding their immense tragedy.[63]

The interesting thing in this case is that the question was not asked by the husband, but rather, by the rabbi of the neighborhood in which the couple lived. The rabbi was uncertain whether it was his responsibility to bring this matter to the attention of her husband, a Torah-abiding Jew, because "he has not himself asked the question," or whether to turn a blind eye to it. The questioner explained his inclination to turn a blind eye to the halakhic matter:

> According to rumor, the woman is very sensitive and does not say anything about what happened to her, even to those closest to her, and if we brought it up it would be a very great tragedy. Hence the esteemed rabbi has asked me to state whether I believe he would be doing his religious duty by keeping silent.

In this case, silence was chosen for the sake of the survivors. It must also be added that not only did the rabbis do all that they could to permit the survivors to marry,[64] but some even ruled that "it is a meritorious act to marry off these orphans"[65] and that it was especially meritorious to marry off widows who lost their husbands in the Holocaust.[66] Beyond that, in their lenient rulings, the rabbis sought to rehabilitate the status of Jewish law, knowing that if they did not find a way to grant permission, the questioners might try to rebuild their home outside the framework of Jewish law.

Engagements

Immediately after the couple was found to be fit to marry according to Jewish law they got engaged. Due to the strong impulse to marry, the interval between engagements and weddings was usually very short.[67] In the DP camps, the process was particularly rapid; however, in countries to which the survivors immigrated, a modest engagement celebration was occasionally held.

Z. Asiriya described her feelings of loneliness at her engagement party, held at the home of Rabbi Shlomo Schwab (1896-1962) in London, when the rabbi mentioned the parents of the bride and groom who had perished in the Holocaust:

My eyes were filled with tears. I had no idea how I could express my gratitude that he [Rabbi Schwab] had succeeded in finding just the right moment and place to mention our parents' souls. For the first time in many years, a crack appeared in my hardened heart, and I was granted, even for a few short minutes, the ability to mourn them. The massive pain had caused me to seal my heart under lock and key, and for all those years, I had not allowed myself to think of them. However, in addition to the mourning I felt their presence, and today I fully understand it. For me, that revived my soul.[68]

Asiriya recounted how she and her betrothed arrived in Israel and were hosted by family members. The families that hosted the groom and the bride planned the wedding as though they were in-laws.[69] As was customary in Haredi society, all the discussions were held without the couple being present, except for that pertaining to the invitation's wording.[70] These "in-laws" accepted the fact that, "because our bride and groom have wandered so much since early childhood, it is very important that they have a corner, however modest, but their own, where they can build their home." They therefore found a tiny apartment for the couple, in exchanged for key money.[71] With the assistance of philanthropists in Israel and abroad, who sought to fulfill the precept of providing for a bride, a small dowry was collected. The wedding was held at the home of the family that hosted the bride – the home of then-Knesset member Meir David Levenstein (1904-1995). In the end, it was decided that their host families would invite the guests as though it were their own children getting married. In addition, the groom helped with the wedding expenses by taking a loan. Moreover, it was decided to invite the rabbi of the Ponevezh yeshiva, accompanied by several of his important students, "to create the atmosphere of a yeshiva, as was fitting for the groom in question, whose aspirations were to learn Torah, despite the conditions that had forced him to work for a living."[72]

In the Ponevezh yeshiva, engagements, weddings, and bar-mitzvahs were held for the survivors in a manner that was relatively festive and grand for the period in question,[73] and Rabbi Kahaneman was punctilious about honoring the event with his presence whenever possible.[74] Rabbi Moshe Munk, the inspector of Youth Aliya on behalf of Agudat Yisrael, described one of these celebrations which he attended with Rabbi Kahaneman:

> I was at an engagement party with him for one of the orphans, and it was celebrated in the yeshiva with all pomp and glory, as though a queen was getting engaged. The school principal, rabbis from the yeshiva, and I, as the representative of Youth Aliya, all spoke. They all stated their hope that the couple would follow the path of Torah and would establish a home devoted to God and His Torah. Of course, they based their words on the portion of the week and rabbinical sayings. In the end, Rabbi Kahaneman got up to speak. He emphasized a totally different point. He wished the couple, and especially the orphaned girl, a life of happiness and tranquility… He delved deep into the soul of the orphan and spoke to her like a father to his daughter.[75]

As a result of the support which the Haredi survivors received from rabbis and educators, marriage in the shadow of grief played the dual role of allowing survivors to process grief and facilitating re-education. The process of establishing oneself as an individual, and the transition from being alone to being the head of a family, led the survivors to look toward the future, to rehabilitate themselves, and to undertake the tasks facing Haredi society – first and foremost, the task of recoupling the generational chain.[76]

The Wedding Ceremony

In the Bergen-Belsen DP camp in the British Zone of Occupation, in which a quarter of the residents belonged to Agudat Yisrael,[77] there were more than one thousand weddings in 1946 alone (approximately seven weddings per day).[78] In Poalei Agudat Yisrael's largest preparatory kibbutz, "Netzach Yisrael" in Hénonville near Paris, which numbered on average several hundred unmarried male and female survivors, some 100 couples were married during the six years of its existence (1946-1952). During the week when Rabbi Hezkiayhu Joseph Mishkovsky visited Hénonville (April 1946),[79] ten weddings were held there.[80]

The unmarried brides lacked even minimal knowledge of the laws of family purity, which, for reasons of modesty, are not discussed before the wedding. In normal times, brides learned these laws on the eve of their wedding, taught orally by a married woman – a mother, the rabbi's wife, or a bridal instructor.[81] In the absence of mothers or rabbis' wives, survivors who wished to marry were compelled to seek the "written law," and to attempt to reconstruct the natural process by which girls become women and mothers. Granatstein delicately cites the embarrassed memories of a woman, subsequently his wife, who was compelled to become a "bridal counsellor" in the Agudat Yisrael kibbutz in Lodz:

> I remember when I received the first request on this subject – my hair stood on end. I refused to even think about it. I was just a young lady, and I had never learned these laws. But needs must be addressed. The girls were about to get married… I asked one of the girls to look for a prayer book that has these laws in Yiddish…I stayed up all night considering and studying, and I arranged the material. In the morning, I invited the first young woman to the lesson… The first discussion is engraved in my memory. We talked about the responsibility toward the next generation: a responsibility which is the lot of all generations, but which had especially great meaning to us, the girls who survived. This mission, the most precious of all, obligated us to keep it all in purity.[82]

Cooperation between dynamic DPs and representatives of the JDC resulted in the establishment and refurbishing of numerous ritual baths in many DP camps in both the British and the American Zones.[83] The many marriage ceremonies conducted in the DP camps, which combined joy and sadness, became the focus of local social life.[84]

Research on the rehabilitation of survivors' lives clearly reflects that during the years in question, personal salvation was sustained by national salvation.[85] In many cases, someone under the wedding canopy spoke about the establishment of a new Jewish family as a victory over the Nazis, invoking the memory of the couples' parents and other relatives who were not able to participate in the event.

Some recited a Jewish memorial prayer (*El Maleh Rahamim*) under the wedding canopy.[86] The various prophets' prophesies of redemption linked the establishment of the family unit to national redemption, as did the marriage ceremony, with the words "thus shall there be heard again in…the cities of Judah and the streets of Jerusalem…the sound of joy and the sound of gladness, the sound of the groom and the sound of the bride" (Jeremiah 33), on which the rabbis based their saying: "Gladdening the groom and the bride is like rebuilding one of the ruins of Jerusalem." Thus, the rabbis decreed that at any joyous occasion, the destruction of the Temple should be mentioned, and as a result, it is customary at the wedding ceremony to place a pinch of ash on the groom's head and to break a glass. After the Holocaust, the wedding canopy was transformed from a traditional Jewish "memorial space" for the destruction of the Temple into a significant "memorial space" commemorating the latest destruction, with both events merging with the same general meaning.[87] Expressing Holocaust commemoration through interweaving layers of basic values and traditional spaces of Jewish memorial of the Destruction (under the wedding canopy, and other family ceremonies such as the Passover Seder and the Sabbath dinner table) cast these family frameworks into what Iwona Irwin-Zarecka has referred to as a "sedimentation of meanings" stacked on top of one another. The oldest and most meaningful bear the new, which, in turn, acquire depth from the older layers.[88]

The departed have always been both present and absent at weddings, and every joyous Jewish occasion integrates some pain over those who are no longer with us. However here, the mourning mentioned under the wedding canopies increased the survivors' sense of obligation to build new Jewish families.

In the absence of family members, incidental guests sought to rejoice with the bride and groom. Yehoshua Eibeshitz attended a wedding conducted by the Klausenberger Rebbe in Fernwald in the autumn of 1945, and he described the event as follows:

> …I was shocked by the scene before my eyes. The study hall was packed from wall to wall, extremely crowded, and the rebbe stood on one of the tables and danced enthusiastically, in a manner befitting a young lad. People told me that this is how he acts at

every wedding and every post-wedding dinner, which he leads for the young couple. He dances for hours until the corporeality has been removed.[89] I was totally amazed by the man, who was not young, and by his superhuman powers. A man who lost his wife and all his children at Auschwitz was able to rejoice, and to gladden with unusual ecstasy every young couple who established their home after the destruction.[90]

"The weddings were modest and took place in meeting halls in the DP camps and in other places where survivors congregated. In Israel, weddings were held in yeshiva buildings and in Pioneer Homes"[91] Many signings of the wedding agreements (*tnoyim*), engagement ceremonies, and post-wedding parties (*sheva brachot*) were held in the homes of rabbis and under their auspices. The invited guests' participation in the weddings and other events of the survivors of past communities, or members of present communities, created meaningful social gatherings for the lonely survivors and provided them with a sense of family and belonging.[92]

Childbearing

The clearest example of the desire for life, creation, and achievement that came to the fore among the survivors was the fact that between 1946 and 1948, the birth rate in the DP camps was among the highest in the world.[93] Having children was a key element of the rehabilitation of Holocaust survivors. Psychiatrist Hillel Klein, himself a Holocaust survivor, described marriage and having children as the survivors' point of "psychological renewal." According to Hanna Yablonka, who has researched the meaning of childbearing for the survivors who immigrated to Israel, two of the most common metaphors used by survivors to describe the birth of their children within their life stories was the light it brought into the lives of the parents and the family tree that had been cut down but sprouted new branches. Yablonka explains that the children lent new certainty to generational continuity, both in terms of the family and the nation. The new generation brought with it not only hope but also the memories of infants and children who did not survive, and the names given to infants commemorated the dead. For the survivors, the parental responsibility was a strengthening factor that prevented them from sinking into loss and despair stemming from memories of the war and the difficulties of absorption in Israel. In addition, the children served as absorption agents in Israel through whom social connections were created.[94]

Haredi survivors who have shared their memories in an orderly manner emphasize that having many children was their answer to and revenge against Hitler.[95] They depict a rapid process of rehabilitation peaking with the establishment of a glorious family living by the light of the Torah and the Jewish commandments. Their children and grandchildren are described as providing satisfaction and serving as the focus of the new life they had built.[96]

However, as Lawrence Langer has noted regarding non-Haredi survivors whose testimonies he analyzed, the establishment of a family did not always compensate for the pain and suffering, which remained present in the survivors' lives. In Langer's words, the past continues to chase the survivors as though the day of liberation never arrived,[97] and therefore "during the Holocaust part of the future was also murdered."[98] The absence of the relatives who perished in the Holocaust was especially troublesome during family celebrations. As one survivor wrote about the circumcision of her son:

> There was great joy, but it was mixed with sorrow. The child (may his light shine) was named for his grandfather who was shot to death together with his wife…. during the liquidation of the Lemberg ghetto in 1942…. At this stage Malka's parents Michael and Yitzhak (the writer and her husband) felt as though their family had started to be rebuilt. The awareness that their role, after remaining alive, was to ensure the continuation of the glorious family tree began to take form.[99]

In most cases, the infants were named after those who perished. This was not only a memorial but also served to expedite future open discourse regarding the past.[100] In the shadow of orphanhood and bereavement, bringing the infant into the covenant of Abraham was seen as a great privilege. The joy mixed with sorrow, together with the intensified "presence" of the dead that accompanied the peak of the family circle of life, again reminded the survivors of the task they had taken upon themselves: to resume and maintain the severed tradition.[101]

An increased birthrate in Haredi society holds symbolic meaning and political power. Bearing and educating children are part of the Jewish religious and social system of beliefs.[102] After the Holocaust, the demographic mission of "filling out the ranks" was regarded as the most significant national task that Jewish women could and must fulfil. This mission's ideological aspect was accompanied by a demographic one: women were called upon to fulfil their traditional mission as mothers, to strengthen the Haredi family unit, and to see this, rather than the Zionist undertaking, as the Jewish national mission.

When Israel's Security Service Law was enacted in 1949, religious circles opposed the compulsory drafting of women not only due to the many halakhic difficulties this presented, such as the bearing of arms and other matters of modesty, but also out of a desire to maintain the women's place in the home.[103] Against the background of the struggle to exempt girls from the requirement of army service, the following proclamation was issued:

> The Jewish people lost 6,000,000 people, and there is no greater national mission than to increase our nation as the dust of the earth, and our descendants as the sand of the sea. Any path that leads to this is a national enterprise, and any step or mobilization that teaches women to think that there are other, higher positions, results in family suicide (God forbid).[104]

Fulfilling this mission, however, involved physical, emotional, and social difficulties. Women, whose practical way of learning and gaining life skills was by observing and imitating their mothers and other female family role models, now faced an immense gap which Haredi society strived to fill.[105] Some of the female survivors in the DP camps had relatives or acquaintances who helped them during childbirth, but the young mothers mainly helped one another. When they reached Israel, many experienced women filled this void, guiding the young women, meeting their needs as brides and then as women giving birth, opening their homes to them during postpartum recovery, and teaching them how to take care of their infants. As most of the young mothers typically had few first-degree biological family members, these adoptive women and friends, as years passed, became 'aunts' who were an inseparable part of their family.

The emotional scars left by the Holocaust refused to vanish and left their mark on the way the children were brought up, as the young mothers lacked a guiding mother figure to emulate when raising their children. Z. Asiriya reconstructed her feelings as an orphaned mother:

> And thus, little Malka (her firstborn daughter) grew up. We knew that it was incumbent upon us to educate her. I was totally fearful – I felt that I didn't have the tools to properly fulfil this undertaking! After all, all my life I wandered from place to place. Most of my childhood was spent among gentiles, and I had never seen how a young Jewish family functions. I felt that I lacked everything a Jewish mother requires in order to educate her children.

In her great distress, she turned to an acquaintance from Tel Aviv who had adopted six refugee families and helped guide them on their path. The young women called her "Mama."[106] Such cases prove that, for the survivors, personal absorption was more important than institutional absorption.

Conclusions

As a result of the prevalent aspiration of building a home and a family characterized by stability and warmth, the search for a match was one of the first undertakings of the Holocaust survivors after the war. The survivors' establishment of new families reflected the satisfaction of a biological impulse, which for the Haredi Holocaust survivors held both religious and moral meaning for the Jewish People as a whole. The large number of weddings that took place after the Holocaust reflected, above all else, the desire to live that pulsed through the veins of the survivors, and the desire to rehabilitate their lives and not sink into despair. The years immediately following the Holocaust have therefore been characterized as a period of confusion during which the personal and the national, destruction and revival, and despair and hope were all mixed together.

It was therefore an unusual period for matchmaking in Haredi society. In a period of blurring of identities, the absence of parents – who were traditionally responsible for matchmaking, and the absence of a substantial pool of unmarried men and women from which to choose, "mixed marriages" between Hassidic and non-Hassidic Jews and between natives of different countries became possible. For a short period, Haredi society became more pluralistic and open, at least in Haredi terms, reflecting the awareness of a minority that could not permit itself to be overly strict or selective, as had been customary in the past.

The emotional scars of the Holocaust remained, leaving their mark on the manner in which the children were raised and on every joyous occasion, which inevitably incorporated an element of grief regarding those who were absent. There were long-term effects for the generation of descendants on the reasons for marriage, the age at marriage, and family relationships. The impact of the memory of the Holocaust on intergenerational relationships in Haredi families still needs to be researched.[107]

The modernization of Jewish society, which has sped up increasingly since the eighteenth century, has eroded the traditional family. Hassidism, and later enlightenment, secularism, socialism, Zionism, and broader processes of urbanization and migration challenged the educational supervision of families, who found it difficult to deal with their children's captivation by exciting movements that presented themselves as alternatives to the traditional world.[108] To contend with these phenomena, Haredi leaders established inclusive family-like institutions – the yeshiva for boys and the *Beit Yaacov* network for girls. These institutions deliberately sought to mold the worldview and lifestyle of their attendees and provided for all of their students' physical and spiritual needs, playing the role of parents, who had themselves undergone a process of modernization.[109] However, between the two world wars, these institutions had met with only partial success.[110] Only after the Holocaust did Haredi society become a stable and fortified Torah society. Saving the world of Torah Judaism was a mission that many Haredi educator rabbis took upon themselves, seeking to continue the "martyrs' heritage." The family was the means to achieve this ideal. Ideals that, prior to the Holocaust, belonged only to the Hassidic or non-Hassidic elite, were demanded of the general public after the Holocaust.

Commitment to an ideological movement always creates an element of tension with the commitment to family, and therefore the ideal of dedication to the study of Torah, and the model of holiness developed by the Gur Hassidim, required that all family members bear the yoke. Similar to Zionist society, Haredi society after the Holocaust was a "mobilized society" that demanded the dedication of its members in order to establish an exemplary society in Israel.

With the world of Torah Judaism in ruins behind them, as their eyes observed the formation of an alternative secular entity in the Holy Land, a deep sense of mission, to strengthen the world of Torah Judaism and to prevent its disruption by secular forces, developed among Haredi Holocaust survivors. This mission was characterized by a self-awareness of being the representatives of the world that was. Through the new families they established, the survivors restored Haredi society, demographically as well as socially and ideologically, when they bestowed upon their descendants the ancestral tradition according to Haredi interpretation.

Establishing new families is a personal, national, and human means of dealing with death and destruction. For Haredi Holocaust survivors, the family was first and foremost a significant framework for commemorating those who perished, communing with the memory of the dead, and working through the mourning. The excitement over and care for the children became the core of the lives of many survivors, while the experiences of the Holocaust remained buried deep within them. But these memories would arise and gush forth, especially during family events and gatherings. It is almost certain that the heavy shadow of the Holocaust, which always hangs over Haredi society and Israeli society as a whole, is one of the reasons that the State of Israel has one of the highest birthrates of all developed countries[111] and that the value of family is considered to be especially important and is never taken for granted.

Endnotes

1   The Haredi (Ultra-Orthodox) world has never been homogenous but rather is composed of subgroups characterized by a number of social divisions, the major one being between "Hassidim" and "Lithuanians" (non-Hassidim). Of the numerous definitions regarding who is a "Haredi," we employ the one advanced by Menachem Friedman in *The Haredi Society: Sources, Trends and Processes* (Jerusalem, 1991), p. 9. The value of family and the memory of the Holocaust are among the shared and unifying factors in this diverse society. Although it can be assumed that part of the discussion in this article is relevant to non-Haredi families (particularly religious families), researchers note that Haredi society is characterized by unique patterns both in terms of establishing families and the memory of the Holocaust. On this basis, the discussion here is dedicated exclusively to these subjects. Moreover, although this study deals specifically with Israel, it can be assumed that part of the discussion is also relevant to Haredi families around the world.

2   This fastidious process, which is conducted according to accepted principles, is a transaction in all senses, in which the emotional foundation between the spouses plays only a marginal role. See Amnon Levi, *The Haredim* (Jerusalem, 1988), pp. 104-119 (Hebrew); Nava Wasserman, *I Never Called My Wife: Intimacy Within the Gur Hassidim* (Sde Boker, 2017), pp. 160-177 (Hebrew); Esther R. Goshen-Gottstein, "Marriage and Pregnancy in 'Geula': A Study of an Ultra-Orthodox Jerusalem Group," *Israel Annals of Psychiatry* 4 (1966), pp. 43-46 (Hebrew).

3   Despite the semantic differences among them, the expressions "survivors," "remnants," and "surviving remnants" are used interchangeably in Hebrew. On the various terms and their meanings see Dalia Ofer, "Introduction: Israel in the Eyes of the Holocaust Remnants and its Survivors," in Ofer (ed.), *Israel in the Eyes of Survivors of the Holocaust* (Jerusalem, 2014), pp. 7-8 (Hebrew).

4   Michal Ganz, "Birthrate and Women's Power in Haredi Society in Israel," M.A. thesis, Bar-Ilan University, 2003 (Hebrew).

5   Researchers of Haredi Society identify it as a traditionalist society, meaning one that consciously sanctifies tradition. See Kimmy Caplan, "Research of the Haredi Society in Israel: Characteristics, Achievements, and Challenges," in Kimmy Caplan and Emmanuel Sivan (eds.), *Israeli Haredim: Integration without Assimilation?* (Tel-Aviv, 2004), p. 231 (Hebrew).

6   Ganz, "Birthrate and Women's Power"; Menachem Friedman, "The Haredi Woman," in Yael Atzmon (ed.), *A Window into the Lives of Women in Jewish Societies: An Interdisciplinary Research Anthology* (Jerusalem, 2005), pp. 276-287 (Hebrew).

7   See Michal Shaul, "The Israeli Ultra Orthodoxy and the Holocaust: Global, Local, and Domestic Dimensions of Memory," in Jacob S. Eder (ed.), *Holocaust Memory in a Globalizing World* (Göttingen, 2016), pp. 114-127.

8   In post-war periods, the value of family increases. This dynamic was especially notable around the world in the initial years following World War II, and the heightened birthrate of this period (known as the "Baby Boom") had far reaching consequences for the history of the twentieth century. See Andrew Cherlin, "Changing Family and Household: Contemporary Lessons from Historical Research," *Annual Review of Sociology* 9 (1983), pp. 51-66; Jesús J. Sánchez-Barricarte, "Measuring and Explaining the Baby Boom in the Developed World in the Mid-20th Century," *Demographic Research* 38 (March 2018), pp. 1203–1204; Jessica Weiss, *To Have and to Hold: Marriage, The Baby Boom, and Social Change* (Chicago, 2000).

9   See: Hagit Lavsky, "Families and Children in the Rehabilitation of Holocaust Survivors from Bergen-Belzen," *Yalkut Moreshet* 81 (April 2006), pp. 23-29 (Hebrew); Beth B. Cohen, "Starting Over: Reconstituted Families after the Holocaust," in Sharon Kangisser Cohen et al. (eds.), *Children in the Holocaust and its Aftermath: Historical and Psychological Studies of the Kestenberg Archive* (New York, 2017), pp. 62-80; Atina Grossman, "Victims, Villains, and Survivors: Gendered Perceptions and Self-Perceptions of Jewish Displaced Persons in Occupied Postwar Germany," *Journal of The History of Sexuality* 11 (1/2) (January-April 2002), pp. 291-318; Uta Larkey, "Transcending Memory in Holocaust Survivors' Families," in Joanna Beta Michlic (ed.), *Jewish Families in Europe, 1939-Present: History, Representation and Memory* (Waltham, MA, 2017), pp. 209-232.

10 The status of women, and particularly of those who were alone, was shaky. Exploitation, sexual licentiousness, and marriage out of despair after only a short acquaintance all took their toll, resulting in unhappy marriages, divorce, abandonment, and a dark and traumatic shadow cast over the lives of the survivors and their descendants. For primary research on the subject see Ruth Balint, "Children Left Behind: Family, Refugees and Immigration in Postwar Europe," *History Workshop Journal* 82 (2016), pp. 151-172; Federica K. Clementi, *Holocaust Mothers and Daughters: Family, History, and Trauma*, (Waltham, MA, 2013); Tara Zahra, *The Lost Children: Reconstructing Europe's Families after World War II* (Cambridge and London, 2011).

11 See Michal Shaul, *Holocaust Memory in the Ultra-Orthodox Society in Israel* (Bloomington, 2021), pp. 20-30.

12 See Yaacov Katz, *Tradition and Crisis: Jewish Society After the Middle Ages*, (Jerusalem, 1978), chapters 14 and 15 (Hebrew); Tamar Shalmon-Mack, *Tan Du: On Marriage and their Crises in Polish-Lithuanian Jewry, 1650-1800* (Tel-Aviv, 2012), chapter 1 (Hebrew); Menachem Friedman, "All of a King's Daughter's Honor is Outwards: The Haredi Woman," in David Y. Ariel et al. (eds.), *Blessed Be He who Made Me a Woman? Women in Judaism: From the Bible until Today* (Tel-Aviv 1999), p. 204 (Hebrew).

13 See Judith Tydor-Baumel, "Prayer Books and Hats: A Chapter in the Religious Rehabilitation of the Survivors in the DP Camps in Germany, 1945-1949," *Yalkut Moreshet* 48 (1990), pp. 55-68 (Hebrew); Tydor-Baumel, "Pioneers, Teachers, and Mothers: Haredi Women among the Holocaust Survivors," *Yad Vashem Studies* 36 (2008), pp. 121-149; Tydor-Baumel, "Kibbutz Buchenwald and Kibbutz Hafetz Hayyim: Two Experiments in the Rehabilitation of Jewish Survivors in Germany," *Holocaust and Genocide Studies* 9 (2) (1995), pp. 242-243; Esther Farbstein, *Hidden*

in Thunder: Perspectives on Faith, Halachah, and Leadership during the Holocaust (Jerusalem, 2007), pp. 513-615.

14 On the various approaches toward research of the history and sociology of the family, see Matat Adar-Bunis, *Families in the View of Sociology and Anthropology* (Raanana, 2007), pp. 15-59 (Hebrew); Adiel Shermer, *He Created Them Male and Female: Marriage at the end of the Second Temple Period and at the Time of the Mishna and the Talmud* (Jerusalem, 2004), p. 21 (Hebrew); Jane Turner-Censer, "What Ever Happened to Family History?" *Comparative Studies in Society and History* 33 (1991), pp. 528-538.

15 The subject of the DPs has been re-examined over the past two decades. See, for example, Yehoyakim Cochavi, *Root for the Uprooted* (Tel Aviv, 1999) (Hebrew); Hagit Lavsky, *Towards New Life: Survivors and DPs in Bergen-Belsen and in the British Occupation Zone in Germany, 1945-1950* (Jerusalem, 2006) (Hebrew); Ze'ev Mankovitch, *Between Memory and Hope: The Holocaust Survivors in Occupied Germany* (Jerusalem, 2007), pp. 30-31; Atina Grossman, *Jews, Germans and Allies: Close Encounters in Occupied Germany*, (Princeton and Oxford, 2007); Daniel Cohen, *In War's Wake: Europe's Displaced Persons in the Postwar Order* (Oxford, 2012).

16 Eliezer Schweid, "The Return to Religious Observance as an Ultraorthodox Response to the Holocaust," *Kivunim Hadashim* [New Directions] 6 (2002), p. 40 (Hebrew).

17 Baumel-Schwartz, "Pioneers," p. 127.

18 See, for example, the attempts of the Chief Rabbi of Celle to separate single Jewish girls from their Polish boyfriends in the Bergen-Belsen DP camp, in Refael Olavsky, *The Tear* (Tel Aviv, 1983), pp. 271-272 (Hebrew); Yehiel Grantstein, *The Days of Genesis: The Wondrous Story of the Spiritual-Faith-Religious Revival by a Small Group of Haredi Survivors after the Holocaust* (Bnei Brak, 1997), p. 136 (Hebrew); Yosef Lev, *These Bones Shall Live*, (Bnei Brak, 1998), p. 249 (Hebrew).

19 See Shulamit Fredricka Michman, *"No One Can Know What the Day Shall Bring": Personal Letters from the Rehabilitation Period in Holland after the Holocaust* (Tel Aviv, 2003), p. 16 (Hebrew).

20 Baumel-Schwartz, "Pioneers," pp. 142-145; Lavsky, "Families and Children," p. 12; Mankovitch, *Between Memory and Hope*, pp. 30-31; Grossmann, *Jews, Germans and Allies*, pp. 184-236.

21 Lavsky, "Families and Children," 9.

22 See: Yizhak (Izak) Liebes, *Beit Avi* (New York, 1971), p. 8 (Hebrew).

23 Lavsky, "Families and Children," 12.

24 See Grantstein, *The Days of Genesis,* p. 155.

25 Wasserman, *I Never Called My Wife*, pp. 194-197; Solomon Poll, *The Hasidic Community of Williamsburg: A Study in the Sociology of Religion* (New York, 1971), pp. 57-58; Linton C. Freedman, "Marriage without Love: Mate Selection in Non-Western Societies," in Graham B. Spanier and Robert F. Winch (eds.), *Selected Studies in Marriage and the Family* (New York, 1974), pp. 54-66.

26 Refael Stern, *Eternal Memory Book* (Jerusalem, 1947), p. 7 (Hebrew).

27 Z. Asiriya (Y. Luxenburg), *We Have a Young Sister* (Bnei Brak, 2003), p. 188 (Hebrew); Y. Segal, *While It Was Still Night: The Rabbi's Wife – Bathsheba Schwartz, Daughter of Rabbi Yehoshua Beckerman of Telz* (Bnei Brak, 1996), pp. 150-151 (Hebrew).

28 Wasserman, *I Never Called My Wife*, p. 161.

29 Ibid., p. 160.

30 See Mordechai Breuer, *The Tents of the Torah: The Yeshiva, Its Structure, and Its History* (Jerusalem, 2004), p. 401 (Hebrew); Shaul Stampfer, *The Evolution of the Lithuanian Yeshiva* (Jerusalem, 2005), p. 320 (Hebrew).

31 Author's interview with Avraham Verdiger, a Poalei Agudat Yisrael activist, May 8, 2007. Rivka Horowitz was a leader of the Beit Yaakov movement in the Bergen-Belsen DP camp and was most active in the field of matchmaking. Every evening, as the representative of the Beit Yaakov movement in the camp, she gave a dress that was sewn for her to women going to meet a potential husband in order to help them look respectable. See Pearl Benisch, *Carry Me in Your Heart: The Life and Legacy of Sarah Schenirer, Founder and Visionary of the Bais Yaakov Movement* (New York, 2003), pp. 346-348.

32 The Klausenberger Rebbe's chief goal was to facilitate the establishment of new families. See Zorach Warhaftig, *A Refugee and a Remnant from the Days of the Holocaust* (Jerusalem, 1984), p. 350 (Hebrew); Farbstein, *Hidden in Thunder*, pp. 355-357; Baumel, "Prayer Books," pp. 81-85; Aharon Sorasky, *The Klausenbuerger Rebbe* (MI and NY, 2003), p. 63. In some cases, there was a significant age difference between the groom and the bride.

33 Avraham Meir Israel, *The Sayings of Avraham* (New York, 1960), pp. 6-7 (Hebrew).

34 See The Testimony of Gita Virzhvinsky, Yad Vashem Archives, File 03/11305. In her testimony, Virzhvinsky stated that in the Gur Shteible in Haifa's lower city, both she (a young single woman at the time) and her widowed father were offered matches at the same time.

35 Rivka Engelard, the director of the Pioneers House in Ramat Gan, was concerned with matchmaking for her female students and after their weddings would throw "*sheva brachot*" parties for them in the Pioneers House. She, herself, was also married there. See Rut Zeidman-Dz'ubas, *When Dawn Breaks* (Jerusalem, 1995), 154 (Hebrew). Engelard's successor in the institution's management, Chava Herman, also made marrying off the girls at the Pioneers House her top priority and availed herself of the services of matchmakers from Bnei Brak. In one of her autobiographical books, she notes that "with every girl [who got married], we were as joyful as if it was our own biological sister." Hava Herman-Bronstein, *I Have Come Home: Absorption Pains in the Holy Land* (Jerusalem, 2006), pp. 47-49 (Hebrew).

36 Over the years, 12 bachelors who lived on Kibbutz Hafetz Hayim in August 1945 set up homes with girls from among the survivors who came to the kibbutz after the war. See Ada Gebel (Campagnano), "Hafetz Hayim: The Kibbutz of the Agudat Yisrael Workers Movement Facing the Holocaust," M.A. thesis, Ben-Gurion University of the Negev, 2007, p. 55 (Hebrew); Meir and Miriam Schwartz described their wedding on the kibbutz as follows: "…We were not alone. We felt as though the entire kibbutz was part of our family. We contributed to the community, and they contributed to us. We did not feel alone, the kibbutz's rabbi, Rabbi Hillel Brukental, performed the marriage ceremony. All the kibbutz members participated in the wedding feast…" See Meir and Miriam Schwartz, *From Generation to Generation*, (Jerusalem, 2005), p. 149 (Hebrew).

37 Lev, *These Bones Shall Live*, pp. 250-251.

38 Author's interview with Penina Basch, Bnei Brak, January 1, 2007. Mrs. Basch grew up in the Batei Ungarin compound in Jerusalem and married Mordechai, an Auschwitz survivor who was originally from Hungary. While her father had reservations regarding the match, her mother viewed Mordechai as a successful young man and encouraged her to marry him.

39 See Judith Hemmendiger-Feist, *The Children of Buchenwald* (Jerusalem, 1990), p. 33 (Hebrew). Eventually, Rabbi Frankel gave his blessing to the match, saying: "I believe that my daughter, with the spiritual endowment with which I have bequeathed her, has the tools needed to lay the foundations of a steadfast Jewish home in Israel. And I trust him that he will know how to make her happy." Ibid. A similar story was told by Rabbi Yehuda Amital about his match with the granddaughter of Rabbi Issar Zalman Meltzer, the head of the "Etz Chaim" yeshiva, who, for several years, chaired Agudat Yisrael's Council of Torah Sages. Amital related that Rabbi Meltzer preferred to follow his heart rather than the accepted rules and that the family was impressed by the refugee's *joie de vivre*. See Elyashiv Reichner, *By Faith Alone: The Story of Rabbi Yehuda Amital* (New Milford, 2011), pp. 129-132.

40 See Menachem Friedman, "Life Tradition and Book Tradition in the Development of Ultra-Orthodox Judaism," in Harvey E. Goldberg (ed.), *Judaism Viewed from Within and Without: Anthropological Studies* (Albany, 1987), pp. 235-255.

41 Bronstein, *I Have Come Home*, pp. 49-50.

42 Hava Bronstein, *Figures I Have Valued*, manuscript on file with the author.

43 See Yosef Shilhav and Menachem Friedman, *Growth and Segregation: The Ultra-Orthodox Community in Jerusalem* (Jerusalem, 1985), p. 50. The data refers to the Haredim in Israel, without differentiation between immigrants and long-time Israelis, Sefaradim and Ashkenazim, and Hassidim and Lithuanians (Lithuanians marry at an older age). It should be noted that, in 1981, the average marriage age dropped drastically to 21.5 for men and 20.0 for women).

44 See Farbstein, *Hidden in Thunder*, pp. 354-355.

45 See Shaul Stampfer, "Marital Patterns in Interwar Poland," in Israel Gutman et al. (eds.), *The Jews of Poland Between Two World Wars* (Hanover and London, 1989), pp. 173-197.

46 Thus, for example, the "Pioneers House" of Poalei Agudat Yisrael in Haifa operated for only a year, with the institution's head, Rabbi Yacobson, ensuring matches for the girls, most of whom married, some even to well-known yeshiva students. In Agudat Yisrael's "Youth House" in Jaffa, 73 out of the institution's 90 girls were married within a year, making the institution no longer necessary. Poalei Agudat Yisrael's Pioneer Houses in Ramat Gan and Jaffa held many weddings for the girls of the institutions. Binyamin Ze'ev Yacobson, *Memories* (Jerusalem, 1953), p. 189 (Hebrew). See also Rivka Wolbe, *Faith in the Night* (New York, 2009); Zeidman-Dz'ubas, *When Dawn Breaks*, p. 154; Ayalah (Hinda) Rottenberg, *Echoes of Yesteryear: Reminiscences of Jewish History in the Making: Eretz Yisrael from 1934 to 2000 through the Eyes and Pen of a Young Girl Growing Up amidst Turbulent Times* (Jerusalem and New York, 2003), pp. 261-262.

47 Meir Schwartz, who immigrated from Germany in 1939, and his wife Miriam Freitag, a Holocaust survivor from Lodz, testified: "We had no relatives left and didn't have anyone to ask whether it was a good match for us." See Schwartz, *From Generation to Generation*, p. 149.

48 In testimony given to Yad Vashem in the late 1990s, Holocaust survivor Zippora Fischer claimed that the high dowry price was a hindering factor for matchmaking in pre-Holocaust Hungary, but that in retrospect, it enabled rehabilitation after the Holocaust. Older unmarried women were saved because they weren't sent to their deaths as young women taking care of children, and after the Holocaust they were the ones who could marry widowers and rebuild the Haredi world. Testimony of Zippora Fischer, born in Hungary in 1933, Yad Vashem Archives (hereinafter, YVA) 0.3/11310 p. 35.

49 On responsa as historical sources, see Haym Soloveichik, *Responsa as a Historical Source* (Jerusalem: 1991) (Hebrew). On responsa during the Holocaust and after, see Yitzhak Avneri, "Halakhic Literature during the Holocaust," *Sinai* 92 (1983), pp. 172-188 (Hebrew); Itamar Levin, *Letters of Fire: Testimony from the Holocaust Period in Halakhic Literature* (Tel Aviv, 2002)(Hebrew); Yechezkel S. Lechtenstein, *And Your Faith at Night: Issues During the Holocaust in the Mirror of Halakha*, (Jerusalem, 2017) (Hebrew); Avraham Fuchs, *The Holocaust in Rabbinic Literature* (Jerusalem, 1995) (Hebrew); Farbstein, *Hidden in Thunder*, pp. 155-323; Y. Shafran, "Questions of Halakha During the Days of Holocaust and the European Destruction," *Sinai* 64 (1969), pp. 190-198 (Hebrew); Hirsch J. Zimmels, *The Echo of the Nazi Holocaust in Rabbinic Literature* (London, 1975).

50 YIVO Archives (hereinafter, YIVO), DP Collection, 209/33.

51 See Yael Fuchs, "The Attitude towards the Holocaust Survivors in the Responsa Literature and its Uniqueness in the Years after the War," seminar paper, David Yellin College (Jerusalem, 2008), pp. 15-16.

52 See Levin, *Letters of Fire*, pp. 203-248; Farbstein, *Hidden in Thunder*, pp. 365-398.

53 Farbstein, *Hidden in Thunder*, p. 365.

54 See Rabbi Yitzhak Isaac Halevi Herzog, *Yitzhak's Temple* (Jerusalem, 1960), Even Ha'Ezer A Section 28 (a response to Rabbi Prato, March 1947) (Hebrew).

55 See also Farbstein, *Hidden in Thunder*, pp. 366-376.

56 See Avigdor Haneman, "The Laws of Agunot (Bound Women): The Changing Halakha – Law, Exegesis, History and Society," Ph.D. dissertation, Ben-Gurion University of the Negev, 2017 (Hebrew).

57 See, for example, Ruth Bondy, *Shevarim Shelemin* [Complete Shards] (Tel Aviv, 1997) (Hebrew); Miriam Harel, *We Are Now Allowed to Cry* (Tel Aviv, 1989) (Hebrew); Esther Dror and Ruth Lynn, *How Did We Survive?* (Bnei Brak, 2016) (Hebrew).

58 Ephraim Oshry, *Responsa from the Holocaust* (New York, 2001), I, 27.

59 Oshry issued a similar ruling regarding the desire of a survivor to remove the number tattooed on her arm. See *Responsa from the Holocaust*, IV, 22 (Originally published in the monthly magazine *Hapardes*, February 1967 (Hebrew). Rabbi Meir Amsel, editor of the periodical *Hamaor* in Brooklyn, New York, strongly opposed Rabbi Oshry's halakhic ruling, permitting the removal of the tattoo and suggested that the woman should remember the salvation as opposed to the enslavement. See: Meir Amsel, "Erasure of Amalek and Erasure of the Nazis," *Hamaor* 150, February 1965, p. 3 (Hebrew).

60 See Levin, *Letters of Fire*, pp. 241-243 (Hebrew).

61 Liebes, *Beit Avi*, I, 134 (Hebrew). The previous question discussed here, which had been put to Rabbi Oshry, is not the only evidence that contradicts this assumption. On the Nuremberg Laws of September 1935, which banned sexual relations between Aryans and non-Aryans, see Shaul Friedlander, *Nazi Germany and the Jews: The Years of Persecution, 1933-1939* (Tel Aviv, 1997), pp. 167-178. See also Judith Tydor Baumel, *Double Jeopardy: Gender and the Holocaust* (London, 1998), pp. 117-138.

62 Yehuda Tuvia Tavyomi, *A Good Land* (Jerusalem, 1947), Section 61 (Hebrew).

63 Tavyomi, *A Good Land*, 188.

64 Rabbis also permitted a woman whose two husbands had died to marry a third, despite the orthodox interpretation of the law as designating such women as "deadly" and not permitted to remarry. See Yekutiel Yehuda Halberstam, *Divrei Yatziv* (Netanya, 1999) (Hebrew), Even Ha`ezer Section 25 (Hebrew); Dov Berish Weidenfeld, *Dovev Meisharim* Part III (Jerusalem, 1970), Section 45 (Hebrew).

65 Liebes, *Beit Avi* (Hebrew).

66 See Yehoshua Menachem Mendel Ehrenberg, *Dvar Yehoshua* [The Word of Joshua], Volume 5 (Bnei Brak, 1987), Section 37, on "Other Matters"; Shmuel Aharon Pardes, *Hapardes* [The Orchard] 19(8), October 1945, pp. 34-36. In contrast, rabbis

were divided on the issue of permitting men who had been castrated or sterilized during the Holocaust to marry. See Issar Yehuda Unterman, *Shevet Miyehudah* [The Scepter of Judah] (Jerusalem, 1984-1994), Volume 4, Section 17 (Hebrew); Mordechai Yaacov Breisch, *Helkat Yaacov* [The Plot of Jacob], Part II (Jerusalem), Part 145. As Levin explains in *Letters of Fire* (p. 248, note 91) (Hebrew), the question originates in the ban prohibiting infertile men from marrying in order to enable their intended wives to become mothers.

67 See Zoë Waxman, *Women in the Holocaust: A Feminist History* (Oxford, 2017), p. 129.

68 Z. Asiriya, *We Have a Young Sister*, p. 196.

69 Ibid., p. 214.

70 This decision was accompanied by significant misgivings on the part of the couple. Ibid., pp. 215, 217-218.

71 Ibid., p. 214.

72 Ibid., p. 215.

73 See Nathan Ortner "Our Great Rabbi," *She'arim*, September 10, 1969, p. 3 (Hebrew); Moshe Prager, "Those Who Weren't Consumed (…) The Life Travails of one of the Orphans of the Holocaust," *Beit Yaacov* 180-181 (January-February 1975), pp. 7-13 (Hebrew); Meir Deutsch, *The Children of the Sabbath: Mattersdorf, Gotha, Zagreb, Italy, Eretz Israel* (Jerusalem 2008), p. 150 (Hebrew).

74 See Gershon Gora, "A Great Scholar and Lover of Israel," *She'arim*, September 10, 1969, p. 3 (Hebrew); Granatstein, *Yemei Bereishit* [New Days], p. 130 (Hebrew). A student at the Ponovezh Yeshiva said that he and four other grooms from the yeshiva received packages from Rabbi Kahaneman in London containing fabric that could be sewn into wedding garments. See Aharon Sorasky, *The Ponevezher Rebbe: Our Rabbi Yosef Shlomo Kahaneman OB"M*, III (Bnei Brak, 1999), pp. 126-127 (Hebrew).

75 See Moshe Eliyahu Munk, *In the Mirror of the Torah: A Collection of Articles on Subjects of Education and Current Questions* (Jerusalem. 1975), pp. 341-342 (Hebrew).

76 See also *The Holy Memory Book: In Memory of our Rabbi Shlomo David Yehoshua Weinberg from Slonim-Baranovitch* (Jerusalem, 1967), p. 23 (Hebrew).

77 See Lavsky, *Toward a New Life*, p 160 (Hebrew).

78 See Lavsky, *Families and Children*, p. 12 (Hebrew).

79 Interview with Avraham Verdiger, one of the repatriated who served as the European General Secretary of Poalei Agudat Yisrael in Paris. Verdiger married a Hungarian Holocaust survivor in Hannonville.

80 See Farbstein, *Hidden in Thunder*, p. 354.

81 Sima Zalcberg "Sources of Information about Menstruation and Sexuality among Hasidic Adolescent Girls," *Nashim* 17 (2009), pp. 60-88 (Hebrew).

82 Granatstein, *Yemei Bereishit*, pp. 136-137. In lessons, discussions and posters, the girls and women were urged to build their homes according to Jewish law. See also Rabbi Snieg's book on the laws of family purity, which was written in Munich and published in the DP camps in Yiddish, Polish, and Hungarian. *Hidden in Thunder*, pp. 355–357, 359–360.

83 YIVO, Schwartz Collection, MK 488, Roll 22, Folder 249, Frame 636, "Reports of Rabbi Rosenberg about JDC Religious Activities in the US Zone, 1946."

84 Lavsky, *Towards New Lives*, pp. 140-147. See also Yehoshua Eibeshitz, *The Uprooted: A Survivor's Autobiography* (Haifa, 2002), p. 490 (Hebrew).

85 Hanna Yablonka, "'The Happiest Day of our Lives': On the Survivors and their Sabra Children," in Dalia Ofer (ed.), *Israel in the Eyes of the Holocaust Survivors and Those Who Outlasted It* (Jerusalem, 2015), p. 480 (Hebrew).

86 Farbstein, *Hidden in Thunder*, pp. 354-355.

87 See Yisrael Samet, "The Meanings of Wedding Customs," *Zohar* 9 (2002), pp. 75-85 (Hebrew). Haredi writer David Zaretsky effectively gave voice to the stream of consciousness of the Holocaust survivors, the protagonists of his story, under the wedding canopy and to the prayer they recited. See: David Zaretsky, *Shimke: Children of the War* (Tel Aviv, 1952), pp. 258-259 (Hebrew).

88 Iwona Irwin-Zarecka, *Frames of Remembrance: The Dynamics of Collective Memory* (New Brunswick, 1994).

89 The "removal of corporeality" is a Hassidic conceptualization of the demand that a person relinquish his individual consciousness in order to reach an awareness that his existence comes from God.

90 Eibeshitz, *The Uprooted*, p. 490. Even after immigrating to the United States, the Klausenberger Rebbe concerned himself with matches for his students whom he brought with him from the DP camps. He was personally involved in all the stages of the process, as a "father" or "father of the bride" in all senses. See Sorasky, *A Torch of Fire*, p. 425 (Hebrew).

91 Mordechai Plevinski , "Remember What Amalek Did To You," in *The Labor of Torah* (Jerusalem, 1984), p. 646 (Hebrew).

92 The author's interview with Zipora Rubin, a student at Agudat Yisrael's refugee center in Jerusalem, Bnei Brak, January 1, 2007.

93 Grossmann, *Jews, Germans, and Allies*, p. 184.

94 Yablonka, "The Happiest Day," p. 470 (Hebrew).

95 For example: Testimony of Hava Hana Guterman, YVA 0.3/12343, p. 74; Testimony of Leah Landau (Feldman), a native of Satmar, YVA 0.3yz.60; Yeshayahu and Miriam Yaacovson, *From Generation to Generation Your Deeds Shall be Praised and Your Might Shall Be Recounted* (Jerusalem, 2004), pp. 111-112 (Hebrew); Michal Shaul, "Testimonies of Ultra-Orthodox Holocaust Survivors: Between 'Public Memory' and 'Private Memory'," *Yad Vashem Studies* 35(2) (2007), pp. 143-185.

96 See Nathan Wachtel, "Remember and Never Forget," *History and Anthropology* 2 (1986), pp. 307-335. At the end of the testimonies of the Haredi Holocaust survivors that were video-taped, the witnesses show the camera joyful photos of families that typically have many descendants and that are dressed in Haredi attire. See Shaul, "Testimonies of Ultra-Orthodox Holocaust Survivors," pp. 143-185.

97 See Lawrence L. Langer, *Holocaust Testimonies: The Ruins of Memory*, (New Haven and London, 1991), p. 119.

98 Ibid., p. 96.

99 Asiriya, *We Have a Young Sister*, p. 228. On parenthood as a formative experience for the survivors see Dan Bar-On, *Parenthood and the Holocaust* (Jerusalem, 2001).

100 Yablonka, "The Happiest Day," p. 468 (Hebrew).

101 See, for example: Hava Herman Bronstein, *After the Earthquake: Descriptions and Testimonies of Holocaust Survivors* (Jerusalem, 1990), pp. 186-188 (Hebrew).

102 Dvora Wagner, "Fathers as Yeshiva Students: Identities and Functions in the Haredi Family in Israel," *Research of Haredi Society* 2 (June 2015), pp. 147-168 (Hebrew).

103 "The Daughters of Agudat Yisrael in the Land of Israel," undated, Poalei Agudat Yisrael Archive, Hafetz Hayim, 20/12 (Hebrew).

104 See Nurit Gilat, "The Attitude of Israeli Society towards Women Serving in the Army, 1948-1967," Ph.D. dissertation, University of Haifa, 2005.

105 On the paradox between the claim of continuity and processes of modernization regarding the education of Haredi women, see Tamar El-Or, "'Are They Like Their Grandmothers?': A Paradox of Literacy in the Life of Ultraorthodox Jewish Women," *Anthropology and Education Quarterly* 24(1) (1993), pp. 61-82; Menachem Friedman, "Back to the Grandmother: The New Ultra-Orthodox Woman," *Israel Studies* 1 (1988), pp. 21-27. On the different ways that Haredi society sought to fill the void, see Michal Shaul, "The Legacy of Sarah Schenirer and the Rebuilding of Ultraorthodox Society after the Holocaust," *Jewish Culture and History* 22(2) (forthcoming 2021).

106 Asiriya, *We Have a Young Sister*, pp. 218-226 (Hebrew); Orit Rozin, "Women Absorb Women: The Role of Veteran Women in the Absorption of the Great Immigration during the 1950s: History and Theory," in Avi Bareli, Daniel Gutwein, and Tuvia Freiling (eds.), *Society and Economy in Israel: A Historical and Current Look*, II (Jerusalem, 2005), pp. 645-670 (Hebrew).

107 For an initial reference, see Hava Baron, "The Second Generation of the Holocaust," place and date not indicated, Kiddush Hashem Archive; Ruth L.N., *Reliable Testimony: The Destruction of European Jewry* (Jerusalem, 2001), pp. 402-408 (Hebrew). See also the spirited virtual dialog between "second generation" Haredim on the Haredi forum on the internet: http://www.bhol.co.il/forum/topic.asp?whichpage=1&topic_id=1364645&forum_id=771

108 See Katz, *Tradition and Crisis*, p. 282; David Biel, *Eros and the Jews* (Tel Aviv, 1995), pp. 159-195 (Hebrew). Compare with Shaul Stampfer, "The Influence of Hasidism on the Jewish Family in Eastern Europe: A Re-evaluation," in David Assaf and Ada Rappoport-Albert, *New Instead of Old: Studies in the History of the Jews of Eastern Europe and their Culture – A Gift for Emmanuel Etkes,* I (Jerusalem, 2009), pp. 165-184 (Hebrew). Stampfer denies this influence and claims that Hasidism did not destabilize the traditional family structure, as such a clash would have harmed its chances of dissemination.

109 Menachem Friedman, "The Family-Community Model in Haredi Society," *Studies in Contemporary Jewry* 14 (New York, 1998), pp. 166-177.

110 Shaul Stampfer, "The Hasidic Yeshivot in Poland between the Two World Wars," in Emmanuel Etkes et al. (eds), *In Hasidic Circles: Studies in Hasidism in Memory of Mordechai Wilensky* (Jerusalem, 2000), pp. 374-375.

111 This factor is not mentioned in the report and in most of the research on the subject. See, for example, Alex Weinreb, Dov Chernichovsky, and Aviv Brill, "Israel's Exceptional Fertility," Taub Center, The State of the Nation Report, 2018. http://taubcenter.org.il/wp-content/files_mf/exceptionalfertilityeng.pdf

Lea Langleben

A Simchat Torah Celebration in the Kovno Ghetto

Rabah bar bar Chanah: I was on a ship, and I saw a fish that had sand on its back. Grass was growing from it. We thought that it was an island [Yisrael thought that Galus was over]. We came up, and were cooking on its back [enjoying the feast of Achashverosh]. When it got hot, it flipped over. Had we not been close to our ship [repented], we would have drowned. (Bavra Basra 73b)

Introduction

Between the two world wars, Jewish youth movements, and especially pioneering Zionist youth movements, flourished in Poland and Lithuania. The education system of these movements, which was simple in form, was self-maintaining: that is, over time, regular movement members would become youth counselors (*madrichim*). Youth counselors were essential, as they devoted their time to expanding the ranks of the movement, teaching its ideology, building its social fabric, and preparing members in preparation for their immigration to *Eretz Israel* (the Land of Israel, then known formally as Mandatory Palestine) and fulfillment of the Zionist idea. Although the youth movements were representative of different ideological camps, and despite the differences between them, which sometimes reached a level of bitter rivalry, there was little difference between their modes of activity. The youth culture in the youth movements was based on social encounters, evening discussions, newspaper publication, agricultural training, ideological seminars, ceremonies, and celebrations reflecting the rousing impact of meetings and discussions and song and dance. The national leaderships of the youth movements were visited by emissaries from the Jewish Yishuv in Palestine, who served as a conduit for conveying and teaching the ideological content of the movements, including songs of Eretz Israel.

After the initial days of fighting during the German conquest and after a period of residing in the ghettos, youth movements in many ghettos managed, in conditions of underground and terror, to get organized and remain operating. The heart of the movement, the local movement headquarters (referred to in Hebrew as a "*ken*," literally meaning nest), again became an enclave of Eretz Israel and a center for discussion on the subject – "What would the future state look like, if it were established?"[1] For a time, movement headquarters protected members from the sights and the experiences of the ghetto.

Regardless, a radical change began to characterize the activity of the youth movements in the ghettos. The youth were suffering from cold and hunger, as well as from fear and the loss of parents, which was the lot of the entire Jewish population of the ghettos. The youth counselors contemplated the changes to the children's lives that had resulted from the war with concern. These changes had transformed their lives into an existence of degeneration and declining self-confidence, which in their view could endanger the next generation of the Jewish People. The members of youth movements in the ghettos, who were taught to bear responsibility, mobilized themselves for the tasks of the hour, for work in the present, and for work in real time in the ghetto. The responsibility was converted into concern for the fate of the entire Jewish community of the ghetto. This included responsibility for spearheading the educational work in the different possible open and underground learning spaces, as well as responsibility for initiatives requiring mental fortitude in the conditions and circumstances of the ghetto. This enabled them to continue adhering to the unique ideals of the movement and to persevere in their cultivation – ideals such as pride, withstanding the temptation of evil, adhering to the principles of faith and hope that the war would come to an end, and "nevertheless, and despite all odds, Eretz Israel."[2] It also involved responsibility in the struggle against the trend of declining morals and in favor of intensifying moral steadfastness, which provided human resilience during the stormy times. With the daring that is characteristic of adolescence, they sought to engage in work that was helpful and to maintain "a stronghold that reinforces the Jewish spirit of freedom."[3]

Members of Irgun Brit Zion in the Kovno Ghetto

The organizational and social infrastructure of the Zionist organization known as Irgun Brit Zion (I.B.Z.) was established in the city of Kovno between 1940 and 1941, during the period of Soviet occupation and governance in Lithuania. It consisted of underground cells of young Jews seeking to express their protest at the collapse of the Jewish and Zionist institutions under Soviet rule. During this year-long period, activities took place on an operative level to rescue the Hebrew book, including studies on topics of Zionist information such as the Hebrew language, the history of the Jewish People, Zionism, and Eretz Israel. These were efforts conducted in underground conditions that facilitated almost complete continuity in the functioning of I.B.Z. in the Kovno Ghetto between 1941 and 1944.

I.B.Z. was founded by young activists of the Zionist youth movements in Kovno and by students of the Real ("Reali") Gymnasium[4] and the Schwabe Gymnasium,[5] two Hebrew institutions that cultivated the values of Jewish and Zionist education and culture among their students during the interwar period. Within these institutions, students studied the purity of the Hebrew language. Hebrew, which unlike the language's prevalent conception as a language in need of revival, had always been the language of religious study, the religious public's language of daily prayer, and the language of Jewish literary writing and Jewish thought. The Hebrew language cleared itself a path among the youth in Zionist circles in Lithuania as a national symbol advocating the Zionist idea of returning to Eretz Israel. Knowledge of the Hebrew language also had added value: it made it possible for the youth to engage in the unmediated reading of the original cultural sources: the Bible and the Hebrew literature and poetry that had been written in the Diaspora and in Eretz Israel.

During the stages of reorganization of the I.B.Z. in the Kovno Ghetto, many students of the two gymnasia resumed filling the ranks of the group. These were primarily teenagers from the religious Zionist camp that had been active during the Soviet period. The I.B.Z. in the Kovno Ghetto encompassed Hanoar Hatzioni, Maccabi Hazair, Bnei Akiva, Betar, and Hashomer Hatzair. It also included many young Jews who had left the Communist "Young Pioneers" movement,[6] which they had joined during the Soviet occupation and to whose influence they were subject in the ghetto, and joined the educational frameworks and institutions of Brit Zion, along with boys from the *Tiferes Bachurim* yeshiva[7] and girls from the Yavneh and Histadrut Batya schools (affiliated with Agudas

Yisroel). Over time, the number of supporters and new members of the I.B.Z. grew, and individuals who had not previously belonged to any movement or party took part in its activities. At its height in 1943, the I.B.Z. had between 150 and 200 members.

The I.B.Z. in Kovno had two primary attributes. The first was its focus on education, culture, and the social realm for the benefit of the children and youth of the ghetto. After the collapse of their basic frameworks (such as property, status, home, and family), I.B.Z. members expressed an intense desire to bypass the suffering of the true present and to create experiences that were worthy of the youth whose future lay ahead of them. It did not ensure physical survival, but it had become urgent for them to nurture their spiritual, emotional, and intellectual resilience. One way to organize life in the ghetto was to create frameworks and cells of youth who both learned and taught. The main subjects of study were Jewish history, Zionism, select topics on Eretz Israel, Hebrew and Hebrew literature, and other topics aimed at enhancing their Jewish identity. The I.B.Z.'s second attribute was its unification of all youth movements under one roof in the Kovno Ghetto, which was possible due to the fact that many young Jews in the ghetto did not toe their movement line. They were dissatisfied with the excessive divisions within the Zionist public in the reality that had emerged in ghetto life under the Nazi regime. The challenges of the hour required joint action through internal unity of the Jewish youth, which was the next generation of a magnificent community and family whose typical identifying marks were adherence to religious tradition and adherence to the tradition of religious study. As noted, the Lithuanian Jewish community had advocated Hebrew culture in its educational institutions for generations, and the youth found its way within the different factions of the Zionist movement, the roots and symbols of which were drawn from Jewish history: landscapes of Eretz Israel, the Hebrew language, the days of the kingdoms and the prophets, the destruction and the Diaspora, longings for Jerusalem, and the like. The I.B.Z. provided the youth of the ghetto with the ideological alternative of preserving traditional cultural values, national values, and Zionist ideology. Based on the idea of unity and Zionist pre-eminence,[8] the Zionist youth movements in the Kovno Ghetto united with one another to overcome the ideological differences between the different camps. The union terminated neither the heritage nor the ideological platform of the individual youth movements, leaving their platforms and the fundamentals of their educational approaches untouched. Each movement continued to exist and to operate according to its own worldview; at the same time, however, it removed divisions and softened positions in order to work together on education and culture within the ghetto. This required emotional and spiritual resilience.

The Ghetto is Burning, Oh the Ghetto is Burning…[9]

An older Gdud Ma`apilim of the I.B.Z. was established in mid-1942. It reached the height of its activity in 1943, when it had approximately 30 members. The Battalion's activities are documented in the five chapters of the *Gdud Ma`apilim Almanac*[10] for the period between January 26, 1943 and January 30, 1944: (1) "The Chronicles of the Gdud, 1942-1944"; (2) "Autobiographies" and "'Articles" by Members of the Gdud, 1944; (3) "Celebrations of the Gdud, 1942-1944"[11]; (4) "The Missing Members"; and (5) "The Chronicles of the Gdud Commanders." 160 pages written in pen by members of the Gdud recount the deeds, the thoughts, and the beliefs of its members in the Kovno Ghetto. Members were required to sign a declaration of identification with and devotion to the principles of the Gdud and to join the Gdud, which advocated "the justness and the sanctity of the ideal of a Jewish state for the Jewish People," and undertook to

> …fight until the final moment for the actualization of this ideal…a spearhead of the war for the revival of our People and the land of our birth, disseminating this idea among the Jewish masses…to train the young youth. For this they develop their skills and constantly fill out their knowledge in all areas…preserve the national culture and the Hebrew language…speak Hebrew and disseminate it among the Jewish masses…believe in the eternal existence of the Jewish People and strengthen hope in our future in the hearts of the People…We will fight against all despair…[12]

Everyday life in the ghetto led to a quest for positive ways to belong and connect to something larger, which, in their eyes, symbolized life. Members of I.B.Z. took upon themselves a mission and a responsibility involving imagination and hope. The content of the cultural activity was replete with historical episodes of the Jewish People and segments of Hebrew literature and poetry. Its goal was to build the young generation and to construct for it a Jewish and Zionist soul that would not collapse before the day of liberation. It was not life-saving activity; but in terms of spiritual life, it preserved humanity in the language and the reality of the ghetto.[13]

I.B.Z. celebrations were a means of expressing the principal idea and the strong belief in what lay beyond the present; in the words of the counselors: "after the enthusiastic singing departed their lips…I said to myself: As long as we have such youth, our hope is not lost."[14]

The *Almanac* documents literary evenings, evenings of song, lectures, plays, seminars for youth counselors, celebrations to mark Jewish holidays (such as Passover, Hanukkah, and Shavuot) and to commemorate historical figures whose intellectual worlds lit up the faces of those imprisoned in the ghetto (in the Jewish month of Tamuz, a celebration was held in honor of Yoseff Trumpeldor and Tel-Hai) and events in the Jewish-Zionist historical memory that held ethical content for the youth of the ghetto.

The autumn of 1943 witnessed the onset of the implementation of a plan to convert the ghetto into a concentration camp.[15] Horror and tumult prevailed among the men, women, and children, and the elderly population. All the residents of the ghetto who had survived the events until that point were placed under the authority of the S.S. and designated to be sent to the labor camps. "Rosh Hashana and Yom Kippur were sad days this year; we can say that they were critical,"[16] wrote Avraham Tory, secretary of the Ältestenrat in the Kovno Ghetto, in the final entry in his diary. At the end of October 1943, the period of relative calm in the life of the Kovno Ghetto came to end, marking the beginning of the transition to a period of upheavals, during which the ghetto residents were condemned to life or death. After the selection, the group of workers was sent to Estonia, and the elderly and the children were sent to Auschwitz.

The Jews of the ghetto understood that the final battle for their lives had arrived. As the dangers increased, they accelerated the activities for rescue and the struggle, the building and preparation of "*melinas*" (hiding places), and their connections with the Lithuanian partisans for those who chose to leave the ghetto and join the groups of partisan fighters in the forests.

The document discussed in this article is the program for the I.B.Z. Simchat Torah celebration that was held on *Shabbat Bereishit* (the Saturday on which the annual cycle of Torah readings recommences with Genesis 1), October 21, 1943. During a week of mourning and grief in the ghetto, members of the Gdud Ma`apilim of Irgun Brit Zion were engaged in preparations for a diverse celebration that reflected considerable work, with speeches, recitations, poems and songs, a choir, and dancing. The success of the Simchat Torah celebration was attested to by the enthusiastic texts on the subject that were written in the *Almanac*[17] by the members who attended the party (see below, "'Ma`apilim' Members Write in the Almanac about the Simchat Torah Celebration").

It is no coincidence that the literary works recounting the history of the never-ending struggle for the survival of the Jewish People – works dealing with generations who had risked their lives and maintained their faith both in Eretz Israel and the Diaspora, and continued to do so in Eretz Israel in the era of new revival – and a tumultuous Jewish history abounding with motifs of freedom fighters, defense, heroism, sacrifice, rescue, and redemption, became materials for study and for use during the artistic segments of the celebrations of the youth movements in the ghettos. The texts were replete with national mottos and images regarding the sanctity of the uprising and the war against national injustice. David Shimoni's poem "We Shall Not Forfeit Our Blood," and poems such as "We Set Out at Dawn," "Five," and "Unknown Soldiers" were more than just history. "On the Slaughter" by Haim Nahman Bialik was read at every party. Their words shouted the everyday coping with life in the ghetto, and "thoughts and ideals based on our rich historical past guided the present."[18] Many texts were received with great affection, such as "Masada," a poem written by Yitzhak Lamdan inspired by the story of Josephus Flavius in *The Jewish War against the Romans*. In the ghetto, the poem generated its own vitality and power: the Jews locked in the ghetto were engaged in a struggle against large and mighty enemy forces, and at a later stage they believed they could be the last survivors. The poem aroused a call to loyally and courageously continue working for the dignity of their People; it was an invitation to contemplate their identity and the fate and purpose of the Jews: "For us, heroism is life itself, a way of life, of not retreating one inch…As long as the blood of our people is spilled in the Diaspora and its youth is driven by despair and filled with faith, the golden chain of heroism will not be broken. We will continue it."[19] An entire generation was raised on literary works containing historical episodes from the remote and the recent past. The works proved to be and were received as the reservoir of the People's strength and spirit. This presence of the past was meant to teach them about themselves: the Jews' journey of torment, humiliation and helplessness revealed their abilities of steadfastness and the preservation of heroism and strength of spirit. The youth counselors called to mobilize the strength of members in order to maximize their steadfastness, because there was no other choice. It was a call for a combination of total devotion and allegiance to themselves and to principles that, in essence, included being Jewish, a deep identification with their connection to Eretz Israel, and a belief in the Jewish return to Zion.

The texts which the youth sang and recited at the celebration reflected the Jews' thirst for rebirth and independence and their yearning to build a homeland and to strengthen their connection with the life that was emerging in Eretz Israel. They opened with prophetic verses and writings of praise for the return to Zion ("Dry Bones" and "Shir Hama`a lot" (A Song of Ascents) and continued with songs such as "The Miracle is Flying on the Flagpole," "Two Letters," "A Multitude Rejoices," "The Song of the Valley," "We Have Been Strengthened," "The Jordan," "Oh, How Long?" "The Song of the Road," "The Song of the New Port," and more.

As noted, emissaries from the Yishuv would teach these songs to the members of the youth movements. However, the selection of songs reflected the feelings and the mood of the members who sang them:

> One of the wishes that is most important to me now concerns my future path. After all, the ghetto is only a preparation for a path to come…It will be a great moment when we go free, as this is the moment we have always been waiting for… How wonderful that moment will be, when we will be able to tell the whole world about our work.[20]

The program of the Simchat Torah celebration in the Kovno Ghetto attests to the defense of the Jewish People's right to exist, reflecting an ancient ancestral legacy of preserving the living historical connection with the People's intellectual and spiritual treasures and the principle of continuity. The program's content is a declaration of allegiance to the essential principles of Jewish life and Zionism as a continuation of Jewish tradition, representing the fact that they are Jewish not out of compulsion or external violence but rather out of conscious choice. Indeed, had they not chosen to connect with and strengthen the values they inherited from their ancestors (a return to the Jewish Prophets, to the days of the Second Temple, to the Hasmoneans, and to the Jewish war against the Romans) – with regard to Jewish consciousness, the strong Jewish spirit for building their future in Eretz Israel, and knowing themselves and their identity in the ghetto – they would have drowned.

On weekdays, the youth in the ghettos sang:

> This evening we demonstrated what we are and what we can accomplish. Club members came with songs and recitations. Until late into the night we sang…songs which tell about youthfulness and hope…We are, as it were, intoxicated with the joy of youth. We do not want to go home. Songs keep bursting forth, they simply will not stop.[21]

They also sang a significant amount on Saturdays and holidays:

> It is difficult to overstate the importance of the role that songs played in our lives. They were like air in our lungs…Following the special celebratory service we would hold on Saturdays, we would sing the typical Sabbath songs…It would penetrate the soul and arouse in us longings and hope for a different life. The songs themselves, their melodies and their lyrics, imbued us with the strength and the desire to overcome difficult reality…We would sing and continue singing, in the depths of our souls.[22]

The singing was accompanied by times of horror and times of hope:

Inspired by the singing, we believed that the evil would pass and that we had something to live for. And so all the *zmiros* [Jewish hymns] and our songs from before the war flowed off of our lips. We would cling to them and sit and sing. We would continue to sing in the depths of our souls.[23]

Singing played a central role in the educational work in the ghettos. To be more precise, it filled the major lack that existed in ghetto life: "We sang in a loud voice, and singing is somewhat useful for warming up the body; we sang a song in praise of the Creator of the Universe."[24]

In her memoirs, I.B.Z. member Masha Greenbaum wrote about the selection of readings from Hebrew poetry on holidays:

> After the meal and the Hagada, the celebratory program began. They read Saul Tchernichovsky's "Baruch from Meinz," David Frishman's "The Messiah," Judah Leib Gordon's "With Our Youth and Our Elderly We Shall Go," and Lamdan's "Masada." It was already late. No one wanted to leave. No one wanted to stop the celebration.[25]

When singing, unlike when speaking, music is added and operates on emotional level, unifying people simply and quickly and arousing and creating a collective experience. In this manner, Zivia Lubetkin effectively described the lessons of teacher Itzhak Katznelson in the Warsaw Ghetto:

> He was our most respected and popular teacher. His specialty was the Bible, and he taught his students to love their People and their heritage, and to strive for national independence. His enthusiasm was contagious and at its height he would start singing and his students and the family in whose apartment they were studying would soon join in. [26]

Singing is an inseparable part of Jewish tradition. The book of psalms, the song book of the Bible, accompanies the entirety of the human events and experiences of the Jews in times of sorrow and hardship, in times of hope and joy, and in times of longing and war:

Music, which is entrenched in the spiritual and moral life of the People, finds a way to be created in its penetration of the soul of every individual, and in doing so it arouses and strengthens the national sentiment – from the songs and the dances of the [Jewish] pioneers to the songs of prayer, to the melancholy tunes of the Diaspora that touch the depths of the soul, to the exhilarating tunes of Hasidic dancing. All of these reflect the spirit and the unique character of our People, and in all of these our national might finds expression. In song and in joy, in lamentation and in wailing. And in this way, playing [music] becomes a source of Jewish nationalism.[27]

•••

The Program for the Simchat Torah Celebration[28]
Shabbat Bereshit 5704 • October 21, 1943

I. Faith and Hope
1. *Opening Speech – Simchat Torah – The Joy of Hope and Faith and the Contempt for the Tortured / The Gduda'i (Battalion Commander)[29]*
2. *The Dry Bones – Ezekiel[30] / M. Ulman[31]*
3. *Bashuv Adonai[32] / The Choir*
4. *Jerusalem[33] – Solo / M. Nadel[34]*
5. *The Chain Has Not Yet Been Broken[35] / The Choir*
6. *On Sukkot and Simchat Torah (speech) / A. Rozin[36]*
7. *We Set Out At Dawn…[37] / The Choir*
8. *Words of Greeting / B. Gurewitz[38]*
9. *I Brought Peace[39] / The Choir*
10. *Words of Greeting / F. Rosenberg[40]*
11. *Techezakna[41] / The Choir*

II. Festive Meal
12. *Shulchan Orech (a Few Words) / The Gduda'i*
13. *Five[42] – Solo / S. Zimon[43]*

14. *Song of the Valley*[44]

15. *Two Letters*[45] / *M. Nadel*

16. *Words of Greeting* / *T. Shapira*[46]

17. *A Multitude Rejoices* / *The Choir*[47]

III. Anger

18. *A Few Words of Anger* / *The Gduda'i*

19. *It Is Not Because Our Enemies Are Many*[48] *(Bialik) / M. Nadel*

20. *To Live and to Suffer…*[49] / *The Choir*

21. *We Shall Not Forfeit Our Blood*[50] *(Shimonovich) / S. Zimon*

22. *Oh, Until When?*[51] *(Solo) / Sachs*[52] *and Finkelstein*[53] *accompanied by the Choir*

23. *Unknown Soldiers…*[54] / *The Choir*

24. *The Sicarius with the Yellow Badge*[55] *(Avishay Ben-Avner) / M. Nadel*

25. *We Forged*[56] *(song) / Sachs-Finkelstein-Zimon-B. Gurewitz*

Five minute break, conclusion of the festive meal in a circle (seated).

26. *The Miracle is Flying on the Flagpole*[57] / *The Choir*

27. *Beneath Horseshoes (Solo) / D. Kurlyandchick*[58]

28. *A Few Things about the Sabbath / S. Jetkonski*[59]

29. *Facing the Seashores*[60] / *The Choir*

30. *I Was Walking in the Valley*[61] / *The Choir*

31. *By the Rivers of Babylon*[62] *(solo) / S. Zimon*

32. *I've Had Good Days*[63] / *The Choir*

33. *A Short Letter*[64] / *L. Finkelstein*

34. *The Joy of Israel…*[65] / *The Choir*

35. *The Messiah*[66] *(Frishman) / M. Kaminsky*[67]

36. *Our Ship Is Wandering…*[68] / *M. Rogol*[69]

37. *About Sukkoth (words of greeting) / A. Rafovsky*[70]

38. *There in the Galilee...*[71] */ The Choir*

39. *The Jordan*[72] *(Solo) / L. Finkelstein, accompanied by the Choir*

40. *That's a Hammer...*[73] */ The Choir*

41. *On the Slaughter*[74] */ M. Ulman*

42. *We Have Strength... / The Choir*

43. *A Gift*[75] *(Recitative Shneur) / S. Zimon*

44. *Song of the New Port*[76] */ The Choir*

45. *To the Levant Fair*[77] */ The Choir*

46. *The Choir / The Choir*

47. *It Is No Wonder,*[78] *everyone starts to sing. The Hora breaks out, [people] dance the Hora.*[79] *Abraham Rafovsky teaches a new dance, "Tashzik," and now they dance it. The Gduda'i concludes with a speech for everyone as words of parting. The celebration concludes with Hatikva.*[80]

•••

The Biblical Verses, Poetry, and Songs of the Simchat Torah Celebration

Ezekiel 37

The hand of the Lord was upon me, and he brought me out in the Spirit of the Lord and set me down in the middle of the valley; it was full of bones. And he led me around among them, and behold, there were very many on the surface of the valley, and behold, they were very dry. And he said to me: "Son of man, can these bones live?" And I answered: "O Lord God, you know." Then he said to me: "Prophesy over these bones, and say to them: 'O dry bones, hear the word of the Lord. Thus says the Lord God to these bones: Behold, I will cause breath to enter you, and you shall live. And I will lay sinews upon you, and will cause flesh to come upon you, and cover you with skin, and put breath in you, and you shall live, and you shall know that I am the Lord.'"

So I prophesied as I was commanded. And as I prophesied, there was a sound, and behold, a rattling, and the bones came together, bone to its bone. And I looked, and behold, there were sinews on them, and flesh had come upon them, and skin had covered them. But there was no breath in them. Then he said to me: "Prophesy to the breath; prophesy, son of man, and say to the breath: 'Thus says the Lord God: Come from the four winds, O breath, and breathe on these slain, that they may live.'" So I prophesied as he commanded me, and the breath came into them, and they lived and stood on their feet, an exceedingly great army.

Then he said to me: "Son of man, these bones are the whole house of Israel. Behold, they say: 'Our bones are dried up, and our hope is lost; we are indeed cut off.' Therefore prophesy, and say to them: 'Thus says the Lord God: Behold, I will open your graves and raise you from your graves, O my people. And I will bring you into the land of Israel. And you shall know that I am the Lord, when I open your graves, and raise you from your graves, O my people. And I will put my Spirit within you, and you shall live, and I will place you in your own land. Then you shall know that I am the Lord; I have spoken, and I will do it, declares the Lord.'"

Psalm 126

When the Lord restored the fortunes of Zion, we were like those who dream. Then our mouth was filled with laughter, and our tongue with shouts of joy; then they said among the nations, "The Lord has done great things for them." The Lord has done great things for us; we are glad. Restore our fortunes, O Lord, like streams in the Negev! Those who sow in tears shall reap with shouts of joy! He who goes out weeping, bearing the seed for sowing, shall come home with shouts of joy, bringing his sheaves with him.

Jerusalem – From the Summit of Mount Scopus

From the summit of Mount Scopus,
I will prostrate myself to you,
From the summit of Mount Scopus,
O Jerusalem, peace unto you.

For a hundred generations I have dreamt of you,
Of beholding the light of your countenance.

Jerusalem, Jerusalem
Light up your face for your son,
Jerusalem, Jerusalem
From your ruins I will build you.

From the summit of Mount Scopus,
O Jerusalem, peace unto you.
Thousands of exiles around the world,
Raise up their eyes to you.
In thousands of blessings may you
Be blessed,
Kingly sanctuary, royal city.

Jerusalem, Jerusalem,
I shall not leave here,
Jerusalem, Jerusalem,
The Messiah will surely come, one day.

The Chain Has Not Yet Been Broken

The chain has not yet been broken
The chain still continues
From ancestors to children
The chain still continues.
This is how our ancestors danced
This is also how we shall dance.
One hand on the shoulder of a friend
And the other on the Torah.
La la la…

We Set Out At Dawn –
The Song of the Three

We set out at dawn
To venture up mountains and into ravines
If the whole world dozes all day and night –
The youth rises alert and alive!

High, high up, we mightily flew
The flag of the great uprising.
Upon the flag of our lives
We engraved:
Fear not death or blood!

If non-Jewish hands take over the fruits
Of our labor and destroy our fields
We set out to throw off the bothersome
Laborious burden from our backs.

If great emotion dies among our People
And the taskmaster's whip strikes –
With our blood we shall redeem
A contemptible and self-restrained disgrace of a People.

If the God of our fate of death
Demands our life, a gift for the People –
From a mass grave, day and night,
Our blood will cry out for revenge.

I Brought Peace unto You

I brought peace unto you
I brought peace unto you
I brought peace unto you
I brought peace, peace, peace unto you.

Techezakna [Strengthen the Hands] – *The People's Blessing*[81]

Strengthen the hands of all our brothers, who cherish
The dust of our homeland wherever they are.
Let not your spirits fall, happy ones rejoice,
Come as one to support the people.

Each trek we enumerate and hold dear,
Each tear drop and drop of sweat upon brow
That falls like dew for Yisra'el, reviving
Its debilitated soul, so weighed upon.

And forevermore may each tear that
Fell into our sea of tears be sanctified, an offering to the people.
Each drop of brow sweat paving
The path of Adonai like sweat and blood.

If to build to the roof a lifetime suffices not
And you lay but the base of your national home
Enough have you wrought; your achievements despise not.
Those who come after will yet lay the line.

What a deliberate people are we! Step by step we raise up
The desolate ruins and rebuild them eternally!
From sea to sea go forth and be amazed
To see what the smallest among nations has wrought, the wandering people.

And why do the laggards take their time dragging their feet?
The workers of Yisra'el, are they an enigma?
Hey! Be strengthened dispersed ones, unite and stand tall!
Work your portion as one with valor and might!

Do not say "We are not worthy" — in short time you will observe
The visage of the Mighty One of Yaaqov going off to battle!

From the days of Zerubavel our hands have not wrought
Deeds as mighty as this or as numerous.

Scorn not small deeds, but, scoffers despising.
Rescue your people with hoe and with plough
Till we hear from the head of the mountains the signal for rising
The time for redemption has come; it is now.

Five

Five set out to build a homeland
Five left a mother, a sister, a baby, and a wife at home.
Hammers beat the mountains. Hammers beat.
Five cut through the morning and paved tracks and roads.

Suddenly shots cut through the morning.
The shots of hammers in their hand, in their healthy souls.
The hills fell and rose,
And rose, and rose, and rose, and rose, and rose.
At night when the men went out to the mountains
They again dreamed of five hammers
And since then they have not fallen silent.

And at times a sigh or a whisper is heard;
At home, they left a mother and a sister and a baby and a wife.
The hands do not rest for even a moment.
Five set out to build a homeland – five.

The Song of the Valley

The weary came to rest
And finish their labors.
Pale night covers
The fields of the Jezreel Valley.
Dew underneath and moonlight above,
From Beit Alpha to Nahalal.

Oh, what a night of nights.
Silence over Jezreel.
Sleep dear Valley, land of glorious beauty
We will guard you.

The sea of grain is swaying,
The song of the flocks rings out.
This is my country and her fields,
This is the Jezreel Valley.
Bless my country reveler
From Beit Alpha to Nahalal.

Oh, what a night of nights…

Mount Gilboa is darkened
A horse gallops from shadow to shadow.
A voice is carried high
Over the fields of the Jezreel Valley.
Who was shot? Who has fallen?
Between Beit Alpha and Nahalal.

Oh, what a night of nights…

Two Letters
Mother:
On a sheet of paper as white and pure as snow
A letter arrives from the Diaspora.
A tearful mother writes:
"To my good son in Jerusalem,
Your father is dead, your mother is ill,
Come home to the Diaspora!
Come home to the Diaspora!
We will constantly await you

From morning to night.
Come home, darling son
Come home to spring
Come home.
Come home
Come, darling son.
Son:
On a simple sheet of paper, grey as ash
A letter goes to the Diaspora.
A tearful pioneer writes
The year 5684 [1923/24] in Jerusalem:
"Forgive me, my ill mother
I will never return to the Diaspora!
I will never return to the Diaspora!
If you love me
Come here and hug me
I will no longer wander!
I will not budge from here!
I will not budge
I will not budge
No!"

A Multitude Rejoices

A multitude rejoices
A multitude of a nation applauds.
Binyamin Ze'ev spoke his words to the People
The hour of freedom has arrived.
Get up, shake it off
The time of exile is over!

Straighten your back, lift your head
You are great-grandchildren of great-grandchildren of the Maccabees.
Turn your face to the ancestral land
Become a nation like all other nations!

If we assimilate, even if we convert our religion
Even if we rely on the grace of nations
Oh, our People will never be redeemed,
And we will be slaves forever.

To Live and To Suffer

To live and to suffer is our life
To live and to suffer for a nation?
That is the fate of the youth of our generation.

We are fed up with being persecuted
And singing with the people of our enemies
Wrapping ourselves in the flags of those who hate us
That are soaked in the blood of Jews.

We shall awaken the strength of our heroes
The strength of the Maccabees, of Bar-Kokhba.
With our blood we shall redeem the land of our ancestors
On one path, war.

We Shall Not Forfeit Our Blood

No! We shall not forfeit our blood
Blood is sacred, human life is sacred.
But we shall also sanctify and respect our lives
And all those lying in wait for us behind every wall shall know
We shall not forfeit our blood!
Our blood is like water for all the world's soil
But here we shall not be like a wilting leaf,
A leaf that falls with every wind.
Here we shall not meet death like sheep
Here our cheek shall not be struck with the rod.
We shall behold death – and we shall live!
You shall not frighten us, what are knives and arrows

To a people that has nothing left?
The torch of the wicked shall not frighten or discourage
A people that has only one remaining path.
Only one path: to be redeemed in our land
In our one land: the Land of Israel.

Oh, Until When?

Oh, until when
Shall our people suffer without a homeland,
Moving and wandering?
Oh, until when shall our people live
Among gentiles, moving and wandering?

Until they unite as a people
Until they learn their language
And return to their homeland, and return to their borders.

Source: Notebook of the composer, Berlin, 1934.
* The song also appears in *Almanac of the Kovno Ghetto*, in the program for the
Herzl-Bialik celebration.

Unknown Soldiers

We are unknown soldiers, uniforms we have none,
In death's shadow we march, in its terror,
Volunteering to serve to the end of our days.
Only by death from our duty can we be severed.

In days red with slaughter, destruction and blood,
Nights black with pain and despair,
Over village and town our flag we'll unfurl,
Love and freedom the message 'twill bear.

Not like slaves brought to heel were we dragged to the fight,

In strange lands our life's blood to squander.
Our desire is to be free forever
Our dream is to die for our country.
And if we must die for our people to be free,
Our lives we are willing to surrender.
In days red with slaughter…

With obstacles rising to block every move,
By fate cruelly sent to entrap us,
Neither enemy, prison or miserable spy
Will we ever permit to divert us.
In days red with slaughter...

Should we happen to fall in some building or street,
To be furtively buried by night,
Many thousands of others will rise in our stead
To defend and continue the fight.
In days red with slaughter...

With the tears of mothers bereaved of their young,
In the blood of pure infants only spilt,
We'll cement the bricks of our bodies for walls
And our homeland will surely be built
In days red with slaughter…

We Forged the Will

We forged the will from iron
We learned the doctrine of defense
We swore to forfeit our lives
For the rebirth of the nation.
Arise pioneer…and build
Our path is not lined with roses
It is filled with mire and blood.

Without fear, without the fright of pioneers
We shall raise the flag of the People.
Arise pioneer…

And should our enemies arise as obstacles
On the road to the rebirth of the People
We pioneers swore
That the blood will not frighten us.
Arise pioneer…

The Miracle is Flying on the Flagpole

The miracle is flying on the flagpole
A campfire ignites.
On the mountain of pine forests
The line is consolidated.

Hey, forward, only forward.
Raise your voice,
Sing, rejoice, ascend [ha`epilu*] the path.

A voice calls from mountain and hill:
Please come!
Come guards, to the heart of nature,
Please come!

Our song is vigor,
A stormy song,
And it breaks through
And smashes everything.

Raise your leg!
Raise a flag!
We will climb, we will ascend [na`apila*]
Despite it all!

* Apparently derived from the Hebrew term used to refer to the unsanctioned Jewish immigration to Palestine at the time: *ha`apala*.

A Sacred Sabbath on the Shore of My Sea

Facing the shore of my sea
All the ships have already lit the Sabbath candles.
Sailors pick up an oar
Boats' sails get no whiter.
A sacred Sabbath on the shore of my sea
Boats' sails get no whiter.

On the shore of my sea, on the shore of my sea
The sacred Sabbath approaches.
Fishermen's wives have dressed in white
The fishing net is drying –
Even the fish in the sea are at peace.
The fishing net is drying.

A sacred Sabbath on the shore of my sea,
See the shore, it is as if it has grown whiter.
And the skies have added blue.
Even the seagull is not paddling
And moving away from the realm of the Sabbath.
Even the seagull is not paddling.

Even the fish in the sea are at peace,
And it is as if the shore has grown whiter.
The sailors pick up an oar,
Boats' sails do not get whiter…
On the shore of my sea
All the ships have already lit the Sabbath candles.

I Was Walking in the Valley

I was walking in the Valley, with the staff of a nomad.

I came upon a village, the village of Ein Harod.

I shall go no further

Here I shall stand

Here, it is good to live

Here, it is good to work.

I shall go no further

This is Ein Harod.

I was walking in the Valley and I grew very thirsty.

I found a spring, Ein Harod.

I shall go no further

Here, I shall stop

Here, it is good to rest

Here, it is good to drink.

I shall go no further

Here I shall stop.

I shall go no further

This is Ein Harod.

By the Rivers of Babylon

By the rivers of Babylon, there we sat down, yea we wept, when we remembered Zion.

We hanged our harps on the willows in the midst thereof.

For there they carried us away captive, required of us a song; and they that wasted us required of us mirth, saying: Sing us one of the songs of Zion.

How will we sing the Lord's song in a strange land?

If I forget thee, O Jerusalem, let my right hand forget [her cunning].

If I do not remember thee, let my tongue cleave to the roof of my mouth; if I prefer not Jerusalem above my chief joy.

I've Had Good Days

I've had good days,
Good days, and especially nights.

Nighttime and stillness doze
Around, around cows.

In the light of the rising moon
Days of memory arise, appearing suddenly.

The path to the *kvutsa* [a small agriculture-based collective settlement type in
pre-state Palestine]
Is neither short nor long
Nighttime, stillness…

My guy, my guy
He hugs, strokes and kisses me
Nighttime, stillness…

On The Slaughter[82]

Mercy O Heavens, beg mercy for me!
If a god be in you, with a way in you,
A way that I never knew
Pray unto him for me!
My own heart is dead, prayer drained from my tongue.
The hands lie limp, and hope undone.
How long?
Until when? How long?

Executioner! Here is a neck to hew
With your mighty axe. Put me down like a dog.
All the world's my chopping block.
And we're just Jews, just a few.
My blood is fair game. From the skull you sever
Bursts the blood of old men, the blood of children.
Murderer's blood be on you forever.

"Ma`apilim" Members Write in the Almanac about the Simchat Torah Celebration

The Simchat Torah Celebration. The Sukkot holiday came and went, and the Gduda'i called a meeting of the Gdud in which he proposed having a celebration on Simchat Torah. Some of the members were opposed to the idea on the grounds that this was not an appropriate time for celebrations. However, the Gduda'i's view prevailed, and the Gdud began to prepare for the celebration, which was held on the day after Simchat Torah, on Saturday evening. None of the members dreamed that the celebration would be so successful. Even now, the party is still spoken of as the most successful celebration ever held by Gdud Hama`apilim.[83]

Additional Words by Gdud Member Shalom about the Simchat Torah Celebration [*Shabbat Bereishit* 5704]
24th of Tishrei, October 23, 1943 • Sunday

There are very special moments in a person's life, ideal moments in which one feels his strength and his humanity. Such moments are so few in our lives, to the point of being insignificant. Spiritual ascension to another world, to a world that is both sacred and dear, shaking off the burden of the mundane and entering a life of sanctity and joy, and connecting to something out of the ordinary and unknown.

The Sabbath is such a moment.

An "internal" celebration is such a moment

And therefore even more so an "internal" celebration held on the Sabbath.[84]

Autobiographies of I.B.Z. Members[85]

Vilijampole-Kovno Concentration Camp
5704 – 1944

Mina Kaminsky

I was born in Kovno in 1927. My parents are free thinking in their views. My father is a difficult and cold person by nature. His coolness had a significant influence on my character, and this may also be why I am so sensitive. My mother is a traditional woman. As a result of her efforts, and especially those of my grandmother, I was sent to attend the strict Yavneh school… When the Germans entered Lithuania and the yellow patch marked me, I realized the oppressed state of my people. I became an enthusiastic Zionist, and after some time I joined I.B.Z. I remain under the flag of this organization today, and I am devoted to it, heart and soul.

Miriam Rogol

I was born in Kaunas in 1927. My father was a nationalist Zionist, but he was not very active. He was a pharmacist by profession…Mother was busy in our shop…I attended kindergarten in the Jewish gymnasium…[Later] they wanted to take me to "Hashomer Hatzair," but I was already doing other activities… During Russia's conquest, I flowed with the tide and joined the Young Pioneers. But I remained a Zionist at heart…They could not extract it from my heart. The first crisis in my life came with the invasion of the Germans and the arrest of my father. Life was very difficult without my father. But you have to get used to everything. And I even got used to that life. I joined the I.B.Z., where I found consolation. It gave me the mental strength and vitality to get through this difficult time. It gave me a new path in an empty life. My private life quickly merged with the life of the organization.

Moshe Nadel

I was born in the city of Kaunas in 1927. My father owns a factory and is free thinking in his views. My mother is a woman who educates more in the Jewish spirit…Until I went to school, I received a modern Jewish education at home. My grandmother was the only one who wanted to educate me in a traditional Jewish spirit, and I still remember the nights I spent with her, when she would tell me stories and anecdotes from the Pentateuch and the Bible. When I was five, I was sent to the kindergarten of the Real Gymnasium, where I encountered the Hebrew language for the first time… In 1938, when I was 11 years old, I already belonged to *Hanoar Hatzioni Bet*…When the Red Army arrived…the propaganda also affected me…My heart was filled with despair, and, albeit not out of my own desire, and perhaps we can say by force, I assimilated among them, that is to say, I signed up for the Young Pioneers. At the beginning of the war, and the onset of the cursed German Eagle's rule in Lithuania, I again had the opportunity to resume my Zionist work…and I have already been working a year and a half in Irgun Brit Zion.

Aharon Rozin

I was born in 1927 in the city of Kovno. My father is the rabbi, and he served as the principal of the primary school. I received a religious education at home. I remember when I was a child, my father would tell me nice fairytales about the Jewish People and the Jewish sages. My grandmother taught me the first prayers. When I got a bit older, I started attending the Yavneh gymnasium. After I finished 4 grades…my father sent me to study at a yeshiva called *Ateret Zvi* in Kovno…In addition to the yeshiva, I participated in Betar. I was active, and I considered myself a loyal Betar member. When the Russians entered [Lithuania], my situation worsened from a spiritual perspective…two spirits collided within me: the moral spirit of Judaism and the Red spirit of assimilation. But the former approach won out over the latter and prevailed…I myself remained a boy who is loyal to the People and to the Torah…The Germans entered the lands of Lithuania and the Jews were forced to move into ghettos…And in the ghettos an important event in my life occurred. The contradiction between the moral spirit of Judaism and the spirit of Betar emerged within me…I worked toward the Betar ideal…I began to understand the latent contradiction in the depths of my heart. For a second time, the spirit of Judaism celebrated victory. The first time, it defeated the spirit of Communism, and the second time it defeated the spirit of Betar. It won out because I was raised on it and I was preparing for life. That is how I was drawn to I.B.Z., on whose behalf I work as a loyal member.

Bilha Gurewitz

I was born in the city of Mazeikiai in 1927. My father is a photographer and my mother is a physician. The education I received from my parents was a Jewish education that was not exceedingly religious and not exceedingly Zionist… At the age of 6 I was sent to the Hebrew-language primary school in the city… During my six years of study at the school I became an enthusiastic Zionist… It was transitory enthusiasm… The Soviets entered Lithuania, which was very depressing…But I was unable to withstand the trial. The Red propaganda and arguments with a few adults influenced me… I signed up for the Young Pioneers association…In the middle of the winter, our family moved to Kovno. I was pleased that there was no border. I was accepted into Jewish gymnasium No. 12… Approximately half a year later the war began…Slowly but surely, my views began to change, especially when I began attending the vocational school… Even after I returned to Zionism…I joined the young Betar members' group. I did it only for the sake of Zionist work… When I learned the main points of I.B.Z. ideology, I moved without any problem to the new recruit organization, and then I was accepted into I.B.Z.

Shoshana Zimon

I was born in Klaipėda in 1927, the daughter of a nationalist but passive Jew. My father owned a knitting factory. In Klaipėda, I attended the German gymnasium and I studied Hebrew privately. Shortly before my 12th birthday, we had to leave Klaipėda out of fear of the Nazis. I came to Kaunas to study… It was only in Kaunas that I was exposed to the life of the Zionist youth. I became a member of Hehalutz Hatzair…At the outset of the Russian occupation…our organization was closed…Under the influence of the poor material conditions I became a Young Pioneer. I thought that no eyes would penetrate my heart. My time in the Pioneers left no traces in me, and the war was about to break out. Once again, my thoughts tended toward Zionism…My sister took me to Hashomer Hatzair; I wanted to be active in the Zionist realm, but I did not relate to their ideals, which were indeed rather remote from me. At the vocational school, I met Sarah L. and I became her new recruit. When I saw the major difference between Sarah's group and Hashomer Hatzair I left Hashomer Hatzair, because it gave me no spiritual satisfaction. On July 22, I was accepted into Irgun Brit Zion.

Yonina Sachs

I was born in 1927. My father was a clerk…Until I was six years old, my childhood was spent in Vilkaviškis. From Vilkaviškis, we moved to Marijampolė, where I attended the Lithuanian gymnasium. I was always distant from Judaism, especially from Zionism, because I was brought up in a Christian environment and did not feel at all like I was a Jew. In 1940, I came to Kaunas and I began attending the Lithuanian gymnasium, which became Russian with the arrival of the Soviets. The Communist spirit quickly found its way into my heart and I became a Young Pioneer…I remained true to my views for the entire first year in the ghetto. However, thanks to a friend from "Ma`apilim," I learned about Zionism, in which I found the right path…Fortunately, at the vocational school, I met a member of Irgun Brit Zion, Sarah L., and I joined the organization as her new recruit on July 22, 1943.

Moshe Ulman

I was born on the 23rd of Nissan, 5687 [April 25, 1927], or Isru Chag Pesach, in the town of Birzai… Until I was five years old I spoke only Russian. When I was five years old, I was sent to the kindergarten of the Schwabe Hebrew Gymnasium. Then I started to speak Hebrew. I spoke only Hebrew with my father and Russian with my mother. My father was a Zionist political functionary and I was raised on Zionism. In the third grade I started selling *Keren Kayemeth* [J.N.F.] stamps…When the Red Army entered Lithuania, I had to move to the Russian gymnasium for national reasons. Like the rest of my friends, I was forced to wear the red tie, although in my heart I remained a loyal [Jewish] nationalist.

We were about six good friends in class. We would meet at the home of our friend Moshe A. and discuss Zionist national questions. When I entered the ghetto, I was left without even one friend, and I remained lonesome and on my own. After approximately a year in the ghetto, I joined the ranks of I.B.Z., and here I found the family for which I had been hoping for some time.

Shalom Yadkowsky

I was born in Kovno on the 27th of Menachem Av 5687 [1926/27]. My father is a Zionist activist. From the beginning of my childhood, he gave me a national education with the intention of my nationality finding a place in my heart. In the year 5693 [1932/33], I visited Eretz Israel…This visit of mine, unbeknownst to me, strengthened my nationalist sentiment and provided it with a great deal of support. In 5695 I was accepted into the Schwabe Hebrew Gymnasium, which I attended until the year 5699, which was the year the Russians seized Lithuania. The [Soviet] regime prohibited study in the Hebrew language by closing the Hebrew-language schools. In Menachem Av 5741 [1940/41] I was pushed behind the fences of the Vilijampolė Ghetto, and at the end of Av 5742 [1941/42], after a year of hardships, I was already standing by in the ranks of I.B.Z.

Photographs of I.B.Z. Members Whose Names Are Mentioned in the Celebration Program

Avraham Rozin • Bilha Gurewitz

Endnotes

1   Dov Levin, *Between Spark and Flame: The "Brit Zion" Organization in World War II* (Ramat Gan, 1987), p. 29 (Hebrew).

2   Diary of Miriam Hatchevsky, a member of the Zionist youth society in Radomsko, Yad Vashem Archive (herein YVA), 0.3/3382, p. 8.

3   "Gordonia in the Warsaw Ghetto Underground," *Davar Hatzeirim*, June 11, 1941, in Yitzhak Arad, Israel Gutman, and Abraham Margalit (eds.), *The Holocaust Documented: Selected Documents* (Jerusalem, 1978), p. 169 (Hebrew).

4   The Real ("Reali") Gymnasium was founded in Kovno by Rabbi Dr. Joseph Hirsch Carlebach in 1915 and closed its doors in 1940.

5   This gymnasium was established in Kovno in 1920 by its namesake, Dr. Moshe Schwabe. It closed its doors in 1940.

6   This is a reference to students from the professional school in the Kovno Ghetto who had previously belonged to the Young Pioneers youth movement, which was run by the Communist Party for children between the ages of 11 and 14. See "Autobiographies of I.B.Z. Members."

7   *Tiferes Bachurim* consolidated yeshiva students in the Kovno ghetto, including those engaged in forced labor, and organized Torah study groups. Many of the students opened *heder* frameworks and served as teachers of Torah study groups for children.

8   Levin, *Between the Spark and the Flame*, p. 19.

9   "The Sicarius with the Yellow Patch," a poem by I.B.Z. member Shraga Aharonowitz. See note 54.

10   "We young members of Irgun Brit Zion have decided to record our chronicles in a book. If we survive, for us I.B.Z. ma`apilim this book will be a book commemorating our Zionist work in the ghetto. For others, it will be an action book about young Zionists and the history of the life of the Jews in the Kaunas concentration camp. However, if it is our fate to die, then in this book we will be presenting a monument in commemoration of our sacred work…Truth be told, in this boo we offer nothing of our ideology or perspective or our programs: only dry history, writings by our members, etc. But all of this is sufficient for providing a clear picture of our work." *Almanac of the Kovno Ghetto*, YVA B/1215, pp. 2-3. The almanac of the members of Irgun Brit Zion in the Kovno Ghetto, of the members of Gdud Ma`apilim, survived the hardships of the war and was entrusted to the Yad Vashem Archive for preservation. The *Almanac*, and another document – the bulletin of Irgun Brit Zion that was written at the Kaufering concentration camp – appear in Zeev Mankowitz (ed.), *"Prepare for liberation!": Documents from the Kaunas Ghetto and the Kaufering Camp: The Ma'apilim Almanac and Nitzotz* (Jerusalem, 2011) (Hebrew).

11   "Celebrations of the Gdud," *Almanac of the Kovno Ghetto*, pp. 85-107.

12   "The Ten Commandments of the Ma`apil," *Almanac of the Kovno Ghetto*, pp. 81-82.

13 The emphasis was on the importance of "being a mensch."

14 *Almanac of the Kovno Ghetto*, pp. 73-74.

15 Following the May 21, 1943 order issued by Heynrich Himler, head of the Gestapo in the Third Reich, to set up concentration camp regimes in the ghettos, the Kovno Ghetto became a concentration camp.

16 Avraham Tory, *The Everyday Ghetto* (Tel Aviv, 1988) p. 419 (Hebrew). The entry is dated October 13, 1943.

17 File of writings and chronicles on the history of Gdud Ma`apilim of Irgun Brit Zion (I.B.Z.) in the Kovno Ghetto that were written between October 1943 and January 1944, YVA B/1215.

18 Reizel (Rozka) Korczak, *Flames in the Ashes*, translated from the Polish by Benjamin Tenenbaum (Merhavia, 1946), p. 88 (Hebrew).

19 Mordechai Tennenbaum-Tamaroff, *Pages from the Fire: Chapters from a Diary, Letters, and Essays* (Tel Aviv, 1984), p. 194 (Hebrew).

20 Liella Finkelstein, *Almanac of the Kovno Ghetto*, pp. 48-52. Liella Finkelstein, a member of I.B.Z., attended the Simchat Torah celebration but not leave behind autobiographical writing. See "Autobiographies of I.B.Z. Members."

21 Isaac Rudashevski, *The Diary of the Vilna Ghetto, June 1941-April 1943* (Ghetto Fighter's House, 1973), p. 105.

22 Sarah Selver-Urbach, *The Bnei Akiva Movement in the Lodz Ghetto during the Years of Destruction and Extermination through the Memories of its Survivors* (Bnei Brak, 1999) p. 76 (Hebrew).

23 Ibid.

24 Shlomi Friedman, *Abraham the Golem in the Lodz Ghetto* (Kibbutz Dalia, 2006), pp. 119-120 (Hebrew).

25 Masha Greenbaum, *Hope at the Abyss: The Jews of Lithuania, between Ghetto and Camp* (Jerusalem, 1999), pp. 58-59 (Hebrew).

26 Zivia Lubetkin, *In the Days of Destruction and Uprising* (Tel Aviv, 1981), p. 69.

27 Jakob Schönberg, *Songs of Eretz Israel* (Berlin, 1935), p. 5 (published in Hebrew in 1947).

28 This program appears in *Almanac of the Kovno Ghetto* in the chapter titled "The Gdud's Celebrations in the Concentration Camp, Slobodka-Williampola, 1942-1944, 5702-5704," pp. 100-102 (Hebrew).

29 The head of Gdud Ma`apilim was Shraga Aharonowitz. The members of I.B.Z. operated in the Kovno Ghetto in "companies" (*plugot*, plural of *pluga*) each containing between 5 and 7 people headed by a company commander (*pluga'i*). The Batallion (*Gdud*) consisted of between three and five companies and was headed by a "battalion commander" (*gduda'i*).

30 Ezekiel 37.

31 Moshe Ulman was born in Birzai in 1927 and died in the Kovno Ghetto in 1944. See "Autobiographies of I.B.Z. Members."

32 Psalms 126. This text was also included in the Hanukkah celebration of 1943, *Almanac of the Kovno Ghetto*, p. 105.

33 According to a comparison with other sources, this appears to refer to the poem "Jerusalem," written in 1928 by Avigdor Hameiri (1890-1970) and composed by Polish opera composer Stanisław Moniuszko (1819-1872). The poem is Meiri's Hebrew rendition of the Yiddish poem "Midnight" or the poem "If I forget Thee Oh Jerusalem" by Bayruch (Benedict) Shafir, which depicts the hardships of the Jewish People in the Diaspora and the eternal longing for Jerusalem. The poem is also known by the title "Above the Peak of Mt. Scopus."

34 Moshe Nadel, a member of Hanoar Hatzioni, was born in Kovno in 1927 and died in the Kovno Ghetto in 1944. See "Autobiographies of I.B.Z. Members."

35 "The Chain Song" or "The Chain Has Not Yet Been Broken" comes from "Night-time Bonfires," one of the six chapters of the epic poem "Masada," which was written by poet Isaac Lamdan (1897-1954) in 1923-1924. In the Kovno Ghetto, "The Chain Song" was also included in the program for the Herzl-Bialik celebration. *Almanac of the Kovno Ghetto*, pp. 86-94. Excerpts from "Masada" were read as part of the review of poems read after the meal and after the reading of the Passover Hagada on the second night of Passover, 1942. See: Masha Greenbaum, *Hope at the Edge of the Abyss* (Jerusalem, 1999), pp. 57-58 (Hebrew). In the Vilna Ghetto, on the eve of the Masada celebration, the youth club's literary group designated the poem "Masada" and studied it in school. See Marek Dworzecki, *Jerusalem of Lithuania in Rebellion and in the Holocaust* (Tel Aviv, 1950/51, pp. 213-214). In one of the Sunday morning *shacharit* services that the schools would hold for the residents of the ghetto, teacher Zelig Kabatchnik devoted the program to listening to the poem "Masada." See: Korczak, *Flames in the Ashes*, p. 88. In the Warsaw Ghetto, "The Chain Song" was selected to be performed as a theatrical play in a competition among the elementary schools in 1941. In his diary, teacher Michael Silverberg wrote about "The Chain Song" and about the educators' hesitations in selecting it: "Rabbi Yitzhak Nissenbaum came immediately to our aid. He suggested "Masada" by Yitzhak Lamdan. It was clear to him that the poem could be performed as a play. We were amazed. Masada, the stronghold at the top of the mountain, the site of the Jews' resistance against the Romans during the great revolt, was a symbol of resistance of the few against the many; however, after three years of rebellion, the war there ended in the mass suicide of the defenders. How can we put on such a play under the present circumstances? Rabbi Yitzhak said quietly: "Take the risk of doing it. At least you will see that the Jews have always known how to fight. This play will instill moral courage. It will show that the People must at least stand strong. He took the book from the shelf and read aloud from it. He stopped at "The Chain Has Not Yet Been Broken." The chain has not yet been broken...The words sounded so current that, after a brief discussion, we concluded that we would put on "Masada" and that the play would be our entry in the competition...All those who knew Hebrew of course enjoyed it the most and had

a unique experience. One could see that the Masada in question was not only that of ancient times: its spirit was aroused in Warsaw of our time. We received second prize, and we were required to perform the play again at the request of the public. To the end, they added "The Chain Has Not Been Broken." Michael Silverberg, *Warsaw Diary, 1939-1945* (Tel Aviv, 1978), pp. 26-28 (Hebrew)

36 Aharon Rozin was born in Kovno in 1927 and later became a member of Betar. From the Kovno Ghetto, he was moved to a labor camp near the city of Kėdainiai, escaped with a group of friends, joined the partisans, and died in battle. See "Autobiographies of I.B.Z. Members."

37 "Song of the Three" was written in Kovno in 1938. It was written by Israel Yivrovitch (1915-2004) and composed by Saul Blecharovitz. The song is also known as "The Song of Three from Rosh Pina," in honor of the members of the Betar work battalion at Rosh Pina: Avraham Shein, Shalom Zuravin, and Shlomo Ben-Yosef, who threw a grenade at a bus that was carrying Arabs, were captured by the British police, and were executed. It is one of the songs of the Betar movement in Lithuania. *The Betar Book: History and Sources* (Jerusalem and Tel Aviv, 1969-1973) (Hebrew).

38 Bilha Gurewitz-Rosenberg was born in Mazeikiai, Lithuania on September 24, 1927, to Zvi and Dr. Fruma Gurewitz, the physician of the Kovno Ghetto. A member of Kibbutz Yagur, Bilha passed away on January 24, 2004. On the history of Dr. Fruma Gurewitz and the rescue of her three daughters, see: Fruma Gurewitz, *The Memories of a Doctor: With the Jews of Lithuania in the Holocaust* (Lochamei Hagetaot, 1981) (Hebrew). See "Autobiographies of I.B.Z. Members."

39 "We Have Brought Peace unto You" was first disseminated during the Third Aliyah. It was discovered in a private notebook belonging to Aya Ruppin, daughter of Arthur Ruppin. Based on the group of songs in which it appears, it was written in or around 1939.

40 Fima Rosenberg (Chaim Rosen) was born in Minsk in 1921. He was a member of the ideological committee of I.B.Z. and a member of its command beginning in 1943. He immigrated to Palestine as part of *Ha`apala* (the clandestine immigration of Jews to Palestine prior to the establishment of the state of Israel) in 1945.

41 "Techezakna" is the popular name for the poem "Birkat Am," which was written by Nahman Bialik in 1894. The musical composition is attributed to Avrhama Zvi Idelson. The song "Techezakna" has six verses, which extol the Zionist enterprise and call for Jewish immigration to Eretz Israel. Immigrants of the Second Aliyah and the Third Aliyah adopted the song as a socialist anthem and sang it at workers' meetings along with "Hatikva."

42 "Five," written by S. Shalom and composed by Mordechai Zeira. The song was written after the murder of five members of a settlement group from the Gordonia movement, who were killed in an Arab shooting attack on November 9, 1937 while paving a road on Mount Haruach near Jerusalem. The five were Aharon Ulishevsky, Arieh Mordechovich, Yehoshua Fochovsky, Yitzhak Migdal, and Moshe Bar-Giora–Baumgarten. Together, they are the namesake of Kibbutz Maaleh Hachamisha. The

song also appears in the program for the Herzl-Bialik celebration, *Almanac of the Kovno Ghetto*, pp. 86-94.

43 Shoshana Zimon-Ekerling was born in Klaipėda in 1927 and was a member of Hechalutz Hatzair. She escaped from the ghetto and went into hiding in a village until the arrival of the Soviets in August 1944. She immigrated to Palestine in 1947 as part of the *Ha`apala*. See "Autobiographies of I.B.Z. Members."

44 "Song of the Valley" (*Shir Ha`emeq*) was written in 1934 by Nathan Alterman (1910-1970) and composed by Daniel Samborski (1909-1977) as the soundtrack for the movie "A New Life," an 80-minute propaganda film for Zionist settlement in Palestine. Produced by Margot Klausner, the film featured Keren Hayesod's activities aimed at encouraging Jews to immigrate to and settle in Eretz Israel.

45 "Two Letters" was written by Avigdor Hameiri and composed by Joel Engel in 1924 in Jerusalem.

46 Tirtza Shapira was killed in an I.B.Z. "*melina*" (hiding place) in the Kovno Ghetto in 1944.

47 The song "A Multitude Rejoices" (*Hamon Tzohel*) was written and composed by Abraham Salman (1911-1976) in honor of Theodor Herzl. It appears in David Niv (ed.), *On the Barricades: Songs of Valour* (Tel Aviv, 1984) (Hebrew). Verses from this song were also performed at the Herzl-Bialik celebration. *Almanac of the Kovno Ghetto*, pp. 86-94.

48 From the Bar Kokhba poems, "It Is Not Because Our Enemies Are Many" was written on the Jewish holiday of Lag Ba`Omer in 1899. This poem, about the revenge taken by members of the Bar Kokhba generation against their Roman enemies, is a song of anger about the murderers and about the desire for vengeance of those who were murdered.

49 "To Live and To Suffer is Our Life," recorded personal testimony of the Ben Stonehill Collection, 1948, National Library of Israel, YC 00977/78. The title of the poem is attributed to Zeev Jabotinsky, although The Jabotinsky Institute Archive in Israel cannot confirm this. This poem also appears in the program of the Hanukkah celebration of 1942, *Almanac of the Kovno Ghetto*, pp. 105.

50 "We Shall Not Forfeit Our Blood" was written by poet David Shimoni (1891-1956). On April 19, 1936, a wave of anti-Jewish violence erupted in Jaffa and in the neighborhoods between Jaffa and Tel Aviv. The poem was written after the severe bloodletting of the first day which left nine dead and 54 wounded. Within a few days, the inferno engulfed the entire country, marking the onset of the Arab Revolt of 1936-1939. David Shimoni, *Poems*, Part 2 (Tel Aviv, 1950) (Hebrew).

51 "Oh, Until When?" was written by Meir Ben-Uri, an architect, artist, and musician who was born in Riga in 1908 and died in Israel in 1983. Ben-Uri was active in the Blau-Weiss nationalist youth movement, and he subsequently became a member and youth counselor in the Zionist student association Kadimah in Berlin. In 1939,

he composed this song as the movement's anthem. The song also appears in the program of the Herzl-Bialik celebration, *Almanac of the Kovno Ghetto*, pp. 86-94.

52 Tania Yonina Sachs was born in Vilkaviškis, Lithuania in 1927 and died in Stutthof in 1945. See "Autobiographies of I.B.Z. Members."

53 Liali (Lela) Finkelstein-Zohar. "About Liali" is a text that was written by Bilha Gurewitz about her friend Liali Finkelstein after learning that Liali had left the ghetto in an effort to save herself: "Liali came to us from a completely different world. At first, it was as if she viewed the world into which they sought to insert her with suspicion. But suddenly, all at once, when nobody thought it possible, she threw herself into the arms of the new world with all her heart and soul and was willing to sacrifice for it all she could sacrifice. Recently, therefore, it was as if she was boiling over with devotion to the IBZ." *Almanac of the Kovno Ghetto*, pp. 145-149.

54 "Unknown Soldiers" was written by Avraham (Yair) Stern, the founder and commander of the underground group *Lehi*. The song, which was put to music by him and his wife Roni Stern, was written in 1932, during the Nebi Musa riots in Jerusalem (and against the background of the 1929 Palestine Riots). The song became the anthem of the I.Z.L. until 1940. Israel Eldad (Scheib) (ed.), *Book of Songs of Avraham Stern* (Tel Aviv, 1946) (Hebrew). The song also appears in the program for the Hanukkah celebration of 1943. *Almanac of the Kovno Ghetto*, p. 105. In her research on this song, Yaira Ginnosar reveals that it was also sung by members of Hashomer Hatzair in the Warsaw Ghetto: "In the Warsaw Ghetto, the song 'Unknown Soldiers' was known, sung, and quoted by the leaders of the Ghetto Warsaw Uprising. A testimony remains in which the line 'we all volunteered to serve to the end of our days' is quoted by Hashomer Hatzair members, Shmuel Breslav, a young Jew in the Warsaw Ghetto...Mordechai Anielewicz's partner in leading the underground and the ghetto. In these difficult days of Nazi fascism, Breslav was the editor of the Hashomer hatzair newspaper *Against the Current*. The well-known Ringelblum Archive contains a manuscript by him...Yad Vashem published the Hebrew translation from the Polish, which concludes with the final line that is originally written in Hebrew: "It needs to change for the sake of everyone, and also for the sake of us Jews. This is our answer, know that despite it all, we exist. We all volunteered to serve to the end of our days!" The documentation expands on the information and confirms that the song was known in the ghetto during the siege: in 1945, a young woman from among the Warsaw Ghetto fighters, Aliza Melamed-Willis, who survived and immigrated to Eretz Israel, gave fresh testimony that is held by the Moreshet Archive. It is documentation of a gathering of the fighters battalion on the eve of the uprising, at which Mira's soft voice is heard, that ends with the following words: ...It is not a big thing to be a person when you rely on others...Your test will come when you are left alone, when each of you remains completely alone, face-to-face with the enemy. And our moto will be that song that our brothers sang far away in Eretz Israel when defending their land, we all volunteered to serve to the end of our days. Only death will release us from this line. The song that

our brothers sang far away in Eretz Israel, lines of 'Unknown Soldiers' from the lips of Hashomer Hatzair members in the Warsaw Ghetto Uprising, as good examples of pioneers from Eretz Israel!" See Yaira Ginnosar, *"Not For Us The Saxophone Sings": The Poems of Yair Avraham Stern* (Tel Aviv, 1998), pp. 521-522 (Hebrew).

55 Written by Avishay Ben-Avner, Shraga Aharonowitz's underground code name. Aharonovitch was born in Kovno in 1923 and attended the Schwabes Hebrew Gymnasium. He was a member of the editorial staff of the newspaper *Nitzotz*, in which he published the poem "The Sicarius with the Yellow Patch." The poem was written after the major action in the ghetto, on October 28, 1941. Sicarius is a reference to the Sicarii, the group of fighters against the Roman conquest at the end of the Second Temple Period. In 1943, Aharonvitch was appointed as commander of I.B.Z. He was killed during the liquidation of the Kovno Ghetto in 1944.

56 "We Forged the Will," a Betar song, was written by Yechezkel Pulerevitch (1914-1995) in 1941 and published under his pen name Avi Shabi Maor. He was exiled to Siberia in 1941, and he immigrated to Israel in 1974. The Hebrew phrase "Arise and Build" (*aleh uvneh*) may have been taken from the chorus of the song "Arise Pioneer," which was popular in Eastern Europe in the 1920s and 1930s. Niv, *On the Barricades*.

57 "The Miracle is Flying on the Flagpole," or "Kadimah," is a song of the youth movement Hashomer Hatzair. It was written by Mordechai Werhaft (Mordechai Amitai, 1914-1993), a children's author and poet from Kibbutz Sarid. The song appears in *Singing Together: A Songbook to Mark the 50th Anniversary of the Hashomer Hatzair Youth Movement, 1913-1963* (Tel Aviv, 1963) (Hebrew).

58 Dvorah Kurlyandchick later immigrated to Israel (date not indicated).

59 Shalom Yadkowsky was born in Kovno in 1927 and was murdered in Kaufering concentration camp on April 27, 1945. See "Autobiographies of I.B.Z. Members."

60 "Holy Sabbath on the Seashores" was written by writer, poet, and journalist Aharon Ze'ev Ben-Yishai (1902-1977) and composed by Joel Engel Engel. Nahum Ben-Ari (ed.), *Songs for Sabbath* (Tel Aviv, 1948) (Hebrew).

61 "I Was Walking in the Valley" was written by Aharon Ze'ev Ben-Yishai and composed by Yariv Ezrachi (1904-2002). It is considered to be the anthem of Kibbutz Ein Harod. The poem is Song No. 254 in *The Notebook of Gershon Gurewitz*, which is currently held by Gurewitz's daughter Dvorah Ben-David of Kibbutz Hazorea. In 1934, Gurewitz (1912-1999) began writing a notebook of songs that emissaries from the Jewish Yishuv in Palestine taught the youth members during their visits to Poland. He immigrated to Israel in 1939.

62 Psalm 137, a psalm expressing the lamentation of the Kingdom of Judea, which was exiled to Babylon following the destruction of the Temple and the kingdom.

63 "Night of Silence" was written by Neomi Brontman (1910-1969) for a school play when she was a 16 year-old student at Moshav Nahalal. It was composed by Moshe Bick (1899-1985). Song No. 172 in *The Notebook of Gershon Gurewitz*.

64 "A Short Letter from the Diaspora to My Brother in Zion" was written by Chaim

Nachman Bialik in 1894. It was also included in the program for the Herzl-Bialik celebration. "Autobiographies of I.B.Z. Members," p. 86-94.

65 "Israeli Joy," written and composed by Abraham-Avrasha Salman in 1939. Niv, *On the Barricades*.

66 "The Messiah" was written by David Frischman (1859-1922) – a poet, editor, translator, writer, feuilletonist, art critic, and Hebrew journalist who was one of the pioneers of Modern Hebrew literature. The poem "The Messiah" was included in the program for the second night of Passover, 1942, as one of a number of selected excerpts that were read aloud following the meal and the reading of the Passover Hagada. See Masha Greenbaum, *Hope at the Abyss: The Jews of Lithuania, between Ghetto and Camp* (Jerusalem, 1999), pp. 57-58 (Hebrew).

67 Mina Kaminsky (Shafir) was born in Kovno in 1927 and immigrated to Israel in 1948. See "Autobiographies of I.B.Z. Members."

68 "Our Ship is Wandering" was written by Emmanuel Lin (Linkowski) (1901-1985) in 1935. Zivia Lubetkin's biography notes that they would sing this song in the bunker of the leadership of the Jewish Combat Organization at 18 Mila Street. Bella Gutterman, *The Life Story of Zivia Lubetkin* (Jerusalem, 2011) (Hebrew).

69 Miriam Rogol Pepper was born in Kovno in 1927 and survived the Holocaust. See "Autobiographies of I.B.Z. Members."

70 Abraham Rafovsky was born in Jonava, Lithuania in 1922 and was killed during the liquidation of the Kovno Ghetto in 1944. He was married to Lea (née Ritavsky) (1924-1944). Both were youth counselors in the Bnei Akiva youth movement in the Kovno Ghetto.

71 "On a Hill, Yonder in the Galilee" was written by Abraham Broides (1907-1979) and composed by Menashe Ravina (1899-1968).

72 "The Jordan," whose writer is unknown, is Song No. 22 in *The Notebook of Gershon Gurewitz*. The song was sung in paroxytone.

73 "The Road Song" was written by Nathan Alterman in 1934 and composed by Daniel Samborsky. It appeared in the film "For a New Life," about the "Labor Battalion" (*Gdud Ha`avoda*) groups that worked paving roads.

74 "On the Slaughter" was written by Chaim Nachman Bialik in 1903 following the Kishinev pogroms in Russia: "Such vengeance for blood of babe and maiden / Hath yet to be wrought by Satan." On April 19, 1903, anti-Jewish pogroms erupted in Kishinev. They lasted two days and resulted in 49 Jews dead and 495 wounded (95 of them seriously). Shortly afterward, Bialik was sent to Kishinev as part of a committee of inquiry on behalf of the Jewish communities for the purpose of documenting the events. The verses of this poem were also included in the program for the Herzl-Bialik celebration. *Almanac of the Kovno Ghetto*, pp. 86-94.

75 "A Gift" was written by Zalman Schneur (1887-1959), the *nom de plume* of Schneur Zelkind, a poet who wrote in Yiddish and in Hebrew. The poem, originally written in Yiddish, was published in *Hashchar* in Warsaw in 5669 (1908/09).

76 "The Song of the Port" was written by Lea Goldberg (1911-1970) in 1936. It was first published on the front page of *Davar for Children* approximately half a year after the Port of Tel Aviv began operations and approximately a year and a half prior to its official opening (February 23, 1938). It was composed by Rivka Levinson (1906-1983), a rhythmics teacher from Jerusalem who immigrated to Mandatory Palestine in 1936.

77 "The Flying Camel" is a poem that was written for the Levant Fair by poet Emmanuel Harussi (1903-1979) and composed by Mordechai Zeira (1905-1968). The flying camel was designed especially for the fair by architect Aryeh Elhanani and became a symbol of the international commercial fair that was held in Tel Aviv in the 1930s, attracting 300,000 visitors.

78 This song was written in the Kovno Ghetto by Yitzhak Katz, a poet and a member of I.B.Z. It was written about forced labor, but in a mischievous manner: "It is no wonder…If one sits in jail." The song may be a paraphrasing of the poem "What a wonder, What a Wonder," which was written by Nathan Alterman and put to a popular melody. Levin, *Between Spark and Flame*, pp. 31-32.

79 "We did not want to make a lot of noise. Still, we danced the 'Hora'. Only the Hora was short, but it came together with resolve. Everyone was gripped with enthusiasm." *Almanac of the Kovno Ghetto*, p. 155. See also the diary of Rutka of the Andrychów Ghetto in Poland, who, on October 4, 1942, wrote: Simchat Torah, and another hour of 'joy' is stolen from life and from the harrowing reality. Today, our youth burst into a Hora. Their legs danced on their own, and a loud and powerful song burst forth from their chests. Girls moved around the Hora circle, and the loud singing rang with strong emotion and intensity. Our hearts rejoiced that we are Jews; Jewish youth is the future of our people. In the notes of Hatikva we found ourselves, until our souls gave way from so much excitement. How good it was for us…" In: Yehoshua Eibeshitz (ed.), "Ruthka Leiblich, Ruthka's Diary," in *Women in the Holocaust: A Documentary Collection of the Courage and Steadfastness of Women during the Holocaust*, VI (Jerusalem, 1989/90) (Hebrew).

80 The song "Hatikva" was the climax of youth parties and celebrations: "We concluded with 'Hatikva.' The singing was very cordial." *Almanac of the Kovno Ghetto*, p. 150. Or the singing of 'Hatikva' to conclude the third Seder for the youth in the Kovno Ghetto, see Tory, *The Everyday Ghetto*, p. 259: "At midnight I stopped the singing, and I asked everyone to stand in silence for the singing of 'Hatikva.' I did so as was customary in Betar. We started to sing the national anthem, my heart beat strongly. I felt as if I was liberated, as if I was no longer anyone's slave. I am proud of my nationalism. I am a Zionist, just like I used to be. Singing 'Hatikva' was a call to the heavens and a last will and testament diluted with the blood of our hearts." Aryeh Segalson, *In the Heart of the Citadel: A View from Within the Destruction of Jewish Kovno* (Jerusalem, 2003), p. 301 (Hebrew): "And Hatikva, which was sung in such a mighty voice and with great emotion, until my spirit was awoken within me, as Jews are brothers…Nevertheless, they have the same characteristics and the same goal: the

desire for freedom and the "Land." In Eibeshitz (ed.), "Ruthka Leiblich," pp. 85-86: "Two wishes could be sensed: the desire for freedom and the aspiration to immigrate to Eretz Israel. At the end, everyone sang 'Hatikva,' and the singing was a reflection of both wishes." This occurred at the party celebrating the end of the school year at the Ohel Moshe synagogue in the Warsaw Ghetto. See Silverberg, *Warsaw Diary*, p. 48.

81 This English translation, by Aharon Varady and anonymous contributors to the Open Siddur Project, can be found at: https://opensiddur.org/prayers/secular-calendar/state-of-israel/yom-haatsmaut/the-peoples-blessing-by-hayyim-nahman-bialik-1894/ (accessed February 17, 2021).

82 Translation by by A.Z. Foreman. http://www.emjc.org/wp-content/uploads/2020/03/Bialik-the-National-Poet-Texts1edited-1.pdf (accessed March 4, 2021).

83 *Almanac of the Kovno Ghetto*, p. 14.

84 Ibid., p. 107.

85 Ibid., p. 16. See "Autobiographies of I.B.Z. Members."

Nir Itzik

Rachel Ronen – The Diary of a Girl from the Lodz Ghetto: A Document from the Moreshet Archive

Introduction

Rachel Ronen (Rachelka Gratz) was born on January 12, 1926 in Lodz, Poland, where her father was the theatre director and manager of the Jewish theatre in the city. When World War II broke out and the destruction of European Jewry began, Rachel's father and brother fled to Russia. Rachel and her mother remained in Lodz and, along with the rest of the local Jewish community, were moved into the ghetto. There, Rachel lived with her mother in a small attic, and both were sent to forced labor. In 1944, when the ghetto was liquidated, Rachel and her mother were sent to Auschwitz to work. Following the death of her mother, Rachel escaped from the camp with a friend, and for a few months the two hid in the homes of farmers in the Sudetenland. After the war, Rachel returned to Lodz and was sad to discover that no one from the Jewish community remained.

Rachel joined a *Bonei Hanegev* (Negev Builders) settlement group and immigrated to *Eretz Israel*. After arriving in the country, the members of her settlement group established Kibbutz Ramot Menashe within the jurisdiction of the Megiddo Regional Council. There, she started a family with Zeev Rosenblat, a fellow member of her settlement group whom she met prior to immigrating and married at the end of World War II on the trip from Europe to *Eretz Israel*. After settling on the kibbutz they had three children: Gila, Naomi, and Amir. Rachel worked in education on the kibbutz and ran the kibbutz library. She died on December 15, 2013.

What follows are the only surviving pages of the diary of Rachel Ronen. During her time in the Lodz ghetto, Rachel wrote a lengthy, comprehensive diary that was stolen when her apartment was broken into. She continued writing on pages that she acquired in various ways. After fleeing from Auschwitz and returning to her hometown of Lodz, she found the surviving pages of her diary in a garbage can and brought them with her when she immigrated to *Eretz Israel*. After settling in Ramot Menashe, she entrusted the pages to the archive of Moreshet, The Mordechai Anielevich Memorial Holocaust Studies and Research Center, where it was recently translated from Polish into Hebrew for initial publication in the Hebrew edition of *Moreshet Journal*. It is being published in English here for the first time.

What remains of Rachel Ronen's diary is relatively short: 10 pages of densely handwritten Polish that were composed between February 21 and April 11, 1943. In the diary, Rachel writes about coping with illness and about life in the ghetto in general. The Lodz Ghetto was one of the larger ghettos in Eastern Europe and contained approximately 160,000 Jews in the spring of 1940, at the time it was sealed. Under the leadership of Mordechai Chaim Rumkowski, the Jews of the ghetto served as forced labor in the service of the Germans.

At the time, Rachel was 17 years old. The following pages contain her intriguing account of her experiences during that terrible period: the alternation of hope and despair, the importance of writing in her diary, the relationships she had, the loneliness she experienced, and the like. Rachel's diary offers a window into the human soul. Though she lived through this harrowing period in which every day could be her last, she grasped tightly onto every shred of hope, and her desire to live overcame all despair.

The Diary (from the Moreshet Archive, A.1319)[1]
The Lodz Ghetto
Sunday February 21, 1943

Oh cruel fate! From a pretty black journal, to a prettier blue one with a sad ending, to a red one filled with audacious complaints, to…a regular notebook. Emotions must be expressed, not restrained, especially when one is suffering. It had been a long time since I wrote in my red journal. It still had many blank pages. I never thought something like that could be taken from someone. That was the first blow after our first move to a different apartment – the theft. They stole all the food (I had a large stock of food), as well as the diary, which was in the same suitcase, and my bracelet (and a thick comb and letters from my father). That was a cruel blow; first, due to the threat of starvation itself; and second, due to the importance of the items – [most notably] the diary. For whom could I tell? To whom could I spill my heart about the fact that I no longer have that pretty silver bracelet and that I have nothing with which to comb my hair with?

What a shame! I grew indifferent and I waited patiently. The period of hunger passed, new rations were distributed, and we were all equal. But my trusted ally,[2] my torn thoughts…There was Tosia, she appeared in a beautiful dream. A small, wonderful room with white windows where we were to move, where we would help each other with the hardships and live, rejoice, and worry together. Yes…the dream. Then I am lying in bed (I had a fever), in the room from the dream, and what happens? The door and the windows are by no means white. The room is pretty, but it is far from the dream. And Tosia herself is so different, for the worse. Where is her former cordiality? It is dark now and we have no light, so I will finish up and hide my pent-up bitterness until tomorrow.

Monday February 22

Indeed, it is more difficult to write what I used to write in the old diary on which I relied in a simple notebook that is meant for something else. I am writing in it for the time being. There is no need to repeat myself and to again write what I wrote in my previous diary. After all, if the past is only memories, doing so is not logical. So, today I woke up and for the first time in a long time I feel terrible. If now I have a fever again, I will have to return to bed. I have started falling ill in general. Is it because of sudden hunger or the difficulties of the move to another apartment? First, my leg hurt. Now, my side, my back, and actually everything hurts. I am filled with a terrible longing. I so regret having left my attic, where I felt free. It is my own fault for giving in to my aunt's attempts to persuade me. I have fallen and gotten stuck. I will not find that bit of freedom anymore. I too have been infected with the anger that lies in wait for us all. Life here holds nothing but evil, and it is the ultimate evil – illness – that is the most mysterious. I do not want to be ill. I try, with all my will, to cast out this demon. My golden age of health has passed. I have destroyed myself, I fear. Everything has changed, and it will never, ever be the same. But I still go about my tasks automatically, and my stomach will continue aching and my head spinning until I prepare the meal.

Wednesday February 24

I am back in bed and I have a fever. Tosia and Abramek went to work. Mother stayed home to take me to the doctor. I am so sad. It is so hard to be ill. Aneke did not come. I asked her to bring me a slip for the doctor. Did she forget? The moment I moved here I started falling ill. It was an inauspicious beginning. I used to have many friends, and it is strange that I now have none. People do not really like the ill. In truth, I would rather not go back to work, to the machine[3] – for it to be some kind of end. When I am lying down alone, I imagine the world no longer exists. My only companions in my loneliness are the notes of the song of the birds, which is always joyful. I am so sad and feel such a strong yearning – emotions as incomprehensible as a beautiful spring itself.

Thursday February 25

I went to see the doctor yesterday. The examination took a very, very long time. In the end, he said that I have pleurisy. He said that he saw a bit of water there and that it is dangerous, especially for youth. My heart sunk. Is there anything related to the lungs that can be happy? He gave me a referral for an x-ray, prescribed medication and an ointment, and suggested we stay in touch. [And] nutritious food, first of all. How will I find it? This being the case, I will again not see father Avram. Oh Lord, it is so natural, after all. How many people have "left"[4] the ghetto in this manner? Both Poldak and Dubcia. Everyone leaves in this manner, and all like thunder on a clear day. But it is so difficult to get used to the idea that I am ill with a lung malady. Me! I am always in perfect health. Will I too take my leave in this way, so quietly, like them? But it will take more time, as it is only a non-remarkable beginning. Apart from that, I will wait for the x-ray. Maybe the war will end before the illness develops. Because I have no hope of overcoming this illness. How? With some fat? With my diet? In addition, I am nauseated by sugar. I simply cannot eat sugar. I would like so much to eat meat – a great, great deal of fatty meat. I can feel the ghetto, which is mistreating me. The illness has me in a strange mood. For example, I can be feeling excellent when I [suddenly] remember "my lungs" – "my lungs for God's sake" – and my hair immediately stands on end, and I immediately begin searching for some kind of imaginary pain in my right shoulder bone, and I have thoughts like: I may not see father [again]. I will not survive the war. Will I die tomorrow? What kind of death will it be? I sometimes feel as if my life will soon be gone, and I try to find beauty everywhere. I want so much to get dressed and to walk, to at least face death walking. But the bed and the fever keep me. The "black line"[5] shows 36, 37, 38 degrees capriciously, again and again. Aneke was here yesterday. I saw her with Tosia when I got back from the doctor's office with mother. I gave her the 10-day illness authorization he gave me. I will be given soup, but I have no idea what to do with it. Should I sell it and buy oil, or should I eat it? For one portion of soup I would receive perhaps half a decagram[6] of oil. So, is it worth it? Is it worth it to live and to suffer? Is it worth it to tend to all of it? But the spring is so beautiful!!!

Friday February 26
Aneke. What strange feelings that girl can arouse in a person. How much trust she has within her. How much innocent sorrow. How much emotion. And ultimately, how much healthy life. How many ideas. How much strength. One has to love Aneke, because we do not possess the happiness that is in her, which we need so much. We need Aneke, and therefore we must protect her. How unaware she is, like a child. In truth, she is a happy, good girl. It is actually strange that she still has not taken notice of the great evil around her, and that she focuses on something else that is happier from her childlike perspective – and more worthy of attention. _____

In any event, it is strange that she has not given up. It is so rare and so good. I still sit alone, the same thing, day after day. Although I no longer have a fever, I am still sitting at home and thinking (of course) about my illness. It is difficult for me because I have been detached from the machine that runs in a uniform manner, from the machine of which I was a part. It is hard for me to be disconnected, because work helped me forget, reach exhaustion, and escape my thoughts. Now I am detached and spurned, and simply ill. Will I return to work? Who would believe it? All year long I did my job and did not leave but rather sewed meticulously. And now, to my great sorrow, I am ill! I know that this is foolishness that I am writing and that my head holds nothing wiser. Perhaps the illness is to blame, perhaps it is due to lack of air, or perhaps I am just becoming a fool. Ultimately, it is sad. This is a very bad period. We are given little, and we have no oil whatsoever. Mother gives me her ration, but not even from the next ration. We are starting to cook separately. I do not cook soups. I have no idea how I will do it. I do not even want to think about it.

Friday March 5

I was at the doctor's on Wednesday. He told me that it is over (the water, the illness – I don't know). It is important that he authorized me to return to work. But I did not return. Aneke forbade me to return because she wants to use her connections with the head supervisor to help me leave the machine. I of course listened to her and did not go to work. I am waiting. Aneke always looks for the "bright ray of light on the dark horizon."[7] I spent all afternoon alone at home. Oh lord, what should I do with myself? I would at least like to work, but in a different position in order to not toil, different work. I would even prefer to return to the machine.

Sunday April 11

I am still writing. I have found the time and desire for this foolishness. Today I picked up a ration. Three grams of yellow turnips, three kilograms of beets for two weeks, 50 decagrams of flour, and milk for porridge. Despite the terrible weather, rations, and mood, I am writing. Aneke's story may have affected me, or perhaps the springtime is to blame. The springtime, which is always beautiful – those overused words, is not for us. Regardless, Aneke survives and continues to breathe. She is so good because she is childlike and therefore lacks judgment. I do not complain to anyone because I have no one. I still have no one. Is this natural? Tosia is living her life. She is introverted, and I too feel self-conscious in her presence. And despite it all, we have nothing in common. It is terrible to sit at the window as a monotonous rain falls outside and to wait for dinner, with a forlorn sense of hunger and a sad loneliness. I will stop writing here. Tosia is coming. God! I am so sad…

Endnotes

1   The diary was translated from Polish into Hebrew by Gosha Kubitsa.

2   Here the author appears to be referring to her diary.

3   This appears to be a reference to a sewing machine.

4   The word "leave" here refers to those who had died, apparently from illness.

5   The "black line" here appears to be a reference to the mercury in a thermometer.

6   Decagram: a metric unit of measure for 10 grams.

7   A Polish expression referring to the positive aspects of a difficult situation.

David Golinkin*

"These troubles trouble me and take my life, literally": a letter from Rabbi Mordechai Ya'akov Golinkin in Danzig to Rabbi Yoseph Lipman Gurewicz in Melbourne

My grandfather Rabbi Mordechai Ya'akov Golinkin (1884-1974) was born in Cherson, Ukraine and studied in the yeshivot of Lomzha, Ticktin, and Lida. There, he was influenced by Rabbi Yitzhak Ya'akov Reines, the founder of Mizrahi; he became an active member of Mizrahi in 1913 until the end of his life. Rabbi Golinkin served as the Chief Rabbi and Av Bet Din of Zhitomir, Ukraine beginning in 1913, where he founded the *Tiferet Bahurim* organization for young men and where he lobbied the authorities on behalf of the Jewish community. After the February Revolution of 1917, he founded the *Ahdut* organization together with Rabbis Yehudah Leib Tsirelson of Kishinev and Shlomo Aronson of Kiev. In the period of the Petliura pogroms against the Jews, Rabbi Golinkin and his wife Chaya Freida fled with their four children – including my father Noah (1913-2003) – to Vilna, where he was very active in Mizrahi, but also a regular visitor at the home of Rabbi Hayyim Ozer Grodzinski (see below), one of the founders of Agudat Yisrael. After serving as rabbi in Dokshitz and Rhuzany, he served as the Chief Rabbi and Av Bet Din of the city of Danzig during the stormy period of 1936-1939. It is from there that he sent the letter which is being published below.[1]

My father Noah succeeded in immigrating to the United States in 1938 as a rabbinical student at Yeshivat Rabbi Yitzhak Elhanan (Yeshiva College), and to bring his parents to the U.S. in May of 1939. It should be stressed that my grandparents did not abandon their community. The members of the Danzig community decided to leave in December 1938 as a result of Kristallnacht the month before, and the Senate of Danzig decided that they had to leave by May 1939. Indeed, most of the members of the Kehillah left by the fall of 1941 when the Nazis stopped all emigration.[2]

Rabbi Yoseph Lipman Gurewicz (1885-1956), the recipient of the letter printed below, was a devoted disciple of Rabbi Hayyim Ozer Grodzinski mentioned above. He travelled to Melbourne, Australia in 1930 in order to raise funds for the *Va'ad Hayeshivot* of Lithuania. The local Jewish community was impressed by him and there he remained as the rabbi of an Orthodox synagogue and the Av Bet Din until his death.[3]

From the letter below by Rabbi Golinkin found in the papers of Rabbi Gurewicz, which I purchased at an auction in New York in July 2020, one can learn a number of important things about the Jews of Danzig and its vicinity in February 1938.

The letter expresses depression about the situation, but there is no feeling of immediate pressure. Rabbi Golinkin asks about the dangers of assimilation and about the Jewish institutions and newspapers in Melbourne. He still expresses a wish for good matches for his children – without imagining a World War and the horrors of the Shoah. He also does not ask about a refuge for himself and his family, something which only happened, as mentioned, in 1939.

The letter is written in fluent Hebrew in a classic rabbinic style, including many Biblical and Talmudic expressions and frequent usage of the third person to address the recipient in a display of respect. In the following translation, I have preserved these elements. I have also listed some of the text's sources in the notes. Finally, as is customary in correspondence between rabbis, Rabbi Golinkin used a large number of abbreviations, which I have translated as complete words.

◆ ◆ ◆ ◆ ◆

Rabbiner		הרב
M.J. Golinkin	ב"ה יום א' לחדש אדר א' תרצ"ח	מרדכי יעקב גאלינקין
Danzig		אבד דק"ק דנציג
Adebargasse 8a		אדעבבארגאססע 8a
Tel. 27291		טלפון 27291

Shalom and Berakhah and all good to my good friend the Rabbi, the famous Gaon, whose "mouth drips pearls", the crown of the Torah, our teacher Rabbi Yoseph Lipman Gurewicz may he live a long life, the Gaon Av Bet Din of the community of Melbourne, Australia, may God protect him; and to all who accompany him Shalom and Berakhah.

After enquiring after his health, friend and exalted rabbi! Many days and years have passed from the day that we last saw each other when his excellency was by me in Dokshitz.[4] In the course of time, his excellency was accepted as the Av Bet Din in Australia, for mazal tov and much success, and I was appointed here for mazal tov in place of Rabbi Sagalowitsch, who relocated to Brussels in Belgium.[5] And all the time that I am here I am occupied, thank God, with the matters of my community and I did not take the time to ask my acquaintances in Vilna the address of his excellency, and to exchange letters of friendship with him, as is appropriate for loyal friends. Even though a few times "my soul yearned"[6] to enquire after him, for from the time I met him "my soul is bound up with him"[7], and I am certain that "as face answers to face in water"[8]. And behold now the Gaon Rabbi Hayyim Ozer [Grodzinski], may he live long, gave me the address of his excellency, and behold I am turning to him regarding a very unpleasant matter. And this is the matter: His excellency surely knows of the spirit[9] of racial hatred which has been wreaking havoc here recently, which cannot be described. And our Jewish brothers are in trouble and distress without any place to which they can escape. And it occurred to the members of our community and they advised me that I should turn to his excellency with both a question and a request, to try to learn correctly and to inform me in detail what are the possibilities at least for individuals, if not for many of our fellow Jews, to enter and support themselves in his country. For "at this time"[10], when all the gates are being locked for general emigration, one should not give up on the emigration of even one individual.

--- The information from HIAS [=Hebrew Immigrant Aid Society] is too general and official. But we must know in detail the appropriate ways for individuals, which cannot be learned from generalities. For example, is there a possibility for young people to enter there as students of some university or seminary? And if there are stipends to support them[11] or whether there can be found there generous communities or individuals who will worry about their support until they have the opportunity to support themselves.

II. What are the possibilities available to merchants and craftsman, and is there room for Hebrew teachers and Cantors and ritual slaughterers and the like? We also need to know what are the prospects for capitalists, and what is the amount considered "capital" in your country. ---- The ritual slaughterers and Cantors that I am asking about are not from my community, but rather immigrants who came here.

III. In general, his excellency should let me know the situation of the Jews there materially and spiritually, if it is worthwhile for me to advise the people of my community to push themselves to get in there. What is the situation of assimilation there, if there is not, God forbid, a danger threatening us from assimilation? If in his country there are all of the institutions needed for our Jewish brothers who are observant,[12] such as: *mikvaot, Talmudei Torah* [=Jewish schools], kosher meat -- in all of the communities or just in some of them? Are there Hebrew or Yiddish newspapers at least with a national spirit or not? Are there prospects that the Jewish community will develop with a national/religious spirit? His opinion and advice.

IV. All the details and conditions of entry, to whom should we turn? And the amount of money with which one should enter? And are there public institutions in his country to which one can turn with all difficult matters? And what are their addresses?

I hope that his excellency will forgive me for bothering him with such a difficult matter, for he should understand that I do not do so out of malice, but rather the necessity of the situation of my community forces me to do this. May his excellency not think that my words written here are in black ink as they appear to the naked eye. The truth is that if the eye could see and the pen could write, he would see the blood of the souls of our fellow Jews hovering between life [and death] under the above-mentioned letters and in between the lines. Surely his excellency was here and knows how our brothers lived here in tranquility and comfort and how they helped those who came here to request their assistance. And now -- millionaires and wealthy people have turned into paupers and poor people overnight.

---- I do not have the strength to write more. In his letter to me, please let me know about his life and health and private situation. How did he succeed in setting himself up and the matters of his community physically and spiritually, for I would like to know this. Where are the members of his household? It seems to me that one of his sons was still in Vilna not long ago. Why? And what is the reason he did not bring him into Australia? ----

About my situation, I can inform him that my two sons finished university, and my two daughters -- one finished university and the second the gymnasium.[13] And now I expect and hope that God will send them good matches. But for now, these troubles trouble me and take my life, literally. May God have mercy. Please may he hasten to reply, for every single hour is saving Jewish lives, literally. His friend who honors him in truth according to his lofty value and who blesses him with all good, together with his wife the honored Rebbetzin.

Rabbi Mordechai Ya'akov Golinkin

[And in the lower right hand corner diagonally:]

Warm regards from my wife and all the members of my household.

Endnotes

* Prof. David Golinkin is a Professor of Talmud and Jewish Law at the Schechter Institute of Jewish Studies in Jerusalem and the President of The Schechter Institutes, Inc. Both the letter and its introduction were translated into English by the author.

1 Regarding Rabbi Mordechai Ya'akov Golinkin, see what I wrote in the *Encyclopaedia Judaica,* second edition, 2007, vol. 7, p. 740; Rafael Medoff and David Golinkin, *The Student Struggle Against the Holocaust,* Jerusalem, 2010, pp. 97-102, 121-123.

2 See Gershon Bacon, "Danzig Jewry: A Short History," in *Danzig 1939: Treasures of a Destroyed Community* (Detroit, 1980), p. 34. My thanks to Prof. Bacon who sent me a copy of his important article, which is based on the literature about the history of the Jews of Danzig.

3 Regarding Rabbi Yoseph Lipman Gurewicz, see Sam Lipski [and Rabbi Ronald Lubofsky], "Chalk and Cheese – Rav Gurewicz et Amicorum," in Anna Rosner (ed.), *Eshkolot: Essays in Memory of Rabbi Ronald Lubofsky* (Melbourne, 2002), pp. 32-46. My thanks to Sam Lipski for sending me a copy of this important article.

4 Rabbi Golinkin served as the rabbi of Dokshitz from the end of the 1920s until the beginning of the 1930s, and Rabbi Gurewicz immigrated to Melbourne in 1930. In other words, the two of them had not seen each other for at least eight years.

5 Regarding the activities of Rabbi Jacob Sagalowitsch in Danzig between the years 1923-1933, see Bacon, "*Danzig Jewry*," pp. 31-32.

6 This phrase is borrowed from Psalms 42, 2: "so my soul yearns for You, Oh God."

7 This phrase is borrowed from Genesis 44, 30: "and his soul was bound up with his soul."

8 The verse in Proverbs 27, 19 ends: "so does one man's heart to another."

9 Perhaps it says "*mei'harei'ah,*" from the odor of.

10 This phrase is borrowed from Esther 4, 14: "And who knows, perhaps for just such a time, you have attained royalty."

11 At the bottom of the page it says "Verte,"(?) which apparently means "verso," turn over the page.

12 The Hebrew original says "*haredim,*" which today means ultra-Orthodox Jews, but here it means religious, observant or Orthodox Jews.

13 Eliyahu, Noah and Rachel finished university; Rivka finished the gymnasium.

Yechiam Weitz

As a Separate Topic?
The Trial of Victims

Rivka Brot. *In the Gray Zone: The Jewish Kapo on Trial*. Raanana, Israel: Open University of Israel and Ben-Gurion University of the Negev, 2019. 461 pp.

In the mid-to-late 1950s and the early 1960s, Israeli society was inflamed by two formative Holocaust trials: that of the victim Israel Kasztner, and that of the murderer Adolf Eichmann. Kasztner's trial and Eichmann's trial differed from one another in fundamental ways.

Eichmann's trial was conducted under the Nazis and Nazi Collaborators (Punishment) Law, 5710-1950. It was nationalist and statist in character, and it unified the Israeli public. It is viewed by scholars as a central link in Israeli society's transition from its primal stage to a stage of maturity and as a major event in the evolution of Israeli attitudes toward the Holocaust and its survivors. A few days after Eichmann's abduction by Israel, David Ben-Gurion, Israel's first prime minister, proclaimed that Eichmann would be tried in an Israeli court. This, he maintained, would fully reveal "the Holocaust for the knowledge and education of the youth in Israel following the Holocaust, as only a weak echo of its horrors has thus far reached their ears."[1]

The Kasztner trial was not conducted under the Nazis and Nazi Collaborators (Punishment) Law. Instead, it was an extremely lengthy defamation trial that lasted exactly four years. It began in the Jerusalem District Court in January 1954 and ended with the conclusion of the appeal proceedings before the Israeli Supreme Court in January 1958. Unlike the Kasztner trial, the Eichmann trial was relatively brief, lasting just over a year. It began in the Jerusalem District Court in April 1961 and ended with the conclusion of the defendant's appeal proceedings before the Israeli Supreme Court in late May 1962.[2]

Unlike the Eichmann trial, the "Kasztner trial," which was actually a defamation trial initiated by the State's Attorney of Israel against Melchior Gruenwald for publically accusing Israel Kasztner of collaborating with the Nazis, was political, subversive, and intensely controversial. Israeli journalists followed the trial incessantly, covering its hearings with detailed reports and massive headlines. The Kasztner trial was a significant part of the public political discourse that was underway in Israel at the time. According to historian Roni Stauber, all the newspapers – party papers and unaffiliated papers alike – covered all the stages of the trial in great detail.

The controversy that surrounded the trial pertained primarily to the conduct and character of Kasztner during the Holocaust in Hungary. It is a controversy that continues to play out today, more than 60 years later. Some maintain that Kasztner was one of the great rescuers of the Holocaust, with his actions resulting in the rescue of tens of thousands of Jews; others argue that Kasztner collaborated with the Nazis and assisted them in the lethal extermination process, whether or not he was aware of doing so. To his dying day, Shmuel Tamir, Gruenwald's defense attorney in the trial, maintained that Kasztner had provided the Germans with substantial assistance in their plot to exterminate the Jews of Hungary.

The trial itself, and the fierce debates regarding the subjects it raised, captivated Israeli society for a significant period of time. During the same period, the country witnessed dozens of trials focusing on victims' collaboration with the Germans. From the perspective of the Israeli public and historical research, however, it was as if these trials did not exist.

Until the mid-1980s, the subject of the Jewish Yishuv's attitude toward the Holocaust was taboo and went unexamined. The first, pioneering study on this volatile topic was Dina Porat's book *An Entangled Leadership: The Yishuv and the Holocaust, 1942-1945*.[3] The release of Porat's book was followed by the publication of numerous studies on related issues, such as the attitude of Mapai (the name of Israel's ruling labor party at the time – Hebrew acronym for the "Workers Party of the Land of Israel") toward the Holocaust[4] and Ben-Gurion's complex approach to the matter.[5] Studies have also been written on the two above-mentioned formative Holocaust trials (which, as noted, inflamed the Israeli public for many years), including Hanna Yablonka's study of the Eichmann trial and my own book on the Kasztner trial.[6]

During the years when research focused on Israeli society instead of on the Jewish Holocaust in Europe, nothing at all was written on the kapo trials; the subject vanished from Israeli hearts and minds and was non-existent for researchers. The first to address the issue was Tom Segev, who devoted four pages to it in his weighty volume on Israelis and the Holocaust that was published in the early 1990s.[7] Segev's discussion focuses on two points: the circumstances that led up to the enactment of the Nazis and Nazi Collaborators (Punishment) Law, and the approximately 30 trials that were conducted under this legislation. In this context, he describes a number of kapo trials, characterizing them as follows:

> Generally, only Holocaust survivors connected to the case at hand visited the courtrooms. Sometimes there were violent outbursts against the defendants and their attorneys. Only a few trials were covered by the press, some not at all. A kapo trial was a filthy and embarrassing story, and the papers did not want to get caught up in it.[8]

Segev, then, viewed these trials as personal matters of survivors. They conducted them in private, and Israeli society at large took no interest in them. His succinct remarks can be regarded as initial seeds presaging the emergence of research interest in the topic, which matured slowly, with articles on the subject being published from time to time.[9] The year 2015 marked the publication of the first book devoted entirely to the kapo trials: Itamar Levin's *Kapo in Tel Aviv: Prosecution in Israel of Jews Accused of Collaboration with the Nazis*.[10] In this book, Levin, an Israeli journalist and historian who authored a number of books on the restitution of the Jewish property that was stolen by the Nazis during World War II,[11] addresses an extremely sensitive question: What was the image of the kapos in the 1950s, when these trials were conducted? In the book's introduction, Levin argues that their image encompassed a notable element of distortion and injustice, but that for the Israeli public it was neither gray nor complicated; it was, rather, unequivocal and completely dark – a symbol of evil, human hatred, and betrayal. "In 1950s Israel," he writes, "anyone who had held a position of any kind under the German regime was referred to as a kapo. This appears to have been the most severe insult that could be leveled at an Israeli Jew at the time."[12] Levin offers the following blunt example of the harsh treatment kapos received during this period. In 1954, Israel Gutman – a survivor of Auschwitz and a member of Kibbutz Lehavot Habashan who would later become one of the most important Holocaust scholars in the world – wrote that he himself had seen the kapos engaging in the contemptible work of predatory animals, hated by all. Devoured by sadism and free of all inhibitions, they constituted obedient tools in the hands of the murderers…They were guided only by the despicable desire to ensure themselves life while entertaining themselves with the illusion of rule, achieved at the cost of the lives of others.[13]

Rivka Brot's 2019 book focuses on the kapo trials based on her doctoral dissertation: "Community and State: Trials of Jewish Collaborators with the Nazis."[14] In her book, titled *In the Gray Zone: The Jewish Kapo on Trial*, Brot addresses the one-dimensional image of these kapos in the public eye, on which Levin had written in an effort to present a picture that was more complex. Brot may be regarded as a researcher who focuses distinctly on this issue of emotionally charged trials, since a decisive majority of her publications deal with this issue.[15] Her book was awarded the prestigious Goldberg Foundation Prize.

In the Gray Zone begins with a personal story. In 1945, following the end of World War II, Zerach Warhaftig travelled from the United States to the Displaced Persons (DP) camps in occupied Germany for his first mission abroad.[16] Prior to his departure he met with Brot's grandfather, Rabbi Shmuel Brot, whom young members of Mizrachi regarded as a moral and religious authority.[17] During the encounter, Rabbi Brot told him explicitly that "his first obligation and activity after the end of the war must be to capture the 'two hundred' Jews who collaborated with the Nazis or did their bidding in the forced labor camps, and to try them with the utmost severity of the law" (p. 11). According to Rivka Brot, this was clearly understood by her grandfather, who passed away more than half a century ago. "For me," she writes, "the choice to contend legally with the Jewish collaborators became a research question" (ibid.).

A major pioneering aspect of this book is its focus on the trials that were conducted in the DP camps of Germany before the establishment of the state of Israel, and not only on the trials of collaborators that took place in Israel under the Israeli justice system. She preferred to study the legal aspect through comparison "between two legal approaches in two social frameworks."

The first framework was the Union of Liberated Jews, an organization founded by the Jews of the American Zone of Occupation in Germany immediately following the war. This organization established a special court known officially as the "Court of Rehabilitation," which tried a few hundred survivors who were suspected of collaborating with the Germans. The second framework was the justice system of the state of Israel. Following the enactment of the Nazis and Nazi Collaborators (Punishment) Law, 5710-1950, which was passed by the Knesset on August 1, 1950, a few dozen Jews were put on trial in the 1950s and the 1960s. The trials were held in Israeli district courts, and primarily in Tel Aviv.

In terms of historical research, Brot's writing about the Union of Liberated Jews is no less than pioneering. A significant number of studies have told the stories of the quarter of a million Jews who assembled in the American Zone of Occupation in southern Germany and, in the process, also discussed the trials that were conducted in the DP camps in this region. However, these trials have not been researched at all. Historian Zeev Mankowitz was a prominent researcher who wrote on the subject of survivors in Germany immediately following the war. Still, his book *Life between Memory and Hope: The Survivors of the Holocaust in Occupied Germany*,[18] a major study dealing with the DPs, says nothing about these trials. Brot explicitly addresses this omission: "This legal phenomenon," she notes, "leaves no trace on the post-Holocaust Jewish-Israeli historiography" (p. 164).

According to Brot, the main attribute of the DPs in the American Zone was activism, reflected in vitality and a powerful desire to grab hold of life: "They refused to be enslaved to despair; instead, they invested in themselves by creating a variety of realms of activity that encompassed all of the Jews" (p. 73). Brot notes that at the beginning of the period of the DP camps, the Jewish DPs succeeded in running an exceptional organizational framework "like nothing seen among the Jewish DPs in the other zones of occupation or among members of other national groups" (ibid.). They took the unique measure of establishing a Jewish court on German soil. From their perspective, establishing courts in the DP camps was not a foregone conclusion; rather, it was an act of extreme importance, "a sign and a symbol of the beginning of the change in the condition of the Jewish People after the great destruction." The Jewish court was a "symbol of the continuity of the Jewish legal culture of the past. At the same time, it was also a symbol of Jewish renewal in the present."

Dr. Samuel Orenstein, the chief prosecutor of the court that was set up in the DP camp in Landsberg, wrote the following: "I had the providence to be part of doing justice – Jewish justice. With reverence, I awaited the moment when the legal hearing would get underway" (p. 89).

The immediate reason for holding the trials in the DP camps was the urgent need to try Jews who were suspected of collaboration with Germany. Severe, violent confrontations were occurring between survivors and those they identified as having held positions and working on behalf of the Germans in the ghettos and the camps. Establishing the courts in the DP camps was justified by emphasizing its goal of bringing an end to the mob attacks that were occurring there. "The documentation shows," writes Brot, "that the immediate reason for establishing these courts was the desire to channel emotions onto the rational route of law, a desire to move the violence from the social to the legal realm" (p. 100). The legal proceedings were conducted with an emphasis on their formality: maintaining the rights of the accused, including the right to legal representation; maintaining the proper rules of evidence; and recording orderly protocols of the court proceedings. A difficult issue related to these trials was that of sentencing. The courts' punitive power was limited, as they were not operating in a sovereign state that possessed all punitive powers. The sentences handed down were not criminal but rather social and declarative – such as halting activity of the defendant for a specific period or in perpetuity, or "declaring the accused a traitor to the Jewish People" (p. 144). "These were not punishments in the standard sense of this word in modern criminal law" (ibid.), it was emphasized, but rather symbolic, educational, and moral punishments. The sentences were not light as far as the accused were concerned: inscribing the mark of Cain on their foreheads was a heavy burden for them and their families to bear.

What was the historical significance of these trials? According to Brot, the trial of camp collaborators "was a trial of social and national cleansing that went beyond regular criminal representation in its focus on the victim, the Jewish People. Although the legal proceedings pertained to the affairs of the individual, they were 'exploited' for the sake of dealing with the Jewish collective." The goal of the trial of collaborators in the DP camps was to "re-demarcate the social and moral boundaries of the Jewish People, which touched the very heart of Jewish identity and belonging after the Holocaust." Brot stresses what for her is a decisive point: the split that was evident in the courts. On the one hand, most of the witnesses at the trials viewed all the defendants as collaborators who had betrayed the Jewish People. On the other hand, the judges offered a different version "of the formative story of betrayal of the Jewish People in the context of the Holocaust": not all of the collaborators were made of the same material, and they could not be regarded as a uniform group of traitors. Rather, the judges regarded the defendants as characters acting not in a black world of darkness but rather in a world that was gray and complex. They refused to see them as monsters and preferred to try to understand the essence of the maze in which they had been living (p. 164).

The second part of the book focuses on some 30 kapo trials that were conducted in the state of Israel. According to Brot, the dual approach to the kapo defendants that had characterized the trials in the DP camps was also manifested in the trials that were held in Israel. The attitude toward the defendants that was held by the witnesses who had testified in these trials was extremely negative. They "saw them as traitors; those who were caught were worse than the Germans, and it was therefore necessary to settle accounts with them before they began doing so with the Germans" (p. 233). Brot maintains that the desire for revenge played a major role in the testimonies. The witnesses who appeared before the court did so not only in order to tell their personal stories, "but rather also to avenge the blood of the dead." They felt immense fury toward the defendants. One witness told a judge that he "came [to the trial] to defend the blood of my brothers who died" and explained that he had survived in order to testify against "this accused murderer" (ibid.).

The judges in these trials were forced to contend with the outbursts of anger in the courtroom. They understood that the witnesses bore a grudge against the defendants, "and, in practice, against all [Jewish] position officials." They clearly understood that the intense emotions being expressed by the witnesses in their testimonies could divert the trials "to emotional channels that could be detrimental to the legal proceedings. As a result, they usually related to these testimonies as a factor that undermined the reliability and credibility of the witnesses" (p. 235). Many of the judges were able to understand the intense anger of the witnesses, who had gone through hell during the Holocaust. The following is an excerpt from the ruling of Judge Shalom Kassen[19] in the trial of Haim Silverberg, a kapo in the Skarzysko labor camp,[20] in reference to the reliability of the witnesses who appeared before him:

> These witnesses testified to extraordinary facts. They felt the Holocaust with their own flesh and bodies. They are seeking revenge, seeking to take vengeance upon someone for what the Nazi creature did to them. Perhaps they found the defendant to be their victim, and therefore he served as their "*forerbeiter*" [labor detail head] during the terrible period (p.237).

Brot shows that the judges, who expressed their sympathy and compassion for the witnesses, tried to understand the defendants and did not view them as traitorous monsters. Some judges "understood that the reality with which they were presented by the testimonies was, first and foremost, legally and historically unprecedented, but primarily a reality that is difficult to translate into legal language" (p. 253). To clarify the essence of this complex subject, Brot quotes the words of Benjamin Cohen[21] from his ruling in the trial of Mordechai Goldstein, who was a member of the Jewish police in the Ostrowicz Ghetto[22] and at the labor camp set up nearby after its liquidation. When he finished reading out the ruling, the judge continued with "a general comment that demarcates the behavior of the defendant in the unusual circumstances of the labor camp." This comment was not part of the "pure" legal determination or the ruling, and was seemingly superfluous. According to Brot, this comment, which was surprising in its candor, brings to the surface the tension between the legal aspect – "the legal decision according to strict legal categories" – and the historical aspect, meaning "broad contemplation of the events regarding which the witnesses provided commentary beyond the legal categories, contemplation beyond the legal categories, contemplation that can reveal the 'historical' reality of life, as opposed to the legal reality." The gap and the tension between these two worlds created a gray reality: policemen who were regular Jews who, in this capacity, used the whip and the club against prisoners who were Jews, like them. These policemen "committed acts which they would never have dreamed of committing in normal times and which, according to the 'laws' of the camp were a necessity." In his decision, Judge Cohen explained the meaning of the gray zone. On the one hand, the formal law may "mark the convicted defendant with a darker than usual stain"; on the other hand, there was no reason to doubt the fact that the defendant, who experienced the horrors of the Holocaust, was "a fair person with an average demeanor and a good Jew all year round." According to the evidence presented before the judge, his conduct did not deviate from the general day-to-day practices of the Jewish police "in the places of detention, which had to maintain proper order" (p. 254). Judge Cohen regarded this figure as neither black nor white but rather gray, which is a point that Brot reiterates repeatedly in her book. The defendants can also be regarded as victims, which is how Brot wrote about them: "The legal proceedings were based on human individuals that cannot be disregarded. Indeed, they were there – human beings, flesh and blood, physically and mentally injured, people whose troubling stories arouse embarrassment, discomfort, and even rejection." Israeli society faced the stories of the defendants via a legal agenda "based on law that had only a slim connection to them" (p. 262).

Rivka Brot's book paints a picture that is fascinating and original, but also extremely troubling. It indicates that Israeli society and the Israeli justice system were unable to cope with the stories of the kapos – a phenomenon that materialized during the days of the horror and chaos of the Holocaust.

Endnotes

1 David Ben-Gurion, "The Eichmann Trial will be Held in Israel," *Davar*, May 27, 1960 (Hebrew).

2 The appeal hearing was held on May 29, 1962, and Eichmann was executed two days later, on May 31, 1962.

3 Porat, *An Entangled Leadership: The Yishuv and the Holocaust, 1942*-1945 (Tel Aviv, 1986) (Hebrew).

4 Two books have been written on this subject: one dealing with the first part of the war (Hava Eshkoli, *Mapai and the Holocaust, 1939-1942* [Jerusalem, 1994] [Hebrew]) and the other dealing with the second part of the war (Yechiam Weitz, *Awareness and Helplessness: Mapai Facing the Holocaust, 1942-1945* [Jerusalem, 1994] [Hebrew]).

5 Tuvia Friling, *Arrows in the Dark: David Ben-Gurion, the Yishuv Leadership and Rescue Attempts during the Holocaust* (Sede Boker, 1998) (Hebrew).

6 Hanna Yablonka, *The State of Israel versus Adolf Eichmann* (New York, 2004), originally published in Hebrew in 2001; Yechiam Weitz, *The Man Who Was Murdered Twice: The Life, Trial and Death of Israel Kasztner* (Jerusalem, 2011), originally published in Hebrew in 1995.

7 Tom Segev, *The Seventh Million: The Israelis and the Holocaust* (Jerusalem, 1991), pp. 243-247 (Hebrew) (the book's Hebrew-language edition has 547 pages). The subject is discussed in the chapter titled "Politics: The Kasztner Trial." In English, see Tom Segev, *The Seventh Million: The Israelis and the Holocaust* (New York, 1993).

8 Segev, *The Seventh Million* (English), p. 262.

9 For example, in 1996, the Hebrew-language journal *Cathedra* published two articles dealing with these trials and with the Nazis and Nazi Collaborators (Punishment) Law. Hanna Yablonka, "The Law for Punishment of the Nazis and their Collaborators: Legislation, Implementation, and Attitudes," *Cathedra* 82 (December 1996), pp. 135-152 (Hebrew); Yechiam Weitz, " The Law for Punishment of the Nazis and their Collaborators as Image and Reflection of Public Opinion," *Cathedra* 82 (December 1996), pp. 153-164 (Hebrew).

10 Levin, *Kapo in Tel Aviv* (Jerusalem, 2015).

11 His major book is *The last chapter of the Holocaust?: The Struggle over the Restitution of Jewish Property in Europe* (Jerusalem, 1998) (Hebrew).

12 Levin, *Kapo in Tel Aviv*, p. 14.

13 Ibid., 13-14.

14 Brot, "Community and State: Trials of Jewish Collaborators with the Nazis," doctoral dissertation, Tel Aviv University, 2015 (Hebrew).

15 Two examples of her publications are the article "The Gray Zone of Collaboration in the Courtroom," *Theory and Criticism* 40 (2012), pp. 157-187 (Hebrew) and "Conflicting Jurisdictions: The Struggle of the Jews in the Displaced Persons Camps for Legal Autonomy," *Dapim: Studies on the Holocaust* 31(3) (2017), pp. 171-199.

16 Zerach Warhaftig was a prominent leader of the religious-Zionist movement. For many years, he served as a member of Knesset and as Israel's minister of religions. In 1983, he was awarded the Israel Prize for Jewish Law. During the war, he fled Europe to the United States via Japan. He wrote about his activities in the displaced persons camps in his book *Survivor and Refugee during the Holocaust* (Jerusalem, 1984) (Hebrew).

17 Samuel Brot (1885-1963) was a leader of the Mizrachi movement. In 1935 he was appointed as a chief rabbi of Antwerp, and during the Holocaust he made his way to New York, where he served as rabbi of *Kehillath Morya*. After immigrating to Israel in 1951, he was selected to serve as a member of the High Rabbinical Court of Appeals in Jerusalem. An admired figure in the religious-Zionist movement, he has been described by Yitzhak Rafael as one of the greatest speakers of the Mizrachi movement. Yitzhak Rafael, *I Did Not Find the Light By Chance* (Jerusalem, 1981), p. 470 (Hebrew).

18 Mankowitz, *Life between Memory and Hope: The Survivors of the Holocaust in Occupied Germany* (Cambridge University Press, 2002).

19 Shalom Kassen (1901-1982) served as district court judge from 1947 to 1971. In 1955, he was appointed rotational president of the Haifa District Court.

20 Skarzysko was a large labor camp in eastern Poland that was established in the summer of 1940. It was intended to exploit its inmates to manufacture weapons for Germany. The conditions in the camp were unbearable.

21 Benjamin Cohen (1913-2006) served as a Tel Aviv District Court judge between 1950 and 1983.

22 The ghetto in Ostrowicz, a city in south-central Poland, was established in April 1941. By the end of the year, its inmate population stood at 15,000 Jews. The last Aktion implemented there took place in January 1943, when some 2,000 Jews were deported to the Treblinka extermination camp.

Sharon Geva

Their Voice Has Been Heard

Review of *Let Me Hear Thy Voice and the Shadows Flee Away: A Selection of Sources on Women in the Holocaust.* Tel Aviv: Moreshet and Yad Vashem, 2018. 378 pp.

At the core of the anthology *Let Me Hear Thy Voice and the Shadows Flee Away* lies tension, and underlying the stories it brings together is an impossible task: that of telling the story of Jewish women during the Holocaust and, in doing so, depict their unique point of view (to use the author's words on the book's cover and in its introduction). However, the motivation of compiling a selection of stories about women in the Holocaust and melding them into an overall story to serve as a useful compass for navigating a theoretical and research path and the biological sex and gender identification of its protagonists, is more of a lighthouse than a target. There is no doubt that the book's editor, Batya Dvir, knew this, as reflected in the book's subtitle: *A Selection of Sources on Women in the Holocaust.* This raises questions, such as who was selected for inclusion in the book. The design of the book's cover – the image of notebook binder bursting with letters, photographs, and scraps of paper – reflects the tension it contains and hints at its content.

The book contains a wide variety of stories about women during the Holocaust from an impressive geographical range that expands from a focus on Poland and Germany to reach as far as Yugoslavia, Bulgaria, Greece, and Libya. The book has six sections, each of which contains stories of varying length. The first section, titled "Strangers in Their Homes," contains primarily stories about women in Germany, with a notable presence of excerpts from the diary of Anna (Paltin) Popper, which she wrote about her daughter Helenka until they were deported to Theresienstadt and murdered at Auschwitz (pp. 48-55). Featured prominently in the second section, titled "Women in the Struggle for Life in the Ghettos of Eastern Europe," are the figures of journalist and documenter Cecilia Slepak from the Warsaw Ghetto (pp. 71-78)[1] and Stefania

Wilczyńska, who is presented as being of equal importance to Janusz Korczak in the management of the orphanage in the city (p. 120).

In the third section, "Women during the Stage of the Final Solution to the Jewish Question," Dvir addresses, among other things, the importance of the stories of women who were children during the Holocaust. One example is the troubling story of Esther (Pasker) Gelbelman, who was 11 years old at the outbreak of the war. Gelbelman spent the Holocaust in Romania and watched the other members of her family die before her eyes (pp. 155-159). These stories have a current dimension: that is to say, the survivors who are still living among us were children at the time. The fourth section, "Women in the Armed Struggle against the Nazis," presents the stories of members of the underground who did not survive, such as Gusta (Justina) Dawidson of Krakow and Zipora Birman of Kibbutz Tel Chai, the Zionist settlement training framework in Bialystok; both women were extolled in Israel at an extremely early stage: *Justina's Diary* was published in Hebrew in 1953,[2] and Birman's writings were included in the anthology *The Book of the Ghetto Wars*.[3] This section also contains a chapter titled "Women in the General Resistance Movements," which contains the stories of women who served with the partisans, most notably Rozka Korczak (pp. 245-250) and Vitka Kovner (p. 251), but also Haya Shapira-Lazar from the Zionist right wing, who later served as a journalist for *Herut* in Israel (p. 252).

The book's fifth section addresses the rescue attempts by Jewish men and women. Its title, "Like a Mother Rushing to the Rescue," is identical to the title of Daniel Ben-Nachum's book about Yishuv parachutist Haviva Reik, which was published during the second half of 1965 (Sifriat Hapoalim). This section contains the stories of women who attempted to effect rescue through negotiations with officials in the Nazi regime, women such as Gisi Fleischmann in Slovakia and Hansi Brand in Hungary, and Reik and Hannah Senesh. The sixth section, titled "After All – Like the Phoenix," contains stories of women who survived and engaged in documentation and commemoration, as well as in child education. Conspicuously absent in this context are Rachel Auerbach, whose story is told elsewhere in the book (in the second section), and Miriam Novitch, a documenter and a prominent figure at the Ghetto Fighters' House, of whom the book makes no mention.

How were the women chosen? The answer appears to be found in the introduction, which explains that the degree to which each story in the collection elaborates on the woman in question is directly proportional to the inventory of sources about her. This explains the elaboration with regard to Rozka Korczak, a partisan and a member of the United Partisans Organization (*Fareynegte Partizaner Organizatsye*, or FPO) in the Vilna Ghetto, a member of Kibbutz Ein Hahoresh, and one of the founders of the Moreshet Institute; and with regard to Gisi Fleischmann, who worked to rescue large numbers of Jews in Slovakia and was murdered at Auschwitz. It is less helpful in explaining the limited attention paid to Lena Küchler-Silberman (p. 329), despite the multiple sources by and about her, not to mention the fact that she was the author of *My Hundred Children*,[4] the first best-seller in Israel to deal with women and family during the Holocaust; the concise discussion of painter Esther Luria (p. 117); and the lack of mention of Dr. Hulda Campagnano, who testified at the Eichmann trial as a representative of Italian Jewry and published her story as an autobiography.[5]

The selection required decisions by the author that shed light on the importance that Dvir ascribes to the activities of woman Holocaust survivors in their later years. For example, the story of Haika Grossman (1919-1996), a partisan and a member of the underground during the Holocaust and subsequently a public activist and member of Knesset in Israel, is not presented alongside that of ghetto fighters Tosia Altman and Regina Fuden, who were killed in 1943 and who like Grossman were members of Hashomer Hatzair, or that of Jewish Combat Organization fighter Hella Rufeisen-Schuepper (1921-2017). Rather, Grossman's story appears in the book's final section, titled "Women Leaders and Artists," alongside those of writer, translator, and journalist Ruth Bondy and writer Alona Frankel.

A visible effort was made to include as many women as possible in the book. Two examples are Irena Sendler, who worked to rescue children in Poland (p. 291), and Elisabeth of Bavaria, Queen of Belgium. (p. 303), both of whom were recognized as Righteous among the Nations, and both of whom were included in the anthology without an explanation of why and how their stories shed additional light on aspects of the lives of Jewish women (p. 10). The same is true of the decision to include Reik and Senesh and women who were not living in occupied countries during the Holocaust, such as Else Lasker-Schüler (p. 56). Also difficult to explain is the decision to address the book's target audience in the Hebrew masculine singular (for example, "*hakoreh*," meaning the male reader, pp. 9-10, 48), as opposed to the more standard masculine plural ("*hakorim*") or the masculine and feminine plural ("*hakorot v'hakorim*").

The book's format is comparable to that of academic research and non-fiction (scientific editing was entrusted to Dr. Naama Shik of Yad Vashem), and it therefore contains a bibliography and footnotes. However, it lacks many references, as in the story of Diamantina (Addadi) Reginano of Tripoli, for example, who was deported to Italy (pp. 176-179). These references are important due to their usefulness to readers who are interested in reviewing sources that contain some story or another in its entirety. Dvir's distinction between primary and secondary sources differs from the norm in historical research in its basic sense – in its definition of primary sources as sources that were written and produced during the Holocaust, and its definition of secondary sources not as research literature but rather as sources that were written and produced after World War II, such as testimonies and memoirs.

The chapter on female members of the Zionist underground reflects the strong political impact of the explicit choice to deal only with Zionist movements. It focuses on women who served as liaisons in the underground and were therefore present on the frontlines of the fighting in this context. The most prominent among the women included here were members of Hashomer Hatzair, which is directly related to Moreshet, one of the publishers of the anthology. The story of the fighter Margalit Landau, who died at the age of 18, starts off the chapter but is presented in the footnotes (p. 129) and for some reason is missing from the overall list of women in the book (pp. 367-370). In any event, in this section there appears to have been no room for other women, and therefore Fela Finkelstein (1921-2008), a member of Betar and the Jewish Military Organization underground who participated in the Warsaw Ghetto Uprising, is recounted in a different section.

In the book's introduction, Dvir writes that the book's source was Moreshet, The Mordechai Anielevich Memorial Holocaust Studies and Research Center: for example, in the case of the story of Rozka Korczak, her activity in the organization;

the exhibit on women in the resistance movement that was curated by Korczak's daughter Yonat Rotbein at the beginning of the 1990s; and a meeting with David (Jurek) Plonsky, who told Rotbein about his mother (p. 8). Another exhibit that reverberates throughout the book is "Spots of Light: To Be a Women in the Holocaust," a 2007 exhibit that was curated by Yehudit Inbar at Yad Vashem – which was also party to the book's publication.[6] The book's title, "Let Me Hear Thy Voice," tells us that its goal is to cause the women's stories to be heard, to recount their methods of resistance, and to have them published.

But the call to "make one's voice heard," in addition to being a somewhat overused figure of speech, emerges as a vehicle for neither the introduction nor the articulation of new voices, but rather for the reverberation and adapting of processes that have already occurred in the recent decades of the research on women in the Holocaust and Holocaust from the perspective of gender. This voice is already in existence and has been established among an entire generation of scholars around the world and in Israel; it abounds with articulations and revelations, and disagreements and struggles – particularly in academia – for the sake of recognizing the distinction between men and women during the Holocaust, but not necessarily in recognition of the women scholars. The latter are documented in a recently published anthology edited by Judith Tydor Baumel-Schwartz and Dalia Ofer, in which women researches describe the path, paved with difficulties and obstacles, they travelled (for the sake of full disclosure, it should be noted that I am one of the women who contributed to this book).[7]

Against this background, the introductory chapter of *Let Me Hear They Voice* (titled "Is your voice heard? Women in the Holocaust"), which is based almost exclusively on the introduction of the anthology *Women in the Holocaust* edited by Dalia Ofer and Linore G. Weitzman,[8] is, simply put, a generation behind. Although this text by Ofer and Weitzman is an extremely important milestone in the history of Holocaust research from the perspective of gender, it was published in Hebrew more than two decades ago.[9] As a result, with the exception of the richness of the stories in this collection, the value of *Let Me Hear Thy Voice* lies in the fact that it is a product of its time: at the end of the second decade of the twenty-first century, the distinction between the experience of women and the experience of men during the Holocaust is already quite clear not only to those engaged in the scholarship; rather, the roots laid down by the initial scholars in this field sprouted long ago.

Reading the book from a gender perspective also sheds light on the manner in which stories about and of women in the Holocaust are presented today, and, perhaps most importantly, the designated purpose of every woman in a patriarchal society, including Jewish society. In this book, too, women are frequently depicted in terms of their relationship to a man, such as a husband, a father, or a son. The sources that provide information about them do so vis-à-vis men, and even heroic stories are translated into the character of a women rushing to the rescue, whether of her biological children or of the Jewish People. At the end of the book's final section, we find a spectacular, enormous family photo of four generations of the family of Hannah and Sarah Tessler, two sisters who survived the Holocaust and built an extensive family in Israel. This photograph (pp. 365-365) immediately reflects how Dvir ultimately melded together all these stories about Jewish women in the Holocaust with no distinction between destruction and heroism, or between rehabilitation and revival. The book's final two pages remind us that every story about a Jewish woman reflects the aim of fulfilling her purpose: after all, every women is always a mother, whether in actuality or in potential, and in this sense the period of the Holocaust is no exception.

Endnotes

1   For a more detailed discussion of Slepak, see Dalia Ofer, "Her View through My Lens: Cecilia Slepak Studies Women in the Warsaw Ghetto," *Yalkut Moreshet* 75 (2003), p. 111-130 (Hebrew).

2   Gusta Dawidson, *Justina's Diary* (Tel Aviv, 1953) (Hebrew). A new edition was published in 2003 by The Ghetto Fighters' House.

3   Zipora Birman, "In Grodno and in Bialystok," in Yitzhak Zuckerman and Moshe Basok (eds.), *The Book of the Ghetto Wars* (Tel Aviv, 1954), pp. 395-397 (Hebrew).

4   Lena Küchler-Silberman, *My Hundred Children* (Tel Aviv, 1959, and other editions) (Hebrew).

5   Hulda Campagnano, *For a Generation That Did Not Know: The Chronicle of a Young Mother during a Critical Year in the Italian Diaspora* (Kvutzat Yavneh, 1981) (Hebrew).

6   Yehudit Inbar, *Spots of Light: To Be a Woman in the Holocaust* (Jerusalem, 2007) (Hebrew).

7   Judith Tydor Baumel-Schwartz and Dalia Ofer (eds.), *Her Story, My Story? Writing About Women and the Holocaust* (Switzerland, 2020).

8   Dalia Ofer and Lenore J. Weitzman (eds.), *Women in the Holocaust* (New Haven, 1998).

9   Dalia Ofer and Lenore G. Weizman, "The Role of Gender in Holocaust Research," *Yalkut Moreshet* 67 (1999), pp. 9-24 (Hebrew).

Eli Tzur

"A Poor Man's Eichmann" or Ivan the Terrible?

Tamir Hod. *Why Did We Remember To Forget? The Demjanjuk Affair in Israel.*
Tel Aviv: Resling, 2020. 387 pp.

On March 17, 2012, Ivan Demjanjuk died in an elderly care facility in Germany in the midst of an appeal of a court ruling that sentenced him to five years in prison. Demjanjuk's death marked the end of a 37-year legal imbroglio that apparently has constituted the longest trial for war crimes committed during World War II. For the sake of comparison, the Nuremberg Trial, which was the first trial of the surviving heads of the Nazi regime, lasted less than a year (from November 20, 1945 to October 1, 1946). Demjanjuk's circuitous legal saga encompassed proceedings in the United States, Israel, and Germany. In *Why Did We Remember To Forget? The Demjanjuk Affair in Israel*, Tamir Hod traces the development of the affair, with a focus on the trial that was conducted in Israel. Hod's book consists of three sections: one on the evolution of Demjanjuk's legal saga from 1975 onward; another on the trial's reverberations in Israel among the different sectors of Jewish-Israeli society; and a third on the collective memory of the trial and a discussion on the disappearance of this memory.

We do not know for certain what Demjanjuk did during World War II. It is clear that he was taken prisoner by the Germans and that he then chose to join the S.S. auxiliary force. At a training base at Trawniki concentration camp in Poland, he was trained as a *wachmann* (guard), a term that encompassed various roles in the concentration and death camps. Trawniki also had an office that monitored the activity of these guards.

At the end of the war, Demjanjuk took refuge in Germany. In the initial months following the war, before the onset of the Cold War, the Allies acted to transfer members of the national groups that populated the Soviet Union into Soviet control, even if they had collaborated with the Nazis. One example were members of the Russian Liberation Army, known also as the Vlasov army, who were sent to the Gulag (that is, those who were not executed).

When the Cold War got underway, the Allies ceased repatriating Soviet citizens and instead began recruiting them to engage in acts of sabotage within the Eastern Bloc. At the beginning of the 1950s, the American occupation forces began granting them the right to immigrate to the United States (a right that had *not* been granted to Jews at the end of the 1930s). These immigrants were required to sign a declaration that they had not taken part in any war crimes of the Nazi regime. Demjanjuk took advantage of this opportunity and immigrated to the United States. There, in the 1970s, internal domestic pressures resulted in the establishment of a special office within the U.S. Department of Justice responsible for identifying individuals who had perpetrated crimes against humanity. This development was related to a broader struggle for human rights, which served as a tool in the ideological struggle against the Communist Bloc, of which the failure to respect human rights was a prominent failing. In 1975, this office launched an investigation of Demjanjuk's wartime past, and after it became clear that he had concealed his past activity his citizenship was revoked. Demjanjuk could not be prosecuted in the United States because U.S. law precluded trying individuals for crimes that had done no injury to American citizens. It was therefore decided to deport him to a country whose constitution permitted it to prosecute individuals for crimes against humanity. Against this background, Demjanjuk arrived in Israel in 1986. His time and his trial in Israel are the focus of the book under review.

Hod's book focuses on three aspects of the Demjanjuk affair: the factors that motivated the Israeli government to request Demjanjuk's extradition and to try him in Israel; the unfolding of the trial as a juridical system; and the trial's impact on the different sectors of Israeli society. These three aspects, Hod maintains, help answer the question that lies at heart of his study: Why did Israeli society "forget" the trial and erase it from its collective memory? To address the dilemmas posed in the book, the author deals not only with the issues themselves but also with their historical and political background.

When the U.S. legal authorities asked Israel to assume custody over Demjanjuk and try him on Israeli soil, they found the small country in the midst of a whirlwind of political and psychological change. During the initial contacts between the Israeli government and the U.S. Justice Department's Office of Special Investigations (O.S.I.), Israel was still licking its wounds and recovering from the Yom Kippur War of 1973. Therefore, although the contacts began in 1975, more than a decade elapsed before Demjanjuk was extradited to Israel. By this time, Israel had undergone a major internal political shift and was already in the midst of another war. The Likud government sought to recreate Israeli history, but with different actors: this time, instead of the leaders of the Mapai party that had governed Israel for its first three decades of statehood, the main roles would played by the leaders of the Likud party – by Menachem Begin instead of David Ben-Gurion. The narrative of the Holocaust served as a powerful psychological instrument in these processes. The state was both the solution to and the antithesis of the history of the Jewish People during the Holocaust, and the Holocaust was used to strengthen the self-image of the state and its people as eternal victims whom others were constantly attempting to destroy. Israel's self-image as a victim had enabled it to employ a militant policy, to oppress, and to conquer and occupy. Israel was deeply involved in Lebanon at the time, and its image as a victim enabled it to engage in activity there that, under other circumstances, would not have been possible.

In addition to the Holocaust's role as such an instrument, there was also the psychological motivation of Prime Minister Begin. Begin, a pre-war leader of Betar, which was the only Zionist youth movement that had not sent a delegation to Nazi-occupied Poland, compensated himself forty years later by comparing Beirut to Berlin and P.L.O. Chairman Yasser Arafat to Hitler. All of these orientations would converge in the Demjanjuk trial.

From its very beginning, the Demjanjuk trial was conducted in the shadow of the Eichmann trial. Both men were tried under the Israeli Nazis and Nazi Collaborators (Punishment) Law, which was enacted by the First Knesset in 1950. The law itself fit into a broader paradigm. The Zionist movement had proposed *Eretz Israel* as a place of refuge for the Jews of Europe, and, since its establishment, the state of Israel had regarded itself not only as a place of refuge but also as the legal heir of the Jewish People, which had been decimated in the Holocaust. On these grounds, the state of Israel viewed itself as entitled to compensation for the property of the Jews that had been killed, and to punish those who had done them harm. These two prerogatives found expression in Israel's 1952 Reparations (*shilumim*) Agreement with West Germany and the Nazis and Nazi Collaborators (Punishment) Law of 1950. Both the politicians and the judges would give the impression of a re-creation of the Eichmann trial. Indeed, at the outset of the Demjanjuk trial, Haim Gouri wrote: "I assume that the Demjanjuk trial will be for this generation…what the Eichmann trial was for its parents and older siblings" (p. 309).

The state of Israel also regarded the trial as "the Likud's Eichmann trial." However, for the trial to bear historical importance, the defendant needed to be an important enough figure to remain the focus of public discourse. Demjanjuk's trial was conducted during the period in which the Holocaust became the central element of Israel's civil religion, and its use was an important aspect of the many political divisions that split Israeli society (p. 137). It is no coincidence that the Holocaust is more typically used by the Israeli right wing, which has sought to strengthen the Jewish dimension of the event at the expense of the Israeli dimension. On the eve of Israel's evacuation of the settlement of Yamit in the Sinai Peninsula, I remember the opponents of the evacuation producing a booklet with a cover bearing a picture of the train tracks to Birkenau. And more than two decades later, during the evacuation of Gush Katif, the children of the evacuees adorned themselves with yellow Jewish stars and raised their hands in the air to resemble the young boy in the well-known photograph from the Warsaw Ghetto.

In this atmosphere in Israeli society, the Demjanjuk trial might have been expected to have resonance similar to that of the Eichmann trial. However, those who initiated the trial clearly understood that Demjanjuk was not Eichmann. Eichmann had been a middle-tier official in the Nazi hierarchy (not a member of the elite, as Hod maintains) who was responsible for the transports and was involved in the extermination of the Jews across the continent, which is why the account of the horrors of the Holocaust not only offered historical context but also had great resonance in Israeli society. Moreover, from the outset of the trial, it was clear that the defendant was Adolf Eichmann, a bureaucrat whose office had dealt with the extermination; for this reason, the witness testimonies were not meant to convince the judges of Eichmann's actions (after all, Eichmann was not involved in the extermination itself) but rather to produce a panorama of the world of evil in which they occurred. In the Demjanjuk trial, on the other hand, only a small number of inmates who had escaped from Treblinka testified, and those who did had resided not in the extermination area but rather in the adjacent service camps. The witnesses recreated the horrors of Treblinka, and the man who symbolized these horrors more than anything else was a Ukrainian *wachmann* known by the nickname "Ivan the Terrible." In their imagination, this man had ceased to be a human being and had become a symbol of these horrors and of evil itself.

In this context, an unplanned coordination occurred between the goals of the Israeli Justice Ministry and the prosecution in the trial on the one hand, and the witnesses in the trial on the other hand. According to Hod, the goal of the Justice Ministry under Justice Minister Moshe Nissim, who remained true to Begin's approach, was for the trial to have an impact on Israeli society and to have reverberations around the world. Therefore, from the moment Demjanjuk was presented as Ivan the Terrible of Treblinka, the trial had fulfilled these expectations as a result of the figure depicted by the testimonies. The motivations of the witnesses were more complex. In their eyes, punishing Ivan the Terrible offered a solution to their suffering and a symbolic expression of the victory of the uprising and the victory of the Jewish People. In a testimony he gave immediately following the war, in 1946, Eliyahu Rosenberg maintained that Ivan the Terrible had been killed during the revolt. This, however, did not stop him from subsequently arguing that Demjanjuk was Ivan the Terrible. This change in Rosenberg's testimony can be attributed to the common memory held by all the witnesses – a memory that was detached from all the historical events and their individual memories. In this context, the following assessment by an American jurist rings true: "During the trial, they created a shared memory of Treblinka that overcame individual memory, which in any event had been only partial" (p. 87).

Even when presented with an authentic exhibit such as the activity report on Demjanjuk that had been filed at Trawniki, the witnesses were not willing to change their position that Demjanjuk and Ivan the Terrible were one and the same. The Trawniki document resulted in the gap in consciousness between the Eichmann trial and the Demjanjuk trial – between the presentation of the historical panorama of the Holocaust and the dry legal discussion of the reliability of the document. The document worked to Demjanjuk's benefit on only one point: the fact that he had not served at Treblinka and therefore was not Ivan the Terrible. According to the report, Demjanjuk had served as a guard at Sobibor extermination camp, which was no better than Treblinka. The authenticity of the document was finally confirmed in January 2020, when a collection of photographs belonging to Sobibor's Deputy Commandant Johann Niemann was put on exhibit in Berlin. The exhibit contained two photographs in which Demjanjuk can be identified with almost complete certainty. Due to the extended discussion of the Trawniki document, which also addressed the presence of staple holes in Demjanjuk's photograph, *Haaretz* referred to the trial as "the trial about the stapler." This aspect of the trial overshadowed the testimonies of the survivors of the camp and resulted in the public's loss of interest. Ultimately, as the prosecution failed to prove that Demjanjuk was Ivan the Terrible, the judges were forced to acquit him. Under the 1950 law, he could have been tried for his actions at Sobibor (as was done in Germany in 2007); however, this would have meant that the remainder of the trial would have become one of a rank and file *wachmann*, and Israel had no interest in such a trial. The Demjanjuk trial was not the Eichmann trial, and Demjanjuk, as characterized by Justice Zvi Tal, was "a poor man's Eichmann" (p. 309).

In addition to the different character of the two trials, the background of the trials also differed from one another, influencing the reverberations of each. The decade between the end of the 1956 Sinai Campaign and the outbreak of the Six-Day War in 1967 was the calmest and most secure decade in the history of the state of Israel. As a result, domestic events that occurred during this period could have intense reverberations that would have been absent from a more politically charged reality. It was during this decade of calm that the Eichmann trial was conducted; the trial occupied the heart of public discourse and shaped the public consciousness regarding the Holocaust, and all public attention could be focused on it. The Demjanjuk trial, on the other hand, occurred during a turbulent period that witnessed the First Lebanon War, far-reaching political changes, and a severe economic crisis. Moreover, in the two years following

Demjanjuk's release, Prime Minister Yitzhak Rabin was assassinated. In the resulting struggle for the focus of public attention, the Demjanjuk trial was at a distinct disadvantage, overshadowed, as it was, by background noise that prevented it from playing the role its initiators had intended. This disadvantage impacted the different sectors of Israeli society, which promptly lost interest in the trial and its place in the collective memory.

Now, twenty-seven years after its conclusion, it is interesting to note how little of it remains of it in the Israeli collective memory. Hod's book asks "Why did we remember to forget?" and engages the topic of collective memory in Israeli society. Maurice Halwachs, who is regarded as the father of collective memory research, argues that memory is formed through and shaped by a selection of historic events that is intended to serve changing interests. Collective memory, then, is a product of the present that reflects the manner in which a society sees itself at a given moment in time. Collective memory is constructed by highlighting some events and erasing others, and both actions are of equal importance. The fact that this is achieved through manipulation prompts us to consider the identity of the lead agent in the production of memory that is an expression of cultural hegemony. This agent sets the dates of the ceremonies and is responsible for instilling the desired content in society. In Israel, the government and the education system were the agents responsible for remembering and forgetting. As an example of such control we can point to the prominence of Israeli Independence Day ceremonies, in the Arab sector as well, as opposed to the forgetting of the *Nakba*. Two years prior to the Eichmann trial, in 1959, the Knesset enacted the Martyrs' and Heroes' Remembrance Day Law, which dealt primarily with ceremonial aspects and, as a result of the Eichmann trial, assumed increasing significance and depth. In the mid-1980s, the Holocaust became a mandatory topic of study in Israeli high schools, and at the beginning of the 1990s Israeli student trips began to visit the death camps in Poland. The Eichmann trial, then, was conducted in a vacuum when it came to inculcating awareness of the Holocaust in Israeli society, whereas the Demjanjuk trial took place at a time when Israel was already suffering from an excess of Holocaust experiences. This excess also resulted in the social cheapening of the Holocaust, especially at the intersection of politics and consciousness. From the perspective of the Ministry of Education, the trips to

Poland provided a sufficient psychological solution, making the Demjanjuk trial an unnecessary event.

Tamir Hod's book is not only the story of a legal saga that encountered complications; it is also the story of how Israeli society has contended with the Holocaust: the most traumatic experience in Jewish history. The book not only touches exposed nerves of twentieth-century Israeli society but also addresses dilemmas with which the state is dealing (or failing to deal) today. Israeli politicians hoped that the story of the Holocaust would serve as the cement that would bond and unify the different sectors of Israeli society. In actuality, however, the Holocaust was the story of European Jewry alone, and a story with which Jews of Eastern origins have had difficulty connecting, as reflected in the recurring refrain of talkbackers: "It's a shame that Hitler didn't kill you all." In collective memory, the Holocaust is a narrative that both unifies and divides. The story of the Demjanjuk trial was erased from this memory.

List of Contributors

Dr. Irit Back is a senior lecturer in Tel Aviv University's Department of Middle Eastern and African History and head of the African Studies Program. Her research interests include contemporary Islam and the regional dimensions of conflict resolution in Africa. Dr. Bak has published numerous books and articles, in academic journals and other venues, on subjects in her fields of expertise. A leading commentator on African issues in the Israeli and global media, her book *From Sudan to South Sudan: IGAD and the Role of Regional Mediation in Africa* was published in 2020. Her current research focuses on reflections of Holocaust discourse in internal state conflicts in post-colonial Africa.

Prof. Judy Baumel-Schwartz is a professor in the Israel and Golda Koschitzky Department of Jewish History and Contemporary Jewry at Bar-Ilan University. She heads the Arnold and Leona Finkler Institute of Holocaust Research and is the current holder of the Abraham and Edita Spiegel Family Chair of Holocaust Research and the Pynchas Brener Chair in Research on the Holocaust of European Jewry. She is the author of numerous studies on the Holocaust and the State of Israel, with an emphasis on gender, commemoration, memory, and, most recently, second and third generation Holocaust survivors.

Dr. Graciela Ben Dror has been the editor of *Moreshet, The Journal for the Study of the Holocaust and Antisemitism* since 2011. She has served as a researcher at an Institute for the Study of Antisemitism at Tel-Aviv University, a lecturer in the Department of Jewish History at the University of Haifa, and Director of Moreshet. Her books include: *The Catholic Church and the Jews: Argentina, 1933-1945* (2000) (Hebrew), which was awarded the Israeli Ministry of Culture's Prize for the year 2000, and was also published in Spanish (2003), and English (2008); *La Iglesia Católica ante el Holocausto. España y América Latina 1933-1945* (2003); *Radical Socialist Zionism on the Banks of Rio de La Plata: The Mordechai Anielevich Movement in Uruguay, 1954-1976* (2016) (with Victor Ben-Dror); and *Christianity without Grace* (2018) (Hebrew).

Dr. Irit Cherniavsky holds a Ph.D. from the Hebrew University of Jerusalem's Institute of Contemporary Jewry (2010). Her books include: *By the Skin of Their Teeth: On the Immigration of Polish Jewry before the Holocaust* (2010) (Hebrew) and *At the Last Moment: The Jewish Struggle for Emigration from Poland before the Holocaust* (2015). Her recent articles include: "The Polish Righteous among the Nations: Statistical Aspects," *Dapim: Studies on the Holocaust* (1997) (Hebrew); "Eretz Israel in the Eyes of Polish Jewry," *Bishvil Hazikaron* (July 2017) (Hebrew); "Polish Jews and Their Descendants in Israel," in Robert Kusek and Joanna Sanetra-Szeliga (eds.), *Does Poland Lie on the Mediterranean* (2012); and "The Emigration of Polish Jews in the 1930s," in Sergio Della Pergola and Uzi Rebhun (eds.), *Jewish Population and Identity* (2018).

Dr. Sharon Geva is a historian, a scholar of gender, and a lecturer at Kibbutzim College of Education and the Women and Gender Studies Program at Tel Aviv University. She researches women and gender in the Holocaust, the memory of the Holocaust from the perspective of gender, the history of women in Israel, and the history of Israeli society during the initial years of statehood. Her book *To the Unknown Sister: Holocaust Heroines in Israeli Society* (Hebrew) was published in 2010 and was awarded the Yad Izhak Ben-Zvi's Mordechai Ish-Shalom Prize. Dr. Geva is also the editor of a collection of articles titled *Lessons of the Holocaust: Humanistic Pedagogical Perspectives* (2017) (Hebrew).

Prof. David Golinkin is the President of the Schechter Institutes and a Professor of Talmud and Jewish Law at the Schechter Institute of Jewish Studies in Jerusalem. He is the author of 60 books on various subjects in the field of Jewish studies, including *The Student Struggle against the Holocaust* (2010), co-authored with Raphael Medoff.

Prof. Aviva Halamish is Professor Emerita of History at the Open University of Israel. Her research encompasses the history of the Jewish people and of Palestine/ Eretz Israel in the twentieth century. Among her publications: *The Exodus Affair: Holocaust Survivors and the Struggle for Palestine* (1998); *A Dual Race against Time: Zionist Immigration Policy in the 1930s* (2006) (Hebrew]; "Palestine as a Destination for Jewish Immigrants and Refugees from Nazi Germany", Frank Caestecker and Bob Moore (eds.), *Refugees from Nazi Germany and the Liberal*

European States (2010), pp. 122-150; *Kibbutz - Utopia and Politics: The Life and Times of Meir Yaari* (2017); "Immigration is Israel's History, So Far", *Israel Studies*, 23/3 (2018), pp. 106-113; "Jewish immigration: The base of the Palestine triangle", in Michael J Cohen (ed.), *The British Mandate in Palestine: A Centenary Volume, 1920-2020* (2020), pp. 172-188.

Nir Itzik earned an M.A. in Jewish history (with honors) from Tel Aviv University. His thesis was titled "Yitzhak (Antek) Zuckerman and his Testimonies about the Jewish Fighting Organization in the Warsaw Ghetto," and he has worked as a research assistant for Prof. Havi Dreifuss of Tel Aviv University's Department of Jewish History. From 2016 to 2020, he worked at Moreshet – The Mordechai Anielevich Memorial Holocaust Study and Research Center, in education, conference organization, and archival research in Moreshet's archive. He currently directs the Ethiopian Heritage Center's research institute.

Dr. Menachem Keren-Kratz earned a Ph.D. in Yiddish literature (with honors) from Bar-Ilan University in 2009. In 2013, he completed another Ph.D. in Jewish history at Tel Aviv University. His first book, *Maramaros, Hungary: The Cradle of Extreme Orthodoxy* (Hebrew), was published in 2013, and his most recent book, *The Zealot: The Satmar Rebbe - Rabbi Yoel Teitelbaum* (Hebrew) was published in 2020. He is the author of dozens of articles, some in journals but most in collections of academic articles or peer-reviewed journals.

Lea Langleben is a graduate of Bar-Ilan University's Department of Jewish History and Land of Israel Studies. She received her master's degree from the Institute of Contemporary Jewry at the Hebrew University of Jerusalem. Her research has examined the life of the Jewish religious population during the Holocaust and the educational and cultural work that was conducted in the ghettos. Her recent articles include: "The Holocaust as a Subject of Study at Bais Yaakov Seminary," *Hagigei Giva* 8 (2000) (Hebrew); "Teaching for a Loaf of Bread: Education Activity in the Słobódka Ghetto, 1941-1944," *Hagigei Giva* 10 (2002) (Hebrew); and "…but neither are you at liberty to neglect it: Teachers in the Struggle to Survive in the Ghettos," *Bishvil Hazikaron* 24 (2016) (Hebrew). She is also the editor of *To Live and Learn – Jewish Education in Poland and Lithuania during the Holocaust: A Collection of Documents* (2014) (Hebrew).

Noam Leibman holds a master's degree from the University of Haifa's Department of Jewish History (research track), for which he was awarded high honors. His thesis, which explored "The Conception of the Role of Jewish Police in the Ghettos of Warsaw and Otwock as Reflected in the Memoirs of Contemporaries," was supervised by Prof. Marcos Silber and Prof. Avihu Ronen. The article that appears in this issue represents the development of one aspect that was not addressed in the thesis itself. Leibman has received funding from Yad Vashem and the Inter-University Program in Russian and East European Studies, and he is currently in the initial stages of his doctoral research. He has been working at the Education Department of Moreshet – The Mordechai Anielevich Memorial Holocaust Study and Research Center, since 2008.

Prof. Dalia Ofer is Professor Emerita of Holocaust and Eastern European research at the Hebrew University of Jerusalem. Her studies and publications deal with the research of everyday life during the Holocaust, women and gender, the memory of the Holocaust in Israel, and the illegal Jewish immigration to Mandate Palestine. She is a recipient of the Izhak Ben-Zvi Prize (1989), the National Jewish Book Award (1992), and the Distinguished Achievement Award in Holocaust Studies from the Holocaust Educational Foundation of Northwestern University (2018).

Dr. Michal Shaul is the head of the History Department at Herzog College. Her book *Beauty for Ashes: Holocaust Memory and the Rehabilitation of Ashkenazi Haredi Society in Israel 1945–1961* was published in 2014, and in 2020 it was translated into English. For this book, Dr. Shaul was awarded the 2016 Zalman Shazar Prize in Jewish History.

Prof. Eli Tzur is Professor Emeritus at the Kibbutz College of Education and is currently the academic advisor to the Yad Yaari Documentation and Research Center at Givat Haviva. He is a graduate of Tel Aviv University and the London School of Economics and Political Science. His research explores the history of the Israeli Left and the history of youth movements, with an emphasis on the history of Hashomer Hatzair in Eastern Europe. His books include: *The Landscapes of Illusion* (1998), *Can't Do without Us* (2000) (Hebrew), *Guardian of Israel* (2001) (Hebrew), *Before Darkness Fell: Hashomer Hatzair in Poland and Galicia* (2006) (Hebrew), and *Nipped in the Bud: Hashomer Hatzair in Poland, 1944-1950* (2017) (Hebrew).

Dr. Moshe Vered received his Ph.D. in physics from the Weizmann Institute of Science's Geophysics Laboratory in 1975 and has spent his entire professional career working in applied research in this scientific field. He is also a master's degree student (research-track) in the Department of Jewish History at Tel Aviv University. The article that appears in this issue was written for a seminar course.

Prof. Yechiam Weitz is Professor Emeritus in the Department of Land of Israel Studies at the University of Haifa and teaches at Bar-Ilan University. His research interests include: Israeli society's attitude toward the Holocaust and its survivors; Holocaust trials; the Israeli public debate surrounding Germany-Israel relations; Israel's Revisionist and civic right wing; Ben-Gurion's role in the history of the Jewish People and Israeli historiography; and patterns of Israeli leadership – Moshe Sharett, Levi Eshkol, Golda Meir, and Menachem Begin. Over the years, Prof. Weitz has supervised the writing of more than 45 doctoral dissertations and master's theses. His upcoming book, *The Life, The Death, and the Commemoration of Yechiam Weitz*, will be published in 2021.

Dr. Efraim Zadoff is a historian. He holds a Ph.D. from Tel Aviv University and is a Spiegel Fellow at the Arnold and Leona Finkler Institute of Holocaust Research at Bar-Ilan University. He is also a secular humanistic rabbi ordained by the International Institute for Secular Humanistic Judaism (IISHJ) – Tmura Israel. Dr. Zadoff has served as a research fellow at Yad Vashem and the Hebrew University of Jerusalem. He is a publisher, editor, and translator of Spanish-language books on the Holocaust, including an encyclopedia of the Holocaust and an Encyclopedia of the Ghettos in the Holocaust, both published by Yad Vashem. He has published dozens of books and academic articles on the history of the Jews in Latin America and on the relations between Latin American countries and the Jews during the Holocaust, and he is a member of AMILAT-Research Association for Latin American Jewry.

INSTRUCTIONS FOR CONTRIBUTORS

MORESHET, THE JOURNAL FOR THE STUDY OF THE HOLOCAUST AND ANTISEMITISM

1. Moreshet Journal, a **peer reviewed publication,** invites researchers to send us scholarly articles and/or review essays relating to topics dealing with the Holocaust and Antisemitism.

2. Articles have to be original, and not published in other publications.

3. Manuscripts should not exceed 12,000 words including notes, and including a short abstract of 150 words. The articles must be sent by email or on CD, must be typewritten, double-spaced, and all pages should be numbered consecutively. Two typewritten, double-spaced copies of the article on A4 paper should be sent to the address of the Moreshet Journal.

4. Details of the author's institutional affiliation, degree, short CV for the list of contributors (3-4 lines), address, phone number and email must be added.

5. To be accepted for publication the articles will pass both internal and external peer review and, if accepted, the author may be requested to make revisions.

6. Articles may be sent in English, French, German, Polish or Hebrew, but in some cases other languages will also be considered.

7. The author will receive 10 offprints of the article and a copy of the volume in which the article was published.

Please send the articles to the following address and e-mail:
Dr. Graciela Ben Dror, Editor
Moreshet, the Journal for the Study of the Holocaust and Antisemitism
Givat Haviva, Doar Na Menashe, 37850
Israel
graciela.moreshet@gmail.com

MORESHET

JOURNAL FOR THE STUDY OF THE HOLOCAUST AND ANTISEMITISM

14 2017

- Graciela Ben-Dror
- Yehuda Dvorkin
- Sharon Geva
- Aviva Halamish
- Liat Meirav
- Dalia Ofer
- Avinoam J. Patt
- Na'ama Seri-Levi
- Zipora Shehory-Rubin
- Ada Schein
- Bilha Shilo
- Yfaat Weiss
- Yechiel Weitzman

MORESHET

JOURNAL FOR THE STUDY OF THE HOLOCAUST AND ANTISEMITISM

15 | 2018

- Judy Baumel-Schwartz
- Graciela Ben-Dror
- Hanoch Ben-Pazi
- Lea Ganor
- Leiky Geronik
- Yossi J. Goldstein
- Yosef Govrin
- Maya Guez
- Nicholas Dreyer
- Ronnen Harran
- Guy Miron
- Rami Nowodworski
- Robert Rockaway
- Aron Shai
- Laurence Weinbaum

MORESHET

JOURNAL FOR THE STUDY OF THE HOLOCAUST AND ANTISEMITISM

16 2019

MORESHET

JOURNAL FOR THE STUDY OF THE HOLOCAUST AND ANTISEMITISM

Historiography of the Holocaust

17  2020

- Yehuda Bauer
- Judy Tydor Baumel-Schwartz
- Graciela Ben Dror
- Havi Dreifuss
- Aviva Halamish
- Dan Michman
- Dalia Ofer
- Avinoam Patt
- Dina Porat
- Roni Stauber
- Esther Webman
- Nikola Zimring

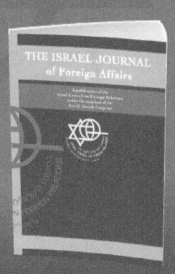

Made in the USA
Middletown, DE
01 May 2022

65061717R00276